AFRICAN-AMERICAN ORATORS

AFRICAN-AMERICAN ORATORS

A Bio-Critical Sourcebook

Edited by
RICHARD W. LEEMAN

Bernard K. Duffy, Advisory Editor

Greenwood Press
Westport, Connecticut • London

Library of Congress Cataloging-in-Publication Data

African-American orators : a bio-critical sourcebook / edited by
   Richard W. Leeman.
       p.   cm.
    Includes bibliographical references and index.
    ISBN 0–313–29014–8 (alk. paper)
    1. Afro-American orators.   2. Political oratory—United States.
   I. Leeman, Richard W.
   E185.96.A447   1996
   808.5'1'08996073—dc20   95–37338

British Library Cataloguing in Publication Data is available.

Library of Congress Catalog Card Number: 95–37338
ISBN: 0–313–29014–8

First published in 1996

Greenwood Press, 88 Post Road West, Westport, CT 06881
An imprint of Greenwood Publishing Group, Inc.

Printed in the United States of America

The paper used in this book complies with the
Permanent Paper Standard issued by the National
Information Standards Organization (Z39.48–1984).

10 9 8 7 6 5 4 3 2 1

CONTENTS

PREFACE

Any volume of this size and scope is by necessity the product of many people's labor. While any errors of subject, tone, inclusion, or focus are surely mine, there are many whose generous contributions of time and talent are responsible for whatever success this book may enjoy.

For the genesis of the book itself, I owe much to Bernard Duffy, Halford Ryan, and Greenwood Press. Their Bio-Critical Sourcebooks on American orators paved the way for this more specialized, but sorely needed, volume. I benefitted very directly from their work when Bernie agreed to serve as Advisory Editor for this volume. His suggestions were particularly invaluable in the early, critical stages of assembling this work.

Greenwood Press has been a professional and cooperative partner in this project. Mildred Vasan, social and behavioral sciences editor, and Ann Newman, production editor, have been especially helpful to me throughout the long process of completing this volume.

The administration and my colleagues at the University of North Carolina at Charlotte have also been supportive. The University provided time as well as financial support for the research and editorial work that I put into the volume. My colleagues provided the departmental environment which I have come to expect, a work environment as conducive to learning as it is to working and—on more than one occasion!—even enjoying.

Of course, without the contributions of the authors whose essays populate these pages, this volume would not exist. I appreciate the time, energy and expertise which they brought to their writing. I also appreciated their many positive comments about the project itself. For all of them, I believe, their scholarship was a labor of love—albeit occasionally a frustrating one, where ethereal sources seemed to lurk just beyond their reach. I believe the reader will find that these authors were *engaged* by the oratory of their speakers, and that this intellectual and emotional engagement contributed positively to the analysis provided in each essay.

I also owe a large debt of gratitude to my family. My wife, Carol, has supported my work with this volume from inception to completion, and I thank her wholeheartedly for that support. My two young sons, Christopher and Gregory, especially loom large as the backdrop to this volume. Neither has known a time when I *wasn't* working on it. More significantly, though, throughout my work with this project my thoughts frequently turned to them. To me, the essays in this volume tell an invaluable and inseparable part of American history, history which my sons and all young Americans should learn by heart as they enter the twenty-first century. I fervently hope that this volume helps teach them that history.

Finally, the deepest gratitude is owed to the speakers whose ideas, words, arguments, and concerns fill this volume. They have persuaded, cajoled, scolded, pleaded, informed and entertained. They have spoken to large audiences and small, domestic audiences and foreign, wealthy audiences and poor. There has been no subject which they were unwilling to engage. They have been the voice of a people and the conscience of a nation. Without them, the world would have been a quieter, duller, less educated, and much less interesting place. To them is owed the largest thanks of all.

INTRODUCTION

Nobody would be surprised at, nor would anyone probably question, the statement that a volume like the one presented here has been long, very long, overdue. The detailed study of all American oratory has been generally neglected, finally experiencing a significant revival only in the past decade or so. African-American oratory, one hardly needs mention, has been even less studied in the American academy, an institution that has traditionally been consumed with the study of the Great (usually Dead) White Male. Such neglect is all the more shameful given the African-American community's history of powerful oratory. From nineteenth-century voices that commanded attention, such as those of Frederick Douglass and Sojourner Truth, to twentieth-century voices of authority, such as those of Barbara Jordan and Thurgood Marshall, public speaking has been a central part of the African-American heritage.

While the academic neglect of African-American oratory has not been total, it has been comprehensive. A survey of communication studies national and regional journals is instructive. Prior to 1963, only three articles had been published that examined African-American oratory: "Old Time Negro Preaching: An Interpretive Study" (1945), "Negro Speakers in Congress, 1869–75" (1953), and "Sojourner Truth: God's Appointed Apostle of Reform" (1962). It might seem that 1963 was a year in which the discipline's attention finally blossomed, when four articles more than doubled the previous half-century's output. Accompanying "Frederick Douglass: Abolitionist Orator," however, were three articles spurred by the already eight-year-old civil rights movement (using the 1955 Montgomery bus boycott as a birthing point that few should have missed): "A Stormy Rally in Atlanta," "Does Non-Violence Persuade?" and "The Future of Non-Violence." It is revealing to note that these three articles *totaled* eight pages in length.

The following year saw the publication of two articles, both of which were pre–civil rights movement in focus. "An Antiphonal Negro Sermon" and "Negro Oratory in the Anti-Slavery Societies, 1830–60" reflected earlier articles, looking at the black church and the abolition era. Through 1964, then, only two individual orators had merited an entire article—Sojourner Truth and Frederick Douglass—and the ensemble studies had been restricted to four subjects: sermons, abolition, congressional Reconstruction orators, and the 1950s/1960s civil rights movement. There had been nothing about the antilynching crusade, African-Americans' work with education, the Great Migrations northward, the post–Depression-era congressional representatives, or early civil rights movement orators, and nothing about Booker T. Washington or W. E. B. Du Bois. Nothing had been written about Thurgood Marshall, Adam Clayton Powell, Jr., Mary McLeod Bethune, or others who, even at the national level, were movers and shakers of their times. Even Martin Luther King, Jr., who by this time had already delivered his famous March on Washington speech, had merited only one article ("A Stormy Rally in Atlanta") about a single demonstration, and it was but four pages in length.

While the period 1966–71 produced a boomlet of articles on African-American oratory, the discipline's myopia was only slightly corrected. From 1966 to 1969, there were thirteen articles published. Five of those examined the civil rights movement generally; the remaining eight concerned themselves with the black power movement specifically. In those thirteen articles, only two individual orators were spotlighted. Martin Luther King, Jr., was the focus of one article ("Martin Luther King, Jr.: In the Beginning at Montgomery," 1968), while Stokely Carmichael was the subject of six.

The next two years, 1970 and 1971, saw the discipline engage African-American oratory a bit more broadly. Of the twelve articles published in those two years, only four analyzed the rhetoric of black power, although a fifth examined black nationalism. Two of the black power articles focused on individual speakers, one on H. Rap Brown and one on Stokely Carmichael. Some of the remaining seven articles returned to traditional ground. One article examined "Black Persuaders in the Anti-Slavery Movement" (1970), while another looked at "The Rhetorical Legacy of the Black Church" (1971). Four of the essays examined the oratory of three speakers. Two critiqued the oratory of Henry Highland Garnet, seeing in him an analog to contemporary black radicalism, while the other two looked at Booker T. Washington and Thurgood Marshall. Finally, one article examined African-American oratory more broadly, discussing the "Socio-Historical Perspectives of Black Oratory" (1970).

Until very recently, however, the period 1967–71 represented the high-water mark (using the term very loosely) of the journals' concern with African-American oratory. Rarely have even three articles devoted to the study of black oratory appeared in any given year; generally the number has been one or two. In the discipline's journals, the most studied individual figure since 1971 has been Barbara Jordan (four articles, of which three critiqued her keynote address at the 1976 Democratic National Convention).

A survey of books with African-American oratory as their focus tells a similar story: a general neglect of the subject during the pre–civil rights movement era, a flurry of activity in the late 1960s and early 1970s, and a marked return to general indifference afterwards. For many years, the standard work in the field was Carter G. Woodson's exhaustive 1925 anthology of African-American speeches, *Negro Orators and Their Orations*. Containing full reprints of seventy speeches, Woodson's book made many famous and not-so-famous orators and their speeches readily available for academic study. Again, however, except for a few collections of individual speakers' papers (e.g., Francis Grimke's *Works*, edited in 1942 by Woodson), the subject of Negro oratory was generally ignored by rhetorical scholars until the 1950s/1960s civil rights movement was well under way.

Following the rise of the black power movement there came, again, a flurry of activity in the field. In 1969, Marcus Boulware's *The Oratory of Negro Leaders, 1900–1968* surveyed the lives and speaking of some fifty-five twentieth-century orators. Boulware's critiques ranged from a single paragraph on speakers such as the Reverend Nathaniel Tross to full chapters on Booker T. Washington and Martin Luther King, Jr. While the analysis was often anecdotal, until the publication of the present volume Boulware's book stood alone in its comprehensive survey of African-American oratory. In the same year, Arthur L. Smith (Molefi K. Asante) published the first book that essayed a broad analytical framework for black rhetoric, although it focused specifically on black revolutionary rhetoric. In *Rhetoric of Black Revolution*, Asante examined the history, strategies, and topics of black revolutionary rhetoric and also discussed the nature of the black audience. While Boulware and Asante broke new ground with their volumes, the largest proportion of books published during these years were anthologies of African-American speeches, including Roy L. Hill's *Rhetoric of Racial Revolt* (1964), Philip S. Foner's *The Black Panthers Speak* (1970), Arthur Smith (Asante) and Stephen Robb's *The Voice of Black Rhetoric: Selections* (1971), Daniel O'Neill's *Speeches by Black Americans* (1971), James Golden and Richard Rieke's *The Rhetoric of Black Americans* (1971), and Philip S. Foner's encyclopedic *The Voice of Black America: Major Speeches by Negroes in the United States, 1797–1971* (1972), which reprinted 198 speeches by African-Americans.

As with the articles, however, and despite the fact that public address anthologies now include representative African-American speeches, books that exclusively examine African-American oratory have dwindled considerably since the early 1970s. General anthologies have been hard to come by, although Robbie Jean Walker added some long-overdue attention to African-American women's oratory with her anthology, *The Rhetoric of Struggle: Public Address by African American Women* (1992), which reprinted thirty-five speeches. Anthologies focusing on a single orator's speeches—for example, Shirley Chisholm's *The Good Fight* or Jesse Jackson's *Straight from the Heart*—have been slightly more plentiful. Two recent textbooks, James Ward's *African American Communications* (1993) and Lyndrey A. Niles's *African American Rhetoric: A Reader* (1995), make available several primary materials (including but not limited to speeches) as well as providing the reader with some critical analyses of black oratory.

Of late, however, three rather unique volumes have appeared that may indicate that the study of African-American oratory has truly commenced. In 1987, Molefi K. Asante published *The Afrocentric Idea*. Although Asante and others had been developing the Afrocentric method for some time (e.g., Asante's *Afrocentricity*, 1980), *The Afrocentric Idea* provided a fuller statement of this perspective. Grounded in an understanding of African discourse as essentially harmony/ balance maintaining, and of the Afrocentric critic as observer and audience, Asante drew his method inductively from his discussion of African and African-American oratory and literature. In 1993, Carolyn Calloway-Thomas and John Louis Lucaites edited the first volume of essays devoted to the study and analysis of a single African-American orator, a book entitled *Martin Luther King, Jr., and the Sermonic Power of Public Discourse*. That same year, in *Crafting Equality: America's Anglo-African Word*, Celeste Michelle Condit and John Louis Lucaites examined "equality" as an ideograph—a single word that serves to summarize and evoke an ideology—and surveyed its evolution across the centuries of American discourse. All three volumes—studying an alternate critical method, a single orator, or a single word—provided marked and significant departures from earlier efforts to critique African-American oratory.

What may be most surprising about this history of scholarly disregard of African-American oratory is the significance of the subject that has been ignored. By all accounts, oratory has been one of the few rhetorical resources available to the African-American community. Black abolitionists, for example, had few weapons to use against slavery except their voices raised in protest. But consider the quality and significance of just some of those voices: Maria Miller Stewart, Charles Lenox Remond, Frederick Douglass, Sojourner Truth, Henry Highland Garnet, William Wells Brown, and Frances Watkins Harper. If we but listen, these are voices that have echoed down through our history even to the present day.

Or consider the Reconstruction era, itself followed quickly by the institution of Jim Crow laws in the South and segregationist practices in the North, maintained through agencies ostensibly charged with enforcing the law as well as through practices of lynching, terror, and ostracism. With little political power, and still suffering economically from the effects of over two hundred years of slavery, African-Americans again found a voice in their oratory. The period 1865–1920 was particularly marked by outstanding and influential women orators, speakers who addressed the problems of civil rights, lynching, women's rights, and social justice generally. Frances Harper, Ida B. Wells-Barnett, Anna Julia Cooper, Fannie Barrier Williams, Mary Church Terrell, and Mary McLeod

Bethune are just a few of those who frequented the platform, speaking to many different groups, organizations, and clubs. The era was also marked by the clash between two of the best-known and most influential of African-American orators, Booker T. Washington and W. E. B. Du Bois. While their debate about the proper strategy for acquiring full civil rights was played out in many arenas, oratory was, for both, a major avenue for articulating their philosophies and reasoning.

Preaching, of course, has long been a training ground for African-American speakers. Barred from most middle-and upper-middle-class occupations, many of the community's brightest entered the ministry. Habituated to the practice of sermonizing, oratory grounded in religious argument was a mainstay for these advocates of reform, including such speakers as Henry Highland Garnet and Alexander Crummell. Some of these ministers preached outside mainstream America, such as Father Divine with his claims of godhood; others, such as Francis Grimke, can be considered solidly traditional. Still others straddled the line, speakers who, like Vernon Johns, created no little discomfort among their own congregations. More recent orators, such as Martin Luther King, Jr., Benjamin Hooks, Andrew Young, and Jesse Jackson, have continued the tradition of combining ministerial training with secular public speaking.

Oratory was also a prominent weapon in the struggle for civil rights that marked the 1950s and 1960s. Some orators, whose eloquence is now well recognized, will forever be inextricably linked with the civil rights movement: Martin Luther King, Jr., Malcolm X, Eldridge Cleaver, and Stokely Carmichael, to name but a few. Others have experienced less fame—for example, Louis Lomax, John Lewis, and Robert Moses—but their oratory represents the vibrant wealth of public speaking that helped constitute the movement of that era. These speakers' oratory illustrates the diversity of tactics, philosophies, arguments, and oratorical styles that emerged from and helped mold the movement. Whatever their differences, however, they shared a common bond of turning to public speaking as a means of engaging the American public—of all races—in a public dialogue that eventually led to the most significant legal reforms since the Reconstruction era.

Many might end their case for the importance of African-American oratory with the civil rights movement of the 1950s and 1960s. Certainly our survey of communication studies articles would indicate that, informally, many scholars have already done so. But public speaking has continued to be a critically important tool for African-American leaders. Some of these orators, such as Jesse Jackson, Marian Wright Edelman, Eleanor Holmes Norton, and Andrew Young, have their oratorical roots in the civil rights movement, but have had their greatest impact in the post–civil rights movement era. Two of these figures amply illustrate the continued importance of oratory for African-Americans. Relying largely on the appeal of his public speaking, Jesse Jackson has mounted two presidential campaigns, both of which have been inarguably influential in American politics. As head of the Children's Defense Fund, lobbyist Marian

Wright Edelman relies heavily on her powers of persuasion to change the minds and hearts of politicians and the public. Her many successes are owed, in large part, to her forceful eloquence.

With these two examples, we have begun making the transition to the larger reason why African-American oratory deserves study: its significant influence on American history. Recent speakers and speeches, quickly apprehended by all, can easily illustrate this point. In government, for example, it is impossible to imagine American history without Shirley Chisholm's voice of conscience raised against the war in Vietnam and on behalf of the traditionally disadvantaged; or Barbara Jordan's clear recitation of the case for impeaching a president; or Colin Powell's articulation of American military policy in the post–Cold War world and the application of that policy in the Persian Gulf War. Outside government, too, African-American oratory is clearly both influential and significant. Some of these voices, like those of Benjamin Hooks and Louis Farrakhan, have helped shape the predominantly black organizations they have led, as those groups have confronted their roles in the post–civil rights movement era. Other leaders have addressed their speaking to organizations that are not predominantly black, such as Edelman with the Children's Defense Fund or Faye Wattleton with Planned Parenthood.

But even in earlier eras, when the influence African-Americans wielded in public life was less than today, there were speakers who helped tangibly to mold the direction of American history. Frederick Douglass, though often frustrated by the prejudice of others, was a significant voice in the Republican party and, even more so, in the reform movement of the late nineteenth century. Although white America did not readily hear her message, Ida B. Wells-Barnett was indeed successful in placing the antilynching crusade on the agenda of existing organizations like the Woman's Christian Temperance Union and in catalyzing the creation of other organizations, such as the Association of Southern Women for the Prevention of Lynching. Whether it ultimately proved beneficial for blacks or not, white America listened to Washington's message, resisted Du Bois's, and feared Garvey's, Malcolm X's, and, lest the myths of history cloud our memories, even Martin Luther King, Jr.'s. What black America has said these past two centuries has indeed been an important force in shaping all Americans' history, not just that of African-Americans.

But what have we to learn about these speakers, or perhaps ourselves, by studying their speeches? We will, perhaps, learn that, as Mark White tells us, we need to be careful about how we mythologize Malcolm X, paying closer attention to what his speeches actually said and less to what others have said they say. Or perhaps we will learn, as Mark McPhail points out, that Louis Farrakhan's message is far less one-dimensional than the media portray it. Perhaps we will read side by side the essays on Angela Davis, Lenora Fulani, Colin Powell, and Walter Williams and come to a greater appreciation for the diversity of voices heard within the African-American community.

We will certainly discover a diversity of styles in the speaking analyzed in this volume. Some of it soars with eloquence, sometimes with the classical tones of a Frederick Douglass, sometimes with the plain speaking of a Sojourner Truth. Some, such as William Whipper or Barbara Jordan, speak with a sharp eye for detail and a keen attention to argument. Others, such as Maria Miller Stewart or Henry Highland Garnet, speak more broadly, capturing in their speaking the emotional truth contained within the issue. Some use the florid style of a Jesse Jackson, some the plain style of an Ida Wells-Barnett, and still others employ the multiple styles of a Frances Harper or an Adam Clayton Powell, Jr.

Accompanying these diverse styles are a complementary variety of arguments and evidence. Alexander Crummell speaks with a voice of moderation, while his colleague Henry Highland Garnet urges revolution. Ida Wells-Barnett uses an avalanche of statistics and quotations, drawn from Southern, white-owned newspapers, while Mary Church Terrell is a storyteller at heart. Marcus Garvey leads a back-to-Africa movement, while W. E. B. Du Bois and Thurgood Marshall articulate the cause of legal integration. A. Philip Randolph brings African-Americans into the union movement, while Mary McLeod Bethune brings education to African-American women. For the orators discussed here, the causes are many, the issues diverse, and their audiences varied.

But while their arguments and their styles are diverse, themes do emerge that unify the essays, common threads that, as Jesse Jackson might characterize it, pull the patches together into a single quilt. These themes are grounded in the experience of being black in America, an element of the rhetorical scene that seems to cross the situational divides of religion, class, occupation, ideology, or issue.

The first identifiable theme is the presence—sometimes in the background, often brought to the fore—of a common exigence: the quest for freedom and equality of treatment. That thread is most readily seen in the pre-1970 oratory, of course, from Frederick Douglass's sarcastic challenge, ''Must I undertake to prove that the slave is a man?'' to Martin Luther King, Jr.'s, famous call that we judge ''not by the color of our skin but the content of our character.'' A deep and abiding interest in freedom and equality can also be discerned in post–civil rights movement public address, however. For example, the search for equality often demanded that earlier orators confront and address the poverty of the race. That concern permeates much of the speaking of Harper, Washington, Du Bois, Garvey, Bethune, and Fannie Barrier Williams, among others. It informs Louis Lomax's call that his audience turn their church basement into a school in order to ''save these children'' from the poverty imposed by a poor education. Post–civil rights movement empathy for the ''damned, disinherited, disrespected and the despised'' is not solely found in Jesse Jackson's address to the 1984 Democratic National Convention. The ''Voice of the People'' (Shirley Chisholm), the ''Children's Champion'' (Marian Wright Edelman), and two-time New Alliance presidential candidate Lenora Fulani are all orators whose discourse is primarily concerned with improving the lot of those—black, white, yellow, brown, or red—stricken by poverty.

The historical search for freedom has sometimes taken a different turn of late, but it, too, can still be quickly discovered in the oratory of contemporary speakers. Although the law was too often used against the African-American, as with Jim Crow segregation, if *all* laws (especially federal statutes) had been rigidly upheld, blacks' lives would have been markedly improved. Thus the speeches of Ida Wells-Barnett and Thurgood Marshall requested plainly that the letter of the law—for example, due process and equal treatment under the law—be strictly enforced. Such enforcement would have provided many essential freedoms for blacks: freedom of speech, assembly, and press, freedom from fear, and freedom to pursue any occupation, political position, or education. Such concern for the enforcement of the law can be found in Barbara Jordan's 1974 Watergate speech to the House Judiciary Committee, in which she noted in her introduction that "my faith in the Constitution is whole, . . . [and] I am not going to sit here and be an idle spectator to the diminution, the subversion, the destruction of the Constitution." A similar valuation of the law grounded Eleanor Holmes Norton's legal defense of George Wallace's right to hold a rally in Shea Stadium.

A second theme that emerges in African-American oratory parallels the search for freedom and equality: the upholding of America's ideals. Indeed, as I read the speakers' addresses discussed in this volume, it does not seem hyperbole to term their collective works "the conscience of America." Rhetorically, such an interest is logical, for America has traditionally professed itself a believer in two moral codes—the principles of democracy and the Judeo-Christian ethic—both of which contain clear imperatives to treat others with fairness and decency.

African-American orators have acted as America's conscience in two ways: by praising America's ideals and condemning America's hypocrisy. Some orators have favored one tack or the other; many have combined both. Colin Powell, for example, in his position of leadership in the American military, primarily emphasized America's lofty principles. His words of praise are found not only in his "official" speeches—those that announce or defend policy—but in his less officious speeches as well. "I believe in this great land that God blessed and called America," he told the 1992 graduating class of Fisk University, "because it is full of young men and women like you. Men and women who will keep this nation moving on down the road to glory, its beacon of freedom lighting up all the dark places of the world until there is no darkness left."

Frances Harper took the opposite approach in "Duty to Dependent Races," a speech delivered in 1891 to the National Council of Women. There she roundly criticized America for its general failure to protect its citizens, its specific failure to enforce the rights guaranteed in its fundamental laws, and its citizenry's failure to live up to their professed Christianity. In regard to lynching and race violence, Harper declared that "a government which can protect and defend its citizens from wrong and outrage and does not is vicious, [while] a government which would do it and cannot is weak." "The strongest nation on earth," she warned, "cannot afford to deal unjustly towards its weakest and feeblest members." To America's belief in itself as a "Christian nation," Harper posed a simple challenge: "What I ask of American Christianity is not to show us more creeds, but more of Christ; not more rites and ceremonies, but more religion glowing with love and replete with life." Whether speaking of America's declarations of political or religious ideals, Harper asked for fewer professions of faith and more faith acts.

Most speakers, however, have combined their praise for America's ideals with their condemnation of its practices. Indeed, two of the most eloquent and best-known speeches were constructed around those twin themes: Frederick Douglass's 1852 Fourth of July speech and Martin Luther King, Jr.'s, 1963 "I Have a Dream." Douglass opened his speech with a long section in which he praised the "founding fathers" of American democracy: "They were statesmen, patriots and heroes," who "seized upon eternal principles [of justice, liberty, and humanity] and set a glorious example in their defence." Throughout his opening, however, Douglass foreshadowed the hypocrisy that marked his contemporaries' celebration of these principles. The founders "had not adopted the fashionable idea of this day, of the infallibility of government"; "their solid manhood stands out the more as we contrast it with these degenerate times." Douglass developed this charge of degeneracy in greater detail in the body of his speech. "What to the American slave, is your 4th of July?" Douglass asked. "To him," he answered, "your shouts of liberty and equality ... your prayers and hymns ... [are] mere bombast, fraud, deception, impiety, and hypocrisy—a thin veil to cover up crimes which would disgrace a nation of savages." By embracing the institution of slavery, "America is false to the past, false to the present, and solemnly binds herself to be false to the future."

King's speech generally reversed Douglass's arrangement, beginning with his criticism and ending with his call to idealism. "One hundred years after the promise of the Emancipation Proclamation," King said, "the Negro is still not free." In one of the speech's famous metaphors, King combined praise and blame: "The magnificent words of the Constitution and the Declaration of Independence" were a "promissory note," which "guaranteed the unalienable rights of life, liberty, and the pursuit of happiness." But, King continued, "it is obvious today that America has defaulted on this promissory note insofar as her citizens of color are concerned." After recounting African-Americans' "trials and tribulations," suffered at the hands of America's hypocrisy, King declared that "I still have a dream" and noted almost immediately that "it is a dream deeply rooted in the American dream." Even his anaphorical peroration—"let freedom ring"—was drawn from a traditional American anthem, "My Country,'Tis of Thee."

Douglass's and King's speeches, as well as those of many of the other speakers included in this volume, were and are clarion calls to the American conscience. At the close of the twentieth century, as for the period in which they were delivered, these speeches remind us of who we profess to be and of how short of that mark we still remain.

The third theme that emerges in the oratory is what has sometimes been called "black pride." While for many whites, and some blacks, black pride seems a phenomenon of the 1960s, it actually extends as far back as our oratorical records go. Said Maria Miller Stewart in a speech delivered on September 21, 1832:

> Take us generally as a people, we are neither lazy nor idle; and considering how little we have to excite or stimulate us, I am almost astonished that there are so many industrious and ambitious ones to be found ... Look at our young men, smart, active, and energetic, with souls filled with ambitious fire; if they look forward, alas! what are their prospects? They can be nothing but the humblest laborers, on account of their dark complexions.

Stewart's complaints were echoed in the oratory of all the abolitionist speakers of the day—such as Brown, Douglass, Garnet, Harper, and Whipper—but probably no one spoke the language of pride as forcefully as an illiterate black woman, born into slavery simply as Isabella, who turned to itinerant preaching and speaking when she was about forty-six years old. Sojourner Truth, for all her apparent "disadvantages" in life, refused to stand behind anyone—white or black, male or female—in matters of rights or respect. In the few speeches of hers still extant, Truth's self-respect permeates her arguments. "Ain't I a woman?" she asked, after recounting the labor and physical difficulties she had endured in her life: she had plowed, planted, reaped, been lashed, and borne children. It was with clearly evident irony that she asked, "Ain't I a woman?" when she knew full well that few whites—male or female—would have then accorded her "womanly" status of their own volition. But it was with pride that she related her accomplishments—"I could work as much and eat as much as a man, and bear the lash as well"—and the irony of her question illuminated the audience's ignorance of what was prideful, not hers. "Nobody has any business with a right that belongs to her," Truth postulated in her speech of May 10, 1867, to the American Equal Rights Association convention. She went on to summarize her argument and her sense of self succinctly, noting simply that "I can make use of my own right."

Abolitionist speakers were hardly alone in reminding their audiences, white as well as black, of African-Americans' worth to themselves and their country. Booker T. Washington, often assailed for his "accommodationist" stand, also preached black pride. In "There Is Still Much to Be Done," delivered in 1915 before the American Missionary Association, Washington ironically observed that "there is sometimes much talk about the inferiority of the Negro. In practice, however, the idea appears to be that he is a sort of superman. He is expected, with about one fifth of what whites receive for their education, to make as much progress as they are making." However, Washington noted with a flurry of statistics that despite this economic disadvantage, "there has been great progress in Negro education during the past fifty years," and he lauded the "transformation" of the race that had "occurred practically within a single generation." Du Bois, often juxtaposed with Washington as his ideological and rhetorical counterpart, also spoke of black pride. In Du Bois's case, however, his discourse usually took the form of a challenge. "Are we not men enough to protest?" he asked in his 1905 address defending the Niagara Movement, forming a question that was eerily reminiscent of Douglass's. He answered the question a year later in an address to the second annual convention of the Niagara Movement, in tones that could easily pass for those of orators of the 1960s: "We refuse to surrender the leadership of this race to cowards and trucklers. We are men; we will be treated as men."

Many other words could be quoted as well—Mary McLeod Bethune's "Last Will and Testament," for example, or Marian Wright Edelman's recollections of her parents' work among the poor of South Carolina. Appeals to black pride do not appear simply in the black nationalist movements of a Marcus Garvey or the religious sects of a Father Divine; they are notes that were sounded regularly and frequently throughout the oratory studied here.

Unquestionably, African-American oratory is worth studying—because of its significance, because of its eloquence, and because it helps tell the story of its people—which makes its virtual omission from the discipline's annals of the academy all the more egregious. Sadly, the reader will find that the tale told by the bibliographic survey that opened this introduction is often repeated in the bibliographic material at the end of each essay. The critical source materials are dominated by histories and essays from the popular press, not by sources drawn from the field of rhetoric. Speech texts are often hard to come by and are frequently found in varied and diverse sources rather than a single anthology or collection. When archival materials can be found, it is depressing in the extreme how frequently they are concentrated in one of two locations: the Schomburg Center for Research in Black Culture in the New York Public Library and the Moorland-Spingarn Research Center at the Howard University Library. Even secondary biographical materials were difficult to locate for some speakers.

There is thus an important difference between this volume and others like it. While most reference volumes of this sort would be summary in nature, surveying the latest and most general conclusions that the discipline has developed, this book must function more as a prologue. Even many of the better-known figures—such as Booker T. Washington, W. E. B. Du Bois, Marcus Garvey, Malcolm X, or Jesse Jackson—have had relatively few of their speeches actually studied, analyzed, and critiqued. While the authors of these essays have made every effort possible to develop an exhaustive (and accessible) bibliography of speeches, many speech texts and sources are undoubtedly yet to be found. The work begun by these authors has hardly been started, much less completed.

Because there is so much to be done in this area of study, it is with regret that so many speakers who deserve study have necessarily been omitted. Indeed, the orators who could or should grace these pages but do not could easily fill another volume equal in size to this one. But it is for reasons of space, as well as the availability of materials and authors, that hard decisions were (and had to be) made regarding which figures were included and which were not. Two aims undergirded those decisions, however. First, speakers were chosen to make the volume as representative as possible, so that, while each speaker is obviously unique in his or her own right, the collection of essays as a whole generally reflects the community's voice in American history. Second, because so little has been done in this area, the number of figures covered was restricted in order to make the essays as comprehensive and insightful as possible. The goal was to provide essays which in their critical analyses and their bibliographic materials, would be springboards for further study of the oratory.

It was, in fact, this desire to stimulate additional study of African-American oratory that motivated the writing and publication of the essays which appear here. Even if modesty did not prevent it, few if any of the authors would consider their work as "authoritative." The common hope, routinely expressed, was that this work would be a catalyst for research by students and scholars alike. Ironically, then, the success of this volume may well be measured by how quickly it becomes outdated. It is the fond hope of the editor and authors alike that this volume will aptly convey to the reader the vibrant oratory that it studies, that it will raise our appreciation as a community for the ideas and ideals these speakers brought to life through their words, and that it will quickly become antiquated, assigned to the category of "early critical works" in future bibliographies of African-American oratory.

BIBLIOGRAPHY

Asante, Molefi K. *The Afrocentric Idea*. Philadelphia: Temple UP, 1987.

Asante, Molefi K. *Afrocentricity*. Trenton: Africa World, 1988.

Asante, Molefi K. *Afrocentricity: The Theory of Social Change*. Buffalo: Amulefi, 1980.

Asante, Molefi K. (Arthur L. Smith). "Henry Highland Garnet: Black Revolutionary in Sheep's Vestments." *Communication Studies* 21 (1970): 93–98.

Asante, Molefi K. (Arthur L. Smith). *Language, Communication, and Rhetoric in Black America*. New York: Harper and Row, 1972.

Asante, Molefi K. (Arthur L. Smith). *Rhetoric of Black Revolution*. Boston: Allyn and Bacon, 1970.

Asante, Molefi K. (Arthur L. Smith). "Socio-Historical Perspectives of Black Oratory." *Quarterly Journal of Speech* 56 (1970): 264–269.

Asante, Molefi K. (Arthur L. Smith). "Some Characteristics of the Black Religious Audience." *Communication Monographs* 37 (1970): 207–210.

Asante, Molefi K. (Arthur L. Smith) and Stephen Robb, eds. *The Voice of Black Rhetoric: Selections*. Boston: Allyn and Bacon, 1971.

Boulware, Marcus H. *The Oratory of Negro Leaders, 1900–1968*. Westport, CT: Negro Universities Press, 1969.

Bowen, Harry W. "Does Non-violence Persuade?" *Communication Quarterly* 11 (1963): 10–11.

Bowen, Harry W. "The Future of Non-violence." *Communication Quarterly* 11 (1963): 3–4.

Bradley, Bert. "Negro Speakers in Congress, 1869–75." *Southern Communication Journal* 18 (1953): 216–225.

Brockriede, Wayne E. and Robert L. Scott. "Stokely Carmichael: Two Speeches on Black Power." *Communication Studies* 19 (1968): 3–13.

Brownlow, Paul C. "The Pulpit and Black America: 1865–1877." *Quarterly Journal of Speech* 58 (1972): 431–440.

Burgess, Parke G. "The Rhetoric of Black Power: A Moral Demand?" *Quarterly Journal of Speech* 54 (1968): 122–133.

Calloway-Thomas, Carolyn and John Louis Lucaites, eds. *Martin Luther King, Jr. and the Sermonic Power of Public Discourse.* 1993.

Campbell, Finley C. "Voices of Thunder, Voices of Rage: A Symbolic Analysis of a Selection from Malcolm X's Speech, 'Message to the Grassroots.' " *Communication Education* 19 (1970): 101–110.

Campbell, Karlyn Kohrs. "The Rhetoric of Radical Black Nationalism: A Case Study in Self-Conscious Criticism." *Communication Studies* 22 (1971): 151–190.

Campbell, Karlyn Kohrs. "Style and Content in Rhetoric of Early Afro-American Feminists." *Quarterly Journal of Speech* 72 (1986): 434–445.

Condit, Celeste M. "Democracy and Civil Rights: The Universalizing Influence of Public Argumentation." *Communication Monographs* 54 (1987): 1–18.

Condit, Celeste Michelle and John Louis Lucaites. *Crafting Equality: America's Anglo-African Word.* 1993.

Daniel, Jack L. "Black Rhetoric: The Power to Define Self in an Age of World Citizenship." *ACA Bulletin* 16 (1976): 39–42.

Dick, Robert C. "Negro Oratory in the Anti-Slavery Societies, 1830–1860." *Western Journal of Communication* 28 (1964): 5–14.

Dickens, Milton and Ruth E. Schwartz. "Oral Argument Before the Supreme Court: Marshall v. Davis in the School Segregation Cases." *Quarterly Journal of Speech* 57 (1971): 32–42.

Di Mare, Lesley A. "Functionalizing Conflict: Jesse Jackson's Rhetorical Strategy at the 1984 Democratic National Convention." *Western Journal of Communication* 51 (1987): 218–226.

Erickson, Keith V. "Black Messiah: The Father Divine Peace Mission Movement." *Quarterly Journal of Speech* 63 (1977): 428–438.

Foner, Philip S., ed. *The Black Panthers Speak.* Philadelphia: Lippincott, 1970.

Foner, Philip S., ed. *The Voice of Black America: Major Speeches by Negroes in the United States 1797–1971.* New York: Simon and Schuster, 1972.

Frye, Jerry K. and Franklin B. Krohn. "An Analysis of Barbara Jordan's 1976 Keynote Address." *Journal of Applied Communication Research* 6 (1977): 73–82.

Fulkerson, Gerald. "Exile as Emergence: Frederick Douglass in Great Britain, 1845–1847." *Quarterly Journal of Speech* 60 (1974): 69–82.

Fulkerson, Gerald. "Frederick Douglass and the Kansas-Nebraska Act: A Case Study in Agitational Versatility." *Communication Studies* 23 (1972): 261–269.

Fulkerson, Richard P. "The Public Letter as Rhetorical Form: Structure, Logic and Style in King's 'Letter from Birmingham Jail.' " *Quarterly Journal of Speech* 65 (1979): 121–136.

Golden, James L. and Richard D. Rieke. *The Rhetoric of Black Americans.* Columbus, OH: Merrill, 1971.

Gorden, William. "An Antiphonal Negro Sermon." *Communication Quarterly* 12 (1964): 17–19.

Hamilton, Charles V. *The Black Preacher in America*. New York: William Morrow, 1972.

Harris, Thomas E. and Patrick C. Kennicott. "Booker T. Washington: A Study of Conciliatory Rhetoric." *The Southern Communication Journal* 37 (1971): 47–59.

Heath, Robert L. "Alexander Crummell and the Strategy of Challenge by Adaptation." *Communication Studies* 26 (1975): 178–187.

Heath, Robert L. "Black Rhetoric: An Example of the Poverty of Values." *The Southern Communication Journal* 39 (1973): 145–160.

Heath, Robert L. "Dialectical Confrontation: A Strategy of Black Radicalism." *Communication Studies* 24 (1973): 168–177.

Hill, Roy L. *The Rhetoric of Racial Revolt*. Denver: Golden Bell, 1964.

Hope, Diana Schaich. "Redefinition of Self: A Comparison of the Rhetoric of the Women's Liberation and Black Liberation Movements." *Communication Quarterly* 23 (1975): 17–25.

Jabusch, David M. "The Rhetoric of Civil Rights." *Western Journal of Communication* 30 (1966): 176–184.

Jefferson, Pat. "The Magnificent Barbarian at Nashville." *The Southern Communication Journal* 33 (1967): 77–87.

Jefferson, Pat. " 'Stokely's Cool': Style." *Communication Quarterly* 16 (1968): 19–24.

Kennicott, Patrick C. "Black Persuaders in the Anti-Slavery Movement." *Communication Studies* 37 (1970): 15–24.

Kennicott, Patrick C. and Wayne E. Page. "H. Rap Brown: The Cambridge Incident." *Quarterly Journal of Speech* 57 (1971): 325–334.

King, Andrew A. "The Rhetorical Legacy of the Black Church." *Communication Studies* 22 (1971): 179–185.

Larson, Charles U. "The Trust Establishing Function of the Rhetoric of Black Power." *Communication Studies* 21 (1970): 52–56.

Logue, Cal. "Teaching Black Rhetoric." *Communication Education* 23 (1974): 115–120.

Lucaites, John Louis and Celeste Michelle Condit. "Reconstructing <Equality>: Culturetypal and Counter-cultural Rhetorics in the Martyred Black Vision." *Communication Monographs* 56 (1990): 5–24.

Mann, Kenneth Eugene. "Nineteenth Century Black Militant: Henry Highland Garnet's Address to the Slaves." *The Southern Communication Journal* 36 (1970): 11–21.

Martin, Donald R. and Vicky Gordon Martin. "Barbara Jordan's Symbolic Use of Language in the Keynote Address to the National Women's Conference." *The Southern Communication Journal* 49 (1984): 319–330.

McFarlin, Annjennete S. "Hallie Quinn Brown: Black Woman Elocutionist." *The Southern Communication Journal* 46 (1980): 72–82.

Mitchell, Henry H. *Black Preaching*. Philadelphia: Lippincott, 1970.

Newsom, Lionel and William Gorden. "A Stormy Rally in Atlanta." *Communication Quarterly* 11 (1963): 18–21.

Niles, Lyndrey A., ed. *African American Rhetoric: A Reader*. Dubuque, IA: Kendall/Hunt, 1995.

O'Neill, Daniel J., ed. *Speeches by Black Americans*. Encino, CA: Dickerson, 1971.

Phifer, Elizabeth Flory and Dencil R. Taylor. "Carmichael in Tallahassee." *The Southern Communication Journal* 33 (1967): 88–92.

Pipes, Williams Harrison. "Old Time Negro Preaching: An Interpretative Study." *Quarterly Journal of Speech* 31 (1945): 15–21.

Richardson, Larry S. "Stokely Carmichael: Jazz Artist." *Western Journal of Communication* 34 (1970): 212–218.

Scott, Robert L. "Justifying Violence—The Rhetoric of Militant Black Power." *Communication Studies* 19 (1968): 96–104.

Scott, Robert L. and Donald K. Smith. "The Rhetoric of Confrontation." *Quarterly Journal of Speech* 55 (1969): 1–8.

Simons, Herbert W. "Patterns of Persuasion in the Civil Rights Struggle." *Communication Quarterly* 15 (1967): 25–27.

Smith, Donald K. "Martin Luther King, Jr.: In the Beginning at Montgomery." *The Southern Communication Journal* 34 (1968): 8–17.

Smith, Donald K. "Social Protest . . . and The Oratory of Human Rights." *Communication Quarterly* 15 (1967): 2–8.

Snow, Malinda. "Martin Luther King's 'Letter from Birmingham Jail' as Pauline Epistle." *Quarterly Journal of Speech* 71 (1985): 318–334.

Stromer, Wayne F. "A Note on Brockriede and Scott on Carmichael." *Communication Studies* 20 (1969): 308–309.

Thompson, Wayne N. "Barbara Jordan's Keynote Address: Fulfilling Dual and Conflicting Purposes." *Communication Studies* 30 (1979): 272–277.

Thompson, Wayne N. "Barbara Jordan's Keynote Address: The Juxtaposition of Contradictory Values." *The Southern Communication Journal* 44 (1979): 223–232.

Thurber, John H. and John L. Petelle. "The Negro Pulpit and Civil Rights." *Communication Studies* 15 (1968): 273–278.

Wagner, Gerald A. "Sojourner Truth: God's Appointed Apostle of Reform." *Southern Communication Journal* 28 (1962): 123–130.

Walker, Robbie Jean, ed. *The Rhetoric of Struggle: Public Address by African American Women*. 1992.

Ward, James, ed. *African American Communications*. Dubuque, IA: Kendall/Hunt, 1993.

Ware, B. L. and Wil A. Linkugel. "The Rhetorical *Persona*: Marcus Garvey as Black Moses." *Communication Monographs* 49 (1982): 50–62.

Whitfield, George. "Frederick Douglass: Negro Abolitionist." *Communication Quarterly* 11 (1963): 6–8.

Woodson, Carter G., ed. *Negro Orators and Their Orations*. New York: Russell and Russell, 1925.

AFRICAN-AMERICAN
ORATORS

MARY McLEOD BETHUNE
(1875–1955), educator, college president

MELBOURNE S. CUMMINGS

Mary McLeod Bethune was a person of uncommon fortitude. She was born on July 10, 1875, in Mayesville, South Carolina, the fifteenth of seventeen children of Sam and Patsy McLeod, who were among the many slaves freed by the outbreak of the Civil War. In the tradition of most Southern blacks during that time, Mary and her family were dirt poor, but she was determined to get the bit of education offered by the Trinity Presbyterian Mission School located a few miles from her family home.

Because she was an excellent student who displayed uncommon leadership potential, Mary was sent on to attend high school at Scotia Seminary, from which she graduated in 1894. Prepared to do missionary work as well as teach, Bethune set out to do both. She was soon rebuffed on racial grounds when her application to go to Africa to do missionary work was rejected by the Presbyterian church. Mary McLeod returned to her native South Carolina, and while working as a teacher at the Presbyterian-run Kendall Institute in Sumter, South Carolina, she married Albertus Bethune. They were the parents of one son, Albert McLeod Bethune. Mary Bethune was known basically for her work for the advancement of black people, but her family life suffered as a result. She and her husband separated, and she became the primary caregiver for her son, whose greatest success in life, it appears, was to present his mother with a grandson whom she adopted and who, unlike his father, took advantage of the opportunity for education. He became a successful librarian and a mainstay at Bethune-Cookman College.

In 1904, Mary McLeod Bethune founded Bethune-Cookman as the Daytona Educational and Industrial Institute. Eventually, the school became one of the most famous normal and preparatory schools for African-American women in the South. Thanks to Bethune's vocal advocacy and successful fundraising, by

1925 Bethune-Cookman College had united with the Cookman Institute for boys, had become a college preparatory institution, and was cited as "the best secondary school for Negroes in Florida." Bethune, continuing to serve as its president, witnessed many of the same fiscal hardships that had closed many other schools, but she maintained for the public an inspiring, confident, and optimistic image as she went about her fundraising to keep the school open and accredited. For this, she won the National Association for the Advancement of Colored People's (NAACP) coveted Spingarn Award in 1935.

Soon after, Bethune took on a demanding government position in Washington, D.C., with the National Youth Administration, while continuing to serve as her institution's chief executive. She was able to keep the college functioning with high-powered solicitations from foundations, government agencies, and individual donors, while trusted colleagues kept the college running academically. Her work took its toll, however, and she began suffering from ill health. The school thrived, however, while continuing to reflect the vision of its founder. Bethune-Cookman cultivated better racial relations, emphasizing strong Christian values and practices. It championed vocational education in areas such as agriculture, secretarial work, cooking, and sewing, as well as in academics.

Bethune felt, however, that she could not simply help to improve the lives of the few students who enrolled in the school, but that she had to help the communities from which these students came. She thus made it the responsibility of the school's students to help to improve their communities, wherever they were. In her daily chapel meetings, Bethune emphasized the important connection between the self-sufficiency of their schools and the self-sufficiency of their communities. In Elizabeth Ihle's interview with Lucy Miller Mitchell, one of Mary McLeod Bethune's former students, Mitchell spoke of how each of them was taught that their education was an obligation "to help the less fortunate of our people." Mitchell quoted an oft-used expression of Bethune's from her speeches at chapel: "You are being trained to serve; go out into our community and be an example of what education training can mean to an individual. . . . Help your fellow man."

Helping fellow human beings was exactly what Mary McLeod Bethune did all her life. Even in ill health, she continued to help African-Americans develop to their fullest potential. Bethune-Cookman became a senior college in 1942, due in no small part to funding from her government agency and from the public and private donations she solicited.

Bethune retired from the presidency of the college in 1942, but continued her work with women. Bethune was a club woman, and she played a leadership role in many local, state, and national clubs for African-American women. One of her greatest accomplishments was the founding of the prestigious National Council of Negro Women (NCNW), an organization that, according to its newspaper, came into being for the purpose of "speaking with one voice and one mind for the highest good of the race." Because of her commitment to the betterment of women in all walks of life, her involvement in clubs was not unusual, nor was her strong association with influential white women's clubs. It was because of this interest and her belief that America's problems could be solved harmoniously if there was better interracial understanding that First Lady Eleanor Roosevelt became acquainted with her. Bethune was able to use her relationship with the Roosevelts to gain membership on the women's advisory council in 1945 for the organizing of the United Nations.

Mary McLeod Bethune was a leader of the first magnitude, securing jobs and positions of advantage for African-Americans with promise of advancement. She traveled throughout the United States, representing the president and fulfilling her childhood dream. After a long and distinguished career, Mary McLeod Bethune died in 1955 of a heart attack. She has long been considered the most influential African-American woman. Of late, however, she has taken her place along with Martin Luther King, Jr., Frederick Douglass, and W. E. B. Du Bois as one of the most important African-American persons in history.

MARY McLEOD BETHUNE: THE TEACHER ORATOR

Though Mary McLeod Bethune was not specifically known for her oratory, there were many organizations, causes, and institutions of which she was a part that owed their success to her support and to her speechmaking. In fact, she was probably one of the best-known black women speakers during her lifetime. Most of her speeches are not extant, for she gave most of them extemporaneously to her students at daily chapel. Of those that still exist, however, the themes of the messages are strikingly similar. All center around education, racial uplift, full freedom for black people, and interracial cooperation. Her messages are practical in nature; they concern what one might refer to as the mundane. In the *Christian Advocate*, Elmer Carter pointed out that usually the purpose for her many talks was utilitarian, that is, to secure contributions for her school, her students, and the work of the organizations of which she was a part.

Bethune's rhetorical style was straightforward, plain, direct, and unencumbered. Because her audiences often included people from all walks of life, she made a point of speaking in such a way that both the least and the most well-educated listener could understand what she had to say. She often spoke to racially mixed audiences, and on those occasions the subject of her remarks was direct and forceful enough that the black audience members could appreciate and feel the sense of dignity and forthrightness of her words. At the same time, white audience members could sense the fervor of her commitment and her belief in the causes she espoused, yet she could evoke a sense of compassion without making them feel as if they were under personal attack. She was a teacher by profession, and in everything she said, she had a way of broadening her listeners' horizons as she spoke.

In her speech "A Philosophy of Education for Negro Girls," Bethune began, as she often did, with a historical overview of the conditions that existed for black people after emancipation that had caused them to live in their present blighted, poverty-stricken situations. In this speech she contended that these conditions would prevail if communities continued to shun the education of the girls. Woman held the key to the development of the race, Bethune argued, but instead of educating her, she was given all the domestic chores to do and virtually forgotten, with very few exceptions. Bethune used these exceptions as examples of what African-American women could accomplish if they were given the chance. She quoted Phyllis Wheatley's poetry; she mentioned the accomplishments of African-American women such as Madam C. J. Walker, Charlotte Hawkins Brown, Nannie Helen Burroughs, and Mary Church Terrell; and she pointed to communities that had been greatly enhanced because they had decided to educate and train their young women.

Bethune believed that God had given her a vision and a mission, and wherever she went, she used her speaking opportunity to rally her audience to the cause of educating young women for the good of the community and the good of the country. Although her specific educational mission focused on her work with women, never did she advocate educating women over men. She wanted both groups to be educationally prepared for the changes in opportunities and status for African-Americans that were sure to come. Her concern was that, through education, men had been given a head start, and she wanted women to be given an equal opportunity to learn.

Educating the youth of both genders would require teachers, and some of Bethune's speeches could be classified as "recruitment" speeches for the teaching profession. Even in speeches with other purposes, the value Bethune placed on education was evident. For example, in a 1926 speech before the National Association of Colored Women, Bethune, as the organization's president, spoke of "representing a greater awakening of our people to the need and virtue of self help in education." She continued: "Education is the solid rock of progress throughout the universe. I want you to think of yourselves as salesmen of a most necessary commodity to the race . . . Education."

In a 1934 commencement speech entitled "The Educational Values of the College-Bred," delivered at both the Hampton Institute and Lincoln University, Bethune unequivocally pronounced the role of teachers in the development of the community: "The future of America is in the hands of [the teacher]. . . . I raise the recruiting trumpet for [the teacher]." As she addressed audiences of potential teachers, she often requested that they pledge along with her "(1) the vow of definite and specific preparation; (2) the vow of sympathetic attitude; (3) the vow of faith; (4) the vow of courage; (5) the vow of industry; and (6) the vow of idealism." Wherever she could find a teacher living up to that pledge, Bethune would extol her work. For example, in a 1928 address given to a large group in West Palm Beach, Florida, Bethune described the work of a "colored" teacher whose own schoolhouse, furniture, and home had been swept away in a recent hurricane, but who had courageously given "wonderful service" and "valuable help to her people."

Mary McLeod Bethune's efforts toward interracial cooperation were legendary. The singular idea behind her founding of the women's college was to prepare women to serve their communities and nation with the purpose of solving the race problems that plagued the United States. In "A Philosophy of Education for Negro Girls," she held that

> Negro girls must be taught to realize their responsibility ... to develop to the fullest extent the inner urges that make them distinctive and that will lead them to be worthy contributors to the life of the little worlds in which they will live. This in itself will do more to remove the walls of inter-racial prejudice and build up intra-racial confidence and pride than any of our educational tools and devices.

Interracial cooperation was the hallmark of her teaching, teaching that occurred everywhere and not simply in the classroom. In the speech marking the hurricane mentioned earlier, Bethune took the opportunity to point out that devastation knew no race, and that assistance had come from all areas of the state. Both black and white women laid wreaths of flowers upon tombs of the unknown dead as they comforted the bereaved, and the Red Cross assisted every victim, regardless of race. These were examples of interracial cooperation during times of crisis that were then overlooked in the daily events of life.

In a speech entitled "Interracial Comradeship," Bethune again noted that teachers would have to play an important role in preparing the world to live together interracially.

> The exact synonym for "missionary" is Negro teacher. The "Gospel" which she carries is that of successful living. Reading and Writing and 'Rithmetic are her main products, but just as many manufacturing companies do a larger business with their by-products than with the chief commodity, so the Negro teacher must, more often than not, do a large percentage of educating along other than purely academic lines.

As a member and leader in the women's organizations, her purpose was to foster good relations between white women's groups and her own. She fostered a good working relationship with the leaders of the white Palmetto Women's Club. This relationship was extremely beneficial to her when she undertook the mammoth job of organizing the NCNW, which was the counterpart to the white General Federation of Women's Clubs. With the founding of the NCNW, Bethune had put in place an organization whose specific aim was to foster intercultural, interracial, and international relationships among women of color.

Besides her undaunted fervor for the education of women and for interracial cooperation, Mary McLeod Bethune was relentless in speaking out against prejudice. In her 1926 "President's Address" to the National Association of Colored Women's (NACW) 15th Biennial Convention, Bethune urged her audience to take a strong, vocal stand against racial prejudice.

It is our duty to stand against segregation and discrimination. This country belongs
to Negroes as much as it does to those of any other race. Our forebears and those
of us living in this time have suffered, agonized, bled for this—our land. We have
helped to make it what it is today. Denied equal share in the fruits of our sacrificing
and suffering, we have protested. We shall protest, and protest again.

Along with Mary McLeod Bethune, women in the Negro women's movement
saw themselves as agents of change. As in this presidential address, Bethune's
speeches to this audience were typically replete with optimistic admonitions to
the women to fulfill their responsibility for service to the community.

America can be changed. It will be changed. Here and there we see bright signs;
stars of hope in the distant heavens. To these we must hitch our wagons and keep
driving. . . . We must uphold the status of the Christian religion, resist the impli-
cation that we constitute a separate part of this nation, invade every field of activity
in America, contribute in every way we can to fostering and perpetuating the
honored National ideals, battle shoulder to shoulder with the Nation's best citizenship for an untarnished service of a free people by public offices of unques-
tioned character and honor in county, city, state and National government.

In Mary McLeod Bethune's early speeches to white audiences, she primarily
delivered a message that admonished white Americans to reassess their thinking
on race relations. She urged whites to work in cooperation with African-
American groups for the common good of the country, both economically and
politically. The problem of race, she said, was primarily due to prejudice, and
the country suffered as a result of it. World War II, however, proved to be a
watershed in her speaking, as blacks returned from fighting for liberty and the
cause of America, but found themselves once again still treated as second-class
citizens. Agitation for full and equal rights accelerated in all quarters of the
black community, and Mary McLeod Bethune was one of the leaders in the
forefront.

In a speech entitled "What Are We Fighting For?" delivered in 1942 at the
Southern Conference for Human Welfare, Bethune castigated those whites who
valued "the ghosts of old prejudices more highly than they do the freedom of
our country." After detailing examples of America's capricious judgment in
regard to how it meted out its wealth, Bethune noted in conclusion that black
people were fighting for liberty and the pursuit of happiness the same as any
white American. "Negroes [were] true, loyal, courageous, unyielding Americans," she said, Americans who sought freedom from poverty, from ignorance,
from discrimination, from religious and racial hatreds, from mob violence
and brutality. She continued: "The fate of America is the fate of the Negro
people . . . we go up or down together." To Bethune as to many others, it was
blind of white America to believe that these black soldiers returning from fighting for America's freedom would consent to live in a system of bondage that
provided them with less than full equality: "These are not the days to consider

from whence one came, nor the traditional customs of social standing, caste and privilege. These are the days for a united front with a united purpose to fight for that victory which we must have, or regardless of caste, creed or position, we will all sink together.''

In 1945, Mary McLeod Bethune was selected to participate as an advisor to the U.S. delegation in the founding conference of the United Nations, and she used that platform to broaden her challenge from a national to an international one. In a speech delivered at the conference in June of that year, she challenged the ideology of the white man's civilization, especially as it related to the ill and inhumane treatment of blacks and other peoples of color. Her address was an exceptionally strong one, as she called for, on behalf of the "millions of little people," a major role in shaping the "new civilization." There could be seen in her statement a veiled threat of revolutionary action as she warned that "this must be a peoples' world if our civilization is to survive." Bethune had spoken boldly about the need for inclusion of African-Americans in solving the problems of the nation before, but her passion seemed to strengthen with age. She spoke of the "Negro in America" as a "subject people" with little more than "colonial status in a democracy." Bethune called for full and equal status regardless of race, color, or religion in all the nations of the world, because "world unity cannot become a reality as long as the old traditional order remains."

Speaking of the participation, hardships, and losses of World War II, Bethune laid the ground for understanding why "the little people" had such a stake in seeing change in the world. She talked about the passion for freedom and justice that could be found among African-Americans and their "counterparts elsewhere in the world." She implored the United States to take this call of unity, peace, and freedom to heart, for the soldiers, returning from having fought for America in foreign lands, would not stand for the same kind of "vicious and tyrannical treatment" that they had endured before leaving for the war. They would, she asserted, return with a new appreciation for freedom and equality and with a will to fight like never before. Her speech was a powerful one, but it ended on a conciliatory note that softened the sound of her virtual call to arms. Closing with a series of rhetorical questions, Bethune called for the production of a "blueprint for [African-Americans'] role in the future." She was, in effect, asking for a full and earnest participation in solving the problem of race relations in the United States by the power structure, by the government, and by the international community.

The educated elite, of which Mary McLeod Bethune was integrally a part, did not want to appear militant or incendiary; they wanted instead to approach the problem of race relations intellectually. Thus, in the earlier speech to the NACW, Bethune had spoken of her vision of a world gathering of "colored women, a conservative, peace-loving body carrying the torch of freedom, equal rights, human love—holding it high and brightening the world with rays of justice, tolerance and faithful service in God's name." She believed that it would be a woman's organization that would "overturn racial intolerance and artificial prejudice."

By the time of the United Nations conference, Bethune's tone had shifted toward militancy and her audience had expanded to become international, but her discourse had always been marked by her dedication to principle. Throughout her life and speeches, Mary McLeod Bethune was concerned with improving the condition of her race for the purpose of seeking full citizenship. She believed that this could best be accomplished through education, and so she worked tirelessly in her effort to educate the youth. She founded and nurtured a school that still enjoys a good reputation today. She labored in women's organizations, private agencies, and the government to further ensure that the benefit of an education would be available to all who desired it. Her relationship with the president of the United States, Franklin Roosevelt, and his wife Eleanor opened many doors that were philanthropically and politically beneficial. These contacts later proved helpful in building interracial cooperation and understanding.

Mary McLeod Bethune's best-known statement was published in 1955, the year of her death, in *Ebony*. Although it is an example of her written discourse, it aptly summarizes the philosophy exhibited throughout her oratory. Addressed to "Negroes everywhere," it was entitled "My Last Will and Testament," but was called, in Bethune's own words, her "legacy."

IF I HAVE A LEGACY TO LEAVE MY PEOPLE IT IS MY PHILOSOPHY OF LIVING AND SERVING. I PRAY NOW THAT MY PHILOSOPHY MAY BE HELPFUL TO THOSE WHO SHARE MY VISION OF A WORLD OF PEACE. HERE, THEN, IS MY LEGACY . . .

> I leave you love . . . I leave you hope . . .
> I leave you the challenge of developing confidence in one another.
> I leave you a thirst for education.
> I leave you a respect for the use of power.
> I leave you faith.
> I leave you racial dignity.
> I leave you a desire to live harmoniously with your fellowmen.
> I leave you, finally, a responsibility to our young people.

INFORMATION SOURCES

Research Collections and Collected Speeches

Few speeches of Mary McLeod Bethune are known to exist, despite the number of speeches she delivered over her lifetime. Those speeches that can be found, in pamphlet or manuscript form, are often without reference to the time or place at which the speech was delivered. Her papers can be found in several collections: the Moorland-Spingarn Research Center at Howard University, Washington, D.C.; the Bethune Foundation and Bethune-Cookman College Archives at Bethune-Cookman College, Daytona, Florida;

and the National Council of Negro Women Papers at the National Archives for Black Women's History in Washington, D.C.

Bethune, Mary McLeod. "My Last Will and Testament." *Ebony*, August 1955:105–110. [*MSRC*] Moorland-Spingarn Research Center, Howard University, Washington DC.

Selected Biographies

Bennett, Lerone, Jr. "The 50 Most Important Figures in Black History." *Ebony*, February 1989:176–178+.
Carter, Elmer. "A Modern Matriarch." *Christian Advocate*, 4 Feb. 1937: np.
Ihle, Elizabeth L. *Black Women's Oral History Project.* (audiotape series). Schlesinger Library, Radcliffe College, Cambridge, MA, 1986.
Leffall, Dolores C., and Janet L. Sims. "Mary McLeod Bethune—The Educator; Also Including a Selected Annotated Bibliography." *Journal of Negro Education* 45 (1976): 342–359.
McCluskey, Audrey Thomas. *We Specialize in the Wholly Impossible: African American Women School Founders and Their Mission.* Bloomington: Indiana UP, 1989.

CHRONOLOGY OF MAJOR SPEECHES

[See "Research Collections and Collected Speeches for source codes.]

"Interracial Comradeship." N.p., n.d. MSRC.
"A Philosophy of Education for Negro Girls." N.p., n.d. MSRC.
"President's Address to the 15th Biennial Convention of the National Association of Colored Women." N.p., 1926. MSRC.
"In the Midst of the Storm." West Palm Beach, FL, 1928. MSRC.
"The Educational Values of the College-Bred" (commencement speech delivered at Hampton Institute and Lincoln University). Hampton, VA, and Oxford, PA, 1934. MSRC.
"Interracial Cooperation in Florida." N.p., 1934. MSRC.
"A Century of Progress of Negro Women." N.p., 1935. MSRC.
"Speech at the Dedication of the Center for Negro Youth." Baltimore, MD, September 1936. Files of the Division of Negro Affairs, National Youth Administration Archives, Washington, DC.
"Clarifying Our Vision with the Facts" (address to the 22nd Annual Meeting of the Association for the Study of Negro Life and History). N.p., 1937. *Journal of Negro History* 23 (January, 1938): 10–15.
"What Are We Fighting For?" (speech delivered at the Southern Conference for Human Welfare). N.p., 1942. MSRC.
"Statement of Mrs. Mary McLeod Bethune" (speech before the United Nations Founding Conference). New York, NY, June 1945. MSRC.
"The Negro in Retrospect and Prospect" (address to the 34th Annual Meeting of the Association for the Study of Negro Life and History). N.p., 1949. *Journal of Negro History* 35 (January, 1950): 9–19.

WILLIAM WELLS BROWN
(c.1814–1884) abolitionist, author

ROBERT L. HEATH

William Wells Brown (c.1814–November 6, 1884) was a noted abolitionist speaker and man of letters. In 1847, he published a narrative of his life to demonstrate the horrors of slave life, especially the cruelty of the slave trade down the Mississippi. Along with others who described their lives in slavery and escape from it, he argued by example that people could arise from the degrading harshness of slavery to achieve intellectual accomplishment. In 1858, he dramatized his escape in a play entitled ''The Escape; or, A Leap to Freedom.'' The first African-American novelist, author of *Clotel; or, The President's Daughter* (1853), Brown committed his life to freedom, equality, and uplift. Like others in the antislavery movement, he captured the attention of thousands of listeners and readers in the United States and abroad by narrating his experiences with slavery.

Born near Lexington, Kentucky, Brown was one of seven children of Elizabeth, a slave, daughter of Simon Lee, one of many slaves who fought in the American War for Independence. As described in Brown's autobiography, Brown's father was George W. Higgins, ''a white man, a relative of my master, and connected with some of the first families in Kentucky.'' While Brown was a child, his owner, Dr. John Young, moved his chattel to St. Charles on the Missouri River, where young Brown became a house servant. Despite this preferred treatment, he recalled hearing ''every crack of the whip, and every groan and cry of my poor mother'' as she was beaten for being tardy to work in the field. His family was at the mercy of a cruel overseer, who could subdue even the most defiant slave.

Such cruelty did not end when in 1827 his owner moved to a 3,000-acre farm near St. Louis and hired out Brown to work in the city. Twelve years old, Brown was fortunate to be hired to Elijah P. Lovejoy, who in 1833 began publishing the *St. Louis Times*, in which he opposed slavery. In that office, Brown began to read and write. Later, Brown was hired to a steamboat captain. Seeing people going freely about their business created a lust to be free, to run to Canada, a dream slowed by his reluctance to leave his family in St. Louis. During this time, his owner, Dr. Young, struggled financially and was forced to sell Brown's mother and several of his siblings to different owners in St. Louis. The worst years of his hire occurred when he worked for a man engaged in the slave trade; Brown was responsible for seeing that the slaves in transit did not escape, drown, or otherwise render themselves useless as chattel. Cruelties of the trade and other atrocities he witnessed in his travels educated him with stories that he later used in his antislavery speeches.

In January 1834, he finally escaped and had the good fortune to come into the protection of a Quaker, Wells Brown, who assisted his passage into Canada, where he entered the antislavery movement, motivated particularly by his experience with the slave trade. He honored this man in his *Narrative* as "his earliest benefactor": "Even a name by which to be known among men, slavery had denied me. You bestowed upon me your own. Base indeed should I be, if I ever forget what I owe to you, or do anything to disgrace that honored name!"

WILLIAM WELLS BROWN AS A VOICE FOR ABOLITION AND UPLIFT

Through various influences, Brown began his involvement with the abolitionist movement in 1836 when he moved to Buffalo, New York, where he and his wife Elizabeth attended meetings and provided comfort for antislavery speakers. By 1843, Brown was engaged in the movement as a full-time agent for the Western New York Anti-Slavery Society. As an agent, Brown organized and publicized meetings, served on boards of directors, delivered speeches, and provided hospitality and comfort for agents who traveled through towns where he lived. His talent earned him an invitation to speak at the American Anti-Slavery Society annual meeting in New York City in 1844. The next five years were devoted to lecturing, writing, and educating himself without benefit of school. He relocated his operations in May 1847 to be part of the Massachusetts branch of the society. Headquartered in Boston, he published his *Narrative* and joined ranks with Frederick Douglass, James W. C. Pennington, Jermin W. Loguen, James McCune Smith, Robert Purvis, Charles Lenox Remond, Henry Highland Garnet, and Henry Bibb. Often reading from narratives of their lives, these men frequently spoke from platforms decorated with panoramas that portrayed scenes of slavery designed to heighten the effect.

As did other African-Americans in the antislavery crusade, Brown traveled his arranged circuit despite discrimination, harassment, and dangers of violence and capture. Slights and overt discrimination also occurred within the Anti-Slavery Society even though it was one of the greatest grass-roots movements in the history of this country. Thousands of people earned money to support the travels of speakers and fund abolitionist publications. A network of families provided modest comfort and security to agents of the society as they traveled on their lecture tours. Brown's progress in the society was steady, and by 1849 he was mentoring other escaped slaves, such as William and Ellen Craft, as they began their service in the society. In the mid-1850s, he experienced the joy of having one of his daughters, Josephine, join him on the lecture circuit.

About his efforts as an agent for the Massachusetts Anti-Slavery Society, the *Liberator* of January 21, 1848, reported that as a speaker he gained "general respect and approbation." Much of what these agents learned about speaking was the result of their intuition and astute observation of tactics that worked for others. Practice was on-the-job training with skills honed in the midst of hecklers. Demonstrating promise in his early years, Brown matured into a polished speaker, especially during his tour of England and Europe. "None could fail to be impressed with the eloquence, wit and pathos with which friend Brown addressed us," wrote an admirer from Peacham, Vermont, to William Lloyd Garrison, "and his dignified, gentlemanly deportment won all hearts."

Throughout this time, Brown was in danger of being captured because he had not gained his freedom, at least to the monetary satisfaction of the owner he had left behind. This risk increased when the Fugitive Slave Law was passed in 1850, as slave hunters had added incentives and authority to patrol states frequented by runaways in search of prey for whose return a bounty awaited. Also, the law formally required all citizens, in the North and the South, to engage in the practice of catching runaway slaves. Speakers on the antislavery circuit were obvious targets because they told stories of their escape and were hated by those who supported slavery.

As many abolitionists did, Brown spent time in England and Europe working to gain support for emancipation of slaves in all countries and to strengthen commitment to the effort in the United States. He traveled to Paris in 1849 for the International Peace Congress as an elected delegate of the American Peace Society. There he met and became friends with Richard Cobden, a member of the British House of Commons and delegate to the congress, and the prominent writer, Victor Hugo, president of the congress. During the five years Brown was abroad, he wrote and traveled extensively, giving as many as one thousand public addresses, and lectured before twenty-three mechanics' and literary institutions.

Shortly before his return to the United States in 1854 after his freedom had been purchased by British philanthropists, Brown spoke at the convention celebrating the emancipation of slaves in the British West Indies, held in the Town Hall at Manchester, England. Samuel Ward and William Lloyd Garrison also participated in the ceremony. The meeting, sponsored by the North of England Anti-Slavery and India Reform League, gave Wells one final occasion to inform the people of England about the atrocities and violations of moral principle that were associated with slavery in the United States. In his introduction, he demonstrated disarming humility by suggesting that others could more adequately speak on this occasion because they were educated and eloquent. In contrast, he stood before the audience, as he said, "without ever having had a day's schooling." Referring to himself as a "piece of property," he acknowledged that he was "a slave according to the laws of the United States." Reporting with delight that conversations were leading to the purchase of his freedom, he noted that until that transaction was complete, "there is not a single foot of soil over which the stars and stripes wave upon which I could stand and be protected by law." Said Brown, "I am liable to be seized at any moment, and conveyed in chains to the Southern States, there handed over to a man who claims me as his property, and to be worked up as he may think fit."

A master of the description of atrocity, he took this celebratory occasion to describe the peril of African-Americans: "By the fugitive slave law, every colored man in that country is liable to be arrested and carried off to the far South, and made a slave of, no matter whether born in New York, Massachusetts, Vermont, or any free State." To prove his point, Brown told of an African-American in Illinois who had been claimed as a fugitive slave, despite the fact that he was free and had himself acquired property. Forced to defend his freedom, in court this man was financially ruined. Brown described another atrocity involving slave hunting:

> Within the last year, two villains from a Southern State arrived in a certain town of Pennsylvania, and attempted to seize a colored man, who was employed there as a waiter in one of the inns. They approached him in a clandestine manner, and threw their chains upon his limbs, but the man, whom they would have made a slave, escaped from his pursuers; he ran out of the house, he ran to the nearest stream, and plunged into it, and there stood immersed up to his neck in the running waters. The slave-hunters came up, and many people gathered around, sympathizing with the hunted fugitive. He exclaimed to his persecutors, "If any of you come near me here, I will drown him in this water that flows about me." The slave-hunters answered him, "If you don't come out of the river, and surrender, we will shoot you where you are." And then, suddenly, to the horror and astonishment of the bystanders, one of the slave-hunters raised his gun or pistol, aimed it at the fugitive, and fired at him. We are told how the water then ran red with the blood of the slave; and how a crowd of four or five hundred people, who stood by and saw this thing done, did nothing more than cry "Shame" upon those who had done it, because it was the law.

Because the Fugitive Slave Law forced all citizens to support the apprehension and return of fugitives, it obliterated all distinctions between slave and nonslave states. "There are none of them free," argued Brown, "because that cannot be a free State which cannot protect the freedom of its inhabitants; and there is no State in this Union now which can give liberty, or even secure his liberty, to the colored man." Expert in the use of narrative, Brown described events clearly, with controlled hyperbole.

On occasions such as this, the firsthand experience of former slaves was a powerful part of antislavery oratory and, for that reason, drew larger antislavery crowds than was possible for white or free African-American speakers. Based on his experiences, Brown could attest, as he said, that the description presented in *Uncle Tom's Cabin* was a true account of the lives of three to four million of "God's children." He reported to this audience in England that "no language which we can use can exaggerate the workings or the evils of the system of slavery as it is carried on in that country." He continued:

> I cannot exaggerate, sir, the effect of this Fugitive Slave Law, and, indeed of everything else that is connected with slavery in the United States. If you had been, as I have been, for twenty years of your life in the Southern States of America, and had seen there, as I have seen, the workings of slavery, the trading in human beings, the buying and selling of them, the whipping and abusing of them, as I have seen all that carried on there,—and if you had seen the dear ones torn from you, and taken to be sold at the auction-block, and handed over to the highest bidder, as I have seen my dear ones taken, never to see them again,—if you had seen all this, you could not think anything, in the statements made at this Conference, or in the publications you may have read, was at all exaggerated.

He damned the inconsistency between the principles in the Declaration of Independence and those reflected in the laws passed to protect persons who owned other people: "The one declaring that all men are created equal, and endowed by their Creator with certain inalienable rights, among which are life, liberty, and the pursuit of happiness, and the other is the history of the encroachment of slavery upon liberty, or legislation in favor of slavery in that country against the cause of freedom." He used historical fact to demonstrate that from the time the principal documents of government were discussed as the rationale for colonial independence through their creation as the basic documents of government, one line of analysis had prevailed: these documents espoused legal and moral rationale for owning slaves. He used the Fugitive Slave Law to demonstrate how offensive American law was to principles of personal and national freedom. He blasted the institution that separated family members in the name of profit: "100,000 slaves are annually taken from the slave-raising States, to supply the Southern markets." He implored listeners to "maintain anti-slavery principles" and to not "give their influence to the side of the oppressor, instead of the oppressed. . . . We do not ask you to take up arms; we do not ask you to do any act, or utter any language, unbecoming Christians; but we ask you to learn the facts and the truth of this matter, and honestly to speak out upon it." Such appeals to identification were intended to reinforce and dedicate people's efforts to end slavery everywhere as it had been destroyed in the West Indies, the basis of the celebration that brought this audience together.

Announcing his return from abroad, the *Liberator* noted that "a public meeting of the friends of emancipation" was scheduled for October 13, 1854, in Tremont Temple to "welcome WILLIAM WELLS BROWN on his return after an absence of five years in Europe—no longer a fugitive slave, but ransomed from American chattelhood by British Philanthropy. For admission of 10 cents, people could hear Brown, along with Wendell Phillips, Wm. Lloyd Garrison, Charles Lenox Remond, and others, on this occasion.'' From this day until the end of slavery, Brown served the American Anti-Slavery Society and various state associations.

To destroy slavery required a commitment to end racism, a thesis Brown voiced in West Chester, Pennsylvania, on October 23, 1854. Such statements posed a substantial rhetorical challenge for African-American antislavery speakers, who risked offending persons who supported antislavery but opposed racial equality. Such arguments could also polarize the fence sitters. The threat of equal and free association of the races was a prospect that frightened many who did not want changes in social and economic mores. Mindful of such quandaries, Brown personalized his arguments: ''Place your wife, daughter or child in their position, to be struck off to the highest bidder, if you would realize their wrongs and sufferings.'' He asked the audience to reflect on the emotions of ''the slave mother who sees her child placed in the market and knows that that child is sold by its father.'' He indicated that he could recount many stories of his own experiences and of other slaves as means for moving the audience, but he insisted that the time for those stories had passed. Now was the time for action.

No longer did the attention of audiences need to be solely directed to the Southern states; many inequities were occurring in Northern states as well: ''Look at the colored people of the free States, thrown out of your schools, your churches and your social circles, deprived of their political rights and debarred from those avenues of employment that are necessary to a proper maintenance of themselves and their families.'' He directed the audience's attention to cases of discrimination in the use of public transportation: ''Foreigners, mere adventurers, perhaps, in this country, are treated as equals, while I, an American born, whose grandfather fought in the revolution, am not permitted to ride in one of your fourth-rate omnibuses.'' Foreigners could earn the right to vote for president of the United States by merely being citizens for five years, whereas others spent a lifetime here without the franchise. Brown described the discrimination he suffered in the United States, but not in England. For instance, he noted that his daughters were denied admission to schools here. Thus he challenged audiences to consider the hypocrisy of laws and morality: ''When you talk about equality and liberty, the land of the free and the home of the brave, the asylum of the oppressed, the cradle of liberty! You have the cradle, but you have rocked the child to death.'' He continued, ''You have allowed them to enslave the black man, to extend the institutions and to make the whole North a hunting ground for their slaves, until the people of the free States can endure it no longer, and the North is now fairly pitted against the South.''

Abolitionists' criticism of church support for slavery also polarized audiences and alienated potential allies. In a speech on April 25, 1855, at the Cincinnati Anti-Slavery Convention, Brown recounted the kindness of a minister and his wife and how it momentarily led him to think about lessening his criticism of the way the church rationalized slavery. Seeing a child of that family, however, he recalled his own family torn apart by slavery and again resolved to criticize all those who did not seek an immediate end to slavery—including churches.

Addressing the 23rd Annual Meeting of the Massachusetts Anti-Slavery Society in Boston, January 24–25, 1856, Brown noted the importance of continued efforts to create a public opinion that despised the institution of slavery and condemned all who supported it by act or deed. His purpose on this occasion was to refute arguments presented on the previous night by Robert Toombs of Georgia regarding the Southern states' views of slavery and the rights of government. Brown voiced disappointment that the audience in Massachusetts did not greet Toombs with silence or hisses, but indeed applauded him. Brown lamented, "I felt last night the want of that public opinion in Massachusetts which shall sustain anti-slavery, and condemn slavery in every form. The remarks of the speaker in favor of slavery, although they were not received with that enthusiasm they would have been five or ten years ago, were yet listened to with manifest respect."

Brown reported that Toombs's aim was "to prove that slavery was compatible with Republicanism, with the interest of America, and with the interest of the African; and during his discourse, he [Toombs] said that it was the duty of the Caucasian to look after and rule the African, and the God of justice would protect the Southern people in so doing." This theme could be articulated because people believed that African-Americans were poor and degraded, a claim that Brown challenged by pointing to the accomplishments of persons of his race. The distinction between the opinions held by those who believed as Toombs did as opposed to what Brown advocated must be held in sharp contrast. Making that point, Brown challenged the audience, "Now, it seems to me that when we shall go to work and labor as I think we can, as I think we ought, and as I hope we shall, to create that public opinion that shall do the cause of liberty and justice, shall prepare the people of Massachusetts to treat the slaveholder who dares come here to lecture as he ought to be treated, and as anyone who goes into any community for the purpose of vindicating an atrocity equal to that of enslaving men ought to be treated." He also characterized Toombs as a slaveholder from a slave-consuming state who told the audience that a clergyman of Boston had encouraged him in his efforts. By seizing this occasion to challenge the audience's values, Brown employed tactics of polarization. He sought to increase the tension produced by the presence of slavery, the audience's doctrines of freedom and equality, and their hypocritical approval of those who defended the institution. This strain laid the foundation for mobilizing opposition against a Union that supported slavery.

Brown assaulted the Southern mores and manners that resulted from slavery when he spoke on May 8, 1856, at the City Assembly Rooms, New York City. His theme was "man cannot inflict upon his fellowman a greater crime than to enslave him, for by so doing he not only injures his fellowman, but himself."

Evidence for this thesis included description of how planters sent their children to Northern schools because the slaveholders' efforts to deny slaves an education necessarily stifled the education of whites. Once the young Southerners went north to school, Brown argued, their degraded spirits weakened those of their Northern counterparts. Southerners were encouraged to strike and degrade slaves, a custom that led them to be brutal to others as well. Discrimination related to slavery reinforced separation of the races in the North. Brown challenged slavery's apologists by recounting tales of his experiences with discrimination in public transportation and eating establishments. He told amusing stories to ridicule the immorality of discrimination such as the time when he kept eating pies even though a waitress kept insisting that he could not be accommodated, to which he replied after eating his fill that he had been accommodated quite well. He described how a white man who had grown wealthy by doing business with an African-American man had invited his friend to church. They sat together in the white man's pew, which unnerved the minister and congregation. One member of the congregation voiced hostility to the presence of the African-American until he learned that the visitor was a millionaire, at which point he sought an introduction. Brown used anecdotes such as these in brilliantly making sharp points in disarming ways.

On August 1, 1860, Brown met with others in Framingham, Massachusetts, for the traditional celebration of the abolition of slavery in the West Indies. This occasion was typically used to praise persons whose untiring efforts had resulted in freedom of slaves. Brown noted that resistance to abolition was not based on moral or social reasons alone, but resulted from the thousands, the millions of dollars that were invested in the trade, which in turn supported cotton, sugar, and rice trade. Of those who toiled for the freedom of others, he said: "Those brave and generous hearts were impelled by pure and philanthropic motives, and onward they went, until their truthful denunciation and fiery zeal melted the chains from the limbs of slaves." He noted that the doctrine of inferiority was used as a rationale for keeping others in bonds. To destroy this rationale, Brown noted how quickly former slaves became part of Jamaica's government after abolition—evidence of their ability to rise. He described, in what may have been autobiographical reflection, the feeling of emancipation: "The first moment he touches the sacred soil of Britain, . . . his soul walks abroad in her own majesty; his body swells beyond the measure of his chains, that burst from around him, and he stands redeemed, regenerated and disenthralled, by the irresistible Genius of Universal Emancipation." Brown continued, "The love of liberty cannot be extinguished by municipal laws or tyrannical mandates." "This love of liberty, fellow-citizens, is universal, and the African possesses his share equally with the Anglo-Saxon. But the American people consider it a crime in the black man to aspire to be free, and upon terms of equality with the whites, and the white American thinks it his duty to strike at the colored man wherever he sees him."

The 1860s brought the war that abolitionists hoped would end slavery, giving voice to the slogan of the antislavery movement: No Union with slavery. The war moved at a frustratingly slow pace for these abolitionists, however. For a variety of reasons, Brown, along with Frederick Douglass, John Mercer Langston, and Charles Lenox Remond, advocated the use of African-American troops. Having gained that end, he joined his voice and pen with others who believed that men who risked their lives in equal danger in behalf of the Union effort should enjoy equal treatment in the ranks. Again turning to examples as rhetorical tools, Brown gave accounts of African-Americans' commitment to die for freedom, thus reasoning that they should be treated as equals. Brown challenged Lincoln's conduct of the war and his unwillingness to extend equal treatment to African-American soldiers. Brown stressed that slavery was the issue of the war and that, therefore, those African-American soldiers who were committed to help gain freedom for their kind should be extended proper military support, responsibility, and treatment.

During the war years, one issue consistently haunted the abolition cause. If the war effort began to cost too much in material and human outlay, support for it could diminish. In a lecture summarized in the *Liberator*, May 30, 1862, Brown addressed that concern. He pointed out how some slaves had acquired enough money to buy their freedom and that of other members of their families. Such free African-Americans in Southern states had prospered despite ''all the odious and unjust laws operating against them.'' They had achieved affluence and respectability. He alluded to a paradox of a former president of the United States owing at his death $12,000 to a free African-American. Reported the *Liberator*, ''From all the above facts, and many more that might be mentioned, Mr. Brown argued that the slaves, when secured their inalienable right to liberty and the pursuit of happiness, would show to the world their ability to take care of themselves.'' Optimistic about the favorable outcome of abolition, Brown knew that part of the realization of that dream was ''that this nation should take its heel from their necks, repeal all unjust and unequal laws, and leave them to find their equality under the laws which govern the Anglo Saxon race.''

On the theme of freedom after slavery, in a speech reported in the *Liberator* of May 16, 1862, Brown documented the virtues of slaves that prepared them for independence. He pointed out that they had learned trade skills and were accustomed to being hired out to practice their craft. Such expertise would readily transfer into self-employment after abolition. He delighted in providing statistics of the success of freed blacks who, in the thousands, had prospered ''in spite of the public opinion and laws of the South, in spite of prejudice, and everything. They have acquired a large amount of prosperity; and it is this industry, this sobriety, this intelligence, and this wealth of the free colored people of the South, that has created so much prejudice.''

However, another fear expressed by Northerners was that former slaves would compete successfully in the labor market by settling for lower wages. In response to such fears, the Tammany Hall Young Men's Democratic Committee passed a resolution that former slaves should be colonized to prevent them from entering the labor market in the United States. Such acts, Brown argued, resulted from fear planted in the minds of Northern laborers. If working people of the North could be persuaded to fear the entry of former slaves into the labor market, their resolve for the Union cause could be weakened. The evidence Brown offered to refute that argument was to note the tendency of free African-Americans to remain in the South. African-Americans' only incentive for migration was the desire to escape slavery; if there were no slavery, Brown noted, they could live in the South, as was their preference.

Brown was confronted, however, with evidence that contrabands—slaves freed by military intervention—were moving north. To resist this movement, states such as Ohio, Pennsylvania, and Illinois began passing laws to prohibit their settling in communities. Brown asked, what rationale do the freed slaves have to leave the South under these circumstances? He answered, to be as far from the threat of slavery as possible. The solution to the migration was to ensure the former slaves' freedom everywhere, which would remove their incentive to leave. What of the slave after freedom? Said Brown, "He is the bone and sinew of the South; he is the producer, while the master is nothing but a consumer, and a very poor consumer at that." A fourth issue raised by the war was the ability of the races to live together in equality and harmony. As he often did, Brown used the experience of the races in the West Indies as an analogy for the United States: "The blacks and the whites live together in Jamaica; they are all prosperous, and the island is in a better condition than it ever was before the act of emancipation was passed."

Brown knew how crucial public support would be to oppose enactment of Jim Crow laws to replace chattel slavery with other means for economic suppression. Arguments presented during the Civil War were a prelude to those that would resound after the war in condemnation of oppression and discrimination. Unwilling to go too far in alienating needed white support for his people, Brown argued that freedom was the immediate issue, not equality. "Why, every man must make equality for himself," he said. "No society, no government can make this equality. I do not expect the slave of the South to jump into equality; all I claim for him is, that he may be allowed to jump into liberty, and let him make equality for himself."

Brown turned white prejudice on its head, however, saying, "I have got some white neighbors around me; they are not very intellectual; they don't associate with my family; but whenever they shall improve themselves, and bring themselves up by their own intellectual and moral worth, I shall not object to their coming into my society." Using his own experience as an example of what African-Americans could achieve, he recalled that he wanted nothing as he fled from slavery except opportunity without restraint. As evidence of African-Americans' resolve to be worthy citizens, he pointed to the speed with which they volunteered for military service. Contrabands supplied intelligence of the conditions of the Southern states and served as guides for military operations in their neighborhoods. Because of this faithfulness to their own people and help for the nation, these humble people deserved to be paid by receiving liberty. The North, Brown challenged his audiences to realize, had conspired to assist the South in its chattel tyranny by not destroying the Fugitive Slave Law. Now the North should at least support the efforts of the former slaves, not shun them out of fear by calling for colonization. The question, Brown argued, was not what should be done with former slaves, but with former slaveholders—a question that Reconstruction answered to the continued detriment of those who had suffered under slavery. Through arguments such as these, Brown supported the war effort and laid the rhetorical groundwork for opposing the racism of Reconstruction. Believing that the future was uncertain and hostile for African-Americans, he used July 4, 1865, to criticize the federal government for "having broken faith with the black man" and leaving him to the mercy of the South.

After the Civil War, his perceptive criticism focused on new issues, such as temperance and discrimination, including suffrage for African-American males—an issue of special importance in the South, where they were a significant portion of the population. His ideas were expressed in plays and historical studies as well as in speeches at occasions such as the anniversary of the Emancipation Proclamation and on tours in the United States and once more to England. In 1863, he published *The Black Man, His Antecedents, His Genius, and His Achievements*, followed by *The Negro in the American Rebellion: His Heroism and His Fidelity* (1867), a pioneering study of African-American military history. These studies lauded the dedication of African-Americans who were offered as exemplars, themes extended in *The Rising Son; or, The Antecedents and Advancements of the Colored Race* (1874) and *My Southern Home; or, The South and Its People* (1880), a response to apologists of slavery. These books are part of a rich legacy by a prominent Boston citizen whose pioneering accomplishments were praised in several local newspapers after his death in November 1884.

INFORMATION SOURCES

Research Collections and Collected Speeches

Brown, William Wells. *Narrative of William W. Brown, a Fugitive Slave*. Boston: Anti-Slavery Office, 1847.
Ellison, Curtis W. and E. W. Metcalf, Jr. *William Wells Brown and Martin R. Delany: A Reference Guide*. Boston: G. K. Hall, 1978.
[*BAP*] Ripley, C. Peter, ed. *The Black Abolitionist Papers. Vol. 4, The United States, 1847–1858*. Chapel Hill: U of North Carolina P, 1991.

Selected Biographies

Farrison, William Edward. *William Wells Brown: Author and Reformer*. Chicago: U of Chicago P, 1969.
Quarles, Benjamin. *Black Abolitionists*. London: Oxford UP, 1969.

CHRONOLOGY OF MAJOR SPEECHES

[See "Research Collections and Collected Speeches" for source code.]

"Speech Celebrating Emancipation of Slaves in British West Indies." Manchester, England, August 1, 1854. *Liberator*, September 1, 1854, 138.

"Speech at the Horticultural Hall." West Chester, PA, October 23, 1854. *BAP*, 245–251.

"Speech before the Cincinnati Anti-Slavery Convention." Cincinnati, OH, April 25, 1855. *Anti-Slavery Bugle*, May 5, 1855, 1–2.

"Speech at the 23rd Annual Massachusetts Anti-Slavery Meeting." Williams Hall, Boston, MA, January 24–25, 1856. *Liberator*, February 8, 1856, 22.

"Speech to the New York Anti-Slavery Society." City Assembly Rooms, New York, NY, May 8, 1856. *BAP*, 339–344.

"Speech Celebrating the First of August." Framingham, MA, August 1, 1860. *Liberator*, August 17, 1860, 130.

"Speech Addressing What Shall Be Done with the Slave If Liberated." City Assembly Rooms, New York, NY, May 2, 1862. *Liberator*, May 16, 1862, 77.

"Fourth of July Address to the Massachusetts Anti-Slavery Society." Framingham, MA, July 4, 1865. *Liberator*, July 14, 1865, 112; *National Anti-Slavery Standard*, July 15, 1865, 2.

SHIRLEY ANITA ST. HILL CHISHOLM
(1924–   ), U.S. congresswoman, U.S. presidential candidate, educator

LEROY G. DORSEY

Shirley Chisholm made history in the 1960s and 1970s as the first African-American woman elected to Congress and as the first African-American woman to run for the presidency. These milestones set the stage for Chisholm's rhetorical expression of her philosophy regarding political advocacy. In her autobiography *Unbought and Unbossed*, she observed that she considered herself a "maverick" unwilling to "play the rules of the game" if it meant allowing the handful of men in power to remain in power. Her goal, she wrote, was to "change the system," to "shake it up" by becoming a major "voice" for those groups that have been neglected by the system. In *Women in the United States Congress, 1917–1972,* Rudolf Englebarts labeled that voice as "fearless," "articulate," and "shrewd." In her 1987 essay "Shirley Chisholm," Susan Duffy described that voice as attempting to "move an audience with rational argumentation and strong evidence" in a sincere call for change. As James Haskins's biography *Fighting Shirley Chisholm* concluded, Chisholm's voice brought about much-needed reforms for many disenfranchised groups.

Chisholm's well-reasoned and hard-hitting oratory, as well as her seeing herself as a champion of the oppressed, stemmed from her educational experiences in the 1930s and 1940s. She excelled in grammar and high school, taking specific interest in American history and the roles of such female advocates as Susan B. Anthony and Mary McLeod Bethune. Having several scholarships to choose from in 1942, Chisholm enrolled in Brooklyn College intending to become a teacher. While she did begin teaching upon graduation, two college experiences served to prepare her for her role as a political advocate. After majoring in sociology, Chisholm realized with horror the extent to which society oppressed and dismissed African-American and other minority groups. Overcoming her shyness and slight lisp, she joined the Debating Society and quickly became known as a fiery debater—particularly on subjects involving discrimination and prejudice. Because of her skill as a consummate debater, one of Chisholm's professors urged her to enter politics.

Despite teaching and administrating at a child-care center during the day and taking night classes at Columbia University to earn a master's degree in education, Chisholm worked in both local and state politics. From 1946 to 1959, she participated in several community political clubs. In 1960, however, she formed her own—the Unity Democratic Club—to replace the white political machine running her district. This organization acted as Chisholm's launching pad into state politics four years later. After getting the club's endorsement and campaigning unceasingly, she won a state assembly seat in 1964. As a New York State assemblywoman for four years, Chisholm introduced fifty bills in the legislature and lobbied successfully to get a record eight bills passed. Two of the more notable bills enacted into law included one that established the state's first unemployment insurance coverage for domestic workers and one that created a program called SEEK (Search for Education, Elevation, and Knowledge) to fund college scholarships for minority students. During her tenure in the assembly, Chisholm gained the reputation of being independent by resisting high-pressure lobbyists as well as other fellow Democrats.

With the creation of a new congressional district in the predominantly African-American Bedford-Stuyvesant area in 1967–68, Chisholm set her sights on Congress. Without the money for a conventional campaign, she addressed her audiences at public housing projects, private homes, parks, and shopping centers. Her fluency in Spanish helped her carry the Spanish-speaking sections of the district. Chisholm's slogan—''Fighting Shirley Chisholm—Unbought and Unbossed'' became her battle cry that rallied women to organize on her behalf, and her debate skills constantly put her opponents on the defensive. In January 1969, Chisholm joined the ranks of the Ninety-first Congress. Her role as a representative, she wrote in *Unbought and Unbossed,* was to promote ''the heart, the humanity, [and] the Christian love'' needed to ''insure justice'' for all people. By the time she left Congress in 1983, Chisholm had proposed and supported scores of bills ranging from preventing discrimination in hiring practices to supporting federally funded abortions for welfare mothers.

Chisholm's run for the presidency in 1972 symbolized her philosophy of ''shaking up the system.'' In *The Good Fight,* an account of her presidential campaign, Chisholm revealed why she undertook this overwhelming challenge. ''I ran for the Presidency,'' she wrote, ''in order to crack a little more of the ice which in recent years has congealed to nearly immobilize our political system and demoralize people.'' As she observed in her book, her campaign speeches— many of which were extemporaneous and impromptu—stressed the fundamental belief ''that our government cannot keep on being primarily responsive to the privileged white upper classes but must serve the human needs of every citizen.''

Following her seven terms in Congress, Chisholm continued to educate her audiences about equality and justice. In the early 1980s, she took a position as a professor at Mount Holyoke College. Today, as an active lecturer, writer, and political activist (most recently touring the country to support Bill Clinton), Chisholm continues to alert a new generation that the problems faced by women and minorities still need determined attention.

SHIRLEY CHISHOLM: CHAMPION OF THE PEOPLE

The idea that an elected official embodies the vox populi was realized most strikingly in the form of Shirley Chisholm. Throughout her political career, Chisholm prided herself as being the "voice of the people." At a time when many disenfranchised groups needed a representative willing to question certain entrenched beliefs and venerated institutions, Chisholm stood ready. As a gifted debater, she constructed each speech so that it made a complete and logical case for her position. As a strategic rhetorician, she adapted her provocative messages to particular audiences by blending pragmatic realizations with moral idealism.

Chisholm quickly illustrated that her tenure in Congress would be marked by anything but docility. In a 1969 address "It Is Time to Reassess Our National Priorities," she used her maiden speech as a congresswoman to attack the Nixon administration. She accused it of spending too much money on military weaponry and too little on programs such as Head Start. According to Chisholm, the military held a "blank check" that it used unreservedly while America's "greatest enemies—poverty, prejudice, and neglect" continued unabated. Attempting to awaken the consciences of fellow congressmen, she painted their actions in harsh tones. Because of their subservience to the military, congressmen fed the "cancerous growth," "monstrous waste," and "shocking profits" of the Defense Department. How could reasonable people, she wondered aloud, continue to fund weapons systems that "are found to be impractical, inefficient, unsatisfactory, even worthless?" Chisholm bombarded her audience with a repetition of accusations: "Two more years of hunger for Americans . . . Two more years of high taxes . . . Two more years of too little being done . . . Two more years of . . . penny-pinching on social programs." If the government failed to address the real enemies of the country, she warned, it would be exposed as a hypocrite in the global community.

Less than two months after her first speech to Congress, Chisholm attacked institutional sexism by supporting the Equal Rights Amendment (ERA). In a later 1969 address "For the Equal Rights Amendment," she again challenged the consciences of House representatives. She asked: "Why is it acceptable for women to be secretaries, librarians, and teachers, but totally unacceptable for them to be managers, administrators, doctors, lawyers, and Members of Congress?" Chisholm noted that an "unspoken assumption" was at work: that women lacked the "executive ability, orderly minds, stability, [and] leadership skills" to succeed in such positions. To prove the allegation that women were not well represented in business and government, she assembled an array of compelling evidence:

More than half of the population of the United States is female. But women occupy only 2 percent of the managerial positions . . . No women sit on the . . . Supreme Court. There have been only two women who have held Cabinet rank, and at present there are none. Only two women now hold ambassadorial rank in the diplomatic corps. In Congress, we are down to one Senator and 10 Representatives. Considering that there are about 3 ½million more women in the United States than men, this situation is outrageous.

Being the consummate debater, Chisholm was not content only with advancing her position in "For the Equal Rights Amendment." She anticipated the arguments of the opposition and offered a refutation of them. One argument against the ERA, she observed, involved the belief that more legislation was not needed since women were already protected under the law. This idea was erroneous, she reasoned, given the "concentration of women in lower paying, menial, unrewarding jobs and their incredible scarcity in the upper level jobs." Known for her sarcastic wit, she inquired that if "women are already equal, why is it such an event whenever one happens to be elected to Congress?" She noted that a second argument maintained that the ERA would interfere with existing marriage and divorce laws and eliminate many existing laws that already gave special protection to women. In terms of the former, she acerbically observed that the marriage laws were "due for a sweeping reform." Regarding the latter, she transcended the issue of women needing protection to all people needing protection equally. "Women need no protection that men do not need," she declared; "what we need are laws to protect working people, to guarantee them fair pay, safe working conditions, [and] protection against sickness and layoffs." This "male supremacist myth," she concluded about her opponents' argument, "is ridiculous and unworthy of respect."

Chisholm's commencement address at Howard University in June 1969 confirmed her as an iconoclastic orator. In "Progress through Understanding," she took to task many highly regarded institutions and their counterproductive actions. She indicted city governments whose methods of operations were antiquated. She accused unions "formed to proclaim and defend the brotherhood of working men" of instead jealously defending the status quo. For Congress, however, she saved her most pointed barbs. Congress, designed to be the bastion of representative democracy, repeatedly ignored its obligation. It no longer represented the interests of "the people," she declared, but the interests of the "oil industry" that received tax breaks for "using up an irreplaceable national resource," and of the makers of military weaponry that perpetuated the "tragic, unjust, wasteful, and illegal war in which we have no national interest at stake." According to her, most representatives ignored the "outpouring of public opinion against the war." Chisholm took the moral high ground for herself by telling her audience that while Congress neglected its constituents, she and a handful of others would "vote for no more military spending bills." As she advocated in so many of her speeches, the time had come to rebel. She implored the

graduating students to "fight the system that has been denying you the opportunity to be a total man or woman" and "build new institutions or reform our
old ones."

One of the best examples of Chisholm's ability to blend pragmatic realizations
with moral idealism came from her "Statement on Abortion" to the Republican
Task Force on Earth Resources and Population in November 1969. This issue
represented one of Chisholm's primary concerns. Her speech, which was also
placed into the *Congressional Record*, discussed bluntly the need for availability
of birth control and abortions for the poor. She warned her audience that she
would be talking about issues that made people "squeamish" but that she did
not "believe in sugarcoating the issue." Using an array of statistics and expert
testimony, Chisholm argued that the needs of minority women were being ignored. Quoting a doctor from the New York County Medical Society, Chisholm
maintained that "80% of maternal deaths are the result of criminal abortions,"
and that the women from minority groups were "hit hardest." Citing another
study, she stated that these criminal abortions proved to be "the cause of [ma-
ternal] death for 25% of the white women, 49% of the non-white women and
56% of the Puerto Rican women." When minority women could not get an
abortion—criminal or otherwise—the children from these unwanted pregnancies
suffered as well. African-American children were condemned to spend their
lives in orphanages since they were four times less likely to be taken in by foster
parents than Caucasian children. Chisholm placed this rational evidence within
a moral context. The fact that poor and minority women had little access to
needed contraceptives and abortions reflected society's immoral attitude that
these women had to "pay the price" for their pleasure. "By forcing a young
girl to have an unwanted child," she admonished, "we are assigning her to
society's trash heap." For Chisholm, given the amount of unwanted pregnancies,
as well as the number of illegal and botched abortions, the public urgently
needed to examine its attitudes and policies regarding family planning in order
to provide more effective birth-control programs.

Anticipating her audience's indifference to an indictment of its sense of morality, Chisholm provided a more basic appeal for helping poor and minority
women. "Some of you gentlemen may think this is all too hearts and flowers,"
she observed, but "an even more practical reason" to be in favor of repeal of
abortion laws was evident. According to her, the audience's callous indifference
cost money:

> About ¼ to ⅓ of all illegitimate children under the age of 18 are on the AFDC
> rolls. Over 70,000 unmarried mothers are receiving aid for dependent children. . . .
> The national average per recipient is $44.30. . . . Think about it, gentlemen, that
> is about $48,730,000 a year and unmarried women are the ones who find it most
> difficult to get off the welfare rolls.

Pragmatically, the audience could save itself money by helping to repeal state
abortion laws. Morally, it could help bring about an ideal state whereby "all

women, for whatever reason, can have abortion [*sic*] performed under safe, healthful conditions by qualified practitioners of medicine.''

Another issue fervently supported by Chisholm involved adequate child-care facilities. In her ''Statement on a National Day Care Program'' before a House subcommittee in May 1971, Chisholm introduced a bill that would ''help families, especially our mothers, feel confident that their children are safe [and] well cared for.'' Having worked in day-care centers for over a decade, Chisholm capitalized on her ethos. She reminded her audience of her ''years of experience as a day care teacher, director and consultant,'' and of her personal visits to many facilities in the preparation of her address. As with many of her speeches, she employed statistical evidence to support her contention that working parents, especially households headed by women, needed financial assistance: ''Among black families 28% are headed by women; the average income for working women . . . is $3091. Black women who are employed mainly as domestics and in low-paying service jobs earn only $1991.'' While the financial considerations of paying for child care were important, she argued, the fact remained that a day-care shortage resulted in only 2% of all working women being able to use such facilities. Her appeals, however, moved beyond the use of statistics. In an appeal to a parent's empathy and compassion for children, Chisholm revealed to her audience the grim truth about child care in America. According to her, most parents faced a ''nightmare hodgepodge of arrangements with elderly relatives'' or were forced to use ''bleak custodial parking lots euphemistically called family care centers.'' Many ''unlicensed'' facilities, she bemoaned, were no better than ''dumping grounds where children are tied to furniture in dismal surroundings and where they are 'looked after' by someone who may be emotionally disturbed, uneducated, alcoholic, or so old they need help themselves.'' As parents themselves, she urged her audience to pass the legislation required to stop day care from being merely a ''*custodial* service'' and to instead provide an ''*educational* environment'' for the children.

Chisholm carried the fight for equality and justice for minorities and women beyond the halls of Congress. On January 25, 1972, she made her formal ''Announcement'' to run for the presidency. According to Judith Trent and Robert Friedenberg's *Political Campaign Communication: Principles and Practices,* candidates employ several strategies in their announcement addresses. These include, for example, using a newsworthy location for the announcement and sharing the spotlight with prominent figures, as well as explaining the reason for the candidacy and its likelihood of success. Other than selecting the site of the largest Baptist church in Brooklyn for her announcement, Chisholm chose to do things her way. Without the endorsements of any important political advocates, she surrounded herself with her friends, office staff, and community representatives. Instead of spending time discussing the potential for victory, Chisholm concentrated on what her candidacy represented. According to excerpts from this address in *The Good Fight,* she ran not as *the* African-American candidate, nor as *the* women's candidate, but as ''the candidate of the people.''

Her candidacy reflected the fact that the American people were "smart enough" to "recognize the talent, energy and dedication which all Americans, including women and minorities, have to offer." By reciting the ills plaguing the country—Vietnam, economic recession, injustice, political corruption, and loss of communal spirit—Chisholm elevated herself as the person with the "vision" and the "courage" to bring the needed changes.

Although Chisholm campaigned for six months, most of her speeches during that time were ad-libbed. As she observed in *The Good Fight,* if "any of them survive, it must be in the form of films or tape," but her book does contain the texts of two campaign speeches: "Economic Justice for Women" and "The Cost of Care." Both speeches were delivered in late 1971 and early 1972. The former, "freely adapted to suit the occasion," she wrote, was given to several women's groups. It charged that women continued to be discriminated against in the workplace. The latter speech, addressed to a group of hospital administrators, called for adequate health care for everyone.

Together, these speeches reflect Chisholm's ability to artfully adapt to her different audiences. "Economic Justice for Women" played to the audiences' growing frustration and rebelliousness. After providing a statistical account of the discrepancy between male and female wages, as well as the inequity in occupations, Chisholm launched into a militant tirade against "male prejudice." According to her, women began responding to their oppression, and "like every other oppressed people rising today, we're out for freedom—by any means necessary." Chisholm called on American women to "stand and fight—be militant even—for rights which are ours." Those rights, she declared, would come "not necessarily on soapboxes," but "in the community and at the polls."

While Chisholm employed an agitative rhetoric in "Economic Justice for Women," "The Cost of Care" reflected her more formal, debate-oriented style. Organizing the speech in a problem-solution format, she began by revealing the double crisis in health care. Chisholm argued that increases in population and inflation strained an already-inadequate health-care system to the point that "millions of Americans had no doctor to turn to." This, coupled with the "quick-fix" reform proposals of various political advocates, offered no "sound solution" to the health-care problem. She then outlined seven reasons why the country's health services were not meeting the needs of a majority of the people and illustrated why several of the reform proposals failed to take these reasons into account. After setting the criteria and judging these proposals wanting, Chisholm offered three solutions of her own. Ultimately, she contended, "I am not proposing any miracles. All it would take is a new attitude toward health—that it is a human right, not a privilege to be purchased."

One other written transcript of Chisholm's presidential campaign speeches exists. "Economic Injustice in America Today," delivered in April 1972 before the students of the Newark College of Engineering, illustrated once again her role as the "voice of the people." For Chisholm, the rising costs of services, goods, and the basic necessities of living were growing out of the reach of young people, old people, minorities, and women. In other words, the government failed to answer the needs of these disenfranchised groups. As evidence, Chisholm provided numerous examples of governmental neglect: the increase in infant mortality among Spanish-speaking immigrants; the prevalence of substandard housing in predominantly minority urban areas; and the fixing of incomes for elderly Americans at a time of runaway inflation. Bluntly, she demonstrated the economic inequity between the ''haves'' and the ''have-nots'':

> I know a lot of Americans who would be glad to settle for better bus service from their home to their jobs, or from poor neighborhoods to areas of the city where jobs are to be found. . . . but President Nixon's answer is to build a space shuttle or an SST with precious public funds, to serve a tiny elite of the population.

Chisholm's unsuccessful bid for the presidency did not alter her determination to be an advocate of change both within and outside of government. Again blending frank realizations with moral idealism to challenge antiquated ways of thinking, she addressed some eight hundred delegates at the National Women's Political Caucus in February 1973. Justificatory in nature, her ''Women in Politics'' speech explained one of the reasons that she believed had led to her poor showing in the presidential primaries. According to Chisholm, narrow-minded thinking by women's groups helped to doom the campaign. She charged that many women wanted her to be the ''feminist'' candidate. Because of this single-mindedness, these groups failed to understand and support Chisholm, who felt the need to discuss ''issues other than equal rights [and] abortion.'' Part of this parochial thinking, she charged, stemmed from the lack of diversity in such activist groups: ''If we are to succeed in uniting ourselves and in attracting the typical woman who is likely to be a housewife and mother who likes living in suburbia, we are going to have to make a concerted effort to articulate issues so that everyone will want to be identified with and active in the movement.'' To that end, Chisholm declared that the function of the National Women's Political Caucus was not ''to be the cutting edge of the women's liberation movement'' but to become the ''big umbrella organization'' that addressed the concerns of the majority of women. After this pragmatic call, she ended with an idealistic plea to her audience: that they ''all try to be respectful and understanding of each other's views.''

In June 1978, Chisholm again showed her independence within the political structure. In ''Vote for the Individual, Not the Political Party,'' she urged the Independent Black Women's Caucus to recognize the political power that African-Americans possessed in a two-party system. Ever the iconoclastic orator, Chisholm attacked the cherished notion that blacks should stay in the Democratic party given its historically tolerant ideology. Taking the moral high ground, she condemned blacks for their ''sin'' of blindly following a party whose actions belied its philosophy. Herself a Democrat, Chisholm declared that she would no longer ask anyone ''to vote for any man or woman because of the party designation that attaches to their name." Instead, she called for the group to support candidates who had something to offer in return. "We will give our votes and support to individuals—not political parties," she commanded her audience, "in *return for* their support of programs which benefit *us*."

Throughout her political and private careers, Shirley Chisholm challenged the rigid thinking of institutional administrators. She questioned traditional policy-making that perpetuated the economic and social inequities among Americans. She took up the banner for the millions of people whom the system had ignored and gave them a voice. With her aggressive debate style, pragmatic solutions, and moral idealism, Chisholm placed issues such as education, day care, and antidiscrimination laws in the forefront of national consciousness. Her thought-provoking oratory and sincere commitment to winning the presidency gave her the opportunity to pave the way for future minority and women politicians. Because of her accomplishments as an educator and political advocate, she has earned a place as one of the most capable female orators of the twentieth century.

INFORMATION SOURCES

Research Collections and Collected Speeches

A considerable amount has been written about Shirley Chisholm in the popular press, and there are two major reference sources that can help guide the interested scholar. A large archival holding of newspaper clippings and audiovisual material can be found in the Schomburg Center for Research in Black Culture, New York Public Library. Susan Duffy has also compiled an excellent bibliography of works by and about Chisholm, *Shirley Chisholm: A Bibliography of Writings by and about Her*. Metuchen, NJ: Scarecrow, 1988.

[*TGF*] Chisholm, Shirley. *The Good Fight*. New York: Harper and Row, 1973.

Selected Critical Studies

Duffy, Susan. "Shirley Chisholm." *American Orators of the Twentieth Century: Critical Studies and Sources*. Ed. Bernard K. Duffy and Halford R. Ryan. Westport, CT: Greenwood, 1987. 63–68.
Handle, Margaret Jean. "A Critical Analysis of Selected Speeches on Women's Rights by Representative Shirley Chisholm." M. A. thesis, California State U at Long Beach, 1976.
Williamson, Dorothy Kay. "Rhetorical Analysis of Selected Modern Black Spokespersons on the Women's Liberation Movement." Ph.D. diss., Ohio State U, 1980.

Selected Biographies

Brownmiller, Susan. *Shirley Chisholm: A Biography*. Garden City, NY: Doubleday, 1971.
Chisholm, Shirley. *The Good Fight*. New York: Harper and Row, 1973.

————. *Unbought and Unbossed*. Boston: Houghton Mifflin, 1970.

Englebarts, Rudolf. *Women in the United States Congress, 1917–1972*. Littleton, Co: Libraries Unlimited, 1974.

Haskins, James. *Fighting Shirley Chisholm*. New York: Dial, 1975.

Hicks, Nancy. *The Honorable Shirley Chisholm, Congresswoman from Brooklyn*. New York: Lion, 1971.

Scheader, Catherine. *Shirley Chisholm, Teacher and Congresswoman*. Hillsdale, NJ: Enslow, 1990.

CHRONOLOGY OF MAJOR SPEECHES

[See "Research Collections and Collected Speeches" for source code.]

"It Is Time to Reassess our National Priorities." U.S. House of Representatives, Washington, DC, March 26, 1969. *Representative American Speeches, 1968–1969*. Ed. Lester Thonssen. New York: H. W. Wilson, 1969, 68–72.

"For the Equal Rights Amendment." U.S. House of Representatives, Washington, DC, May 21, 1969. *Contemporary American Voices: 1945–Present*. Ed. James R. Andrews and David Zarefsky. New York: Longman, 1992, 302–303.

"Progress through Understanding." Howard University, Washington, DC, June 6, 1969. *Congressional Record* 115.12 (June 16, 1969): 15972–15973.

"Statement on Abortion." Republican Task Force on Earth Resources and Population, Washington, DC, November 1969. *Congressional Record* 115.27 (December 3, 1969): 36765–36767.

"Statement on a National Day Care Program." Select Subcommittee on Education, Washington, DC, May 17, 1971. *Hearings on H.R. 6748 and Related Bills to Provide a Comprehensive Child Development Program in the Dept. of Health, Education, and Welfare,* May 17, May 21, and June 3, 1971, 71–75.

"Announcement." Excerpts of her speech announcing her presidential candidacy, Brooklyn, NY, January 25, 1972. *TGF,* 71–73.

"Economic Justice for Women." Campaign speech delivered throughout late 1971–early 1972. *TGF,* 188–192.

"The Cost of Care." Campaign speech delivered throughout late 1971–early 1972. *TGF,* 193–199.

"Economic Injustice in America Today." Newark College of Engineering, Newark, NJ, April 15, 1972. *Representative American Speeches, 1971–1972*. Ed. Waldo W. Braden. New York: H. W. Wilson, 1972, 27–36.

"Women in Politics." National Women's Political Caucus Convention, Houston, TX, February 9, 1973. *Representative American Speeches, 1972–1973*. Ed. Waldo W. Braden. New York: H. W. Wilson, 1973, 79–85.

"Vote for the Individual, Not the Political Party." Independent Black Women's Caucus, New York, NY, June 24, 1978. *Vital Speeches of the Day,* August 15, 1978:670–671.

LEROY ELDRIDGE CLEAVER
(1935–), civil rights activist, reformer

JOHN C. HAMMERBACK AND RICHARD J. JENSEN

Leroy Eldridge Cleaver was born on August 31, 1935, in Wabbaseka, Arkansas. He was named after his father, a waiter on railroad dining cars and a weekend piano player in local clubs. His mother was a devout Christian who frequently used biblical imagery to teach her children about life. Such religious zeal fit easily in her immediate family, for one of young Eldridge's grandfathers was a Methodist minister and the other a circuit-riding fundamentalist preacher.

Young Eldridge had a happy early childhood in rural Arkansas, but the secure foundation for his pleasant life crumbled in 1945. His family moved to an inner-city section of Phoenix, where the love between his mother and father seemed to disappear. His father began to abuse his mother physically as well as emotionally, deeply disturbing Eldridge. Eventually he and his father engaged in a violent fight, and the father left home soon thereafter.

In Phoenix, Cleaver received his first lessons in street survival. That education continued when the family moved to Los Angeles, where it eventually settled in an area called Rose Hill near South Pasadena. There Cleaver was influenced by streetwise young blacks and Latinos. At age twelve he was arrested for stealing a bicycle, the first in a series of offenses that eventually led to his incarceration in reform schools and then to an almost unbroken stretch of imprisonment from 1954 to 1966.

Cleaver's early years established a lifelong pattern. During each period of his life he joined male-dominated organizations in which he would serve as a leader but not the primary leader, and he would eventually reject the group's dogma before repeating the pattern. Most of the organizations could be defined as religious in nature. Thus, after growing up in a family heavily influenced by the religion of the black Protestant church, he joined the Catholic church while in reform school. After a confrontation with a priest and the realization that preachers could do little to improve the lives of prisoners, he rejected Catholicism and became an atheist for a short time until he was converted to the Nation of Islam, or Black Muslims, and became a follower of Malcolm X.

While in prison, Cleaver developed his rhetorical skills. In 1958 he began the essays that later formed his autobiographical *Soul on Ice.* He completed most of the essays during 1965 and 1966, a period between the death of Malcolm X—and Cleaver's consequent alienation from the leader of the Muslims, Elijah Muhammad—and his parole from prison. Upon his parole in 1966, his lawyer, Beverly Axelrod, helped Cleaver obtain a job with *Ramparts* magazine. There he met a fellow activist, Kathleen Neal, who soon became his wife.

After leaving prison, Cleaver tried unsuccessfully to revive Malcolm X's Organization for African Unity. His doubts about the Nation of Islam increased when he determined that it had failed to carry out its promises to black prisoners. In February 1967 he made his final break with the Muslims during an experience he had with the Black Panthers. In *Post Prison Writings,* Cleaver recounted a meeting he had attended, where this dramatic incident precipitated his conversion:

> From the tension showing on the faces of the people before me, I thought the cops were invading the meeting, but there was a deep female gleam leaping out of one of the women's eyes that no cop who ever lived could elicit. I recognized that gleam out of the recesses of my soul, even though I had never seen it before in my life: the total admiration of a black woman for a black man. I spun around in my seat and saw the most beautiful sight I had ever seen: four black men wearing black berets, powder blue shirts, black leather jackets, black trousers, shiny black shoes—and each with a gun.

Cleaver immediately joined the Panthers.

The publication of *Soul on Ice* made Cleaver a national celebrity and opened a vast audience for his controversial message. Because of his literary fame, he became the Panthers' minister of information. He quickly added to the already-considerable media attention paid to the Panthers by participating in a series of highly publicized incidents, including one in which a group of heavily armed Panthers traveled to the state capitol in Sacramento to protest restrictions on guns. "The press was enchanted by the Panthers," wrote Kathleen Rout, "perhaps most of all by Cleaver, who was photogenic, tall, handsome, charismatic, and articulate." On April 6, 1968, Cleaver and other Panthers were involved in a dramatic shootout with Oakland police. He was jailed, then freed, and later ordered to prison. Rather than return to jail, he fled the country, first going to Cuba, then Algeria, and eventually France, an exile that lasted seven years. Before he left the United States, however, Cleaver had been nominated by the Peace and Freedom party as its candidate for president with Jerry Rubin as his vice-presidential running mate.

During Cleaver's exile, political, personal, and religious changes in his life were preparing him to return home. His strong belief in Marxist-Leninist doctrines gave way to a staunch anticommunism, a drastic change that he attributed to his travels in Communist countries where, according to Bartlett, he discovered "no humanity, no love." The birth of his two children also seemed to motivate his repatriation. In his later book, *Soul on Fire*, Cleaver claimed that a dramatic religious conversion gave him the courage to end his exile in November 1975.

Once back in the United States, Cleaver returned to prison to carry out the terms of his 1968 conviction. Here he experienced another powerful spiritual conversion, this one leading to his affiliation with fundamentalist Christian groups and a final split with the Panthers. He was released on bail during the summer of 1976, was ordered to do community service while on parole, and soon began touring the country as an evangelist/preacher. From 1976 to 1978 his standard speech detailed his rebirth as a Christian and his dissatisfaction with communism. Meanwhile, he formed the Eldridge Cleaver Crusades in Stanford, California, and completed *Soul on Fire*, which summarized his journey from convicted felon to reborn Christian.

In the early 1980s Cleaver continued to speak prolifically even as he made two additional religious changes. In 1980 his relationship with the Unification Church of Reverend Moon surfaced, and he traveled the college lecture circuit representing a Unification Church campus organization, the Collegiate Association for the Research of Principles (CARP). In 1981 his wife moved to New Haven, Connecticut, to become a student at Yale, a separation that led to a later divorce; he remained in California working for a Mormon tree surgeon and studying that religion. Although he joined the Mormon church in 1982, he continued to speak for the Unification Church. According to Rout, his standard speech at this time was entitled "America's Future and the World Revolution."

Cleaver evolved politically as well as religiously. In 1976 he supported Jimmy Carter, but in 1980 he backed Ronald Reagan, whom he had lambasted during his Black Panther years. He ran as a conservative in a 1984 congressional campaign against Representative Ron Dellums for Congress and again in 1986 for the U.S. Senate. In 1992 he ran for a spot on the Bay Area Rapid Transit Board. Since 1986 he has made a living by lecturing on conservative issues, making flowerpots and other ceramic items, and operating a recycling pickup service.

Cleaver's intermittent spiritual conversions and active rhetorical crusade for his religious causes did not prevent him from serious skirmishes with the law. He was arrested for cocaine possession in 1987 and for burglary in 1988, each time describing himself as a victim of police harassment. In March 1994 a dazed and seemingly intoxicated Cleaver was arrested in Berkeley for possession of crack cocaine. He later claimed that he had been robbed and beaten by thieves. While in jail he suffered a seizure and was rushed to a hospital where he underwent nearly five hours of emergency surgery for a brain hemorrhage.

ELDRIDGE CLEAVER: ETHOS OF AN ACTIVIST

Although Cleaver is best known as a writer, he has also been a powerful speaker who, writes Kathleen Rout, was "arguably the most charismatic figure of the late sixties." While in prison he realized the need to acquire training in speaking. In *Soul on Ice* he described how he joined the Gavel Club, "where I'm gaining some valuable experience and technique in public speaking." After the publication of *Soul on Ice* he was invited to speak throughout the United States, addressing audiences on numerous college campuses and in many cities. Upon returning from exile, Cleaver changed his rhetorical purpose. As a Christian evangelist he sought to spread the word of Christ to those he felt needed a spiritual awakening and conversion, including former Black Muslims. Later he spoke for the purpose of teaching the doctrine of the Unification Church and then that of the Mormon church.

Although Cleaver's purpose for speaking shifted over time, his profile as a rhetor remained consistent in two important ways. First, Cleaver always grounded his case in moral principles as he sought to end injustice for blacks in the United States and to improve their lives. As an activist in the 1960s he argued that the lives of blacks could best be improved by confronting the establishment as a member of organizations outside the power structure. When he returned from exile, the reborn Cleaver told audiences that the lives of blacks could more effectively be improved by working within the system. The second rhetorical constant in Cleaver's discourse was his unwavering faith in the power of words, whether written or spoken, to achieve his goals.

Cleaver's rhetorical manner as an orator reflected the unconventional man and his purpose. Robert Scheer described Cleaver's speeches during his Panther years:

> He spoke out front during these always extemporaneous speeches. He proved an uneven though brilliant speaker. As he spoke, he moved around his subject, darting in and out until he had uncovered some key points, and then he poured it on. When it didn't happen, when he hadn't got hold of the essential truth, then the pouring on didn't help—the invective or obscenity was sour and Cleaver knew it, and his mind turned for relief to less serious, though perhaps more bizarre, comments.

Don A. Schanche, who observed Cleaver deliver several speeches during that period, attributed part of Cleaver's credibility to his prison record and "outlaw status." Schanche identified an additional source of Cleaver's charisma by describing his physical build as being "finely muscled and tapered like a funnel" and his green eyes "as cool and impervious . . . as the steel bars of a prison." Cleaver's use of language, according to Schanche, complemented his physical magnetism:

His platform presence was so much a matter of physical and oral style that it is literally impossible to convey the truth of it by recounting his speeches, because the verbal content of so much of his "political" campaigning was so appalling that no person can read the words in cold print and believe that the man who uttered them did so in such an inoffensive way that they seemed not only believable but unprovocative.

Schanche quotes Cleaver's explanation for his often-abusive manner of speaking:

I go around talking like this in public not because I have a five-word vocabulary— I could straighten up on a few words—but because I know it puts a lot of these chumps uptight, and I want to keep them uptight in every way I can. If you don't like the way I walk, I'm gonna walk more like that. If they don't like the way I talk, I'm gonna talk more like that. That's why you young people should let your hair grow long so they can freak out some more. If there's anything we can do to put them uptight, let's do it. Keep them uptight. Make them nervous until they have to stay drunk in order to relate.

The means and goals in Cleaver's speaking, concluded Arthur Smith (Molefi Asante), paralleled those of his writing in *Soul on Ice*. Cleaver acted as a social critic with "an overpowering need to explain, to cut through the muddled concepts and symbols he sees in society." He used his prison experiences to build his credibility and create an intimate relationship with his audience as well as to make ideas more concrete and immediate. Because he relied on personal experiences, Cleaver employed many personal pronouns; for example, he often referred to himself, frequently used "you" when attempting to establish rapport with his audience, and consistently invoked "they" or "them" when drawing distinctions between good and evil. To Asante and Robb, Cleaver's unusual speaking style resulted from his disregard for "established stylistic rules" and preference for "Black English, slang, and the language of the streets."

During Cleaver's period as a vitriolic critic of the United States, the substantive content of his public discourse urged blacks to separate from and confront whites. Verbally excoriating whites, whom he made responsible for every problem suffered by blacks, he urged his black audiences to unite against their oppressors. He depicted whites as clever foes who continually tricked unsuspecting blacks. In a letter to Stokely Carmichael he wrote: "The enemies of black people have learned something from history even if you haven't, and they are discovering new ways to divide us faster than we are discovering new ways to unite." The division succeeded, Cleaver said, because many blacks were easily deceived by whites who treated them in a friendly manner or passed laws that appeared to help blacks but were never enforced. Cleaver cited specific cases in which whites kept blacks in subordinate positions by skillfully using the military and criminal justice systems, the black middle class, the economics of the ghetto, and misleading media coverage.

Cleaver identified blacks as the cannon fodder used in the wars fought by the United States. In Vietnam, for example, black troops supposedly fought for freedom of the Vietnamese, but were denied many basic freedoms in their own country. Battlefield deaths deprived the black community of talented individuals who could have helped their own people had they remained at home. The remedy for these problems was decidedly radical, as Cleaver called for soldiers to desert, return home, and form a people's militia to challenge the power structure.

On the domestic battlefields blacks were again little more than cannon fodder for whites. A discriminatory legal system arrested and imprisoned them at a rate far beyond their numbers in society; and police formed a standing army that harassed them constantly while incarcerating them within the boundaries of ghettos. Those few blacks who made their way into the middle class received power and rewards from whites in return for helping to keep the remainder of the black community subordinate and passive. Cleaver cited Roy Wilkins and Martin Luther King as well-known examples of those whom whites manipulated in order to subordinate blacks generally.

In Cleaver's analysis, economic motives underlay much of white oppression. Like the colonial nations in the Third World, American whites used ghettos as a source of cheap labor, as a place to exploit workers. Cleaver divided the United States into the "black colony" and the "white mother country" that exploited that colony. His use of these terms illustrated the basic polarization he saw in the United States, a sharp division encapsulated in his famous statement "What we're saying today is that you're either part of the solution or you're part of the problem. There is no middle ground."

Moving from what he saw as the truth to those responsible for communicating that truth, Cleaver taught that the press was a part of a designed plan to portray blacks negatively and distort or ignore the economic and physical brutality they suffered. For example, the news media intentionally created negative images of the Black Panthers. In "A Word to Students" he explained that "this is part of their program of distortion, designed to perpetuate confusion so the people of America will look at each other as enemies instead of focusing on the enemies of the people."

Cleaver directed blacks to respond forcefully and vigorously to white oppression. First, blacks must unite. This unification would channel black anger and frustration away from fellow blacks and toward the whites who created the conditions that bred that anger and frustration. Unified black action would force whites to confront their immoral mistreatment of blacks. Once unified, blacks should join with other groups advocating change, particularly other minority groups and white students. This cohesion could in turn lead to ties with Third World nations. In particular, Cleaver aligned himself with revolutionary socialist groups in the Third World, advocating that necessary programs for blacks required that socialism replace capitalism. This political solution would be attained only when whites granted basic rights to blacks. Eventually, he forecast, the

United Nations would serve as an appropriate forum for the debate over his case for change.

Cleaver's specific proposals called for violent confrontation with whites, a war of liberation through violence, with the wealthy and the capitalist system as particular targets. In "The Land Question and Black Liberation" he stated that in order to achieve his goals, "black men know they must pick up the gun, they must arm black people to the teeth, they must organize an army and confront the mother country with a most drastic consequence if she attempts to assert police power over the colony."

Whereas the radical Cleaver of the 1960s stressed separation, confrontation, and violence, the reborn Cleaver of the 1970s and 1980s urged blacks to work within the established structure and harmoniously cooperate with whites. The foundation for his dramatically altered agenda was his belief that the United States and its white residents had been transformed during his years in exile. As evidence he cited the end of the Vietnam War, the increased opportunities for blacks, and the exposure of the Watergate conspiracy. He even claimed that the color line had been eliminated, that there was no "black thing, white thing anymore." His witnessing of racism in other parts of the world, he related, had shocked him and led to his conclusion that the United States alone among nations had attempted to confront racial issues. Equally striking was his assertion that the police in the United States, and indeed the entire justice system of the nation, were far superior to any others in the world.

Turning to economics, he again rendered a startling reversal of claims. He contended that capitalism was far superior to communism, that the United States must therefore be strong militarily to defeat any challenges to its free-market system, and that the Communists were clever as well as evil foes who would attack militarily if their enemies became weak. In his new version of his home country, blacks could participate successfully in the economic as well as the religious and political mainstream.

Cleaver replaced his longtime enemy and rhetorical symbol for all evil, the capitalist whites, with an equally hated and vilified foe, the Communists and their ideology. To explain this complete reversal, he related that as he had traveled through Communist countries during his exile, he had observed the corruption and questionable actions of Communist leaders. In *Soul on Fire* he stated: "I would silently compare that reality with my memories of home. Quietly America started winning." Meanwhile, the birth of his children and the realization that they had souls had caused him to reject Communist teachings that people had no souls; and he had been stunned by the prevalent racism he had observed in Communist countries, particularly in Cuba and North Korea.

Not surprisingly, the reborn Cleaver renounced his earlier commitment to Marxist dogma and specifically to the Panthers' plan to adopt the tactics of leaders like Castro in forming groups of minority veterans who would operate in the cities and mountains of the United States as guerrilla bands fomenting revolution. "I was wrong," Bartlett quotes him as confessing to his audiences, "and the Black Panthers were wrong. We had a totally political and economic approach, without giving any consideration to the more civilizing influences.'' According to Otis, Cleaver also felt that he and the Panthers had been excessive in their language: ''I think we scared a lot of people. . . . If I had to do it over again, I would do it differently.''

Cleaver's sudden and unpredictable shift in themes, arguments, and explanations led many observers to question his sincerity. Former supporters accused him of selling out or being a con man who used a phony religious conversion to gain reentry into the United States. He confronted these charges by relying on his personal experiences as he moved the burden of proof to his critics. In *Soul on Fire* he stated, ''I feel that I had an experience that has not kept me locked in the 1968 slogans and rhetoric. I am free, but I know a lot of people who are trapped. They are the ones in need of liberation, not me.'' Notwithstanding his rhetorical countercharges, most of his former associates in the Panthers and the Nation of Islam continued to reject him. In his speaking tours for the Unification Church he was often booed and on several occasions was physically attacked.

Although Cleaver changed organizations, arguments, and themes, his rhetorical crusade contained significant elements that remained stable. Whether working outside the system as a proponent of violence or inside as a reborn Christian, he produced a morally grounded rhetoric that attempted to improve the lives of blacks in America. His fame as a speaker and writer made it possible for Cleaver to reach large audiences, and the characteristics that formed his rhetorical profile persisted through much of his career. He customarily invoked experiences from his own life to prove his claims. Coupled with his personal history as one who had been there and done it, his powerful physical presence added to his charisma and credibility as an advocate of revolution and rebirth—he appeared to be a person who could accomplish what he asked of audiences. Moreover, his longstanding ability with language allowed him to express his ideas strikingly and vividly.

Cleaver's steadfast commitment to rhetorical discourse rather than to any of his particular and passing ideologies or doctrines holds the key to explaining his career as an activist. His life as a rhetor reveals his fundamental nature and many of his guiding motives, needs, and values (see Jensen and Hammerback). When one views him as a fundamentally rhetorical being who always believed in and was dedicated to using his words to achieve his ends, the coherence and meaning of his career emerge clearly.

INFORMATION SOURCES

Research Collections and Collected Speeches

There is no single collection of Cleaver's writing and speaking. The *Black Panther*, a publication of the Black Panthers, contains numerous writings and speeches by Cleaver. The following sources are also valuable in studying Cleaver and his discourse:

Foner, Philip, ed. *The Black Panthers Speak.* Philadelphia: Lippincott, 1970.
Heath, G. Louis, ed. *The Black Panther Leaders Speak.* Metuchen, NJ: Scarecrow, 1976.
[*PPW*] Scheer, Robert, ed. *Eldridge Cleaver: Post-Prison Writings and Speeches.* New
       York: Random House, 1969.
[*VBR*] Smith, Arthur, and Stephen Robb, eds. *The Voice of Black Rhetoric: Selections.*
       Boston: Allyn and Bacon, 1971.

Selected Critical Studies

Jensen, Richard J. and John C. Hammerback. "From Muslim to Mormon: Eldridge
       Cleaver's Rhetorical Crusade." *Communication Quarterly* 34 (Winter 1986): 24–
       40.
Schanche, Don A. *The Panther Paradox: A Liberal's Dilemma.* New York: David Mc-
       Kay, 1970.

Selected Biographies

Bartlett, Laile E. "The Education of Eldridge Cleaver." *Reader's Digest*, September
       1976: 65–72.
Cleaver, Eldridge. *Soul on Fire.* Waco, TX: Word Books, 1978.
———. *Soul on Ice.* New York: McGraw-Hill, 1968.
Otis, George. *Eldridge Cleaver: Ice and Fire!* Van Nuys, CA: Bible Voice, 1977.
Rout, Kathleen. *Eldridge Cleaver.* Boston: Twayne, 1991.

CHRONOLOGY OF MAJOR SPEECHES

   [See "Research Collections and Collected Speeches" for source codes.]

"Revolution in the White Mother Country and National Liberation in the Black Colony."
       N.p., n.d. *North American Review,* July/August 1968. This speech is an elabo-
       ration of Cleaver's article "The Land Question and Black Liberation," *Ramparts,*
       April/May 1968; *PPW,* 57–72.
"Stanford Speech." Palo Alto, CA, October 1, 1968. *PPW,* 113–146.
"Farewell Address." N.p., November 22, 1968. *VBR,* 286–295.
"Political Struggle in America." N.p., n.d. *Black Panther,* March 16, 1968; Arthur L.
       Smith. *Rhetoric of Black Revolution.* Boston, MA: Allyn and Bacon, 1969, 166–
       174; *Contemporary American Voices: Significant Speeches in American History,*
       1945–Present. Ed. James R. Andrews and David Zarefsky. New York: Longman,
       1992, 108–113.
"Pronunciamento." Berkeley, CA, November 1, 1968. *Black Panther,* December 21,
       1968.
"Community Imperialism." N.p. n.d. *Black Panther,* April 20, 1969:14.
"A Word to Students." A standard speech delivered on various college campuses. *The
       University and Revolution.* Ed. Gary R. Weaver and James H. Weaver. Engle-
       wood Cliffs, NJ: Prentice-Hall, 1969, 153–164.

ANNA JULIA COOPER
(1858–1964), educator, feminist

Born Annie Julia Haywood in 1858 in Raleigh, North Carolina, Anna Julia
Cooper was the daughter of a slave woman, Hannah Stanley Haywood, and her
white master, George Washington Haywood. In a brief autobiographical statement of her early years, Cooper wrote that "my mother was a slave and the
finest woman I have ever known. . . . Presumably my father was her master, so
I owe him not a sou and she was always too modest and shamefaced ever to
mention him." Mary Helen Washington contended that Cooper knew for a fact
that Haywood was her father, because family records indicated that "Wash"
Haywood, a prominent and successful lawyer in Raleigh until the Civil War,
had "one child by his slave Hannah without benefit of Clergy." When in 1868
the Episcopal church opened St. Augustine's Normal School and Collegiate
Institute for the newly freed slaves, Annie Haywood, then about nine years old,
was among the first of the "colored" children to enter St. Augustine's.

It was at St. Augustine's that, as a teenager, Cooper first began protesting
sexism after she realized that men, as candidates for the ministry, were given
preferential treatment. Women students were steered away from studying theology and the classics. Washington writes that Cooper complained to the principal that "the only mission open before a girl . . . was to marry one of those
candidates." She did, in fact, marry one of those candidates, George Cooper.
Ironically, his death two years later allowed her to pursue a career in teaching,
for at that time no married woman—black or white—was permitted to teach.
Two years after her husband's death, Cooper began writing letters to Oberlin
College in Ohio, requesting free tuition and applying for employment so that
she could earn her room and board. Upon entering Oberlin, Cooper rejected the
"Ladies Course" in favor of the "Gentleman's Course," as she had also done
at St. Augustine's. There Cooper earned a B.A. and later an M.A., and in 1887,

DULANY LIBRARY
WILLIAM WOODS UNIVERSITY
FULTON, MO. 65251

as one of the few blacks with a graduate degree, she was recruited by the District of Columbia's superintendent of colored schools to teach at the only black high school in the city, first known as Washington Colored High School, then as M Street High School, and finally as the famous Dunbar High School.

For several decades, the school educated the children of the aspiring black middle class and gained a reputation for having both high academic standards and a deep-seated snobbery based on class and color. In her early years at M Street, Cooper taught mathematics, science, and Latin. She eventually became principal, and it was in this capacity that, according to her own testimony, she experienced untold instances of sexism that ultimately resulted in her expulsion from the school. In 1905 Cooper was brought before the Board of Education and met several trumped-up charges to the effect that (1) she refused to use a textbook authorized by the board; (2) she was too sympathetic toward weak and unqualified students; (3) she was unable to maintain discipline; and (4) she had not maintained a ''proper spirit of unity and loyalty.'' The dispute dragged on for nearly a year, until the board voted to dismiss her in 1906.

Annette Eaton, a former student at the school, is quoted by Washington as recalling that Cooper might have expected such male hostility:

> The idea of a woman principal of a high school must account in some part for any reaction Dr. Cooper felt against her. . . . It was O.K. for women to be elementary school teachers and principals, but they were not supposed to aspire to any higher rank.

Eaton's letter also attests to the white racism apparent in Cooper's dismissal:

> If you could smell or feel or in any way sense the aura of D.C. in those days, you would know that it only took her daring in having her students accepted and given scholarship [sic] at Ivy League schools to know that the white power structure would be out to get her for any reason and for no reason. It was pure heresy to think that a colored child could do what a white child could.

Cooper returned to M Street School in 1910 when a new superintendent rehired her to teach Latin. She was fifty-two years old then, and the next fifty years of her life were as active as the first. Washington suggested that it was perhaps to assuage the humiliation of her ouster that Cooper began studying for her doctorate at Columbia. Before she could complete Columbia's one-year residency requirement, though, she adopted five orphaned children, ranging in ages from six months to twelve years, who were the grandchildren of her half-brother. She brought all five children from Raleigh to Washington, where she had bought a new home ''to house their Southern exuberance.'' In 1915, at the age of fifty-seven, Anna Julia Cooper thus acquired a mortgage and began parenting five children, even as she continued a full schedule of teaching and work on her doctorate.

When the children's school was not in session, Cooper enrolled them in boarding schools, spending her own summers in Paris. In 1924, after requesting sick leave from her teaching job, she went to Paris to fulfill the residency requirements for the doctorate. Washington reported that apparently the sick leave had not been granted, and after fifty days in Paris Cooper received this cable from a friend: "Rumored dropped if not returned within 60 days." Not wanting to risk losing her retirement benefits or income, Cooper returned to her classroom "5 minutes before 9 on the morning of the 60th day of my absence," greeted by the applause of her students. Despite the malicious interference of her supervisors at M Street, Cooper defended her dissertation in the spring of 1925 and was awarded a doctorate in philology from the University of Paris. At the age of sixty-seven, Cooper was the fourth African-American woman to receive a Ph.D.

Upon her retirement from Paul Laurence Dunbar High School in June 1930, Cooper assumed the presidency of Frelinghuysen University. Frelinghuysen was a small institution, founded in 1907 and intended to provide adult education to working African-Americans. Never placed on a sound financial footing, however, and subject to endemic managerial infighting among its trustees, the university continued to experience fiscal difficulties throughout Cooper's tenure as president. She resigned as president in 1940. While her physical health declined during her retirement years, she remained mentally alert until her death in 1964 at the age of 105.

ANNA JULIA COOPER: EARLY BLACK FEMINIST SPEAKER

One of the more historically significant speaking engagements for African-American women "on the threshold of woman's era" was in 1893 at the World's Congress of Representative Women. As part of the Columbian Exposition in Chicago, the forum provided women in general, and black women in particular, a space to exert a national presence. The struggle for black women's equal representation within the women's suffrage and temperance movements had been continually undermined by white women's persistent racism, and the struggle for representation by black women at the World Congress proved no exception. That there were only six black women representatives in attendance is evidence that even at the dawning of the woman's era, black women were still not welcomed as participants in white women's organizations.

After much debate and controversy, six black women were finally selected as representatives from various African-American women's organizations to speak before the World's Congress of Representative Women. The black women who addressed the predominantly white delegation were Fannie Barrier Williams, Anna Julia Cooper, Fannie Jackson Coppin, Sarah J. Early, Hallie Quinn Brown, and Frances Watkins Harper. According to Loewenberg and Bogin, Fannie Williams spoke about the intellectual progress of "colored women of the United States since the Emancipation Proclamation" and asserted that "less is known

of our women than of any other class of Americans.'' Williams argued that if
the black woman was ever to develop her full intellectual potential, white
women would have to join their black sisters in dismantling the charges of
inferior intelligence and sexual immorality that were persistently leveled at the
latter.

Williams was not alone in arguing against the age-old claims of sexual promiscuity among black women. Following Williams's speech, Cooper spoke to
the congress about the status of black women and their struggle for sexual
autonomy.

> All through the darkest period of the colored woman's oppression in this country
> her yet unwritten history is full of heroic struggle, a struggle against fearful and
> overwhelming odds that often ended in horrible death. . . . The painful, patient,
> and silent toil of mothers to gain a free simple title to the bodies of their daughters,
> the despairing fight . . . to keep hallow their own persons. The majority of our
> women are not heroines—but I do not know that a majority of any race of women
> are heroines. It is enough for me to know that while in the eyes of the highest
> tribunal in America she was deemed no more than a chattel, an irresponsible thing,
> a dull block . . . the Afro-American woman maintained the ideals of womanhood
> unashamed by any ever conceived.

Cooper seemed to have captured the essential issue of gravest concern to black
women of the ''era'' when she contrasted ''the white woman who could at least
plead for her own emancipation'' to ''the black women of the South who have
to suffer and struggle and be silent.'' Her concluding appeal was made to the
''solidarity of humanity, the oneness of life, and the unnaturalness of injustice
of all special favoritisms, whether of sex, race, country or condition.''

These were arguments that Cooper had developed a year earlier in her first
and only full-length book, A Voice from the South, and it is reasonable to conclude that the arguments contained within this work are representative of many
of the arguments raised in her speeches. There are few speech texts of Cooper's
now extant, but many of the speeches she gave took the form of lectures, sometimes to learned societies, sometimes to conventions, and sometimes to the
public. Indeed, the first essay included in A Voice from the South, ''Womanhood:
A Vital Element in the Regeneration and Progress of a Race,'' was originally
a speech delivered in 1886 to a convocation of the African-American clergy of
the Episcopal church. Thus a look at A Voice from the South may provide some
insight into Cooper's oratorical voice.

A Voice from the South is one of the earliest feminist discussions of the social
status of black women. At the heart of Cooper's analysis was her belief that the
status of black women is the only true measure of collective racial progress.
Because the black woman was the least likely to be among the eminent of
society and the most likely to be responsible for the nurturing of families, it
was she, wrote Cooper, who represented the entire race: ''Only the black woman

can say when and where I enter, in the quiet, undisputed dignity of my womanhood, without violence and without suing or special patronage, then and there the whole Negro race enters with me.''

Early on, *A Voice from the South* posed a dramatic challenge to the prevailing ideas about black women, and Cooper never softened her uncompromising tone. She criticized black men for securing higher education for themselves through the avenue of the ministry and for erecting roadblocks to deny women access to those same opportunities: ''While our men seem thoroughly abreast of the times on almost every other subject, when they strike the woman questions they drop back into sixteenth century logic. . . . I fear the majority of colored men do not yet think it worth while [*sic*] that women aspire to higher education.''
If black men were a ''muffled chord,'' then black women, wrote Cooper, were the ''mute and voiceless note'' of the race, with ''no language—but a cry.''

Cooper was equally critical of the white women's movement for its elitism and provinciality, and she challenged white women to link their cause to that of all the ''undefended.'' Always, she measured the ideals and integrity of any group by its treatment of those who suffered the greatest oppression.

The feminist essays that comprised the first half of *A Voice from the South* remain compelling for contemporary readers. Yet, as Mary Helen Washington noted, while Cooper spoke *for* ordinary black women, she rarely spoke *to* them. It is easy to wonder, wrote Washington, how Cooper imagined the relationship between herself, an articulate, powerful speaker and writer, and the woman she described as a mute and voiceless note, ''the sadly expectant Black Woman.'' Clearly, she saw herself as the voice for these women, but nothing in her essays suggests that they existed in her imagination as an audience or as peers. Thus Washington argued that

[Cooper's] voice is not radical, and she writes with little sense of community with a black and female past. But in the light of her special vulnerabilities—and that is how her life and work must be examined—it is all the more remarkable that she develops in *A Voice from the South*, with her critique of dominant groups, an analysis that asserts black womanhood as the vital agency for social and political change in America.

Yet Anna Julia Cooper's voice was indeed radical as she struggled against the public perception that the Negro race's ''talented tenth'' existed only among its males. In her critique of American society, she identified an intimate link between internal and external colonization, between domestic racial oppression and imperialism, and it is here that her analyses were distinct from those of her male counterparts at the turn of the century and indeed can be called ''radical.''

Cooper recognized the role expansionism played in creating ideologies of racial hierarchies. She argued that such flagrant abuse had to be questioned, challenged, and opposed. Thus she condemned the increasing imperial expansion to Asia and the Pacific, a movement that found its appeal in the contemporary philosophy of manifest destiny:

> Whence came this apotheosis of greed and cruelty? Whence this sneaking admiration we all have for bullies and prize-fighters? Whence the self-congratulation of "dominant" races, as if "dominant" meant "righteous" and carried with it a title to inherit the earth? Whence the scorn of so-called weak or unwarlike races and individuals, and the very comfortable assurance that it is their manifest destiny to be wiped out as vermin before this advancing civilization?

By confronting her readers with a series of rhetorical questions, Cooper suggested a reassessment of the history that "produced the self-congratulation of 'dominant' races."

Cooper understood the patriarchal power manifest in imperialism, and she understood equally that its influence and range were nurtured and sustained at home. In her essay "One Phase of American Literature," she attacked the white patriarchy evidenced in American literary culture. As Mary Helen Washington contended, "If Cooper was unwilling to have women's lives subordinated to male texts, she was equally unwilling to have black lives subordinated by white texts." As a literary critic, Cooper leveled her criticism against a system of white male power that had control over the "image of the black," and she was uncompromising in berating such establishment figures as William Dean Howells, Joel Chandler Harris, and George Washington Cable. In *A Voice from the South*, she blasted Howells's and Harris's arrogance and ignorance "for attempting to portray black people and black culture in their work." "[They] have performed a few psychological experiments on their cooks and coachmen, and with astounding egotism, and powers of generalization positively bewildering, forthwith aspire to enlighten the world with dissertations on the racial traits of the negro."

In "Woman versus the Indian," one of the most passionately written chapters, Cooper challenged white women to resist the influence of the long arm of patriarchy. She chastised white women for being preoccupied with maintaining racial castes at the expense of oppressed groups. She began the essay with an anecdote about Wimodaughsis, a woman's culture club in Kentucky, whose name was made up of the first few letters of the four words *wives, mothers, daughters,* and *sisters*. When a black woman approached the club's secretary about membership, the latter was, according to Cooper, "filled with grief and horror that any persons of Negro extractions" should aspire to join this organization and benefit from any advantages it offered women. Indeed, concluded Cooper ironically, the secretary had not calculated that there were any wives, mothers, daughters, and sisters except white ones. "With all her vaunted independence," wrote Cooper, "the American woman of to-day is as fearful of losing caste as a Brahmin in India."

Later in the chapter, Cooper returned to a less satiric rhetorical posture when she confronted the suffrage movement with putting forth arguments that "seem to disparage what is weak." Cooper specifically attacked a paper read by Anna Howard Shaw at the 1891 National Women's Council meeting. In that paper, Shaw had compared the Indian's right to vote with woman's lack of that right. In Shaw's comparison Cooper detected a clear, even if not conscious, ethnocentric attitude. "If woman's own happiness has been ignored or misunderstood," Cooper reprimanded, "let her rest her plea, not on Indian inferiority, nor on Negro depravity, but on the obligation of legislators to do for her as they would have others do for them were relations reversed." In this way, Cooper challenged white suffragists to transform their rhetoric.

Cooper believed that a rhetoric of transformation or, perhaps, a transformation of society through rhetoric would take place when white women reform leaders revolutionized their own thinking and practices. Because she did not believe that black women could wait for radical transformation to occur within the larger women's suffrage movement, Cooper felt strongly that the only effective way to counter patriarchal influence was via education. Education held possibilities for the empowerment of women, who could then shape the course of the future.

Contrary to Mary Helen Washington's assertion that Cooper was disconnected from the black and women's communities, Cooper aligned herself with other black women who were outspoken about racism in general and, in particular, the racism that dominated white women's organizations. She, along with a community of black feminist activists, was well aware that black women had been compromised in an unholy alliance between Northern and Southern white women. Cooper was convinced that the key to understanding the unwritten history of the United States was the dictation and dominance of Southern "influence, ideals and ideas" over the whole nation. Cooper characterized the situation as a preoccupation that was transmitted from Southern women to those of the North. The South, she stated, represented not red blood but blue:

> If your own father was a pirate, a robber, a murderer, his hands are dyed in red blood, and you don't say very much about it. But if your great great great grandfather's grandfather stole and pillaged and slew and you can prove it, your blood has become blue and you are at great pains to establish the relationship. . . . [The South] had blood; and she paraded it with so much gusto that the substantial Puritan maidens of the North . . . began to hunt up the records of the Mayflower to see if some of the passengers thereon could not claim the honor of having been one of William the conqueror's brigands, when he killed the last of the Saxon kings and, red-handed, stole his crown and lands.

Cooper used the juxtaposition of red blood with blue blood as a political indictment of the narrative of national heritage, a narrative that disguised a history of unrestrained murder and theft. Her work provided the frame for an alternative reading of American history that exposed the piratical methods of expansionism inherent in its imperialist ventures. Cooper also reinterpreted the history of

Northern and Southern compromise as the North's courting of a "Southern belle" who was finally allowed to keep the institution of slavery under another name—Jim Crow. In much the same way, she described the suffrage movement as "courting the southern lady." It was the courting of the lady at the expense of the woman, she is quoted by Carby as saying, that was the direct cause of "a constrained, restricted, and provincial outlook in the constituency of the white women's movement."

But, asserted Cooper, in *A Voice from the South*, the movement could be shifted and transformed in a revolutionary and visionary way. It was possible, she concluded, for the American (white) woman to wield power that was felt throughout society; the hierarchical structure of white social organizations ensured that the "leading women" had an influence over men that touched "myriads of church clubs, social clubs, culture clubs, pleasure clubs and charitable clubs." As she saw it, white American women were responsible for American manners and moral codes, "the oil of social machinery."

> [T]he working women of America in whatever station or calling they may be found, are subjects, officers, or rulers of a strong centralized government, and bound together by a system of codes and countersigns, which, though unwritten, forms a network of perfect subordination and unquestioning obedience. . . . At the head and center in this regime stands the Leading Woman in the principality. The one talismanic word that plays along the wires from palace to cook-shop, from imperial Congress to the distant plain, is *Caste*.

Cooper concluded that this talisman—racism—was perpetuated and transmitted to future generations by women who instilled it in their children with their first food. She asserted that white women, unlike black women, exercised a significant influence in shaping the country's social formation even though they could not hold legislative office. She characterized this influence as an ability to be "the teachers and moulders of public sentiment," a sentiment that, she argued, preceded and was the source of "all laws, good or bad," including Jim Crow.

Cooper understood and exposed the divisive tactics of the American suffrage movements and redefined a woman's cause as not that of "the white woman, nor the black woman, but the cause of every man or woman who has writhed silently under a mighty wrong." She intended to expand the rubric of concerns of women to include "all undefended woe," and to encompass an ideal and a set of practices that could become a movement for the liberation of all oppressed peoples, not remain a movement of the defense of parochial and sectional interests in the name of "woman."

By linking imperialism to internal colonization, Cooper provided black women intellectuals with the basis for an analysis of how patriarchal power establishes and sustains gendered and racialized social formations. White women were implicated in the maintenance of this wider system of oppression because they challenged only the parameters of their own domestic confinement. Cooper, however, placed her faith in a transformed woman's movement that would address all aspects of the social organization of oppression:

> It is not the intelligent woman vs. the ignorant woman; nor the white woman vs. the black, the brown, and the red,—it is not even the cause of woman vs. man. Nay,'tis woman's strongest vindication for speaking that the world needs her voice. It would be subversive of every human interest that the cry of one-half the human family be stifled. Woman in stepping from her pedestal of statue-like inactivity in the domestic shrine and daring to think and move and speak ... is merely completing the circle of the world's vision. Hers is every interest that has lacked an interpreter and a defender. Her cause is linked with that of every agony that has been dumb—every wrong that needs a voice.

Recalling her speech before the World's Congress of Representative Women, we are reminded of Cooper's concern for the poorest black women and her belief that they were waging a heroic struggle for the necessities of life—for knowledge, for bread, for dignity, and for the simple right of possession of their own bodies. As a forceful articulation of African-American feminist thought during woman's era, Anna Julia Cooper's discourse, along with that of other nineteenth-century black female intellectuals, did the work of "uplifting" that neither black men nor white women were either willing or able to do. It is in this wider view of service to the humanity of all oppressed peoples that Cooper's written and spoken messages must be read in order to understand her connection to both the black and the female communities.

INFORMATION SOURCES

Research Collections and Collected Speeches

The Anna Julia Cooper Papers are housed in the Moorland-Spingarn Research Center, Howard University, Washington, D.C. There are no published collections of speeches.

Cooper, Anna Julia. *A Voice from the South*. Xenia, OH: Aldine, 1892.

Selected Critical Studies

Carby, Hazel. " 'On the Threshold of Woman's Era': Lynching, Empire and Sexuality in Black Feminist Theory." *"Race," Writing, and Difference*. Ed. Henry Louis Gates, Jr. Chicago: U of Chicago P, 1986, 301–316.

Loewenberg, Bert James, and Ruth Bogin. *Black Women in Nineteenth-Century American Life: Their Words, Their Thoughts, Their Feelings*. University Park: Pennsylvania State UP, 1976.

Tichi, Cecelia. "Women Writers and the New Woman." *Columbia Literary History of the United States*. Ed. E. Elliott. New York: Columbia UP, 1988, 589–606.

Washington, Mary Helen. "Introduction." Anna Julia Cooper. *A Voice from the South*. New York: Oxford UP, 1988, xxvii–liv.

Selected Biographies

Gabel, Leona C. *From Slavery to the Sorbonne and Beyond: The Life and Writings of Anna J. Cooper.* Northampton, MA: Dept. of History, Smith College, 1982.
Hutchinson, Louise Daniel. *Anna J. Cooper: A Voice from the South.* Washington, DC: Smithsonian Institution, 1981.

CHRONOLOGY OF MAJOR SPEECHES

"Womanhood: A Vital Element in the Regeneration and Progress of a Race." (Address to the Convocation of Clergy at the Protestant Episcopal Church). Washington, DC, 1886. *A Voice from the South*, 9–47.

"The Higher Education of Women" (Address to the American Conference of Educators). Washington, DC, March 25–27, 1890. Described in Hutchinson, 89.

"Address to the World's Congress of Representative Women." Chicago, May 15–22, 1893. *The World's Congress of Representative Women.* Vol. 2. Ed. May Wright Sewall. Chicago: Rand, McNally, 1894, 711–715.

"Address to the Second Hampton Negro Conference." Hampton, VA, 1894. Described in Hutchinson, 60–61.

"Address before the First National Conference of Colored Women." Boston, MA, July 29, 1895. Described in Hutchinson, 94.

"The Preservation of Race Individuality" (Lecture delivered to the Pan-African Conference). London, England, July 23–25, 1900. Described in Hutchinson, 110–111.

"The Ethics of the Negro Question" (Address to the Biennial Session of Friends' General Conference). Asbury Park, NJ, September 5, 1902. Described in Hutchinson, 115.

ALEXANDER CRUMMELL
(1819–1898), minister

He did his work,—he did it nobly and well; and yet I sorrow that here he worked alone, with so little human sympathy. His name to-day, in his broad land, means little, and comes to fifty million ears laden with no incense of memory or emulation. (W. E. B. Du Bois, *The Souls of Black Folk*)

In 1827, many Americans hailed the Fourth of July, the traditional American independence holiday, as sacred—a time to promulgate American values in celebrations around the country. The exception was the African-American population. In New York and other Northern cities, African-Americans protested Fourth of July celebrations, celebrating their own state emancipation on July fifth, as they denounced Southern bondage. African-Americans could only hope for freedom in the South and equal opportunity in the North. A society of several youths from the New York African Free School protested the institution of slavery that supplied labor for Southern aristocrats on the Fourth of July. One of them was Alexander Crummell.

Crummell, the then eight-year-old son of New York City African-American activist Boston Crummell, began to develop his voice of protest early. It was a continuous voice of hope for the restoration of Africa and its descendants that he maintained through a rhetorical career that lasted more than fifty years. At the African Free School in New York City, where several emerging black leaders studied, including Henry Highland Garnet, Samuel Ringgold Ward, and James McCune Smith, Crummell began his pursuit of knowledge in the academy and the development of rhetorical skills. His rhetorical finesse was visible internationally as he served as an Episcopal minister, civil rights movement crusader, intellectual, and moralist. His experience at the African Free School gave him a superb start as a leader, scholar, and orator.

Though Crummell was a contemporary of leading black abolitionists and former slaves such as Frederick Douglass, he was less noted as one of the black abolitionist orators during the antebellum years. Instead, he was one of the earliest recognized speakers who aimed to subvert racism and discrimination, for he was born of a free middle-class black family in New York and became actively involved in battling racism in the Episcopal church in his attempt to enter the profession as an Episcopal clergyman. During his effort to enter a traditionally white ministerial order, he became well known among the abolitionist elite. While Frederick Douglass was calculating an escape from slavery in 1835, Crummell grappled with racism at the all-white preparatory school for youth in Canaan, New Hampshire, where townspeople physically dragged the school into a swamp to protest the attendance of three black youths: Alexander Crummell, Henry Highland Garnet, and Thomas Sidney. Just months after the incident, Crummell gained entrance into Oneida Institute in Whitesboro, New York, and successfully completed a program of study at the school abolitionist Beriah Green operated. However, he faced one of his most memorable encounters with discrimination when the Episcopal diocese, especially its head, Bishop Benjamin T. Onderdonk, denied him admission to General Theological Seminary because of race rather than ability. He was finally ordained a priest in Philadelphia in 1844 but became a minister in New York. His struggles with Onderdonk began his rhetorical battle with religious institutions, especially the Episcopal church, and his social activism against racism, a battle that tried his faith, but one through which he asserted his hope for the death of discrimination and the restoration of African dignity.

Like many of his African-American contemporaries of all political walks, Crummell adopted standards of European culture and constructed goals for improving the conditions of people of color based upon European values and social, economic, and political norms. However, unlike many of his African-American contemporaries, he received training in Britain at Queens College, Cambridge, where he completed a degree in 1851, making him one of the first African-Americans to receive a degree from a British university, and he worked as a missionary in Liberia, West Africa, for more than twenty years. These combined experiences made him unique among African-American activists. Crummell was a contemplative man, burdened by religious and philosophical questions about human destiny and race and the moral imperatives of humans in his attempt to understand the reasons for the plight of black people and to advocate practical solutions for advancement.

CRUMMELL'S RHETORIC OF HOPE AND SELF-DETERMINATION

Most of Crummell's preserved discourses were sermons addressed to congregations in Liberia and America. More than three hundred of these sermons were published during Crummell's lifetime. His rhetorical career evolved over four stages in his professional career: 1841–47; 1848–53; 1853–72; and 1873–98. His discourse in the first stage of his rhetorical career included sermons and commentaries during his difficult battle with acceptance in the Episcopal church. The second stage of his rhetorical career included sermons and lectures during his years in England as a student at Queens College, Cambridge. The third stage consisted of published sermons and lectures while he was a minister and leader in Liberia, West Africa. Finally, the fourth stage of his rhetorical career included lectures given during the final years of his life in the United States.

Crummell's work in Liberia removed him from a crucial period of African-American social protest (1848–72). However, respect for his character and acknowledgment of his eloquence were clear from black leaders with whom he frequently communicated. His writings and speeches, all of which were in manuscript form, reveal that he was one of the most lucid African-American writers and thinkers of the period. He avoided the bombastic writing and speaking style characteristic of the period and instead opted for simplicity, directness, and brevity. This refreshing style was atypical of intellectuals of his time. His speaking voice was equally as eloquent. The content of Crummell's rhetoric ranged from fundraising appeals to the denunciation of slavery, from proper educational models to moral guidelines for living.

Throughout all four eras of Crummell's rhetorical career, he was preoccupied with the theme of hope as a source for survival and of pride in God's special hand in black affairs. Crummell shared the hope for a better day when humanity would reach a higher level of perfection with numerous other African-American leaders of the day. This thought, expounded in the discourse of many black orators, both clergy and lay leaders, is explained by black clergy who have sought doctrinal answers to oppression and have ultimately turned to liberation theology. Liberation theology is the view that God participates in an oppressed group's situation. God is not a distant, hierarchical authority, but, rather, participates in the experience of each person. The God of righteousness does not reside in a separate and definitive location or period. In other words, there is no gulf between God and the world where God is static and the world fluent.

Crummell's vision was of an enlightened America that embraced all of humankind. Black orators of the time sought ways to motivate blacks beyond their condition. Consequently, they stressed survival despite thwarting conditions. Crummell's theology confronted the issue of race in God's divine plan. He concluded that the suffering of people of African descent had strengthened rather than weakened the race, and that African survival despite conditions of slavery proved divine guidance toward a destiny of prosperity for people of African descent. Blacks should move beyond their feelings of shame to a feeling of pride and dignity, since God would prevail in bringing African-Americans out of darkness. As such, blacks should feel pride rather than degradation, because divine providence would personally uplift blacks from their current state.

Crummell's "Hope for Africa" sermon preached in 1852 in England for the benefit of the Ladies' Negro Education Society is an important example of his liberation theology. The sermon has parallels with those of his contemporaries because it roots the burden of oppression of African peoples in biblical deliverance and prophecies of the imminent restoration of Africa and her people to a state of prosperity. The scriptural text of the sermon is the most commonly preached of African-Americans, Psalm 68:31: "Ethiopia shall soon stretch out her hands unto God."

> Just look at these facts—note the great progress of the African race. See the civil and religious improvement they have made alike in Africa and in the lands of their captivity. Mark the religious solicitude they are manifesting on every hand. Observe the peculiar providences which are just now occurring in connection with them; and then remember that nearly all these events, all this progress, has taken place during the short period of fifty years.

In his speech "The Need of New Ideas and New Motives for a New Era" to the graduating class of 1885 at Storer College, Harper's Ferry, West Virginia, Crummell stressed hope for the future and urged caution in returning to thoughts of the past. He said, "The urgent needs of the present, the fast-crowding and momentous interests of the future appear to be forgotten. Duty for to-day, hope for the morrow, are ideas which seem oblivious to even leading minds among us." In other words, Crummell was concerned about an African-American preoccupation with victimization rather than plans for the future and making progress toward regeneration and rejuvenation. His vision was long-range, yet he felt that some within the African-American rank and file were consumed with the short term and preoccupied with the devastation of slavery. For this reason, Crummell frequently lectured to youth when he permanently returned to the United States in 1872. During this period, Crummell focused on hope realized through specific goals and progressive efforts implemented through a new generation of blacks. As he told the Storer College graduating class, "For 200 years the misfortune of the black race has been the confinement of its mind in the pent-up prison of human bondage. The morbid, absorbing and abiding recollection of that condition—what is it but the continuance of that same condition, in memory and dark imagination?" Crummell proceeded to offer solutions: "The only means by which its formidable difficulties may be overcome are time, and arduous labor, and rugged endurance, and the quiet apprenticeship in humble duties, and patient waiting, and the clear demonstration of undoubted capacities."

Crummell's theme of hope was echoed from America to England to Liberia. Wherever he went, he preached on pride, perseverance, and posterity, each of which was intertwined with hope for change. He worked diligently to offer a foundation of long-term planning and a vision of future prosperity for Liberia. In his speech "The Responsibility of the First Fathers of a Country, for Their Future Life and Destiny," delivered before young men in Monrovia, Liberia, on December 1, 1863, Crummell spoke of the fulfillment of hope and prosperity through vision and careful planning for the future:

> We have placed our feet in the hard, the toilsome, the blood-stained track which we trust will bring to our descendants the grand realities, and the noble fruits we desire in a nation. But all this a future thing which we, of this day, are to anticipate and provide for. . . . What is the future life and character that you would fain secure this country? How would you characterize the ideal national existence which you crave for your posterity? What is the status, the substance, the features of the commonwealth which, say a hundred years hence, you would have as the result and outgrowth of your present aims, activities, and aspirations?

The marked distinction in African-American freedom rhetoric at this time was its focus on the imminence of freedom—a near-immediate change in circumstances for black people and belief in imminent justice for all. Liberation was forthcoming. However, Crummell added to this liberation theology that blacks should prepare for a long-term future whether in Africa or America, one that would plant the seeds for economic, social, and religious prosperity. He did not simply offer an abstract hope for an imminent change. He offered philosophical and practical prescriptions for implementing a successful program of effective intellectual leadership coupled with physical work in both Africa and America, themes that his African-American followers, W. E. B. Du Bois and Booker T. Washington, expanded upon in separate programs.

Without the burden of experience as a slave, Crummell's world was paradoxical. He was first and foremost an intellectual who preferred research and teaching over the grueling tasks of the ministry. As a conservative, he believed in an intellectual elite and in the moral depravation of slaves. His rhetoric adhered to a view that the circumstances of slavery created moral, social, and intellectual depravation. As such, it was incumbent upon the free black population and its leaders to raise slaves out of their darkness by ensuring their education. Thus he argued that African-American self-improvement was the surest means to overcome race prejudice, and that blacks must not succumb to white paternalism. His study of the classics, philosophy, and the condition of slavery, especially that of African peoples, jointly influenced his thinking about the dilemma of blacks in the United States. While he argued that the abolitionist movement would be a crucial vehicle for the ultimate emancipation of slaves through moral suasion, he also cautioned against too much emphasis upon treating African-Americans as victims. His solution to illiteracy and lack of education for slaves was to cultivate free blacks morally and socially, an argument he frequently expounded upon throughout his oratory. His rhetorical appeals always offered a source of hope in the struggle for racial progress.

The other side of Crummell's rhetorical paradox was his strong black nationalism stance. While Crummell had studied the great ideas of Western philosophers such as Plato and Aristotle and had adopted some of their views as a student at Cambridge, his experience in Liberia demonstrated his other side: a man determined to reclaim an African past and to uplift people of African descent to a state of prosperity and the African continent to a strong and healthy nation. His speeches on Africa such as "Hope for Africa" anticipated a religious reawakening in Africa and demonstrated that he considered it his duty to bring all Africans to a renewed state of moral and social consciousness. But his dilemma was that his education and training instilled the values of European culture, and it was the European cultural view of morality and social consciousness that he advocated for African adoption.

The theme of moral regeneration through Christianity as a means toward eliminating racial castes was prevalent in his discourse. Racial self-improvement was gained through education and the ability to disseminate information within the community. As early as the 1840s, Crummell was an advocate of separate black institutions, including a black college and a national black press. However, he was unable to continuously advocate these projects, as his career took him to England from 1848 until 1853, then to Liberia from 1853 until 1872, two paths that prohibited his activism in the United States for nearly twenty-five years. While these ventures kept Crummell from social activism in the United States, they uniquely shaped his discourse upon his return to the United States for his final years—more than twenty years of work that ended only with his death. His published sermons and lectures from 1872 until his death demonstrate that Crummell's hope for Africa and African-Americans was lodged in the future generation of his people. Many of his sermons and lectures upon his permanent return from Africa were directed toward African-American youth. Furthermore, upon Crummell's return to the United States, he acted on his belief in separate institutions as founder of the American Negro Academy and supporter of numerous black organizations aimed at uplifting blacks intellectually and socially. Crummell's rhetorical agenda was committed to building a strong African-American infrastructure, an independent black nation.

As a thinker, Crummell anticipated Booker T. Washington and W. E. B. Du Bois. Crummell's rhetoric advocated black nationalism to the extent that he promulgated black social and economic independence through self-help. He also advocated the traditional values of self-help through manual-labor programs for the masses and black intellectual leadership. Washington later took up Crummell's philosophy of self-help manual-labor education in an effort to increase skilled labor in black communities. Several of Crummell's *Africa and America* speeches focused on the importance of skilled labor as opposed to liberal arts training for blacks. In his 1884 speech "Excellence, an End of the Trained Intellect" before a Washington, D. C., high-school class, he said, "You will remember just here that utility, though somewhat crude and homely, compared with excellence, is the end and object of life. For doing duty, accomplishing work, applying knowledge to useful ends, carrying on enterprises in the world; all this is *the* work of life." In 1886, just nine years before Booker T. Washington's "Atlanta Exposition Address," Crummell argued in his sermon

"Common Sense in Common Schooling" that "if you begin your child's school life by the separation of books and learning from manual labor, then you begin his education with poison as the very first portion of his intelligent life!" W. E. B. Du Bois hailed both Crummell's intellectualism and his emphasis upon the important role of the black elite in leading and educating the masses of blacks. Moreover, unlike Booker T. Washington, Crummell's black nationalist rhetoric instilled racial pride, an important goal of W. E. B. Du Bois.

This essay is written in the spirit of Crummell, perhaps ambivalent and ambiguous in his attempt to battle with issues of race, class, nationalism, and separatism during the nineteenth century. For in his voice, there was what W. E. B. Du Bois made clear in *The Souls of Black Folk*, a decided double-consciousness: a divide between conservatism and radicalism—charging against racism and discrimination in hundreds of sermons and speeches, and on the other hand embracing European values that foster caste according to race. Racism forced Crummell to renounce and battle his opponents at the same time that he embraced traditional European values and teachings as solutions for his people. The rhetorical thread that unified Crummell with other African-American leaders of the time was his uplifting theme of hope for a regeneration of Africa and the restoration of African peoples to full prosperity. He offered a vision for survival despite thwarting conditions. Crummell offered a problem-solution rhetoric, seldom engaging in long philosophical exposition, but often presenting practical principles from which to live whether a sermon or a lecture. He was consistently an advocate for long-range planning devised from lessons of the past. He did not condone commiserating about slavery and hailed strategies for fulfilling a prosperous destiny for African-Americans. Optimism through hope was conveyed through his plain, lucid writing and speaking style that often laid out scripture followed by a clear division of points. Crummell rarely searched for ideas in his treatises on morality and education, nor did he offer strong emotional pleas. His most passionate pleas were constructed around visualizations of what black life could be, the "ought," through hope, a vision of a common destiny, and work toward practical solutions for racial uplift. His plan called for effective leaders trained as intellectuals, for this was a fundamental requirement for leadership, but also leaders trained in manual labor. His rhetoric, both sermons and lectures, denounced pure intellectual pursuits as an answer to the African-American dilemma, for such training alone fostered nonproductive citizens.

The ambivalence between advocating black nationalism and holding Eurocentric values, religious principles, and general philosophy that Crummell faced is no less than that of any black leader and writer in 1990s American society. We might begin with the academy as an example of the ambivalence that forced Crummell's rhetorical dilemma. For instance, this essay appears in a work that embraces the voice of African-Americans from the perspective of rhetoricians. The discipline of rhetorical studies has traditionally excluded voices of minority participants who have actively participated in the practice of rhetoric and have helped shape American policies and values. But academic careers are made from works that participate in the latest tide of writings, and the present tide is that of multiculturalism and ethnic studies, whether the scholar who serves as author has training or expertise in the area or not. This essay is published within such a current.

There is personal ambivalence about participating in the political tide within an exclusionary discipline, touting African-American culture because it is a politically hot topic. But the aim here is not to offer Crummell as a sacrificial lamb to this tide of interest from academicians who have a passing interest in African-Americans out of political necessity. Instead the purpose of participation is to support those who are conducting serious scholarship in the area of black studies and rhetoric, those who intend to highlight the rhetorical worth of innovative African-American activists who have established and are establishing rhetorical standards in the context of their time. Grappling with such a rhetorical dilemma is vintage Crummell.

INFORMATION SOURCES

Research Collections and Collected Speeches

[ACP] Alexander Crummell Papers. Arthur A. Schomburg Collection, New York Public Library.

[AAA] Crummell, Alexander. *Africa and America: Addresses and Discourses*. Springfield, MA: Willey, 1891.

[FOA]——. *The Future of Africa: Being Addresses, Sermons, Etc., Etc., Delivered in the Republic of Liberia*. New York: Charles Scribner, 1862.

[GCO]——. *The Greatness of Christ and Other Sermons*. New York: Thomas Whittaker, 1882.

[DAR] Moses, Wilson Jeremiah, ed. *Destiny and Race: Selected Writings, 1840–1898*. Amherst: U of Massachusetts P, 1992.

Selected Critical Studies

Heath, Robert L. "Alexander Crummell and the Strategy of Challenge by Adaptation." *Central States Speech Journal* 26 (Fall 1975): 178–187.

Scruggs, Otey M. "We the Children of Africa in This Land: Alexander Crummell." *Africa and the Afro-American Experience*. Ed. Lorraine A. Williams. Washington, DC: Howard UP, 1977, 77–95.

Wahle, Kathleen O'Mara. "Alexander Crummell: Black Evangelist and Pan-Negro Nationalist." *Phylon* 29 (1968): 388–395.

Selected Biographies

Moses, Wilson Jeremiah. *Alexander Crummell: A Study of Civilization and Discontent*. Amherst: Univ. of Massachusetts Press, 1992.

Rigsby, Gregory U. *Alexander Crummell: Pioneer in Nineteenth-Century Pan-African Thought*. Westport, CT: Greenwood, 1987.

CHRONOLOGY OF MAJOR SPEECHES

[See "Research Collections and Collected Speeches" for source codes.]

"Address to the Albany Convention." Albany, NY, August 18–20, 1840. *A Documentary History of the Negro People in the United States*. Ed. Herbert Aptheker. New York: Citadel, 1971. 201–205.

"Eulogium on the Life and Character of Thomas Clarkson, Esq., of England." New York, NY, December 26, 1846. *AAA*, 199–267.

"Address before the British and Foreign Anti-Slavery Society." *Anti-Slavery Reporter*, June 2, 1851:87–89; *DAR*, 158–164.

"Address of Rev. Alexander Crummell at the Anniversary Meeting of the Massachusetts Colonization Society." *Liberia: The Land of Promise to Free Colored Men*. Ed. Edward Wilmot Blyden and Alexander Crummell. Washington, DC: American Colonization Society, 1861.

"Hope for Africa." Bristol, England, April 21, 1852. *FOA*, 285–323.

"The Responsibility of the First Fathers of a Country, for Their Future Life and Destiny." Monrovia, Liberia, December 1, 1863. *AAA*, 127–163.

"Eulogium on Rev. Henry Highland Garnet, D.D." Washington, DC, May 4, 1882. *AAA*, 269–305.

"Excellence, an End of the Trained Intellect." Washington, DC, June 6, 1884. *AAA*, 343–354.

"The Need of New Ideas and New Motives for a New Era." Harper's Ferry, West Virginia, 1885. *AAA*, 11–36.

"Common Sense in Common Schooling." Washington, DC, September 13, 1886. *AAA*, 325–341.

ANGELA YVONNE DAVIS
(1944–   ), activist, professor

CINDY L. GRIFFIN

Although Angela Y. Davis was once labeled a dangerous, hardened criminal, she describes herself as a Black woman who is a Communist, a woman who has dedicated her "life to the struggle for the life of Black people," the struggle against racism and sexism. Her rhetoric is both radical and revolutionary, and as an orator, she captures the devastating impacts of both immediate and long-term oppression. In her speeches, Davis identifies and examines the myriad interconnections between past and present; she explores the connections between racism and sexism, economic oppression and violence, and the impending nuclear annihilation brought about by the government's domestic and foreign policies. Throughout her speeches, she presents a vision of a world without any of these foes: a world in which African-American women and men live in health, safety, and respect; a world in which children are free to grow, play, and learn without physical or mental harassment and harm; and a world in which the human spirit is strong not because it refuses to be broken but because it is nurtured, valued, and encouraged. Davis's skill and contribution as an orator rest in her ability to call attention to the subtle and the overt oppression that occurs in the present and the past while simultaneously building a vision of a safer and healthier future.

Born on January 27, 1944, Davis grew up in the neighborhood known as Dynamite Hill in Birmingham, Alabama. The nickname "Dynamite Hill" was given to the area because of the numerous bombings that took place in it—bombings designed to prohibit African-Americans from moving and living there. As a young child, she writes in her autobiography, Davis learned the lessons of racism and poverty well and vowed to herself that she would never wish she were white, regardless of the privileges afforded to those with the "right" skin color. In elementary school, she learned more than the mechanics of reading, writing, and arithmetic; she learned "that just because one is hungry, one does not have the right to a good meal; or when one is cold, to warm clothing, or when one is sick, to medical care."

Davis attended high school in Birmingham until her junior year and then, looking for greater academic challenges, entered Elizabeth Irwin High School in New York City. In her history classes there, Davis was exposed to communism, where the theories in the *Communist Manifesto* hit her "like a bolt of lightning." In the *Manifesto*, she found answers to the dilemmas of racial oppression with which she had struggled as a young child and began to get a sense of how emancipation for black people might become a reality. In 1961, Davis entered Brandeis University to study French literature and spent her junior year abroad in France. From an American newspaper in France, she learned of the murder of four young girls in the bombing of the 16th Street Baptist Church in Birmingham, Alabama—three of whom were friends of her family. She described her grief and fury over these brutal and senseless killings: "No matter how much I talked, the people around me were simply incapable of grasping it. They could not understand why the whole society was guilty of this murder— why their beloved Kennedy was also to blame, why the whole ruling stratum in their country, by being guilty of racism, was also guilty of this murder."

Committed to social change and possessing a burning desire to study philosophy, Davis, after her return to Brandeis, scheduled a meeting with Herbert Marcuse, who was teaching at Brandeis. This first meeting grew into weekly discussions of her readings on the philosophers he suggested. In her last year at Brandeis, Davis applied for and received a scholarship to study philosophy in Frankfurt. After graduating Phi Beta Kappa and magna cum laude from Brandeis, she left to study in Germany. The civil rights struggle in America and her intense desire to be a part of it brought her home from Germany in 1967, before she completed her graduate studies, but not before Marcuse had agreed to direct her dissertation at the University of California in San Diego. Davis took her first teaching job at the University of California, Los Angeles, in 1969 before completing her degree. Engaged in the civil rights movement in Southern California, a member of the Black Panthers, and a member of the Communist party, she apparently was more than the Board of Regents could handle. Fired from her teaching position at UCLA because of her political views, reinstated, and then fired again, Davis's life became more dramatic, public, and revolutionary. In 1970, Davis was placed on the FBI's "Ten Most Wanted" list on charges of murder, kidnapping, and conspiracy after guns registered in her name were used in a failed attempt to take hostages from a Marin County courthouse in exchange for several black political prisoners. She was incarcerated without bail for twenty months and finally was acquitted of all charges in 1972. All of Davis's papers were seized by the FBI at the time of her arrest, including her work on her dissertation, and she has yet to see any of them returned to her.

Since the 1970s, Davis has been a lecturer at Claremont College in California, Stanford University, and San Francisco State University. She is currently a professor in the History of Consciousness program at the University of California, Santa Cruz. Davis explained her life of public activism and struggle as follows: "For me revolution was never an interim 'thing-to-do' before settling down; it was no fashionable club with newly minted jargon, or new kind of social life—made thrilling by risk and confrontation. Revolution is a serious thing. . . . When one commits oneself to the struggle, it must be for a lifetime."

ANGELA DAVIS: REVOLUTIONARY POLITICS, RADICAL CONNECTIONS

Throughout her career as a speaker, Davis has relied on her revolutionary politics and her Communist perspective to weave together seemingly disparate and disconnected themes. At the core of her rhetoric is her powerful and relentless argument for the end of racism and sexism as well as a recognition of the interconnections between both forms of oppression. Each of her speeches contains, in some form, a call for the recognition of the relationships among racism, sexism, economic oppression, and violence against women and all people of color. Her speeches reflect her vision of a world without racism—a world without the daily reality of danger, harassment, and death for African-Americans. Davis asks her audiences to recognize and resist racism in its most subtle and blatant forms, to speak out against sexism, and to protest economic oppression in as many ways as they are able.

Although texts of Davis's speeches prior to 1983 are not available, her work from the 1980s and beyond is marked by a consistency that likely applies to her earlier oratory. From her prison cell in 1971, for example, Davis issued a tribute to be read at the funeral of George Jackson, one of the Soledad Brothers killed by prison guards in San Quentin Prison in 1971. Jackson was a close friend of Davis's, the author of the militant book, *Soledad Brother*, and a powerful voice in the fight against racism in the late 1960s and early 1970s. This early text reads similarly to Davis's later rhetoric, as Davis made connections across themes and between experiences in ways that foreshadowed her published speeches of the 1980s. In her eulogy to Jackson, Davis linked the imprisonment of Black and Third World people to racism and classism, using the prison sentence of one year to life given to Jackson at the age of eighteen for a robbery involving seventy dollars—and the eleven years served until his murder—as her example. Jackson's imprisonment and death, she explained, was a sign of the intense need to strengthen the mass movement against oppression, and his memory and legacy must fuel the fires of resistance within the African-American community. While not as intricately developed as her later speeches, this early text suggests Davis's recognition of interconnections and her ability to locate individual experiences within the larger issues of race and class.

In one of her earliest published speeches, "Imagining the Future," addressed to the 1983 graduating seniors of Berkeley High School, Davis created a vision of a world free from oppression for her audience. Once believing that the youth of the 1980s were more concerned with MTV than political issues, she apologized for accepting uncritically the "propagandistic notions" that caused her to misjudge her audience. Davis surmised that "unconcerned and apolitical young people obviously would not have invited a woman who is a Communist and activist in radical political struggles" to act as their keynote speaker. Rather than continuing to doubt their abilities, Davis placed her faith in these young women and men and encouraged them to engage in the struggle for political and personal freedom. She asked them to imagine a world in which they could live with dignity and to imagine a future of justice, equality, and peace.

The future, Davis explained, belonged to these graduating seniors—young people who certainly could run the country much more efficiently and peacefully than it currently was being run. She asked them to envision a world in which everyone had a home, enough food to eat, a well-paying job, and respect. She asked her audience to imagine a shorter work week, free education, equal opportunities for women and men, no homophobia, no sexism, and no Ku Klux Klan. She asked them to dream a world without the draft, without war, without capital punishment, without prisons, and without the "oppression of people of color." Imagining a future was not enough, however, and she explained that "we must do more than engage in such flights of imagination." The future depended on her audience's willingness to "march, protest, petition, and pursue whatever other avenues of collective resistance will guarantee that one day all people will live together in total peace." They must do this, she explained, because each person is responsible for the future; "All of us, the young and the old alike, women as well as men, must stand up, speak out, and fight for a better world."

As she addressed the graduating Black students at the University of California at Los Angeles two years later, Davis reminded her audience that, while they might have a vision for their own futures, they, too, must recognize their role in creating change and must never forget the relationship between the past and the future. In her 1985 speech, "Reaping Fruit and Throwing Seed," she asked the members of her audience to link themselves to their history and to remember "that people marched and organized, were arrested and lost their jobs—some even lost their lives—in order to clear the way for this victorious moment" of graduation: "I urge you to reflect not only on your own time and efforts, but on the struggles of our forebears as well, which made it possible for you to attend this university, to gain an education, and to collect your diplomas here today." While the struggles before them would be daunting at times, and oppression and discrimination surely awaited them, connections to other oppressed peoples must remain at the center of their visions. Just as the people of South Africa would prevail, so, too, would these students. They must remember, however, the poverty of others, the oppression and violence leveled against their children and people of color, Reagan's racist policies, and the marginalization of their own communities. By highlighting these particular issues and experiences, Davis reminded her audience of the connections among the past, the present, and the future as well as oppression in other parts of the world. She concluded that as "you reap the fruit of past struggles, you must also throw the seed for future battles."

Regardless of her topic, Davis's speeches brought to the forefront the centuries-long struggle against oppression and the violence and harassment African-American people had endured. In her 1984 address to the conference on Women and the Struggle against Racism, "Facing Our Common Foe," Davis not only identified the marginalization Black women experienced as a result of the insensitivity of many of the white women involved in the women's movement, but she expressed the need to unify struggles against sexism and to place black women's experiences at the center of this struggle. Historically as well as currently, white leaders of the women's movement had ignored the needs of their black sisters, considering the "triple oppression" felt and voiced by black women as "at best of marginal relevance to their experiences." What women of all colors needed to recognize, Davis argued, was that in the "pyramid" of oppression, black women resided at the bottom, while white women, depending on their economic status, resided at or near the top. Changes at the top of the pyramid affected only those who resided at the top, but changes at the bottom of the pyramid affected all who resided within this structure. "The forward movement of women of color almost always initiates progressive change for all women," she explained.

Davis linked advances made in the present to African-American women and men of the recent past. The national political campaigns of Shirley Chisholm, Charlene Mitchell (the 1968 Communist party's presidential candidate), Charlotta Bass (the 1952 Progressive party's vice-presidential candidate), Davis herself (who was the vice-presidential candidate for the Communist party's 1980 and 1984 campaigns), and Jesse Jackson had all pushed the boundaries of racism and oppression, she asserted, making the path that others would follow a little easier. Jesse Jackson might have "opened the door," Davis reminded her audience, but Geraldine Ferraro "walked through!" While advances had been made, she cautioned, Black women still remained discredited and marginalized. "If it was necessary for Sojourner Truth to exclaim, 'Ain't I a woman?' in 1851, Black women are still compelled to expose the invisibility to which we have been relegated, in both theory and practice, within large sectors of the established women's movement."

Davis did more than recognize the interconnections of past and present; she offered solutions to the oppressive conditions she saw. Rather than continue to perpetuate this marginalization, she argued, the women's movement must place the concerns and experiences of African-American women at the very core of their agenda: "In order for the women's movement to meet the challenges of our time, the special problems of racially oppressed women must be given strategic priority." Women of color and working-class women "confront sexist oppression in a way that reflects the real and complex objective interconnections between economic, racial, and sexual oppression." For these reasons, issues of women's poverty, welfare benefits, teen pregnancy, safe contraception, abortion, child care, education, affirmative action, and well-paying jobs "must be given strategic priority" within the women's movement. Although these issues might be faced by women of all colors, Davis explained, the recognition that these were issues that Black women faced in a more devastating way would facilitate the elimination of racist structures within the women's movement itself. The "process of exorcising racism from our ranks," she argued, "will determine whether the women's movement will ultimately have a part in bringing about radical changes in the socioeconomic structures of this country."

Not only must white women recognize the oppression perpetuated by marginalizing African-American women, but they must eradicate the racist structures within their own movement by being especially clear about the sexist and racist structures embedded in society as a whole. In her speech "We Do Not Consent: Violence against Women in a Racist Society," presented in 1985 at Florida State University, Davis identified these structures by arguing that a web of interconnections existed between the past and the present, between global violence and localized racist actions. With sexual assault as her focus, Davis carefully identified the interconnections between global and local violence. Sexual assault, she explained, must be situated "within its larger sociopolitical context. If we wish to comprehend the nature of sexual violence as it is experienced by women as individuals, we must be cognizant of its social mediations" at the global level.

Davis reminded her audience that the "imperialist violence imposed on the people of Nicaragua, the violence of South African apartheid, and the racist-inspired violence inflicted on Afro-Americans and other racially oppressed people here in the United States" are linked to "[r]ape, sexual extortion, battering, spousal rape, sexual abuse of children, and incest." Citing June Jordan's "Poem About My Rights," Davis suggested that Black women were considered "the wrong people of the wrong skin on the wrong continent." The violence that occurred against women of color in South Africa, Namibia, Angola, Zimbabwe, and numerous other countries meant that for the Black woman, the message was still "I was wrong I was wrong again to be me being me where I was/wrong to be who I am." For Davis, "sexual violence against individual women and neocolonial violence against people and nations" had clear parallels.

In her speech, Davis brought her argument from this global level down to the local, domestic level and then moved back again to the question of global violence. She explained that at the local level, "one out of three women will be sexually assaulted in her life time." In addition, "one out of four girls will be raped before she reaches the age of eighteen. Despite these startling statistics, there is only a 4 percent conviction rate of rapists—and these convictions reflect only the minute percentage of rapes that are actually reported." More rapes were committed by white men than Black, but "there are a disproportionately large number of Black men in prison on rape convictions"—a testament to the racist U.S. penal system. The myth of the Black man raping the white woman,

Davis continued, was simply that—a myth. Davis reminded her audience that "proportionately more white men rape Black women than Black men rape white women." The final irony of this oppressive situation lay in history because "Black women's bodies were considered to be accessible at all times to the slave master as well as to his surrogates" during slavery. White men rape Black and white women, but Black men go to jail.

Leaving this local level and returning to the larger global political arena, Davis argued that as imperialist aggression increased, so, too, did domestic and racist violence against women. As violence around the world became more wide-spread, women could "expect that individual men will be more prone to commit acts of sexual violence against the women around them." Men are socialized to rape, she argued, and the level of violence inflicted on women is often a result of official policy. Her audience need only consider the atrocities of Viet-nam to be reminded of this. In Vietnam, she argued, "U.S. soldiers often re-ceived instructions for their search and destroy missions that involved 'searching' Vietnamese women's vaginas with their penises." Sexual assault, she argued, "bears a direct relationship to all of the existing power structures in a given society. This relationship is not a simple, mechanical one, but rather involves complex structures reflecting the interconnectedness of the race, gender, and class oppression that characterize the society." Foreign policy condoned and even encouraged sexual assault, and domestic actions followed in kind.

Davis continued to develop the theme of interconnectedness by relating global violence to local violence. She argued that the "explosion of sexual violence" in the United States was happening at a time when the government had "de-veloped the means with which to annihilate human life itself." The government spent millions and millions of dollars an hour on "the most devastating instru-ments of violence" the human race had ever known, taking that money from programs that assisted people living in or near poverty; just five hours of military spending—$200 million—"could provide annual support for sixteen hundred rape crisis centers and battered women's shelters." Davis's strategy was not only to expose the myth of sexual assault but to link military destruction and spending to women's abuse and oppression. Violence against women occurred at the local and the global level, and activists must contextualize the rape epi-demic in order to dismantle the structures that perpetuated this atrocity. From police violence against African-American women in the United States to the policies of Vietnam, South Africa, and Central America, "sexual violence can never be completely eradicated until we have successfully effected a whole range of radical social transformations in our country."

In 1987, Davis turned her attention from sexual violence to questions of violence against African-American women's health. In a speech delivered to the North Carolina Black Women's Health Project at Bennett College in Greens-boro, North Carolina, "Sick and Tired of Being Sick and Tired: The Politics of Black Women's Health," Davis drew interconnections not between global and local issues but between health and poverty. Never fond of Ronald Reagan, in this address Davis used statistic after statistic and example after example to illustrate the damage that Reagan's policies had done to African-American women, revealing the absurdity of Reagan's domestic cutbacks and the impossible situation these reductions created for African-American women and children.

Davis began by explaining that politics "do not stand in polar opposition to our lives. Whether we desire it or not, they permeate our existence, insinuating themselves into the most private spaces of our lives." As an example, she cited cases of Black women being turned away from doctors and hospitals because they were assumed not to have insurance coverage when they actually did. She noted that although Black women were less likely to get breast cancer, they were more likely to die from it. Fewer Black women received prenatal care, and more Black than white infants died as a result. Violence against Black women's health was the result of racism, for which much of the blame lay with Reagan. She attacked his domestic policies, his racist stance, and his willingness to eliminate the small amount of financial assistance Black women received: "[H]ealth ought to be universally recognized as a basic human right. Yet in this society, dominated as it is by the profit seeking ventures of monopoly corporations, health has been callously transformed into a commodity—a commodity that those with means are able to afford."

She presented a string of statistics in order to make her point: Black women were twice as likely as white women to die of hypertensive cardiovascular disease; they had three times the rate of high blood pressure; Black women were twelve times more likely to contract the AIDS virus than white women; where usually there was one doctor per fifteen hundred people, in "Central Harlem, there is only one doctor per forty-five hundred people"; infant mortality for Black children was twice that of white infants; lupus was "three times more common among Black women than white"; and Black women were far more likely to die of diabetes and cancer than their white counterparts. As numbers and comparisons continued, Davis painted a graphic picture of the obstacles Black women faced under the Reagan administration.

In this speech, Davis again intertwined the global with the local, explaining that while Reagan's policies funnelled millions of dollars into military spending, few Black people—especially women—were employed in this arena. Returning to an earlier theme from her speaking career, Davis explained that "[s]ince 1980, the military budget has more than doubled, taking approximately $100 billion from social programs that were underfunded to begin with." Davis concluded by suggesting that once again, the larger social and political context of racism and sexism must be recognized if poverty, sickness, and joblessness were to be challenged and eliminated. Reagan's global focus on military spending and defense had been devastating locally and had left Black women in very difficult situations. Subsidized programs must be reinstated, Davis concluded—programs that "emphasize prevention, self-help, and empowerment."

Speaking earlier in 1987, to the National Women's Studies Association annual conference at Spelman College, Davis had addressed the themes of unity as well as the necessity of recognizing the interconnectedness of racism and sexism. In her speech, "Let Us All Rise Together: Radical Perspectives on Empowerment for Afro-American Women," Davis brought together each of the issues on which she had touched throughout her speaking career. Empowerment of African-American women, she argued, only would come when individuals recognized the connection of human dignity with global responsibility. Citing Gerda Lerner's *Black Women in White America*, Davis explained: "We are not drawing the color line; we are women, American women, as intensely interested in all that pertains to us as such as all other American women."

In this speech, Davis argued that empowerment for African-American women should be linked to their history and guided by the principle called for by the National Association of Colored Women's clubs of the early 1900s: "Lifting as we climb." African-American women, Davis argued, brought to the women's movement "a strong tradition of struggle around issues that politically link women to the most crucial progressive causes." African-American women brought a concern for homelessness, joblessness, repressive legislation, "homophobia, ageism, and discrimination against the physically challenged." Davis explained that while these were the issues with which Black women had concerned themselves, these were the issues that "should be integrated into the overall struggle for women's rights," and these were the issues that united individuals on a local and global level. To break the "historical pattern" of oppression meant that individuals must merge the local with the global, recognize the links between racism and sexism, and move toward a "revolutionary, multiracial women's movement."

Davis argued that "lifting as we climb" meant that Reagan and his administration—"the most racist, antiworking class, sexist" administration in the recent past—must be stopped. "Lifting as we climb" meant that "sexist-inspired violence—in particular, terrorist attacks on abortion clinics"—must be stopped. "Lifting as we climb" meant jobs, union organizing, affirmative action, pay equity, an end to sexual harassment, paid maternity leave, and funding for AIDS research. "Lifting as we climb" meant "grass-roots organizing" and the "transformation of the socioeconomic conditions that generate and persistently nourish the various forms of oppression we suffer." "Lifting as we climb" meant that we "learn from the strategies of our sisters in South Africa and Nicaragua," that we "forge a new socialist order—an order which will reestablish socioeconomic priorities so that the quest for monetary profit will never be permitted to take precedence over the real interests of human beings."

For Davis, an orator with radical politics and a revolutionary commitment to eliminating oppression, "lifting as we climb" meant that those "who are women of color must be willing to appeal for multiracial unity in the spirit of our sister-ancestors. Like them, we must proclaim: We do not draw the color line. The only line we draw is one based on our political principles." She explained that if "we are not afraid to adopt a revolutionary stance—if, indeed, we wish to

be radical in our quest for change—then we must get to the root of our oppression. After all, *radical* simply means 'grasping things at the root.' '' African-
American women must take the lead in the movement against racial oppression
and violence, they must call attention to the issues that affect women at all
levels, they must make the connections between the global and the local, and,
as their sister-ancestors did generations ago, they ''must lift as we climb.''

Although her life and her rhetoric have been revolutionary, in her autobiography Davis sees herself as belonging to a ''community of humans—a community of struggle against poverty and racism.'' While some might disagree,
Davis also views her life as quite unexceptional. She explained that the ''forces
that have made my life what it is are the very same forces that have shaped and
misshaped the lives of millions of my people. . . . I am convinced that my response to these forces has been unexceptional as well, that my political involvement, ultimately as a member of the Communist Party, has been a natural,
logical way to defend our embattled humanity.'' This commitment to relationship, interconnection, confrontation, and vision informs her rhetoric and her life.
As a rhetor in a sexist and racist society, Davis's life and words present the
global through the lens of the local, the past through the lens of the present and
the future, and the humanness and dignity of African-American individuals
through the harshness of a racist society.

INFORMATION SOURCES

Research Collections and Collected Speeches

[*WCP*] Davis, Angela Y. *Women, Culture, and Politics*. New York:Random House, 1989.
[*VBA*] Foner, Philip S., ed. *The Voice of Black America: Major Speeches by Negroes in
    the United States, 1797–1971*. New York: Simon and Schuster, 1972.

Selected Critical Studies

''Angela Davis Speaks: An Interview with the Controversial Marxist Leader in the Black
    Movement.'' *Today Like It Is* (cassette recording). The Center for Cassette Stud-
    ies, 1973.
Aptheker, Bettina. *The Morning Breaks: The Trial of Angela Davis*. New York: Inter-
    national, 1975.
Davis, Angela Y. *If They Come in the Morning: Voices of Resistance*. New York: Third,
    1971.
Ginger, Ann F. *Angela Davis Case Collection: Annotated Procedural Guide and Index*.
    Berkeley: Meiklejohn Civil Liberties Institute, 1974.
Major, Reginald. *Justice in the Round: The Trial of Angela Davis*. New York: Third,
    1973.
Parker, J. A. *Angela Davis: The Making of a Revolutionary*. New Rochelle, NY: Arling-
    ton, 1973.
Timothy, Mary. *Jury Woman*. San Francisco: Glide, 1975.

Selected Biography

Davis, Angela Y. *Angela Davis—An Autobiography*. New York: Random House, 1974.

CHRONOLOGY OF MAJOR SPEECHES

[See "Research Collections and Collected Speeches" for source codes.]

"The Legacy of George Jackson." Marin, CA, August 25, 1971. *VBA*, 1191–1194.

"Imagining the Future." Berkeley, CA, June 16, 1983. *WCP*, 171–178.

"Facing Our Common Foe," (Address to the Conference on Women and the Struggle against Racism). Minnesota, November 15, 1984. *WCP*, 16–34.

"Reaping Fruit and Throwing Seed." University of California at Los Angeles, June 15, 1985. *WCP*, 179–185.

"We Do Not Consent: Violence against Women in a Racist Society." Florida State University, Tallahassee, FL, October 16, 1985. *WCP*, 35–51.

"Peace Is a Sisters' Issue Too: Afro-American Women and the Campaign against Nuclear Arms." Los Angeles, November 16, 1985. *WCP*, 66–72.

"Let Us All Rise Together: Radical Perspectives on Empowerment for Afro-American Women." Spelman College, June 25, 1987. *WCP*, 3–15.

"Sick and Tired of Being Sick and Tired: The Politics of Black Women's Health." Bennett College, Greensboro, NC, August 29, 1987. *WCP*, 53–65; "The Politics of Black Women's Health," *Vital Signs* 5 (February 1988).

"Children First: The Campaign for a Free South Africa." Harare, Zimbabwe, September 27, 1987. *WCP*, 104–108.

FATHER DIVINE
(c.1879–1965), religious leader

MINA A. VAUGHN

In the early 1930s, during the Great Depression, a number of religious cults developed in Harlem. They were headed by leaders such as Daddy Grace, Mother Horne, and Madame Fu-Fu-Tan, who offered black Americans, in one way or another, a feeling of ethnic self-worth, a new sense of group identity, and a psychological escape from the physical conditions of everyday life. One of the most successful, enduring, and widely known of these unique religious cults was the Peace Mission movement headed by Father Divine. As a social critic, reformer, and civil rights leader, he helped shape society. Sadly, the focus on Divine as a "cult leader" has obscured the importance of his religious leadership and his profound and unique oratory in the struggle for racial equality.

Father Divine denied any earlier life and maintained that he had been "combusted" in his present adult form onto the streets of Harlem in 1900. Most biographical accounts, however, note that he was born George Baker, Jr., around 1879, somewhere in the Deep South, the son of poor Southern sharecroppers. Young Baker's childhood was similar to that of many black Americans of the era—one characterized, physically, by poverty, disease, and malnutrition, and psychologically, by discrimination and segregation. Religion provided the only reprieve for these oppressed people and became the core of the black American community. Baker's childhood experiences in the Methodist church, which imbued him with a dedication to his spiritual convictions, and the memories of his impoverished childhood had a profound impact on the person who later called himself Father Divine.

As a young adult, Baker left home, embarking on an evangelical speaking career that took him to street corners and storefront churches from Baltimore to California, Georgia and the South to New York. Though uneducated and without formal training, he captivated audiences with his compelling voice and mesmerizing gaze. Baker's oratorical style, impassioned and informal, was similar to that of other Black Belt preachers. His language was uniquely his, however, as he created words that were not found in the dictionary. While witnesses described him as a balding, small man, barely five feet tall, he was said by many to have a commanding presence.

During his years on the preaching circuit, George Baker's spiritual development was influenced by his Methodist upbringing, as well as by the ideologies of other religions such as Catholicism, the Unity School of Christianity, and, most importantly, New Thought, which advocated positive thinking. He developed a theology that was, however, uniquely his own. Baker's beliefs about the equality of each in the eyes of God and the social degradation of black Americans he witnessed intensified his religious commitment. As he preached his way across the country, he eventually adopted the title "the Messenger."

The Messenger, along with a handful of disciples, settled down in New York City around 1917. To escape what he considered to be the negative influences of the city, he moved himself and his followers to an apartment in Brooklyn. The familial commune, with the Messenger as the spiritual father and leader, provided a safe haven for his flock. It was at this time that he assumed a new title, Reverend Major Jealous Divine. Although he was known to his business associates as Reverend Divine, his devoted disciples began addressing him as Father Divine.

In 1919, Divine purchased a home in Sayville, Long Island. He, along with his handful of followers, moved to this house in a white, middle-class neighborhood. One of his disciples, and a valued assistant, was a woman named Peninniah. Although there are various accounts of her background and involvement with the movement, it is generally agreed that she and Divine became man and wife around this time. It was in Sayville that Father Divine began holding his Holy Communion banquets, which became a hallmark of his ministry and the center of communal activity in every Peace Mission branch. All were welcome to attend—followers, special guests, and people who were passing by or simply curious. For the physically hungry, the banquets were lavish feasts, typically having dozens of different dishes. The poor paid nothing; the cost of the food was generally covered by donations from the more affluent attenders. Each dish was passed around family style after first passing through Father Divine's hands.

The spiritually hungry were nourished as well. Following the meal, testimonies of broad subject matter, such as renouncing the evils of wicked and sinful behaviors, recounting Divine's healing powers, or glorifying his divinity, were given. In between each testimony there was laughing, crying, clapping, and singing. Finally, there was a sermon from Father Divine, which sometimes lasted for as long as two hours. All of his sermons began, "Peace Everyone," and ended, "I thank you, Peace." His spiritual messages, based on an imaginative but practical approach to religion, along with the banquets, attracted large numbers of people to his house. Many of them became converts; some were white, but the majority were unskilled black Americans. It was the circumstances brought on by the Great Depression, however, that catapulted Father Divine's movement to prominence.

In 1929, conditions in Harlem were particularly severe. Fifty percent of black families were out of work, yet only 9 percent received government relief jobs. Median black income was less than one-half that of the median white income. Housing conditions were terrible: the buildings were run down and overrun with rats, many had defective lighting, and few had plumbing. Despite these appalling conditions, rents were 20 percent higher in Harlem than in the rest of Manhattan. The rate of disease was significantly higher, and the infant mortality rate for blacks was twice that of whites.

The traditional black churches, especially those in Northern urban areas, already faced a crisis on the eve of the Depression. The Great Migration northward of the 1910s and 1920s had been accompanied by a rapid increase of black churches, but there was also an insufficient amount of the leadership required to meet the needs of African-Americans in these cold, impersonal, and strange environments. The Depression's economic collapse only exacerbated the inadequacies of the traditional black church to meet the changing social scene. Furthermore, many religious leaders appeared to be insensitive to the extreme hardships of the time and continued to preach a doctrine of salvation in the "hereafter." It was Father Divine's theology, centered on ideas of self-help, positive thought, and a promise of a brighter future, that set his religious oratory apart from that of his contemporaries.

In 1932, Father Divine moved the Peace Mission movement headquarters to Harlem and, within a short time, distinguished himself from the other cult figures as a spiritual leader with considerable business acumen. Beginning with several restaurants, by the mid-1930s the Peace Mission was the largest real estate holder in Harlem, owning markets, apartment houses, dry cleaning stores, and a coal business. The Mission was financially successful because it delivered high-quality goods and services for low prices. It relied on its high volume of sales for its profits, which reverted to the Peace Mission's common funds and were then reinvested. Followers' outside wages, too, were placed in the common fund. Some followers were provided food and shelter in exchange for their labor, while others were given modest wages by the Mission. Shared housing and low-priced goods purchased from the Mission's various businesses meant that followers needed comparatively little money to live far better than they had previously been accustomed.

The movement's membership continued to grow. Father Divine did not keep records of membership, and accounts by various biographers vary greatly, but according to the *New York Times*, in 1933 Divine had over twenty million followers. Peace Mission branches, or "Heavens," opened across the United States, and by 1935 followers had opened branches in Europe, Canada, and Australia. Success, however, was accompanied by criticism and opposition. In 1934, Faithful Mary, a devoted follower and chief administrator for Father Divine, had a falling out with him and was expelled. She founded a rival sect and assailed Father Divine verbally, claiming, among other charges, sexual and financial misconduct within the Peace Mission. In 1935, Verinda Brown and her husband decided that they wanted to live together and left the movement. They filed a lawsuit against Divine after he refused to return their life savings, which they had given the movement when they had become followers. The New York City courts began pursuing other complaints that had been filed, and the Hearst press especially gave Faithful Mary's and the Browns' allegations wide coverage.

Although they initially had little impact on the Peace Mission movement, the lawsuits, investigations, and decreased public support eventually took their toll. Perhaps to protect his ministry, Father Divine incorporated the Peace Mission by 1941, and the resulting structural rigidity stimulated internal dissension. Too, the rebounding economy diminished the economic power of the Mission that had attracted so many of its followers. In 1942, having rejected all of his appeals in the Verinda Brown lawsuit, the court forced Father Divine to make restitution. Tired, disillusioned, and beyond the prime of his life, Divine, along with his wife and a few hundred followers, left New York and relocated in Philadelphia.

Father Divine continued his work with the Peace Mission, but more as a corporate executive than as an activist. Membership in the movement declined in the early 1940s, mission branches and businesses closed, and at some point Peninniah passed away, although Divine did not acknowledge this for some time. In 1946, he married Sweet Angel, a white woman fifty years his junior. She became his equal partner in running the Peace Mission movement; the disciples called her "Mother Divine." In 1965, Father Divine, then in his eighties, died, still believing, as he wrote in a letter to President Lyndon Johnson, that a universal, Utopian democracy, based on American ideals was still imminent.

FATHER DIVINE AS RELIGIOUS ORATOR

While many religious leaders, both past and present, have claimed that they were messengers of God, Father Divine's rhetoric was unique in that he claimed that he was God and the Peace Mission movement was "God's Movement." In his sermons he reminded his followers, whom he often referred to as Children, of his divine authority: "How marvelous it is to dwell in the ACTUAL PRESENCE OF GOD"; "My followers recognize GOD'S ACTUAL PRESENCE"; "The LOVING KING, as JESUS, came to redeem the children of men and call them HIS." His followers acknowledged his claim of divinity and showered him with loving and godly epithets, such as "HOLY FATHER," "KING OF KINGS," and "BEAUTIFUL REDEEMER."

In many of his sermons, Father Divine reinforced the legitimacy of his divinity through the mystification of circular reasoning. Reminding his followers, and explaining to any skeptics, why God was present in his own bodily form, he declared: "They should not have the slightest thought to question why did I come in the likeness; For GOD formed man in HIS own image; therefore to men and among men I must come in the likeness of them even when and wheresoever I come again." Divine contended that he would rather appear the "same as any other man and still be GOD," but repeated time and time again in his sermons that his bodily form, or anyone else's, was unimportant: "[It is] absolutely immaterial to Me whether I have a BODY or not; with or without a BODY, I will accomplish all of My endeavors." He enjoined his followers to surrender both mind and body ("the manifestations of our mental and spiritual conceptions") to him—God. In doing so, he (God) guaranteed his followers the joys of life.

Divine was also believed to hold the "power of retribution," a power to be used against those who dared to challenge his deity or interfere with his work. The origin of the belief appears to have been an incident that purportedly occurred in 1932. A judge found Divine guilty of disturbing the peace and imposed the maximum sentence on him: a $500 fine and a year in jail. During the trial Judge Smith, an apparently healthy man in his mid-fifties, had exhibited prejudice toward Divine and the followers testifying on his behalf. Three days after sentencing, Smith keeled over dead. A visitor to Father Divine's cell informed him of the death, to which Divine replied, "I hated to do it." The story, and stories with similar themes, were shared among his followers throughout the years.

As during other periods in American history, religion in the early 1900s was the cornerstone of black American lives. It provided, perhaps, the only relief from the pain and despair the black communities endured on an ongoing basis. Father Divine skillfully appealed to the needs and beliefs of those who had been socialized to turn to religion for solace. The "I am God" notion was a function of the highest ethos for a people who believed in God. The concrete value of God in the person of Divine was persuasive, for there was the evidence to support the claim: Father Divine was empowered to inflict retribution. Whether or not the stories of Divine's retributive powers were true was less important than the functions they served: they increased his credibility with his audiences and legitimized his deific claims.

A second belief Divine demanded that his followers accept was that the ultimate rewards of faith were to be experienced immediately and not delayed until entrance to the heavenly kingdom after death. He promised his Children eternal life on earth, arguing that heaven was here and now for those who believed in him and followed his teachings. A real God, Divine maintained, is "not a GOD afar off, But GOD is a GOD at hand." Claiming that he "wouldn't give five cents for a God who would not help me out on earth," Divine stated, "If GOD cannot prepare HEAVEN here for you, you are not going anywhere."

The "here and now" postulate was instrumental in attracting many people to his movement. Although some of the movement's members were white, educated, and financially secure, Divine drew mainly from the traditionally downtrodden and displaced groups in American society. He nourished their physical needs by providing them with food, clothing, and shelter: "You have beautiful homes, you have clothes to wear, I say, you have plenty to eat and drink, you have plenty of nice comfortable automobiles to ride in." His arguments on the "here and now," grounded in his ability to provide for his followers, legitimized the Peace Mission movement and its goals. He also nourished their emotional and spiritual needs. As Father Divine maintained, the people drawn to his heavens "were sick; they were afflicted; they were in lacks, wants, and limitations, until they called on ME, and by their calling on ME sincerely, I came to their rescue." To many of Divine's followers they were indeed participating in heaven on earth.

While Father Divine's two presumptions appeared to be outrageous and bizarre to many people, when examined in context, they were audience centered. His oratory claiming himself as God and promising heaven on earth offered the members of the Peace Mission movement a spiritually, materially, and socially utopian existence, an existence antithetical to the day-to-day racial discrimination and poverty that alienated his followers from society.

Father Divine's ultimate goal was to create full equality for everyone, which became a primary theme embedded in many of his speeches and writings. His printed sermon in *The New Day* of October 5, 1939, affirmed his commitment to equality:

> I have come to give you victory over difficulties, over races, creeds and colors, over segregation, over prejudice. Righteous believers accept the equality of races. To recognize and realize E PLURIBUS UNUM, where there will be no more divisibility of the children of men but all will live in unison together.

Father Divine's positive affirmations of equality were supported by his condemnation of equality's opposite: segregation. Divine considered segregation an evil that prevented the "bringing of all peoples together, that they might recognize and respect each other." He fought to stamp out this evil, actively lobbying to eliminate the Jim Crow laws that segregated and discriminated against black Americans, fighting for antilynching legislation, and writing businesses that practiced segregation, threatening boycotts—including the threatened boycott of New York bus companies twenty years before the Montgomery bus boycott. In many respects, Father Divine's words and actions foreshadowed those of Martin Luther King twenty years later: He advocated and struggled for social change, and, like King, Divine promoted nonviolence, claiming that his true followers would "refuse to fight their fellowman for any cause whatever."

Of particular concern to Divine in his fight for equality was the use of language that kept "localization and segregation existing in all parts of the country." He recommended making it a crime for any publication to use "segregated or slang words referring to any race, color, or creed," or to "write abusively concerning any." Father Divine did not adhere to a tenet of equality that was "regardless of color" because he did not recognize the existence of color. In his sermons he repeatedly stated that he had no conception of himself in terms of color and told his followers that such words as "negro" or "colored" were "segregated terms which they use for the purpose of loweration." His sermon reprinted on August 27, 1936 demonstrated this rejection of a color-conscious society:

> Now the word that you call ME and anyone else as you see ME to be, either one of those words are VULGAR; they are UNINTELLIGENT; they are PREJUDI-CIAL; they are UNDERMINING. . . . [They are] used for the purpose of disgracing people, for dishonoring people, I say, for low-rating people and discounting people and disrecognizing the people.

While Divine's style and language of addressing this issue were different from present conventions of rhetorical effectiveness, the content was similar to what is termed "political correctness" today. He understood that words were symbolic in that they implied more than their immediate meaning and that they contributed to the preservation of the hegemonic relationship that existed between his Children and other groups in society. He linked his rhetorical messages on language to the experiences of his followers in his sermon of August 8, 1940.

> You hear some call people WOPS; you hear some call some GUINEAS, and every other CURSED, VULGAR name for the purpose of segregating the nation and bringing division among them! But I, as the DEAN OF THE UNIVERSE, came to teach you WISDOM, AND BRING AN END TO VULGARITY AND OB-SCENITY.

Father Divine's discourse on equality was warranted by his desire to eliminate racism and discrimination forever, although he did not advocate anarchy. His aim was to perpetuate "true Americanism . . . the hope of the survival and preservation of Democracy" and to build a "RIGHTEOUS GOVERNMENT in which there will be equality for all mankind." Divine's beliefs were grounded in the mainstream democratic principles associated with the American way of life, but he sought to broaden them to include the oppressed and disenfranchised. He was able to blend his rhetoric of Americanism with his rhetoric of reform: Divine appealed to his followers to exemplify his teachings so as to "show the politicians of other countries and of this one, how to produce REAL DEMOC-RACY, a REAL UTOPIA where each person will live according to the CON-STITUTION and its AMENDMENTS, expressing REAL EQUALITY."

While equality provided an interpretive structure for the Peace Mission's collective goals, independence was one of the goals established for the individual. Father Divine's rhetoric embraced an unwavering belief in personal independence, as indicated in one of his many sermons, reprinted on September 2, 1937, on the issue:

> How can we be independent as a nation if we are not independent individuals? Can you not see the mystery? Can you not SEE the mystery? My followers, Hearers, and Friends must produce and bring to fruition within the very spirit and the meaning of the Declaration of Independence by becoming independent individually, severally, and collectively, but especially stressfully I stress the significance of becoming independent as an individual.

Divine claimed that his followers could achieve independence by adhering to prescribed behavioral guidelines that centered around the value of honesty, which included actions such as not hitching a ride on a streetcar or accepting money without working for it. His goal was to create and maintain "a doctrine to be so honest that they [Divine's true believers] will not steal a pin, a penny or even one minute's time from an employer." There were no gray areas regarding the scrupulous adherence to the value of honest conduct. According to Father Divine, those followers keeping anything not belonging to them, "the greedy gains of filthy lucre," were "worse than Judas." He appealed to the traditional value of hard work, arguing that true believers must work hard to "give the world the best you can," and he spoke out against trying to get something for nothing: "You must express your independence individually and prove it conclusively, once and forever by refusing to be solicitors, beggars, borrowers or stealers. Only then can you express REAL CITIZENRY according to my convictions." Father Divine's oratory served as a critique of dramatic changes occurring in American society during this period. He advocated independence and responsibility at a time when people were turning to the government for the resolution of "personal" crises brought on by the Depression. The conservative Divine was against the rise of the welfare state, and his response to it was to offer repressed social groups a seemingly viable alternative.

In addition to prescribing strict fidelity to honesty, Father Divine espoused a rigid code of moral excellence—self-denial, sacrifice, and consecration—and demanded absolute adherence to it. For example, one of the tenets of the Peace Mission movement's philosophy was that followers remain celibate. Although racial integration was practiced in the Heavens (in that white and black members ate, slept, and worked together), males and females lived separately. Divine demanded that members refrain from even casual associations with one another, claiming that "real followers of mine will not even ride in an automobile correspondingly together with the opposite sex."

As he discussed in a sermon in The *New Day* of November 11, 1941, sexual intercourse was considered to be an act of selfishness, one that interfered with his followers consecrating their lives to him:

> And those of the "Crusaders" who live according to MY Teaching they have made sacrifices to this end, that they might present themselves unto GOD as

though they are the church without a spot or wrinkle, without a blemish. Cleanliness is next to Godliness; but when they express truthfully GODLINESS, they have cleanliness and holiness and they also in turn express true VIRTUE.

Father Divine acknowledged that his followers would be tempted and advocated fasting as a means of resisting all temptations: ''By fasting you will overcome the enemy. . . . CHRIST will take the place of tendencies within you . . . and will cause you to praise the SAVIOR in the place of all of your human affection, lust and passion and all mortal tendencies.''

The Bible was cited to support Father Divine's oratory opposing sex. He referred to the Book of John and reminded his audiences that those on Mount Zion with ''their Father's name written on their foreheads were not defiled by women. They are redeemed from among men, for they are not mortal-minded.'' He called upon the women to ''dispel from among them the beguilation of Eve by which Adam and all mankind had been deceived.'' For the majority of his religious followers, Divine's argument from authority warranted the acceptance of his position on the value of adhering to celibacy. Their religious background had conditioned them to believe that promiscuity was sinful; Divine appealed to them to take moral excellence to a higher level.

Despite his own marriages, Father Divine forbade his followers to marry. He called marriage a ''legalized crime'' and claimed that it was a sin. Sin was a ''rascal'' even though ''it may come through and by the way of legality.'' In banning marriage, Father Divine argued that ''it is a wonderful privilege; and there is no small degree of pleasure observed and obtained by making a sacrifice for righteousness sake.'' Divine defined both birth and marriage as equivalent: ''They are closely connected Dear Ones; therefore, the one who is born again, just as he is born mentally and spiritually, he is also married the same.''

Father Divine called for his followers to give him their spiritual, mental, and physical energy: ''The SOUL, the MIND, and the BODY; I came to unite them together.'' As God, he rejected the human distinctions made between men and women; he was all things to all people and spurned gender distinctions in others. That premise, along with his oratory on sex and marriage, was liberating for his female audiences. He offered them an alternative to the ongoing reality of disease, ill health, and infant mortality that were widespread because of poor (or nonexistent) prenatal and follow-up medical care. They were no longer bound by tradition to the roles of wife and mother; they had choices. His ideology broadened his audience appeal by breaking down the barriers that were grounded in racial differences and economic status.

Other vices, such as smoking, drinking, and the use of profanity, were also forbidden in the Heavens. Such behaviors were self-indulgent, the antithesis of self-denial. Followers were commanded by Divine to resist these mortal temptations: ''Not a true follower of mine would indulge in intoxicating liquors, would indulge in profanity, would indulge in obscenity nor any such tendency of mortality, for they know such would not be according to the life and teachings of JESUS.'' Even "gossiping" and "accusing and faultfinding" were considered to be sinful: "You are committing adultery; adulterating your standard of thinking mentally and spiritually.''

In his sermons, Father Divine supported his arguments by citing biblical scriptures advocating abstinence from "strong drink" and taking care of one's body. In addition, testimonies from members, an important part of the Peace Mission movement's religious services, provided additional evidence to reinforce the worth of living a virtuous life. Exuberant speakers emotionally recounted the debasement of their pasts as a result of adultery, debauchery, and other sinful actions and bore witness to how their lives had been rejuvenated through the acceptance of Father Divine's teachings. Living a virtuous life had its rewards; adherents received the grace of God himself: "The person who makes the greatest sacrifice is the nearest to GOD! This is not a supposition! This is not an imagination! This is not what someone else is merely telling you, but GOD HIMSELF has told you!''

Independence and virtue were integrally connected in Father Divine's belief system. Hedonistic, or even natural, behavior created a barrier that inhibited personal independence, which was a condition for achieving equality. One of his most basic and often-repeated arguments was that the price of social justice was to be self-reliant, take full responsibility for one's own choices, and renounce self-indulgent, "earthly" desires. The true believers did not believe that the price was too high to pay. Who in their lives had treated them with such respect? Who in their lives had believed in their worth as human beings? Who in their lives had fought for their rights and offered them hope? In testimony after testimony, audience members asked these questions or the speakers raised them rhetorically. The answer was always the same: Father Divine.

Divine was not the only religious leader of his age to hold out a vision of hope to the poor and desperate. The devotion called for and given by followers of Father Divine, however, exceeded that which can be explained by "hungry people"; one needs to look at his oratory for an answer. He was able to adapt his messages to his audiences in such a way as to help them make sense of a world that by all outward appearances was unrelentingly hostile. He prescribed a well-devised plan of action that, supported by positive values, would guide members to the desired end state of equality. It was not the number of values that determined the oratorical appeal, but the degree to which Divine was able to persuade his followers to identify with the values he espoused.

Divine's vision was one of a reformer, not a revolutionary, and he was in some ways ahead of his times. His activities and oratory stand as prophetic enactments of the civil rights movement that would come years later. He was quintessentially American in a period when many social reformers leaned to the left politically: he accepted capitalism, a strong work ethic, pietism, and the U.S. Constitution. His oratory spoke to what America should be—the America where everyone is equal and in which everyone is guaranteed life, liberty, and the pursuit of happiness.

INFORMATION SOURCES

Research Collections and Collected Speeches

The New Day was an independent paper published by the Peace Mission between 1936 and 1987. It reprinted not only Father Divine's sermons delivered during those years, but also many sermons that had been given before 1936, dating as far back as 1929. Establishing the precise date on which a sermon was delivered is often difficult, as that date is not included in the reprint, and all of the speeches are identically titled "OUR FATHER'S MESSAGE." *The New Day* is available on microfilm.

[*ND*] *The New Day*, 1936–1987.

Selected Biographies

Braden, Charles Samuel. *These Also Believe: A Study of Modern American Cults and Minority Religious Movements*. New York: Macmillan, 1949, 14–17.
Horshor, John. *God in a Rolls Royce: The Rise of Father Divine, Madman, Menace or Messiah*. New York: Hillman-Curl, 1936.
Parker, Robert Allerton. *Incredible Messiah: The Deification of Father Divine*. Boston: Little, Brown, 1971.
Weisbrot, Robert. *Father Divine and the Struggle for Racial Equality*. Urbana: U of Illinois P, 1983.

CHRONOLOGY OF MAJOR SPEECHES

[See "Research Collections and Collected Speeches" for source code.]

"OUR FATHER'S Message." New York, NY, n.d. *ND*, August 27, 1936.
"OUR FATHER'S Message." New York, NY, n.d. *ND*, December 12, 1936.
"OUR FATHER'S Message." New York, NY, n.d. *ND*, February 7, 1937.
"OUR FATHER'S Message." New York, NY, n.d. *ND*, September 2, 1937.
"OUR FATHER'S Message." New York, NY, n.d. *ND*, November 4, 1937.
"OUR FATHER'S Message." New York, NY, n.d. *ND*, February 17, 1938.
"OUR FATHER'S Message." New York, NY, n.d. *ND*, March 3, 1938.
"OUR FATHER'S Message." New York, NY, n.d. *ND*, July 14, 1938.
"OUR FATHER'S Message." New York, NY, n.d. *ND*, December 3, 1938.
"OUR FATHER'S Message." New York, NY, n.d. *ND*, October 5, 1939.
"OUR FATHER'S Message." New York, NY, n.d. *ND*, June 6, 1940.
"OUR FATHER'S Message." New York, NY, n.d. *ND*, August 8, 1940.
"OUR FATHER'S Message." New York, NY, n.d. *ND*, November 11, 1941.
"OUR FATHER'S Message." New York, NY, n.d. *ND*, December 25, 1941.
"OUR FATHER'S Message." New York, NY, n.d. *ND*, July 19, 1942.

FREDERICK DOUGLASS
(1818–1895), abolitionist, reformer

GERALD FULKERSON

Frederick Douglass is widely acknowledged as the most significant black figure in nineteenth-century America. In a lifetime that spanned most of the century (1818–1895), Douglass emerged from slavery to become an influential participant in the most important social and political struggles of his age. He reached the zenith of his career between 1847 and 1860, becoming not only the most prominent African-American in the abolition crusade but arguably the most versatile and effective agitator in the entire movement. In the 1850s, especially, he displayed a remarkable virtuosity as orator, autobiographer, and journal editor. Both before and after the Civil War, Douglass involved himself in a variety of reforms such as civil rights, women's equality, and temperance. He was accorded stature then, as now, however, mainly because he demonstrated unusual courage, tenacity, and eloquence in the crusade against slavery.

The antislavery career of Frederick Douglass, or at least his preparation for it, began the day he was born, for he was born a slave. During his twenty years as a victim of the "peculiar institution," he experienced slavery in virtually all of its basic settings: he lived on an elaborate plantation on Maryland's Eastern Shore until the age of eight, in Baltimore for two periods totaling ten years, in a village, and on a small farm. He served in each of the three fundamental slave roles—as a domestic servant, as a field hand, and as a skilled laborer. He also came to experience all of the typical slave/master relationships, for he was variously owned, borrowed, rented, and accepted on consignment to be "broken."

After Douglass's mistress in Baltimore taught him to read, he developed his own creative tactics for learning to write. In Baltimore, too, he purchased a copy of a 1797 public speaking textbook, Caleb Bingham's *Columbian Orator*, making what Dickson Preston called "possibly the best investment in his life."

Frederick would consciously apply Bingham's recommendations regarding a natural approach to speech delivery in the years ahead, but several model essays and speeches that emphasized the concepts of freedom, independence, and emancipation were of greater immediate significance. He was most profoundly affected by a "Dialogue between a Master and Slave," which forever altered his perception of his world and stimulated him to begin the development of his own antislavery voice.

In both Baltimore and the Eastern Shore, the young Douglass manifested a bent for leadership: he organized secret "Sabbath schools" in which he taught his peers to read and write; he led five other slaves in plotting an abortive escape attempt; and he helped form a secret debating society, the East Baltimore Mental Improvement Society. In September 1838, Frederick escaped to freedom by riding trains from Baltimore to New York in the persona of a free seaman.

Shortly after escaping, Frederick married Anna Murray, a free woman whom he had courted in Baltimore, and settled in New Bedford, Massachusetts. New Bedford, with its active community of black abolitionists, provided a milieu in which he could flourish as a speaker and leader. As Douglass became assimilated into New Bedford's antislavery community, he came to share its loyalty to William Lloyd Garrison and his radical reform agenda, which included feminism, nonresistance, anticlericalism, and antipolitical action. In 1841, Garrison heard Douglass narrate his life in slavery and recruited him to lecture for the Massachusetts Anti-Slavery Society. Between 1841 and 1845, Douglass toured relentlessly, speaking to tiny county antislavery societies, to the larger Garrisonian societies in Boston and New York, and to diverse audiences in towns of every size from Pennsylvania to Maine and from Massachusetts to Indiana.

In the fall and winter of 1844–45, Douglass wrote his first autobiography, *Narrative of the Life of Frederick Douglass, an American Slave.* Laying his slave past open to public scrutiny had become necessary because his audiences were beginning to question the apparent incongruity between his eloquence and his claim to be a self-educated fugitive slave. The *Narrative* sustained Douglass's credibility, but it also revealed his identity and whereabouts, thus increasing the likelihood that he would be pursued by slave catchers. Haunted by the possibility of capture, Douglass fled to Great Britain in August 1845.

Douglass's twenty-month exile in Great Britain changed the course of his career. Wherever he spoke, he attracted large audiences by his self-possession, eloquence, and status as an authentic fugitive slave. He departed the United States a protégé of Garrison but returned as an emergent leader. He also returned as a free man, his freedom having been purchased for $750 by British admirers. British friends also gave him a $2,000 "testimonial" that he used to establish the *North Star* as a weekly journal in Rochester, New York, where it would not compete with the *Liberator.* The move to western New York removed Douglass from Garrison's oversight and brought him into regular contact with antislavery's other major faction, the more moderate political abolitionists led by Gerrit Smith. Between 1847 and 1851, as Douglass interacted with Smith and other moderates, he revised his view of the constitutionality of slavery and the viability of political action. In May 1851, Douglass finally burned his Garrisonian bridges by announcing that he no longer subscribed to a proslavery interpretation of the Constitution.

From the early 1850s through the beginning of the Civil War, Douglass flourished as an increasingly independent and versatile leader. His unequalled versatility made his career a virtual microcosm of antislavery reform. In a crusade that pursued its aims through speaking tours, journals, pamphlets, political pressure, and direct action, Douglass toured and lectured indefatigably, edited both a weekly (*North Star* [1849–51]; *Frederick Douglass' Paper* [1851–60]) and a monthly (*Douglass' Monthly* [1860–63]) journal, published pamphlet texts of some of his major speeches, involved himself in the emergence of the Free Soil and Republican parties, and made his Rochester home a station in the Underground Railroad. He exploited his rhetorical prowess not only as editor and itinerant agitator but also as a debater, epideictic orator, lyceum lecturer, stump speaker, and, for the second time, an autobiographer in *My Bondage and My Freedom*.

Throughout the 1850s, Douglass wrote and spoke on issues affecting Northern blacks with the same intensity with which he pursued his antislavery agenda. He regularly lectured in black churches, became one of the prime movers behind the black convention movement, sought to convince Harriet Beecher Stowe to fund a manual-labor school for black youth, opposed colonization efforts, campaigned for equal suffrage, urged forcible resistance to the Fugitive Slave Law, and preached the doctrine of self-reliance.

As the momentous decade of the 1850s ended, Douglass was wrongly implicated in the John Brown affair, fled to Great Britain yet again to avoid capture, and returned home after six months to mourn the death of Annie, his thirteen-year-old daughter. He returned home in time for the campaign of 1860, but in choosing to sit it out he foreshadowed the ambivalence that he would feel toward Lincoln for the duration of his presidency. Throughout most of the Civil War, Douglass sought to counter Lincoln's conservative positions on the aims of the war and the role of blacks in the Union army.

In the early years of Reconstruction, Douglass invested much of his rhetorical energy in the movement toward black suffrage that culminated in the ratification of the Fifteenth Amendment in 1870. The attainment of constitutional status for black voting rights, however, marked the apex in Douglass's postwar career. He was able to make a considerable income on the lecture circuit in the 1870s, and he continued to be a respected spokesman for the rights of blacks and women up to the time of his death, but his radical reform voice became somewhat muted. He often functioned as a partisan Republican apologist, mythologizing Lincoln and waving the bloody shirt. As he watched a succession of Republican administrations, including those in which he held minor patronage offices, ignore the plight of Southern blacks, he tended to moderate his criticism with a tone of hopeful optimism.

Douglass managed to articulate a rhetoric of hope in the 1870s and 1880s despite a good deal of personal disappointment as well as criticism from his black peers. His home in Rochester, where he stored his journal files, burned in 1872. In 1874, he gave up on a three-year effort to reinvigorate a black journal, the *New National Era,* and in the same year he presided over the death throes of the Freedman's Savings and Trust Company. His desire for important posts in Republican administrations was frustrated by such appointments as marshal of the District of Columbia in 1877 and recorder of deeds in 1881. He absorbed intense criticism in 1879 for speaking out in opposition to the Exoduster movement, a migration of oppressed Southern blacks to Kansas. Even the publication in 1881 of the last of Douglass's autobiographies, *Life and Times of Frederick Douglass,* turned into a disappointment when it sold few copies. After Anna died in 1882, he endured criticism again when he married Helen Pitts, a white woman, a year and a half later. After campaigning for Benjamin Harrison in the election of 1888, Douglass accepted appointment as minister to the Republic of Haiti, but he resigned after Haiti refused to cede a naval base to the United States. On February 20, 1895, after participating in a meeting of the National Council of Women, Frederick Douglass died of a heart attack at Cedar Hill, his Washington home.

FREDERICK DOUGLASS AND THE RHETORIC OF IRONY

Frederick Douglass's rhetorical career developed in four stages: (1) the early years as a Garrisonian neophyte, 1841–45; (2) his successful tour of Great Britain, 1845–47; (3) the years of independent leadership in the political wing of the antislavery movement, 1847–60; and (4) his efforts to represent the interests of black Americans during the Civil War and its aftermath, 1860–95. In the remainder of this essay, I shall examine representative speeches from each of these stages in Douglass's career.

In a democracy the rhetorical stock-in-trade of virtually all social reforms is the irony of unfulfilled cultural and political ideals. Inconsistencies and contradictions between the promised and the real, if sufficiently egregious, contain the power to goad people into action. It is hardly surprising, therefore, that the rhetoric of Frederick Douglass, like that of his peers in antislavery, women's rights, and other reform movements, was fundamentally ironic. What distinguished him from his colleagues in the abolition movement was his persona as a victim of the system he sought to eradicate coupled with an extraordinary combination of physical presence, intellectual acumen, and verbal skill. From the beginning of his career, his audiences saw him as an almost unique personification of the ironies that he illuminated with logical precision, wit, and sarcasm.

When Douglass began touring with the Garrisonians in 1841, they urged him to take advantage of the natural interest that Northerners would have in hearing an authentic fugitive describe his experience in slavery, and for the first several months he largely obliged. In the earliest of his speeches for which we have a text, he addressed an audience in Lynn, Massachusetts, sometime in October 1841. In "I Have Come to Tell You Something about Slavery," Douglass began by describing the embarrassment and trembling he experienced when addressing whites, a fear, he explained, that he had learned as a slave. His audience must have considered it ironic that this strong, imposing man over six feet tall with a deep, powerful voice should reexperience old racial fears as he stood before them. Some of the individuals who wrote descriptions of Douglass's speaking over the years noted that he began deliberately, even nervously, with few gestures, gradually increasing his intensity, volume, and physical activity until the speech culminated in a dynamic climax. He followed such a pattern in the Lynn speech.

Douglass then affirmed that he had "come to tell you something about slavery—what *I know* of it, as I have *felt* it." Although white abolitionists, he suggested, could recount the history and suggest the horrors of slavery, "they cannot speak as I can from *experience;* they cannot refer you to a back covered with scars, as I can; for I have felt these wounds; I have suffered under the lash without the power of resisting. And yet my master has the reputation of being a pious man and a good Christian." Douglass typically coupled the irony of brutal bondage existing in a "free" country with the equally ironic support of slavery by apparently pious Christians.

Douglass next assured the abolitionist audience that a large portion of the slaves "cherished with gratitude" the existence of a movement in the North to free them. He urged continued agitation on the ground that emancipation was the only cure for the evils of slavery. He then focused on two of those evils: "Ah! how the slave yearns for [emancipation], that he may be secure from the lash, that he may enjoy his family, and no more be tortured with the worst feature of slavery, the separation of friends and families. The whip we can bear without a murmur, compared to the idea of *separation.*"

As he ended, Douglass reached beyond his assigned sphere, as he would increasingly do, by surmising that emancipation would expose the severity of racial prejudice in the North. When they were free to live where they chose, black residents and runaway slaves would return to the South, where, ironically, racial prejudice was less intense. Discrimination in the North had been so troubling to him personally that it hung from his neck "like a heavy weight." Throughout his career, Douglass demanded that his audiences, even abolitionist audiences, look with clear eyes not only at Southern slavery but also at prejudice and discrimination among themselves.

Douglass delivered a speech in Boston's Faneuil Hall on January 28, 1842, that reveals a skill in satirical parody and mimicry that he effectively used to entertain audiences and lampoon foes for the duration of his career. Four thousand people, including a substantial number who were not abolitionists, attended a meeting called to support abolition in the District of Columbia and heard Douglass present "The Southern Style of Preaching to Slaves." After Garrison dramatically introduced him as a chattel transformed into a man, Douglass began in typical fashion, reminding his audience of the two primary ironies of American life—a system of slavery supported by both law and religion. He stood before them by the law still a slave, he exclaimed, scarred in both body and soul, representing the two and a half million slaves remaining in bondage. After listing rights and privileges denied the bondmen, Douglass urged the auditors in rhythmic, parallel sentences to accept responsibility for helping to free them: "It is to save them from all this, that you are called. Do it!—and they who are ready to perish shall bless you! Do it! and all good men will cheer you onward! Do it! and God will reward you for the deed; and your own consciences will testify that you have been true to the demands of the religion of Christ."

Reference to the legitimate demands of Christianity allowed Douglass to introduce his famous "Slaveholder's Sermon" as an example of the pseudo-Christianity often preached in the South. As he assumed the persona of the Southern preacher explicating the Golden Rule for masters and slaves, Douglass exploited the flexible resources of his voice, face, and gestures. The result was a delightful performance that etched in the auditors' minds a visual image of rich ironic appeal. In one passage of the sermon, for instance, Douglass had the preacher addressing the slaves: "And spreading his hands gracefully abroad, he says (mimicking,) 'And you too, my friends, have souls of infinite value. . . . Oh *labor diligently* to make your calling and election sure. Oh, receive into your souls these words of the holy apostle—'Servants, be obedient to your masters.' (Shouts of laughter and applause.)" Shifting out of role at the end of the sermon with "shouts of applause" still resounding, Douglass affirmed that this "gospel" was more effective in perpetuating slavery than "chains, whips, or thumb-screws."

Although only eight brief texts of Douglass's speeches from 1841 through 1844 (four of which were delivered in a single meeting in 1841) are extant, the reactions of those who heard him make it clear that he experienced rapid development and growing celebrity as an antislavery speaker. By mid-1844, he was speaking with such poise that he felt compelled to write an autobiography largely to convince skeptical audiences that he was not an educated imposter. After the publication of his *Narrative* in the summer of 1845, Douglass sailed to Great Britain to avoid being captured by slave hunters.

Approximately a dozen complete or nearly complete stenographic speech texts as well as an abundance of testimony from fascinated auditors attest to the high level of rhetorical virtuosity that Douglass displayed in Britain. Everywhere he went during his twenty-month exile, large, "respectable" audiences that usually included civic dignitaries attended his meetings. Most of his meetings were sponsored by local emancipation societies that had originally been formed to oppose slavery in the British West Indies. In Ireland, where he toured first, Douglass emphasized the brutality of American slavery and the need for the Irish to bring their public opinion to bear on a morally impotent American society.

Shortly after entering Scotland in January 1846, Douglass became involved in a struggle that allowed for the full deployment of his rhetoric of irony. After separating from the established church in 1843, the Free Church of Scotland had solicited financial aid from Presbyterians in the United States, including the South. When Presbyterians in South Carolina contributed $15,000, American and British abolitionists began a campaign to force the Free Church to return the "blood-stained" offering. The "Send Back the Money" campaign had been in progress for several months when Douglass arrived in Scotland, but after a promising beginning it had lagged and was almost dead.

By the time Douglass went to Arbroath for a series of meetings in mid-February, he had managed to resuscitate the campaign. On February 12, in Abbey Church, one of the largest in Arbroath, he addressed a capacity crowd of several hundred on "The Free Church Connection with the Slave Church." Douglass began his introduction by seeking to repair any damage done to his credibility by recent charges in a Free Church journal that he was being paid and sanctioned by rival denominations. Asserting his desire to be fair as well as candid, he labeled the *Warder*'s accusation "an unblushing falsehood." His real mission, he said, was to "plead the cause of the perishing slave" and to enlist the aid of "the good people of Old Scotland in behalf of what I believe to be a righteous cause—the breaking of every yoke, the undoing of heavy burdens, and letting the oppressed go free!" The biblical allusion to slavery and freedom, a common feature of his antislavery style, heightened the irony inherent in the idea of a church colluding with slaveholders. Douglass then finished the introduction in a fashion further calculated to embellish his credibility. After naming several ministers who supported him, he affirmed, in effect, that he possessed the conviction and courage to condemn the Free Church even if he stood alone. "To the last" he would maintain that since slaveholding and true religion were incompatible, the "Free Church should have no fellowship with a slave church." The irony that the colluding church should of all things be called "Free" was irresistible to Douglass, who used it repeatedly in his anti–Free Church speeches. Punning and playing with words and titles at his opponents' expense was a rhetorical pleasure in which he often indulged.

Douglass developed three themes in the body of the speech, the first of which was stated as a question and answer. In response to his inquiry into the character of the Southern churches endorsed by the Free Church, he quoted Isaiah: "Their hands are full of blood." To elaborate the answer, he listed the horrors of slavery in a long, complex sentence consisting of short, vivid phrases in a staccato rhythm, quoted John Wesley's reference to slavery as "the sum of all villainies, and the compendium of all crime," and argued that fellowship churches that supported slavery privileged creed over practice, thus further entrenching slavery by quieting the consciences of slaveholders.

"Now," said Douglass as he articulated his second theme, "let us look at the circumstances under which this deed of Christian fellowship was consummated." He underscored the irony that the Free Church had broken away from the Church of Scotland in defense of Christian "liberty." Its members felt "so *free*" that they looked upon the remaining members of the established church "as mere slaves." Then, "with all this profession of freedom and purity," they sent a delegation to the United States to solicit contributions from slaveholding churches. Upon arriving in New York, they were publicly beseeched not to solicit funds in the South, but "reason gave way to avarice" and "purity yielded to temptation."

Douglass's third theme was the culpability of the Free Church, which admitted soliciting funds from slaveholding churches but denied any wrongdoing. The Free Church agreed that slavery was a sin, but its leading theologian, Thomas Chalmers, had posited a distinction between the slavery system and "the character of the person whom circumstances have implicated therewith." Douglass sought to reduce Chalmers's distinction to absurdity by applying it to lying, swearing, murder, and adultery. Such moral and logical absurdity, proffered, ironically, by a prominent British theologian, deserved a dose of Douglass's sarcasm: "What an excellent outlet for all sinners! Let slaveholders rejoice! Let a fiendish glee run round and round through hell! Dr. Chalmers, the eloquent Scotch divine, has, by long study and deep research, found that 'distinction ought to be made between sin and sinner.' " The irony was compounded by the fact that Dr. Chalmers shared his exculpatory "doctrine of circumstances" with "the infidel, Robert Owen," a prominent British social reformer notorious among churchmen for his rejection of prevailing forms of religion.

To create an emotional climax in the conclusion, Douglass used mass responses, which he often sought from sympathetic audiences. When he asked his listeners whether Chalmers and the Free Church represented their views, they shouted "No!" in unison. He thanked them for "speaking out" and challenged others who silently opposed the Free Church to "speak in tones not to be misunderstood." He then proposed to lead the auditors in chanting "Send back that money!" and they again "made the welkin ring." Douglass finished with a spirited appeal to Scottish Christians to agitate until the Free Church not only sent the money back (which it never did) but also confessed its error. As he sat down, the audience responded with "loud applause."

Three months later, on May 22, 1846, Douglass responded effectively to a different sort of rhetorical situation. Invited by the British and Foreign Anti-Slavery Society to be the featured speaker in a widely advertised meeting in one of London's largest churches, Finsbury Chapel, Douglass faced an audience of between two and three thousand, many of whom were unaccustomed to antislavery meetings. In "American Slavery, American Religion, and the Free Church of Scotland," he chose to present a general indictment of slavery that was designed to enlighten and shock the more naive members of the audience. The high-quality stenographic text, coupled with Douglass's apparent effort to be at the top of his form on a special occasion, makes this speech particularly useful for a study of his style.

Douglass appears to have been in full control of an elegant, flexible style that held the attention of his large audience for approximately three hours. When, at the end of two hours, he commented that he was "proceeding at too great a length," he was reinforced by cries of "No! No!" The stenographer's indications in the text show that the audience voiced approval 120 times. Douglass's mature antislavery speeches vary greatly in length, but when he was the primary speaker, he often continued for two hours or more.

The classical rhetorical doctrine of three levels of style—plain, middle, and grand—affords a useful scheme for describing Douglass's style in the Finsbury Chapel speech. Throughout the introduction, his language exemplified the plain style. As he explained "the nature of the American Government" and the "geographical location of slavery in the United States," he used simple language in relatively uncomplicated sentence structures. His effort to provide orienting explanation and his calm tone resulted in little overt audience response.

Immediately after making the transition into the body of the speech with a terse statement of his subject ("I am about to answer the inquiry, what is American slavery?"), Douglass also made a transition into the middle style by beginning to choose language that was both more intense and more entertaining; in so doing he escalated the emotional involvement of the auditors and kept them in a state of delighted anticipation. The combination of his ideas, delivery, and language evoked regular outbursts of "loud cheers," "laughter," "loud applause," "great sensation," and cries of "Shame!" at his depictions of the inhumanity of slavery. Douglass's middle style included sarcasm, humor, alliteration, graphic metaphors, extended narrative examples of cruelty, parallelism (sometimes coupled with anaphora and sometimes with isocolon), rhetorical questions, concrete visual images, antithesis, climax, paradox, synecdoche, irony, and hyperbole.

Douglass concluded the speech with a compressed version of his anti–Free Church appeals. The immediacy, concreteness, and irony of the Free Church issue allowed him to attain an emotional sublimity that manifested itself in both language and delivery and is the defining characteristic of the grand style. About halfway through the thirty-minute conclusion, he declared that he felt compelled to bring charges against the Free Church. With the excited audience repeatedly cheering, Douglass articulated in climax order six charges in intensely emotional language. His second charge, for instance, was that the Free Church had "taken the produce of human blood" to build Free Churches and to pay Free Church ministers. The emotional intensity reached its peak when the audience responded to Douglass's request to shout "Send back the money!" three times.

The speech for which Douglass is best known, "What to the Slave Is the Fourth of July?" was delivered on July 5, 1852, in Rochester, New York, where he had moved in 1847 after returning from exile in Britain. Invited by the Rochester Ladies' Anti-Slavery Society to deliver the main address in its second annual Fourth of July celebration, he addressed approximately six hundred abolitionists who paid twelve and a half cents each to hear him. This speech, like his address in Finsbury Chapel, represents Douglass at his stylistic best and illustrates his facility with the three levels of style. Unlike the Finsbury Chapel speech, it is an epideictic address, and unlike most, if not all, of Douglass's previous epideictic speeches, it was meticulously written and delivered from manuscript. Writing and reading epideictic speeches and lyceum lectures would gradually become Douglass's preferred method of preparation and delivery. He would, however, continue to deliver most of his antislavery lectures extemporaneously from obvious necessities of time and circumstance.

"What to the Slave Is the Fourth of July?" stands out in Douglass's oratorical corpus not only as a stylistic masterpiece but also as the most striking example of his rhetoric of irony. No abolitionist taking a platform on the Fourth of July could ignore the overwhelming irony involved in the situation, but probably none ever exploited it as eloquently as Douglass in 1852. Making use of the classical organizational pattern for forensic speeches (an indication of the care that Douglass took with this speech), he employed the exordium (his own label for his introduction) to feign humility in the conventional manner and to plead for indulgence. He then loosely narrated the efforts of the founding fathers to win independence from Britain, affirming as he did so his respect for the founders' patriotism, honesty, and courage. But the rhetorically significant feature of the narration was the ironic tension he created by eulogizing the founders on the one hand while pointedly excluding himself from participation in the blessings accruing from their accomplishments on the other. Thirty-three times in the narration alone he used "you" or "your" instead of "we" or "our" to emphasize his sense of estrangement as a representative of black Americans. In the partition, Douglass made his indirectly suggested exclusion the explicit point of a carefully crafted passage: "This Fourth [of] July is *yours,* not *mine. You* may rejoice, *I* must mourn. To drag a man in fetters into the grand illuminated temple of liberty, and call upon him to join you in joyous anthems, were inhuman mockery and sacrilegious irony. Do you mean, citizens, to mock me, by asking me to speak to-day?" Hearing the "mournful wail of millions" over the "national, tumultuous joy," he risked becoming "a reproach before God and the world" if he ignored the slaves' plight. His subject, then, was "American Slavery" as seen from the slaves' perspective, and in the name of all that was holy he would dare to denounce everything that perpetuated "the great sin and shame of America!"

At this point in the partition, Douglass articulated a rationale for his rhetoric of irony. To the hypothetical criticism that he and other abolitionists tended to denounce rather than argue, he responded that "where all is plain there is nothing to be argued." Should he argue that the slave is a man, or that men were entitled to liberty, or that slavery was not divinely ordained? The time for reasoning on such propositions was past:

> At a time like this, scorching irony, not convincing argument, is needed. O! had I the ability, and could I reach the nation's ear, I would, to-day, deal out biting ridicule, blasting reproach, withering sarcasm, and stern rebuke. For it is not light

that is needed, but fire; it is not the gentle shower, but thunder. We need the storm, the whirlwind, and the earthquake. The feeling of the nation must be quickened; the conscience of the nation must be roused; the propriety of the nation must be startled; the hypocrisy of the nation must be exposed; and its crimes against God and man must be proclaimed and denounced.

Douglass carried out his intention to expose the nation's hypocrisy in the confirmation section of the speech. He first denounced the internal slave trade and the role of politics and religion in sustaining it. After horrifically depicting a "human flesh jobber" driving a hundred slaves from Washington to New Orleans, he reminded the audience that he grew up amid such sights in Baltimore and that the "murderous traffic" was still "in active operation." Douglass claimed that his second target, the Fugitive Slave Law, was even more disgraceful than the slave trade because it nationalized slavery and defied ordinary principles of justice. Under the law, forty fugitives had been returned to the South in less than two years by judges under no compulsion to hear both sides and who received ten dollars for each person they returned but only five for each one they protected. Douglass managed to wring every drop of irony out of the filthy rag: "Let this damning fact be perpetually told. Let it be thundered around the world, that, in tyrant-killing, king-hating, people-loving, democratic, Christian America, the seats of justice are filled with judges, who hold their offices under an open and palpable *bribe,* and are bound, in deciding in the case of a man's liberty, *to hear only his accusers!*" The third object of Douglass's derision was the church, which bore guilt for silence in the face of the slave trade and the Fugitive Slave Law and for at least passive support of the entire slavery regime. His fourth attack was directed against the political system, which, no less than religion, was "flagrantly inconsistent": Americans claimed a love for liberty but bound three million in their midst in slavery; they hurled anathemas at foreign tyrants while consenting to do the bidding of the tyrants of Virginia and Carolina; they were on fire for liberty abroad but were "cold as an iceberg" at the thought of freedom for their own slaves; they proclaimed the dignity of labor but supported a system that denigrated it; they held in a revered national document that "all men are created equal" but allowed some men to hold others in abject bondage.

Noting that some would respond to his denunciations by claiming that the Constitution sanctioned the holding and hunting of slaves, Douglass attempted to refute the proslavery interpretation of the Constitution. His brief refutation utilized the "plain reading" theme developed by Gerrit Smith and other political abolitionists: while the Constitution contained no explicit reference to slavery, it clearly articulated principles that were hostile to its existence.

In his epilogue, Douglass urged hope and optimism. "There are forces in operation," he asserted, "which must, inevitably, work the downfall of slavery." He believed that God would intervene. He took encouragement from the principles embedded in the Declaration of Independence, and he believed that new technologies that were increasing the speed and frequency of commerce and travel would link nations in such a way that knowledge and moral enlightenment would drive out slavery and oppression.

Within a few months after his Fourth of July address in Rochester, Douglass began exploiting a theme, the existence and effects of the "Slave Power," that would remain prominent in his speeches and editorials throughout the decade. He realized that to elicit the attention of Northern whites who were attracted to emerging antislavery political parties, he needed to convince them of the irony that slavery, in addition to its noxious effects on slaves and free blacks, threatened their own freedom and security. Douglass thus appropriated for his own purposes the venerable notion that proslavery interests had evolved a political and religious metanetwork whose activities were subverting the national welfare. "In the concept of the Slave Power," wrote David Blight, "he found a means to convert the enemy of black people into the enemy of all Americans."

Douglass employed the Slave Power concept in "Northern Ballots and the Election of 1852," which he delivered on October 14 in Ithaca, New York, at a Free Democrat rally. Noting that the Whigs and Democrats had stated their intention to resist the agitation of the slavery issue, Douglass inferred that the Slave Power intended to pass legislation that would limit freedom of speech. "It is idle and short-sighted," he warned, "to regard this question as merely relating to the liberties of the colored people of this country. The wrong proposed to be done touches every man." If the freedom to discuss the rights of black men could be abridged today, freedom to discuss the rights of white men could be abridged tomorrow. Furthermore, through passage of the Fugitive Slave Act the Slave Power had nationalized slavery, weakened the idea of trial by jury, made every Northern man a potential hunter of slaves, and undermined religious liberty.

In "A Nation in the Midst of a Nation," a speech delivered at the annual meeting of the American and Foreign Anti-Slavery Society in New York on May 11, 1853, Douglass used most of his address to respond to challenges posed by the Slave Power. The Compromise of 1850 and the presidential election of 1852 were ample proofs that the Slave Power was waging war on free speech, conscience, and the presence of God in the national councils. The election, in particular, revealed "the extent to which Slavery has shot its leprous distillment through the life-blood of the nation." The postelection efforts to bring state laws in the North into compliance with the Fugitive Slave Law clearly emanated from one well-organized source and thus stood as proof of the existence of the Slave Power.

Douglass addressed a lyceum audience possibly for the first time when he appeared before the New Lyceum of Manchester, New Hampshire, on January 24, 1854. In "God's Law Outlawed," he spoke briefly about the nature of slavery before turning to the theme that he believed would seem more pertinent to a general audience. There was, he asserted, "a purely slavery party in the United States" about which he wished to speak. Its membership transcended political-party identity and was especially influential in the Northern states, "over which slavery has spread its death-like pall." The point he wanted to make was that "slavery is here. The men who hold three millions in bondage yonder, are *here.*" The Slave Power had so effectively nationalized slavery that slaves were no safer in Massachusetts and New Hampshire than in the South.

The passage in mid-1854 of Illinois senator Stephen A. Douglas's Kansas-Nebraska bill was for Frederick Douglass additional evidence of the audacious ambition of the Slave Power. Invited to stump for Republican candidates in the senator's home state during the fall congressional campaign, Douglass arrived in northern Illinois in mid-October. Two weeks later, on October 30, fifteen hundred anti-Nebraskaites filed into Chicago's Metropolitan Hall to hear Douglass deliver the final speech of his Illinois tour, "Slavery, Freedom, and the Kansas-Nebraska Act." As usual, he sought to convince his white auditors that their own vital interests were at stake in the contest between the Republicans and the Slave Power. The South must be made to give up slavery, he asserted, or "the North must give up liberty." Liberty, with its "just demands," was "inconsistent with the overgrown exactions of the slave power." The ascendancy of the Slave Power would put at risk freedom of speech, the work ethic, a free gospel, the free movement of mail, and the security of Northern travelers in the South.

Due to his recurring throat soreness, Douglass's first opportunity to respond in a speech to the Dred Scott decision, which was handed down by the Supreme Court on March 6, 1857, came on May 14 when he delivered "The Dred Scott Decision" to the first anniversary meeting of the American Abolition Society in New York. Douglass appealed to an audience of white abolitionists to understand that the Slave Power, which included the Taney wing of the Supreme Court, was their enemy as surely as it was the enemy of the nation's blacks. The Slave Power step by step had grown so imperious that it had marked out "the white man's liberty" for burial "in the same grave with the black man's."

The climax of Douglass's career as an abolitionist was not the North's victory in the Civil War; it was, rather, the ratification of the Fifteenth Amendment in 1870. For Douglass, blacks in the South were not fully invested with human dignity and rights until they were guaranteed the opportunity to vote. Since the ratification of the Fifteenth Amendment seemed to be their ultimate triumph, Douglass and his abolitionist colleagues proceeded to disband the last of their antislavery organizations and to abandon, at least to a significant extent, their fiercely ironic rhetoric. On May 11, 1869, when the ratification of the Fifteenth Amendment seemed inevitable, Douglass poignantly articulated the new rhetorical milieu in "Let the Negro Alone," a speech to the annual meeting of the American Anti-Slavery Society. "The arguments which I once could use with some little skill and effect on occasions like this," he noted, "are no longer pertinent. We stand tonight amid the bleaching bones of dead issues. . . . I have nothing to kick against."

On April 22, 1870, only three days after he had helped disband the American

Anti-Slavery Society, Douglass addressed a meeting in Albany, New York, that had been called to celebrate the ratification of the Fifteenth Amendment, one of several such meetings in which he participated. His extemporaneously delivered speech, ''At Last, at Last, the Black Man Has a Future,'' expressed the exhilaration of victory as well as a mixture of emotions that were naturally stimulated by the dissolution of the movement that had defined and dominated his life for nearly thirty years. This melding of victory into consummation and of consummation into dissolution generated a complex rhetorical situation that called not for customary agitational irony directed toward enemies but for an inwardly directed epideictic rhetoric of celebration and closure. Merely to celebrate victory was insufficient; he needed to celebrate so as to frame the victorious movement in a way that would help its adherents cope with disengagement.

Douglass responded to the situation appropriately. He articulated the dimensions of a significant legacy to be left to future generations of black Americans, honored abolitionists past and present who had struggled to create the legacy, recalled examples of courage and perseverance in the face of persecution and opposition, and sought to develop a sense of transcendent solidarity designed, perhaps, to mute the memory of internecine strife and schism. Douglass served the need for closure by refusing to balance celebration with critique of the amendment's shortcomings.

After 1870, Douglass reduced the ironic bite of his reform rhetoric and at the same time increased the frequency of his appearances on the lecture circuit, where his speeches, as one might expect, were essentially devoid of substantive irony. He lectured on a variety of subjects, but ''Self-Made Men'' was his most famous and most frequently presented lecture. His development of this lecture began as early as 1859. On October 18, 1859, for instance, he delivered ''Self-Made Men'' to the Philadelphia Library Company and received ''deafening applause'' when he asserted that John Brown's raid on Harper's Ferry, which had been terminated by Colonel Robert E. Lee that morning, was a legitimate fruit of slavery. From 1859 until his death in 1895, Douglass delivered ''Self-Made Men'' approximately seventy-five times. His last documented presentation of the lecture occurred in March 1893 at the Indian Industrial School in Carlisle, Pennsylvania. The two-hour lecture retained its basic substance and structure over nearly thirty-four years even though Douglass revised elements of it from time to time to keep it current. The students and teachers in the Indian Industrial School did not hear the reference to Harper's Ferry, but they heard Douglass urge the country to ''give the Negro fair play and let him alone.''

''Self-Made Men'' bears a similarity to Douglass's antislavery rhetoric in that both exploited his image as the quintessential self-made man who is somehow motivated to rise from the worst of circumstances by dint of native talent and hard work. Despite its indirect but obvious self-reference and self-praise, ''Self-Made Men'' attracted responsive audiences who saw Douglass as living proof that first the slaves and later the freedmen were worth saving. Even if ironic verbal appeal had little place in ''Self-Made Men,'' he could continue to take advantage of the nonverbal irony implicit in his imposing physical and intellectual presence behind a lectern. The same irony worked in the background of all of Douglass's rhetorical transactions, including his postbellum lectures, but the theme of ''Self-Made Men'' made it especially salient.

INFORMATION SOURCES

Research Collections and Collected Speeches

Several speech texts are included in the Frederick Douglass Papers at the Library of Congress, which are available on microfilm. The most significant sources of Douglass's antislavery speech texts, however, are several abolition journals that regularly printed stenographic reports of his rhetorical efforts. The most useful journals are the *Liberator* (1831–65), the *National Anti-Slavery Standard* (1840–70), and Douglass's own journals, *The North Star* (1847–51) and *Frederick Douglass' Paper* (1851–60).

[*FDP*] Blassingame, John W., et al., *The Frederick Douglass Papers.* Vols. 1–5. New Haven: Yale UP, 1979–92.
[*FDAC*] Fulkerson, Gerald. ''Frederick Douglass and the Anti-Slavery Crusade: His Career and Speeches, 1817–1861.'' Ph.D. diss., U of Illinois, 1971.

Selected Critical Studies

Blassingame, John W. Introduction to Series One. *The Frederick Douglass Papers,* Vol. 1. Ed. John W. Blassingame et al. New Haven: Yale UP, 1979, xxi–lxxii.
Fulkerson, Gerald. ''Exile as Emergence: Frederick Douglass in Great Britain, 1845–1847.'' *Quarterly Journal of Speech* 60 (1974): 69–82.
———. ''Frederick Douglass and the Kansas-Nebraska Act: A Case Study in Agitational Versatility.'' *Central States Speech Journal* 23 (1972): 261–269.
Leroux, Neil. ''Frederick Douglass and the Attention Shift.'' *Rhetoric Society Quarterly* 21.2 (1991): 36–46.
Martin, Waldo E., Jr. ''Frederick Douglass.'' *American Orators before 1900: Critical Studies and Sources.* Ed. Bernard K. Duffy and Halford R. Ryan. Westport, CT: Greenwood, 1987, 139–145.
Sundquist, Eric J., ed. *Frederick Douglass: New Literary and Historical Essays.* Cambridge: Cambridge UP, 1990.

Selected Biographies

Blight, David W. *Frederick Douglass' Civil War: Keeping Faith in Jubilee.* Baton Rouge: Louisiana State UP, 1989.
Fulkerson, Gerald. ''Frederick Douglass and the Anti-Slavery Crusade: His Career and Speeches, 1817–1861.'' Ph.D. diss., U of Illinois, 1971.
Huggins, Nathan Irvin. *Slave and Citizen: The Life of Frederick Douglass.* Boston: Little, Brown, 1980.

Martin, Waldo E., Jr. *The Mind of Frederick Douglass*. Chapel Hill: U of North Carolina P, 1984.

McFeely, William S. *Frederick Douglass*. New York: W. W. Norton, 1991.

Preston, Dickson J. *Young Frederick Douglass: The Maryland Years*. Baltimore: Johns Hopkins UP, 1980.

CHRONOLOGY OF MAJOR SPEECHES

[See "Research Collections and Collected Speeches" for source codes.]

"I Have Come to Tell You Something about Slavery." Lynn, MA, October, 1841. *FDP*, 1: 3–5.

"The Southern Style of Preaching to Slaves." Boston, MA, January 28, 1842. *FDP*, 1: 15–17; *FDAC*, 448–451.

"The Free Church Connection with the Slave Church." Abroath, Scotland, February 12, 1846. *FDP*, 1:156–164; *FDAC*, 487–494.

"American Slavery, American Religion, and the Free Church of Scotland." London, England, May 22, 1846. *FDP*, 1: 269–299; *FDAC*, 503–526.

"What to the Slave Is the Fourth of July?" Rochester, NY, July 5, 1852. *FDP*, 2: 359–388; *FDAC*, 719–740.

"Northern Ballots and the Election of 1852." Ithaca, NY, October 14, 1852. *FDP*, 2: 397–420; *FDAC*, 752–766.

"A Nation in the Midst of a Nation." New York, NY, May 11, 1853. *FDP*, 2: 423–440; *FDAC*, 771–784.

"God's Law Outlawed." Manchester, NH, January 24, 1854. *FDP*, 2: 454–460; *FDAC*, 785–791.

"Slavery, Freedom, and the Kansas-Nebraska Act." Chicago, IL, October 30, 1854. *FDP*, 2: 538–559; *FDAC*, 821–839.

"The Dred Scott Decision." New York, NY, May 14, 1857. *FDP*, 3: 163–183; *FDAC*, 875–892.

"Let the Negro Alone." New York, NY, May 11, 1869. *FDP*, 4: 199–213.

"At Last, at Last, the Black Man Has a Future." Albany, NY, April, 22, 1870. *FDP*, 4: 265–272.

"Self-Made Men." Carlisle, PA, March, 1893. *FDP*, 5: 545–575.

WILLIAM EDWARD BURGHARDT DU BOIS
(1868–1963), professor, editor, civil rights leader

STACY L. SMITH AND MARTHA SOLOMON WATSON

In the struggle for African-American civil rights and equality, William Edward Burghardt Du Bois was undoubtedly one of the most influential as well as controversial figures. As an author, editor, sociologist, and founding member of both the Niagara Movement and the National Association for the Advancement of Colored People (NAACP), Du Bois was in the forefront of agitation for civil rights for his race. To alleviate the racism and oppression in the United States, he proposed a host of remedies, the most provocative of which was his endorsement of the Russian social model in his later life. However, throughout his life, Du Bois remained consistently committed to eradicating the color line, which he saw as a central question of the twentieth century.

Born in Great Barrington, Massachusetts, on February 23, 1868, Du Bois was raised by his mother, Mary Burghardt Du Bois, who ensured that her son had a sound education. In his autobiography, Du Bois wrote that he led a happy childhood, only vaguely aware of his African heritage that distinguished him from his playmates. A hint of his own future direction, his high-school graduation oration extolled Wendell Phillips, noting his New England heritage, his work with abolition, and his social ideals.

With financial support from the local community, Du Bois enrolled at Fisk University, where he came in contact with the segregated South, a confrontation that became the emotional and intellectual genesis of his lifelong quest for equality. Also, for the first time, he was part of a substantial community of talented, intellectual African-Americans, whose companionship he particularly welcomed.

With recommendation letters from the president of Fisk and other professors, Du Bois was awarded a grant to attend Harvard in the fall of 1888. Although the intellectual climate of Harvard challenged him, his continued experiences with racism affected him psychologically. His mentors in history and philosophy there, Albert Bushnell Hart and William James, respectively, encouraged Du Bois toward pragmatism and a social scientific approach. Their emphasis on the testing of ideas through careful observation of data provided Du Bois with a methodology he employed repeatedly during his lifelong struggle against racism.

In the summer of 1892, before writing his dissertation, Du Bois began a two-year sojourn in Europe. There he also studied with some distinguished social scientific scholars from whom he gleaned a synthesis of theories of history, sociology, and economics that shaped his later thoroughgoing critique of American institutionalized racism.

Du Bois returned to America in 1894 for a position at Wilberforce University in Ohio, where he spent two unhappy years, due mainly to his conflicts with the conservative leadership of the school. Then he accepted a fifteen-month appointment with the University of Pennsylvania to do field research on the quality of life for black residents of the city. Employing careful empirical methods, *The Philadelphia Negro* (1899) focused on environmental and historical rather than genetic explanations for the condition of blacks in the United States, a social scientific approach that differed sharply from previous work. With this project completed, Du Bois accepted a position with Atlanta University, where he remained for thirteen years, during which time he edited *Atlanta University Studies*.

Increasingly, Du Bois's views about the solutions to racism differed sharply from those of Booker T. Washington. At first unwilling to criticize Washington directly for fear of the repercussions, in 1903 Du Bois finally offered a succinct explication and criticism of Washington's views in his widely read *Souls of Black Folk*.

In 1905, Du Bois helped found the Niagara Movement, an organization dedicated to agitating actively for social and political equality for blacks in clear opposition to the accommodationist stance of Washington. Never fully successful, in part because of the efforts of Washington, the movement became a precursor to the NAACP, of which Du Bois was also a founding member. In 1910, Du Bois left Atlanta University to work for the NAACP full-time as director of publications and research. His work with the NAACP included editing its newsletter, the *Crisis*, which by 1919 had over 100,000 subscribers. He frequently used this forum to oppose Marcus Garvey, whom he saw as a misguided and even dangerous demagogue. Although his independence of mind and radicalism frustrated some leaders of the NAACP and eventually forced his resignation as editor in 1934, Du Bois's work with *Crisis* was crucial in the organization's success.

Du Bois also became closely involved in Pan-Africanism, a movement that struggled to secure independence for colonized African nations and pushed to relocate American blacks to countries in Africa. In 1919, he organized the first Pan-African Congress in Paris; he remained actively involved with the cause throughout much of his life, and in 1945 he was honored by the Pan-African Congress in London for his contributions.

After World War II, Du Bois became increasingly vocal about issues of world peace and Russia. In 1950, he ran on the American Labor party ticket for senator from New York. In his speech "I Speak for Peace" in 1950, he advocated peace in Korea, identified economic disparities between classes as "the fundamental problem of the age," and castigated the press, education, and other institutions for their role in diverting attention from this critical issue. Although Du Bois was never a classic Marxist, he joined the American Communist party in 1961 in part because of his frustration with other alternatives to social change.

Because of his views, in 1951 a federal grand jury indicted him for failing to register as an agent of a foreign principal. The case was quickly dismissed, but Du Bois was refused a passport until 1958. Then he traveled extensively in Europe and China for two years. At the invitation of President Kwame Nkrumah of Ghana, he traveled there to work on the *Encyclopedia Africana*. In 1961, he became a citizen of Ghana and died there on August 27, 1963.

DU BOIS AS RHETOR

During his career, Du Bois was a prolific author, publishing work of some kind from the time he was a teenager until he died at the age of ninety-five. He wrote at least twenty-three book-length works, as well as literally hundreds of pamphlets, essays, addresses, lectures, works of fiction, newspaper editorials, chapters in books, and opinion columns. In his *Dusk of Dawn*, he described his rhetorical role accurately:

> My leadership was a leadership solely of ideas. I never was, nor ever will be, personally popular. This was not simply because of my idiosyncrasies but because I despise the essential demagoguery of personal leadership. . . . I think I may not be boasting that in the period from 1910 to 1930 I was a main factor in revolutionizing the attitude of the American Negro toward caste. My stinging hammer blows made Negroes aware of themselves, confident of their possibilities and determined in self-assertion.

His first major published work, *The Suppression of the African Slave-Trade to the United States of America*, was from his dissertation. This careful historical account of the slave trade in America is notable for its meticulous, systematic analysis, based on the sociological methodologies Du Bois had mastered during his graduate training. A similar approach pervaded *The Philadelphia Negro*, published in 1899, for which, according to Moore, Du Bois personally "knocked at the door of each domicile in the Seventh Ward, sat down with whomever answered his knock, and asked questions for ten minutes to an hour," seeking precise answers to his lengthy questionnaire. In 1903, he published what is now probably his most famous work, *The Souls of Black Folk*, which many scholars mark as the beginning of his leadership in the African-American civil rights movement. In 1907, as the founding editor of *Horizon*, a small monthly "Journal of the Color Line,'' Du Bois turned his journalistic experience explicitly to the service of the advancement of his race. His selection as editor of the *Crisis*, where he enjoyed a twenty-four-year tenure, gave him a broader venue to comment frequently on issues and situations of importance to the African-American community.

In addition to his many other writings, Du Bois wrote three autobiographies that chart the development of his thinking and life against the backdrop of contemporary events. The first, *Darkwater: Voices from within the Veil*, which appeared in 1920, reflected his views on pragmatism, African-American nationalism, and Pan-Africanism as well as socialism, all forces that would continue to shape his thinking. His second autobiographical work, *Dusk of Dawn: An Autobiography of a Race Concept*, as its name suggested, continued his reflections on race as illumined by his own life. Although Du Bois worked on his final autobiography, *The Autobiography of W. E. B. Du Bois: A Soliloquy on Viewing My Life from the Last Decade of Its First Century*, while living in Ghana, it appeared after his death edited by Herbert Aptheker. In conventional autobiographical form, Du Bois claimed ''to review my life as frankly and fully as I can.'' Because of Du Bois's perceived ideological commitment to communism, the work was not published in the United States until 1968, five years after his death.

Du Bois's thinking underwent dramatic change during his life as he struggled to find solutions to the deeply embedded racism in America. With growing frustration, Du Bois proposed various alternatives as remedies; but throughout his career and writings he struggled with the persistence of racial discrimination. Consequently, some recurrent themes have become closely associated with his name.

Scholar Robert Michael Franklin suggested that Du Bois's copious writings explore one central question: ''How might blacks achieve personal wholeness and societal power without ignoring their cultural indebtedness to Africa, America, and Europe?'' Du Bois himself described this problem as a central tension in the consciousness of black people in a famous passage from his work *The Souls of Black Folk*:

One ever feels his two-ness,—an American, a Negro; two souls, two thoughts, two unreconciled strivings; two warring ideals in one dark body. . . . The history of the American Negro is the history of this strife,—this longing to attain self-conscious manhood, to merge his double self into a better and truer self. In this merging he wishes neither of the old selves to be lost. He would not Africanize America, for America has too much to teach the world and Africa. He would not bleach his Negro soul in a flood of white Americanism, for he knows that the Negro blood has a message for the world. He simply wishes to make it possible for a man to be both a Negro and an American, without being cursed and spit upon by his fellows, without having the doors of Opportunity closed roughly in his face.

Because he believed that racism had no firm basis in scientific fact, Du Bois insisted that the efforts of blacks themselves were crucial to resolving this tension as well as attaining their rightful place in society. His view of the appropriate direction for those efforts, whether integration into the economic system of the country or the development of black nationalism, changed over time. But he consistently believed that all blacks had the obligation to use their abilities and opportunities to advance the race as a whole. Although Du Bois did not underestimate the problems that confronted his fellow blacks, he was initially optimistic. He strongly believed that as a cohesive group, they could and must better the race as a whole by prizing their collective potentials, history, and contributions.

Early in his career, Du Bois's hopes for the advancement of his race rested with what he termed the Talented Tenth. For him, the key to the elevation of his race was the proper education of the best and the brightest members of that race, who could become leaders and role models for those who did not have the same opportunities and abilities. He believed that once these people were properly educated, any avenue in life was open to them if they worked diligently. In "The Talented Tenth," published in 1903 in *The Negro Problem*, he argued that the elevation of this portion of his race would carry others along:

> The Negro race, like all races, is going to be saved by its exceptional men. The problem of education, then, among Negroes must first of all deal with the Talented Tenth; *it is the problem of developing the Best of this race that they may guide the Mass away from the contamination and death of the Worst*, in their own and other races.

Du Bois's rhetorical vision derived from his philosophical underpinnings. He sought to lead the members of his race to their rightful place in American society—attaining for them, and they for themselves, moral, social, and cultural equality. Although he was not committed to any religious institution, Du Bois had imbibed a strong moral sense from his Puritan background. Thus his writings often have a distinctly moralistic tone. Pointing out the depravity of many groups of African-Americans, he often urged the potential leaders—the tenth— to be the moral examples for those who had fallen short of his ideal. In "The Conservation of Races," delivered in Washington, D.C., in 1897, he said:

> We must unflinchingly and bravely face the truth, not with apologies, but with solemn earnestness. . . . The Academy should seek to gather about it the talented, unselfish men, the pure and noble-minded women, to fight an army of devils that disgraces our manhood and our womanhood. There does not stand today upon God's earth a race more capable in muscle, in intellect, in morals, than the American Negro, if he will bend his energies in the right direction.

In a commencement address at Fisk in 1898, he laid out his view of the role of these leaders:

> And we serve first for the sake of serving—to develop our own powers, gain the mastery of this human machine, and come to the broadest, deepest self-realization. And then we serve for real end of service, to make life no narrow, selfish thing, but to let it sweep as sweeps the morning—broad and full and free for all men and all time, that you and I and all may earn a living and earn, too, much more than that—a life worth living.

His vision for his race also required these talented persons to sacrifice willingly their own personal needs and desires for the good of the race. Later in the commencement address, he averred:

> To choose a life calling is a serious thing: first, you must consider not so much what you want to do as what wants to be done; secondly, you cannot wander at will over all the world of work that wants workers, but duty and privilege and special advantage calls to the work that lies nearest your hands. The German works for Germany, the Englishman serves England, and it is the duty of the Negro to serve his blood and lineage, and so working, each for each, and all for each, we realize the goal of each for all.

But Du Bois did not believe that service to their compatriots was the only goal of these talented leaders. They must also become advocates for their brothers and sisters in the larger world, seeking to combat the forces of deception and denigration. In a commencement address at Baltimore Colored High School, reprinted in the *Horizon* in June 1910, he described the work of the graduates as a crusade like that of Godfrey of Bouillon initiated to rescue Jerusalem; but their joint crusade was "for human freedom and the abolition of the last refuge of Barbarism: the Color line." This "Last Crusade, the crusade to deliver from the Heathen the Sacred Truth of Human Equality and Brotherhood," was also "to beat back the hateful heresy that the world and its joys and opportunities belong to people of any one race or color; to lift high the banner which guides all humanity of every race and color; to the kingdoms of culture and courtesy and liberty—the rightful heritage of all men everywhere."

Clearly, Du Bois himself was a member of that Talented Tenth in whom he placed such great faith. Because of the educational opportunities and advantages he had enjoyed, Du Bois frequently saw himself as a teacher, instructing his audiences about his race and the problems it confronted. For example, in his 1898 commencement address at Fisk, his concise if simplistic view of the influences on young blacks provided a framework for understanding the challenges that confronted them:

> Young Negroes are born in a social system of caste that belongs to the middle ages; they inherit the moral looseness of a sixteenth century; they learn to lisp the

religious controversies of the seventeenth century; they are stirred by discussions of the rights of man that belong to the eighteenth century, and it is not wonderful if they hardly realize that they live upon the threshold of the twentieth century.

In "The Conservation of Races," his analytical view of the concept of racial differences sounds strikingly like a college lecture in a beginning anthropology class:

> Many criteria of race differences have in the past been proposed, as color, hair, cranial measurements, and language. And manifestly, in each of these respects, human beings differ widely. They vary in color, for instance, from the marble-like pallor of the Scandinavian to the rich, dark brown of the Zulu, passing by the creamy Slav, the yellow Chinese, the light brown Sicilian and the brown Egyptian.

His later delineation of the physical differences among the world's major races was factual and precise. His persona was the scientifically objective teacher, intent on explicating a complex subject carefully. Throughout his discourse, Du Bois interwove historical facts, statistics, and sociological observations to enlighten his audience and support his analysis.

Rhetorically, as a teacher, Du Bois analyzed the problems confronting his race, placed the issues in a larger context, and then offered solutions to them. He was not, however, solely a detached observer. In a notable passage in "The Conservation of Races," his clear-eyed assessment of the state of many of his race was coupled with an urgent plea for action by leaders:

> The Negro Academy ought to sound a note of warning that would echo in every black cabin in the land: *unless we conquer our present vices they will conquer us*; we are diseased, we are developing criminal tendencies, and an alarmingly large percentage of our men and women are sexually impure. The Negro Academy should stand and proclaim this over the housetops, crying with Garrison: *I will not equivocate, I will not retreat a single inch, and I will be heard.*

Because Du Bois's corpus is so large, any complete inventory of his rhetorical strategies is impossible. Still, certain features are prominent enough to merit some consideration. First, Du Bois was a master of argument. His most compelling works are models of careful analysis, clear organization, and cogent reasoning. His erudition is apparent in both the variety and the quality of the evidence he educed to support his arguments.

Du Bois's meticulous organization reflected both his analytical skills and his systematic thinking. Frequently, he signposted his thoughts with numbers (first, second, and so on). Alternatively, he carefully used logical connectors (if, then, thus, and so on) so that the structure of his argument was transparent. Maintaining a sharp focus on the relevant issues, he presented his arguments so clearly that he developed a logical stronghold. For example, in "The Conservation of Races," he argued for "race organizations" like the American Negro

Academy to which he delivered this address at its founding meeting. He began his argument with a question that suggested his approach: "The question, then, which we must seriously consider is this: what is the real meaning of race; what has, in the past, been the law of race development, and what lessons has the past history of race development to teach the rising Negro people?" To answer this question, he developed a concise definition of race and then discussed the factors that distinguished each racial group. He concluded that some of the "great races of today—particularly the Negro race—have not as yet given to civilization the full spiritual message they are capable of giving." This fact led him to insist that the only way for the distinctive, valuable contribution of his race to emerge was not through absorption into white America, but rather in developing its own path, guided by race organizations like the academy. He concluded by offering a creed for the academy that articulated its central principles. Characteristically, the items were numbered; they moved from underlying assumptions to recommendations for action to a resolute commitment.

Du Bois's keen sense of argument and his cogent reasoning allowed him to lay out his arguments so they became almost ineluctable. For example, in a debate with Lothrop Stoddard in 1929 regarding a resolution about cultural equality for blacks, Du Bois followed meticulous debate form and order. He first defined his terms, then set up his own ideological premise, then laid out the expected arguments of the yet-to-be-heard opponent, and finally refuted these arguments. A carefully organized opening speech and rebuttal indicate that Du Bois understood the process of debate; his reasoning throughout was meticulous and clear.

Du Bois was equally skillful in refutation. Perhaps nowhere is his skill as a debater more apparent than in his address at the annual meeting of the National Woman Suffrage Association in 1912. In this speech, Du Bois compared women's struggle for the vote to blacks' and in so doing crafted a refutative argument that was compact and persuasive. He framed the speech argumentatively by including in the first paragraph a list of the reasons why anyone was denied the right to vote. Du Bois then noted the importance of engaging in refutation for the purpose of gaining assent: "What is then the essential argument for extending the right to vote? We may possibly reach it by clearing away the misapprehensions that lurk in the arguments mentioned above."

Du Bois then crafted refutations that confronted each of the antisuffrage arguments. For example, he compared the position that ignorant blacks were protected by the votes of benevolent whites to the similar argument that women did not need suffrage because they were "protected" by the votes of their husbands, sons, and fathers:

> So too with American Negroes: the South continually insists that a benevolent guardianship of whites over blacks is the ideal thing. They assume that white people not only know better what Negroes need than Negroes themselves, but are anxious to supply those needs. As a result, instead of knowledge they grope in

ignorance and helplessness. They cannot "understand" the Negro, they cannot protect him from cheating and lynching and in general instead of loving guardianship, we see anarchy and exploitation. If the Negro could speak for himself in the South instead of having to depend on the chance sympathy of white citizens, how much healthier growth of democracy the South would have.

For each argument, Du Bois delineated the position of the South and then refuted it through logic. This strategy was employed throughout his speeches, but especially in those that addressed a specific policy issue such as voting or peace.

Du Bois was also a careful stylist. While he was sometimes poetic, more frequently his style was marked by precise, forceful language. In this style, he crafted his discourse into lists of brief facts. A paragraph composed of simple sentences with simple structure carries force, and Du Bois took advantage of that force often. In "The Negro Citizen," delivered at the Interracial Conference in Washington, D.C., on December 19, 1928, Du Bois utilized this style with great skill:

Political ignorance in the South has grown by leaps and bounds. The mass of people in the South today have no knowledge as to how they are governed or by whom. Elections have nothing to do with broad policies and social development but are matters of the selection of friends to lucrative offices and punishment of personal enemies. Local administration is a purposely disguised system of intrigue which not even an expert could unravel.

He carried his argument further, with precise emotion, as he summed up:

And yet, of all this, there must be no criticism, no exposure, no real investigation, no political revolt, because the decent white South lacks the moral courage to expose and punish rascals even though they are white and to stand up for democracy even if it includes black folk.

In passages about racism such as this one, Du Bois's language and his substance often combined to produce a caustic and biting tone.

At times, however, Du Bois's tone became still more biting. For example, in his debate with Lothrop Stoddard in 1929, he was caustic in his passionate arguments for cultural equality. He invoked morality and historical example in an overall biting style marked by rhetorical questions, specific accusations in the use of the second-person pronoun "you," and sarcasm. He asserted:

You decry lawlessness. Where do you get the lawlessness of Chicago and of the United States? You began it when as a nation you disregarded the 13th, 14th and 15th amendments and then are vastly surprised when you cannot enforce the 18th. You have organized your life so as not to carry out the laws which you yourselves made and you have the heritage of lawlessness to pay for it. You have created here in the United States, which today pretends to the moral leadership of the world, a situation where on the last night of the old year you can slowly and publicly burn a human being alive for the amusement of Americans who represent some of the purest strains of Nordic blood in that great place, Mississippi, which has done so much for the civilization of the world!

This harsh and biting quality added to his refutative strength and precisely forceful style. Taken together, the features of Du Bois's style produce a powerful eloquence that may remind the modern reader of passages in Frederick Douglass and William Lloyd Garrison.

Du Bois's view, cited earlier, regarding his rhetorical role was quite accurate: he was an intellectual force in the debate over race relations in this country. His keen intellect and broad education provided him with the resources both to critique institutionalized racism effectively and to propose often-valuable remedies. But Du Bois's considerable rhetorical talents were also invaluable to his cause. His argumentative prowess, his forceful style, and his impassioned advocacy made his rhetorical voice particularly notable. Because of his abiding commitment and his fearless confrontation, Du Bois became a beacon light for others; he spoke eloquently to both supporters and opponents. Unfortunately, the problem he addressed has resisted solution and continues to perplex the United States thirty years after his death.

However, while Du Bois's vehemence and sarcasm are entertaining to the modern reader and undoubtedly intriguing to some contemporary supporters, his rhetorical persona is daunting rather than attractive. His biting wit and adamancy made him less persuasive to those outside his camp. His propensity for confrontation and his unrelenting critique of American institutions doubtless alienated some fellow citizens; his repudiation of capitalism intensified that problem. His refusal to compromise is admirable ethically but limited his rhetorical effectiveness.

Probably Du Bois's most significant contributions to his cause were his reiteration of the potentials of his race, his reaffirmation of his strengths, and his absolute denial of its innate inferiority. In his life, he enacted the model of the responsible, talented, and dedicated African-American that he urged so strongly in his discourse. In the end, Du Bois's life of abiding commitment, strong advocacy, and persistent interrogating of social practices may be his greatest contribution to his cause. As he said, his "stinging hammer blows" made his race "aware of themselves, confident of their abilities, and determined in self-assertion."

INFORMATION SOURCES

Research Collections and Collected Speeches

The papers of W. E. B. Du Bois are housed at the University of Massachusetts, Amherst, and are open to scholars for study or may be purchased on seventy-three reels of microfilm. The collection includes correspondence, four hundred articles, newspaper columns, novels, plays, poetry, motion pictures, audio and video tapes, and memorabilia. This collection also includes the manuscripts of over three hundred different speeches, ranging from those he gave at his college commencements at Fisk and Harvard to the ones delivered near the end of his life. The speeches address topics such as world peace, colonialism, and political and social development in Africa and America. The collection also includes speeches made during his 1950 campaign for the U.S. Senate. Early drafts and speeches never published are located in the collection.

Fisk University in Nashville, Tennessee, has a collection containing pamphlets, newspaper and journal clippings, manuscripts, research material used for the preparation of manuscripts, and correspondence. The W. E. B. Du Bois Papers, part of the James Weldon Johnson Memorial Collection at Yale University, contain manuscripts, correspondence, articles, and poems. The Schomburg Center for Research in Black Culture of the New York Public Library holds a small collection in the Hugh Smythe Papers, including several essays, articles, and speech drafts, along with material from Du Bois's days as a student. The NAACP Papers at the Library of Congress contain information on Du Bois's work with that organization.

[*CPA*] Aptheker, Herbert, ed. *The Complete Published Works of W. E. B. Du Bois: Pamphlets and Leaflets*. Millwood, NY: Kraus-Thomson, 1986.
[*CPB*]———. *The Complete Published Works of W. E. B. Du Bois: Writings in Non-Periodical Literature*. Millwood, NY: Kraus-Thomson, 1982.
Du Bois, W. E. B. *Darkwater: Voices from within the Veil*. New York: Harcourt, Brace and Howe, 1920.
———. *Dusk of Dawn: An Essay toward an Autobiography of a Race Concept*. New York: Harcourt, Brace and Howe, 1940.
———. *The Souls of Black Folk: Essays and Sketches*. Chicago: A. C. McClurg, 1903.
[*DBS*] Foner, Philip S., ed. *W. E. B. Du Bois Speaks*. 2 vols. New York: Pathfinder, 1970.
[*DBW*] Huggins, Nathan, ed. *W. E. B. Du Bois: Writings*. New York: Library of America, 1986.
Lester, Julius, ed. *The Seventh Son: The Thought and Writings of W. E. B. Du Bois*. 2 vols. New York: Random House, 1971.
McDonnell, Robert W. *The Papers of W. E. B. Du Bois*. Sanford, NC: Microfilming Corporation of America, 1981.

Selected Critical Studies

Butler, Broadus N. "Booker T. Washington, W. E. B. Du Bois, Black Americans, and the NAACP—Another Perspective." *Crisis* 85 (August 1978): 222–230.
Champion, Danny. "Booker T. Washington versus W. E. B. Du Bois: A Study in Rhetorical Contrasts." *Oratory in the New South*. Ed. Waldo W. Braden. Baton Rouge: Louisiana State UP, 1979. 174–204.
Daniels, Walter C. "W. E. B. Du Bois at Lincoln University: Founders' Day Address, 1941." *Missouri History Review* 74 (1980): 343–355.
Harding, Vincent. "W. E. B. Du Bois and the Black Messianic Vision." *Freedomways* 9 (1969): 44–58.
Howard-Pitney, David. "The Jeremiads of Frederick Douglass, Booker T. Washington,

and W. E. B. Du Bois and Changing Patterns of Black Messianic Rhetoric, 1841–1920.'' *Journal of American Ethnic History* 6 (1986): 47–61.

Marable, Manning. *W. E. B. Du Bois: Black Radical Democrat*. Boston: Twayne, 1986.

Meier, August. ''From Conservative to Radical: The Ideological Development of W. E. B. Du Bois, 1885–1905.'' *Crisis* 66 (November 1959): 527–536.

Selected Biographies

Broderick, Francis. *W. E. B. Du Bois: Negro Leader in a Time of Crisis*. Stanford, CA: Stanford UP, 1959.

Clarke, John Henrik, Esther Jackson, Ernest Kaiser, and J. H. O'Dell, eds. *Black Titan: W. E. B. Du Bois*. Boston: Beacon, 1970.

Du Bois, Shirley Graham. *His Day Is Marching On: A Memoir of W. E. B. Du Bois*. Philadelphia: J. B. Lippincott, 1971.

Horne, Gerald. *Black and Red: W. E. B. Du Bois and the Afro-American Response to the Cold War, 1944–1963*. Albany: State U of New York P, 1986.

Isaacs, Harold R. *The New World of Negro Americans*. New York: John Day, 1963.

Lewis, David L. *W. E. B. Du Bois: Biography of a Race, 1868–1919*. New York: Henry Holt, 1993.

Moore, Jack. *W. E. B. Du Bois*. Boston: Twayne, 1981.

CHRONOLOGY OF MAJOR SPEECHES

[See ''Research Collections and Collected Speeches'' for source codes.]

''Jefferson Davis as a Representative of Civilization.'' Cambridge, MA, 1890. *DBW*, 811–814.

''The Conservation of Races.'' Washington, DC, 1897. *CPB*, 1–8; *DBW*, 815–826.

''Careers Open to College-bred Negroes,'' (Commencement Address at Fisk University). Nashville, TN, June 1898. *CPB*, 1–10; *DBW*, 827–841.

''The Niagara Movement: Declaration of Principles.'' Buffalo, NY, July 11, 1905. *CPA*, 55–58.

''The Niagara Movement: Address to the Country.'' Harper's Ferry, WV, August 16, 1906. *CPA*, 63–65.

''Speech at High School.'' Baltimore, MD, June 1910. *Horizon*, June 1910.

''Disfranchisement.'' National Woman Suffrage Association Annual Meeting, 1912. *DBS*, 1:231–238.

''The Negro Citizen.'' Interracial Conference, Washington, DC, December 19, 1928. *DBS*, 2:32–42.

''Report of Debate Conducted by the Chicago Forum: 'Shall the Negro Be Encouraged to Seek Cultural Equality?' '' Chicago, IL, March 17, 1929. *CPA*, 222–229.

''I Speak for Peace.'' New York, NY, September 24, 1950. *CPA*, 287–291.

MARIAN WRIGHT EDELMAN
(1939–), lawyer, children's advocate

BETH M. WAGGENSPACK

An impassioned and relentless champion of needy children and families, Marian Wright Edelman has exemplified her parents' teachings, dedicating her life to helping others as a vocal child advocate. Edelman recalled in her book, *The Measure of Our Success*, that "the legacies that parents and church and teachers left to my generation of Black children were priceless but not material: a living faith reflected in daily service, the discipline of hard work and stick-to-it-ness, and a capacity to struggle in the face of adversity." Today, she crusades for children with the passionate advocacy skills she developed while an attorney on the tumultuous civil rights front lines in Mississippi thirty years ago. Then the goal was minority freedom and recognition. While these remain her general goals, their focus has shifted: her "must have" list includes universal health care for all children, full funding for Head Start, and a host of other laws that emphasize reform, family preservation, or intervention.

Marian Wright grew up in segregated South Carolina, with service to others an essential part of her upbringing; she described that public service legacy "as the rent we pay for living." Named after Marian Anderson, the great contralto, Edelman was the youngest of five children. She credits her parents for providing her with strong values, high expectations, and steady support. Her father, Arthur J. Wright, a Baptist minister in Bennettsville, South Carolina, was the strong family head who provided out-front community leadership and lived his faith every day. His church was the hub of Marian's childhood social existence. In the segregated South, Black children could not play in public playgrounds or sit at lunch counters to get a drink, so Arthur Wright built a playground and a canteen behind the church. There were no Black homes for the elderly, so he began the Wright House for the Aged, which continues today. Marian's mother, Maggie Bowen Wright, worked in the background until Arthur died in 1954, when she extended the family tradition of service by opening her home to twelve foster children and continuing the operation of the Wright House.

Marian Wright was raised on a regimen of study, discipline, self-development, service to others, and community support. She told Norman Atkins that when she went off to predominantly Black Spelman College, neighbors sent her shoe-boxes stuffed with biscuits, chicken, and greasy dollar bills. As a student she was at the center of the sit-ins and the early civil rights movement, as well as being the president of the student body. Her education concentrated on international pursuits: during her junior year at Spelman, she received a Merrill scholarship to study at the University of Paris and in Geneva, Switzerland. That summer, she participated in a student exchange study tour of East Germany, Poland, Czechoslovakia, and the USSR. Following her 1960 graduation, Marian attended Yale University, where she received her law degree in 1963. During the summer of 1962, she worked in Crossroads Africa, a work project in the area of the Ivory Coast of West Africa.

In 1963, her civil rights involvement increased when she joined the National Association for the Advancement of Colored People (NAACP) as a staff attorney. She worked in the Mississippi race war in 1964, a few months before the Neshoba County killings of three civil rights activists by Ku Klux Klan members. She drew national attention to and obtained relief for the starving children of the Mississippi Delta by taking Senator Robert Kennedy on a personal tour. She later recalled this meeting to Norman Atkins:

> I'll never forget. He walked into this really dark, dank shack with dirt floors in Cleveland, Mississippi. And there were no television cameras there. In the back room, the mother was washing the tub. And sitting on the ground was this baby with a bloated belly. I remember him sitting there, stooping down with the baby and really trying to get a response. He was just visibly shaken. He said he had not realized that there was anything like this in this country. I'm ashamed to say that it took me so long to realize the importance of simply personalizing suffering.

This method of personalizing the crisis of children would later become a hallmark of Edelman's rhetoric. A year later she founded the NAACP Legal Defense and Education Fund in Jackson, Mississippi, serving as its director until 1968. In 1965, she was the first African-American woman admitted to the Mississippi bar. It was while working for the fund that she met Peter Edelman, a Harvard-educated Jewish lawyer who was then a legislative assistant to Senator Kennedy. Their 1968 wedding was one of Virginia's first interracial marriages.

Founded by Edelman in 1973, the Children's Defense Fund (CDF) owes its birth to the disturbances of Mississippi's summer of 1964 and the Head Start battles of 1965, where both the great need for and the limits of local action were apparent. In *The Measure of Our Success*, Edelman noted, "As a private civil rights lawyer I learned that I could have only limited, albeit important impact on meeting epidemic family and child needs without a coherent national policy

and investment strategies to complement community empowerment strategies.''
Today, the CDF is the strongest and most persistent clearinghouse for information on children in the United States.

The goal of the CDF is to educate the nation about the needs of children in
order to encourage investment before they get sick, drop out of school, suffer
due to breakdowns in the family structure, or get involved in criminal activity.
The CDF is a private, nonprofit organization with a $9-million annual budget
and 120 employees, including specialists in health, education, child welfare and
development, family income, youth employment, and adolescent pregnancy prevention.

As director of the CDF, Edelman has forged an almost legendary reputation
as a tenacious lobbyist. *Time* quoted Edward M. Kennedy as calling her the
''101st Senator on children's issues,'' and one senator told *60 Minutes* that there
were dozens of senators who ''blanch and try to hide in the men's room when
they hear'' that Edelman is roaming the Senate Office Building. Her detractors
accuse her of bullheadedness and a shortsighted perspective on political realities.
Others charge that she is an old-fashioned 1960s-style liberal, overly loyal to
out-of-date premises that government money solves social problems. Edelman
likes to admit to and to illustrate her persistence and determination with a story
about one of her role models, Sojourner Truth, which she often suggests reflects
herself. To a heckler who announced that he ''cared no more for her anti-slavery
talk than for a flea bite,'' Truth retorted, ''Maybe not, but the Lord willing, I'll
keep you scratching.'' Edelman is renowned for her ability to maintain her anger
at injustice after decades of dueling duplicitous politicians, armed mainly with
words. As she explained her style to Joseph Shapiro, ''If political credibility
rests on being a doormat or not feeling strongly about what you do, then I think
we're in the wrong business.''

Edelman's political focus has continued with the advent of the Clinton administration. Hillary Clinton made her first postelection appearance at a CDF
fundraiser, and she is a former CDF staff attorney and chairperson. Just as Mary
McLeod Bethune focused Eleanor Roosevelt's eyes on the plight of Blacks and
the poor, Andrew Young suggested that one might hope for Marian Wright
Edelman's profound impact on the Clinton administration.

Edelman is the author of many articles and several books, including *Families
in Peril*, based on a series of lectures she delivered for Harvard's 1986
W. E. B. Du Bois lecture series. *The Measure of Our Success* shares her commitment to service and the values she used while raising her three sons, and it
is an adroit example in many ways of the rhetorical style that Edelman employs
in both her oratory and her writing. She wrote the book to convey to her own
children what she thought was meaningful as they crossed the threshold of
adulthood. In a subsequent interview with Eleanor Clift, she disclosed that ''I
realize that there's this psychic tape that goes off in my head in every situation.
I instinctively say, now what would Daddy do here, what would Mama say? I
realized what clear internal anchors our parents had left us.'' Marian Wright

Edelman's many awards include a MacArthur Foundation Fellowship (1985); a Rockefeller Public Service Award; the Albert Schweitzer Humanitarian Prize from Johns Hopkins University (1987); the AFL-CIO Humanitarian Award (1989); and honorary degrees from over sixty-eight American colleges and universities.

MARIAN WRIGHT EDELMAN: THE RHETORIC OF SERVICE

Edelman's character as a rhetor is marked by a personality that is both spiritually optimistic and unwilling to compromise too easily. Calling herself "a determined optimist" in *Families in Peril*, she believes that effective action "requires thorough fact-finding and analysis, a capacity to see a problem whole and then to break it into manageable pieces for action, to delineate clear long-term, intermediate, and short-term goals; and to pursue those goals through a range of strategies that must be constantly evaluated and adapted to changing political and community needs." Reflecting these standards, Edelman's speeches, essays, and books are marked by a staggering compilation of statistics, homey aphorisms, startling challenges, fear-provoking images, religious allusions, tenacity, and value statements learned in her youth. She employs aphorisms, catchy little sayings, condensed thoughts, signposts for life, and dollops of dime-store wisdom in her attempt to put a face on her constituents. While few full texts of any of her speeches are currently available, several examples from speeches, interviews, and printed works illustrate the tenor of Edelman's rhetoric.

Edelman's basic message does not change much from medium to medium. Her issues are framed as a "children's approach" to politics, with the recurring theme that children are not being treated fairly or equally. Relying heavily on the values she herself was taught as a child, Edelman regularly voices the belief, as phrased in *The State of America's Children 1992*, that we must "struggle to live our national and family values in our private and public lives and insist that our leaders do so." Edelman wants America to understand that an investment in children is wise because, as she said in "The Forgotten Children," "the cost to the public of sickness, ignorance, neglect, dependence, and unemployment exceeds the cost of preventive investment in health, education, employed youth, and stable families." At the CDF conference in March 1993, however, Edelman noted that "over the past ten years we have witnessed the American dream shifting into reverse." She pointed out that nutrition, immunization, and quality day care were increasingly urgent needs and that the outlook for America's children was grim.

Edelman's rhetoric is often dramatic, combining a sense of urgency with an understanding of her audience. She developed a formula to give the fight against child poverty the same cast of morality as the fight for civil rights. Many of her strategies, such as her righteousness and a tendency to cast the poverty debates as a conflict between good people and bad or between "helpless" and the forces of "callous" neglect and greed, parallel the rhetorical strategies of the civil rights movement from which Edelman emerged. For example, in an interview with Matthew Scott she claimed that ignorance is one of the biggest obstacles that may keep her from reaching her goals: "There's ignorance in people who just don't know that we have a national child emergency. And there are a lot of people who are conveniently ignorant—they don't want to know." In the Atkins interview, she compared the two crusades: "The struggle of the Nineties is to reframe the civil rights agenda to be about economic empowerment. It's clear that whatever project you label 'black and poor' is going to get a smaller constituency. Which is why we focused on children and prevention." In "The Forgotten Children," pointing out the economic disparity that exists for children in poverty, Edelman asserted, "We can either pay now to prepare our children to be healthy, well-educated, and employable or pay a great deal more later to cover the costs of their ailments and diseases, unemployment and homelessness. We need to make a down payment on the nation's economic future by investing in our children and families today."

Edelman uses a number of strategies to accentuate the crisis of children's rights. She frequently uses the commonplace images of a battle, crusade, and imminent crisis. In several of her 1991 commencement addresses, Edelman noted that twelve million children lack the basic amenities of life, and she challenged the United States to work as hard to overcome poverty as it did to win the Persian Gulf War. In part, she said, "The nation must turn from its recent battle abroad to confront the deadly war against children and the poor at home." In her essay "Of Many Things" she asked, "When are we going to mobilize and send troops to fight for the 100,000 American children who are homeless each night or for the thousands of young families who are struggling to buy homes, pay off college loans, find and afford child care?" In a *Los Angeles Times* interview, she summarized the urgency of the problem: "We face the worst crisis since slavery with the breakdown of our families, the number of out-of-wedlock births, the hopelessness of our young people, particularly black males, many of whom have been pushed out of the mainstream economy and have no hopes of forming healthy families and no positive alternatives."

Edelman always has statistics at her fingertips to demonstrate the extent of problems and the effectiveness of every dollar spent in reacting to those problems. Her 1986 Du Bois lecture "The Black Family in America" is representative. In supporting the claim that "black children in young female-headed households are the poorest in the nation," Edelman noted that "while a black child born in the United States has a one in two chance of being born poor, a black child in a female-headed household has a two in three chance of being poor. If that household is headed by a mother under twenty-five years of age, that baby has a four in five chance of being poor." Edelman uses statistics to give her audience a clearer sense of the problem, often challenging some parts of the "common wisdom" while reinforcing other parts: "Black teens are having fewer rather than more babies: 172,000 births in 1970; 137,000 in

1983. . . . However, the percentage of those births that were to unmarried teens soared 50 percent—from 36 percent in 1950 to 86 percent by 1981.''

Edelman also decries the amount of violence and the negative images that come from television and movies, what she calls a cacophony of cultural messages that bombard children about what they must buy and how they must act. In *The State of America's Children 1994*, Edelman vividly juxtaposed the violence in children's lives with the images portrayed on television: ''Violence romps throughout our children's playgrounds, invades their bedroom slumber parties, terrorizes their Head Start centers and schools, frolics down the streets they walk to and from school, dances through their school buses, waits at the stop lights and bus stop, lurks at McDonald's, . . . and tantalizes them across the television screen every six minutes.'' In the Gayle Terry interview, Edelman lamented that ''we're losing two generations, the younger parents and the young families. Look at the violence against and by children. I cannot believe a child is murdered in this country every three hours; a classroom full of 25 children every two days, and we're standing for it.'' When asked how the killing could be stopped, Edelman responded:

> By confronting this obsession with violence in this culture and the media. . . . We produce a handgun every 20 seconds. Semi-automatic weapons have no socially redeeming purpose. Hunters don't need semi-automatic weapons. We've got to have serious gun control. We have to deal with the signals, the glamorization of violence in our culture, on TV and in the movies. Surely we can be more creative in producing programs that don't laud violence as a way in which we resolve disputes.

As she said in *The State of America's Children 1994*, Edelman's wrath is extended to all variety of media: ''While I am sick of record companies profiting from the violent rap they find a ready market for . . . I am just as sick of Rambos and Terminators, and of video games like 'Mortal Kombat' and 'Night Trap' that portray decapitation, murder, and other violence as fun and entertainment.''

Of course, the religion of her youth plays a foundational role in much of Edelman's rhetoric, but it is a religious value system that promotes self-sufficiency and public service. Edelman told Atkins, ''My reading of Christ is that you help people, not judge them—the judgment doesn't belong to us. . . . I believe very much in the Gospel that says you help people who are hungry and you help people who are suffering and you help people who need help. And I believe very deeply in private charity and in personal service, but I also understand that those are not substitutes for public justice.'' In a 1986 Du Bois lecture entitled ''Leadership and Social Change,'' she reminded listeners that ''the Bible is replete with the images and power of small things which achieve great ends when they are grounded in faith: a mustard seed, a jawbone, a stick, a slingshot, a widow's mite.''

Edelman's religious theme is often combined with prophecies of doom, as in the 1992 Atkins interview with *Rolling Stone*:

> It is evil to let children die when you have the capacity to save them. It is wrong, for example, not to immunize children and to have them dying of measles in the richest nation on earth. We have about 10,000 babies who die from preventable infant mortality each year, and we know how and have the means to save them and choose not to because it doesn't have a political payoff. And I cannot believe for a moment that God's not going to punish a nation that has the capacity to save young lives and chooses not to.

While Edelman might profess not to judge others, she does expect that a higher power is sitting in that judgment.

Edelman does condemn that which she sees as evil. In "Leadership and Social Change," for example, she identified the "weasels" in public life, including the greedy military weasel, the unfairness weasel, the bystander weasel, and the ineffectiveness weasel, all of whom have gnawed away at the rights of children and the moral underpinnings of our democracy. She believes, as she said in *The State of America's Children 1992,* that it is time for adults to stop the hypocrisy and to accept responsibility for the breakdown of society: "Is our social and moral development so arrested that we cannot see, hear, feel, and respond to the killing and injuries of our children or curb the gun and drug driven violence blanketing America? Are we too weak to stand up to the National Rifle Association [NRA] even when the prey is not helpless animals but helpless children?"

As Edelman points out the wrongs done by society to children, her use of vivid images, credible sources, and strong language is tempered by offering practical solutions. She often suggests contacting elected officials, getting involved in community organizations that help with tutoring or homeless people, or simply taking one personal caring act for a child. The CDF's yearly reports *The State of America's Children* propose pragmatic answers, including peer mediation programs in the public schools, standing up to the NRA, and family-life education.

Edelman binds her audience through vows, prayers, or pledges, a practice that probably reflects her early legacy of church and service. In her 1992 "Washington Seminar Speech," Edelman abruptly suggested to her audience of "sociological sightseers" that they join her in her version of a schoolteacher's prayer:

> We pray to accept responsibility for children who steal popsicles before supper, erase holes in the math notebooks and can never find their shoes. We're also going to pray to accept responsibility for children who don't have any rooms to clean up, whose pictures aren't on anybody's dresser and whose monsters are real. . . . In 1992 let's decide to vote for and pray for and speak for those children in

America whose nightmares come in the daytime, who'll eat anything, who have never seen a dentist, who aren't spoiled by anybody, who go to bed hungry and cry themselves to sleep. . . . Let's commit this year to starting a movement that cares and votes and organizes for those children whom we smother, but also for those children who will grab the hand of anybody kind enough to offer it.

Perhaps Edelman's greatest rhetorical strength is in putting a face on poverty, disease, and the inherent, underlying unfairness of the state of children today, as she did with Robert Kennedy in 1964. As she told Atkins, she likes to relate to her audience the outcomes of the Child Watch Visitation Program, one of CDF's attempts to make the extent of the problems known to the larger community:

One distinguished woman was very upset when she went to see the boarder-baby ward at DC General and realized that there was no place for these children to play. Her response was to raise money and build a play area. Union members were taken to some of the homeless shelters and decided to start a clothing drive. We took a bunch of Atlanta ministers to a neonatal intensive-care unit. After their visit, we asked the hospital what it wanted. It turned out that it was very hard to get pauper's burials at the time that babies died, so they wanted the ministers to bury the babies so that the mothers didn't have to go through two bouts of grief. It became very practical and immediate.

Edelman's ability to make the never-imagined real, whether through word or deed, has resulted in action by encouraging others to contribute their service.

Marian Wright Edelman's oratory is legendary for two additional factors: her soft-spokenness and the fountain of facts that she spurts out with breathtaking speed. She tends to speak primarily from notecards, and her remarks often stray from time constraints. French described Edelman as a trim fifty-two-year-old woman who manages to peer down her nose at people even though she is shorter than most. Journalists are warned to bring a tape recorder, because no one on the face of the earth "can write as fast as Edelman can talk." According to Mary Ann French, Edelman delivers facts with devastating speed: "Sometimes her speech takes a geographic turn, but it's hard to tell whether you're hearing the south of her youth or the New England of her early married years. If the audience is lucky, they follow about every third line she delivers. The rest of the time they look stunned, both by the velocity of the delivery and by the content of what words they can catch."

Marian Wright Edelman has spent her entire life calling for public justice for those whom society treats unfairly. She successfully uses challenges and entreaties to a public that is ignorant and apathetic, rather than unfeeling. She employs homey aphorisms and religious allusions that call to mind a simpler time when "family values" was more than just a politically correct phrase. Her command of startling and staggering statistics, as well as realistic portrayals of the face of poverty, illustrates the exigence of civil rights violations maintained by society in its treatment of children. Her rhetoric is neither gentle nor inflammatory, instead being infused with an absolute certainty of the rightness of her cause. Marian Wright Edelman has exemplified the legacy of service and the spirit of social responsibility that was passed on to her in childhood.

INFORMATION SOURCES

Research Collections and Collected Speeches

Currently, no speech manuscripts are readily available, either from the Children's Defense Fund or from traditional sources.

[*FIP*] Edelman, Marian Wright. *Families in Peril: An Agenda for Social Change*. Cambridge, MA: Harvard UP, 1987.
————. *The Measure of Our Success: A Letter to My Children and Yours*. Boston: Beacon, 1992.
————. "On This Mother's Day, A Message." *Parade Magazine*, May 8, 1994: 4–6.
The State of America's Children (published yearly). Washington, DC: Children's Defense Fund.

Selected Critical Studies

Atkins, Norman. "Marian Wright Edelman: On the Front Lines of the Battle to Save America's Children." *Rolling Stone*, December 10–24, 1992: 127–129+.
Clift, Eleanor. "A Mother's Guiding Message." *Newsweek*, June 8, 1992: 27.
"The Forgotten Children." *Progressive*, April 1993: 9.
French, Mary Ann. "The Measure of Her Success: Marian Wright Edelman's Lessons on Raising Kids and Raising Consciousness." *Washington Post*, May 10, 1992: F1+.
Kaus, Mickey. "The Godmother: What's Wrong with Marian Wright Edelman." *New Republic*, February 15, 1993: 21–25.
"Of Many Things." *America*, June 8, 1991: COV1.
Scott, Matthew S. "The Great Defender." *Black Enterprise*, May 1992: 67–69.
Shapiro, Joseph P. "The Unraveling Kids' Crusade." *U.S. News and World Report*, March 26, 1990: 22–24.
Terry, Gayle Pollard. "Marian Wright Edelman: Crusading for Children with This Aggressive Defense Fund." *Los Angeles Times*, November 21, 1993: M3.
Traver, Nancy. "They Cannot Fend for Themselves." *Time*, March 23, 1987: 27.

CHRONOLOGY OF MAJOR SPEECHES

[See "Research Collections and Collected Speeches" for source code.]

"Children's Legislative Issues" (Speech delivered to the National Education Association's 23rd Annual Conference on Human and Civil Rights in Education). N.p., February 22, 1985. Available on audiocassette through the NEA.

"The W. E. B. Du Bois Lectures." Cambridge, MA, 1986. *FIP.*

"Washington Seminar Speech." Washington, DC, 1992. Excerpted in French.

"Commencement Speech at Duke University." Durham, NC, May 17, 1992.

"Opening Remarks at the Children's Defense Fund National Conference." (Yearly).

LOUIS ABDUL FARRAKHAN
(1933–   ), religious leader

MARK LAWRENCE MCPHAIL

Although an active voice in the African-American community since the mid-1960s, Louis Abdul Farrakhan, leader of the Nation of Islam, did not receive national exposure until twenty years later, following his support for Jesse Jackson's bid for the Democratic presidential nomination. Outspoken, controversial, and charismatic, Farrakhan was described at that time by the *National Review* as "*the* black leadership—the cutting edge, the storm center, the presence against which others are measured." Since then he has increasingly been recognized as a leader and spokesman whose message, as *Current Biography Yearbook* phrases it, "articulates the hurt of much of the African American underclass left behind in the progress of civil rights," and whose "refusal to court the approval of the white establishment draws the admiration of many better off blacks. Outside the African-American community, he is widely viewed as a racist demagogue, especially by Jews." Farrakhan's message of black independence, self-reliance, and self-affirmation has drawn criticism and praise, yet both his adherents and opponents admit that he is a skilled and eloquent speaker whose oratory has had an important impact on the African-American community. As William Pleasant observed, "No other Black leader commands larger, or more loyal, audiences than Louis Farrakhan."

Louis Abdul Farrakhan was born Louis Eugene Walcott on May 11, 1933, in New York's Bronx. His parents emigrated from the Caribbean to New York, where his father worked as a schoolteacher and Baptist preacher and his mother as a domestic worker. Walcott's father died when Louis was only three, and he spent his youth growing up in the Roxbury section of Boston, Massachusetts, where he attended St. Cyprian Episcopal Church and served as a choirboy. As a teen he attended Boston English High School, where, as an honor student, he actively participated in track and music and, despite having had a stuttering problem as a child, also excelled in drama. After graduation he attended Winston-Salem Teachers College for two years and continued to pursue his interest in athletics and music. As a young man, he appeared on Ted Mack's "Original Amateur Hour" as an aspiring violinist, and during his twenties he performed in nightclubs, singing, dancing, and playing guitar, alternately appearing under the names "Calypso Gene," "The Charmer," and "The Calypso Charmer."

It was after one such performance in Chicago in 1955 that Walcott was recruited to the Nation of Islam by Malcolm X, then national spokesman for Elijah Muhammad and founding minister of Temple No. 11, the Black Muslim mosque in Boston. Upon joining the Nation of Islam, Walcott changed his name first to Louis X and later to Louis Farrakhan. He served first as an understudy to Malcolm X in the Boston mosque and then succeeded him as its minister when Malcolm left for Harlem's Temple No. 7. During the 1960s, Farrakhan continued to pursue his interests in music and drama, writing and recording the Black Muslim anthem "A White Man's Heaven Is a Black Man's Hell" and writing and directing two plays that were featured in Nation of Islam mosques across America. As minister of the Boston mosque, Farrakhan became an ardent spokesman for, and defender of, the teachings of Elijah Muhammad, founder of the Nation of Islam.

During the early 1960s, the Nation of Islam became divided over accusations that Elijah Muhammad had violated his own moral codes by having illicit affairs with six of his female secretaries. Upon hearing that these accusations were true from Elijah Muhammad's son Wallace, Malcolm X expressed his criticism of the Nation's founder and contacted other ministers in the organization to inform them of Elijah Muhammad's transgressions. At about the same time Malcolm made his infamous "chickens coming home to roost" remark following the assassination of John F. Kennedy and was silenced by Elijah Muhammad. It was, according to Lawrence Mamiya, Louis Farrakhan and the commander of the Boston mosque's security force who reported that Malcolm was "spreading false rumors" about Elijah Muhammad, and it was this event and not his comments concerning Kennedy that Malcolm believed led to his silencing. Malcolm X then broke with the Nation of Islam and shortly afterwards was assassinated. Subsequently, Louis Farrakhan was named minister of the Harlem mosque and later became the national spokesman for Elijah Muhammad.

As national spokesman for the Nation of Islam, Farrakhan had the responsibility of introducing Elijah Muhammad at the Nation of Islam's annual Savior's Day celebrations and also served as a proxy for Muhammad at speaking engagements across the country. In 1970, he addressed the Pan-African Congress, and throughout the decade he spoke at national political gatherings and on college campuses, where he became increasingly popular. After the death of Elijah Muhammad in 1975, Farrakhan was called to Chicago by Elijah Muhammad's son W. Deen Muhammad, who began to restructure the organization by departing from his father's doctrines and moving toward the orthodox teachings of Islam. During 1975 and 1976, Farrakhan traveled to Africa, Asia, and the Middle East and underwent a spiritual "sleep." Upon awakening, Farrakhan rejected the directions pursued by W. Deen Muhammad in favor of the original teachings of his father Elijah. In 1978, Farrakhan publicly announced his departure from the organization and the next year began publishing *The Final Call,* the organ of a new Nation of Islam that remained true to the doctrines of Elijah Muhammad.

Farrakhan's rebuilding of the Nation of Islam was undoubtedly facilitated by his rhetorical skills. During the late 1970s and into the 1980s, he traveled well over 250,000 miles a year on speaking engagements, and by the mid-1980s he drew crowds of up to 25,000. While he has continued to promote the original teachings of Elijah Muhammad, under his leadership the Nation of Islam has become more politically active, as evidenced by Farrakhan's support for Jesse Jackson in 1984 as well as his attempts to promote Nation of Islam representatives in political races across the nation. At the same time, membership in the Nation of Islam has increased dramatically. As Mary Johnson noted, the organization's membership is estimated by experts "at nearly 20,000 registered worshipers and nearly 300,000 more people who follow [Farrakhan's] teachings." Today Louis Farrakhan lives with his wife Khadijah and their nine children and twenty-nine grandchildren in the home of his former teacher, Elijah Muhammad, in Chicago, Illinois. There he continues to rebuild both the Nation of Islam and the philosophy of its founder.

Although his message has changed in temperament over the years, the rhetoric of Louis Farrakhan has persistently focused on the dynamics of identification and division that circumscribe the Nation of Islam's calls for self-reliance, self-definition, and self-defense. As James Spady observed, "[T]he rhetoric of Minister Farrakhan is best seen within the context of the teaching of the honorable Elijah Muhammad, The Nation of Islam and their self defined mission." That mission is the liberation of black people from white domination through the creation of an independent black nation, the rejection of white racism and social control, and the acceptance of Islam as the true religion of black people. Interestingly, the rhetoric used by Louis Farrakhan to fulfill this mission reflects many of the same themes that appear in the rhetoric of war. Thus his oratory is best considered in light of his use of what Ronald Reid calls the "topics of war": territoriality, ethnocentricity, and appeals to optimism in pursuit of war aims.

LOUIS FARRAKHAN AS RHETORICAL WARRIOR

In *A Rhetoric of Motives,* Kenneth Burke described war as a "disease of cooperation" because the act of war can only be sustained by a united community, and this depiction offers important insights into the divisive and conflicting responses to Louis Farrakhan's rhetoric. Not since Malcolm X has an African-American leader's rhetoric elicited such diametrically opposed responses from black and white audiences. Like Malcolm before his split with the

Nation of Islam, Farrakhan subscribes to the teachings of Elijah Muhammad that call for the unity of black people and a commitment to spiritual warfare against white supremacy. In his essay ''Message to the Black Man in America,'' Muhammad made it clear that this warfare is spiritual: ''I am not trying to get you to fight. That is not necessary; our unity will win the battle! Not one of us will raise a sword. Not one gun would we need to fire. The great cannon that will be fired is our unity.''

Although Muhammad did not induce his hearers to engage in physical violence, he clearly believed that blacks and whites are participants in a war between good and evil that will be decided by divine intervention:

> For God to fulfill his promise to deliver us from our enemies, He must go against the enemy and break up the enemy's power of resistance to free us. War is inevitable. The so-called Negroes must come to the knowledge of truth, that they have no future in their enemies who are enemies of Almighty God, Allah. God must come to put an end to war and, that is to say, destroy those who love to make war and delight in making mischief.

Muhammad believed that whites and blacks would never be able to live together in America, for the unity of black people only increased white resistance and violence: ''They hate unity among the so-called Negroes. A continued war is made upon us by the white devils in America.'' This ''message to the black man'' outlined the basic themes that would inform the oratory of Louis Farrakhan the rhetorical warrior, with its emphasis on territorial, ethnocentric, and optimistic appeals.

Farrakhan's rhetoric of war invokes two dominant strategies in the symbolic war against white domination. First, Farrakhan views white people as oppressive warmongers whose desire for territory and control of people of color is motivated by injustice and hypocrisy. In his ''Black Solidarity Day Address,'' delivered in New York City on November 2, 1970, Farrakhan pointed to the international condemnation of postcolonial oppression and warfare as evidence that people of color agree with this assessment: ''The dark clouds of war are hanging over every part of the planet,'' he explained, ''and America is involved everywhere on the planet in war. The guns of China are trained on the West. After first declaring violent revolution against her colonial oppressor, the people of Central and South America are rising up against the robbers of her land and of their mineral resources.'' Farrakhan views Western colonialism as a war waged by whites against peoples of color around the world, and he contends that the dismantling of the vestiges of colonial rule portend a more dramatic and divinely prophesied war.

In his ''Warning to the Government of America,'' delivered in Washington, D.C. a decade later, Farrakhan implied that just such a war looms on the horizon, that the Armageddon prophesied in the Bible shall soon come to pass. Suggesting that President Ronald Reagan might in fact be the beast of Revelations, he said that "the President knows what he is doing. The President sees what you don't see. He sees war on the horizon, and he wants to get prepared to fight the final war which the Bible calls the 'War of Armageddon.' " The development of the neutron bomb was another sign of the biblical nature of Reagan's evil: "[W]henever a man will make a weapon that will slay people and save property, then he has more love for material things than he has for human things—and that is the sign of a beast." America's love for the material over the human, Farrakhan suggested, was further reflected in the country's mistreatment of African-Americans.

Farrakhan pointed to the injustice inherent in a government that demands that African-Americans defend a country in which they are not welcome. He observed that "even though America's army is full of young black men and women willing right now to pour their life's blood out on foreign battlefields for this country, America still evilly mistreats the people of those soldiers." This same appeal was echoed in Farrakhan's October 17, 1990, endorsement of Dr. Lenora Fulani for governor of New York in a speech delivered in New York City. He extended his critique of American injustice from Vietnam to the Persian Gulf, arguing again that African-Americans risk their lives overseas to protect a territory that is not their own. Farrakhan contrasted the deaths of black soldiers in Vietnam with the observation that "in two years time we will have lost more of our people in the streets of America than we lost in nine years in Viet Nam." "What does that say?" he asked rhetorically and then answered: "It says that it is safer for us in an actual war zone than to try to live day to day in the inner cities of America." American injustice was further amplified by Farrakhan in his observation that "there is a disproportionate number of young Black men and women in the Persian Gulf, ready to breathe their life blood out for the vital interests of a nation that has not made us their vital interest." White America's failure to meet the needs of its African-American citizens reflected the injustice and hypocrisy of a race that would never accept African-Americans as equals and even regarded them as enemies.

This depiction of whites as the enemies of African-Americans fuels Farrakhan's second rhetorical strategy, his use of appeals to the topics of war. Farrakhan invokes territorial appeals to persuade his audience of the need for a black nation, separate from and independent of white control. He uses ethnocentric appeals to enhance the affirmation of black identity and to negate the detrimental effects of racism. Finally, he invokes a prophetic optimism to persuade people of color that faith in the one true God, Allah, will guarantee success in the worldwide war against white supremacy. Over time his emphasis has changed from material and external influence to spiritual and internal motivations, but throughout his career Farrakhan's oratory exemplifies a rhetorical war, one that creates divisions within the body politic even as it constructs a communal identity for his followers.

Territorial appeals persistently emerge in Farrakhan's speeches in the form of calls for independence from whites and the building of a black nation. His adherence to the principles articulated by Elijah Muhammad recurs throughout his major speeches and public statements regarding the role and directions of the resurrected Nation of Islam. Lawrence Mamiya noted that Farrakhan "has placed strong emphasis upon the demand for a separate territory or land for black people," and Adolph Reed concurred: "Under Muhammad that goal remained inchoate, appearing mainly as a millenarian dream, but for Farrakhan it figures more directly into programmatic rhetoric." Farrakhan's early speeches clearly indicated this emphasis, which, although changed over time, has continued to be one of his dominant rhetorical appeals. In his "Black Solidarity Day Address," he remarked: "When we talk of independence Black man, we've got to talk in terms of building for self, making homes for self. How can we be independent if we have no land? Land is the basis of all independence." When asked in an interview with Barbara Kleban Mills if he believed "in a separate nation for black people, in Africa," he responded:

> Blacks are already separate. If America does not have the will to bring about a change within a permanent underclass, then—just as the Germans are paying reparations to the Jews and the United States government has agreed to pay reparations to Japanese Americans [placed in internment camps during World War II]— what is the labor and lives of black people worth? What does America owe us? Reparations must include freeing of all blacks from state and federal penitentiaries. Then let us ask our brothers and sisters in Africa to set aside a separate territory for us, and let us take the money that America is spending to maintain these convicts and [invest it in] a new reality on the African continent.

In response to criticism that separation is not a realistic option for black people, Farrakhan's message has shifted from material to moral concerns and has begun to emphasize economic and community development as vehicles for the creation of a nation within a nation. Farrakhan began this shift of emphasis by first arguing that the prospects of developing a separate black nation would be undermined by white fear and black apathy. In "P.O.W.E.R. at Last and Forever," a speech given at the John F. Kennedy Center in Washington, D.C., on July 22, 1985, he remarked that "there is a great fear on the part of some powerful white Americans that if we separate there is the possibility that we might join on to an enemy and come against them. . . . So physical separation is greatly feared, and it is not now desired by the masses of black people, but America is not willing to give us eight or ten states, or even one state." Farrakhan also recognized that countries on the African continent would not provide land for an independent black nation, but he then queried, "If we cannot go back to Africa, and America will not give us a separate territory, then what can we do here and now to redress our own grievances?" The solution Farrakhan offered was economic empowerment of the African-American community.

Farrakhan argued that only through economic self-sufficiency can African-Americans experience moral and material development. He chastised his audience for their failure to take advantage of economic opportunities and suggested that the financial and ethical impoverishment that plagued the black community was the fault of the community itself: "You should not blame the Jews. You should not blame the Arabs. You should not blame the Koreans or the Southeast Asians. You have a breast but you don't put yourself on your own breast." According to Farrakhan, African-Americans had failed to nurture their own financial interests by refusing to invest in their own communities, and instead functioned only as consumers in a society that privileged producers. This "slave mentality," he argued, was a part of the historical legacy of African-Americans, and Farrakhan sought to turn it around: "So we propose that we use the blessing we received from our sojourn in America to do for ourselves what we have been asking the whites in this nation to do for us."

Farrakhan's shift of emphasis from physical to psychological notions of territory is evident in his speech "Self Improvement: The Basis for Community Development," delivered in Phoenix, Arizona, on August 21, 1986. The struggle for self-improvement is the foundation for economic and social development according to Farrakhan, who explained to his audience that it is also a prerequisite to positive social interaction: "And so until we can face ourselves, until we struggle for self-improvement, self-development, then we cannot see the good in ourselves: therefore we will not see the good in others." Farrakhan saw community development not simply in terms of material realities but more importantly in terms of symbolic mentalities, and the state that he attempted to build was first and foremost a state of mind: "We must become moral and act upon that which is morally right. Community development is not building buildings. Community development is building people and linking people with people." In his call for developing positive self-images and moral character, Farrakhan blended territorial appeals with his concern with a second topic of war: ethnocentricity.

Farrakhan's use of ethnocentric appeals is characteristic of the two-sidedness of war rhetoric in its simultaneous emphasis on self-affirmation of the community and on negation of the enemy. Ethnocentric appeals dominate Farrakhan's oratory and are a fitting rhetorical response to a situation circumscribed by the exigency of racism and the oppression of African-Americans. In several speeches presented during the 1970s, Farrakhan sustained the beliefs of Elijah Muhammad that whites are "devils" and the natural enemy of black people. In "Woe to the Hypocrites," he explained that the "devil is the white man, and we are commanded to deny him," and in "Message at the East" he pointed to the essential differences that exist between the two races: "The white man is not the same as the Black Man. We just don't see out of the same eyes. We don't think the same way. We don't feel the same way because by nature we're not the same people." This natural antagonism that exists between blacks and whites complements Farrakhan's belief that the races are indeed engaged in a state of warfare.

His speech at a rally for Angela Davis further amplified this belief and illustrated the Nation of Islam's emphasis on actions over words:

> The enemy of the Black Man's freedom is an old warrior. . . . You can't meet that kind of enemy with rheteric [*sic*]; you can't meet that kind of an enemy with anger. You must meet that kind of enemy with a strategy which unifies our oppressed people, which gives our oppressed people the leverage needed to do what they will for their freedom and their justice.

Farrakhan's strategy for unifying his people called for self-affirmation and self-love. He argued that the enemies of black people had taught African-Americans self-hatred, and he refuted those who would attack African-Americans as racist when they affirmed their own ethnic identity. "I don't feel bad when Jews love Jews. They're supposed to love each other. I don't feel bad when Italians love Italians. Well don't you Jews and you Italians and you Greeks feel bad when a Black man says he wants to love his own Black brother." By contrasting black self-affirmation with white racism, Farrakhan depicted the enemy as both evil and hypocritical and facilitated identification among his constituents and division among his critics.

Just as his territorial appeals have shifted from the external to the internal, so, too, have his appeals to ethnocentricity. In his later speeches Farrakhan equally emphasizes the depiction of whites as the cause of African-American suffering and injustice and the legacy of self-negation that whites have created in the minds of African-Americans. Speaking in 1984 before students at Princeton University, he claimed unequivocally that "America's foreign policy is Eurocentric, it deals with white people. Her whole manifestation and policy is racist and white supremacist to the core." Yet speaking the previous year at Morgan State University, a historically African-American institution, Farrakhan explained that the enemy was no longer white people but "[i]gnorance of the nature of yourself and the nature of your enemy. You must cast off ignorance it is your worst enemy [*sic*]. Not the white people, ignorance. Not the white people, fear of white people. Nobody can help you if you are afraid." Farrakhan suggested that only African-American affirmation of self would lead to the fearlessness needed to overcome the mindset created by years of slavery and injustice.

Despite this shift in emphasis, however, Farrakhan still invokes strong ethnocentric appeals in his indictment of white people in general and Jewish people in particular. His discussion of racism exemplifies an ironic reversal of responsibility in order to facilitate self-definition and affirmation among African-Americans. Speaking at Morgan State University, Farrakhan stated, "I want to end racism what about you? [*sic*] Don't you think we ought to end this superior, inferiority madness? Do you think it's fair to white people that they should walk around in 1985 thinking that they are superior to black people simply because they are white?" For Farrakhan, the failure of African-Americans to challenge white beliefs and institutions contributed significantly to the continuation and perpetuation of racism. "It's terrible that you are doing this to white people. And you are doing it to them. You see they're going to continue to think this way until you are strong enough to challenge that crazy thinking of theirs." Farrakhan's reversal serves a dual purpose: it incites his audience into actions that challenge racist thought, and it counters charges of racism aimed at him because of the negative depiction of whites in much of his oratory.

Such charges were not widespread, however, until the mid-1980s, when Farrakhan allegedly made his now-infamous remarks describing Hitler as "wickedly great" and Judaism as a "gutter" or "dirty" religion. Since then, his Jewish critics have continued to maintain that Farrakhan is an anti-Semite who disguises his racism by claiming that he represents the concerns of African-Americans. "For nearly a decade," explained Mary Johnson of the *Chicago Sun Times*, "Farrakhan has been embroiled in a battle of words with Jewish leaders over remarks he made that, to some, suggested that he was praising Hitler and defiling Judaism as a 'gutter religion.' Farrakhan has said his remarks were taken out of context, misconstrued and misquoted." In his interview with Johnson, Farrakhan argued that Jews are complicitous in the oppression of African-Americans, and that his indictment against them was not anti-Semitic, but the result of the inequitable relationship that exists between the two groups:

> I do want to break up the old Black-Jewish relationship, I don't like it. I don't like that old relationship, where they're the landlord and we're the tenant. They own the house and we make the bed, and cook the food, and clean the floor. I don't want them to be the manager and we the talent. They the movie mogul, and we're just the actor and the actress. We produce something and they're the distributor, and they do this as they please. No, no, no, no, no, we got to break up that old relationship and establish a new one based on mutual respect.

Farrakhan recently reaffirmed his position that he is not anti-Semitic but only concerned with the welfare of African-Americans: "I want you to know," he told Johnson, "as God is my witness, in my heart I don't have that much desire to harm one Jew. I want to see black people free." The pursuit of that goal, however, illustrates a second issue that has led to conflict between Farrakhan and Jewish Americans and reveals the connection between his use of ethnocentric and optimistic appeals: the claim that African-Americans are the chosen people of God.

Farrakhan's depiction of African-Americans as the chosen people enhances his calls for African-American self-affirmation and at the same time creates a powerful optimism. In "P.O.W.E.R. at Last and Forever," he stated: "I declare to the world that the people of God are not those who call themselves Jews, but the people of God who are chosen at this critical time in history is you, the black people of America, the lost, the despised, the rejected." In addressing the Congress of the African Peoples, his optimistic appeals were undergirded by the rhetorical concerns of a chosen people at war: "And when the Black Man comes into unity of Black Man, then the unity of Black Man is the greatest weapon that we could produce the world over. And when we fire the cannon of our unity, what enemy do you think could oppose us. There is none." In "Politics without Economics Is Symbol without Substance," an address given in Washington, D.C., in 1987, he asserted that with "God on our side we'll have to go to war with this nation for freedom." In the earlier "Self Improvement: The Basis for Community Development," he made a similar call to African-Americans to follow in the path of a righteous God: "You have no excuse, Black people. Nobody to blame; look within and conquer the enemy of self that makes you an opposer of your own journey toward God, and you put that internal enemy to flight. There is no external enemy that could handle you." Farrakhan's invocation of God [Allah] elevates the social conflict between races to the level of spiritual warfare between the forces of good and evil.

According to Farrakhan, in this final battle African-Americans will ultimately be on the side of good. For Farrakhan, speaking in Chicago in 1987, the time had come for African-Americans to learn "How to Give Birth to a God": "Come on Black man this is our day, this is your time. God is with you to bless your womb, and fill you with his spirit that you will produce spirit filled children. Children of great vision. Prepare yourself." The preparation that Farrakhan called for is for nothing less than the responsibility of world leadership, since the result of this final war against evil will make African-Americans the "Future World Rulers." But Farrakhan admonished his followers not to make the same mistakes that the world's present rulers have made: "But we will not rule because we are Black, we will rule because God says he wants to try you now, and see how you act. If you act like the people that he is deposing then your rule will be short lived, but according to history it says that this is the time when God himself will rule." Farrakhan's final call reverberates with the optimism characteristic of war rhetoric, and his use of appeals to territoriality and ethnocentricity, as well as his invocation of the war metaphor, clearly characterizes him as an oratorical warrior.

Farrakhan's aggressive oratory has stimulated diverse and often-divisive responses. He has been described as a deliverer by some and a demagogue by others. Jabril Muhammad called him "the fulfillment of what we read in the bible of Peter and Paul," while Michael Kramer referred to him as a "bigot" and a "racist." Coretta Scott King, in a speech at the National Press Club in September of 1985, noted that his statements were "extremely harmful" but described Farrakhan as "a tremendous orator and a very persuasive person." Julius Lester condemned popular support of Farrakhan with the observation that "no amount of poverty, deprivation, or suffering justifies hatred, anti-Semitism, or the elevation of Louis Farrakhan to the position of Spokesman and leader." Yet Manning Marable argued that Farrakhan cannot simply be dismissed as an anti-Semite, and that "a careful analysis of Farrakhan's public address reveals a strong commitment to an anti-racist and anti-imperialist politics, which parallels the late social thought of Malcolm X.''

Andrew Sullivan called his oratory ''hateful,'' noting that ''traditional black 'leaders' don't have a following anything like Farrakhan's and they're afraid to take him on.'' Roger Rosenblatt and Fred Barnes both accused Farrakhan of demagoguery, the former noting that he ''is a demagogue, though not much of one,'' and the latter contending that Farrakhan ''has figured out the secret to demagoguery,'' as evidenced by his ''peppering his speech with racist and anti-Semitic slurs.'' Adolph Reed called Farrakhan ''a masterful performer,'' a ''spellbinding orator,'' and ''a talented demagogue,'' and Jabril Muhammad noted that he is ''just about the most sought after Black Speaker in America, if not the most. Certainly he is a most gifted speaker, who entertains (without intending to) as he informs.'' Clearly the responses to Louis Farrakhan are contradictory: although his followers see him as a deliverer, to his critics Farrakhan is a demagogue.

Steven Goldzwig's depiction of the Nation of Islam leader's rhetoric as a strategy of ''symbolic alignment'' offers one explanation for this contradiction. Goldzwig suggested that rhetoric often labeled demagogic, or as a ''sore'' on the body politic, ''might more profitably be envisaged as a special kind of lesion that precedes healing and renewed health in public debate. The adoption of this view is neither dangerous nor naive: It is a response to an emerging rhetorical reality.'' Goldzwig contended that '' 'demagogic' tactics are often key stylistic devices in the agitation of those leaders and groups in society who feel more disaffected and disenfranchised vis-à-vis the dominant culture.'' His analysis of Farrakhan's rhetoric focused primarily on how orators create social reality: ''Farrakhan's 'truth' creates 'noise' in the dominant culture and his discourse represents a serious attempt to reform and/or reverse the ontological and epistemological premises of black audiences.'' Goldzwig's analysis offers important lessons for those who would condemn Farrakhan without considering the social and historical contexts from which his message emerges.

The fact that Farrakhan's message is unpopular in the American mainstream can just as easily be seen as a criticism of the society in which the speaker lives as a criticism of the speaker. Indeed, simply labeling Farrakhan a demagogue, as so many mainstream critics have done, fails to account for the conditions that give rise to his message and passes judgment on the speaker without recognizing that the rhetoric of those whom we would label demagogic is in some ways a reflection of ourselves. Goldzwig concluded:

> As consummate manipulators of the verbal symbol, their discourse is truly symbolic. It stands for what it is not. It is trick and chicanery and fluid motion; it is also a sometimes marred and sometimes marvelous portrait of ourselves. To realize this, we must listen before we judge and exercise judgment in our attempt to listen.

In attempting to understand the words of Louis Abdul Farrakhan, we are certainly confronted with the difficulty of passing judgment, for his oratory is circumscribed by one of the most divisive and destructive rhetorical situations in human history. Perhaps Mary Johnson explained it best: "To understand Minister Louis Farrakhan's words, you must first understand that he leads an organization that many African Americans refer to as the 'black nation.' And if many white Americans have trouble understanding his words, to much of black America they are crystal clear." Louis Farrakhan's words remind us that the problem of our century continues to be the color line. Regardless of which side one stands on that line, it is important that we recognize his contribution to the legacy of Africans in America. The oratory of Louis Abdul Farrakhan singularly highlights the characteristic of rhetoric to divide even as it creates identification, and his speeches point to the divisions of symbolic and social conflict and material and metaphorical warfare that have informed race relations in America for over four hundred years.

INFORMATION SOURCES

Research Collections and Collected Speeches

Audio and video tapes and transcripts of Louis Farrakhan's speeches may be found in the Simon Wiesenthal Center in Los Angeles, California, and the Final Call, Inc., in Chicago, Illinois. Video and audiotaped interviews and other archival materials may be obtained from the Schomburg Center for Research in Black Culture at the New York Public Library.

[*BWB*] Eure, Joseph D., and Richard M. Jerome, eds. *Back Where We Belong: Selected Speeches by Minister Louis Farrakhan*. Philadelphia: PC International Press, 1989.
[FC] Farrakhan, Louis. Audio and videotaped copies of Minister Farrakhan's speeches can be obtained from the Final Call, 734 W. 79th Street, Chicago, IL 60620.
[*SS*]————. *Seven Speeches by Minister Louis Farrakhan*. Chicago: WKU and the Final Call, 1992.
[*IBL*] Kurlander, Gabrielle, and Jacqueline Salit, eds. *Independent Black Leadership in America*. New York: Castillo International Publications, 1990.

Selected Critical Studies

Barnes, Fred. "Farrakhan Frenzy: What's a Black Politician to Do?" *New Republic*, October 1985: 13–15.
Goldzwig, Steven R. "A Social Movement Perspective on Demagoguery: Achieving Symbolic Realignment." *Communication Studies* 40 (1989): 202–228.
Johnson, Mary A. "I Will Never Bow Down: But Farrakhan Says He Seeks Dialogue." *Chicago Sun Times* July 18, 1993: 1+.
Kramer, Michael. "Loud and Clear: Farrakhan's Anti-Semitism." *New York*, October 1985: 22–23.
Lester, Julius. "The Time Has Come: Farrakhan in the Flesh." *New Republic*, October 1985: 11–12.

Mamiya, Lawrence H. "From Black Muslim to Bilalian: The Evolution of a Movement."
    Journal for the Scientific Study of Religion, June 1982: 138–152.
Marable, Manning. "In the Business of Prophet Making." *New Statesman*, December
    1982: 23–25.
Mills, Barbara Kleban. "Predicting Disaster for a Racist America, Louis Farrakhan En-
    visions an African Homeland for U.S. Blacks." *People Weekly*, September 1990:
    111+.
Muhammad, Jabril. *Farrakhan the Traveler*. Phoenix, AZ: Phnx Sn and Co, 1985.
———. *A Special Spokesman*. Phoenix, AZ: Phnx Sn and Co, 1984.
Pleasant, William. "Introduction." *Independent Black Leadership in America*. Ed. Ga-
    brielle Kurlander and Jacqueline Salit. New York: Castillo International
    Publications, 1990. 1–23.
Reed, Adolph. "The Rise of Louis Farrakhan." *Nation*, January 2, 1991: 36+.
Rosenblatt, Roger. "The Demagogue in the Crowd." *Time*, October 21, 1985: 102.
Spady, James G. "Introduction." *Back to Where We Belong: Selected Speeches by Min-
    ister Louis Farrakhan*. Ed. Joseph D. Eure and Richard M. Jerome. Philadelphia:
    PC International Press, 1989. 1–12.
Sullivan, Andrew. "Call to Harm: The Hateful Oratory of Minister Farrakhan." *New
    Republic*, July 1990: 13–15.

Selected Biographies

"Farrakhan, Louis." *Current Biography Yearbook 1992*. New York: H. W. Wilson Com-
    pany, 1992. 190–194.
"Farrakhan, Louis." *Who's Who among Black Americans*. 7th ed. Detroit: Gale Re-
    search, 1992–93.

CHRONOLOGY OF MAJOR SPEECHES

[See "Research Collections and Collected Speeches" for source codes.]

"Congress of African People." Atlanta, GA, September 1970. *SS,* 123–136.
"Black Solidarity Day Address." New York, NY, November 2, 1970. *SS,* 111–120.
"Minister Farrakhan on the Black Woman" (Message at the East). Brooklyn, NY, Jan-
    uary 1971. *SS,* 13–39.
"Woe to the Hypocrites." N.p., n.d. *SS,* 66–93.
"Minister Farrakhan Speaks at Rally for Angela Davis." N.p., n.d. *SS,* 97–108.
"Warning to the Government of America." Washington, DC, August 15, 1981. FC, 1–
    35.
"Minister Farrakhan Speaks at Morgan State University." Baltimore, MD, October 30,
    1983. *BWB,* 115–141.
"Minister Farrakhan Speaks at Princeton University" (What Is the Need for Black His-
    tory?). Princeton, NJ, 1984. *BWB,* 47–79.
"P.O.W.E.R. at Last and Forever." Washington, DC, July 22, 1985. *BWB,* 143–167.
"Self Improvement: The Basis for Community Development." Phoenix, AZ, August 21,
    1986. *BWB,* 169–199.

"Are Black People the Future World Rulers?" Chicago, IL, April 12, 1987. *BWB,* 225–
    255.
"How to Give Birth to a God." Chicago, IL, July 26, 1987. *BWB,* 83–113.
"Politics without Economics Is Symbol without Substance." Washington, DC, 1987.
    BWB, 201–223.
"Minister Farrakhan's Endorsement of Dr. Lenora Fulani for Governor of New York."
    New York, NY, October 17, 1990. *IBL,* 51–53.

LENORA FULANI
(1950–   ), psychologist, political activist, U.S. presidential candidate

MARY ANNE TRASCIATTI

Lenora Fulani is an active and outspoken public figure who poses a series of challenges to well-established American ideas and institutions. Born and raised in Chester, Pennsylvania, she attended Hofstra University, Columbia University's Teachers College, and the City University of New York, where she earned a Ph.D. in developmental psychology. As a practicing psychologist working with poor people of color in Harlem, she continually challenges psychotherapy to move beyond its white, middle-class, heterosexual, individualistic assumptions of normality. As a single parent with two children, who was herself raised in a very poor family, she offers an alternative to the dominant image of the white woman from a middle-class background who successfully combines marriage, family, and career.

Fulani's political career includes numerous bids for elected office. As an independent candidate for mayor, lieutenant governor, and governor of New York, and as a founder of the black-led, multiracial, progay New Alliance party (NAP), under whose banner she ran for president of the United States in 1988 and 1992, Fulani challenged the Democratic party's hold on black, Latino, and white liberal voters. She also exposed the inequities of the American electoral system when, despite being the first African-American and the first woman on the ballot in all fifty states, she was denied participation in the presidential debates.

When she is not campaigning for office, Fulani remains politically active, leading voter-registration drives, participating in public protests against police brutality, and speaking at various conferences and colleges as well as on numerous television and radio programs. She has written an autobiography, *The Making of a Fringe Candidate, 1992*, and has contributed to other books on independent black politics, black empowerment, and psychotherapy. She hosts a weekly cable television show, "Fulani!" and authors a weekly syndicated column, "This Way for Black Empowerment." Like her political allies Louis Farrakhan and Al Sharpton, Fulani has been criticized for her views on racism, black-Jewish relations, presidential politics, relations between the United States and Africa and the Caribbean, and an array of other important issues. Indeed, she provides a distinct and often-controversial alternative to the ideas of mainstream black political leaders.

Although Fulani is quite active in speaking and writing for social and political change, she has been virtually ignored by mainstream scholars and journalists. However, her energy, intelligence, and commitment to racial justice and political reform ensure that she will continue to challenge commonly accepted ideas about politics and political issues, and that she will remain a vital force in progressive, black-led independent politics for years to come.

LENORA FULANI: VOICE AGAINST OPPRESSION

Like any contemporary political figure, Fulani speaks and writes on a wide variety of issues. Despite topical variations, however, a single argumentative thread runs throughout her discourse. Fulani's central argument is that racism pervades American society, causing relentless economic, political, and physical oppression of all African-Americans and other people of color. According to Fulani, this oppression will continue to permeate the lives of people of color until society itself is transformed.

In laying out her argument, Fulani follows a problem-solution model. First, she outlines the problem, including its causes: African-Americans and other people of color are oppressed because American society is based on a system whose continued existence depends upon their degradation and endangerment. This racist system is rooted in economic exploitation. As Fulani stated in "Understanding Racism," a speech from her 1988 presidential campaign, "Keeping us and other people poor is what keeps the rich in business." Racial inferiority, she avers, is merely a myth propagated by those whose business interests are served by the continued impoverishment of people of color.

Fulani's solution does not involve changing the hearts and minds of racist Americans. Instead, she seeks an end to institutionalized economic exploitation, a goal that requires a transformation of American politics, not American economics. This political transformation can be achieved only through the abolition of the stagnant two-party system and the subsequent election of progressive, independent politicians. In a 1992 letter to the editor of the *New York Times,* Fulani offered a succinct statement of her view of the relationship between racism and the American two-party system: "There can be no solution to poverty, police brutality, inadequate schools, drug-generated violence and indifferent health care within the existing political structure. Racism and the two-party system are married to each other."

Despite her radical rhetorical posture, Fulani's solution is actually one of moderate political reform. Although she seeks to break with certain American political traditions, specifically with the continued dominance of two-party electoral politics, she remains strongly committed to the overall structure and principles of the American political and economic system: democracy and private enterprise. Fulani's ultimate goal is not to overthrow the system, but to make it better by electing progressive, independent candidates who will provide just and equitable solutions to familiar and nearly intractable problems: welfare reform, drug abuse, universal health care, and school reform. The reformist nature of Fulani's program is evident in her 1992 presidential campaign brochure, "When Democracy Is on the Job, America Works," where she distanced herself from radical economic restructuring to embrace a program of political reform:

> The ordinary people of America—middle class people, working class people and poor people—must have access to the decision-making process. We must be in a position to use the political process in our interests, so that the very wealthy come to recognize that it is ultimately more profitable for them to respond to our demands—to invest in jobs and job training, adequate housing, quality health care and education for every American—than it is for them to continue their reckless, deadly profiteering in dead-end non-productive paper trading and gun running. I'm not talking about top-down socialism; I'm talking about the redistribution of wealth through the democratic process.

Fulani initially impresses one as a spokesperson for militant African-Americans with little chance for successfully reaching beyond her relatively narrow constituency. Closer analysis reveals that while her central argument about racist oppression remains constant, Fulani adapts important rhetorical elements—evidence, ethos, tone, and persona—to fit broader constituencies. The remainder of this analysis examines her efforts to use these rhetorical elements to make her reformist agenda attractive to diverse audiences.

When speaking to her grass-roots constituency of poor, working-class, and militant African-Americans, Fulani relies on personal experience as a source of evidence for her claim that racism pervades American society. For example, she frequently begins speeches by telling how her own father died prematurely because, like other African-Americans in the racist society in which he lived, he was denied access to medical care. Very often, however, as in a 1988 campaign speech, "Drugs versus Empowerment," she offers no evidence at all, assuming that her audience needs no convincing of the racism that permeates their lives: "Our children are dying of drugs, of poverty, and of despair because there is no room for them in white America and the Powers That Be would rather see them dead . . . than alive, angry and empowered."

Fulani derives her ethos from her personal experience as an African-American single parent from a poor family, her professional training in psychology, and her political experience. Drawing on this background, she is qualified not only to speak frankly about the issue of racial oppression, but also to propose a political "cure" for it. The introduction to one of her 1988 presidential campaign speeches, "From Endangerment to Empowerment: Speaking as an Independent Black Woman," illustrates Fulani's use of experience and professional credentials as a source of ethos:

> As a developmental psychologist practicing in Harlem, as the mother of an eleven year old Black son, and as a political activist . . . who speaks for the Black Agenda, I have a profound and lifelong commitment to the transformation of the Black man from an "endangered" species to an empowered one. . . . My father, who was an alcoholic, held down two jobs. . . . When I was almost 12 he died. . . . I sat with my father while he was dying. . . . It shocked and hurt me terribly to see that my father might have lived if only someone in authority—which meant someone white, someone who wore a coat and tie—had cared whether he lived or died. But no one in authority did care.

Her combined personal experiences and professional qualifications enable Fulani to craft for herself a rhetorical persona of advocate for African-Americans. This is evident in "From Endangerment to Empowerment" when Fulani explains:

> I became a psychologist because . . . I was determined to help our people out of the pain and degradation that make us, Black women and Black men, an "endangered species." And I became a political activist because I came to recognize that . . . we needed . . . to change the conditions—the profoundly unfair and degrading and DANGEROUS conditions—of all of our lives.

Fulani's rhetoric disavows competing class interests among African-Americans. Instead, she unites blacks into a monolithic group sharing a common, oppressive experience. Moreover, she chastises financially successful African-Americans who believe that they have overcome the color barrier. Her 1988 campaign speech "Black Empowerment: The Struggle Continues" is illustrative:

> And there is the black man who has "made it"—allowed to be somebody in the white man's world on the condition that he forgets his Blackness, on the condition that he ignores the Blackness of his Black sisters and brothers, on the condition that he agrees to keep silent about what it is really like to be Black in America.

This sense of African-American unity is further enhanced by Fulani's strong defense of Reverend Al Sharpton and Minister Louis Farrakhan, African-American leaders steeped in controversy within the black community as well as the larger society. Fulani refers to Sharpton and Farrakhan as important allies in the struggle for black liberation, and she iterates staunch support for the Black Agenda, first articulated in 1988 by Farrakhan at the Wheat Street Baptist Church in Washington, D.C. The Black Agenda comprises demands for housing, health care, and an end to police brutality against minorities to be made of any candidate seeking black electoral support. "Proud to Be in History," a speech Fulani delivered in her 1990 run for the governorship of New York State, evidences her close alliance with Sharpton and Farrakhan as well as her support for Farrakhan's Black Agenda:

> I am deeply proud and deeply honored to receive the endorsement of these two extraordinary Black leaders, Minister Louis Farrakhan and Reverend Sharpton. It is clear that these brothers have lived their lives involved in a passionate fight for the Black Agenda and that they have fought ruthlessly to free our people from oppression.

Although her first loyalty is undeniably to black Americans and the Black Agenda, Fulani depicts herself as a leader, empowered by experience and education, in the struggle to free all Americans from race-, class-, or sex-based oppression. Her advocacy is inclusive of Latinos, women, laborers, Native Americans, and homosexuals; analogous to her depiction of black Americans as a unified group, Fulani unites these disparate groups under the rubrics "outsiders" or "the oppressed." She asserts her own and her party's appeal to a broad-based constituency of minority groups in "Speaking for Black and Puerto Rican Unity," a speech delivered during the 1989 New York City municipal elections in support of grass-roots Puerto Rican candidate Pedro Espada:

> You see, NAP is supported by tens of thousands of people—African American people, Latino people, Native American people, progressive white people, lesbians and gays. Last year NAP made history when I became the first woman and the first African American Presidential candidate ever to be on the ballot in every state and in the District of Columbia. Last year two percent of the national Black vote and two percent of the national gay vote went to me, the independent New Alliance Party candidate.

Fulani's grassroots style is straightforward and direct. Simple sentence structure and forceful vocabulary lend a sense of certainty, passion and bellicosity to her written and oral discourse. These characteristics are evident in her 1988 speech "Tawana Brawley and the Central Park Jogger:"

> The case of Tawana Brawley was a prime example of the racist double standard that is practiced in America. Tawana was not only gang raped by six white men, some of whom had ties to the local police—she was raped again by the corporate media. . . . millions of words were published and broadcast "proving" that the rape story was a hoax perpetrated by someone who was no better than a slut and habitual liar. There was no anonymity. There was no compassion. And there was no justice.

Indeed Fulani is not one to equivocate; as the preceding example illustrates, she depicts life in contemporary America in stark terms. Often she refers to an active conspiracy of powerful, white, male elites, aimed at crushing African-Americans and all other people of color. She calls these elites "Those Who Rule," "The Powers That Be," or simply "They," and she uses active voice to implicate "Them" in concrete acts of aggression against black Americans. This strategy is evident in a 1988 campaign speech, "A Tribute to Reverend Sharpton":

> Phony exposes are part of a long tradition in the effort to intimidate and punish independent Black leaders. They did it to Marcus Garvey. They did it to Adam Clayton Powell. They did it to Dr. Martin Luther King, Jr. and to Malcolm and to the Black Panthers. They are doing it to Minister Farrakhan.

In essays and speeches to her more moderate middle-and upper-class black audiences, Fulani adapts her rhetorical strategies accordingly. Personal examples are still offered as evidence, but the examples refer primarily to Fulani's experiences with politics. Other evidence is gleaned from her perceptions of broader political issues, such as the Democratic party's rebuke of Jesse Jackson in the 1988 presidential campaign, or the discrepancy between black voters' loyalty to the Democratic party and the party's poor record on issues of importance to the black community.

Fulani also adjusts her rhetorical persona to this audience. She calls directly on middle-and upper-class African-Americans to reject cooptation by the corporate interests of white America and exhorts them to put the needs of their race before their individual personal or political needs. In "Black Representation Is Not the Same as Black Leadership," a 1993 speech delivered in Denver, Colorado, on the state of black America, she urged her audience to "take this issue of the difference between Black representation [fulfilling one's personal needs] and Black leadership [putting the needs of the entire black community before one's personal needs] to heart" and to "take leadership in building the new movements, the policies and the new democratic process which will better the state of Black America today, tomorrow, in the year 2,000 and beyond." With such exhortations Fulani constructs her persona as a call to conscience for middle-class African-Americans.

Although her style in these speeches remains forceful and direct, Fulani's tone is noticeably softened. For example, militant metaphors, prevalent in her grass-roots discourse when she refers to the "struggle" and "fight" for black "liberation," are juxtaposed with much less aggressive tropes. In "Black Representation," references to black militancy combined with a baseball metaphor where Fulani chided black elected officials to learn how to "play hardball politics" so they could more effectively be "part of the [Democratic] team."

Fulani speaks very differently to her third constituency, the American voting public. To convince a primarily white electorate, assertions, personal experience, and observations about racial oppression are supplanted by historical references. In a 1993 speech at the University of Alabama, Fulani outlined the discrepancy between the principles articulated in the Constitution and the financial interests of American corporations in order to demonstrate that American society is fundamentally inequitable. Thus, for example, she argued that while the Constitution embodies the principle of government by the people, business and financial interests have sought—and won—"discriminatory ballot access laws in virtually every state, elimination of the fairness doctrine and equal-time provisions in the media, and the erosion of due process and civil liberties in the judicial system." The triumph of American business interests has severely eroded the democratic rights of the people, leaving them with virtually no control over economic policies that foster chronic unemployment by diverting capital from socially constructive uses to pure speculation and permitting factories to close down or relocate without any advance notice. Fulani drew evidence from a poll by *U.S. News and World Report* to prove that Americans desire an end to this state of affairs.

Fulani crafts yet a different persona, adopts a less belligerent tone, and employs a less aggressive style with this audience. She casts herself as a political outsider with the clarity of vision to enact a genuine program of change in American politics. However, Fulani is not merely an aberration, a colorful candidate with popular appeal; instead, she embodies the hopes and desires of Americans who seek to establish a viable, independent third party as a means of breaking political gridlock. Moreover, as she indicated in the 1993 speech at the University of Alabama, Fulani is not just a symbol of America's desire for political reform; she is a driving force for its implementation:

> Bill Clinton can't solve the problems of the nation . . . because he's caught up in a bureaucratic machine that can't move, that can't change, that actually cannot *see* the real problems or the solutions. . . . If the independent movement can articulate that new politic [*sic*] . . . then the independent movement will be the force that will choose the next President of the United States. . . . In my opinion, the American people need to grab this historical opportunity. I will do everything in my power to make that possible.

By pledging herself to the cause, Fulani is the ultimate patriot, transcending ideological and color boundaries with her willingness to sacrifice herself for the betterment of her country. Her ethos is derived not only from her independent political status but also from her position as the most recent in a long line of patriotic, self-sacrificing American reformers. Yet Fulani does not invoke W. E. B. Du Bois, Martin Luther King, or Malcolm X, as she frequently does to predominantly black audiences. Instead, she refers to reformist groups without naming controversial individuals, and when she does refer to individuals, she selects premiere figures from the pantheon of American heroes. In her 1988 campaign brochure "When Democracy Is on the Job, America Works," she linked her political activism to the efforts of "abolitionists, reformers, women, people of color, and other people at the grassroots'' and compared her version of democracy to that of Samuel Adams and Thomas Jefferson:

> My campaign has the potential to be an important step in turning the U.S. around. But to fight for democracy takes guts. Thomas Jefferson said our country would benefit from a rebellion every 20 years. We are long overdue for an electoral rebellion.

Fulani's strategies of audience adaptation attest to the difficulties rhetors confront when they advocate for disempowered groups. While articulation of forceful, passionate ideas about the effects of racism on the status of African-Americans may be highly effective in motivating a militant black audience, such appeals may be perceived as too radical or dangerous for other segments of the population. Thus Fulani, who needs the support of moderate liberals in order to seriously threaten the status quo, walks the delicate line between retaining the integrity of her challenge to oppression while simultaneously broadening its appeal.

INFORMATION SOURCES

Research Collections and Collected Speeches

No speech manuscripts or archival materials are currently available except those obtained by the author from New Alliance party headquarters, 200 West 72nd Street, Room 35, New York, NY 10023. In addition to the works cited herein, Fulani authors a weekly syndicated column, "This Way for Black Empowerment," which appears in 120 African-American papers nationally.

[*IBLA*] Farrakhan, Louis, Lenora B. Fulani, and Alfred Sharpton. *Independent Black Leadership in America*. New York: Castillo International Publications, 1990. No indication is offered as to whether texts in *IBLA* are culled from speeches, statements to the press, or printed essays. However, in a few cases, tentative judgments can be made based on context.

Fulani, Lenora B. " 'All Power to the People!' but How?" *The Psychopathology of Everyday Racism and Sexism*. Ed. Lenora B. Fulani. New York: Harrington Park Press, 1988, xi–xix.

——. *The Making of a Fringe Candidate, 1992*. New York: Castillo International, 1993.

[DJAW] Fulani, Lenora, and Phyllis Goldberg. "When Democracy Is on the Job, America Works." Campaign brochure, 1992.

Pleasant, William. "Introduction." Louis Farrakhan, Lenora B. Fulani, and Alfred Sharpton. *Independent Black Leadership in America*. New York: Castillo International Publications, 1990, 7–23.

CHRONOLOGY OF MAJOR SPEECHES

[See "Research Collections and Collected Speeches" for source codes.]

"From Endangerment to Empowerment: Speaking as an Independent Black Woman."
     1988. *IBLA*, 56–58.
"Drugs versus Empowerment." 1988. *IBLA*, 59–60.
"Understanding Racism." 1988. *IBLA*, 60–62.
"New Alliances." 1988. *IBLA*, 62–65.
"Black Empowerment: The Struggle Continues." 1988. *IBLA*, 65–75.
"A Tribute to Reverend Sharpton." 1988. *IBLA*, 75–77.
"Tawana Brawley and the Central Park Jogger: Down with the Double Standard!" 1988.
     IBLA, 81–83.
"The ADL's Problem: NAP Is Not 'Deceptive' But Attractive." 1988. *IBLA*, 83–85.
"A New Kind of Voter." 1988. *IBLA*, 85–87.
"Speaking for Black and Puerto Rican Unity." 1989. *IBLA*, 77–81.
"Proud to Be in History." 1990. *IBLA*, 87–89.
"Who Killed the Economy?" 1992. DJAW, 18–29.
"African Americans Can't Win Justice in the Two-Party System." *New York Times*,
     August 11, 1992: A18.
"Black Representation Is Not the Same as Black Leadership." Denver, CO, 1993.
"Speech at University of Alabama at Birmingham." Birmingham, AL, 1993.

HENRY HIGHLAND GARNET
(1815–1882), minister, abolitionist,
U.S. ambassador

CYNTHIA P. KING

In 1843, Reverend Henry Highland Garnet delivered a fiery address before the audience of African-Americans attending the National Negro Convention in Buffalo, New York. Garnet's passion and eloquence so captivated the assembly that not until his powerful conclusion did the audience realize that the speaker had called for a slave revolt; a bitter debate then ensued between conservative and militant conventioneers. No stranger to political strife, Garnet often articulated controversial stances that were characterized by fire and eloquence working in tandem to produce powerful orations. Armed with arguments grounded in Christian theology and libertarian principles, trained in classical eloquence, and with a flair for the dramatic, Garnet launched vicious attacks against his avowed foes: slavery and discrimination. Personal memories of enslavement also fueled his passionate attacks.

Born on December 23, 1815, in Kent County, Maryland, Garnet was enslaved for the first nine years of his life. In 1824, assisted by abolitionists, his parents fled with him and his sister to New York City. His formal education began in 1826 at the New York African Free School. In *Henry Highland Garnet: A Voice of Black Radicalism in the Nineteenth Century,* Joel Schor reported that although Garnet was a bright student, his studies were impeded by the pain of a "useless leg," which eventually had to be amputated. In his *Eulogy of Henry Highland Garnet,* classmate Alexander Crummell noted how Garnet's illness inadvertently shaped his reasoning processes. Chronic pain prevented Garnet from studying laboriously; therefore, his mind, recalled Crummell, "was more the product of intuition than scholarship"; "without any labored processes of reasoning . . . he invariably reached . . . the clearest conception of his argument." Garnet's cognitive skill was complemented by a vivid imagination that fostered a talent for writing poetry. Though he later abandoned poetry writing, his speeches reflected that poetic influence in their rhythmic and metaphorical qualities.

Garnet pursued higher education in 1835 at Noyes Academy, an integrated school formed by progressive abolitionists in New Hampshire. In 1836, Garnet began his training for the ministry at Presbyterian-affiliated Oneida Theological Institute. His curriculum, which included Greek, New Testament, Hebrew poetry, and logic and rhetoric, sharpened his writing and speaking skills. According to Schor, one of Garnet's teachers lauded him as "a refined scholar, writer and speaker of touching beauty."

Garnet ascended to prominence in abolitionist circles in the 1840s. He moved to Troy, New York, in 1841, where he divided his time between pastoral duties at the Liberty Street Presbyterian Church and abolitionist agitation. During this decade, he edited two short-lived newspapers, the *Clarion* and the *Anglo-African*. He also participated in the Negro Conventions, which met intermittently from the 1830s though the Civil War to discuss ways to elevate the African-American community. Garnet played especially prominent roles in the Negro Conventions of 1843, 1848, and 1864.

The following decade, Garnet carried his fiery antislavery message to Europe. In the early 1850s, he was a delegate to the World Peace Congress in Frankfurt, Germany, and addressed many antislavery societies in England and Scotland. Garnet so impressed the United Presbyterian Church of Scotland that in 1853 it sent him to pastor a church in Jamaica. He returned to the United States three years later, only to be disillusioned by the worsened plight of African-Americans, which prompted him to found the African Civilization Society, through which he promulgated his controversial advocacy of limited emigration of blacks to Africa. At the outset of the Civil War, Garnet left for a speaking tour of England, but returned a year later to urge African-Americans to enlist in the Union army. After the Civil War, he served briefly with the Freedman's Bureau. In 1865, while pastoring an upscale congregation in Washington, D.C., Garnet became the first African-American to deliver a sermon before the House of Representatives. During the 1870s, Garnet remained active in protest efforts. He participated in a small movement for Cuban independence and also agitated against the oppression of Southern blacks. In 1881, President Garfield appointed him minister and consul general to Liberia. Garnet departed for those shores in January 1882, but died two months later in Liberia of a severe asthma attack.

PASSION AND ELOQUENCE

By age twenty-eight Garnet had earned the reputation of a master orator. Newspaper accounts praised his oral presentations as "powerful," "intelligent," and "eloquent." In *History of the Negro Race in America, 1619–1880,* George Washington Williams extolled Garnet's oratorical skills as "equaling" those of Frederick Douglass. Despite an amputated leg, Garnet's physical appearance enhanced his orations. Describing Garnet's personal appeal, scholar Carter G.

Woodson reported that at six feet, Garnet was "tall and majestic in stature . . . [he had] complete command of his voice and used it with skill."

Like most members of the antebellum African-American community, Garnet was profoundly disturbed over Southern slavery and Northern discrimination against free blacks. Though united in their goals to abolish slavery and secure equal rights, African-Americans disagreed over the means by which these goals could be realized. Garnet often adopted positions that put him at odds with other influential members of the community, most notably Frederick Douglass, who staunchly advocated moral suasion as the only respectable weapon to fight oppression. Though not averse to moral suasion, Garnet believed that strategies such as political action, physical resistance, and African emigration could empower the spoken word.

Like many of his abolitionist contemporaries, Garnet grounded his arguments against slavery and discrimination in two powerful nineteenth-century appeals: Christian theology and libertarian political principles. These rhetorically forceful concepts framed his discussions of the immediate exigencies of an oration and provided internal evidence for his arguments; Garnet did not use an abundance of external factual and statistical evidence to substantiate his claims. His orations were exhortative and depended on the stirring of his audiences' emotions to produce belief.

Garnet's formal education versed him in Christian theology. Though he seldom explicitly quoted Scripture in political speeches, his orations were replete with biblical themes such as the punishment of sin, the blessings of righteousness, God as protector and avenger, and Christian duty. In his 1843 "Address to the Slaves of the United States of America" touted simultaneously as being his most famous and most radical speech, Garnet grounded his advocacy of physical resistance to slavery in Christian principle. His central argument was that slavery, with its base and evil nature, is a sin; therefore, he warned slaves, "To such degradation it is sinful in the extreme for you to make voluntary submission." Refuting a popular proslavery claim that Christian slaves must obey their masters, Garnet informed them that all God requires of Christians is to keep "divine commandments . . . to love him supremely, your neighbor as yourself—and to keep the Sabbath day holy—to search holy Scriptures." In a rhetorically shrewd move, Garnet then deductively established a link between his central thesis and the action he proposed: physical resistance to slavery. He commanded, "Therefore it is your solemn and imperative duty to use every means, both moral, intellectual, and physical that promises success [in breaking the bonds of slavery]."

Christian principle similarly grounded his argument in the "Speech Delivered at Cooper's Institute" given in New York City in 1860. Championing the controversial cause of limited emigration of African-Americans to Africa, Garnet appealed to his audience "on the broad grounds of humanity and Christian love," holding it "the duty of Christians and philanthropists in America either to send or carry the Gospel and civilization into Africa." He believed that limited emigration would be mutually beneficial to both Africans and African-Americans. The former would benefit by having the Gospel diffused among its inhabitants and by using African-American commercial knowledge to establish positive trading practices with other parts of the world; the latter, Garnet asserted, would profit by working with Africans to economically undermine slavery in America.

Consistent throughout Garnet's Christian appeals was the assertion that "God is no respecter of persons." He charged with hypocrisy those claiming to be Christian who debased men because of their skin color. In his 1842 "Speech Delivered at the Liberty Party Convention" given in New Bedford, Massachusetts, Garnet reacted to attempts by whites to make color a qualification for citizenship, averring, "The spirit of Christianity, while it is as extensive as the universe, in its desire to do good to man, it is also as impartial as the light of heaven. It does not stop to consider the complexion of its adorers." Similarly, Garnet levied a charge of hypocrisy against the propagators of slavery in "Address to the Slaves," where he lamented the years of oppression of Africans since they first encountered "men calling themselves Christian." In like fashion, in "The Wrongs of Africa," delivered in Homer, New York, in 1845, Garnet decried the "iniquities . . . sanctioned by many of the professing Christians, and by many of the ministers in the land." A charge of hypocrisy was also implied in his 1865 "A Memorial Discourse," delivered in the House of Representatives. In this oration, Garnet drew an analogy between those in government who acquiesced to the slave system and the "Scribes and Pharisees" of "Matthew 23:4." Both epitomized hypocrisy in their misguided "intelligence," which permitted their acceptance of slavery.

Garnet's political arguments invoked the sentiments of the Declaration of Independence, with its embodiment of the egalitarian spirit of the Revolutionary War. In "Address to the Slaves," he revered the Declaration of Independence as a "glorious document" with "God-like sentiments." Echoing the Declaration's universalist statement of equality, in his "Speech Delivered at the Seventh Anniversary of the American Anti-Slavery Society," Garnet proclaimed, "All men are created free and equal."

A central component of Garnet's political arguments is his emotive deification of the founding fathers. His "Speech Delivered at the Seventh Anniversary of the American Anti-Slavery Society" is representative. In the introduction of the oration Garnet immediately denounced the denial of citizenship to "the people of color" as "a pile of wrongs," a "national disgrace," and antithetical to the libertarian spirit of the founding fathers. He extolled the "solid materials" from which the "foundations of this government were formed" and praised the founders because they "had no communion with tyranny and oppression." Garnet continued his exaltation by recalling the love of liberty that caused the founders "to press forward with holy and patriotic zeal in the road to that national independence." He contrasted the "noble" image of these patriots with the "base conduct of their degenerate sons." While he acknowledged that the founders bore some blame for allowing slavery to flourish, he was willing to "possibly pardon them for neglecting our brethren's rights" because the "nation was newly formed" and the "patriots' duty did not appear plain." On the other hand, he castigated his white contemporaries for their role in perpetuating the institution, insisting, "Now that we have reached the midday of our national career, this nation is guilty of the basest hypocrisy."

Garnet's arguments are normally expressed in abstract terms using emotive language and forgoing external evidence. A notable extant exception is "The Past and Present Condition, and the Destiny of the Colored Race," delivered at the Female Benevolent Society in Troy, New York, in 1848. About eight thousand words long, this three-part speech is distinct in its scholarly tone and the inclusion of external evidence.

Stylistically, Garnet's orations are generally endowed with vivacity and rhythm. He often used figurative language such as metaphors and personification to enable those who had no firsthand knowledge of slavery to visualize the dark nature of the "nefarious institution." Indeed, these metaphorical images of slavery are one of the most prominent features of Garnet's orations. Buttressing his appeals to Christianity, he often conferred lifelike, profane characteristics upon the institution, as in the "Speech Delivered at the Liberty Party Convention." Here he condemned the ominous nature of slavery, describing how its "Dark Spirit . . . hovers . . . over our whole Union. . . . She is casting her huge shadow over our whole domain." In "Address to the Slaves," he noted the devilish torments of slavery, charging that it "shuts out . . . relief and consolation . . . affects and persecutes you with a fierceness not seen in the fiends of hell."

Garnet did not limit his use of metaphorical language to sinister depictions; he also portrayed more picturesque images metaphorically. Imaging the ascendent movements of the heavenly bodies in "The Past and Present Condition," he imparted his optimism for the future of African-Americans:

> The star of our hope is steadily rising above the horizon. As a land that had long been covered by storm and clouds, and shaken by the thunder, when the storms and clouds had passed away, the thunder was succeeded by a calm, like that which cheered the first glad morning.

In "Speech Commemorating West Indian Emancipation," delivered at the Methodist Episcopal Church, Troy, New York, in 1839, Garnet celebrated the sweetness of freedom in the Caribbean Islands: "But however sweet the music of the streams . . . far sweeter are the anthems of freedom. . . . it is the shouts of the islanders of the sea, that come careening upon every wave that rolls westward."

A second stylistic feature common to Garnet's orations is the use of anaphora. By employing this trope of repetition, Garnet created compelling rhythmic passages that generate momentum and emphasize key ideas. For example, in the "Address to the Slaves," imploring slaves to contemplate the horrors of slavery, he entreated, "Think of your wretched sisters. . . . of the undying glory that hangs around the ancient name of Africa. . . . how many years you have poured out." Likewise, in his discourse delivered in the House of Representatives, describing the noteworthy character of modern-day Scribes and Pharisees, he anaphorically declared: "They are intelligent and well-informed. . . . They are acquainted with the principles of the law. . . . They are teachers of common law. . . . They acknowledge . . . a just and impartial God." Later in the "Discourse," Garnet used anaphora to frame his response to the rhetorical question "When and where will the demands of . . . reformers . . . end?": "When all unjust and heavy burdens shall be removed from every man in the land. When emancipation shall be followed by enfranchisement. . . . When our brave and gallant soldiers all have justice done unto them." Likewise, in the conclusion of the "The Wrongs of Africa," delivered in Homer, New York, in July 1845, anaphora was used to list the complaints of African-Americans and their supporters:

> We complain that . . . ministers . . . and their deeds are evil. We complain that this connection with sin hinders the growth of undefiled religion. . . . We complain that those who sit in Moses' seat do not rebuke this sin. . . . We complain we are subjected to all these misfortunes.

Garnet frequently contrasted the base nature of slavery and its propagators with the honorable character of the institution's adversaries. These contrasts generated images that served his larger rhetorical goal of defaming black enslavement and exalting abolitionism and egalitarianism. In the "Address to the Slaves," he labeled those who enslaved as "incarnate devils," "heartless tyrants," "guilty soul thieves," and "God cursed." He intensified the evil image of slavery and its propagators by featuring African-American "martyrs of freedom": Nat Turner and Denmark Vesey, among others, whom he celebrated as "noble," "God-fearing" men who died in "freedom's conflict," and whose "names are surrounded by a halo of glory." He made similar use of labels in "Speech Delivered at the Seventh Anniversary of the American Anti-Slavery Society," calling the founding fathers "patriots" and "noble" despite their accommodation of slavery. Such labeling serviced Garnet's larger argument that the institution of slavery was fundamentally antithetical to both Christianity and the political principles upon which America was founded.

A speaker of tremendous force, Garnet used his oratorical skills to denounce the oppression of nineteenth-century African-Americans. The high praise rendered in the *Washington Daily Morning Chronicle* after his "A Memorial Discourse" is typical of the reports that followed his orations: "This is but a faint sketch of his [Garnet's] able discourse, and several times during its delivery, the audience was so thrilled by the power of his logic that it was with difficulty their enthusiasm was restrained."

While Garnet's contribution to nineteenth-century American oratory has been generally overlooked, his oratory is noteworthy from both an ideological and a rhetorical perspective. He often unabashedly challenged the views and methods of popular abolitionists such as William Lloyd Garrison and Frederick Douglass. Rhetorically, his orations were fueled by a passion and eloquence that enthralled his many nineteenth-century audiences.

INFORMATION SOURCES

Research Collections and Collected Speeches

According to Earl Ofari, most of Garnet's private papers were destroyed by fire. In fact, only a few of his sermons are extant. Many of Garnet's documents are found among the private papers of his contemporaries, most notably Alexander Crummell and Frederick Douglass. Extracts from Garnet's speeches and his written editorials can be found in nineteenth-century newspapers, such as the *Emancipator, Anglo-African*, the *Colored American, Douglass' Monthly*, the *Anti-Slavery Reporter*, and the *Clarion. The Minutes of the Proceedings of the National Convention of Colored People* contain the speeches Garnet made before those assemblies.

[*MSRC*] Moorland-Spingarn Research Center, Howard University, Washington, DC.

Selected Critical Studies

Bell, Howard. *A Survey of the Negro Convention Movement, 1830–1861.* New York: Arno, 1969.
Brewer, William. "Henry Highland Garnet." *Journal of Negro History* 13 (January 1928): 36–52.
Crummell, Alexander. *The Eulogy of Henry Highland Garnet, D.D., Presbyterian Minister, etc., in Africa and America.* Washington, DC: n.p., 1882.
Ofari, Earl. *Let Your Motto Be Resistance: The Life and Thought of Henry Highland Garnet.* Boston: Beacon, 1972.
Schor, Joel. *Henry Highland Garnet: A Voice of Black Radicalism in the Nineteenth Century.* Westport, CT: Greenwood, 1977.

Selected Biography

Woodson, Carter G. "Henry Highland Garnet." *Dictionary of American Biography.* Vol. 4. Ed. Allen Johnson and Dumas Malone. New York: Charles Scribner's Sons, 1932, 154–155.

CHRONOLOGY OF MAJOR SPEECHES

[See "Research Collections and Collected Speeches" for source codes.]

"Speech Commemorating West Indian Emancipation." Troy, NY, 1839. *Herald of Freedom*, November 18, 1839; Schor, 21–22.

"Speech Delivered at the Seventh Anniversary of the American Anti-Slavery Society."
    New York, NY, 1840. *Emancipator*, May 22, 1840.

"Speech Delivered at the National Convention of Colored Citizens." Troy, NY, 1840.
    Minutes of the State Convention of Colored Citizens. New York: Peircy and Reed,
    1840.

"Speech Delivered at the Liberty Party Convention." New Bedford, MA, February 1842.
    Ofari, 138–144.

"Address to the Slaves of the United States of America." Buffalo, NY, August 1843.
    Afro-American History: Primary Sources. Ed. Thomas R. Frazier. New York:
    Harcourt, Brace and World, 1970, 113–119; and Ofari, 144–152.

"The Wrongs of Africa." Homer, NY, July 1845. Extracts reprinted in *Emancipator and
    Free American*, August 6, 1845.

"The Past and Present Condition, and the Destiny of the Colored Race." Troy, NY,
    February 1848. Reprinted as a pamphlet of the same title. *MSRC*.

"Address of the Liberty Party to the Colored People of the Northern States." Buffalo,
    NY, 1848. *Proceedings of the National Liberty Party Convention, Buffalo, New
    York, June 14th and 15th*. Utica, NY: S. W. Green, 1848.

"Eulogy of John Brown." New York, NY, December 1859. Ofari, 186.

"Speech Delivered at Cooper's Institute." New York, NY, 1860. Ofari, 183–185.

"A Memorial Discourse" (Speech before the House of Representatives). Washington,
    DC, February 1865. Reprinted as a pamphlet of the same title. *MSRC*; Ofari, 187–
    203; and James McCune Smith, *A Memorial Discourse*. Philadelphia: Joseph M.
    Wilson, 1965.

MARCUS MOZIAH GARVEY
(1887–1940), black nationalist

HAL W. BOCHIN

W. E. B. Du Bois described him in the *Crisis* as "the most dangerous enemy of the Negro race . . . either a lunatic or a traitor." An African-American writer for the American Communist party called him "the greatest confidence man of the age." J. Edgar Hoover considered him a notorious agitator and tried to deport him. In spite of, or perhaps because of, such opposition, Marcus Moziah Garvey led the largest grass-roots movement in African-American history. The exact number of his followers will never be known, but during the peak years of the Garvey movement (1920–28) as many as four million blacks on four continents (North and South America, Europe, and Africa) considered themselves Garveyites, while possibly 25 percent of that number contributed dues to the United Negro Improvement Association (UNIA), the organization that Garvey founded and led for twenty-six years. For the most part Garvey's success as a leader of a mass movement can be attributed to his editorial pen and to the dynamic speaking ability that led his followers to tout him as the "greatest orator of the Negro race."

Born on August 17, 1887, in St. Ann's Bay, Jamaica, British West Indies, Marcus Garvey learned at an early age what it meant to be black on an island ruled by a white elite, willing to share their power only with the lightest-skinned of the black majority. His father was a mason who worked when he felt like it and forfeited most of the family property by losing lawsuits to his neighbors. His mother cooked for neighboring families and farmed a small garden until it was destroyed by a tropical storm. When he was fourteen, Garvey began an apprenticeship in the printing trade with his godfather, Alfred E. Burrowes, a master printer. Noting his limited prospects in his small hometown, the nineteen-year-old Garvey moved to the capital city of Kingston, where he worked as a printer. The animated political discussions he found in the streets of the city impressed him immediately; but according to Amy Garvey in *Garvey and Garveyism*, the first time he tried to participate, his dialect called attention to his rural background and he was told in no uncertain terms to "shut your mouth, country boy." Determined not to be embarrassed by his speech again, Garvey spent his Sundays observing different preachers to discover what speaking techniques seemed most effective. He also read aloud in his room in front of a mirror so that he could work on proper gestures as well as on his pronunciation and grammar. He eventually joined discussion groups on Victoria Pier every Saturday evening, talking about ways to improve the lot of Kingston's poor. As he gained confidence in his own speaking ability, Garvey organized elocution contests for youths in Kingston.

In 1912, Garvey traveled to London to learn more about the treatment of blacks throughout the British Empire. There he met Duse Mohammed Ali, a black Egyptian editor, who stimulated in him an interest in Africa, its culture and history, and its exploitation by colonial powers. In London, Garvey read Booker T. Washington's autobiography, *Up from Slavery,* and decided to introduce Washington's industrial-school model to Jamaica.

Returning to Jamaica in the summer of 1914, Garvey reported in an autobiographical article in *Current History:* "My brain was afire" with the dream of "uniting all the Negro peoples of the world into one great body to establish a country and Government absolutely their own." To that end, Garvey founded the Universal Negro Improvement and Conservation Association and African Communities League. Its motto was "One God! One Aim! One Destiny!" Garvey became the first president of the organization, which called for the improvement of job opportunities for blacks in Jamaica through the establishment of industrial schools modeled after the Tuskegee Institute in Alabama. When he found that local blacks were indifferent to what he was trying to do and that Jamaica's mulattoes opposed his project, Garvey decided to go to the United States to seek support for his Jamaican program.

On March 24, 1916, Garvey arrived in New York, where he settled in Harlem. His first pulpit was a stepladder on Lenox Avenue from which he addressed ever-increasing crowds of passersby. On June 12, 1917, Garvey was offered the opportunity to address his largest single audience to that time, several thousand persons attending a mass meeting at the Bethel AME Church, for the purpose of organizing a group called the Liberty League. His impassioned plea brought the audience to their feet, and, perhaps for the first time, Garvey realized the power he could hold over a large audience. Biographer Elton Fax reported in *Marcus Garvey: The Story of a Pioneer Black Nationalist* that "for days afterward, his performance was the talk of Harlem."

In 1917, Garvey started a New York division of the UNIA, becoming its president-general. By the middle of 1919, he claimed that UNIA membership had reached two million, with thirty branches in the United States and the West Indies. Adding to Garvey's increasing prominence was the *Negro World,* the newspaper he published as the voice of the UNIA. The paper, whose slogan was "Up You Mighty Race," was started in August 1918 and, within two years, claimed a paid circulation of 50,000. With articles in French and Spanish for its West Indian readership, the *Negro World* continued to spread Garvey's views until 1933.

In June of 1919, Garvey launched the Black Star Shipping Line. Chartered to operate ships that would carry passengers and freight to all parts of the world, the Black Star Line was owned solely by African-Americans, who bought shares of stock at five dollars each. While skeptics scoffed, thousands of Garvey's followers used what little money they could spare to become part of the enterprise, and on September 17, 1919, the line purchased its first ship, the freighter *Yarmouth,* for $168,000. The sale of stock increased dramatically, and within months the company bought two additional ships, the excursion boat S.S. *Shadyside* and the yacht *Kanawha.*

On July 27, 1919, Garvey presided at the dedication of a large auditorium (originally the first floor of an unfinished Baptist church) that provided seating for 3,000 listeners. He named the building Liberty Hall, and it became the international headquarters of the UNIA and the scene of weekly speeches by the stocky Jamaican to his supporters. In August 1920, Garvey organized the first international convention of the UNIA, which attracted delegates from thirty-five nations to Liberty Hall for a one-month session to draw up a Negro Declaration of Rights.

In January 1922, federal authorities arrested Garvey for using the mails to defraud stockholders in the shipping line. He was indicted and a short time later had to announce that the operations of the Black Star Line had been suspended. In fact, the three ships had been financial disasters, and by late 1922 they all had been either sunk or sold for scrap, at a loss to the UNIA of $600,000.

Following a trial in which he unwisely served as his own attorney, Garvey was convicted and sentenced to five years in the Atlanta Federal Penitentiary. In November 1927, President Calvin Coolidge commuted Garvey's sentence to time served with the stipulation that he would be immediately deported as an undesirable alien. Garvey attempted to run the UNIA from Jamaica, but the international organization was never the same.

Garvey visited Europe in the spring of 1928 to establish a European headquarters in London and a branch of the UNIA in Paris. His first major speech in England proved to be a disaster. Despite promotional material promising the "Greatest Orator in the World," only 200 listeners filed into the 10,000-seat Royal Albert Hall to hear what the Jamaican had to say. Returning home, the irrepressible Garvey founded the People's Political Party, seeking land reform, prison reform, and improved public health. Garvey himself ran for the island's Legislative Council but lost.

Almost totally destitute and forced to sell his furniture to pay off his debts, Garvey left Jamaica for London in March 1935 to set up permanent UNIA headquarters there. Every Sunday he spoke in Hyde Park, often to large crowds, but he never gained the kind of following he had in America. He published a

monthly magazine, the *Black Man,* through which he caused considerable controversy by blaming Haile Selassie for the defeat of Ethiopia by Italy.

On June 10, 1940, Garvey died from a cerebral hemorrhage and was buried
in London. His second wife, Amy Jacques–Garvey, and two sons survived him.
His body was returned to his native land in 1964, where Jamaicans honored him
as their first "national hero."

ORATOR OF BLACK NATIONALISM

Alphonso Pinkney wrote in *Red, Black, and Green: Black Nationalism in the
United States* that three elements form the basis of contemporary black nationalism: unity, pride in cultural heritage, and autonomy. These elements were the
core of Marcus Garvey's speaking from the time he came to Harlem in 1916
until his last published speech in 1938. Uniting practical ideas with dramatic
visions, he preached the doctrine of black nationalism to an attentive audience
for more than twenty years.

Garvey arrived on the American scene at an opportune moment. With the
death of Booker T. Washington in 1915, no black leader commanded a mass
following, yet leadership was sorely needed. Southern violence, often in the
form of lynching, together with the promised economic opportunities of wartime
employment up North, had led to a massive redistribution of the African-
American population from the rural South to Northern cities between 1910 and
1920. Although economic conditions improved for the newly settled African-
Americans during the war, postwar race riots in Northern cities and increased
unemployment, as war production ceased and white veterans returned, left many
African-Americans frustrated and despairing. Thus when Garvey landed in New
York, according to Pinkney, "he found a leaderless people, a people despised
by whites at all levels, and a people in desperate need of assurance of their
human worth." Starting with street-corner rallies, but eventually filling Liberty
Hall every week, and occasionally speaking to tens of thousands at Madison
Square Garden, Garvey provided such assurance with his program of black na-
tionalism.

That a "new Negro," "out to get what has belonged to us, politically, socially, economically, and in every way," had arrived provided the central theme
of Garvey's speech to a mass meeting of the UNIA at Carnegie Hall on August
25, 1919. Garvey pictured this new Negro as militant and united: "If any white
American man thinks that the new Negro is going down on his knees to beg
anything today, he makes a big mistake. . . . We are fifteen millions in America;
we are fifteen or twenty millions in the West Indies; and two hundred and eighty
millions on the continent of Africa, and we have declared for a free and independent race."

Garvey declared that "the one country in the world that has wealth . . . the
great continent of Africa" belonged to the new Negro. He justified black nationalism by comparing it to other contemporary struggles for self-determination:

"As the Irishman is struggling and fighting for the fatherland of Ireland, so must the new Negro of the world fight for the fatherland of Africa." He issued a militant warning to "the white man who now dominates Africa, that it is to his interests to clear out of Africa now, because we are coming, not as in the time of Father Abraham, 200,000 strong, but we are coming 400,000,000 strong; and we mean to retake every square inch of the 12,000,000 square miles of African territory belonging to us by right divine." To gain an African homeland, Garvey thundered, "we will continue to fight, and fight until we make ourselves a great people—the new race that is to be." "Africa for the Africans, at home and abroad" became the great rallying cry of the UNIA.

Garvey reported that the new Negro no longer believed that everything white was good or that black signified evil. On the contrary, he observed that now "the black man is saying that everything that is pure is black." Economic independence was an important goal of the UNIA, and Garvey closed his address by asking his audience to buy stock in the newly capitalized Black Star Shipping Line because "we want to see our men occupying positions in the world as white men are occupying."

In January 1920, Garvey started the Negro Factories Corporation, which offered loans and business expertise to Negro entrepreneurs. Using the slogan "Be Black, Buy Black, Build Black," the corporation eventually established a chain of cooperative markets, a restaurant, dressmaking and tailor shops, a steam laundry, and a publishing house. Black dolls and calendars with pictures of blacks began to appear in the black community. In his speeches as well, Garvey often stressed pride in racial heritage, as he did on January 1, 1922, in an address at Liberty Hall commemorating the fifty-ninth anniversary of the Emancipation Proclamation: "This race of ours gave civilization, gave art, gave science, gave literature to the world. . . . The Negro once occupied a high position in the world, scientifically, artistically, and commercially."

In August 1920, Garvey organized the first international convention of the UNIA. Delegates from thirty-five nations came to Liberty Hall for one month to discuss mutual problems and to draw up a Negro Declaration of Rights. Twenty-five thousand enthusiastic delegates and guests crowded into Madison Square Garden on the evening of August 2 to hear Marcus Garvey, dressed in an academic robe of green and red, offer the keynote address to "a people who are determined to suffer no longer."

Again Garvey compared the Negroes' quest for self-determination with that of other peoples in the world: "Ireland is striking out for freedom; Egypt is striking out for freedom; India is striking out for freedom; and the Negroes of the world shall do no less than strike out also for freedom." Like the others, the Negroes not only wanted a homeland, they were willing to fight for it: "If the Englishman claims England as his native habitat, and the Frenchman claims France as his native habitat, and if the Canadian claims Canada as his native habitat, then the time has come for four hundred million Negroes to claim Africa as their native land. . . . [W]e pledge our life's blood, our sacred blood to the battlefields of Africa, to plant there the flag of Liberty, of Freedom and Democracy.''

Often accused by his critics of advising all Negroes to leave for Africa immediately, Garvey clarified his position in a speech delivered on August 8, celebrating the opening of the second week of the convention: ''We are not preaching any doctrine to ask all the Negroes of Harlem and of the United States to pack up their trunks and leave for Africa. . . . But we are asking you to get this organization to do the pioneering work. The majority of us will stay here, but we must send our scientists, our mechanics, and our artisans and let them build railroads, let them build the great educational and other institutions necessary and when they are constructed, the time will come for the command to be given, 'Come Home.' '' Over the next few years, Garvey negotiated with the government of Liberia for enough land to house a sizable settlement. He thought that they had reached an agreement, but the Liberian government, facing pressure from African colonial powers and fearing that the Garveyites might attempt to gain political control over its country, reneged on its offer and leased the promised acreage to the Firestone Company for a rubber plantation. Garvey never visited Africa.

In late February 1921, Garvey left the United States for a five-week promotional tour of the West Indies to raise funds for the Black Star Line. He addressed friendly crowds in Jamaica, Cuba, Costa Rica, British Honduras, and Panama, selling stock and gaining members for the UNIA. J. Edgar Hoover, who had long sought evidence to deport Garvey, encouraged the State Department to refuse to readmit him. At first Hoover was successful. Garvey was twice refused a visa to return to the United States because of his activities ''in political and race agitation.'' The State Department eventually rescinded its opposition, however, and Garvey received a visa on June 25. He returned to New York, where the second international convention of the UNIA began in August.

At the convention, Garvey continued an ongoing battle with an old nemesis, W. E. B. Du Bois, whom Garvey had earlier accused of being a spokesman for white men. Garvey attempted to discredit Du Bois, who was then leading a Pan-African Congress in London, by offering, as part of his opening address to the delegates, a resolution declaring: ''W. E. B. Du Bois, Secretary of the so-called Pan-African Congress, and those associated with him, are not representatives of the struggling peoples of the world, and . . . the men who have called the said Congress have not consulted the Negro peoples of the world of their intention, and have received no mandate from the said people to call a Congress in their name.'' He deplored ''a desire among a certain class of Negroes for social contact, comradeship and companionship with the white race.''

But Du Bois was just one of many critics with whom Garvey had to contend. Tony Martin in *Race First* described the opposition Garvey faced: ''The United States government was against him because they considered all black radicals subversive; European governments were against him because he was a threat to the stability of their colonies; the communists were against him because he successfully kept black workers out of their grasp; the National Association for the Advancement of Colored People and other integrationist organizations were against him because he argued that white segregationists were the true spokesmen for white America and because he in turn advocated black separatism."

It is not surprising that Hill found that during the 1921–22 period, Garvey's speeches "reflected a desire to placate the United States government while simultaneously assailing his black critics and denouncing European colonizers of Africa." In "The Statesmanship of President Harding," delivered at Liberty Hall on October 30, 1921, Garvey praised Harding as "one of the greatest statesmen of the present day" for a speech the president had given in Birmingham, Alabama, in which he had said, "Race amalgamation, there can never be; but . . . unless our democracy is a lie, you must recognize that equality." The president continued, "The black man should be encouraged to be the best possible black man, and not the best possible imitation of the white man." Garvey claimed that Harding's statement was "a direct slap or hit at Dr. Du Bois . . . the Chief Executive of this nation made us understand that trying to imitate white men, trying to be white, will in no way bring better appreciation from the white man than if we try to be what we are."

Because of the severe financial losses suffered by the Black Star Line, Garvey had to delay the purchase of a fourth ship, tentatively named the S.S. *Phyllis Wheatley.* He continued, however, to feature the ship in promotional literature for the sale of stock in his shipping line; and in January 1922, Garvey was arrested for using the mails to defraud. He immediately defended himself and attempted to shift the blame for the line's problems onto his associates in a speech presented at Liberty Hall on January 13, 1922. "I have never defrauded a man in my life," he said, "but it is not the Post Office Department's fault; they are only instruments being used to carry out the designs of those who have been fighting the Universal Negro Improvement Association for the last four years." Garvey blamed his arrest on the activities of unnamed officers of the organization whom he had left in charge during his West Indian speaking tour.

On November 25, 1922, in "The Principles of the Universal Negro Improvement Association," a speech at Liberty Hall, Garvey contrasted the UNIA with other black organizations and offered an eloquent statement against racial prejudice. He said that "the difference between the Universal Negro Improvement Association and the other movements of this country, and probably the world, is that the UNIA seeks independence of government, while the other organizations seek to make the Negro a secondary part of existing governments." Garvey felt that true equality of opportunity was impossible in a white-dominated country and asked, "If I am as educated as the next man, if I am as prepared as the next man, if I have passed through the best schools and colleges and universities as the other fellow, why should I not have a fair chance to compete with the other fellow for the biggest position in the nation? I have feelings, I have blood, I have senses like the other fellow; I have ambition, I have hope. Why should he, because of some racial prejudice, keep me down? . . . This is where the UNIA differs from other organizations.''

A jury found Garvey guilty of one count of mail fraud in June 1923. Following a lengthy appeals process, his bail was revoked and he was incarcerated in the Atlanta Federal Penitentiary on February 8, 1925. A flood of petitions, telegrams, and letters appealing for pardon was directed at President Calvin Coolidge, including one from Earl Little, the father of Malcolm X. Garvey remained in prison until the president commuted his sentence in November 1927.

Back in Jamaica, large crowds greeted Garvey as a returning hero, but he failed in his attempts to influence island politics because property restrictions prevented many of his supporters from voting. Nevertheless, in a speech offered in Kingston on September 9, 1929, Garvey announced the formation of a new political party, the People's Party, and offered a fourteen-point program ''that will bring you better conditions and an improved country generally.'' He demanded a minimum wage for the working class, land reform, a national university, and the creation of a national park, modeled after London's Hyde Park. Garvey's call for ''a law to impeach and imprison such judges who . . . will illicitly enter into agreements and arrangements with lawyers and other persons of influence to deprive other subjects in the Realm of their rights in such courts of law, over which they may preside'' resulted in his arrest for contempt of court, a finding of guilty at trial, and a sentence of three months in prison.

To earn a living, Garvey promoted the Edelweiss Park Amusement Company, which offered concerts, vaudeville shows, debates, and elocution contests. He also published the *Blackman,* later called the *Black Man: A Monthly Journal of Negro Thought and Opinion.* By giving strong editorial support to Franklin Roosevelt, Garvey hoped to win readmission to the United States, at least on a temporary basis, so that he could engage in much-needed fundraising. His efforts, however, proved unsuccessful. With Garvey permanently out of the United States, local UNIA units split into rival factions, and other movements, such as the Peace Mission of Father Divine, began to compete successfully for the support of Garveyites.

In addition to his UNIA problems, Garvey lost his printing press, the Edelweiss property, and even his home to creditors, so he decided to attempt a new start in London in early 1935. He became a fixture at Speakers' Corner in Hyde Park and continued publishing the *Black Man.* Robert Hill noted an important change in Garvey's political position: ''Cut off geographically and emotionally from old supporters, Garvey became increasingly conservative in his political opinions, taking stances that were incongruent with the main currents of political action central to other members of the Pan-African community.'' Despite some unpopular positions, such as his criticism of Haile Selassie, Garvey presided over three UNIA regional conventions in Canada (1936–38), and in 1937, after the convention adjourned, he offered a workshop, which he called a ''School of African Philosophy,'' to prepare younger members of the UNIA for leadership positions in the organization.

Following the workshop, he made an extensive speaking tour of the Caribbean. On the island of St. Kitts on October 24, 1937, Garvey presented the same type of self-help message that he had offered in Jamaica twenty years earlier: "If you do not train and protect your mind, men with trained minds will subjugate you. . . . My friends, you have to buck up and make your civilization what it ought to be. Read, read, read and never stop until you discover the knowledge of the Universe. . . . Spend a little less on food and a little more on your brain. Eat less and think more."

In what may be his last recorded speech, delivered in Toronto, Canada, on August 14, 1938, to a UNIA regional conference, Garvey repeated his call for racial unity and racial separateness: "A race's place in the world is independent from that of any other race because God made you a race when He made man." He asked, "If God intended that we should mix and lose our identity, why should he have originally made you separate and distinct from the other man?"

A number of studies have attempted to discover what made Garvey's rhetoric so effective. Shirley Weber outlined Garvey's use of four agitational rhetorical strategies—mythication, legitimation, objectification, and vilification—that kept "his audience believing and working for the goals of the UNIA." She described his style as "eloquent, and yet simple and pleasing. His language was rhythmic, with repetitious sentence structure, imagery, and metaphors." She argued that Garvey's greatest asset was his ability to relate to an audience and have them identify with him—an ability that other contemporary black leaders lacked.

Using an Afrocentric analysis of four speeches delivered by Garvey at the UNIA conventions and one editorial letter written while he was in prison, Francis Dorsey found that Garvey's speeches contributed to the "unity of the occasion," the "elimination of chaos," the "making of peace among disparate views," and the creation of "harmony and balance." Based on these four values and on seven African principles, Garvey's rhetoric resulted in the establishment of "the most controversial, emotional, and nationalist organization in the history of Black Americans."

Ware and Linkugel argued that Garvey's "auditors perceived him as a Black Moses," a type of "cultural symbol that ultimately subsumed and stood for the ideas of election, captivity, and liberation." Because of this persona, Garvey was "without peer as a mobilizer of black masses."

Clearly, Garvey succeeded because he offered his listeners a message they needed, and he presented it in a dramatic and compelling fashion. Moreover, Garvey made his followers important people in their own environment. E. Franklin Frazier, a contemporary observer, wrote in the *Nation* of August 18, 1926:

> He invented honors and social distinctions and converted every social invention to his use in his effort to make his followers feel important. While everyone was not a "Knight" or "Sir" all of his followers were "Fellow-men of the Negro Race." . . . The women were organized into "Black Cross Nurses," and the men became uniformed members of the vanguard of the Great African Army. A uni-

formed member of a Negro lodge paled in significance beside a soldier of the
Army of Africa. A Negro might be a porter during the day, taking his orders from
white men but he was an officer in the black army when it assembled at night in
Liberty Hall. Many a Negro went about his work singing in his heart that he was
a member of the great army marching to "heights of achievements."

Garvey presented his message of black nationalism in a dramatic fashion.
Those who heard Garvey speak always mentioned his strong delivery as a factor
in his success. William Sherrill was quoted in *Garvey and Garveyism* recalling
the first time he heard Garvey:

I squeezed in, until I could get a good look at him; then suddenly he turned in
my direction, and in a voice like thunder from Heaven he said, "Men and women,
what are you here for? To live unto yourself, until your body manures the earth,
or to live God's Purpose to the fullest?" He continued to complete his thought in
that compelling, yet pleading voice for an hour. I stood there like one in a trance,
every sentence ringing in my ears, and finding an echo in my heart.

Perhaps because of his first unsuccessful attempts at public speaking, Garvey
recognized the importance of a lively presentation. In offering advice to potential
leaders of the UNIA as part of his series of lessons in leadership, reprinted in
More Philosophy and Opinions of Marcus Garvey, Garvey told them, "If you
are honest in what you are saying you will feel it and it will move you. Always
be enthusiastic over your subject. The way to do that is to know it well. . . .
You must hypnotize your audience by expression. Stare into their eyes and
firmly express yourself. You must not shiver from their glare, you must make
them shiver from yours."

Marcus Garvey's message of racial unity, cultural pride, and economic independence brought him millions of followers. As "fellow men of the Negro
race," they were part of a group "400 million" strong about to recapture a
homeland that had an important cultural history. He made them proud of their
color and taught them that they could do anything a white man could do, even
run a shipping line. His speeches at Liberty Hall reached a worldwide audience
through their transcription in the *Negro World*. It was even said that his message
was carried by drum across Africa. If his rise was meteoric, so too was his fall.
After his imprisonment, his audiences never approached the size of those in the
early years, and all his business enterprises went bankrupt. But as his old opponent W. E. B. Du Bois wrote in his autobiography, *Dusk of Dawn,* "It was a
grandiose and bombastic scheme, utterly impractical as a whole, but it was
sincere and had some practical features; Garvey proved not only an astonish-
ing[ly] popular leader, but a master of propaganda. Within a few years, news
of his movement, of his promises and plans, reached Europe and Asia, and
penetrated every corner of Africa."

INFORMATION SOURCES

Research Collections and Collected Speeches

The major sources of unpublished materials on Garvey are the Schomburg Center for Research in Black Culture at the New York Public Library; Fisk University Library, which houses the Amy Jacques–Garvey papers; and the Marcus Garvey Project at the University of California, Los Angeles (see *MGP* below). A good source for printed materials is Lenwood G. Davis and Janet Sims, eds. *Marcus Garvey: An Annotated Bibliography*. Westport, CT: Greenwood, 1980.

[*MPO*] Essien-Udom, E. U., and Amy Jacques-Garvey, eds. *More Philosophy and Opinions of Marcus Garvey*. London: Frank Cass, 1977.

[*VBA*] Foner, Philip S., ed. *The Voice of Black America: Major Speeches by Negroes in the United States, 1797–1971*. New York: Simon and Schuster, 1972.

Garvey, Marcus. "Negro's Greatest Enemy." *Current History Magazine* September 1923: 951–957.

[*MGP*] Hill, Robert A., ed. *The Marcus Garvey and Universal Negro Improvement Association Papers*. 7 vols. Berkeley: U of California P, 1983–91.

[*P&O*] Jacques-Garvey, Amy, ed. *Philosophy and Opinions of Marcus Garvey*. New York: Atheneum, 1969. Reprinted 1992.

[*VBR*] Smith, Arthur L., and Stephen Robb, eds. *The Voices of Black Rhetoric: Selections*. Boston: Allyn and Bacon, 1971.

Selected Critical Studies

Dorsey, Francis E. "A Rhetoric of Values: An Afrocentric Analysis of Marcus Garvey's Convention Speeches, 1921–1924." Ph.D. diss., Kent State U, 1990.

Frazier, E. Franklin. "Garvey: A Mass Leader." *Nation*, August 18, 1926: 147–148.

Pennington, Dorothy L. "Marcus Garvey." *American Orators of the Twentieth Century*. Ed. Bernard K. Duffy and Halford R. Ryan. Westport, CT: Greenwood, 1987, 167–172.

Ware, B. L., and Wil A. Linkugel. "The Rhetorical *Persona:* Marcus Garvey as Black Moses." *Communication Monographs* 49 (1982): 50–62.

Weber, Shirley Nash. "The Rhetoric of Marcus Garvey, Leading Spokesman of the Universal Negro Improvement Association in the United States, 1916–1929." Ph.D. diss., University of California, Los Angeles, 1975.

Selected Biographies

Clarke, John Henrik, ed. *Marcus Garvey and the Vision of Africa*. New York: Random House, 1974.

Cronon, E. David. *Black Moses*. Madison: U of Wisconsin P, 1969.

———, ed. *Marcus Garvey*. Englewood Cliffs, NJ: Prentice-Hall, 1973.

Fax, Elton C. *Garvey: The Story of a Pioneer Black Nationalist*. New York: Dodd, Mead, 1972.

Jacques–Garvey, Amy. *Garvey and Garveyism*. London: Collier Macmillan, 1970.

Lewis, Rupert, and Patrick Bryan, eds. *Garvey: His Work and Impact.* Trenton, NJ: Africa World Press, 1991.

Martin, Tony. *Race First.* Westport, CT: Greenwood, 1976.

Pinkney, Alphonso. *Red, Black, and Green: Black Nationalism in the United States.* Cambridge: Cambridge UP, 1976.

Stein, Judith. *The World of Marcus Garvey.* Baton Rouge: Louisiana State UP, 1986.

CHRONOLOGY OF MAJOR SPEECHES

[See ''Research Collections and Collected Speeches'' for source codes.]

Speech at UNIA Mass Meeting. Carnegie Hall, New York City, August 25, 1919. *MGP,* 1:500–509.

Opening Speech at First UNIA International Convention. Madison Square Garden, August 2, 1920. *MGP,* 2:499–502.

Speech by Marcus Garvey. Liberty Hall, New York City, August 8, 1920. *MGP,* 2:557–560.

''Opening Speech of the Convention.'' Liberty Hall, New York City, August 1, 1921. *MGP,* 3:576–585.

''The Statesmanship of President Harding.'' Liberty Hall, New York City, October 30, 1921. *MGP,* 4:141–151.

Speech Delivered on Emancipation Day. Liberty Hall, New York City, January 1, 1922. *MGP,* 4:322–327; *P&O,* 1:78–82.

''Garvey Explains Motives of Arrest.'' Liberty Hall, New York City, January 13, 1922. *MGP,* 4:344–352.

''The Principles of the Universal Negro Improvement Association.'' Liberty Hall, New York City, November 25, 1922. *MGP,* 5:143–149; *P&O,* 2:93–100; *VBA,* 749–757; *VBR,* 101–109.

''Speech by Marcus Garvey.'' Royal Albert Hall, London, England, June 6, 1928. *MGP,* 7:193–206; *MPO,* 44–58.

''Speech by Marcus Garvey.'' Cross Roads, Kingston, Jamaica, September 9, 1929. *MGP,* 7:328–338.

''Speech by Marcus Garvey.'' Basseterre, St. Kitts, October 24, 1937. *MGP,* 7:804–810.

''Can the Negro Find His Place?'' Toronto, Canada, August 14, 1938. *MGP,* 7: 885–890; *MPO,* 27–34.

FRANCIS JAMES GRIMKE
(1850–1937), minister

DANIEL ROSS CHANDLER

In his introduction to Francis James Grimke's published sermons, Carter Woodson explained that the minister's birth was determined by the peculiar relations between master and slave in the South. Nancy Weston Grimke was compelled by master Henry Grimke to serve him as wife and to bear three sons: Archibald Henry, Francis James, and John. Henry Grimke was descended from a prominent South Carolina family, from which also came the white aunts Angelina and Sarah, abolitionists who had freed their slaves and moved north, where they actively campaigned for the antislavery movement.

Francis Grimke was born in Charleston, South Carolina, on November 4, 1850. His father, who died when Francis was five years old, stipulated in his will that the boy should be freed, but he also placed Francis under the guardianship of Henry's eldest son, E. Montague Grimke. Although Francis's half-brother fulfilled this responsibility for five years, he attempted to reenslave ten-year-old Francis. The boy attempted to avoid this scheme by joining the Confederate army and serving as valet to an officer for two years, but Montague arranged for Francis's imprisonment in the Charleston workhouse when Francis returned to the city with his regiment. Becoming dangerously ill, he might have died; however, he was rescued and taken to his mother's home, where he was nursed and restored to health. Before he had recovered completely, Montague sold him to another Confederate officer, and there Francis worked until the Civil War ended.

Through the intervention of a woman who administered the Morris Street School in Charleston, Francis and his brother Archibald were sent north to receive an education. Intending to pursue a career in medicine, Francis resided temporarily with Dr. John Brown's family in Stoneham, Massachusetts, where he slept in the hayloft of a barn. Mr. and Mrs. Lyman Duke took him into their shoe factory, where he started learning that trade. However, the school administrator who had sent the Grimke brothers north advised Francis to move to Chester County, Pennsylvania, where preparations were made for continuing his education at Lincoln University. In 1870, Francis graduated as valedictorian from the college department of Lincoln, and the following year he began to study law. In 1872, he worked as the financial agent of the university, resuming his legal education the following year. Francis then moved to Washington, where he continued his legal training at Howard University. However, growing increasingly interested in theology and intending to enter the ministry, he enrolled at Princeton Theological Seminary in 1875 and graduated in 1878.

From Princeton, Francis was called to serve the Fifteenth Street Presbyterian Church in Washington, D.C. Soon after commencing his ministerial career, Grimke married Charlotte Forten, granddaughter of Philadelphia businessman James Forten, who had assisted in organizing the African-American freedom movement during the early nineteenth century. Grimke served the Fifteenth Street Church for seven years, until in 1885 he moved to the Laura Street Church in Jacksonville, Florida. He was recalled to the Washington church in 1889, however, and remained there as pastor until his death in 1937.

Throughout his life, Grimke conducted a prominent public ministry. He regularly contributed articles to the *New York Independent* and the *New York Evangelist*. He served as a trustee of Howard University and the public schools of the District of Columbia and as chairman of the committee on morals and religion of the Hampton Negro Conference. For several summers, he preached at the Hampton Conference and preached and lectured at Tuskegee Institute in Alabama. In 1891, he was offered a professorship in Christian evidences and in mental and moral philosophy at Biddle University in Charlotte, North Carolina, but he chose to remain in the ministry. Later, he was offered the presidency of Howard University, but similarly declined, insisting that he was a minister rather than an administrator.

Grimke was a distinguished minister serving the people in the nation's capital and was especially effective in reaching an educated audience with a socially relevant discussion of the crucial issues of the day. Although Grimke was never an agitative preacher, he was drawn inevitably into the battles for human rights because he was pledged to champion human dignity by preaching the Christian gospel. Woodson noted that Grimke "alienated the genuflecting, compromising, and hypocritical leaders within both races" because he remained an "uncompromising and unyielding agent of righteousness and truth." Grimke worked to abolish lynching, establish equal educational opportunities, improve the resources of health and recreation, encourage the exercise of suffrage, increase whites' appreciation for blacks' contributions to culture, and improve race relations.

Francis Grimke commenced a gradual but prolonged prelude to retirement when he reached his seventieth birthday. He resigned from the board of Howard University and submitted his resignation to the session and members of the

Fifteenth Street Church on May 13, 1923. The church refused to accept his letter, however. Insisting that Grimke maintain his pastoral office, the congregation called an associate pastor who assumed the administrative responsibilities. Although Grimke's uncompromising disposition and physical presence made this relationship problematic, this dual arrangement continued until his death on October 11, 1937.

FRANCIS GRIMKE: PREACHING RACIAL JUSTICE

Grimke's published sermons reveal the preacher's principal preoccupation with racial issues and reflect his concern for securing racial justice and the betterment of the African-American community. Sermons contained in *The Works of Francis James Grimke* suggest that his congregation-centered speaking directly addressed the serious, sustained issues that confronted his audiences. Using specific events and biographies as his topics, Grimke believed that effective preaching not only responds to and reflects the times but provides a force for influencing those times.

Grimke delivered powerful sermons and scholarly lectures to his Washington congregation and addressed many college audiences about marriage, divorce, parental responsibilities, and creative living. The first volume of Grimke's *Works* contains twenty speeches and sermons that examine the lives of specific individuals, five that analyze racial problems, a three-part series discussing lynching, and twenty-two addresses that probe issues of race, evangelism, post–World War I America, and African-American social organizations. The second volume contains thirteen sermons and addresses about marriage, twelve that discuss the training of children, twelve based on Christ's parable of the prodigal son, eleven that examine specific social concerns, and four that describe a "worthy woman." Eventually Grimke refused to speak at those schools that emphasized practical training for African-Americans rather than the liberal education that Grimke strongly supported. He denounced the industrial education that some advocates presented as the *summum bonum* suited especially to African-American students.

Preaching during the transitional era from the end of Reconstruction through America's post–World War I ascendancy, Grimke saw African-Americans reach their lowest social position and economic level since emancipation. Responding directly to this situation, he became an architect of social protest and reform and emerged within an enduring tradition of ministers who encouraged African-Americans' struggles toward the complete realization of their constitutional guarantees. Sometimes serving as an unpopular and controversial prophet, Grimke condemned racial prejudice with a historic biblical faith and a resolute social conscience. As Woodson summarized:

He knew no compromise and did not listen to any excuses offered by so-called Christians who were too weak to stand up for the principles of the fatherhood of

God and the brotherhood of man. Very often he had to stand by himself, for there
were not a few Negro ministers who, in order to enjoy the profits of segregation,
sealed their lips on the matter of the unfair treatment of the Christian Church.

With considerable courage and immeasurable integrity, Grimke discussed
African-American progress, Christianity, and racial prejudice.

As a pastor serving a relatively wealthy, well-educated Washington congregation, Grimke observed the federal legislators who planned to reduce African-
Americans to their pre-Civil War status. When he criticized religious
denominations in which constitutional rights of African-Americans were compromised, he discovered himself excluded from many prominent pulpits from
which he had previously preached. Grimke protested when the ministerial meetings involving African-American and white clergy became segregated. The
Washington minister was deeply disturbed when some denominations that had
advocated abolition and supported freed persons withdrew into silence and submission. In a sermon titled "Christianity and Race Prejudice," preached on June
5, 1910, Grimke noted that racism remained rampant, that prejudice paralyzed
some Southern churches, and that many Northern congregations were infested
with intolerance toward blacks. "Everywhere this hydra-headed monster has not
only intruded itself," he declared, "but is in control." He continued:

> Why should there be churches made up of white Christians, and churches made
> up of colored Christians in the same community . . . if they are all Christians, if
> they all believe in the Fatherhood of God, and the brotherhood of man, in doing
> by others as they would be done by, in loving each other as they love themselves,
> in their oneness in Christ Jesus, and if the same Holy Spirit dwells alike in their
> hearts?

Churches that transgressed the Christian principles of love and community were
criticized as "so-called Christian churches" and the congregations censured as
"so-called Christians." Emphatically, the provocative preacher refused to identify genuine Christianity with the prejudice and discrimination that infested some
congregations. Grimke claimed that genuine Christianity is not powerless before
prejudice and argued that white congregations could abolish racism simply by
applying Christian principles. Challenging the white clergy and the congregations, he declared that these teachings should be preached from the pulpits and
extended throughout the community.

Simultaneously, Grimke admonished African-American clergy that character
was essential in elevating African-Americans, and that social progress within
the community required that they develop Christian morality. In his 1892 sermon
"The Afro-American Pulpit in Relation to Race Elevation," Grimke emphasized
that ministers should serve as moral examples: "[The minister's] duty is to
rebuke wrong, and to keep steadily before his hearers the right. His work,
mainly, is character-building; to give the right direction to the budding and

expanding life about him—in a word, to develop and strengthen Christian character.'' Grimke maintained that the ultimate achievement of racial justice required that a moral foundation undergird African-Americans' material and intellectual progress. Christian character was more important to African-Americans than anything else, he argued, and was essential in making the race morally strong. Grimke condemned three undesirable characteristics found among African-American clergy that prevented them from fulfilling their ministry as moral teachers: appeals to pathos, inappropriate use of humor, and too great a concern for the financial contributions made by congregations. Grimke insisted that a ministry ''whose chief characteristics are emotionalism, frivolity and greed for money is not a ministry to inspire hope, and is not a source of strength but of weakness. . . . [T]he Afro-American pulpit today . . . is frittering away its energies . . . to the neglect of those things which are fundamental, and without which we cannot hope for permanent prosperity.'' Using sermonic discourse, Grimke condemned the practices he thought undermined the pulpit as a source of power for improving the condition of the African-American.

Events and occasions often guided Grimke's preaching. Within specific circumstances or conditions, the audible ''word'' of God was as much a historic happening as a sentence gleaned from the sacred Scripture. The secular revealed the spirit's movements as unmistakably as any sacred source. In ''The Atlanta Riot,'' a sermon preached on October 7, 1906, Grimke noted that four or five assaults were apparently against white women by African-American men, but he indicted the white community's condemnation of and reprisals against the entire black population:

> The Negroes of Atlanta, as a class, had no more responsibility for those assaults than the whites as a class had. The fact that the assailants were black, furnished no justification or excuse, for assailing the other members of the race who had nothing to do with them, and no knowledge of them. It is only a subterfuge, a lying device, behind which to hide their hatred of all Negroes. According to their own statement, the probabilities are that of all those who were brutally murdered, not one guilty person suffered.

The Southern lynching of African-Americans provided another secular situation that commanded the attention of Grimke's Christianity in a series of sermons delivered on June 4, June 18, and June 25 in 1899. In the initial sermon, he cited two contributing factors in explaining the frequent outbreaks of Southern lawlessness: a low state of civilization and race hatred:

> The Southern white man believes that the Negro has a place,—not a place which he may carve out for himself by dint of perseverance and hard work, by the development of intellectual, moral, and financial strength, just as in the case of any other race; but a place in spite of whatever qualities he may develop, however praiseworthy, or whatever his achievements might be, in which he must be kept;

and that is a position of inferiority. As long as the Negro is willing to occupy that
position the Southern white man is ready to befriend him, and to go to any length
in showing his friendship for him; in other words, it is the old time Negro that
the Southern white man loves, the Negro of the ante-bellum days, the Negro that
stands with hat in hand, and that knows his place.

Sermons preached for the purpose of encouraging Christian compassion and
charity in whites risked provoking bitterness and resentment, but Grimke was
careful in the particular blame he assigned. In the sermon analyzing the Atlanta
riot, the preacher did not blame whites for protecting their women or feeling
indignant. Grimke acknowledged that these "unspeakable infamous" assaults
"cannot be too severely condemned." However, he chastised white men because
their concern was only for protecting white women, because white men took
the law into their own hands, and because they did not discriminate between
those who had committed the assaults and those who were innocent.

Throughout his sermons and speeches, Scripture was a rich resource for seeking black enfranchisement, securing African-American liberation, and promoting
racial justice. Employing Scripture to define and justify the principle of justice,
Grimke called prejudice an adverse feeling that indicated antipathy and evidenced a lack of charity by assuming that one race is superior to another. On
October 12, 1902, in a sermon entitled "A Resemblance and a Contrast between
the American Negro and the Children of Israel in Egypt," Grimke noted that
while the Hebrews' enslavement was in some ways different, it was similar to
that of the African-American in some significant respects. Perhaps most important, he argued, the Hebrews' subjugation "was due also to a sense of race
superiority, and the assumption that if they [the Egyptians] were in any way
civil, if they treated the Jews with the common courtesies that one human being
owes to another, it might create within them a desire for social equality." Continuing his thinly veiled analogy, Grimke asserted that "the fact remains that
the policy inaugurated by them was an utterly heartless and brutal one . . . until
God's righteous indignation was excited, and the angel of death was sent forth
and smote the first-born throughout the land, and overthrew the tyrants in the
Red Sea." He then warned: "It is only a matter of time when all such oppressors
the world over, will meet a similar fate."

The seventy-fifth anniversary of the Fifteenth Street Presbyterian Church provided the preacher an auspicious opportunity for surveying the past and anticipating the future. In an address delivered on November 19, 1916, he stated that
through these passing decades the church had championed a pure unadulterated
Gospel, promoted temperance, sanctioned the sanctity of the Sabbath, protested
sexual immorality, sent missionaries to the heathen, insisted upon the intelligent
preaching of the Gospel, practiced the orderly worship of God, and remained a
race-loving church where people squarely and uncompromisingly sought their
human rights as American citizens. Turning from the past to the future, Grimke
summarized his philosophy of the demands and rewards of Christian living:

It is a great thing to be a member of a Christian church! It is a greater thing to be a worthy member of it—to be in it in such a way as to make others think more highly of religion—in such a way that when we are gone the sweet influence of our character and lives will remain to cheer and comfort and bless those who remain.

Throughout his sermons and speeches, Francis Grimke forthrightly promoted his Christian faith. His speeches were not, however, otherworldly theological; they were in and of the community in which he preached. To black and white alike he illuminated the shortcomings of their Christianity and pointed out the path by which we might achieve that "sweet influence of our character." His was always a call to conscience, timely in its observations but timeless in its message of justice, community, and Christian love.

INFORMATION SOURCES

Research Collections and Collected Speeches

Grimke donated his library to Howard University, where this contribution was designated as the Dr. Grimke Collection. Subsequently, other books were given to Lincoln University.

[W] Woodson, Carter G., ed. *The Works of Francis J. Grimke*. 4 vols. Washington, DC: Associated Publishers, 1942.

Selected Critical Studies

Handy, Robert T. "Negro Christianity and American Church Historiography." *Reinterpretation in American Church History*. Ed. Jerald C. Brauer. Chicago: U of Chicago P, 1968, 91–112.
Kerr, Hugh T. *The Sons of the Prophets*. Princeton, NJ: Princeton UP, 1963.
Luker, Ralph E. *The Social Gospel in Black and White: American Racial Reform. 1885–1912*. Chapel Hill: U of North Carolina P, 1991.

Selected Biographies

Ferry, Henry Justin. "Francis James Grimke: Portrait of a Black Puritan." Ph.D. diss., Yale, 1970.
Weeks, Louis B., III. "Racism, World War I, and the Christian Life: Francis J. Grimke in the Nation's Capitol." *Black Apostles: Afro-American Clergy Confront the Twentieth Century*. Ed. Randall K. Burkett and Richard Newman. Boston: G. K. Hall, 1978, 57–75.
Woodson, Carter G. "Introduction." *The Works of Francis James Grimke*. Washington, DC: Associated Publishers, 1942, 1:vii–xxii.

CHRONOLOGY OF MAJOR SPEECHES

[See "Research Collections and Collected Speeches" for source codes.]

"The Afro-American Pulpit in Relation to Race Elevation." Washington, DC, 1892. *W*, 1:223–234.

"Some Things That Lie across the Pathway of Our Progress." Hampton, VA, July 1897. *W*, 2:550–566.

"The Negro, His Rights and Wrongs, and the Forces for Him and against Him." Washington, DC, November 20, November 27, and December 4, 1898. Washington, DC: n.p., 1898.

"The Lynching of Negroes in the South: Its Causes and Remedy." Washington, DC, June 4, June 18, June 25, 1899. *W*, 1:291–333.

"The Roosevelt-Washington Episode, or Race Prejudice." Washington, DC, October 27, 1901. *W*, 1:334–347.

"A Resemblance and a Contrast between the American Negro and the Children of Israel in Egypt." Washington, DC, October 12, 1902. *W*, 1:347–364.

"The Things of Paramount Importance in the Development of the Negro Race." Washington, DC, March 29, 1903. *W*, 1:378–391.

"God and the Race Problem." Washington, DC, May 3, 1903. *W*, 1:364–378.

"Religion and Race Elevation." New Haven, CT, February 11, 1906. *W*, 3:566–588.

"The Atlanta Riot." Washington, DC, October 7, 1906. *W*, 1:406–418.

"The Progress and Development of the Colored People of Our Nation." Galesburg, IL, October 21, 1908. Washington, DC: n.p., 1909.

"Christianity and Race Prejudice." Washington, DC, May 29 and June 5, 1910. *W*, 1: 442–473.

"An Anniversary Address on the Occasion of the Seventy-Fifth Anniversary of the Fifteenth Street Presbyterian Church, Washington, D.C., 1841–1916." Washington, DC, November 19, 1916. *W*, 1:531–554.

"Theodore Roosevelt." Washington, DC, February 9, 1919. *W*, 1:174–189.

"The Religious Aspect of Reconstruction." Washington, DC, February 19, 1919. Washington, DC: n.p., 1919.

"A Phase of the Race Problem Looked at from within the Race Itself." Washington, DC, March 6, 1921. Washington, DC: n.p., 1921.

"The Brotherhood of Man, the Christian Church, and the Race Problem in the United States of America." Washington, DC, March 20, 1921. Washington, DC: n.p., 1921.

"The National Association for the Advancement of Colored People: Its Value, Its Aims, Its Claims." Washington, DC, April 24, 1921. *W*, 1:618–627.

"A Message to the Race." Washington, DC, March 1, 1925. Washington, DC: n.p., 1925.

FRANCES ELLEN WATKINS HARPER
(1825–1911), poet, author,
abolitionist, lecturer, reform leader

RICHARD W. LEEMAN

Called an "orator poet" in *Early Black American Poets* by literary critic William Robinson, Frances Ellen Watkins Harper was also thought of as a poetic orator. Best known today for her poetry, during her lifetime Harper was also a highly respected, widely traveled platform speaker of middle and late nineteenth-century America. Displaying an equal ability to woo her audiences or challenge them, Harper lectured on behalf of abolition, civil rights, women's rights, temperance, and "self-improvement." In his 1872 book *The Underground Rail Road*, William Still called her "one of the ablest advocates of the Underground Rail Road and of the slave." William Nell, writing in the *Liberator*, called her "eloquent."

Only a general outline of Frances Watkins Harper's life is known, but it is an outline diverse in experiences and rich in accomplishments. Born a free black in Baltimore in 1825, Frances Watkins was orphaned at the age of three. She was raised by her aunt and uncle, William Watkins, who ran the William Watkins Academy for Negro Youth. She was enrolled in her uncle's school, studying the Bible, the classics, and elocution until the age of thirteen. Then going to work as a live-in domestic, Frances was given free run of the family library by her employers. In this way both formally schooled and self-taught, in 1846, at the age of twenty-one, she published her first book of poetry, *Forest Leaves*. With the passage of the Fugitive Slave Act of 1850, Watkins left Maryland to move north. In the early 1850s, she was employed as a teacher, but continued to write and publish her poetry, including *Poems on Miscellaneous Subjects* (1854) and *Poems* (1857).

In 1854, she left teaching in order to work for the abolition of slavery. By August of that year she was lecturing for the Maine Anti-Slavery Society, touring New England to speak on behalf of abolition. As a well-known poet, essayist, and lecturer she raised money for and donated liberally from her own earnings to support the Underground Railroad. After leaving the Maine Anti-Slavery Society in 1857, she was retained by the Pennsylvania Anti-Slavery Society to speak to audiences in the Great Lakes states. Of frail health and considering retirement from the lecture circuit, in 1860 she became engaged to and married Fenton Harper. The couple settled on a farm near Columbus, Ohio, purchased partially from money earned by Frances as a lecturer and poet. Four years later, Fenton Harper died. Frances sold the farm to pay off outstanding debts and moved to New England with her daughter, Mary. There she resumed lecturing.

With the battle for abolition a cause of the past, Harper's lectures turned primarily to Reconstruction. Touring the South as well as the North, she spoke on behalf of "moral law," such as the importance of marriage, industry, thrift, and temperance, as well as "political law," such as universal suffrage for blacks and women and equality under the law. She was a member of many organizations, including the Congress of Colored Women in the United States, the National Council of Negro Women, the National Council of Women, the American Equal Rights Association, and the Woman's Christian Temperance Union. As a member of the executive board for many of these organizations, she was a prominent speaker at their conventions. As a poet (*Sketches of Southern Life*, 1872; *Moses: A Story of the Nile*, 1889; *The Sparrow's Fall and Other Poems*, 1894; *Atlanta Offering: Poems*, 1895), novelist (*Iola Leroy; or, Shadows Uplifted*, 1892), and speaker, Harper worked for the improvement of America throughout the last decades of the nineteenth century. In 1901, she retired from public life, quietly living out her remaining years until her death in 1911 at the age of eighty-five.

FRANCES HARPER AS POETIC ORATOR

With her national reputation as a poet, Harper was commonly viewed as a poetic orator. However, the defining characteristic of Frances Harper's oratory is its mastery of diverse substance and styles. While her language was always polished, her speeches were at some times poetic and at other times prosaic. Her appeals could be romantically reassuring or radically challenging. She echoed many of the themes voiced by other African-American orators, but developed other themes less frequently heard from nineteenth-century African-Americans as well. She was a poetic orator not because she utilized a single, lyrical style, but because, like a good orator, she could artfully adapt her style to her purpose and audience.

Harper began her speaking career by addressing the two most common themes of antebellum African-American oratory: slavery and prejudice. "The Colored People in America" and "Could We Trace the Record of Every Human Heart" provide representative examples of her oratory in this period as they utilize

Harper's poetic skill. Both were speeches designed to reinforce the beliefs of and move to action audiences who were already in fundamental agreement with the abolition movement. A poetic language, polished and elegant, was not only a natural style for Harper to use, it was also appropriate to her purpose.

In "The Colored People in America," a standard abolition lecture of Harper's probably delivered several times around the year 1857, Harper advanced two of the standard arguments against prejudice. First, she argued that if African-Americans were not as "advanced" as white Americans, it was because of the conditions under which they had suffered. Slavery and prejudice kept blacks uneducated and poor. Second, Harper argued that despite such a punishing environment, the African-American race had still exhibited cultural and intellectual successes. African-American children were attending private and public schools, African-Americans owned and operated newspapers, and there had developed a national African-American church. Implicitly, the prejudice of white America had ignored the explanation presented in the first argument and undervalued the meaning of the successes described in the second.

"Could We Trace the Record of Every Human Heart," delivered in 1857 at the fourth-anniversary meeting of the New York City Anti-Slavery Society, attacked slavery by focusing on the evils of the institution. Harper began by noting that every human heart aspires to freedom: "The law of liberty is the law of God, and is antecedent to all human legislation." Through description, Harper then indicted the selfishness and greed of the slave states as they deprived African-Americans of this God-granted gift. There, "instead of listening to the cry of agony, they listen to the ring of dollars and stoop down to pick up the coin." Having condemned the Southern states, Harper moved her attention northward to berate the "free states" for their role in sustaining the institution of slavery. "When you [the Southerner] fail to catch the flying fugitive [slave], ... the ready North is base enough to do your shameful service." She concluded her speech by calling on the audience's shared belief in Christian doctrine. "The message of Jesus Christ," she said, "is the message of freedom."

Harper's arguments in these speeches consisted primarily of standard abolitionist fare, whether delivered by whites or blacks. What distinguished these early speeches was the poetic language. Such poetic style not only lent grace and charm to her speeches, it also made them very visual. Harper's metaphors, for example, invited her audience to "see" the effects of slavery and prejudice. Slavery "dwarfs the intellect" and was a "fearful alchemy by which this blood [of slaves] can be transformed into gold." Synecdoche, the substitution of a symbolic part for the larger argument, was a poetic tool frequently used by Harper. In the passage just quoted, "blood" and "gold" substituted synecdochically and poetically for "labor and pain" and "wealth." Similarly, Northern prejudice condemned free blacks to menial labor, that is, to be "hewers of wood and drawers of water." Taken together, Harper's visual metaphors and rhythmic meter painted a compelling portrait of the African-American's lot:

> Born to an inheritance of misery, nurtured in degradation, and cradled in oppres-
> sion, with the scorn of the white man upon their souls, his fetters upon their limbs,
> his scourge upon their flesh, what can be expected from their offspring, but a
> mournful reaction of that cursed system which spreads its baneful influence over
> body and soul?

Where Harper's poetry of this period was frequently rhetorical, her early oratory
was conversely poetic.

Harper's lyrical language did more than simply add style to her speeches,
however. First, poetic devices provided subtextual commentary within her economy of language. For example, Harper's "fearful alchemy" suggested evil sor-
cery as well as pecuniary interest at work within the slave trade. Second, Harper
used poetic language to provide unique points of view by which to challenge
the audience's perspective. In her poem "The Slave Mother," she used a second-person perspective to place the audience at the scene of a slave auction:
"Heard you that shriek? It rose / So wildly on the air. . . . Saw you those hands
so sadly clasped—/ The bowed and feeble head?" Harper's speeches used point
of view for similar purposes. In "Could We Trace the Record of Every Human
Heart," for example, she personified the slave states in order to engage them
in dialogue:

> Ask Virginia, with her hundreds of thousands of slaves, if she is not weary with
> her merchandise of blood and anxious to shake the gory traffic from her hands,
> and hear her reply: "Though fertility has covered my soil, though a genial sky
> bends over my hills and vales, though I hold in my hand a wealth of water-power
> enough to turn the spindles to clothe the world, yet, with all these advantages, one
> of my chief staples has been the sons and daughters I send to the human market
> and human shambles."

Third, poetic language served the purpose of enactment in Harper's oratory. As
she made claims for African-Americans' cultural and intellectual advancements
despite all odds, the grace and elegance of her language implicitly served as an
exemplar of what Harper's race could achieve if given the opportunity. More
than simple adornment, Harper's poetic oratory was style in the service of substance.

Harper's postwar speeches can be divided into two general categories: her
self-improvement speeches and her addresses before major women's conventions. The first type represented a continuation of her earlier platform lecturing.
Her language was poetic, her themes were traditional reform messages, and her
purposes were primarily motivational. The second type of postwar speaking
represented a departure from this more traditional, nineteenth-century style. In
these speeches she urged predominantly white audiences to extend their defense
of women's rights to include full civil rights for blacks. Here her language turned
prosaic, her arguments challenged her audiences, and her purpose was to con-

vince and persuade. During this postbellum era, Frances Harper matured as an orator, demonstrating a skillful mastery of diverse rhetorical styles.

Few of Frances Harper's everyday lectures were written down or survive to the present day. Of those that have, "Enlightened Motherhood," delivered in 1892 to the Brooklyn Literary Society meeting in New York City, probably best represents Harper's series of moral-law lectures. Most of her postwar speaking— for example, her 1866–67 Southern speaking tour during which she sometimes spoke twice a day—consisted of such lectures, which promoted temperance, education, thrift, industry, and general self-improvement. These were themes often heard from late nineteenth-century reformers, and they solidly place Harper's work within the tradition of American reform.

"Enlightened Motherhood" was a lecture that encouraged mothers to teach their sons temperance and sexual purity. She grounded her speech in the nineteenth-century American doctrine of the spheres, that is, that men and women each had unique "spheres" of interest and influence. There was a romantic perspective to this doctrine, and "Enlightened Motherhood" echoed that tone. Being a wife and a mother, Harper argued, is the greatest possible achievement: "You may place upon the brow of a true wife and mother the greenest laurels; you may crowd her hands with civic honors; but, after all, to her there will be no place like home, and the crown of her motherhood will be more precious than the diadem of a queen." Indeed, so natural was the role of motherhood to a woman that "the moment the crown of motherhood falls on the brow of a young wife, God gives her a new interest in the welfare of the home and the good of society."

However, while men and women had different, traditional spheres of interest, Harper argued for a single standard of behavior for their sexual mores, a position known euphemistically as "social purity." "I hold," she argued, "that no woman loves social purity as it deserves to be loved and valued, if she cares for the purity of her daughters and not her sons." The attitude "O, well, boys will be boys, and young men will sow their wild oats" was rejected out of hand.

For Harper, as for most nineteenth-century reformers, virtue was not literally its own reward. Social purity and temperance were important lessons for mothers to teach because vice led to poverty, illness, and death, while virtue led to health, wealth, and success. "Enlightened Motherhood" was full of stories about "young men awaiting death as physical wrecks," Annie and Minnie, who inherited "thin, pinched faces, with vulgar mouths . . . and skin, so wrinkled and yellowed" from their alcoholic father, and a binge drinker whose "wife was telegraphed from an obscure neighboring village, where she found him dying of *mania a potu*." Vice, whether sexual or alcoholic, was a disease, and as such it was a mother's responsibility to warn her son away from those dangers that lay beyond the safe confines of the home.

Virtue, in contrast, led to success. The foundation for virtue was laid through right living by the parents and right instruction in the home by the mother.

Harper's romantic tone was clearly displayed in her examples of virtue's success:

> But we turn from these sad pictures to brighter pages in the great books of human life. To Benjamin West saying: "My mother's kiss made me a painter." To John Randolph saying: "I should have been an atheist, if it had not been for one recollection, and that was the memory of the time when my departed mother used to take my little hands in hers and sank me on my knees to say: 'Our Father, who art in heaven.'"

If you would have "strong men, virtuous women, and good homes," argued Harper, "then enlighten your women, so that they may be able to bless their homes by the purity of their lives, the tenderness of their hearts, and the strength of their intellects."

If it suited her purpose, however, Frances Harper could just as quickly abandon the lyrical style as employ it. Where lectures like "Enlightened Motherhood" were traditional, romantic, and poetic, Harper's convention addresses were challenging, pragmatic, and prosaic. Two speeches, "Coloured Women of America" and "Duty to Dependent Races," provide complementary examples of Harper's prosaic style. Significantly, both were speeches delivered at national conventions of women's organizations rather than to general lecture-going audiences. Both speeches challenged white women who were interested in women's rights to extend their logic of equal rights to the African-American population. In each case, Harper recognized that prosaic argumentation, rather than poetic motivation, was the more appropriate style.

While similar in theme, each speech was developed differently. "Coloured Women of America," delivered in 1877 to the Women's Congress, created an argument for equal rights anecdotally and statistically. In story after story, Harper detailed the accomplishments of African-American women. Mrs. Montgomery managed a cotton farm of 130 acres; Mrs. Brown and Mrs. Halsey "formed a partnership . . . leased nine acres and a horse, . . . and are living independently." Mrs. Henry, an invalid, had still managed to make "600 bushels of sweet potatoes, . . . has 100 hogs, thirty dozen chickens, a small lot of ducks and turkeys, and also a few sheep and goats." Such accomplishments were not restricted to agricultural successes, however. As Harper noted in the second half of her speech, "In higher walks of life too, the coloured women have made progress." She noted that the principal of the Coloured High School in Philadelphia was an ex-slave, that "nearly all the coloured teachers in Washington are girls and women," and that two women were studying law at Howard University while two others were studying at the Woman's Medical College of Pennsylvania. Harper's style was direct, simple, and to the point, that "women as a class are quite equal to the men in energy and executive ability."

While "Coloured Women of America" was prosaic in its anecdotes and use of statistics, "Duty to Dependent Races" employed a nonpoetic style in its development of reasoning and argument. In this later speech, delivered in 1891 to the National Council of Women convention meeting in Washington, D.C., Harper began by laying a ''claim'' upon the United States of America on behalf of African-Americans: ''Our first claim upon the nation and government,'' she said, ''is the claim for protection to human life.'' Grounding this claim on the ''basis of our civilization,'' Harper proceeded to put her white audience on the horns of a dilemma: ''A government which can protect and defend its citizens from wrong and outrage and does not is vicious. A government which would do it and cannot is weak.'' In this fashion, she developed a rationale against lynching and for renewed federal intervention in the Southern states.

Harper next constructed a rebuttal to Southern arguments that African-Americans were poor and ignorant and thus, if truly allowed to exercise their right to vote, would be a dangerous force. Harper began her refutation by noting that African-Americans had not yet proved such a danger, and she asked, ''Does any civilized country legislate to punish a man before he commits a crime?'' Tartly rebuffing Southern arguments, she noted that ''it comes with ill grace from a man who has put out my eyes to make a parade of my blindness.'' More importantly, she went on, ''there are some rights more precious than the rights of property and claims of superior intelligence: they are the rights of life and liberty, and to these the poorest and humblest man has just as much right as the richest and most influential man in the country. Ignorance and poverty are conditions which men outgrow.'' Harper then described a few of the accomplishments of African-Americans, but she particularly detailed their contributions in times of war: in the American Revolution, the War of 1812, and, of course, the Civil War. Such demonstrations of patriotism, Harper argued, entitled African-Americans to ''share citizenship with others in the country.'' Finally, she challenged white Americans: ''Instead of taking the ballot from his [the African-American's] hands, teach him how to use it, and to add his quota to the progress, strength, and durability of the nation.''

In her final line of prosaic reasoning, Harper laid claim upon the nation's professed Christianity, arguing that ''Jesus Christ has given us a platform of love and duty from which all oppression and selfishness is necessarily excluded.'' Touching a theme common to African-American oratory, Harper concluded her speech: ''When His religion fully permeates our civilization, and moulds our national life, the drink traffic will be abolished, the Indian question answered, and the negro problem solved.''

While her platform lectures combined a poetic style with a romantic tone, Harper's convention addresses had a more pragmatic tenor. For example, where ''Enlightened Motherhood'' presented a romantic vision of women, ''We Are All Bound Up Together,'' delivered in 1866 at the Eleventh Women's Rights Convention, was more realistic: ''I do not believe that giving the woman the ballot is immediately going to cure all the ills of life. I do not believe that white women are dew drops just exhaled from the skies. I think that like men they may be divided into three classes, the good, the bad, and the indifferent.'' She explicitly contrasted her audience and herself: "You white women speak here of rights. I speak of wrongs." In her concluding sentences, Harper summarized her unique argument on behalf of women's suffrage, one very different from the usual defense of suffrage:

> Talk of giving the white women the ballot-box? It is a normal school, and the white women of this country need it. While there exists this brutal element in society which tramples upon the feeble and treads down the weak, I tell you that if there is any class of people who need to be lifted out of their airy nothings and selfishness, it is the white women of America.

Through poetic oratory, Frances Harper had gently challenged abolitionists to free themselves from their prejudice and realize the moral hypocrisy of honoring the Constitution above the Bible. Changing to a more prosaic style, her postwar speeches to women's rights groups lost the earlier gentleness, chiding the women to extend the logic of gender equality to racial equality.

Historians and literary critics have provided only passing commentary regarding Frances Harper's oratory. Most scholars comment on Harper's advocacy of change. Maxwell Whiteman noted that Harper's work contained seeds of the concept "black power," while Paula Giddings in *When and Where I Enter* classified Harper as an early feminist. Maryemma Graham argued that through both her poetry and oratory, Harper provided a "profound challenge to American democracy."

While these scholars are correct, only Frances Smith Foster has touched upon the diversity that marked Harper's oratory:

> As a writer and lecturer, [Harper] was a complex and confounding figure. Her language was "chaste," her literature was "moral," and contemporary reporters rarely failed to note her "slender and graceful" form and her "soft musical voice." Watkins was by all accounts very ladylike in her public appearances. However, on the podium, as William Wells Brown says, "Her arguments are forcible, her appeals pathetic [full of emotion], her logic fervent, her imagination fervid, and her delivery original and easy."

In one regard, it was this ability to adapt her oratory to her purpose that made Frances Harper a distinguished African-American orator. However, beyond her skillful ability to forge a variety of oratorical styles for her wide-ranging purposes, what also distinguished Frances Harper's oratory was the seriousness of those purposes. She spoke to the issues that concerned African-Americans most immediately—slavery, prejudice, and civil rights—but she also addressed problems that confronted black and white Americans generally—education, temperance, women's suffrage, and gender equality. In both areas, her oratory strove to better the society in which she found herself, and she fashioned that oratory with a grace and elegance that definitively marked it as her own.

INFORMATION SOURCES

Research Collections and Collected Speeches

No speech manuscripts are known to still exist, but related archival materials may be found in the Frances E. Watkins Harper Collection at the Schomburg Center for Research in Black Culture, New York Public Library.

[*BCD*] Foster, Frances Smith, ed. *A Brighter Coming Day: A Frances Ellen Watkins Harper Reader.* New York: Feminist Press at the City University of New York, 1990.

Selected Critical Studies

Boyd, Melba Joyce. *Discarded Legacy.* Detroit: Wayne State UP, 1994.
Foster, Frances Smith, ed. *A Brighter Coming Day: A Frances Ellen Watkins Reader.* New York: Feminist Press at the City University of New York, 1990.
Graham, Maryemma, ed. *Complete Poems of Frances E. W. Harper.* New York: Oxford UP, 1988.
Still, William. *The Underground Rail Road.* Philadelphia: Porter and Coates, 1872. Reprint. New York: Arno, 1968.
Whiteman, Maxwell. "Introduction." Frances Ellen Watkins Harper, *Poems on Miscellaneous Subjects.* Philadelphia: Rhistoric, 1969.

CHRONOLOGY OF MAJOR SPEECHES

[See "Research Collections and Collected Speeches" for source code.]

"The Colored People in America" (Elevation and Education of Our People). 1857. *BCD*, 99–100.
" 'Speech of Miss Watkins' at the Fourth Anniversary of the New York City Anti-Slavery Society" (Could We Trace the Record of Every Human Heart). New York, NY, May 13, 1857. *BCD*, 101–102 (abridged); *National Anti-Slavery Standard*, May 23, 1857:3 (abridged).
"Speech to the Eleventh Woman's Rights Convention" (We Are All Bound Up Together). May 1866. *BCD*, 217–219.
"Speech to the Centennial Anniversary of the Pennsylvania Society for Promoting the Abolition of Slavery" (The Great Problem to Be Solved). Philadelphia, PA, April 14, 1875. *BCD*, 219–222; *Centennial Anniversary of the Pennsylvania Society for Promoting the Abolition of Slavery.* Philadelphia: Grant, Faires and Rodgers, 1876, 29–32.
"Speech to the Women's Congress" (Coloured Women of America). 1877. *BCD*, 271–275 (abridged); *Englishwoman's Review*, January 15, 1878: 10–15 (abridged).
"Work among the Colored People." Philadelphia, PA, October 30–November 3, 1885. *Minutes of the National Woman's Christian Temperance Union.* Chicago: Woman's Temperance Publishing, 1885, cx–cxiv.
"Work among the Colored People." Atlanta, GA, November 14–18, 1890. *Minutes of*

the National Woman's Christian Temperance Union. Chicago: Woman's Temperance Publishing, 1890, 213–221.

"Duty to Dependent Races." Washington, DC, February 3, 1891. *Transactions of the National Council of Women of the United States.* Ed. Rachel Foster-Avery, Philadelphia: J. B. Lippincott, 1891, 86–91.

"Enlightened Motherhood." Brooklyn, NY, November 15, 1892. *BCD*, 285–292.

"Woman's Political Future" (Speech delivered to the World's Congress of Representative Women). Chicago, IL, May 15–22, 1893. *The World's Congress of Representative Women.* Vol. 1. Ed. May Wright Sewall. Chicago: Rand, McNally, 1894, 433–437.

BENJAMIN LAWSON HOOKS
(1925–   ), lawyer, minister, NAACP director

EDE WARNER, JR., AND BERNARD L. BROCK

Benjamin Hooks moves people when he speaks. He chooses to revel in the rhetorical style of historical African-American oratory as the newer generation of African-American speakers move toward more contemporary styles of oratory. Hooks told Les Payne of *Newsday* magazine on July 11, 1977, "Some intellectuals feel ashamed of the Southern Baptist tradition. . . . To me that is insincere. Blacks have a rich tradition in speaking and singing." When Benjamin Hooks speaks to a crowd, his rhetoric is grounded firmly in the past with an eye toward the future. Many have described his oratory as eloquent, but what makes Hooks special as a rhetorician is his ability to combine his eloquence with pragmatism.

Benjamin Lawson Hooks was born in Memphis, Tennessee, on January 31, 1925, the fifth of seven children of Robert B. Hooks, Sr., and Bessie (White) Hooks. He was raised in a very disciplined home, where the children were taught to strive for perfection in everything they did. Even as a child, Hooks was attracted by professions that required oratorical skills. Following his boyhood hero, Reverend G. A. Long, an outspoken African-American leader in Memphis at the time, Hooks was drawn to the ministry. However, his father, Robert, refused to support a career in organized religion, so Benjamin first chose a legal career instead. Through his choices of the pragmatic career of law and the eloquence of a fiery Baptist minister, Hooks had planted the seeds for the development of an oratory that was eloquently pragmatic.

A brief but significant stint in the service during World War II was sandwiched between studies at LeMoyne College in Memphis, Tennessee, and Howard University in Washington, D.C. One of the many instances of segregation and racism that confronted young Hooks throughout his life occurred during his military experience, when he was not allowed to eat at certain "white-only" restaurants, although the white Italian prisoners he was transporting were served. In 1948, Hooks graduated from DePaul University in Chicago with a J.D. degree, having gone North for his studies because no law school in Tennessee would admit him. Although he had many more career opportunities in the North, Hooks returned to the South on a mission to stop the racial injustice prevalent in that region. Being an African-American practicing law in the South in the 1950s and 1960s was difficult, however. On December 21, 1972, Hooks told *Jet* magazine: "At that time you were insulted by law clerks, excluded from white bar associations and when I was in court, I was lucky to be called 'Ben.' Usually it was just 'boy.' But the judges were always fair."

Hooks was appointed assistant public defender of Shelby County, the Memphis jurisdiction in 1961. Although he failed to win public election for several legislature seats and judgeships that came up over the next five years, in each successive campaign he garnered an increased number of white votes. In 1965, Governor Frank G. Clement appointed Hooks to fill a vacancy for a criminal-court judgeship, making him the first black criminal-court judge in Tennessee, and he subsequently won election to a full term in the position.

At the same time, Hooks began to answer his call to the ministry. Indeed, he claims that it was through the ministry that he overcame his fear of speaking. Preaching regularly at the Middle Baptist Church in Memphis, in 1961 he joined Martin Luther King's Southern Christian Leadership Conference. Working actively in the SCLC, in Memphis he led boycotts and sit-ins in segregated establishments. By 1965, Hooks was serving his judgeship while presiding as minister at Middle Baptist. After a guest sermon at Greater New Mount Moriah Church in Detroit, Michigan, he also took over the pastorship there, alternating weekends between Memphis and Detroit for over a year.

In 1972, Richard Nixon appointed Hooks to the board of the Federal Communications Commission. During this period, he produced and appeared in several local television productions, and many of his speeches addressed issues of minority ownership and employment in broadcast communications and the image of blacks in the mass media.

In November 1976, Hooks was elected executive director of the National Association for the Advancement of Colored People (NAACP). He made it his mission to reinvigorate a civil rights movement that many had taken for dead. Hooks broadened the agenda of the NAACP while strengthening its commitment to traditional issues of voting, civil rights, and integration. He was one of the first to discern the changing face of racism and how its newfound complexity would impose new and flexible strategies on the movements. Hooks retired in 1992 after delivering thousands of speeches and written messages not only aimed at the half a million NAACP members, but intended for the entire American community, black and white.

BENJAMIN L. HOOKS AS THE ELOQUENT PRAGMATIC ORATOR

For most orators, the stylistic components of eloquence and pragmatism work at cross-purposes that prevent a single speaker from mastering both. Cicero, who was remembered not for the content of his speech, but as an eloquent and grand speaker, wrote that language choices and delivery were secondary to the idea. Benjamin Hooks, however, had the ability to transcend and combine these two elements of oratory.

Benjamin Hook's oratorical style was developed in both the pulpit and the courtroom. Influenced by traditional Southern Baptist preachers, he embraced this style with open arms. The great ministers of the day, including Martin Luther King, Jr., were the models from which Hooks molded his style and delivery. Hooks acknowledged in *Time* magazine on November 22, 1976, that at first glance, a style predicated as the ''old country preacher'' might imply to some a lack of sophistication and education, but he dismissed such elitist assumptions. Because he recognized the strength of an appeal grounded in pathos, the emotion that marked his sermons can later be seen in his lay public addresses. Indeed, at first glance, one could easily mistake his soft-spoken, everyday conversation as that of a quiet man whose persuasive appeals are nondemonstrative. However, given a lectern or a pulpit, he becomes a ''fiery orator who delivers his speeches and sermons in a vibrant, ringing tenor voice.''

Hooks's eloquence employs vivid language choices, a lyrical content, and a simple narrative style of address. One stroke of his rhetorical brush and Hooks captures the vision of a younger audience with a powerful use of metaphors, while simultaneously interesting an older audience by relating his message to traditionally popular black musical standards. Both are evident in the introduction of his inaugural address to the 68th NAACP Annual Convention hosted by St. Louis in July 1977:

> The train is running toward freedom. We invite you to get on or off at your pleasure, but for God's sake don't stand on the track unless you want to be run down.
>
> We are singing an old tune but with new lyrics. I'm coming, I'm coming and my head ain't bending low—I'm walking hard, I'm talking loud, I'm America's New Black Joe.

Hooks creates his vision through simple rhetorical techniques, while at the same time choosing examples that have broad appeal for a diverse audience. This vision, combined with a delivery grounded in the rhythmic nature of the black church and the black communities' historical connection to music, provides the foundation for captivating an audience.

The lyrical nature of Hooks's style can especially be found in his use of anaphora and epistrophe, which are the repetition of similar clauses at the beginning and ending of sentences or paragraphs. Speaking at a press conference only a couple of days after the 1992 Los Angeles uprising in the wake of the verdict in the Rodney King beating case, Hooks utilized these traditional devices of the Baptist minister in order to contextualize the emotionally tense event:

> Never, at this point in time, did we ever believe any jury in this country could return such a verdict. If it had been in the 1930s and the Scottsboro Boys had been wrongly convicted, we would have not been surprised.
> Had it been in the 1950s and the killers of Emmett Till had walked free, we would not have been as surprised.
> Had it been in the 60s, and the accused had been given the gift of two hung juries in the murder of our own Medgar Evers, we would not have been surprised.
> But in the 1990s, when from every quarter, we hear demands for law and order, when increasingly harsh sentences are meted out to defendants in criminal cases, the verdicts stunned and sickened us.

A similar rhetorical strategy employed by Hooks is the use of crescendo, reminiscent of King and in the tradition of the black preacher. A Hooks address builds gradually, invoking the imagery and drama of the black condition, then eloquently concludes by proclaiming the ultimate victory over those conditions. In 1977, he ended his first keynote address, by saying:

> Black Americans are not defeated. The civil rights movement is not dead. If anyone thinks that we are going to stop agitating, they had better think again. If anyone thinks that we are going to stop litigating, they had better close the courts. If anyone thinks that we are not going to demonstrate and protest . . . they had better roll up the sidewalks.

The most common rhetorical device in Hooks's arsenal is the utilization of the simple narrative. Hooks transcends the rule that eloquence demands complex verbosity and instead offers a simple, graceful persuasion that is not only forceful but reaches varied audiences. He begins the communication act by introduction of a concept that the audience may find complex or even oppose, then offers a simple narrative that not only generates interest, but illuminates the issue, and concludes by reinforcing his persuasive message. In a 1976 speech to a group of historians about the post-bicentennial century of America, he discussed the black self-help movement, amazingly, over a decade before most mainstream African-American leaders began discussing it, during a time of predominantly integrationist-led civil rights leadership:

> Will the third century be any better or different?
> I think that to a large extent, in spite of the dimness and darkness we see all around us, that what happens in the third century in America to black people will to a great extent depend upon us. And how we seize the opportunities and how we meet the challenges of the partial successes that we have achieved.

You will recall the story, the legend of the Indian chief, who was challenged for leadership by the young brave. And one of the things that had to be done was to ask the question which the chief could not answer.

And so the young brave got a small bird and put it in his hand. And the question that he asked was, "Is the bird living or is the bird dead?" And he already prepared himself to prove that the chief did not have so much wisdom. For had he [the chief] said that the bird was alive, he [the brave] had planned to squeeze the bird to death, and drop a dead bird. And if the chief had said the bird were dead, he planned to simply open his hands and let the bird fly to freedom. But as he stood there before the chief with his hands clasped together, with the small bird in his hand, and asked him was the bird living or was the bird dead. The chief looked at him and said, "My son, the answer is in your hands." . . .

Will we be able to indebt the future to us, as our foreparents have made us indebted to them?

I think, my brothers and sisters, that the third century of American way of life will not depend so much on the institutional white racism that has been a pervasive part of American way of life, but will depend on the challenges that we will have or what we will do.

Hooks's unique style provides for diversity in language choices in recounting the narrative, choices that avoid a complicated sentence structure and thus maintain a high level of interest in the story.

When Hooks combines these rhetorical techniques, oratory of the highest eloquence results. One example is "Jubilee Day," Hooks's 1979 address to the NAACP National Convention, in which he concluded:

As I look out on this sea of faces, most of you hard working, unpaid, unhonored, and unsung volunteers, my heart leaps with joy. God bless every one of you, for because of your noble selfless devotion and dedication, this nation has moved forward and generations as yet unborn will rise up and call your name Blessed.

So, we chart the NAACP ship into the uncertain waters of the future.

It has been our tower of hope, amidst the blinding disappointments of yester-years.

It has been our anchor, amidst the surging seas and howling winds of racial conflict.

It has been the mighty shelter of a rock in a weary land, in the sea of despair, and 2nd class citizenship.

It has been our harbor and our refuge.

This is not only the ship of the past, it is the ship of the present and it is the ship of the future.

Don't weep—Don't mourn—Don't despair—the NAACP is the ship of our future.

The NAACP is the fruition of our weary years.

So, go tell it—tell it on the mountains
Go tell it on the plains;
Go tell it in the cities;

Go tell it in the village—every hamlet;
Go tell it in every City Council chamber;
Go tell it in every State House;
Go tell it in every Congress;
Go tell it in the White House;
Tell it on the mountains, over the hills, everywhere—
Go tell it, that the NAACP is here.

The impact of Hooks's oratory was illustrated on May 17, 1979, on the steps of the South Carolina State Capitol in Columbia, where he addressed a crowd assembled to celebrate the twenty-fifth anniversary of the Supreme Court's *Brown v. Board of Education*. Paul Delaney wrote in the *New York Times Magazine*:

Mr. Hooks delivered a sermon that made use of one of the most effective preaching techniques of the black church: bringing each sentence, each successive paragraph, to a crescendo and climaxing with a familiar parable or hymn (Dr. King did it in 1963 with "Free at last . . ."). Mr. Hooks paraphrased the folk song, "Old Black Joe." . . . he shouted to wild cheers and applause.

Without question, the eloquent style of Benjamin Hooks's rhetoric is demonstrated throughout his speeches. Beyond that eloquence, however, Hooks never loses sight of his goals for the NAACP and the practical applications of his oratory. As stylistically eloquent as his oratory is, his rhetoric always reveals the pragmatist behind the preacher.

In 1976, when Hooks became the executive director of the NAACP, interest in civil rights and activism was on the wane. The membership of the organization had fallen dramatically, and the gains of the 1960s had sapped much of the vitality and urgency that had defined the civil rights movement at its peak. The organization was struggling to define its new role. African-Americans had achieved legal civil rights, but the struggle had shifted to the implementation of those rights. The NAACP now was fighting complex legal battles in the desegregation of schools and housing. The movement's language of rights had lost focus and had been replaced by complacency as the movement had become disoriented. Hooks brought a new vision that redefined the struggle for civil rights.

Hooks made two goals central to his leadership while he was executive director of the NAACP. The first was a clear recognition that the passage of legislation and judicial decisions of the 1960s were not the ultimate prize, but merely another link in the chain in the fight for equality. For example, at the 1990 NAACP National Convention, Hooks challenged black Americans to find ways to help themselves. He suggested that African-Americans were at a crossroads: "No longer can we proffer polite, explicable reasons why black America cannot do more for itself. I'm calling for a moratorium on excuses. I challenge black America today—all of us—to set aside our alibis.'' During his tenure in office, Hooks sought to revitalize the NAACP by redefining the organization's direction. The rights that had been promised in the 1960s and gained in the 1970s were being eroded in the 1980s. Vigilance and active protection of these gains were imperative if these gains were not to be lost.

For his second goal, Hooks expanded the NAACP's interests beyond the traditional civil rights issues. For example, in the *New York Daily News*, July 31, 1977, Hooks announced to the world that many national issues, not normally considered NAACP issues, needed to be addressed through a diverse perspective: ''We will take stands . . . on the environment, ecology, and energy . . . the problems of the cities, national health insurance, welfare, and the criminal system.'' Broadening the NAACP mandate was important for two reasons. First, it acknowledged that the needs and interests of African-Americans reached far beyond the issues of discrimination and race relations. Second, attention to nontraditional issues allowed people with diverse interests to feel that the NAACP had something to offer them as well.

The signature speech encompassing Hooks's efforts to redirect the organization was his inaugural address at the 1977 NAACP National Convention. The new priorities suggested previously were outlined, and by the end of the speech the audience was in a fervor over the endless possibilities that the organization had in store. The list of priorities he announced included empowerment tactics; building new relationships beyond government with business and other liberal organizations; image building; and the need for the organization to enter into foreign policy issues of significance to African-Americans, such as South Africa.

Hooks's vision for reinvigorating the NAACP found resistance among the old guard inside the organization who still believed in the traditional role of the association's purpose, and these differences forced serious discussions of the organization's future. In Hooks's sixteen years as NAACP executive director, rarely a week went by when he did not formally address an audience. In these speeches and in essays published in the NAACP's *Crisis*, he initiated public debate over topics of interest to the African-American community, such as the lack of opportunities for African-Americans in Hollywood, the exploitation of the African-American athlete, or the need for a more ''communal'' approach to the rejuvenation of urban America. In the end, Hooks's persuasiveness and the effectiveness of his leadership secured his vision as the one that would guide the NAACP into the twenty-first century.

While the pragmatism of Hooks's eloquence is exemplified throughout his work, no single set of addresses better exemplifies his merger of these two elements than his response to the Los Angeles uprising. The *Crisis* issue that followed the Rodney King verdict began with a statement that outlined the African-American community's sense of outrage and injustice. Comparing the King verdict and the Scottsboro case of the 1930s, in which an all-white jury convicted nine innocent African-American males of rape, Hooks wrote that the King decision should have come as no surprise:

> We see little difference in injustices perpetrated against human decency in both instances. The not guilty verdicts in the King case are outrageous, a mockery of justice. Clearly, they send an inviting sign to other law enforcement officers so inclined, that anything goes in the name of law enforcement. . . .
>
> African-Americans and many others are grieved by this inexplicable miscarriage of justice, that will reinforce the belief there is a double standard of justice when race enters the picture.

Despite his scathing indictment of the verdict, however, Hooks then described the need for a calm response and a positive channeling of anger. Hooks saw self-destructive impacts to the African-American community in the riots and spoke directly both to the issue of injustice and to how the community must respond to that injustice:

> We are bitter and disappointed at the outcome, but we urge that the decision be met with calmness. Any anger felt should be directed in constructive channels, such as we have done by holding a series of public hearings to compile information on the status of relations between the African-American community and the police.

Returning to the community's anger, Hooks warned that ''there is a towering wall of distrust between African-American citizens and the police, built in large measure by the historical mistreatment of the former by the latter.'' Hooks recognized the need not merely to condemn the verdict, but also to speak to those who had committed violence as a result of the verdict. By combining eloquent outrage with pragmatic concerns, Hooks gave voice to the reasons for the uprising, but not to the particular response itself.

In a subsequent speech on June 23, 1992, during a NAACP retreat at the University of California in Los Angeles, Hooks developed a similar argument, detailing the blame. Hooks began by telling the federal government, ''We told you so.'' He referred repeatedly to NAACP prognostications of urban conflict, including a 1989 conference paper entitled ''The Present Crisis'' in which the NAACP prophesied conflict as a result of the current condition of the underclass, directly caused by years of ''neglect, indifference, and ignorance.'' The media and government response had been that the organization was ''alarmist.'' The violence in Los Angeles had vindicated Hooks and his organization's conclusions. By emphasizing the accuracy of the NAACP's analysis, Hooks reinforced the credibility of the organization. He again, however, balanced restraint and condemnation of the verdict. Hooks made note that ''we urged calmness and restraint, and acceptance of the verdicts, which even though they stink to the high heaven with racism, are tragically irreversible.'' He continued: ''The justifiable revulsion at what has occurred must not be allowed to push into the background the real nature of this situation in which African Americans have been wronged.''

Again searching for a positive channel for the community's righteous anger,

Hooks announced a march designed to protest the relationship between the law-enforcement community and African-Americans. He clearly defined the goal of the march—to send a message to the nation that police brutality must cease—and outlined the demands of the protesters. By enumerating the protesters' bill of complaints, Hooks redirected attention away from the violence and onto the march. He thus severed justifiable outrage from unproductive action in order to reunite it with productive action.

Hooks concluded the press conference by refocusing attention on the underlying causes of the Los Angeles uprising—the economic decay and neglect of the African-American community. Throughout the discussion of the injustice of the verdict and the Los Angeles community's response, Hooks reminded his audience that the critical issue went beyond these sidelights to a greater issue, that of equal opportunity for the nation's underclass. The underlying message was that no matter what was done to address the issue of police brutality, the problem of economic and educational equality was inescapable and of the highest order.

The final address in this set, ''Why Are We Here,'' is the opening remarks of a retreat held two months after the violence. After another discussion of the 1989 conference where the NAACP predicted the Los Angeles conflict, Hooks again addressed the root causes of the revolt and pointed the finger squarely at the Reagan-Bush administration for not heeding their warnings as he noted: ''We warned the Administration and the representatives of government that the seeds for social disorder and social strife had been planted.'' The importance of this rhetoric lay in a commitment by Hooks to provide solutions to the problems that he had isolated in the earlier speeches. Hooks avoided the trap of indicting the system without making any attempt at reforming it. In his concluding recital, he made detailed and explicit suggestions about combatting the urban blight and neglect, including cooperative job and training programs, a massive overhaul of the educational system to begin training earlier in life, and a greater emphasis by law enforcement on prevention, as opposed to punishment. Here Hooks emphasized that the NAACP had been active in proposing positive change, thus pointing to the possibility of the organization acting as a proactive bridge between the government and the African-American community.

Taken together, these three statements by Hooks move on a continuum from directly addressing the Rodney King verdict to providing solutions for the economic injustices being perpetrated in society by institutionalized racism. With a clear agenda in hand, this is not a haphazard journey. The problem of equality in opportunity is developed as the root cause for the reaction to the verdict, and Hooks's practical discussion of the causes of the revolt never loses sight of his ultimate goal: tangible improvements for the African-American community. Hooks understood that if the focus was placed solely on the judicial system, a repetition of the Los Angeles incident was likely. He used the crisis to spotlight the true evils of the condition of the African-American community at a time when white and black Americans had more questions than answers.

Vivid imagery, a lyrical cadence, simple, yet powerful language, and a forceful delivery are all components of the eloquence that Benjamin Hooks displays throughout his oratory. This grand style, however, walks hand in hand with a rhetoric of purpose, always keeping one eye on the practical interests of the African-American community. Benjamin Lawson Hooks considers himself "just an ol' country preacher," and that may be true, but Dr. Hooks is one preacher who could move an entire nation with both his wisdom and his compelling style. He played a central role in the revitalization of the United States' largest civil rights organization and helped lead the first post–civil rights movement generation through the turbulent waters that followed the legal successes of the 1960s. In that work, Hooks has notably created an oratory marked by pragmatic eloquence.

INFORMATION SOURCES

Research Collections and Collected Speeches

The National Association for the Advancement of Colored People national headquarters at 4805 Mount Hope Dr., Baltimore, MD 21215, houses a library and archives of speeches and materials.

[*CRI*] *The Crisis.* Published by the NAACP, this magazine contains excerpts from many of Hooks's speeches.
[*SEA*] Hooks, Benjamin L. *Seasons of a Leader—Ben L. Hooks on. . . .* New York: NAACP, 1993. A book of excerpts taken from Hooks's addresses to the annual NAACP conventions and other speeches.

Selected Biographies

Delaney, Paul. "The Struggle to Rally Black America." *New York Times Magazine*, July 15, 1979: 84 +.
Deleon, Robert A. "Man Behind Changes to Make Radio TV Relate to Blacks." *Jet* December 21, 1972: 20–26.
Douglas, Carlyle C. "Watchdog of the Air Waves—Benjamin L. Hooks Helps the FCC Regulate the Nation's Radios, TVs, Telephones, Satellites." *Ebony*, June 1975: 54–56+.
"Hooks, Benjamin L[awson]." *Current Biography*, 1978: 198–202.
"Hooks, Benjamin Lawson." *Who's Who in Black America*, 1983: 443–444.
Kram, Mark. "Benjamin L. Hooks: Executive Director of the NAACP, Attorney, Clergyman." *Contemporary Black Biography* 2 (1993): 109–112.
"NAACP's Country Preacher." *Time,* November 22, 1976: 22.

CHRONOLOGY OF MAJOR SPEECHES

[See "Research Collections and Collected Speeches" for source codes.]

"Speech before the Fourth General Session: America: The Third Century." Audiotape. Northridge, CA: On-the-Spot Duplicators, 1976.

"1977 Keynote Address to the NAACP National Convention." St. Louis, MO, July 1977. *SEA,* 11.

"1978 Keynote Address to the NAACP National Convention." Baltimore, MD, July 1978. *SEA,* 13–17.

"Jubilee Day" (Keynote Address to NAACP Convention). Lexington, KY, June 29, 1979. *CRI,* October 1979, 345–348.

"Struggle On!" (Keynote Address to the NAACP Convention). New Orleans, LA, July 12, 1983. *Representative American Speeches, 1983–1984.* Ed. Owen Peterson. New York : H. W. Wilson, 1984, 81–91.

"Address to the Black Business Advocacy Conference." Charlotte, NC, 1983. *CRI,* October 1983: 10–11.

"1984 Keynote Address to the NAACP National Convention." Kansas City, MO, July 4, 1984. *CRI,* August/September 1984: 22–23; *SEA,* 37–41.

"1990 Keynote Address to the NAACP National Convention." Chicago, IL, July 1990. *SEA,* 75–77.

"Press Conference on Rodney King Verdict." Los Angeles, CA, May 4, 1992. *CRI,* April/May 1992: 2–3.

"Why Are We Here? (Leadership Retreat Opening Statement)." Los Angeles, CA, June 23, 1992. *CRI,* June/July 1992: 4–15.

"1992 Keynote Address to the NAACP National Convention." Nashville, TN, July 12, 1992. *CRI,* August/September 1992: 4–12; *SEA,* 87–96.

JESSE LOUIS JACKSON
(1941–　　), minister, civil rights activist, U.S. presidential candidate

LYNDREY A. NILES AND CARLOS MORRISON

Few other public speakers of the latter half of the twentieth century have been ranked in the category of Jesse Louis Jackson, preacher, civil rights activist, and presidential contender. His fluent delivery, rhythmic sentences, forceful style, and vivid portrayals have all combined to leave listeners with Jackson's words replaying in their ears.

Jesse Jackson was born on October 8, 1941, to a high-school student in Field-crest Village, Greenville, South Carolina. He described himself as having been "born in occupied territory, and having lived all my developing years under apartheid." His mother, Helen Burns, was living at home with her mother, who worked as a maid for a white family. Jesse later said that "the cycle of pain" was repeated when his sixteen-year-old mother got pregnant by a married man, their next-door neighbor Noah Robinson, a relatively wealthy black man. Later, Helen married Charles Jackson, a janitor, of whom Jesse once remarked: "He adopted me and gave me his name, his love, his encouragement, discipline and a high sense of self-respect."

In 1959, Jackson graduated from Sterling High School, where he was president of his school's chapter of Future Teachers of America. He was also the versatile quarterback of the football team, who additionally won letters in baseball and basketball and who shortly thereafter left Greenville with an athletic scholarship to the University of Illinois. Soon he learned that he would not become the first black quarterback at a big-time university because he had been shifted to play halfback or end.

The next school year, Jackson transferred to North Carolina Agricultural and Technical College at Greensboro. It was here that he met Jacqueline Davis, whom he married in 1962 and with whom he raised five children. At A & T Jackson became actively involved in the civil rights movement, taking part in both sit-ins and marches. His participation and leadership resulted in the deseg-regation of downtown Greensboro and a leadership role in the local Congress of Racial Equality (CORE) chapter. It also led to his meeting Dr. Martin Luther King, Jr., whom he would later join in the Southern Christian Leadership Conference (SCLC). After graduating with a bachelor's degree in sociology, Jackson accepted a Rockefeller grant to attend the Chicago Theological Seminary.

By 1967, the SCLC was moving ahead expeditiously with the expansion of its self-help and economic programs in the black community. In an effort to facilitate this expansion, King appointed Jackson to the position of executive director of Operation Breadbasket. As a major economic program of the SCLC, Operation Breadbasket, which was based in Chicago, focused on finding jobs for blacks in bakeries, milk companies, and other firms that had a large black consumer base. As head of the program, Jackson was very successful—probably through his oratorical skills and his ability to lead protests—in getting Chicago businesses to end their discriminatory practices in hiring. He was able to find over 2,200 jobs for blacks in white-owned companies within a twelve-month period. Jackson's continued success with Operation Breadbasket was praised within the leadership ranks of the SCLC, while an emerging image of self-serving and self-promoting behavior was not.

After the death of King in April 1968, tension arose between Jackson and the SCLC leadership. At issue was the question of who would assume the mantle of leadership within the organization. There was concern among members of the SCLC that Jackson was trying to take control of the organization but was not the rightful heir. There was also some opposition within the organization to the accession of Rev. Ralph Abernathy to the leadership post. The confrontation between Abernathy, King's second-in-command, and Jackson, King's appointee to Operation Breadbasket, ended in a stalemate until *Playboy*, in 1969, billed Jesse Jackson as "King's heir apparent." By 1970, Jackson had also appeared on the cover of *Time*, in an issue devoted to black America. Thus the media had cast the deciding vote, and, for the time being, the winner was Jackson. Also at issue within the SCLC was Jackson's apparent lack of regard for organizational protocol. In December 1971, the SCLC's board suspended him for a period of sixty days because he had failed to get its permission to organize trade fairs for black businesspeople. These trade fairs were called "Black Expos" and were organized to bring black businesses together with the black community in order to improve their networking.

Because of "bruised pride," Jackson resigned as executive director of Operation Breadbasket, left the SCLC, and started his own organization, Operation PUSH. Initially, the acronym stood for People United to Save Humanity, but was later changed to People United to Serve Humanity. The guest list for the kickoff of Operation PUSH at New York's Commodore Hotel indicated Jackson's influence even at an early age. Reading like a celebrity's who's who, the roll of attendees included singers Aretha Franklin and Roberta Flack, politicians Carl Stokes and Richard Hatcher, actor-director Ossie Davis, Junius Griffin of

Motown Records, bandleader Reuben Phillips, Loretta Long of "Sesame Street," Harvard psychiatrist Alvin Poussaint, and members of the press such as Ed Lewis, publisher of *Essence*, Clarence Jones of the *Amsterdam News*, and free-lance writer Ernest Dunbar. Chicago car dealer Al Johnson and SCLC board member W. A. Saunders were also among Jackson's supporters. This cadre of entertainers and professionals provided Jackson and Operation PUSH with a solid base of support, morally as well as financially.

The goals of PUSH were very similar to those of Operation Breadbasket: to increase minority employment and minority businesses. For example, PUSH would negotiate and monitor agreements, or "covenants," with major corporations that committed these companies to hiring more minorities. Anheuser-Busch, the Southland Corporation, Coca-Cola, and Kentucky Fried Chicken were some of the corporations that signed such covenants with PUSH after negotiating with Jackson. Using the stick as well as the carrot, PUSH would also threaten to boycott businesses that engaged in unfair hiring practices. An affiliate organization called PUSH for excellence, or PUSH-Excel, would later come under severe criticism from the media and the government because of its failure to submit acceptable financial reports as required by law. However, Operation PUSH grew rapidly to over seventy chapters with more than 80,000 members.

It was during Jackson's years as head of PUSH that he began to promote his theme of education and excellence to students throughout the world. Through the power of his oratorical skills, Jackson was able to inspire students to higher levels of achievement. He spoke to students about education, self-discipline, and self-esteem. In an effort to empower the young people, Jackson would intone the words that later became the hallmark of his political campaign: "I am somebody . . . respect me . . . I am somebody . . . My mind . . . is a pearl . . . I can learn anything . . . in the world . . . down with dope . . . up with hope . . . I am somebody."

Throughout the 1970s, Jackson's fame spread. The *1970 Harris Survey Yearbook* reported that Jackson was in ninth place in name recognition among black leaders and organizations. By 1978, however, he had attained even wider national acclaim and was featured on the "NBC Evening News" as having the highest name recognition of any American civil rights leader.

The summer of 1983 marked the twentieth anniversary of the March on Washington. Amid a feeling that the Reagan administration was turning back the clock in areas such as jobs, housing, education, and affirmative action, the "celebration" of King's famous speech was titled "Dreaming New Dreams." Speaking to the gathering, Jackson focused his speech on the need for blacks to gain political power and referenced the 1980 presidential campaign as an example of how blacks could have changed the outcome:

Reagan won Alabama by 17,500 votes, but there were 272,000 unregistered blacks. He won Arkansas by 5,000, with 85,000 unregistered blacks. He won Kentucky by 17,800 votes, with 62,000 unregistered blacks . . . the numbers show that Reagan won through a perverse coalition of the rich and the registered. But this is a new day. Hands that picked cotton in 1884 will pick the president in 1984.

Jackson repeated this message throughout his travels across the country, and it became clear that he had his sights on the 1984 Democratic presidential nomination. Two major goals emerged in conjunction with his presidential campaign: voter registration and voter participation. Despite criticism from some black leaders such as John Jacob of the National Urban League, Benjamin Hooks of the National Association for the Advancement of Colored People, and Coretta Scott King that a black presidential candidate would split the Democratic vote, Jackson was convinced that he would invigorate the Democratic party through the creation of the Rainbow Coalition.

The coalition consisted of various ethnic groups such as blacks, whites, Hispanics, Asian-Americans, and Native Americans and made special appeals to the poor, the downtrodden, and the disaffected. Jackson's Rainbow Coalition represented those groups living on the margins of society who, for all practical purposes, had been locked out of the political process under the Reagan administration. Jackson encouraged these various groups to seek political and economic power and better educational opportunities and to believe in themselves. Because of Jackson's commitment and political savvy, he was extremely successful in drawing together the coalition he envisioned. For example, in the New York State primary Jackson won 34 percent of the Puerto Rican vote. He received significant support from the Native American community for having addressed the National Congress of American Indians. Jackson also gained considerable support among white voters who were liberal-left peace activists and among unemployed and low-income blue-collar workers. Blacks also strongly supported Jackson, particularly the black clergy. Throughout the country, as the spokesperson and political candidate of this coalition, Jackson made these peoples' voices heard.

JESSE JACKSON'S ELOQUENCE

As a speaker, Jackson has commanded the attention of hundreds of audiences throughout the nation with his eloquent and dynamic speeches. He has become "the most feared, loved, powerful, articulate, and controversial national political figure in our time." His discourse has addressed a wide variety of issues such as coalition building, education, economics, homelessness, and poverty.

Jackson began his speaking career during his formative years when he was initially influenced by his pastor, Rev. D. F. Sample, his speech teacher, Mrs. Bates, and Dr. Benjamin Mays. As a child, Jackson's speechmaking consisted of presentations he made before his elders at state conventions and public speeches given at Christmas and Easter programs. These early speeches emphasized delivery over content, brought Jackson a great deal of recognition and respect within the black community, and prepared him well for the challenges he would meet at North Carolina A & T. As a college student, Jackson made ample use of his oratorical experience by becoming a leader in the sit-in movement. He led students in various protest marches against the business establishments in Greensboro, North Carolina, and spoke out against segregation and discrimination. After college, Jackson made full use of his oratorical skills in his leadership positions in SCLC, Operation Breadbasket, PUSH, and the Rainbow Coalition.

In characterizing Jackson's 1984 address to the delegates of the Democratic National Convention in San Francisco, California, Soloman and Stewart noted that it blended religious appeals, self-promotion, attacks on the opposition, compliments to the party leadership, appeals to the disaffected, and an apology for his past statements into an intoxicating brew spiked with rhymed slogans and vivid images. Indeed, it was all of these. His address focused primarily, however, on criticizing the Reagan administration for having "created a good economy 'on the backs' of poor America." In developing his message, Jackson relied heavily on two complementary forms of argument, both of which typify the black oral tradition: comparison/contrast and analogy.

In one instance in the speech, Jackson employed the comparison/contrast strategy in regard to the handicapped in U.S. society and Reagan. Jackson argued that "the disabled have their handicap revealed and their genius concealed; while the able-bodied have their genius revealed and their disability concealed; but ultimately we must judge people by their values and their contribution. Don't leave anybody out. I would rather have Roosevelt in a wheelchair than Reagan on a horse." Jackson also used the comparison/contrast strategy in reference to "Reagan being a false prophet." Jackson held that Reagan did not truly understand prayer: "Apparently he is not familiar with the structure of prayer. You thank the Lord for the food you are about to receive, not the food that just left. I think we should pray. But don't pray for the food that left, pray for the man that took the food to leave."

Analogies were also plentifully used in Jackson's address and can be categorized into three types: explanatory, substantive, and root metaphor. Of particular interest was the root metaphor in which he argued that "the Democratic party is a family." Jackson emphasized that "we must be unusually committed and caring as we expand our family to include new members." Jackson used this root metaphor of the family to argue for unity between the Rainbow Coalition participants and the Democratic party as they combined to fight the common foe: the Reagan administration.

The theme of unity was continued in Jackson's 1988 address to the Democratic National Convention held in Atlanta, Georgia, a speech entitled "Common Ground and Common Sense." In this speech, Jackson argued for "common ground" to be established between members of the Rainbow Coalition and all Americans regardless of race, creed, or religion. He also argued for the need for "common ground" within the Democratic party, claiming that

Mike Dukakis' parents were a doctor and a teacher. My parents were a maid, a beautician and janitor. . . . He studied law and I studied theology. There are differences of religion, region and race, differences in experiences and perspectives, but the genius of America is that out of the many we become one. Providence has enabled our paths to intersect. His foreparents came to America on immigrant ships. My foreparents came to America on slave ships, but, whatever the original ships, we are in the same boat tonight.

While calling for common ground to be established within the Democratic party and throughout the nation, Jackson employed the strategy of identification. By using this strategy, he was able to attract a variety of political constituents to his message of unity. According to Makay, ''He called for their mutual identification by challenging audience members, calling them by political, economic, religious, and social labels; and he urged them to come together and find common ground.''

In addition to his use of identification, Jackson employed ''several different kinds of arguments in the 1988 address . . . [such as] comparison/contrast, analogy, sign, argument within an argument, and groundless claims'' (Hallmark). However, his most compelling argument was the quilt analogy, where ''he argues that each interest of the Democratic party cannot win alone. It was only through compiling all of the interests together through mutual support that each interest will see victory.'' Jackson said that

America is not a blanket woven from one thread, one color, one cloth. When I was a child growing up in Greenville, South Carolina, and grandmama could not afford a blanket, she didn't complain and we did not freeze. Instead, she took pieces of old cloth-patches, wool, silk gabardine, crokersack. Only the patches—barely good enough to wipe your shoes with, but they didn't stay that way very long. With sturdy hands and a strong cord, she sewed them together into a quilt, a thing of beauty and culture.

Noting the strength that could be found in each of the various groups represented at the convention, Jackson continued:

When you fight for what you believe, right-wing, left-wing, hawk, dove—you are right, from your point of view, but your point of view is not enough. But don't despair. Be as wise as my grandmama. Pull the patches and the pieces together, bound by a common thread.

Jackson's quilt analogy symbolized his call for unity through the establishment of ''common ground.'' Each group was identified as a part of the collective that, because of its unity, acquires a ''stronger voice.'' The message was simple: united we stand, divided we fall.

Jesse Jackson's style of delivery is grounded in the African-American oral tradition, making effective use of alliteration, rhyme, and antithesis. As Evelyn

Dandy noted, in *Black Communications: Breaking Down the Barriers*, "The culture of African-Americans has been preserved in the oral language—the music, stories, folk sayings, jokes, [rap] and most especially in the way words are used." Jackson uses words for effect and "lasting pleasure," moving skillfully from so-called standard English to contemporary African-American English style and vocabulary. In essence, he is always preaching, as he engages his audience in the call-and-response, an interactive communication process in which the sender and receiver encourage the other to greater participation. Call-and-response exchanges often conclude in a rich vocal celebration, not only of the occasion, but of the "special message of the hour."

One such occasion occurred during Jackson's speech "It's Up to You," delivered at the What's Happening Teen Conference held in Atlanta, Georgia, on June 19, 1978. In his introduction, Jackson engaged his youthful audience in the "I am somebody" dialogue and then focused on the four main points of his speech: (1) service to others, (2) making responsible choices in life, (3) delaying gratification of material wealth, and (4) concentrating on lifelong goals. Within these themes, he placed great emphasis on teenage pregnancy and charged the youths to work toward educating themselves about sex because it was "too beautiful to be made ugly by ignorance, greed and lack of self-control." He repeated this theme often so that no one could miss the point. Later, on building self-esteem, he advised: "If my mind can conceive it, my heart can believe it, I know I can achieve it. Down with pill power; up with willpower. Down with dope; Up with hope. You can either use willpower and cope, or use pill-power and cop out." Rhyme, rhythm, analogy, antithesis, cadence, clarity: Jackson combines all these verbal elements of the oral tradition with a forceful, animated delivery.

Jesse Jackson was, and still is, a very effective public speaker. He structures his arguments well and uses a variety of strategies such as comparison/contrast, analogy, illustration, and short story. His theses are clearly stated because he believes that a speech should have a point, and his proofs are rational, often employing life experiences. Jackson's style is appropriate to his audiences, employing a plain usage of English and creating word pictures for his audience to recall long after the event is over. Jackson once commented that he reads widely, every night. His wide reading makes him knowledgeable about the subjects he addresses, while his eloquence and dynamic delivery demand attention, aid the memory, and generate a rousing response from his audience.

INFORMATION SOURCES

Research Collections and Collected Speeches

Speech texts and other information may be obtained from the Rainbow Coalition, Inc., 1700 K Street, NW, Washington, DC 20006.

[*KHA*] Clemente, Frank, and Frank Watkins, eds. *Keep Hope Alive: Jesse Jackson's 1988 Presidential Campaign.* Boston: South End, 1989.

[*SFH*] Jackson, Jesse L. *Straight from the Heart.* Ed. Roger D. Hatch and Frank E. Watkins. Philadelphia: Fortress, 1987.

Selected Critical Studies

Colton, Elizabeth O. *The Jackson Phenomenon: The Man, the Power, the Message.* New York: Doubleday, 1989.

Hallmark, James R. "Jesse Jackson's Argumentation: A Comparison of Jackson's 1984 and 1988 Addresses to the Democratic National Convention." Paper presented at the Speech Communication Association Convention, San Francisco, CA, 1989.

Hatch, Roger D. *Beyond Opportunity: Jesse Jackson's Vision for America.* Philadelphia: Fortress, 1988.

Hunt, Barbara Ann. "The Use of Television by the Rev. Jesse Louis Jackson, 1968–1978." Ph.D. diss., Northwestern U, 1988.

Landess, Thomas, and Richard Quinn. *Jesse Jackson and the Politics of Race.* Ottawa, IL: Jameson, 1985.

Makay, John. "An Analysis of Jesse Jackson's Convention Speech, 1988." *African American Rhetoric: A Reader.* Ed. Lyndrey A. Niles. Dubuque, IA: Kendall/Hunt, 1995. 124–131.

Morris, Lorenzo, ed. *The Social and Political Implications of the 1984 Jesse Jackson Presidential Campaign.* New York: Praeger, 1990.

Reynolds, Barbara A. *Jesse Jackson: The Man, the Movement, the Myth.* Chicago: Nelson-Hall, 1975.

Solomon, Martha A., and Paul B. Stewart. "The Rainbow Coalition." *Great Speeches for Criticism and Analysis.* Ed. Lloyd Rohler and Roger Cook. 2nd ed. Greenwood, IN: Alistair, 1993.

Stanford, Karin L. "Citizen Diplomacy: An Analysis of Rev. Jesse Jackson's Diplomatic Efforts from 1984–1986." Ph.D. diss., Howard U, 1993.

Selected Biographies

Collins, Sheila D. *The Rainbow Challenge: The Jackson Campaign and the Future of U.S. Politics.* New York: Monthly Review, 1986.

Faw, Bob, and Nancy Skelton. *Thunder in America: The Improbable Presidential Campaign of Jesse Jackson.* Austin, TX: Texas Monthly, 1986.

Kimball, Penn. *Keep Hope Alive!: Super Tuesday and Jesse Jackson's 1988 Campaign for the Presidency.* Washington, DC: Joint Center for Political and Economic Studies, 1992.

Niles, Lyndrey A., and Frank W. Hale. "An Interview with Jesse Jackson." *African American Communications.* Ed. James Ward. Dubuque, IA: Kendall/Hunt, 1993. 251–260.

"Pride and Prejudice," *Time,* May 7, 1984:30–40.

White, John. *Black Leadership in America: From Booker T. Washington to Jesse Jackson.* 2nd ed. New York: Longman, 1990.

CHRONOLOGY OF MAJOR SPEECHES

[See "Research Collections and Collected Speeches" for source codes.]

"The Ten Commandments for Excellence in Education" (Speech before Operation PUSH's Community Forum). October 23, 1976. *SFH,* 183–188.

"Political Votes, Economic Oats" (Speech before the Republican National Committee). Washington, DC, January 20, 1978. *SFH,* 23–36.

"It's Up to You" (Speech before the "What's Happening" Teen Conference). Atlanta, GA, June 19, 1978. *SFH,* 205–212.

"In Search of a New Focus and New Vision." Washington, DC, May 17, 1980. *SFH,* 96–102.

"Black Americans Seek Economic Equity and Parity." March 16, 1982. *SFH,* 277–281.

"From Battle Ground to Common Ground to Higher Ground" (Speech before a joint session of the Alabama legislature). Montgomery, AL, May 24, 1983. *SFH,* 137–145.

"Dreaming New Dreams." Washington, DC, August 27, 1983. *SFH,* 19–22.

"Foreign Policy—But Not Foreign Values" (Speech before the United Nations General Assembly). New York, NY, January 27, 1984. *SFH,* 224–231.

"Binding Up the Wounds" (Address at Temple Adath Yeshurun). Manchester, NH, February 26, 1984. *SFH,* 132–136.

"The Call of Conscience: Redemption, Expansion, Healing, and Unity" (Speech to the Democratic National Convention). San Francisco, CA, July 17, 1984. *SFH,* 3–18.

"Protecting the Legacy: The Challenge of Dr. Martin Luther King, Jr." (Sermon at Ebenezer Baptist Church). Atlanta, GA, January 15, 1986. *SFH,* 122–131.

"Saving the Family Farm." Greenfield, IA, January 25, 1987. *KHA,* 159–161.

"Invest in America: Rebuild Our Cities" (Speech to the U.S. Conference of Mayors). Nashville, TN, June 15, 1987. *KHA,* 95–100.

"A Chance to Serve" (Presidential campaign announcement). Raleigh, NC, October 10, 1987. *KHA,* 27–32.

"The Challenge of Our Day: Confronting Environmental and Economic Violence." Mendocino Headlands, CA, March 20, 1988. *KHA,* 179–182.

"A New Realism in Foreign Policy" (Speech to the American Society of Newspaper Publishers). Washington, DC, April 14, 1988. *KHA,* 187–191.

"An Economic Program to Make America Better and to Keep America Strong." Cleveland, OH, May 2, 1988. *KHA,* 57–61.

"The Promise and Politics of Empowerment" (Speech to Ward AME Church). Los Angeles, CA, June 5, 1988. *KHA,* 209–211.

"Keep Hope Alive" (Sometimes titled "Common Ground and Common Sense," Address to the Democratic National Convention). Atlanta, GA, July 20, 1988. *KHA,* 33–39.

"The Struggle Continues" (Speech to the Jackson delegates at the conclusion of the Democratic National Convention). Atlanta, GA, July 22, 1988. *KHA,* 213–218.

VERNON JOHNS
(1892–1965), minister

ROBERT INCHAUSTI, WARREN OBERMAN, AND JAMES K. WEST

It is good to be present when the ordinary is transformed; when the dull plain garments of a peasant become shining white, and the obscure "mountain place, apart," comes into the gaze of the centuries. ("Transfigured Moments")

Vernon Johns was an American original, a man ahead of his time, representing a road not taken for the civil rights movement in his emphasis upon economic self-development as an integral part of aggressive political activism. He advocated a "visionary pragmatism" for black America—Emersonian self-reliance tied to an unwavering agenda of political reform. He stubbornly insisted upon the dignity of labor, the equality of all men, and the necessity of fighting for one's rights and one's dignity. He was a fierce advocate of the common people—not in their commonness, but in their Christian capacity to be reborn and transfigured. An ordained Baptist minister and renowned orator, his fiery character and example—and the legends that evolved out of them—were as much a part of his influence as his publications and sermons.

Vernon Johns was born in Farmville, Virginia, in 1892, growing up on his father's farm and receiving very little formal education as a child. His origins—like the accounts of his life—teem with legend and controversy. His father's father, a slave, was reputedly hanged for cutting his master in two with a scythe. His maternal grandfather, a white man named Price, maintained two families, one white and one African-American. Price himself spent time in the Virginia State Penitentiary for killing another white man who assaulted his slave mistress. Later, when Price's African-American "wife" died, he took their children into his household to be raised by his childless white wife.

John's mother was one of those children. She eventually met and married the son of the hanged slave, and a few years after, their first child Vernon was born. All three later attended Price's funeral "in a separate-but-equal family section, just across the gravesite from the white relatives."

Largely self-taught, as a youth Vernon would read any book he could find, using his prodigious mind to memorize the poems of Wordsworth and Byron, passages from the works of Shakespeare, Plato, and Aristotle, and long biblical passages, including the entire Book of Romans. He eventually attended the Virginia State Seminary at Lynchburg but was subsequently expelled for rebelliousness.

Finally, Johns managed to talk his way into Oberlin College. As legend has it, Dean Fiske at Oberlin was openly skeptical about the young man's night-school credits and unofficial preparation. In the face of this, Johns quipped, "Do you want students with credits or students with brains?" Fiske then handed Johns a book in German and challenged him to read it—which he did. Impressed, Fiske sent Johns to the dean of the seminary, Dr. Edward Increase Bosworth, who challenged Johns to translate a passage of biblical Greek. He read that too, apologizing that his Greek was actually not as strong as his Latin. Bosworth enrolled Johns on the spot as a provisional student, and within a year he had replaced Robert M. Hutchins, future president of the University of Chicago, as the top student in his class.

Upon hearing the news that he was no longer the top student, Hutchins complained that the "country Negro" must have somehow cheated. Johns hunted Hutchins down, demanded an apology, and when Hutchins resisted, flattened him with a right to the jaw. The two eventually became close friends, and years later Hutchins tried to get Johns to accept a teaching position at the University of Chicago, but Johns refused the offer.

After graduating from Oberlin, Johns enrolled in the Graduate School of Theology at the University of Chicago, which at the time was nationally known as the home of the Social Gospel Theologians. Johns was ordained a Baptist minister in 1918, and after teaching homiletics and New Testament hermeneutics at the Virginia Theological Seminary for a year, he became pastor of the Court Street Church in Lynchburg. Soon after, his fame as a religious scholar and preacher brought him offers from the best churches and universities around the country, though he lost or left every position he accepted in short order—usually returning to the family farm in Virginia. Johns was a man who needed space, open territory in which to think and move, and thus tenured positions or pastorships did not hold his interest for long. His most famous pastorship was at Dexter Avenue Baptist Church in Montgomery, Alabama (1948–52), where he was an outspoken opponent of segregation and the immediate predecessor of Martin Luther King, Jr. However, Johns preferred instead to preach and lecture at African-American churches and schools up and down the east coast, earning a meager but passable living in this manner. Historian Taylor Branch wrote, "Johns would catch the Richmond train and rumble off, wearing a tattered suit with books stuffed into the pockets. On his return from these trips his brother would often meet him with a fresh horse, and Johns would farm for a few days before his next lectures.''

PREACHING FOR THE PLEBEIAN SUBLIME

Philosophically, Vernon Johns was a spokesman for what might be called ''the plebeian sublime.'' In 1926, Johns's sermon ''Transfigured Moments'' was the first work by an African-American to be published in the annual *Best Sermons* anthology that included works by such luminaries as Reinhold Niebuhr, Henry Sloane Coffin, Harry Emerson Fosdick, and Willard L. Sperry. The sermon's topic was the transformation of the mundane and quotidian into the exalted and sublime, and its key image was the mountain-top experience—an image later to reverberate throughout several of Martin Luther King, Jr.,'s most memorable speeches.

As Johns phrased it in ''Transfigured Moments,'' it is ''good to be present when the ordinary is transformed.'' In this sermon, he remarked that ''the lowly ones of earth need to experience this transformation. The great majority of our lives must be lived apart from any elaborate or jeweled settings; must plod along without any spectacular achievements. . . . In the humblest routine, we must discover our task as part of the transforming enterprise of the Heavenly Father.'' He also believed that it was ''good to be in the presence of persons who can kindle us for fine heroic living.'' With a rolling, aphoristic style, marked cadences, and telling antitheses, he carried this idea to its climax:

> Mr. Roosevelt's criticism of his Progressive Party was that it meant well, but meant it feebly. That is often the trouble with our righteousness. It lacks intensity. It does not make itself felt. We are trying to grind great mills with a quart of water; we would set great masses of cold and slimy material aglow with a wet match. Wave our hands full of halfway measures. We scrap a part of our navies. We enthrone Justice in places where there is no serious objection to it. We practice brotherhood within carefully restricted areas. We forgive other people's enemies. We carry a Bible but not a cross. Instead of the Second Mile, we go a few yards and then wonder that Christian goals are not realized. ''O fools and slow of heart to believe all that the prophets have spoken!'' When we lift ourselves, at last, from the ruin and entanglements of our diluted and piecemeal righteousness, it will be under the leadership of persons for whom righteousness is a consuming and holy fire instead of a mere luke-warm and foggy something.

Vernon Johns embodied this ''consuming and holy fire'' and saw it as his vocation to rekindle sentiments for ''fine and heroic living.''

By the late 1920s, Johns had become as famous in the world of the black American church as Mordecai Johnson, then president of Howard University in Washington, D.C., and Howard Thurmond, an internationally known theologian. But unlike these exemplary men of the African-American aristocracy, Johns was a maverick who seldom published and, wrote Branch, "who thought nothing of walking into distinguished assemblies wearing mismatched socks with farm mud on his shoes." These eccentricities shocked and finally angered the conservative members of Dexter Avenue Baptist, who did not care to see their learned minister selling watermelons or fish off the back of a truck. This was no affectation or lack of manners on Johns's part, however, but a reflection of his authentic plebeian perspective—his celebration of the virtues of practical labor and the doctrines of self-sufficiency, and his whole-hearted identification with God's "Good Earth," which he espoused in his sermon "Mud Is Basic."

Johns also believed in economic self-development, as well as a full-fledged campaign for political rights, and these radical views eventually ran afoul of the more conservative beliefs of his Dexter patrons. As a result of this opposition, Johns's later sermons lost some of their lyricism, becoming more didactic and confrontational as he challenged his well-mannered congregation to acknowledge the harsh sociopolitical and economic realities of African-American life in America.

One Sunday, as Johns rose to the pulpit, the whole church noticed with great amusement that he had forgotten to lace his shoes. Johns quickly made use of this oversight. "I'll wear shoestrings when Negroes start making them!" he thundered back at the tittering congregation. As Branch put it: "Johns was both the highest and the lowest, the most learned and the most common, the most glorious reflection of their intellectual tastes and the most obnoxious challenge to their dignity."

In 1951, Johns delivered a sermon titled "It's Safe to Murder Negroes in Montgomery," and the next day a cross was burned on the church lawn. Nevertheless, he continued undaunted as prophet and fishmonger until an exasperated Dexter finally replaced him in 1952 with the younger, more dignified Martin Luther King, Jr.

Johns then retired to a life of obscurity, where he lived close to the land, venturing out on speaking tours from time to time but still avoiding the various permanent positions that were offered him. Instead, he farmed and occasionally drove around the Southern states by himself, reciting aloud the vast amounts of Scripture, poetry, and history that were committed to memory.

Although his tenure at Dexter was over, his powerful sermons were not soon forgotten. Branch told the moving story of how King, at the zenith of the civil rights struggle, sent Chicago tax attorney Chauncey Eskridge to locate Johns and the texts of his sermons to use as ammunition in the war for civil rights. Eskridge found Johns, without socks or shoelaces, tending a vegetable stand next to a vacant lot thirty miles from Richmond. Branch described the encounter:

> It took some time for Johns to adjust to the gravity of the request. When he did he began ticking off sermon titles, then reciting snatches of sermons, and finally he began preaching in full animation on the dangers of drinking Pharaoh's wine. Eskridge stood there in the mud for the better part of an hour, deeply moved.

Later, he recovered enough of his legal skepticism to suspect correctly that the notebooks Johns promised to send did not exist—always his sermons returned to the air from which they had come.

A few months later, in 1965, Johns died after delivering his lecture, "The Romance of Death."

Johns's style as an orator, much like his life, was a mixture of high rhetoric and direct moral challenge. Intensely intellectual and blessed with that powerful memory, he would extemporaneously move through centuries of human thought from Genesis to Wordsworth to contemporary theology, applying ideas and quotations to any and every subject at hand, from the genealogy of the public sign and its Roman origins to the relevance of his beloved "mountain-top experience" in biblical history. Yet through it all, his advocacy of the "plebeian sublime" remained intact: that is, the lowly were the source of God's inspiration, in the common people were the seeds of the great, and what we should live for are those "transfigured moments" when the "ordinary is transformed" and the "obscure 'mountain place, apart' comes into the gaze of the centuries." Such moments were soon to occur on a bus in Montgomery, in a school in Little Rock, and at a lunch counter in Nashville.

Johns's published works bear these same marks of sweeping overview, insightful synthesis, radical juxtaposition, and passionate moral insistence—these ideas carried by his rolling, aphoristic, antithetical, and always profoundly engaging prose. But one senses that the full thrust of his witness was felt more deeply while in the presence of Johns himself, for who Vernon Johns *was* mattered as much as what he said. What he did was consistent with what he recommended, and thus his sermons should not be read in isolation from their autobiographical context or the history that gives them their power, their edge, and their significance as documentation of a life of heroic witness.

His themes were simple and direct: the dignity of labor, the sacredness of the earth and nature, the need for heroic leadership, the equality of all men and women before God, the immorality of segregation, the importance of social justice, and the value of plebeian self-pride—all of this delivered in the simple but penetrating style of a brilliant and learned man who was close to the earth and to the needs of his people. He was, in many ways, a John the Baptist figure, crying out an eloquent but forceful message in the wilderness, tilling the spiritual soil of black America for the leaders who would follow, planting the seeds for those "transfiguring moments" that would occur with increasing regularity throughout the modern civil rights movement.

INFORMATION SOURCES

Research Collections and Collected Speeches

A collection of sermons, essays, and literary pieces, known as the "Vernon Johns crib," is located in the Moorland-Spingarn Research Center in Founders Library, Howard

University. Oberlin College in Ohio, one of Johns's alma maters, has his student file and a collection of his speeches made while attending there.

Gandy, Samuel Lucius. *Human Possibilities: A Vernon Johns Reader*. Hoffman, CA: Hoffman Press, 1977.

Selected Biography

Branch, Taylor. *Parting the Waters: America in the King Years, 1954–63*. New York: Simon and Schuster, 1988.

CHRONOLOGY OF MAJOR SPEECHES

"Transfigured Moments." *Best Sermons 1926*. Ed. Joseph Newton Fort. New York: Harcourt, Brace, 1926, 335–350.
"What Ails the World." Religious Educational Center, New York City, 1927.
"A Negro Agrarian Culture." N.p., n.d. *Opportunity Magazine*, November 1933.
"Religion and the Open Mind." N.p., n.d.
"To Boycott or Not to Boycott." N.p., n.d. *Crisis Magazine*, September 1934.
"Creative Homicide." N.p., n.d.
"Money Answereth All Things." N.p., n.d.
"Rock Foundation." N.p., n.d.
"The Christian Sermon." N.p., n.d.
"The Foundation of Immortality." N.p., n.d.
"The Men Who Let Us Drink." N.p., n.d.
"Mud Is Basic." N.p., n.d.
"Segregation after Death." Dexter Avenue Baptist Church, Montgomery, AL, 1949.
"When the Rapist Is White." Dexter Avenue Baptist Church, Montgomery, AL, 1951.
"It's Safe to Murder Negroes in Montgomery." Dexter Avenue Baptist Church, Montgomery, AL, 1951.
"The Romance of Death." N.p., 1965.

BARBARA CHARLINE JORDAN
(1936–1996), lawyer,
U.S. representative, professor

CARL R. BURGCHARDT

Barbara Charline Jordan's career was marked by distinctive milestones. Jordan was the first African-American woman to be elected to the Texas Senate, to preside as governor for a day in Texas, to be elected to Congress from a Southern state, to serve on the House Judiciary Committee, to address a national political convention, and to deliver a commencement address at Harvard. Jordan's perseverance and indomitable spirit vaulted her into national prominence and made her one of the most admired women in the United States. Yet she chose to forgo higher political office for a professorship, where her independent voice for fairness could be heard unimpeded by political exigencies and compromises.

Barbara Jordan was born in 1936 in Houston, Texas, a member of a poor but nurturing family. Before Jordan's birth, wrote Patricia Witherspoon, her mother had been "a respected orator in church circles," while her "father worked as a warehouse employee during her childhood and became a Baptist minister in 1949." It was only natural, then, that Jordan's first public performances occurred in church, where she recited poetry and sang, and her religious upbringing was a major influence on her values and beliefs. As well, Jordan's father stressed the importance of education. According to David E. Rosenbaum, Jordan's father was not satisfied with less than perfect grades in school, and he was a stickler for correct language. Thus Jordan developed early "the precise diction that has become her hallmark."

Jordan attended a segregated public high school in Houston, where she developed into a talented orator. As a student, she took top honors in local and state speaking events, as well as winning first place in the National Ushers Convention Oratorical Contest. According to David Henry, Jordan's participation in these speech competitions convinced her of the importance of a captivating delivery, a skill at which she excelled.

Jordan continued her participation in forensics at Texas Southern University, where she led her debate team to success against both black and white competitors. After graduating magna cum laude from TSU in 1956 with a degree in political science, Jordan pursued a law degree at Boston University. Law school proved challenging for Jordan, but she persisted. Most importantly, Jordan noted in her autobiography, legal study honed her abilities to "think and read and understand and reason," capacities that she would display in future public speaking.

After receiving her LL.B. degree in 1959, Jordan practiced law in Houston out of her family's home. However, she soon became active in the local Democratic party, working for John F. Kennedy's election in 1960. At first, Jordan labored behind the scenes to help organize a block-worker program. One evening, however, Jordan was asked to fill in for an absent campaign speaker. Jordan's impromptu talk was such a success that the party put her "on the speech-making circuit for the Harris County Democrats." This experience thrilled Jordan and started her thinking about a political career of her own.

In 1962 and 1964, Jordan campaigned for the Texas House, but was defeated both times. In 1966, she ran successfully for the Texas Senate after the Supreme Court forced her district to be reapportioned. Thus Jordan became the first black woman to be seated in the Texas State Senate, and in 1968 she was reelected to a four-year term. Jordan's effectiveness as a senator was demonstrated by the fact that about one-half of the bills she submitted became law. She concentrated on legislation concerning employment practices, the state minimum wage, and voting rights. Jordan was willing to work patiently and cooperatively for reform goals, although this approach was not without its critics. Nonetheless, she won the honor of outstanding freshman senator after completing her first year. In 1972, Jordan was elected president pro tempore of the state senate. As a consequence, she was honored as governor for a day on June 10, 1972, which made her, however briefly, the first African-American female governor in the United States.

In 1972, Jordan was elected overwhelmingly to the U.S. House of Representatives, which was another first: no other woman had ever represented Texas in Congress. She was reelected in 1974 and 1976 by large margins. In Congress Jordan advocated the rights of the poor, women, minorities, consumers, and the elderly; she opposed escalating military spending; and she sponsored an extension of the Voting Rights Act of 1965. Some African-American legislators criticized her for not taking more militant stances on civil rights, but Jordan believed that pragmatic legislation would eventually provide equal opportunities for all Americans.

Jordan played a prominent role in Jimmy Carter's successful bid for U.S. president in 1976. Afterwards, the press and public speculated that Jordan would be nominated for attorney general or another high-ranking post, but such an offer was not extended. After a period of contemplation, Jordan chose to leave politics altogether. In her autobiography, she reasoned that her national fame created an opportunity for her to address the public without the encumbrances of running for office: "I thought that my role now was to be one of the voices in the country defining where we were . . . [and] where we were going. . . . I felt I was more in an instructive role than a legislative role."

In 1979, Jordan accepted a professorship at the Lyndon B. Johnson School of Public Affairs, University of Texas. According to Jordan, "The idea of play-ing a definitive role in educating young people to go into government was very attractive to me." After 1988, Jordan used a wheelchair or walker because of multiple sclerosis, but she continued an active career. In her words, reported Karen Zauber, "I felt I should treat the limitations as irrelevant and refuse to let them be an impediment."

Throughout her career, Jordan received numerous awards, distinctions, and honorary degrees. To name a few, in 1984 the International Platform Association named her "Best Living Orator." The National Women's Hall of Fame inducted her in 1990, and the following year Texas governor Ann Richards appointed her special advisor on ethics in government. In January of 1996, Barbara Jordan died from complications of pneumonia and leukemia.

BARBARA JORDAN: VOICE FOR FAIRNESS

Barbara Jordan was thrust into the national spotlight in 1974 as a member of the House Judiciary Committee, which, during the spring and summer, con-ducted hearings concerning the possible impeachment of Richard Nixon. On the evening of July 24, the committee made its deliberations public. Each member was asked to make a fifteen-minute opening statement before a national tele-vision audience. As a junior member of the committee, Jordan did not speak until the second day, July 25. Prior to the speech, she was determined to be fair in her remarks about Nixon. She had studied the legal precedent and reviewed the testimony. Jordan had asked her assistant to prepare a chart that listed all of Nixon's suspect actions and matched them against criteria for impeachment obtained from historical precedent. Ultimately, Jordan decided to support im-peachment, but she did not actually organize her statement until three hours before the committee was scheduled to reconvene on Thursday evening. When her turn came, she spoke extemporaneously from a four-page outline, in addition to the chart that her assistant had assembled.

Jordan began the speech reflexively by noting that the Constitution originally excluded black women from full participation in society: "I was not included in that 'We the people.' . . . But through the process of amendment, interpreta-tion, and court decision, I have finally been included in 'We the people.' " Despite this original exclusion, Jordan stated, "My faith in the Constitution is whole. It is complete." Jordan made a wise strategic decision to address the people of the United States rather than her committee colleagues who were already well versed in the law and the facts of the Nixon case. In the body of the speech, Jordan systematically explained to the public how Nixon's actions fit reasonable standards for impeachment. The impeachment criteria were grounded in historical authority, including James Madison, Justice Story, and the Carolina Ratification Convention. According to David Henry, Jordan arranged her speech "in a fashion strikingly similar to the dictates of the classical stasis system, which established standard lines of legal argumentation." Jordan concluded by declaring, "If the impeachment provision in the Constitution of the United States will not reach the offenses charged here, then perhaps that eighteenth-century Constitution should be abandoned to a twentieth-century paper shredder."

The reaction to her address was as immediate as it was positive. When Jordan left the Rayburn building later that evening, she was cheered by an appreciative crowd. The press lauded her efforts the following day. R. W. Apple, Jr., opined in the *New York Times*, "In her booming voice, with her elegant articulations, she delivered a lecture in constitutional law." The didactic nature of her speech was not lost on the public. One man from Houston paid to display the following message on twenty-five billboards: "THANK YOU, BARBARA JORDAN, FOR EXPLAINING THE CONSTITUTION TO US." In addition, Jordan, received scores of letters from admirers who praised her for being honest, eloquent, intelligent, cogent, logical, sincere, and dignified.

The positive reaction to Jordan's "We the People" speech made her a celebrity and attracted the attention of national Democratic party leaders, who invited her, along with Senator John Glenn, to be a keynote speaker for the 1976 Democratic National Convention in New York. On July 12, Glenn delivered a sincere but dull speech to an inattentive audience at Madison Square Garden. Jordan's speech was preceded by a short film clip that traced her remarkable career. When Jordan finally appeared on the stage, she was cheered for three minutes. As she began to speak, the delegates became silent immediately and continued to give her their full attention, which is unusual for contemporary political conventions. Her twenty-five-minute oration was interrupted repeatedly by applause.

When Jordan gazed upon her audience, it was the first time an African-American woman had ever addressed a Democratic National Convention, and she alluded to this fact: "There is something special about tonight. What is different? What is special? I, Barbara Jordan, am a keynote speaker. . . . [M]y presence here is one additional piece of evidence that the American dream need not forever be deferred." At that moment Jordan "embodied" the words she expressed. As Campbell and Jamieson put it, "She herself *was* the proof of the argument she was making."

In the body of the speech, Jordan warned about the dangers of the nation collapsing into competing "interest groups" and instead called for "national community." But Jordan did not stop with appeals for unity. In an unusual move, she criticized the past actions of her party. Although the Democrats had "made mistakes," these were "mistakes of the heart." At the same time, Jordan insisted that "the Democratic Party can lead the way" to greater "national community." According to Johannesen et al., Jordan criticized "her own party, but in such a moderate way as to freshen the speech without weakening her praise of party principles or generating negative audience reaction.'' Wayne Thompson argued that Jordan skillfully coupled generally accepted national values such as patriotism and traditional morality with values more specific to the Democratic party such as ''change and progress,'' ''ethical equality,'' ''equality of opportunity,'' and ''rejection of authority.''

When Jordan concluded her speech, cheers of ''we want Barbara'' reverberated throughout the hall. Her speech was so impressive that many urged Jimmy Carter to put Jordan on the ticket as the vice-presidential candidate. Jordan's keynote address proved to be successful outside the convention hall, as well. *Time* magazine of July 26, 1976, reported that Jordan's speech would ''take its place among Democratic convention oratorical classics,'' and Wayne Thompson noted that a public opinion poll revealed that more than half of the national audience reacted positively toward the address.

The 1976 keynote speech increased Jordan's fame and created a strong demand for her as a speaker. Jordan turned down most requests, but she was intrigued by an invitation to receive an honorary degree and become commencement speaker at Harvard, the school she had originally dreamed of attending while a student at Texas Southern University. Jordan agreed to appear and worked hard on topic selection, finally settling on a main theme of her political career: citizen involvement. She argued that the people ''want to be insiders on America'' and appealed for ''the re-inclusion of the people in their government,'' which ''would be a return of a right which we once considered unalienable.'' Her speech at Harvard broke another precedent: in June 1977, Jordan became the first African-American woman to deliver a commencement address at Harvard. The immediate impact of the speech was positive, as audience members approached her to obtain an autograph or handshake. But the experience had an important, personal, long-term consequence: it crystallized her intention to leave politics and to become an impartial national voice.

In the 1970s, Jordan gave several notable addresses on women's issues. On November 10, 1975, during the International Women's Year, she delivered a speech at the LBJ School of Public Affairs in Austin. Jordan argued that women must change their concept of themselves: ''The problem remains that we fail to define ourselves in terms of whole human beings.'' The solution was to ''act out the equality we say we feel.'' Women must exercise leadership to insure ''justice for everybody.'' She sounded much the same theme in a keynote speech delivered at the National Women's Conference in Houston, November 19, 1977. Martin and Martin quoted Jordan as stating, ''We endorse personal and political freedom as a national right of human pride.''

In 1992, Jordan was again named a keynote speaker for the Democratic National Convention. On July 13, Jordan shared the platform with Senator Bill Bradley of New Jersey and Governor Zell Miller of Georgia. According to *Congressional Quarterly Weekly Report*, Senator Bradley delivered a ''serious but uninspiring speech, often having trouble overcoming the buzz of conversation in the hall," while Governor Miller had some applause lines, but the delegates continued to be restless. Jordan, however, "held their rapt attention." As Daniel Henninger observed, "When she began to talk, the hall quieted, and save for the applause, it stayed quiet."

Jordan opened the speech by reminding her audience, "It was at this time; it was at this place; it was at this event, 16 years ago, I presented a keynote address to the Democratic National Convention." And, she added, "we won the presidency" in November 1976. She stated that the Democrats could reclaim the White House, but they would have to change their approach: "Why not change from a party with a reputation of tax and spend to one with a reputation of investment and growth?" Such an economic policy would provide educational and job opportunities to impoverished individuals. In order to create economic growth and reduce the deficit, however, "everybody must join in the sacrifice, not just a few." Significantly, she advised the convention, "The American electorate must be persuaded to trust us, the Democrats, to govern again." Jordan concluded with the words of Franklin Roosevelt, who, during the depths of the Depression, called for "a leadership of frankness and vigor."

According to Leslie Barnes, the arrangement of ideas in the 1992 speech was virtually identical to that in the 1976 address. Jordan opened both speeches by referring to a positive historical event; she conceded that the party had made mistakes in the past; she argued that despite the mistakes, the Democratic party was still the one to assume leadership when the nation called for change; she explained how the party would bring about the needed change; she claimed that in order to be successful, all American citizens must participate; finally, she concluded with a quotation from a national hero.

Henninger noted that Jordan received hearty applause for much of the speech, but only polite responses for other parts. She drew a warm ovation when she praised the presence of women candidates for Congress, but when she called for programs "which help us help ourselves," the applause was "tepid." The least applauded sentence in the speech was when she insisted that Democrats must admit their "complicity in the creation of the unconscionable deficit."

Jordan's speech received an uncertain reaction from delegates and virtual silence from Democratic officials, the press, or television commentators. Obviously, this address was not as celebrated as the 1976 keynote speech. Why did this happen? One reason is that the situation was no longer novel. In 1976 Jordan's appearance was unprecedented, but by 1992 many of the delegates had seen Jordan before and heard a similar message. Moreover, Jordan had been out of Congress for thirteen years. Another reason for the subdued reaction is that the Democratic party was more sensitive to criticism, even constructive criticism, because of the adversities of the Clinton candidacy. Although change was the central theme in Bill Clinton's presidential campaign, Jordan called for profound conversion within the Democratic party itself, not just a partisan victory over the Republicans. While delegates were eager to cheer standard Democratic themes and welcomed the symbolism of an African-American woman on the podium, they were less receptive to the honest criticism of Democratic failures.

No discussion of Jordan's oratory would be complete without considering her physical presence and resonant voice. Throughout her career, Jordan was self-conscious about her weight. At various times, journalists described her as "hulking," "massive," and "ample," although they also reported her charisma and great dignity. By far Jordan's most distinctive physical trait was her voice, however, which she considered her strongest oratorical feature. Patricia Lasher and Beverly Bentley provided an excellent summary of Jordan's delivery skills:

> The sheer power of her rhetoric often caused otherwise inattentive legislators to sit up and listen. Her voice is that of a seasoned actress, an impassioned missionary, a righteous headmistress, a lecturing parent. It can sound arrogant, soothing, indignant, supportive, reproving or understanding, depending on her intent. She is a diva who provides her own chorus, often repeating key words and phrases with a rhythmic cadence that gives her speeches an evangelical quality.

Jordan emphasized points through the use of inflection, pitch, varied rate, dramatic pauses, and rhetorical questions. Her exaggerated enunciation of words was a technique that held the attention of distracted delegates at chaotic political conventions.

A unifying theme in Jordan's rhetoric was "the people." Indeed, her indictment of Richard Nixon was grounded in the constitutional authority of the people. Her Harvard commencement speech stressed the importance of citizen involvement in a democracy, as did her 1976 and 1992 keynote addresses. Another common thread of Jordan's discourse was her status as a female African-American. Most of her speeches began reflexively with references to her race and gender. Yet, ironically, she stated repeatedly that she did not wish to become a symbol for blacks or women.

Rather than focusing exclusively on a particular group or cause, Jordan strived for balance and fairness. During her legislative career, she advocated the rights of the disadvantaged, but she also stressed the importance of individual drive, responsibility, and initiative. Her reform goals were not revolutionary, but simply asked for equal justice to all. Although Jordan condemned Richard Nixon in 1974, she agonized over her decision and struggled to objectively weigh the facts of the case. Indeed, her "We the People" speech is strongly analytical and exhibits thorough research and attention to detail. Jordan's two Democratic National Convention speeches promoted victory for her party, yet she offset praise with honest criticism of past faults and excesses. Because of her balanced, well-supported arguments, Lasher and Bentley argued that Jordan "has come to represent uncompromising rectitude, moral authority, judicious reasoning and strength." In short, Barbara Charline Jordan became a determined voice for fairness in the United States.

INFORMATION SOURCES

Research Collections and Collected Speeches

Speech manuscripts and other archival materials are located in the Barbara Jordan Collection at Texas Southern University. Jordan's speeches are widely anthologized. The sources listed here contain the most accurate, printed versions.

[*CQ*] *Congressional Quarterly Weekly Report*, July 18, 1992.
[*BJ*] Jordan, Barbara, and Shelby Hearon. *Barbara Jordan: A Self-Portrait*. Garden City, NY: Doubleday and Company, 1979.
[*GS*] Rohler, Lloyd E., and Roger Cook, eds. *Great Speeches for Criticism and Analysis*. Greenwood, IN: Alistair Press, 1988.

Selected Critical Studies

Barnes, Leslie. "Barbara Jordan, Then and Now: A Comparison of Jordan's 1976 and 1992 Keynote Addresses." Paper delivered at the Colorado Speech Communication Association Convention, Greeley, CO, April 24, 1993.
Campbell, Karlyn Kohrs, and Kathleen Hall Jamieson. "Form and Genre in Political Criticism: An Introduction." *Form and Genre: Shaping Rhetorical Action*. Ed. Karlyn Kohrs Campbell and Kathleen Hall Jamieson. Falls Church, VA: Speech Communication Association, n.d., 9–32.
Henninger, Daniel. "A Woman of Substance." *Wall Street Journal*, July 15, 1993:A-12.
Henry, David. "Barbara Jordan." *American Orators of the Twentieth Century*. Ed. Bernard K. Duffy and Halford R. Ryan. Westport, CT: Greenwood, 1987, 233–238.
Johannesen, Richard L., R. R. Allen, and Wil A. Linkugel. "Democratic Convention Keynote Address: Barbara Jordan." *Contemporary American Speeches*. 7th ed. Ed. Richard L. Johannesen, R. R. Allen, and Wil A. Linkugel. Dubuque, IA: Kendall/Hunt, 1992, 369–374.
Martin, Donald R., and Vicky Gordon Martin. "Barbara Jordan's Symbolic Use of Language in the Keynote Address to the National Women's Conference." *Southern Speech Communication Journal* 54 (1988): 319–330.
Rosenbaum, David. "Black Woman Keynoter." *New York Times* July 13, 1976: 24.
Thompson, Wayne N. "Barbara Jordan's Keynote Address: The Juxtaposition of Contradictory Values." *Southern Speech Communication Journal* 44 (1979): 223–232.
Witherspoon, Patricia D. " 'We the People': Barbara Jordan's Statement before the House Judiciary Committee on the Impeachment of Richard M. Nixon." *Great Speeches for Criticism and Analysis*. Ed. Lloyd E. Rohler and Roger Cook. Greenwood, IN: Alistair Press, 1988, 183–194.

Selected Biographies

"Barbara Jordan." *1993 Current Biography Yearbook*.
Bryant, Ira B. *Barbara Charline Jordan: From the Ghetto to the Capitol*. Houston, TX: D. Armstrong Co., 1977.

Duckworth, James. "Barbara Jordan." *Notable Black American Women.* Ed. Jessie Carney Smith. Detroit: Gale Research, 1992, 609–612.

Jordan, Barbara, and Shelby Hearon. *Barbara Jordan: A Self-Portrait.* Garden City, NY: Doubleday and Company, 1979.

Kennedy, Patricia Scileppi, and Gloria Hartmann O'Shields. "Barbara C. Jordan." *We Shall Be Heard: Women Speakers in America.* Ed. Patricia Scileppi Kennedy and Gloria Hartmann O'Shields. Dubuque, IA: Kendall/Hunt, 1983, 327–336.

Lasher, Patricia, and Beverly Bentley. "Barbara Jordan." *Texas Women: Interviews and Images.* Austin, TX: Shoal Creek Publishers, 1980, 98–103.

Zauber, Karen. "Meet: Barbara Jordan." *NEA Today,* December 1992: 9.

CHRONOLOGY OF MAJOR SPEECHES

[See "Research Collections and Collected Speeches" for source codes.]

"Statement on the Articles of Impeachment" (We the People). Washington, DC. July 25, 1974. *GS,* 179–182 [transcribed from videotape]; *BJ,* 186–192.

"International Women's Year Address." Austin, TX, November 10, 1975. *BJ,* 215–220.

"Democratic Convention Keynote Address" (Who Then Will Speak for the Common Good?). New York City, July 12, 1976. *GS,* 76–79 [transcribed from videotape].

"Commencement Address." Harvard University, Cambridge, MA, June 1977. *BJ,* 260–266.

"Keynote Address" (Change: From What to What?). New York City, July 13, 1992. *CQ,* 2117–2118 [unedited version].

MARTIN LUTHER KING, JR.
(1929–1968), minister,
civil rights activist

JOHN H. PATTON

Martin Luther King, Jr., consistently referred to himself as a "simple preacher," yet his voice became one of the most significant influences in American culture. His sound was distinctive, a different and penetrating tonality that carried with it the full drama of racial relations in America. His was a voice that could not be ignored, despite strong efforts by many to do so. Once heard, King's voice continued to reverberate within the moral and social consciences of diverse persons for the duration of the civil rights movement in the 1950s and 1960s. The combination of his roles as preacher, leader of a major social movement, and international symbol of nonviolence for social change made him an unparalleled figure in many respects. His oratory, which sometimes took the form of sermonic addresses, sometimes the form of philosophical and reflective social commentary, and sometimes the shape of major policy and value arguments on ceremonial occasions, gave King a memorable place in the history of those who have practiced the art of spoken discourse. Moreover, King's oratory was almost always accompanied by action, usually in the form of demonstrations to protest the evils of segregation and racial discrimination. It is important to remember King's rhetorical heritage as a creative blending of words and deeds, a synthesis that he attempted to carry out himself and that he correspondingly made accessible to the public audiences who heard his message.

The major events and episodes of King's life are well known. He was born on January 15, 1929, in Atlanta as the second child in the black middle-class family of Martin Luther King, Sr., and Alberta Williams. King, Sr., was assistant pastor of Atlanta's Ebenezer Baptist Church and soon became pastor in a family tradition that Martin Luther King, Jr., would continue. King, Jr., attended Morehouse College in Atlanta, eventually majoring in sociology and participating in oratorical contests and a variety of interracial organizations. David Garrow described the latter as especially formative in helping King deal with strong antiwhite feelings derived from experiences of discrimination in his childhood. After deciding to enter the ministry, King enrolled in Crozer Theological Seminary in Philadelphia and gradually became immersed in the writings of social gospel theologians such as Walter Rausenbusch. He graduated from Crozer in 1951 as class valedictorian and that fall began doctoral studies at Boston University School of Theology, where he was deeply influenced by the personalist theology of Edgar Brightman and Harold DeWolf.

In 1953, before completing his dissertation, a document that has retrospectively become a matter of considerable academic controversy, King made the crucial decision of accepting the pastorate of Dexter Avenue Baptist Church in Montgomery, Alabama. There he succeeded the highly polemic Vernon Johns and soon became involved in civil rights organizations. With Rosa Parks's act of resistance and the ensuing Montgomery bus boycott, King helped form the Montgomery Improvement Association and began to articulate the themes that characterized the soul and substance of the civil rights movement. He adapted and refined the strategy of nonviolent resistance and, after the eventual success of the Montgomery boycott, formed the Southern Christian Leadership Conference to guide and direct a full-fledged civil rights movement throughout the South.

Pivotal episodes in King's oratorical career are intertwined with the history of the movement. The virtual failure of the movement in Albany, Georgia, followed by its rebirth largely through the power of King's sermonic oratory in Birmingham and Selma, Alabama, are landmarks of major importance. This phase of the movement was highlighted by King's most memorable speech, "I Have a Dream," delivered at the culmination of the March on Washington, D.C., on August 28, 1963. King celebrated the progress of the movement and tried to fashion a transition to larger themes in his address accepting the Nobel Peace Prize in 1964. A different phase of the movement evolved as King began campaigns in Chicago and Boston, where his oratory shifted toward issues of economic justice, the details of fair-housing provisions, and poverty. The final stages of his life were marked by continued emphasis on economic themes along with prophetic and penetrating appraisals of American foreign policy in Vietnam. King became one of the earliest and strongest voices against U.S. involvement in the war. His opposition was proclaimed in such major addresses as "A Time to Break Silence" and "A Christmas Sermon for Peace" in 1967. King's last campaign in Memphis, Tennessee, focused on the sanitation workers' economic and employment needs and produced his climactic "I've Been to the Mountaintop" address. The day after that remarkable address, King was assassinated on the balcony of the Lorraine Motel in Memphis, on April 4, 1968.

MARTIN LUTHER KING, JR., AS TRANSFORMATIONAL ORATOR

King's rhetoric was transformational because it created new understandings and possibilities for many different audiences. This was especially the case for

African-American audiences, for whom King provided a new sense of self-understanding, definition, and direction. King's rhetoric established the framework for a different pattern of structural and interpersonal relationships between African-Americans and whites, and it recast legal and political issues into questions of morality and conscience. Many important features of King's oratory in carrying out these transformational functions could be discussed. Two qualities, however, were central to the transformational process: (1) the nature and significance of orality in King's discourse and (2) his reflection of African traditions and performative patterns in oratory.

King's oratory profoundly affected African-American audiences in several major ways. First, his discourse shaped the individual and collective self-identities of African-Americans. Many of his arguments and narratives provided grounds for a renewed version of self-worth, while simultaneously creating confidence that social change could actually become reality. Second, his discourse created a pluralistic framework for validating and reconciling conflicting views about civil rights within the African-American community. Third, his discourse enacted and developed an essentially African oral tradition that engaged and energized African-American publics in significant ways.

The realities of historic slavery and legalized segregation had left African-Americans not only in conditions of material oppression, but also in a state of considerable self-doubt. Prior to King's emergence in Montgomery and the beginnings of the civil rights movement, few had suggested that African-Americans could bring about significant social or political changes. Change, if it occurred, would have to come through beneficent individuals or by exceptional circumstance. From the beginning, King argued in his sermons that African-Americans had the inherent capacity to constructively and collectively confront the system of segregation. In doing so, he focused attention on the inner qualities, the spiritual strength of the African-American community, and linked those qualities to the model of nonviolent social resistance. For example, in "A Tough Mind and a Tender Heart," delivered at Dexter Avenue Baptist Church in Montgomery, King argued against softmindedness as "one of the basic causes of race prejudice." The use of "softmindedness" here is King's encompassing symbol for the compliant self-concepts of many African-Americans who had been conditioned to accept a sense of inferiority from the legacy of slavery and separateness. This same sense of "softmindedness" resulted in a consequent inability of many to visualize, much less plan for, social change. In contrast, King urged that "we as Negroes must bring together toughmindedness and tenderheartedness, if we are to move creatively toward the goal of freedom and justice. Softminded individuals among us feel that the only way to deal with oppression is by adjusting to it. They acquiesce and resign themselves to segregation. They prefer to remain oppressed." In contrast, King pointed, as he frequently did, to "a third way," one "that combines toughmindedness and tenderheartedness and avoids the complacency and do-nothingness of the softminded and the violence and bitterness of the hardhearted." This third way allowed him to articulate the principles of nonviolent resistance and even to link them with the very nature of God. Thus he remarked, "The Bible, always clear in stressing both attributes of God, expresses his toughmindedness in his justice and wrath and his tenderheartedness in his love and grace." This and many similar passages displayed the positive alternative of nonviolence as a form of resistance that activated the stored-up power of African-Americans.

Similarly, King frequently used reversal images to communicate with African-American audiences that the very things that may appear as weaknesses could now become strengths. An especially vivid example is his use of the "well-adjusted–maladjusted" theme as a reversal image. An early version appears in his sermon "Transformed Nonconformist," also delivered originally as a Dexter Avenue Church sermon. King argued that "there are some things in our world to which men of goodwill must become maladjusted. I confess that I never intend to become adjusted to the evils of segregation and the crippling effects of discrimination, to the moral degeneracy of religious bigotry and the corroding effects of narrow sectarianism, to economic conditions that deprive men of work and food, and to the insanities of militarism and the self-defeating effects of physical violence. Human salvation lies in the hands of the creatively maladjusted."

Another dimension of the restoration-of-confidence imagery is reflected in an early passage King aimed at "Negro youth." This passage is found in "Three Dimensions of a Complete Life," a pivotal sermon that appeared in its original version as his trial sermon at Dexter Avenue Baptist Church. It contains key images and examples King would later weave into many public addresses. He admonished younger listeners that "you must not wait until the day of full emancipation before you make a creative contribution to the life of this nation. . . . We are challenged on every hand to work untiringly to achieve excellence in our lifework. Not all men are called to specialized professional jobs . . . but no work is insignificant." He went on to argue that "if a man is called to be a street sweeper he should sweep streets even as Michelangelo painted, or Beethoven composed music, or Shakespeare wrote poetry," ending with a quotation from Mallock's poem: "If you can't be a pine on the top of the hill, be a scrub in the valley—but be the best little scrub by the side of the rill, be a bush if you can't be a tree."

Moreover, in the classic "I Have a Dream" speech in 1963, King spoke at times directly to the rank-and-file participants in the civil rights campaign. He did so in order to validate the experience of African-American publics, while at the same time enlarging the boundaries of their experience of oppression to envelop all persons who heard the call of conscience. In that address a powerful passage is tucked in between the series of "we can never be satisfied" urgings and the memorable "I still have a dream" section that concludes the address. King remarked, "I am not unmindful that some of you have come here out of excessive trials and tribulation. Some of you have come fresh from narrow jail cells. Some of you have come from areas where your quest for freedom left you battered by the storms of persecution and staggered by the winds of police brutality. You have been the veterans of creative suffering. Continue to work with the faith that unearned suffering is redemptive.'' These words publicly affirmed and reinforced the sacrificial efforts of participants in the movement. They held special significance for African-Americans because they provided a symbolic transformation of the unbroken legacy of suffering, changing the hopelessness of persecution into the positive notion of ''creative'' and ''redemptive suffering.'' This passage and many others like it throughout King's oratorical career helped African-Americans make sense of their history and supplied a fresh foundation for belief in the future.

Finally, King's discourse provided grounds for confidence within the African-American community by envisioning a sense of inevitable victory. A representative example comes from King's address culminating the 1964 voting rights campaign march from Selma to Montgomery, Alabama. Dimensions of orality and performance were clearly at work in King's exhortation to the demonstrators: ''We are on the move now. The burning of our churches will not deter us. We are on the move now. The bombing of our homes will not dissuade us. We are on the move now. The beating and killing of our clergymen and young people will not divert us. We are on the move now. The arrest and release of known murderers will not discourage us. We are on the move now. Like an idea whose time has come, not even the marching of mighty armies can halt us. We are moving to the land of freedom.'' This led to the famous ''how long?—not long'' sequence of phrases that bonded King, audience, and moment of experience together in a unity of experience and expression. Placing himself in the frame of the audience as he frequently did, King asked rhetorically, ''I know you are asking today, 'How long will it take?' I come to say to you this afternoon however difficult the moment, however frustrating the hour, it will not be long, because truth pressed to earth will rise again. How long? Not long, because no lie can live forever. How long? Not long, because you still reap what you sow. How long? Not long, because the arm of the moral universe is long but it bends toward justice.'' The sermonic speech ended with the quotation of the Battle Hymn of the Republic, also a frequent staple in King's addresses.

In these and other passages King carried out a significant enactment of many crucial features of what Walter Ong described as primary orality within the context of a visually dominated world. Orality is directly linked to African traditions and patterns throughout King's public discourse, a connection that is essential for understanding important forms and functions of his messages. In saying this, I am mindful of the dangers of excessive revisionism, and I am not suggesting that King was consciously articulating an Afrocentric view of the world, which would have been counter to much of his approach. He was, we remember, exceedingly uncomfortable with the emerging language of ''black power'' and continued to use the accepted terminology of ''Negro'' in his own discourses. Nonetheless, an understanding of African rhetorical traditions provides an extremely important lens for explaining and interpreting much of

King's oratory, especially the impact of his addresses on African-American audiences at a particularly pivotal moment of social and cultural identity.

Among the central qualities of African oratory are functionality, creativity of the artist, and the participatory nature of oratory as a performed social action. Arthur Smith (now Molefi Asante) has underscored the unity of the speaker as creative artist and the participation of the audience in the moment of communication as a central feature of African rhetoric. He noted that "what are conventionally labeled reactions and responses of the audience might be better understood if we spoke of these phenomena as collective actions of participants." He further argued that "Africans highlight the creative process of the artist. . . . The African sees the discourse as the creative manifestation of what is *called to be*. That which is *called to be* because of the values and mores of society becomes the created thing; and the artist, or speaker, satisfies the demands of the society by calling into being that which is functional."

This perspective is grounded in what Asante and others have elaborated as the African concept of *Nommo*, "the generating and sustaining powers of the spoken word." The significance of the word as a source of power is central to grasping virtually all of the creative activities within Africa and, most important for our purposes, throughout the African diaspora. The voice with all of the associated aspects of tonality, rhythm, inflection, emphasis, and pace becomes an inherent part of the act of communication, an indelible substance inseparable from the message. Smith-Asante made the comparison in this regard that "the almost methodical pathos of Martin Luther King can be viewed alongside the mournful utterances of Ray Charles; the vocal expressions of both simply reflect different parts of the same fabric."

King's approach to public discourse was essentially sermonic, heavily theological, and deeply experiential. It was drawn from his experiences in the African-American church, which were in turn extensions and manifestations of African oral traditions. Fortunately, we have a fairly clear record of King's process of refining his sermonic oratory, a process that came largely from his training in homiletics at Crozer Seminary. Significantly, Branch reported that "King perfected minute details of showmanship, such as tucking away his notes at the podium in a manner just unsubtle enough to be noticed, and his general style was extremely formal." He noted that King called his orations " 'religious lectures' instead of sermons," partly reflecting an inner conflict "over such issues as knowledge versus zeal." King was clearly influenced by his homiletics professor Robert Keighton, whom Branch said "brought to the classroom a preoccupation with style and the classical form of argument, which suited King perfectly." According to Branch,

Keighton taught that a preacher should first prepare an outline based on one of the proven sermon structures. There was the Ladder Sermon, the Jewel Sermon, the Skyrocket Sermon, the Twin Sermon, the Surprise Package Sermon, and many others. The Ladder Sermon climbed through arguments of increasing power toward the conclusion the preacher hoped to make convincing. The Jewel Sermon held up a single idea from many different angles, as a jeweler might examine a precious stone. The Skyrocket Sermon usually began with a gripping human interest story leading to a cosmic spiritual lesson, followed by a shower of derivative lessons falling back to earth among the congregation.

These sermonic patterns became highly heuristic experiences for King and his classmates. Branch observed that "the Negro students shared much merriment in contrasting Keighton's highly formal structures with their own homemade preaching formulas. Keighton might have his Ladder Sermon, they joked, but they had Rabbit in the Bushes, by which they meant that if they felt the crowd stir, they should repeat the theme, just as a hunter shoots into the shaking bush on the assumption that a rabbit might be there." Similarly, Keith Miller commented that "on hundreds of occasions he [King] organized speeches and sermons by rearranging parts of old addresses in new combinations. . . . Instead of dissolving his homiletic patterns when he mixed and matched, King usually opened the forms and stirred part of one address into another." Miller also contended that "like folk homilists before him, King created himself and introduced sacred time by using typology, borrowing sermons, and embedding quotations." This practice allowed "ministers [to] dissolve chronological time and reenact important moments." Miller held that this approach to the use of biblical passages is precisely what energized King's sermons and allowed him to connect with African-American audiences. He observed that by "extracting the Bible from the straitjacket of the past, he [King] explained that archetypal Biblical acts continually spiral through history. . . . King's interpretation of the Bible recapitulates and reenacts the archetypal, typological view of slave religion and the folk pulpit. From late 1956 until his death, he electrified his followers by reawakening the slaves' sense of sacred time and archetypal view of the Bible."

In *Martin and Malcolm and America*, James Cone illuminated this point further by emphasizing King's reliance on the form and content of black experience. Cone argued that "the influence of the black church and its central theme of freedom and hope can be seen in the language of King's speaking and writing. Everything he said and wrote sounds like a black sermon and not rational reflection." This is especially important in analyzing King's oral discourse "because the theme of freedom and hope had to be reflected in the movement and rhythm of his voice, if he expected a black congregation to take his message seriously. . . . In the black church, the meaning is found not primarily in the intellectual content of the spoken word but in the *way* the word is spoken and the effect on those who hear it." Cone extended this argument by noting that what black audiences "understood was the appropriate tone and movement of his [King's] speech which the people believe is the instrument for the coming of God's spirit, thereby empowering them with the hope for freedom. The people believe that freedom is coming because a foretaste of it is given in the sermon event itself." In this view, King's rhetoric constituted a virtual enactment of the African concept of *Nommo* and the narrative functions associated with it.

Indeed, one of the most crucial features of King's rhetoric was his narrative ability both to function in complete unity with his audience and also to operate as a leader strategically demarcated from his audience. In the unified or harmonious role, King was able to articulate, affirm, and reinforce the deepest feelings and strongest expectations of African-American audiences. In the demarcated role, King was able to critique and provide guidance and pragmatic direction by helping confront his audiences with the questions, issues, and risks central to the further life of the movement.

One of the paramount examples of the unifying function of King's narrative is found in his 1963 eulogy for the young girls killed in the bomb-blast attack on Sixteenth Street Baptist Church in Birmingham. Speaking both to grieving families and to the national conscience, King argued that the children did not die in vain: "The innocent blood of these little girls may well serve as the redemptive force that will bring new light to this dark city. . . . These tragic deaths may lead our nation to substitute an aristocracy of character for an aristocracy of color. Indeed this tragic event may cause the white South to come to terms with its conscience." He went on to affirm his understanding of and unity with his listeners by urging them not to despair. He acknowledged that "it is almost impossible to say anything that can console you at this difficult hour and remove the deep clouds of disappointment which are floating in your mental skies." Quickly King affirmed a continuing sense of hope: "At times, life is hard, as hard as crucible steel. It has its bleak and painful moments. Like the ever flowing waters of a river, life has its moments of drought and its moments of flood. . . . But through it all God walks with us. Never forget that God is able to lift you from fatigue of despair to the buoyancy of hope, and transform dark and desolate valleys into sunlit paths of inner peace." Here King becomes one with his immediate audience and, by extension, with the shocked consciences of a watching and listening nation responding to the tragic deaths of children.

As the movement matured and developed, King frequently spoke in a more demarcated narrative, confronting loyal audiences with issues and concerns about which they had not yet come to terms. No better example remains than his speeches linking civil rights to American policy on the war in Vietnam. In his 1967 speech "A Time to Break Silence," delivered on April 4 at Riverside Church in New York City, King argued that there was a direct connection from his original sermons at Dexter Avenue Baptist Church in Montgomery to his voice of opposition to U.S. policy on Vietnam. He took the perspectives of both the poor and the minorities who were "sending their sons and their brothers and their husbands to fight and to die in extraordinarily high proportions relative to the rest of the population." He critiqued the civil rights movement and maintained that "I knew I could never again raise my voice against the violence of the oppressed in the ghettos without having first spoken clearly to the greatest

purveyor of violence in the world today—my own government.'' In these and
similar terms, which were very difficult for mainstream leaders and ordinary
supporters of civil rights to accept, King held that ''the true meaning and value
of compassion and nonviolence'' occurs ''when it helps us to see the enemy's
point of view, to hear his questions, to know his assessment of ourselves.'' After
these stinging critiques, King sought to provide a new synthesis that he termed
a ''revolution of values.'' In the final analysis, he contended, ''there is nothing,
except a tragic death wish, to prevent us from re-ordering our priorities, so that
the pursuit of peace will take precedence over the pursuit of war. There is
nothing to keep us from molding a recalcitrant status quo with bruised hands
until we have fashioned it into a brotherhood.''

As a demarcated voice, King experienced a sense of distancing from some of
his public audiences. Yet his voice on this and other issues involving value
conflicts provided an anchor point for moral arguments about the war and added
to the public's sense for new directions on this and related issues. That King
was able to move effectively between the dual roles of harmonious and demarcated voices in relation to his audiences reflected the essential qualities of oral
performance in African traditions. Martin Luther King, Jr.,'s capacity to create
a synthesis of the unified and demarcated narrative roles remains one of the
most significant and enduring qualities of his oratory and public discourse.

INFORMATION SOURCES

Research Collections and Collected Speeches

Carson, Clayborne, ed. *The Papers of Martin Luther King, Jr.* 2 vols. Berkeley: U of
    California P, 1992–1994.
[*STL*] King, Martin Luther, Jr. *Strength to Love.* New York: Harper and Row, 1963.
———. *The Trumpet of Conscience.* New York: Harper and Row, 1967.
[*TOH*] Washington, James M., ed. *A Testament of Hope: The Essential Writings of
    Martin Luther King, Jr.* New York: Harper and Row, 1986.

Selected Critical Studies

Ansbro, John J. *Martin Luther King, Jr.: The Making of a Mind.* Maryknoll, NY: Orbis,
    1982.
Baldwin, Lewis V. *There Is a Balm in Gilead: The Cultural Roots of Martin Luther
    King, Jr.* Minneapolis, MN: Fortress, 1991.
Calloway-Thomas, Carolyn, and John Louis Lucaites, eds. *Martin Luther King, Jr., and
    the Sermonic Power of Public Discourse.* Tuscaloosa: U of Alabama P, 1993.
Cone, James H. *Martin and Malcolm and America.* Maryknoll, NY: Orbis, 1991.
———. ''Martin Luther King, Jr.: Black Theology—Black Church.'' *Martin Luther
    King, Jr.: Civil Rights Leader, Theologian, Orator.* Vol. 1. Ed. David J. Garrow.
    Brooklyn, NY: Carlson, 1989.

Lentz, Richard. *Symbols, the News Magazines, and Martin Luther King.* Baton Rouge: Louisiana State UP, 1990.

Lischer, Richard. *The Preacher King.* New York: Oxford UP, 1995.

Miller, Keith D. *Voice of Deliverance: The Language of Martin Luther King, Jr., and Its Sources.* New York: Free Press, 1992.

Patton, John H. " 'I Have a Dream': The Rhetoric of Theology Fused with the Power of Orality." *Martin Luther King, Jr. and the Sermonic Power of Public Discourse.* Ed. Carolyn Calloway-Thomas and John Louis Lucaites. Tuscaloosa: U of Alabama P, 1993, 104–126.

Reagon, Bernice J. "Songs of the Civil Rights Movement, 1955–1965: A Study in Culture History." Ph.D. diss., Howard U, Washington, DC, 1975.

Smith, Arthur L. (Molefi Asante). *Language, Communication and Rhetoric in Black America.* New York: Harper and Row, 1972.

Smith, Donald H. "Martin Luther King, Jr.: In the Beginning at Montgomery." *Southern Speech Journal* 34 (1968): 8–17.

Spillers, Hortense J. "Martin Luther King and the Style of the Black Sermon." *Black Scholar*, September 1971: 14–27.

Selected Biographies

Branch, Taylor. *Parting the Waters: America in the King Years, 1954–63.* New York: Simon and Schuster, 1988.

Garrow, David J. *Bearing the Cross: Martin Luther King, Jr., and the Southern Christian Leadership Conference.* New York: William Morrow, 1986.

Lewis, David L. *King: A Biography.* 2nd ed. Urbana: U of Illinois P, 1978.

Oates, Stephen B. *Let the Trumpet Sound: The Life of Martin Luther King, Jr.* New York: Plume Signet, 1982.

CHRONOLOGY OF MAJOR SPEECHES

[See "Research Collections and Collected Speeches" for source codes.]

"Three Dimensions of a Complete Life." Montgomery, AL, January 17, 1954. *STL*, 67–77.

"A Tough Mind and a Tender Heart." Montgomery, AL, n.d. *STL*, 1–7.

"Transformed Nonconformist." Montgomery, AL, n.d. *STL*, 8–15.

"I Have a Dream." Washington, DC, August 28, 1963. *STL*, 217–220.

"Eulogy for the Martyred Children." Birmingham, AL, September 1963. *TOH*, 221–223.

"Nobel Prize Acceptance Speech." Oslo, Norway, December 10, 1964. *TOH*, 224–226.

"Our God Is Marching On." Montgomery, AL, March 25, 1965. *TOH*, 227–230.

"A Time to Break Silence." New York, NY, April 4, 1967. *TOH*, 231–244.

"A Christian Sermon for Peace." Atlanta, GA, December 24, 1967. *TOH*, 253–258.

"I've Been to the Mountaintop." Memphis, TN, April 3, 1968. *Texts in Context*, Ed. Michael C. Leff and Fred J. Kaulfield, Davis, CA: Hermagoras, 1989, 311–321.

JOHN ROBERT LEWIS
(1940–   ), minister, civil rights activist, U.S. representative

KURT RITTER AND GARTH PAULEY

The man who would become a civil rights orator, a voting rights advocate, and a U.S. congressman was born as John Robert Lewis on February 21, 1940, in deepest black Alabama. His farm home near the rural community of Dunn's Chapel was so isolated in southeast Alabama that Lewis did not recall seeing white people as a young child. The son of sharecroppers, he was the third of ten children who grew up in a house without plumbing or electricity. His father farmed and his mother did laundry. By the time Lewis was four years old, his parents had been able to save $300—enough to buy a farm of 102 acres, where the family grew cotton, corn, and okra and raised chickens.

Lewis attended the segregated public schools in Pike County, Alabama, and although his speech was afflicted with a stammer, in 1957 he became the first member of his family to complete high school. The nearest town was Troy, Alabama, home of the then-segregated (white) Troy State College. Unable to challenge the segregated status of that college and unable to afford the tuition at black colleges in Atlanta, Georgia, Lewis enrolled in the American Baptist Theological Seminary, a tuition-free black school in Nashville, Tennessee. After graduating from the seminary in 1961, he continued his education at Fisk University, another historically black school in Nashville, completing a B.A. degree in religion and philosophy in 1963.

The formative influences on Lewis as a youth were religion and the embryonic civil rights movement. Raised in the tradition of the black Christian church, Lewis developed a religious commitment at about the age of eight. Lewis was responsible for raising the chickens on his family's farm, which provided an outlet for his religious interests. In recalling his childhood to Gregory Kearse, Lewis remarked: "I wanted to be a minister when I grew up, so I preached to the chickens." In *Parting the Waters,* Taylor Branch reported that "soon young

Lewis was . . . sneaking out to the henhouse whenever he could to holler and pray for them in long incoherent sermons, loosening the stammer from his tongue. Bedtime became a religious ritual in the henhouse, with Lewis in contemplation of his clucking congregation as he preached them to a peaceful roost.'' In an interview with journalist Milton Viorst, Lewis recalled that his preaching was not limited to chickens: ''Between the ages of six and twelve . . . I would get together with my brothers and sisters, my first cousins and my friends, and we would literally play church''—with Lewis as the minister.

In February 1956, just a week before his sixteenth birthday, Lewis preached his first church sermon. He later reported in his autobiography: ''I've never forgotten the response. I was really overcome by it.'' Soon he was preaching regularly at small black Baptist and Methodist churches near his home. His model both for preaching and moral suasion was Martin Luther King, Jr. Quite by accident, Lewis had listened to a radio sermon by King in 1955, when Lewis was a fifteen-year-old high-school student. Branch reported that years later ''Lewis still remembered being heartshaken in front of the radio.'' Shortly afterward, Lewis was impressed with King's nonviolent philosophy in the Montgomery bus boycott, which took place fifty miles north of Lewis's home. Later Lewis would hear King speak in person, and in 1959 he met and visited with King as part of his unsuccessful effort to gain admission to Troy State College.

Lewis was profoundly influenced by King's philosophy of nonviolent confrontation, direct action, civil disobedience, and passive resistance. As a college student in Nashville in the late 1950s, Lewis faithfully attended the nonviolence workshops of one of King's disciples, Rev. James J. Lawson. Those workshops led Lewis to study the history and philosophy of nonviolence and civil disobedience in the tradition of Christ, Thoreau, Gandhi, and King. Lewis became deeply committed to nonviolence, seeing it as a moral force for social reform.

Close on the heels of the first sit-ins in Greensboro, North Carolina, in 1960, Lewis led the Nashville Student Movement in nonviolent sit-ins of lunch counters and other public facilities. As one of the thirteen original ''Freedom Riders'' in May 1961, Lewis was repeatedly arrested and attacked as he attempted to desegregate the facilities at bus stations across the South. Due largely to his commitment and courage in those actions, Lewis became a leader of the Student Nonviolent Coordinating Committee (SNCC). As a SNCC representative, Lewis was one of the principal speakers at the March on Washington on August 28, 1963—the event that featured Martin Luther King, Jr.,'s famous speech, ''I Have a Dream.'' Lewis presented hundreds of speeches throughout the nation as he represented SNCC, raised funds for the organization, and recruited student volunteers for its projects, such as the 1964 ''Freedom Summer'' voter-registration drive in Mississippi.

When the revolutionary ''black power'' faction took over SNCC in 1966, Lewis was deposed as chair. Lewis subsequently held a series of positions in which he worked for community action, civil rights, and especially voting rights. These included work with the Field Foundation in New York (1966–67), the

Southern Regional Council in Atlanta (1967–70), and the Voter Education Project in Atlanta (1970–76). In 1977, Lewis entered elective politics, running unsuccessfully for the congressional seat vacated when Andrew Young was appointed U.S. ambassador to the United Nations. During the presidency of Jimmy Carter, Lewis was an administrator in the federal antipoverty agency ACTION (1977–80).

When Carter lost his bid for reelection as president in 1980, Lewis returned to Atlanta. Following two years as the community affairs director for a bank, Lewis was elected to the Atlanta City Council—a position he held until 1986, when he was elected to the U.S. Congress from the Fifth District of Georgia. As of 1995, Lewis had served nine years in Congress. Before the Republican party winning control of the U.S. House of Representatives in 1994, Lewis rose rapidly in the Democratic party's congressional leadership. In 1991, he was appointed as one of three chief deputy whips, which caused a fellow member of Congress to predict, prior to takeover in 1994, that Lewis would eventually become Speaker of the House.

JOHN LEWIS: REVOLUTIONARY VERSUS REFORM RHETORIC

John Lewis's place in the history of American civil rights oratory seems, at first glance, to be paradoxical. He was committed to nonviolence, to social reform, and to racial integration. Yet he is remembered primarily as the author of a revolutionary speech that the moderate leaders of the 1963 March on Washington would not allow to be delivered. Indeed, that address is the only one of his SNCC speeches that has been widely published. But three years after the march, Lewis was removed from his leadership role in SNCC because black revolutionaries accused him of being a moderate. Any attempt to unravel these contradictions must begin with Lewis's address on August 28, 1963, at the March on Washington.

The original version of that speech declared: "We are now involved in a serious revolution." At an event that many hoped would build political pressure on Congress to pass Kennedy's civil rights bill, the speech rejected JFK's public accommodations legislation as "too little, and too late." The speech denounced the politicians of both the Republican and Democratic parties as "cheap political leaders who build their careers on immoral compromises and ally themselves with open forms of political, economic and social exploitation." It accused the federal government of being "part of a conspiracy" with local Southern politicians to suppress the civil rights movement and accused Kennedy of appointing "racist judges."

The original text of the speech proclaimed that "the revolution is at hand," and that if changes were to occur, "the people, the masses must bring them about." It literally declared revolution: "We will take matters into our own hands." Addressing the political establishment, the speech commanded: "Listen, Mr. Kennedy, Listen Mr. Congressman, listen fellow citizens, the black masses are on the march. . . . The black masses are on the march! We won't stop now. . . . We will march through the South, through the heart of Dixie, the way [Civil War General] Sherman did. We will pursue our own 'scorched earth' policy and burn Jim Crow to the ground. . . . We will make the action of the past few months look petty.''

Social and rhetorical critics (including one of the authors of the present entry) have erroneously cited this speech as evidence that John Lewis embodied the revolutionary challenge that would eventually displace the reform rhetoric of Martin Luther King, Jr. With the publication in the past decade of a number of interviews, memoirs, and other primary materials from the civil rights movement as well as the availability of definitive texts of the initial draft and the final version of the speech, a rather different portrait emerges: Lewis was never a revolutionary rhetor. Instead, he was trying to carry on a religiously based reform rhetoric in the face of a rising revolutionary spirit within SNCC.

Lewis had been elected chairman of SNCC in large part because of his years of activism in sit-ins, freedom rides, and other demonstrations. At the time of his election in June 1963, he was twenty-three years old, had been arrested twenty-four times, and had been savagely beaten on numerous occasions. In 1963, wrote Danny Lyon, the more radical members of SNCC viewed Lewis as a ''physically brave figurehead.''

Because Lewis had been elected chairman of SNCC less than three months before the March on Washington, many SNCC activists and supporters took it upon themselves to contribute to his address at the march. Clayborne Carson understated the case when he reported that the speech was drafted ''with the help of other SNCC leaders.'' In fact, according to Taylor Branch, the more radical SNCC activists repeatedly inserted their revolutionary ideology into the address. Courtland Cox, one of Stokely Carmichael's classmates at Howard University, inserted the attack on the Kennedy administration's civil rights bill. Tom Kahn, a white socialist and also a former student from Howard University, inserted the claim that progress could only be achieved by ''the masses.'' James Forman, executive secretary of SNCC, added a list of atrocities that local police had inflicted on civil rights demonstrators, as well as the closing phrases about marching through the South like General Sherman and using a ''scorched earth policy.'' Julian Bond, Eleanor Holmes, and others contributed to what had become not a speech by John Lewis but a collective manifesto of SNCC.

Rather than merely being a figurehead, Lewis was a serious moral advocate who contributed his own views to the address. The multiple authorship of the manifesto created an odd juxtaposition of Lewis's nonviolent sentiments with the revolutionary ideology of others. The speech alternately used the words ''revolution'' and ''nonviolent revolution,'' creating ambiguity about its true character. Similarly, the announcement of a march through Dixie and the declaration that SNCC would ''burn Jim Crow to the ground'' were qualified with the word ''nonviolently'' at the end of the sentence. Elsewhere Lewis inserted:

"In the struggle we must seek more than mere civil rights; we must work for the community of love, peace and true brotherhood." In an implicit rejection of the rising black nationalism in SNCC, Lewis added: "Our minds, our souls, and our hearts cannot rest until freedom and justice exist for *all the people*" [emphasis in the original].

Despite Lewis's moderating phrases, the initial version of the manifesto was radically out of character with the reform spirit of the March on Washington. The day before the march, reported Branch, Courtland Cox mimeographed the speech so that advance copies of the SNCC manifesto could be distributed along with those of some other speakers, such as Whitney Young. Later, Julian Bond would personally distribute copies of the speech to the press. The SNCC speech soon reached Attorney General Robert Kennedy, who was unamused with its attacks on the Kennedy administration and the administration's civil rights bill. Garrow wrote that Kennedy arranged for moderate participants and supporters of the march to demand that the speech be toned down.

SNCC at first refused to modify the speech. Lewis's own reluctance seemed to be rooted in his sense that the student group's autonomy was at stake. He later recalled to Carson that he was "angry that someone would tell me what to say and what should be deleted." After considerable negotiations with A. Philip Randolph, Roy Wilkins, and others, SNCC agreed to moderate its manifesto. Lewis was influenced by Randolph, who defended SNCC's use of language such as "revolution" and "the masses," but urged the removal of the attacks on the Kennedy administration, saying, "John, we've come this far together, let's stay together." Perhaps the key moment, however, came when Martin Luther King, Jr., turned to Lewis and pointed to the passage about marching through the South like Sherman. As Lewis recalled to Garrow, King said: "John, I know who you are. I think I know you well. I don't think this sounds like you." With that observation, King had redefined the speech: it was not just a SNCC manifesto; it was also the personal speech of John Lewis. In the rush of negotiations on the morning of the march several versions of the speech evolved, with James Forman editing the next-to-last version, while Lewis participated in the opening ceremonies. Four different preliminary versions of the speech have been published, but none reflect what John Lewis actually said at the March on Washington.

The final version of the speech was created by John Lewis, whose changes while delivering the speech completed the transformation of a revolutionary speech into a powerful reform speech. The final version of the speech has never been published, but is preserved on videotape. Instead of describing the civil rights revolution as "a serious revolution," Lewis called it "a serious *social* revolution," stressing the word "social" as he delivered the speech. Attacks on the Kennedy administration were omitted, as was the vision of marching through the South like Sherman. Where the original draft had charged that both the Democratic and Republican parties had "betrayed the basic principles of the Declaration of Independence," in his speech Lewis called upon his audience to demonstrate "until the revolution of 1776 is complete." With that revision, Lewis redefined the revolution discussed in his speech. It was no longer an overthrow of America, but the fulfillment of the American Revolution. His next words were "We must get in this revolution and complete the revolution."

In drafting the penultimate version of the speech, James Forman had intended Lewis to declare: "We do not want to go to jail if that is what we must pay for love, brotherhood and peace." But Lewis reversed the sentiment: "We do not want to go to jail. But we will go to jail if this is the price we must pay for love, brotherhood, and true peace." The original criticisms of the federal government and the Kennedy administration portrayed the national government as so morally corrupt that the only hope for African-Americans was a literal revolution. In contrast, the final version of the speech argued that the federal government should and could live up to its constitutional obligations to protect the civil rights of blacks in the South and elsewhere. Such revisions in his speech allowed Lewis to find common ground with the moderate wing of the civil rights movement.

For radicals who opposed the March on Washington, the controversy over the SNCC manifesto merely confirmed that the entire event was "a sellout." About two months after the march, Malcolm X made direct reference to the Lewis address in his famous speech, "Message to the Grass Roots." White bosses, he charged, had told the blacks at the march "what signs to carry, what song to sing, what speech they could make, and what speech they couldn't make." SNCC activist Mary King recalled that the 1963 march "produced a canker that never healed and inflicted pain on the organization for years to come." She attributed that to the "changes [in the speech] that John made under pressure from other figures participating in the event."

The difficulties occasioned by the SNCC manifesto at the March on Washington heralded continuing struggles within SNCC between revolutionaries and reformers, between those who saw nonviolence as a tactic and those, like John Lewis, for whom nonviolence was a philosophy of life. In many ways, this conflict was between those such as Lewis who were motivated by Christian convictions and the secular members of SNCC such as Stokely Carmichael whose Marxist ideology made them scornful of those they called "preachers." By 1966 Lewis and Carmichael had clashed repeatedly over philosophy and tactics. Carmichael recalled to Viorst: "I wanted his blood." When Lewis stood for reelection as chairman of SNCC on May 14, 1966, Carmichael outmaneuvered him in a marathon election meeting. In ousting Lewis, SNCC abandoned his reform rhetoric and his commitment to nonviolence and adopted the revolutionary rhetoric of black power. SNCC had been an integrated organization with at least as many whites as blacks, but in short order whites were expelled from the group. Lewis did not hesitate to denounce the advocates of "black power." The rhetoric of black power was adopted, he charged, "to scare the hell out of the white people. . . . No good can come of it. I agree with Dr. [Martin Luther] King that racism is implied in the slogan." In a *Los Angeles Times* interview, Lewis asked: ''What is scaring the hell out of the people going to do for the Negroes in the long run?''

Stokely Carmichael was accurate in charging that Lewis was a ''preacher.'' In fact, the tradition of black preaching strongly influenced Lewis as a speaker from the time of the civil rights movement through his congressional years. That influence was clear in perhaps the most thoughtful and sophisticated of John Lewis's civil rights speeches—his address at Vanderbilt University on May 3, 1968. This speech was presented amid the incredible turmoil of 1968, almost exactly one month after the assassination of Lewis's mentor, Martin Luther King, Jr., and slightly more than a month after Lyndon Johnson announced that he would not seek reelection as president. In his address Lewis quoted Senator Robert F. Kennedy on how violence overseas in the Vietnam War was legitimizing violence as an instrument of change at home—words that foreshadowed Robert Kennedy's own assassination one month after Lewis's speech.

Lewis's address was striking in its parallel to the first sermon he had ever heard by Martin Luther King, Jr. Taylor Branch reported that in King's radio address in 1955, titled ''Paul's Letter to the American Christians,'' he had ''assumed the style and theology of St. Paul to criticize Christians for selfishness and failures of brotherhood.'' Thirteen years later Lewis criticized the white church for its failures, just as he had been criticizing the federal government for not protecting the civil rights of its citizens. Lewis made his purpose clear by explaining the roles that he and his Vanderbilt audience would have during his speech: ''If I may presume to stand today as a surrogate for these people [of color in America and abroad] and if you are prepared to represent the living [white Christian] Church, then this last plea can be made in good conscience.'' Speaking as an Old Testament prophet, Lewis presented a jeremiad warning that ''the judgment of Almighty God is upon all of us, Black and white, Catholics, Protestants and Jews. Woe unto a nation that prefers to wage war. . . . Woe unto the political leaders who listen to the voices of expediency. . . . Woe unto the churches that . . . [fail to] cast their lot with the hopeless and starving.''

The influence of the black Christian church could be seen in both the style and the substance of Lewis's public speeches. Such characteristics transcended the type of address, appearing in speeches that were essentially political as well as those with religious dimensions. Lewis's speeches abounded with the stylistic devices commonly used from the black pulpit to achieve emphasis, namely, repetition, rhyme, and alliteration. Through these techniques of language, Lewis made his ideas not only identifiable and memorable, but urgent.

Whether in a convention hall or the chamber of the U.S. House of Representatives, Lewis brought with him the cadence and rhythm of the black church. In speaking, he frequently repeated words and phrases to stress a particular element of an address. For example, in his speech at the 1992 Democratic National Convention in New York City that seconded the nomination of Albert Gore for vice president of the United States, he proclaimed that Gore would give America ''a sense of vision, a sense of purpose, a sense of direction.'' In the same speech, Lewis argued that Gore would create "a community of justice, a community of opportunity, and a community of peace itself."

A year later, when Lewis believed that the Clinton-Gore administration was neglecting the concept of community by proposing the North American Free Trade Agreement (NAFTA), he marshalled his rhetorical skill of repetition against NAFTA:

> Can we turn a deaf ear to the working conditions in Mexico? Can we turn a deaf ear to the starvation wages that many people are receiving? Can we turn a deaf ear to political oppression? Can we turn a deaf ear to the large number of people who have been arrested and detained for no good reason? Can we turn a deaf ear to the number of people who have turned up missing? I ask you today, can we turn a deaf ear to the large number of political assassinations?

Lewis often reinforced the rhythm of repetition with rhyming and alliteration. In praising Gore, for example, Lewis spoke of a "community of opportunity," of a world that would be "a little greener and a little cleaner," and of his conviction that Gore "cannot only talk the talk, but Al Gore can walk the walk." Elsewhere in the same speech, Lewis praised Bill Clinton and Al Gore as a "creative, compassionate, and courageous team" and described Gore as a "caring and compassionate man, a man of courage and a man of conviction." On the other hand, when opposing Clinton and Gore's NAFTA legislation, Lewis announced that Congress had "a moral obligation, a mandate, and a mission" to reject the agreement.

Lewis's personality and credibility were projected most clearly through the delivery of his speeches. Because he was by nature a quiet and reflective person, his forceful speaking style was all the more effective because of the contrast with his manner when not speaking in public. James Farmer, the director of the Congress of Racial Equality (CORE) and organizer of the 1961 "Freedom Ride" in which John Lewis was a leading participant, recalled that in working with the six members of the Council on United Civil Rights Leadership, Lewis "was the soul of decorum and gentlemanliness. Small in stature, he was huge in dignity, and that dignity was matched by a quiet courage and flawless integrity. John was not very talkative. . . . He did not speak to 'get things off his chest.' He kept those things inside. Only when he believed that his intervention would be of genuine usefulness to the entire group did he share his thoughts with the rest of us."

When SNCC photographer Danny Lyon encountered John Lewis for the first time at a SNCC project meeting in Cairo, Illinois, in the summer of 1962, he could not determine whether Lewis was "bored or dreaming" as he sat quietly in the back of the room. Lyon, a young white man from New York, recalled: "Then John came to the podium. I had seldom been in a church before and had never heard a black preacher. The speech, delivered in a heavy, rural Alabama accent, seemed to come up out of him, out of centuries of abuse, and explode from this unassuming young man. His voice was high pitched and trembling with emotion. John's speech would have converted anyone, and it converted me.''

Lewis has never completely lost the vocal traces of his youth. When he has spoken in the U.S. House of Representatives, his enunciation has sometimes been indistinct, even as his delivery has been powerful. According to his press secretary, those who knew of the many blows to his head that he received in sit-ins, in the freedom rides, in the marches of Selma, Alabama, and elsewhere, wondered whether Lewis's sometimes slurred speech resulted from those injuries. But that was not the case. In Lewis's own words, he still has the "heavy tongue'' of black, rural Southern speech.

Although not particularly refined, Lewis's delivery is effective. In reporting on Lewis's bitter election campaign for Congress against his old friend Julian Bond in 1986, *Black Enterprise* noted their contrast of styles: "The patrician Bond'' was described as "a skilled orator'' who used his "eloquence and debating skills to out talk Lewis,'' but it was the "scrappy, less articulate Lewis [who] appealed to a poor and working-class constituency'' and ultimately won the election.

Lewis's oratory has been strikingly consistent. His speeches challenge his audience, sometimes sounding a strident tone, but ultimately seeking reform rather than revolution. These contrasting characteristics were clearly evident in his 1965 address honoring Paul Robeson. Like Robeson, Lewis declared, SNCC had "rejected gradualism and moderation.'' Because it spoke out "independently and radically,'' SNCC was being attacked by "The Establishment.'' Yet later in the speech Lewis offered his liberal and reformist solution to the violation of voting rights in the South: depositions would be submitted "to a Congressional subcommittee for consideration.'' This pattern has continued for three decades. No matter how critical Lewis is of the status quo, his speeches include the hope of redemption. The government, the churches, the people are all portrayed as capable of correcting their errors and fulfilling the ideals of democracy and community.

As a member of Congress Lewis has spoken on a host of liberal issues: gun control, the homeless, health care, trade policy with China, opposing the nomination of Clarence Thomas to the Supreme Court, and supporting the nomination of Dr. Henry Foster as surgeon general. But the greatest proportion of his congressional speeches have been devoted to using the power of the federal government to promote voting by all citizens and thereby to achieve the nation's democratic ideal. Such speeches underscore the essentially reformist character of Lewis's oratory: they portray the government as capable of being an agent for reform.

The unifying ideology of Lewis's oratory, however, is not just democracy, but the kind of society a democracy seeks to achieve. In a self-conscious effort to keep alive the aspirations of Martin Luther King, Jr., Lewis holds forth the goal of creating a "beloved community.'' This is the community of "love, brotherhood, and true peace'' that he mentioned in his address to the March on

Washington in 1963. In his 1968 address at Vanderbilt University, Lewis anguished over the prospect that King's assassination might end all hope for such a community: King's "goal was the 'beloved community,' a community at peace with itself. . . . He used the gentle teachings and tools of Christ and Gandhi. He was so black and so American. . . . A nation conceived and born in violence could not deal with a prophet of love and non-violence, so it destroyed him."

But Lewis's hopes for a "beloved community" did not die with King; those hopes have continued to find expression in his speeches. When addressing a 1993 meeting of Americans for Democratic Action, Lewis declared: "We must create a society and a world community that is at peace with itself." Such a society could be achieved, Lewis believed, if people took "responsibility to eliminate war from the global village" and unified "a society divided by race and class." Lewis has only scorn for those who abdicate responsibility for creating such a community. In criticizing the civil rights bill signed by President George Bush, Lewis asked Bush: "Is it right for you to tamper with the very moral fiber which holds this nation together? Is it right to move us closer to chaos rather than toward the building of the beloved community? And is it right to pander to the worst fears, to the racist elements?"

Directly and indirectly, many of Lewis's speeches in the 1980s and 1990s have been concerned with the legacy of the civil rights movement of the 1960s. That legacy, Lewis has argued, is the progress American society has made toward becoming a beloved community. He sees the civil rights movement as "almost like a Holy Crusade" (1984) that has helped to create "a better country, a more humane country, a more caring country" (August 6, 1987). The religious implications of Lewis's comment were clear when he commemorated those who had died in the movement: "They shed their blood, they gave their lives, in their own land, not on foreign soil, to create a true interracial democracy" (June 21, 1989).

At root, the goal of all of Lewis's oratory is to help build a beloved community. Such a community would transform American society; but Lewis has sought to achieve that transformation by reforming American society, rather than by destroying it. As he explained on the occasion of the twenty-fifth anniversary of the March on Washington: "My brothers and sisters, let me say, it is important to remember that our struggle is not for a month, a season, or a year, but for a lifetime—if that's what it takes to build what Martin Luther King, Jr., often called the beloved community, a community of peace, justice, and brotherhood."

INFORMATION SOURCES

Research Collections and Collected Speeches

John Lewis holds his own private papers, but several libraries have manuscript collections with material on his activities. The King Library and Archives of the Martin

Luther King, Jr., Center for Nonviolent Social Change, Atlanta, GA, holds manuscript collections on the Southern Christian Leadership Conference, of which Lewis was a board member in the 1960s, and on the Student Nonviolent Coordinating Committee. The King Center's SNCC collection is also available on microfilm (seventy-three reels) from University Microfilms International.

The State Historical Society of Wisconsin, Madison, WI, holds a number of small collections related to the Student Nonviolent Coordinating Committee, including the papers of SNCC activist Mary King. The Moorland-Spingarn Research Center at Howard University, Washington, DC, has an oral history by John Lewis recorded on August 22, 1967. Scholars may read the oral history, but may not photocopy, quote, nor cite the material during the lifetime of John Lewis. The authors hold a transcript of an interview with John Lewis by John Tindell, April 29, 1994, as well as notes of an interview with Ronald Roach (Congressman Lewis's press secretary) by Kurt Ritter, January 6, 1994.

[CO] Congressional Office of John R. Lewis, U.S. House of Representatives.
[CR] *Congressional Record*, 1987–1995.
[PAVA] Public Affairs Video Archives, Purdue University.
[SV] *The Student Voice, 1960–1965: Periodical of the Student Nonviolent Coordinating Committee*. Compiled by Clayborne Carson et al. Westport, CT: Meckler, 1990.

Selected Critical Studies

Branch, Taylor. *Parting the Waters: America in the King Years, 1954–63*. New York: Simon and Schuster, 1988.

Carson, Clayborne. *In Struggle: SNCC and the Black Awakening of the 1960s*. Cambridge, MA: Harvard UP, 1981.

Farmer, James. *Lay Bare the Heart: An Autobiography of the Civil Rights Movement*. New York: Arbor House, 1985.

Forman, James. *The Making of Black Revolutionaries: A Personal Account*. New York: Macmillan, 1972.

Garrow, David J. *Bearing the Cross: Martin Luther King, Jr., and the Southern Christian Leadership Conference*. New York: William Morrow, 1986.

Hampton, Henry, and Steve Fayer with Sarah Flynn. *Voices of Freedom: An Oral History of the Civil Rights Movement from the 1950s through the 1980s*. New York: Bantam, 1990.

King, Mary. *Freedom Song: A Personal Story of the 1960s Civil Rights Movement*. New York: William Morrow, 1987.

Lyon, Danny. *Memories of the Southern Civil Rights Movement*. Chapel Hill: U of North Carolina P, 1992.

Mills, Nicolaus. "Heard and Unheard Speeches: What Really Happened at the March on Washington?" *Dissent* 35 (1988): 285–291.

Ritter, Kurt, and James R. Andrews. *The American Ideology: Reflections of the Revolution in American Rhetoric*. Annandale, VA: Bicentennial Monograph Series, Speech Communication Association, 1978, 93–117.

Sellers, Cleveland, and Robert Terrell. *The River of No Return: The Autobiography of a Black Militant and the Life and Death of SNCC*. New York: William Morrow, 1973.

Stoper, Emily. *The Student Nonviolent Coordinating Committee: The Growth of Radicalism in a Civil Rights Organization*. Brooklyn, NY: Carlson, 1989.

Viorst, Milton. *Fire in the Streets: America in the 1960s*. New York: Simon and Schuster, 1979.

Zinn, Howard. *SNCC: The New Abolitionists*. Boston: Beacon, 1965.

Selected Biographies

"[Congressman John Lewis and the] Fifth District [of Georgia]." *Almanac of American Politics 1994*. Ed. Michael Barone and Grant Ujifusa. Washington, DC: National Journal, 1993, 342–345.

Kearse, Gregory S. "John Lewis: He's Still 'On the Case.' " *Ebony* 32 (November 1976): 133–142.

Lewis, John. "A New Day Begun." *Growing Up Southern*. Ed. Chris Mayfield. New York: Pantheon, 1981, 189–204.

Salaam, Kalamu ya. "John Lewis: An Agent for Social Change." *Black Collegian* 9 (March–April 1979): 148–153.

CHRONOLOGY OF MAJOR SPEECHES

[See "Research Collections and Collected Speeches" for source codes.]

"Address by the Chairman of SNCC at the March on Washington." Washington, DC, August 28, 1963. Initial Version:". . . a Serious Revolution," *Liberation* 8 (September 1963): 8; and Lyon, 86–87 (photocopy of original manuscript). Second Version: *Nonviolence in America: A Documentary History*. Ed. Staughton Lynd. Indianapolis, IN: Bobbs-Merrill, 1966, 482–485. Third Version: *Black Protest: History, Documents, and Analyses, 1619 to the Present*. Ed. Joanne Grant. New York: Fawcett World Library, 1968, 375–377; and *The Voice of Black America: Major Speeches by Negroes in the United States, 1797–1971*. Ed. Philip S. Foner. New York: Simon and Schuster, 1972, 975–977. Fourth Version: "Text of Lewis's Speech at Washington," *SV*, October 1963, 73, 75–76; and Forman, 336–337. Final Version (as delivered): Videotape from the television broadcast of the March on Washington, CO.

"Paul Robeson: Inspirer of Youth." New York, NY, April 22, 1965. *Freedomways* 5 (1965): 369–372.

"Religion and Human Rights: A Final Appeal to the Church." Nashville, TN, May 3, 1968. *New South* 23 (Spring 1968): 57–61.

"Mississippi Freedom Summer—20 Years Later." Circa 1984. *Dissent* 32 (Winter 1985): 14–15.

"Anniversary of the Voting Rights Act of 1965." Washington, DC, August 6, 1987. *CR* 133. 132:H7276.

"Address at the 25th Anniversary of the March on Washington." Washington, DC, August 27, 1988. PAVA, ID# 4138.

"Anniversary of the Slaying of Civil Rights Workers." Washington, DC, June 21, 1989. *CR* 135.84:H2983.

"Opposing the Nomination of Clarence Thomas to the Supreme Court." Washington, DC, September 9, 1991. PAVA, ID# 21780.

"Address Denouncing the Civil Rights Act of 1991." Washington, DC, November 21, 1991. PAVA, ID# 22911.

"Address Supporting the National Voter Registration Act." Washington, DC, June 16, 1992. *CR* 138.86:H4715–4716.

"Address Seconding the Nomination of Albert Gore for Vice President of the United States." New York, NY, July 16, 1992. PAVA, ID# 27155.

"NAFTA Must Be Defeated." Washington, DC, February 17, 1993. *CR* 139.160 (Part II):H9907–9908.

"Address to the Annual Meeting of Americans for Democratic Action." Washington, DC, June 19, 1993. CO.

"Supporting the Nomination of Dr. Henry Foster for Surgeon General." Washington, DC, February 9, 1995. *CR* 141.26:1533–1535.

LOUIS E. LOMAX
(1922–1970), journalist, author, professor

DALE G. LEATHERS

On February 5, 1994, a jury in Jackson, Mississippi, composed of eight African-Americans and four whites, convicted Byron De La Beckwith of the murder of black civil rights leader Medgar Evers. Medgar Evers was shot down from behind in his driveway after midnight on June 12, 1963. One must, therefore, be struck by the fact that Evers's murder occurred over thirty years ago. Significantly, De La Beckwith had been tried twice previously by all-white juries who failed to convict him of murder.

The trial and conviction of De La Beckwith (arrogant white supremacist and racist) serves to focus our attention on the memorable decade of the 1960s. On the one hand, this was a decade of significant advances in civil rights for African-Americans. Not coincidentally, this was also a decade marked by conflict, physical assault, and murder. Thus the two African-Americans who were arguably the most eloquent spokespersons for their race in the 1960s—Martin Luther King, Jr., and Malcom X—were both assassinated during the decade. Similarly, the two most powerful white liberals who used armed force in the interests of integration—President John F. Kennedy and Attorney General Robert Kennedy—were also victims of assassination in the 1960s.

The 1960s was also the decade of major race riots in Detroit, New York, and Los Angeles as well as near riots in many other locations. Violent as the decade proved to be, the potential for even greater and much more destructive violence was ever present. This was true because the pro– and anti–civil rights forces frequently confronted each other face-to-face. On one side, African-American groups and organizations and their white supporters used such high-risk and confrontational, direct-action efforts as bus boycotts, freedom rides into segregated Southern cities, lunch-counter sit-ins, and campus sit-ins. On the other side, the intransigent forces of racism and segregation fought organized efforts to secure civil rights for African-Americans with police dogs, water hoses, brutal beatings, and ultimately with murder.

In this decade of violence, Louis E. Lomax proved to be one of the most thoughtful and articulate proponents of black civil rights and integration. Indeed, Lomax is remembered as a distinguished interpreter of and participant in the civil rights movement. Although he made many white liberals uncomfortable by constantly prodding them to move more aggressively, he was on balance a voice of reason and moderation for African-American rights in the 1960s.

Lomax was a brilliant man who described himself as a member of the "black bourgeois." By virtue of his intellect, education, and varied accomplishments, he led a life of relative privilege where he consistently associated with—and influenced many of—the top African-American and white liberal intellectuals of his time.

Louis E. Lomax was born into a middle-class existence on August 16, 1922, in Valdosta, Georgia. His mother Sarah died shortly after his birth, and he was raised until the age of ten by his grandparents. His grandfather was a noted Negro Baptist minister, and his father was a high-school principal. At the age of ten, Lomax's uncle, the Reverend James L. Lomax, took over his rearing and bore the total responsibility for his not-inconsiderable education. It was because of his uncle's longtime association with the minister Martin Luther King, Sr., that Louis Lomax developed close ties with the King family. A life-long friend of Martin Luther King, Jr., Lomax was also a close personal friend of Malcolm X.

Lomax graduated from Paine College in Augusta, Georgia, in 1942. He received M.A. degrees from American University in 1944 and from Yale in philosophy in 1947. After completing his education, Lomax joined the faculty of Georgia State College in Savannah, Georgia, for a short time as assistant professor of philosophy. He returned to the academic world (as a faculty member at Hofstra University) just before his untimely death in 1970.

The multitalented Lomax described himself as a "social critic." He achieved national recognition for his activities as a newsman, reporter, teacher, and author. As well, Lomax was a highly skilled communicator who excelled in his multiple roles as a lecturer, debater, television host, and public speaker. His national prominence was documented in part by the frequency with which his strong advocacy of integration was covered in such white publications as *Time, Newsweek,* and the *New York Times* and such major African-American publications as *Ebony, Jet,* the *New York Amsterdam News,* the *Journal of Negro Education,* and *Freedomways.*

Lomax began his career as a professional writer with the newspaper the *Afro American.* Then he became a staff features writer for a number of years for the *Chicago American.* While he remained a newspaperman from 1941 to 1958 and a free-lance writer thereafter, Lomax may have been at his most eloquent during his many television appearances and during the uncounted number of speeches he gave throughout the United States. In the early part of the decade, Lomax joined Mike Wallace's staff at CBS. He participated with Wallace in some high-visibility interviews such as one with Malcolm X, parts of which were reproduced in Lomax's book *To Kill a Black Man*. From 1964 until 1968 Lomax had his own twice-weekly television program on KTTV in Los Angeles.

In his book *The Negro Revolt* (1962), Lomax asserted boldly that the NAACP had nearly become an anachronism. He was appalled by the NAACP's unwillingness to lead direct-action programs to secure civil rights for African-Americans. He therefore aligned himself with the most liberal African-American organizations of the 1960s that organized and led direct-action programs designed to achieve integration, that is, the Student Nonviolent Coordinating Committee (SNCC) and the Congress of Racial Equality (CORE).

Lomax realized that it was necessary for him to exhibit a delicate balance in his civil rights speeches. On the one hand, he was forced to come close to advocating black violence in his condemnation of the insensitive and racist practices of many whites. Lomax consistently implied in his speeches that more violence from blacks was imminent unless whites immediately started working harder to secure the civil rights of blacks. The implied threat of black violence was a tactic Lomax had to use to appeal effectively to the black youth of his day. At the same time, Lomax realized that he could go only so far in threatening and condemning white liberals; his condemnation focused on their alleged hypocrisy and their lack of more forceful action on behalf of civil rights. He knew only too well—as did other mainstream African-American leaders such as Martin Luther King, Jr., and Whitney Young, Jr.—that African-American civil rights organizations were heavily dependent on white liberals and their organizations for financial support.

Lomax knew too that he had to be careful if he was to avoid being labeled a hypocrite himself. For example, he showed no reluctance to accept speaking fees from the same liberals he attacked as economic exploiters of blacks. Moreover, Lomax's rather opulent lifestyle contrasted strikingly with the lifestyle of economically depressed blacks about whom he expressed so much concern.

In 1963, in "I Am Somebody," a speech delivered to a predominantly black audience in Pacoima, California, Lomax said sarcastically that "my cup has just about run over with these bourgeois Negroes on the West Coast who get their $35,000 and $40,000 homes and move away from the black masses." Within a year of this speech the notably successful Lomax had moved from New York to Los Angeles. Opponents such as former John Birch Society official John Rousselot were quick to point out that unlike members of the "underprivileged class" that he championed, Lomax lived neither in substandard housing nor in the black areas of Los Angeles. When he debated Lomax at UCLA on May 10, 1967, Rousselot chided Lomax for living in his luxurious, $75,000 "house on a hill." Stuttering noticeably, Lomax replied that he had sold his house on the hill, that it was not worth as much as his critics said, and that he "was now living in an apartment in Bel Air''—one of the most expensive and exclusive white enclaves in Los Angeles in the 1960s.

Throughout his brief life, Lomax remained committed to the concept of integration even though he was considered to be dangerously liberal by many white conservatives. Ironically, a number of black activists considered Lomax to be unacceptably conservative. Thus, Lomax recounted in *The Reluctant African,* a black activist acquaintance of his once told Lomax, ''You are going to die from an overdose of integration yet.''

As a free-lance writer, Lomax was a remarkably productive author during the decade of the 1960s. In fact, one must be familiar with his books and magazine articles in order to fully appreciate one source of inspiration that distinguished his public speaking. In addition to his award-winning books, *The Reluctant African* (1960) and *The Negro Revolt* (1962), Lomax was the author of three other books: *When the Word Is Given* (1963), a treatment of the persuasion of Malcolm X and the Black Muslim movement, *Thailand: The War That Is* (1967), and *To Kill a Black Man* (1968), a comparative biography of Martin Luther King, Jr., and Malcolm X. At the time of his death in 1970, Lomax was working on a history of the African-American.

Lomax's articles appeared frequently in top national magazines such as *Harper's, Life, Pageant,* the *Nation,* and the *New Leader.* Lomax was commissioned by *Harper's* to fly to Castro's Cuba in 1962 to report on how nonwhites in Cuba felt about whites in the United States. He was the first American newsperson to visit North Vietnam. While there, he interviewed both Ho Chi Minh and Premier Pham Van Dong. Lomax subsequently traveled extensively worldwide. Indeed, his insightful observations on behavioral predilections of Third World peoples provided grist for both his writings and public speeches.

There can be little doubt that Lomax's strong and eloquent advocacy of full civil rights for African-Americans was influential at the national level. Lomax's was one of the most respected voices of African-American intellectuals in the decade of the 1960s. When *Harper's* magazine ran a special issue in April 1965 entitled ''The South Today, 100 Years after Appomattox,'' this issue featured the articles not only of leading white intellectuals such as Vann Woodward and James J. Kilpatrick but of many of the most prominent African-American intellectuals of the time, including Whitney M. Young, Jr., Langston Hughes, Walker Percy, and Louis E. Lomax. Similarly, *Ebony* magazine published a special issue entitled ''The White Problem in America'' in August 1965. Once again Louis E. Lomax joined some of the most noted white intellectuals of the decade as well as such prominent African-American intellectuals as James Baldwin, Whitney Young, Jr., and Carl T. Rowan as an author of an article.

LOUIS E. LOMAX AS THE INTERPRETER OF THE CIVIL RIGHTS MOVEMENT

Lomax's public speeches cannot be found in a single book or collection or repository. This may be because Lomax died suddenly and unexpectedly in a car accident in 1970 at the young age of forty-seven. Parts of his speeches may be found quoted in mainstream publications such as *Newsweek* and the *New York Times*. However, the exact title, date, and place of delivery are usually not given. The following analysis will focus on four major public addresses that Louis Lomax delivered during the 1960s.

Louis Lomax's speeches echoed one theme of overriding importance: the 1960s was the decade when the Negro must necessarily revolt. In his most penetrating and insightful book, *The Negro Revolt,* Lomax articulated exactly why the Negro was in revolt:

> This hurt and disappointment are vital factors underlying the Negro revolt. While in the South, I talked with the Negro masses—the cooks, the butlers, the maids, and the shoeshine men. They still serve white people but they no longer trust, respect, nor love them. . . . This, I submit, is the main reason why the Negro revolt has come now and as it has.

Lomax's speeches were built on a central, compelling argument: African-Americans of the 1960s were damn mad because of their mistreatment by whites. They simply were not going to take it any more. Although the law of the land in the 1950s said "separate but equal," African-Americans were treated then, and continued to be treated in the 1960s, as "separate and unequal." They were still forced to endure an almost endless list of indignities as the 1960s began: they were forced to sit at the back of the bus, they could not eat at the same lunch counters with whites, segregation in housing prevailed, they frequently could not find overnight accommodations when they traveled, and a number of the South's largest public universities were still segregated. Most of all, African-Americans were discriminated against economically; Lomax pressed this point in his 1964 speech at the University of California at Santa Barbara entitled "Have Slums—Will Travel." There Lomax proposed that "educational cities" be established just outside major urban areas to which young people from both the "overprivileged" and "underprivileged" communities would be bussed in the interest of total integration.

The Negro revolt represented more than a strong rejection of the segregationist attitudes and racist practices of many whites, however. It also represented a strong rejection by Lomax and many other African-Americans of the old-line, conservative Negro leadership that refused to use direct, mass-action programs to get full civil rights immediately. Thus Lomax noted in *The Negro Revolt* that "as a result, established Negro leadership is in the position of the oddly dressed man who said to a bystander, 'please tell me which way the parade went; after all, I'm leading it.' "

In "Roots of Prejudice," a 1968 speech delivered at San Mateo College in California, Lomax hammered away at his contention that the African-American was not going to endure mistreatment by whites any longer. Said Lomax, "You cannot run a free and open society with upwards of 25 million angry people running around. That's too damn many mad people. They bring it down every time.'' This speech was constructed skillfully around the Old Testament story of Samson, who was robbed of his strength, power, and essential masculinity before his eyes were gouged out; then he was placed in chains in the center of the city so that he could be publicly ridiculed. The analogy to the mistreatment and degradation of American blacks was obvious. Finally, Lomax said that a friend came along and ''Samson said just take me to the temple and put my hands on the pillars. The friend said 'What are you going to do?' He said, 'I am going to pull it down.' ''

According to Lomax, African-Americans were not most concerned about the danger of beatings and death in the 1960s, although the threat was a very real one. Indeed, Lomax, who was a superb storyteller, described the threat of physical violence to African-Americans in chilling terms in a chapter he wrote for a book entitled *Race Awareness*. In his brilliant chapter, ''Road to Mississippi,'' Lomax provided a detailed account of the murder of two white and one black civil rights workers in rural Mississippi in the summer of 1964. In the end they were entombed in an earthen dam. Lomax wrote:

> The frogs and the varmints are moaning in the bayous. By now the moon is midnight high. Chaney, the Negro of the three, is tied to a tree and beaten with chains. His bones snap and his screams pierce the still midnight air. But the screams are soon ended. There is no noise now except for the thud of chains crushing flesh—and the crack of the bones.

Lomax's speeches made clear that the Negroes of the 1960s were not revolting primarily because of fear of violence, however. They revolted because their demand that they be treated with dignity by whites remained unfulfilled. In ''Tale of Three Cities,'' delivered in 1963 at Augsburg College in Minneapolis, Lomax demonstrated graphically via extended anecdotes and personal experiences that the nonwhites of the world were angry and restive. They were angry because they had been treated by whites for decades as their inferiors. Thus Lomax encountered strong antiwhite sentiment in the three cities he described in the speech, and which he had visited within the past six months: Havana, Berlin, and Birmingham.

Many miles out into the Cuban countryside Lomax met a Cuban farmer who was in charge of a collective farm. As he had coffee with the Cuban and ''his woman,'' the Cuban remarked, ''The Yankees came with their flashy clothes, cars, and women. They threw coins into the streets and laughed as we danced after them. We did not respect them. You are the first American who ever asked me about my needs. You are the first American who ever had coffee with my woman and me.'' Similarly, Lomax found in Berlin that both Germans and white servicemen from the U.S. Army treated black servicemen as their inferiors. Thus the only place where African-American members of the U.S. Army were allowed to relax and seek recreation was in a small, segregated, five-block area known derisively as ''Niggerstrasse.''

Finally, Lomax emphasized in "Tale of Three Cities" that in Birmingham, Alabama, in 1963 the mistreatment of blacks by whites was even more oppressive than in Havana or Berlin. Not only did whites treat blacks as their inferiors in Birmingham, but they did so with a brutality and viciousness that almost defied description. In Birmingham Lomax "stood with Martin" [Luther King, Jr.,] and watched bored firemen spray water from their hoses into the air. Lomax went on to say:

> Finally, about 5 o'clock in the afternoon some old, black woman, her face drawn, her hands white almost from washing somebody's clothes . . . came shuffling between two houses onto the sidewalk. And as she came, one fireman said 'there she is, a black, nigger bitch—let's get her.' And they brought the fire hoses down out of the air, played the stream upon her body, and knocked her down, and rolled her down the street—as if she were a rubber ball.

Besides skillfully enumerating and describing the African-Americans' discontent, Lomax did a devastatingly effective job of exposing the hypocrisy of white Americans. He came down hardest on the white liberal, knowing that the white liberal was much more likely to support civil rights organizations as a result of guilt feelings than was the white conservative. Thus Lomax stressed in an *Ebony* article entitled "The White Liberal," that "the white liberal is not a happy man. I know; I have encountered him in a hundred lecture halls and plush restaurants across the nation. . . . He is the white Anglo-Saxon protestant marching along the road from Selma while his eyes dart furtively toward the rising Negro crime rate; . . . he is the parent welcoming the new Negro neighbor and praying to God that his daughter will marry one of her own kind."

In both "Tale of Three Cities" and "Roots of Prejudice" Lomax denounced the hypocrisy of white Christians and their churches. In "Roots" Lomax spoke derisively of the white male Christian whose "life is consumed by unction and being withdrawn," and "yet he will go out and hang a black man from a tree and sing 'Jesus created all. All to him I owe.' " In the "Tale" speech Lomax told his audience at Augsburg College that if they drive from Minneapolis to Mississippi, the closer "[you] get to Mississippi you will get the most sanctified radio stations you have ever heard in your life." Then, speaking with great conviction, Lomax asked, "What is the damnable correlation between your Christian religion . . . and the mistreatment of people all over the world?"

Lomax excoriated white Christians for their hypocritical attempt to create God in their own image—"all of em blonde, blue-eyed, white, middle-class—without an exception." Lomax said sarcastically, "You know what you are looking at is perhaps one of the greatest exercises in anthropomorphic reasoning man has ever carried out. We have created God in our image. And, you see, here is the trick—once we have made God look like us, then we can make him think like us." Turning to humor to reinforce his point, Lomax noted that "now Mrs. Lomax and I have just come home from the Holy Land—from Israel and from

Jordan. And verily verily I say unto you, there is no way in the world for anybody to come out of Bethlehem of Judea looking like George Wallace— impossible!'' [much crowd laughter followed].

Finally, Lomax repeatedly condemned white Americans for their hypocritical attitude toward ''freedom.'' He asserted that many citizens sat by passively as the freedoms of blacks in the South were repressed repeatedly and egregiously, but were willing to vigorously support a Vietnamese war that was allegedly designed to protect the freedoms of a people many considered to be their inferiors. Lomax bore down hard on this hypocrisy in a 1963 speech in Los Angeles that was entitled ''Theology of Americanism.'' With great conviction Lomax noted that ''we claim we are fighting and dying for the yellow man in Viet Nam whom we love, and yet we have to swallow hard and be dry in our throats when he reminds us that he is the same yellow, slant-eyed man whom we have deliberately kept out of this country for a hundred years by our immigration quota.''

Lomax's speeches to predominantly black audiences were similar to his speeches to white audiences in at least three ways: whites in general were denounced for treating blacks as their inferiors, liberals were criticized for their hypocrisy and failure to move quickly enough in support of black civil rights, and conservative black organizations were condemned for their failure to support direct-action programs to secure black civil rights. Lomax's speeches to black audiences were different, however, in that he emphasized two distinctive, major themes that did not appear in his speeches to white audiences.

Lomax emphasized these two themes in his 1963 speech ''I Am Somebody.'' The first theme was that ''we must tell our young people that they are somebody. We must tell them to wipe the stigma of inconsequentialness from their brow.'' In developing this theme of the importance of taking pride in one's race, Lomax again attacked whites for equating their color with everything that is good while conditioning African-Americans to believe that ''black'' has an almost endless number of negative connotations. Moreover, Lomax charged that ''most of you Negroes don't want to admit this but . . . [you] really believed what white people told us about ourselves. We went around straightening our hair, putting conk (and we still do it) in our hair, trying to be like what we thought beauty is.'' Lomax went on to stress in graphic terms that blacks had been conditioned by whites to identify the label ''black'' with things that were ''bad'' and ''evil'':

Examine the language of your society. Everything black is associated with something evil, isn't it? And everything white is associated with something good. To be kept out of an organization is to what?—be blackballed. To be put on a bad list is to be black-listed. . . . You love cats, but the one cat you don't want to walk in front of you is a black cat. Anything involved with being black, we've associated it with being evil.

Lomax was thus one of the first prominent black orators of the 1960s to develop the theme of black pride.

The second theme that Lomax articulated to his black audience was the need to develop a sense of responsibility. In "I Am Somebody" Lomax emphasized that blacks must not only have "pride in our race" but must develop "a sense of responsibility." "You see, freedom and responsibility are twins. You can't have one without the other." At the time Lomax was speaking to black audiences, responsibility for blacks in his view began with exercising their right to vote.

Lomax generated his credibility in part from his friends. He could claim accurately that he knew well virtually all of the major African-American civil rights figures of his time. He was an incorrigible name dropper; for example, he noted that he personally advised sports activist Harry Edwards on how to organize the black protest of the Olympics, Lomax and his "close friend, 'Jimmy' Baldwin" were trying to keep black youth from rioting, and Lomax "stood with Martin [Luther King, Jr,]" watching Birmingham firemen flatten blacks with their fire hoses. Though Lomax may have overdone his name dropping, his friendship with the many prominent black luminaries he named in his speeches is not a matter of dispute.

Finally, Louis Lomax's style featured the use of the carrot-and-stick strategy. In the speeches proper, he used the stick with rather strident warnings to white audiences that more, uncontrollable black violence was imminent. Professor Charles Lomas in his book *The Agitator in Society* characterized this technique as "calculated antagonism." In contrast, Lomax used the carrot in the question/answer sessions that followed his speeches. There he was charming, conciliatory, and highly optimistic about the future.

Lomas stressed that Louis Lomax was skilled at adapting his speaking style to his audience. When Lomax addressed white audiences, he spoke virtually without trace of a Southern accent; in fact, he spoke with the clipped enunciation that one might associate with a well-educated member of the upper classes in England. In contrast, "Before Negro audiences, especially in emotionally toned passages, he often lapses into a modified dialect of his native Georgia. Whether or not it is intentional is not apparent, but it has a favorable effect on Negro audiences."

Sociology Professor Joel Torstenson was present when Lomax gave his 1963 speech at Augsburg College, "Tale of Three Cities." He recalled Lomax's speech as "very impressive" and "very moving." In a phone conversation with the author Torstenson noted that Lomax had a major and highly positive impact on his audience at Augsburg College. Although he concluded that Lomax was perhaps not "quite as eloquent as Martin Luther King, Jr.," Torstenson echoed many contemporary observers in considering Louis Lomax to be an eloquent and influential orator.

INFORMATION SOURCES

Research Collections and Collected Speeches

No complete speech manuscripts from Lomax's public speeches are known to be available to researchers currently, although audiotapes of the four major speeches analyzed in this chapter may be obtained from the university and colleges identified. In 1968, alone, Lomax made seventy-five appearances on college campuses. Many of his speeches to students were followed by lengthy question/answer sessions in which Lomax was particularly impressive. A question/answer session followed his speech at Augsburg College in 1963. Lomax also excelled in debates with leading national personalities. Copies of his debates with William Buckley (1965) and with John Rousselot in 1967 at UCLA may be used only by researchers who visit UCLA personally. Related materials on Lomax may be found in *The Kaiser Index to Black Resources, 1948–1986* from the Schomburg Center for Research in Black Culture of the New York Public Library.

Selected Publications

Lomax, Louis E. "Georgia Boy Goes Home." Special Supplement entitled "The South Today; 100 Years after Appomattox," *Harper's,* April 1965: 151–159.
———. *The Negro Revolt.* New York: Harper and Row, 1962.
———. *The Reluctant African.* New York: Harper, 1960.
———. *Thailand: The War That Is, The War That Will Be.* New York: Random House, 1967.
———. *To Kill a Black Man.* Los Angeles, CA: Holloway House, 1968.
———. *When the Word Is Given.* Cleveland, OH: World, 1963.
———. "The White Liberal: Man of Power and Guilt, Fear and Promise." Special Issue of *Ebony,* August 1965: 60–68.

CHRONOLOGY OF MAJOR SPEECHES

"Tale of Three Cities." Augsburg College, Minneapolis, MN, November 21, 1963. Audiotape.
"I Am Somebody." Pacoima, CA, 1963. *The Agitator in American Society.* Ed. Charles Lomas. Englewood Cliffs, NJ: Prentice-Hall, 1968, 121–135.
"Have Slums—Will Travel." University of California at Santa Barbara, December 7, 1964. Audiotape.
"Roots of Prejudice." San Mateo College, San Mateo, CA, November 1, 1968. Audiotape.

THURGOOD MARSHALL
(1908–1993), lawyer,
Supreme Court justice

STEPHEN A. SMITH

"Mr. Civil Rights," Thurgood Marshall, was one of the heroes in the battles to secure the constitutional rights of black Americans, and he had a leading role in that drama on the stage of public life for almost sixty years. Marshall is most remembered as the first African-American justice of the U.S. Supreme Court, on which he served from 1967 to 1991, but his earlier career as a legal advocate for civil rights forever changed the nation far more than his opinions on the Court. "When I think of great American lawyers, I think of Thurgood Marshall, Abe Lincoln and Daniel Webster," said Georgetown law professor Thomas G. Krattenmaker. Marshall, he said, "is certainly the most important lawyer of the 20th century." As an attorney in private practice and later leading the NAACP Legal Defense Fund assault on segregation, Marshall fought and won the hard legal cases throughout the South, culminating in the landmark *Brown v. Board of Education*, and provided the rhetorical structure and the constitutional warrant for the political success of the civil rights movement.

Thurgood Marshall was born in Baltimore in 1908, a place and time that reflected the segregated praxis of American life, but his family was securely among the middle class on the black side of the color line. His mother, Norma Williams Marshall, was a teacher in the segregated elementary schools. A graduate of Coppin Normal who had completed additional graduate work at Morgan State and Columbia, she emphasized the value of education and hoped that Thurgood would become a dentist, but it seems that he was adept with his own mouth in other ways. One neighbor recalled that Thurgood was "a jolly boy who always had something to say"; however, his jovial nature and quick wit were not always appreciated in school. His grade-school principal often required him to remain after school and memorize portions of the Constitution as a consequence of his conduct, recorded Richard Kluger, although his high-school history teacher remembered him more charitably as "a good, earnest, argumentative student."

His father, Will Marshall, had been the first black to serve on a grand jury in Baltimore, and he often took his son to watch the trial courts there. The elder Marshall was known for his "tendency to disputation," and that must have been infectious. According to Randall Bland, Thurgood later remarked, "He never told me to become a lawyer, but he turned me into one. He did it by teaching me to argue, by challenging my logic on every point, by making me prove every statement I made."

Graduating from high school with an admirable record in 1925, but barred from the University of Maryland and not quite qualified for an Ivy League institution, Thurgood enrolled at Lincoln University, "the black Princeton," at Oxford, Pennsylvania. There he first engaged the writings of W. E. B. Du Bois, Carter Woodson, and Langston Hughes, and he participated in an action to integrate the seating at the local movie theater. While he maintained a B average in his coursework for a humanities degree, he worked to project an image of never studying and was even suspended for a fraternity prank. Nonetheless, he was active in the Forensic Society and was an outstanding debater, leading the Lincoln squad to numerous victories over such schools as Bates, Bowdoin, and Colby. In a letter to his father, he claimed, "If I were taking debate for credit, I would be the biggest honor student they ever had around here."

During his senior year at Lincoln, Marshall decided on law school because he "loved speaking in public and thinking on his feet and dealing with people face to face," but again his choices were limited by law. Returning to Baltimore, he commuted by train to attend Howard Law School in Washington, DC. There he came into his own, being mentored by Dean Charles Hamilton Houston, working with professors William Hastie and James Narbit preparing cases for the National Association for the Advancement of Colored People, and attracting the attention of the organization's executive secretary, Walter White. The legal curriculum was enriched during his student days by a guest lecture series that included Justice Felix Frankfurter and Clarence Darrow, and he sometimes cut classes to watch legal giants like John W. Davis argue cases before the Supreme Court.

After graduating as valedictorian in 1933, Marshall hung out his shingle in Baltimore and developed a broad, if not particularly lucrative, private practice. His personal qualities helped him to rise quickly to prominence in the community. As A. J. Payne recalled, "He showed his courage and tenacity, and the people liked him, the common people and the professional people both. . . . People in the community looked up to him. He was never arrogant and always accessible." He also helped reorganize the local NAACP, and he was retained to handle the civil rights cases of interest to Carl Murphy, the editor of the local *Afro-American* newspaper. Murphy's daughter remembered him during that time and said, "He gave you the impression that he had taken the time to think over what he said. . . . He exuded confidence and seemed very solid—a born leader.

His very size helped him give that impression, that and his outgoing personality. He was a bundle of energy—and never a stuffed shirt.''

Marshall joined the NAACP field staff in 1936 as assistant counsel, and in 1938 he followed Houston as counsel, becoming, at age thirty, the most important and most visible black attorney in the United States. He became director-counsel of the Legal Defense Fund (1940–61), planning and winning the legal assault on segregated America. In 1961, he was appointed by President Kennedy to the U.S. Court of Appeals for the Second Circuit, and in 1965 he was appointed by President Johnson as solicitor general of the United States, serving for two years as the government's advocate before the Supreme Court. In 1967, President Johnson nominated Marshall as the first black associate justice of the Supreme Court, a position he held for twenty-four years until he retired in 1991, less than two years before his death on January 24, 1993.

THURGOOD MARSHALL AS CONSTITUTIONAL CRITIC

Marshall had memorized the Constitution as a schoolchild, but his entire adult life was spent giving meaning to the dry words of the text—in public speeches in the community, as an advocate at the bar, in his extrajudicial speeches to legal organizations, and in his opinions from the bench. He spoke from his own experiences, and he always held that the Constitution was a living document to be read and interpreted through the lens of real-life experiences.

As an attorney in private practice in Baltimore, Marshall was active in bringing the Constitution to life in the community. A. J. Payne recalled, ''He spoke around at the churches a lot, and when he talked it would be about our rights.'' During that period, working with Charles Houston from the NAACP national office, Marshall challenged the University of Maryland Law School's racial admission policies on behalf of Donald Murray in 1934. The victory in the state courts was the first such test of segregated education in a legal strategy that would occupy most of his public career as an attorney. It was a personal victory for Marshall, who had been barred from attending the school, and it was an important public victory as well. Juanita Jackson Mitchell, a local activist, later said of the case, ''He brought us the Constitution like Moses brought the people the Ten Commandments.''

Joining the NAACP field staff in 1936 and later heading the legal efforts for the national office and the Legal Defense Fund (LDF), Marshall continued to bring the Constitution to the people through public speaking while he argued its meaning and application in the courts. In 1940, for example, the first year of his twenty-one-year tenure as director-counsel of the LDF, he gave twenty-four public speeches, eighteen of which were in Baltimore and points south. During a three-week period in May of that year he gave speeches in Louisville, Dallas, Corpus Christi, Houston, New Orleans, Mobile, Birmingham, Atlanta, and Asheville to mass meetings organized by state and local NAACP branches.

Marshall's legal strategy to secure rights relied on a parallel public campaign to recruit both lawyers and plaintiffs. His speeches during this period, wrote Mark Tushnet, were meant to "push the members along a path he wanted them to follow, while their responses suggested some limits to the pace and direction of the litigation." In an extemporaneous speech to the National Bar Association on the "Federal Civil Rights Statutes" (1940), he urged Negro attorneys to join the "struggle to obtain full citizenship rights for all American citizens" and to secure legal redress "through intelligent use of the federal [civil rights] statutes." Elaborating on the importance of the civil rights statutes in a speech entitled "The Legal Attack to Secure Civil Rights" (1942) to the NAACP Wartime Conference, Marshall again drew public attention to the effective use of existing federal legislation—and the Fourteenth Amendment—in overcoming barriers to voting, serving on juries, equalizing teacher salaries, and purchasing property despite restrictive covenants. Although the NAACP had not yet successfully challenged public school segregation, he stated his position that the Constitution and existing statutes could "be used to attack *every* form of discrimination against Negroes by public school systems." In addressing the delegates he reminded them that they could "move no faster than the individuals who have been discriminated against," and that "the real job has to be done by the Negro population with whatever friends of the other races that are willing to join in."

Soon after the end of World War II, Marshall and the NAACP were ready to engage the legal assault on segregated education. In a speech to Negro educators, "The Real Party of Interest Must Be the Child" (1945), Marshall seemed to reject Booker T. Washington's "Atlanta Compromise" and the arguments of W. E. B. Du Bois, contending, "There is little use in removing the barriers to economic security so as to place the Negro in fair competition with other citizens unless at the same time we make provision for educational facilities which will give our Negro youth the necessary educational background to stand their ground." Furthermore, Marshall believed that equal educational rights could not be achieved without equal political rights. When he accepted the Springarn Medal for his contribution to advancing the status of the Negro population at the NAACP National Convention the following year, Marshall's speech, "The Essence of Democratic Government" (1946), reminded his audience and the nation that the victory over fascism abroad had not secured full freedom for the victors: "The body of America must throw off the disease of segregation and second-class citizenship or give up the spirit of democracy." He held that American citizens possessed certain rights merely by being born in a democracy, and he stressed the importance of political rights in both securing other freedoms and enjoying them.

Marshall presented eloquent testimony to the President's Commission on Civil Rights on April 17, 1947, calling for broad federal action to assure civil and political rights for all Americans, but there was only passing mention made of the fact that Negroes did not enjoy equal educational facilities. However, in June the NAACP Annual Conference unanimously adopted a resolution signaling a new position on the concept of separate but equal public education. That fall Marshall addressed the Texas State Conference of the NAACP and articulated the meaning of that resolution in a speech entitled "Complete Opposition to All Forms of Discrimination" (1947). The resolution had declared, "Complete equality of educational opportunity cannot be obtained in a dual system of education," and Marshall told his audience, "It no longer takes courage to fight for mere equality in a separate school system." Negroes had been "fighting for equality of education in separate schools for more than eighty years," he said, but "segregation and discrimination are so tied up together that you can't tell one from the other." Segregation meant second-class citizenship, and it was time for a new strategy. The obvious conclusion, he said, was "that the only sane approach is a direct attack on segregation *per se.*"

The direct attack on segregated public schools soon came in five cases that would forever be remembered as *Brown v. Board of Education.* Each of the cases was argued separately, allowing the NAACP team to develop different points in each, and Thurgood Marshall was the legal strategist without peer. Marshall had litigated the case from South Carolina at the trial level, and Robert Carter said, "In the courtroom, Marshall was the consummate professional. I heard him make several splendid arguments before the Supreme Court. But perhaps the best courtroom performance I ever saw him give was his cross-examination . . . in *Briggs v. Elliott.*" That performance both devastated the state's chief witness and exhilarated the black audience in the courtroom. Nonetheless, to no one's surprise, he lost at the trial level in South Carolina.

Marshall was again responsible for the argument in *Briggs* when the cases came before the Supreme Court, but South Carolina relied upon the venerable John W. Davis. Davis had been the Democratic presidential nominee in 1924, had served as U.S. solicitor general, had argued more than 140 cases before the Court, and was a member of a prominent Wall Street firm. Their arguments before the Supreme Court were high drama. Oral arguments in the cases consumed ten hours on December 9–11, 1952, and approximately 300 people packed the Supreme Court chamber, with another 400 lined up waiting to get in.

Each of the cases was important, but the rhetorical encounter between Davis and Marshall was the main act. Davis was confident, and his florid eloquence captured the attention of the justices as he presented his case almost uninterrupted. Marshall's presentation was equally compelling for different reasons. His colleague, Jack Greenberg, described it well: "He hovered imposingly over the lectern as he addressed the justices familiarly, but respectfully. He had been before the Court many times, and the justices knew him well and trusted him." Some of them, Greenberg said, "may well have considered this appearance a continuation of dialogues they had had over the years. While the case was specifically *Briggs v. Elliott,* the subject was a long-standing one between Thurgood and the Court—the status of blacks and the role of the Constitution in defining, perhaps advancing, that status to one of full equality." In terms of delivery, he noted, "Thurgood spoke slowly, for him, on this occasion, making sure to articulate his words in an educated Southern way, rather than in the country style he often used." Richard Kluger, the foremost historian of the case, also commented on the effectiveness of Marshall's oral argument: "In some of his appearances before the Court, he was good; in others, he tended to be a bit on the dull side. On this day, he was at his best. He took the offensive from the start, and he held it throughout the argument."

Even after these historic arguments, the Supreme Court remained reluctant to reach a decision and requested reargument the following year on a number of points. Marshall's performance during reargument was somewhat uninspiring, but the Court had been presented with reasons that would require it to decide whether segregation was constitutional. Changes in the composition of the Court, including the appointment of Earl Warren as chief justice, were fortuitous, and Tushnet noted that Marshall had "adopted a powerful rhetorical strategy," providing the Court with a plausible framework for overruling *Plessy v. Ferguson* "and, more important, [arguing] that overruling it was the right thing to do." On May 17, 1954, the Supreme Court unanimously declared that separate educational facilities were inherently unequal.

The momentous and historic victory in *Brown*, the highlight in Marshall's career as a legal advocate, made him in great demand as a speaker and provided him with a much larger audience beyond the meetings of the NAACP. The opportunity to explain the meaning of *Brown* was a welcome one, and he accepted both traditional speaking engagements and numerous appearances on the new medium of television to tell the story. Yet one of the most important speeches of this period was delivered at Jackson, Mississippi, to the NAACP State Conference. In his speech, "Emmett Till, Mississippi Justice, and the Rest of Us" (1955), Marshall confronted the horror of violence and placed the blame on all who tolerated it. Recapping the racial hatred and perverted justice in Mississippi, he asserted defiantly, "One thing we are certain of: Nothing that has occurred to date and indeed nothing more can happen which will prevent us from using every lawful means of attaining our rights. We will continue to put emphasis on the lawful means. In other words," he said for those who might not understand, "all of the White Citizens Councils, all of the state officials, and all other groups cannot intimidate American citizens who happen to have been born black."

Marshall's entire career had been devoted to achieving legal redress, and he was deeply committed to continuing the struggle through the instrument of law. The victory of the *Brown* decision and the outrage over the unpunished killing of Emmett Till, however, combined to bring forth a civil rights movement with an ambivalent attitude toward law and justice in the South. Marshall was upset by the confrontational approach employed in the Montgomery bus boycott and other efforts to achieve change through civil disobedience. He called Martin Luther King, Jr., an "opportunist" and a "first rate rabble-rouser," but King was allowed to address the NAACP convention in January

1956, and Marshall prepared the brief that spring for the Montgomery Improvement Association in the case that declared the segregated bus system to be unconstitutional.

Continuing to wage the legal battle against segregation, Marshall was victorious in twenty-nine of the thirty-two Supreme Court cases on which he worked during his years with the NAACP. He was appointed to the U.S. Court of Appeals by President Kennedy in 1961, serving in that position until he was appointed solicitor general in 1965 by President Johnson. None of his appellate opinions were overruled by the Supreme Court, and he had an impressive record as solicitor general, winning fourteen of the nineteen cases he argued for the government before the Supreme Court.

President Johnson nominated Marshall as associate justice of the Supreme Court in 1967, only thirteen years after his victory in *Brown,* and he served in that position for twenty-four years. As a member of the Court, Marshall limited his public speaking to legal groups, and most of these addresses dealt with the broad issues before the Court during his tenure.

The last major formal speech of Marshall's career was, perhaps, the most memorable, and it was certainly the most controversial. Justice Marshall's address, "Reflections on the Bicentennial of the Constitution" (1987), delivered to about 150 attendees of the San Francisco Patent and Trademark Law Association annual seminar in Maui, Hawaii, on May 6, 1987, caught the nation's attention, drawing both harsh criticism and strong praise. The speech made the front page of the *Washington Post,* the *New York Times, USA Today,* and most major newspapers. Daniel Popeo of the Washington Legal Foundation called for Marshall's resignation; Eugene Thomas of the American Bar Association called the comments inappropriate; and Assistant Attorney General William Bradford Reynolds devoted a major speech to countering Marshall's views.

At first, Justice Marshall had planned to avoid participation in the bicentennial celebration, even though it was being organized by former Chief Justice Warren Burger; however, in early 1986 he contacted his old friend, Professor John Hope Franklin, for materials documenting the role of slavery in constitutional history and the ways in which it had been finessed by compromise. When Franklin complied with the request, Marshall replied, "Thanks so much for the material on the Bicentennial celebration or whatever else it is. You have given me just the material which will be used when the appropriate time arrives. As of now, everything is so hush hush around here. I don't know what is going on about the anniversary. I think I will wait to be asked to do something and let them have it" (PTM, Box 574, Folder 10).

As Marshall approached the podium to address his audience more than a year later, there was no indication that his speech would be anything but another formulaic recitation of platitudes about the glory of the founding. He had been asked to "recall the achievements of our Founders and the knowledge and experience that inspired them, the nature of the government they established, its origins, its character, and its ends, and the rights and privileges of citizenship, as well as its attendant responsibilities,'' he said, slyly quoting from reports prepared by the commission. Then he declared, ''I cannot accept this invitation, for I do not believe that the meaning of the Constitution was forever 'fixed' at the Philadelphia Convention. Nor do I find the wisdom, foresight, and sense of justice exhibited by the framers particularly profound. To the contrary,'' he said, ''the government they devised was defective from the start, requiring several amendments, a civil war, and momentous social transformation to attain the system of constitutional government, and its respect for the individual freedoms and human rights, that we hold as fundamental today.''

While Frederick Douglass had praised the Declaration of Independence and the Constitution in 1852, charging that the promises of the texts had been betrayed by prejudice in execution and interpretation, Marshall's faith was less in the original writing of the text and more in the political wrenching and judicial rendering of its subsequent life. Anticipating his critics, Marshall acknowledged that ''when the unpleasant truth of the history of slavery in America is mentioned during this bicentennial year,'' it would be claimed that ''the Constitution was a product of its times and embodied a compromise which, under other circumstances, would not have been made.'' Marshall did not intend to let the celebrants off so easily, reminding them that ''the effects of the framers' compromise have remained for generations. They arose from the contradiction between guaranteeing liberty and justice to all, and denying both to Negroes.''

Indicative of his views on both the official celebration and the appropriate way to read the Constitution, Marshall explained, ''I plan to celebrate the bicentennial of the Constitution as a living document, including the Bill of Rights and the other amendments protecting individual freedoms and human rights.'' The Constitution was now much more than it had been two hundred years earlier, and Thurgood Marshall—as a private attorney, as counsel for the NAACP Legal Defense Fund, as a judge on the Court of Appeals, as solicitor general, and as associate justice of the Supreme Court—had done as much as anyone to make it so, to read the dearly amended text as a document of freedom, and to translate the promise of its ideas into the order of the day.

After twenty-four years on the Supreme Court, Thurgood Marshall resigned in 1991, and less than two years later he was dead, buried in Arlington National Cemetary after services in the National Cathedral. In reflecting upon Marshall's contribution to the nation, Judge Irving R. Kaufmann said that he ''achieved national prominence as a staunch advocate of racial equality and social justice at a time when it was essential, but not fashionable, to be one.'' Through his honest oratory and the reason of his rhetoric, opined Carl Rowan, Thurgood Marshall ''was able to sear the nation's conscience and move hearts formerly strangled by hoary intransigence. And because of him, we are all more free.''

INFORMATION SOURCES

Research Collections and Collected Speeches

Columbia University, Oral History Collection, New York, NY. Holdings include an extensive audiotaped interview with Justice Marshall covering his life before appointment to the Supreme Court, conducted by Ed Erwin on February 15, 1977, 199 pp.; two interviews primarily focusing on Marshall's work with the NAACP, conducted by Mark Tushnet on May 23 and August 2, 1989, 34 pp.; and an interview regarding Marshall's work on cases of racial discrimination in the military, conducted by Thomas Buell, April 9, 1980, 73 pp.

The Federal Judicial Center, Washington, DC, holds twenty-seven hours of digital audiotape interviews with Justice Marshall. Stephen Carter was the interviewer, and the taping was done in nineteen sessions in Marshall's chambers at the Supreme Court from March to November 1992. The interviews covered his whole career, although most of them focused on his work before he joined the Supreme Court. Neither tapes nor transcripts are available to researchers at the time of this writing.

National Archives, Washington, DC, holds audiotapes of oral arguments before the Supreme Court of the United States beginning from October 10, 1955. The collection is conveniently indexed, and researchers can make copies of the tapes for educational purposes. Marshall's presentations as director-counsel for the NAACP from 1955 to 1961 are available, as are his arguments for the government as solicitor general of the United States, 1965–67.

[NAACP] National Association for the Advancement of Colored People Collection, Manuscript Division, Library of Congress, Washington, DC. This collection includes manuscript and typescript copies of speeches by Thurgood Marshall from 1940 to 1961 and press clippings relating to his speeches.

[PTM] Papers of Thurgood Marshall, Manuscript Division, Library of Congress, Washington, DC. This collection contains Marshall materials from 1949 to 1991; however, the bulk of the materials are from the years 1961 to 1991, documenting Marshall's career as a judge of the Second Circuit Court of Appeals, solicitor general, and associate justice of the Supreme Court. It contains approximately 173,700 items in 580 boxes.

Selected Critical Materials

Arizona State Law Journal 28 (1994). Special Issue on Thurgood Marshall, with articles by Ralph S. Spritzer, Bruce Green, Daniel Richman, Gerald F. Uelman, Owen M. Fiss, Gay Gelhorn, J. Clay Smith, Jr., Scott Burrell, Calvin William Sharpe, Rebecca Tsosie, and Wendy Brown-Scott.

Bland, Randall W. *Private Pressure on Public Law: The Legal Career of Justice Thurgood Marshall*. Port Washington, NY: Kennikat, 1973.

Fordham Law Review 61 (October 1992). *Brown v. Board of Education* and Its Legacy: A Tribute to Justice Thurgood Marshall, with articles by Michael Treanor, Constance Baker Motley, Louis H. Pollak, Mark Tushnet, Paul R. Diamond, Drew S. Days, III, Conrad K. Harper, Nathaniel R. Jones, Theodore M. Shaw, and Maria L. Marcus.

Georgetown Law Journal 80 (August 1992). Symposium: Honoring Justice Thurgood
    Marshall, with articles by Susan Low Bloch, Stephen B. Cohen, Owen M. Fiss,
    Geoffrey C. Hazard, Jr., Randall Kennedy, Martha Minow, and Mark Tushnet.

Goldman, Roger, with David Gallen. *Thurgood Marshall: Justice for All.* New York:
    Carroll and Graf, 1992.

Greenberg, Jack. *Crusaders in the Courts: How a Dedicated Band of Lawyers Fought
    for the Civil Rights Revolution.* New York: Basic Books, 1994.

Harvard Blackletter Journal, Spring 1989. A Tribute to Justice Thurgood Marshall, with
    articles by Constance Baker Motley, Percy R. Luney, Jr., Linda S. Greene, Derrick
    Bell, David B. Wilkins, Regina Austin, Kathleen M. Sullivan, Karen Hastie Wil-
    liams, Randall Kennedy, Martha Minow, Robert Belton, Charles J. Ogletree, and
    William W. Fisher, III.

Harvard Law Review 105 (November 1991). A Tribute to Justice Thurgood Marshall,
    including articles by William J. Brennan, Jr., Robert L. Carter, William T. Cole-
    man, Jr., Owen Fiss, A. Leon Higginbotham, Jr., and Martha Minow.

Hines, Erma Waddy. "Thurgood Marshall's Speeches on Equality and Justice under the
    Law, 1965–1967." Ph.D. diss., Louisiana State U, 1979.

Howard Law Journal 35 (1991). Thurgood Marshall Commemorative Issue, with articles
    by Benjamin Hooks, Theodore McMillian, Mark Tushnet, Luke C. Moore,
    Thelma Wyatt Cummings, Oliver W. Hill, Ronald H. Brown, Sharon Pratt Kelly,
    L. Douglas Wilder, Jesse L. Jackson, Derrick Bell, and Cynthia Burns.

Kluger, Richard. *Simple Justice: The History of Brown v. Board of Education and Black
    America's Struggle for Equality.* New York: Knopf, 1976.

Malakoff, Burton. "A Comparison of the Strategies in Three Oral Arguments before the
    United States Supreme Court." Thesis, Pacific Lutheran U, 1976.

New York University Law Review 68 (May 1993). In Memory of Thurgood Marshall,
    with articles by Robert L. Carter, Harry T. Edwards, Constance Baker Motley,
    William L. Taylor, Derrick Bell, Ronald L. Ellis, Sherrilyn A. Ifill, Anthony G.
    Amsterdam, Richard L. Revesz, and Annette E. Clark.

Rowan, Carl T. *Dream Makers, Dream Breakers: The World of Justice Thurgood Mar-
    shall.* Boston: Little, Brown, 1993.

Stanford Law Review 44 (June 1992). A Tribute to Justice Thurgood Marshall, with
    articles by William H. Rehnquist, Byron R. White, Sandra Day O'Connor, An-
    thony M. Kennedy, Warren E. Burger, Lewis F. Powell, Jr., Janet Cooper Al-
    exander, Lucius J. Baker, Julius L. Chambers, Deborah L. Rhode, Cass R.
    Sunstein, and Mark Tushnet.

Temple Political and Civil Rights Law Review 2 (1993). Thurgood Marshall and His
    Legacy: A Tribute, with articles by Debra Leanne Wrobel Conn, William H.
    Rehnquist, Vernon E. Jordan, Jr., Karen Hastie Williams, and Harris Wofford and
    the transcript of a ceremony involving judges and attorneys of the Third Circuit
    Court of Appeals in Philadelphia.

Texas Law Review 71 (May 1993). In Memoriam, with articles by William Wayne Jus-
    tice, Louis H. Pollak, Scott Brewer, Elena Kagan, and Jordan Steiker.

Tushnet, Mark V. *Making Civil Rights Law: Thurgood Marshall and the Supreme Court,
    1936–1961.* New York: Oxford UP, 1994.

Williams, Jayme Coleman. "A Rhetorical Analysis of Thurgood Marshall's Arguments
    before the Supreme Court in the Public School Segregation Controversy." Thesis,
    Ohio State U, 1959.

Williams, Juan. "Marshall's Law." *Washington Post Magazine*, January 7, 1990: W12+.
Yale Law Journal 101 (October 1991). A Tribute to Justice Marshall, with articles by
Stephen L. Carter, William T. Coleman, Jr., Paul Gerwirtz, Constance Baker
Motley, and Ralph K. Winter.

CHRONOLOGY OF MAJOR SPEECHES

[See "Research Collections and Collected Speeches" for source codes.]

"Federal Civil Rights Statutes." National Bar Association Convention, Columbus, OH,
August 3, 1940. NAACP, Group II, Box A533.

"The Legal Attack to Secure Civil Rights." NAACP Wartime Conference, Chicago, IL,
July 13, 1942. NAACP, Group II, Box A534.

"The Real Party of Interest Must Be the Child." Association of College and Secondary
Schools for Negroes, Nashville, TN, December 6, 1945. NAACP, Group II, Box
A534.

"The Essence of Democratic Government." NAACP National Convention, 1946.
NAACP, Group II, Box A534.

"Complete Opposition to All Forms of Segregation." Texas State Conference of NAACP
Branches, Denison, TX, September 5, 1947. NAACP, Group II, Box A535.

"Recent Supreme Court Decisions and the History of the Fourteenth Amendment." Fisk
University Institute on Race Relations, Nashville, TN, July 5, 1950. NAACP,
Group II, Box A535.

"The Effect of Recent Supreme Court Decisions on the American Way of Life." National Dental Association Convention, Chicago, IL, August 8, 1951. NAACP,
Group II, Box A535.

"The Bill of Rights for Negro Labor in America." National Convention of the Congress
of Industrial Organizations, Atlantic City, NJ, December 3, 1952. NAACP, Group
II, Box A535.

"The Remaining Vestiges of Slavery." National Urban League Conference, Philadelphia,
PA, September 8, 1953. NAACP, Group II, Box A536.

"Oral Argument before the Supreme Court of the United States in *Briggs v. Elliot.*"
*Argument: The Oral Argument before the Supreme Court in Brown v. Board of
Education of Topeka, 1952–55*. Ed. Leon Friedman. New York: Chelsea House,
1969.

"The Meaning of the Decisions: Bringing the Practice of Democracy in Line with Our
Democratic Principles." National Association for the Advancement of Colored
People Annual Convention, Atlantic City, NJ, June 22, 1955. NAACP, Group II,
Box A536.

"Towards the Final Phase of the Anti-Segregation Struggle." American Teachers Association Meeting, Houston, TX, July 24, 1955. NAACP, Group II, Box A536.

"Brainwashing with a Vengeance." Virginia State Conference of the NAACP Branches,
Charlottesville, VA, October 9, 1955. NAACP, Group II, Box A536.

"Emmett Till, Mississippi Justice, and the Rest of Us." Mississippi State Conference of
NAACP Branches, Jackson, MS, November 6, 1955. NAACP, Group II, Box
A536.

"The End of the Segregated Solid South." South Carolina State Conference of NAACP
Branches, Columbia, SC, November 27, 1955. NAACP, Group II, Box A536.

"The Real Task: Bringing Established Principles of Law into Everyday Practice in Local Communities." AFL-CIO Convention, New York, NY, December 7, 1955. NAACP, Group II, Box A536.

"The Fifty Year Fight for Civil Rights." Freedom Fund Report Dinner, New York, NY, July 16, 1959. PTM, Box 579, Folder 16.

"Individual and Human Dignity." Commencement Address, Kalamazoo College, Kalamazoo, MI, June 4, 1961. PTM, Box 579, Folder 16.

"Our Goal: World Peace through Law." Philippine Constitution Association, Manila, Philippines, February 8, 1968. PTM, Box 579, Folder 4.

"The Continuing Challenge of the Fourteenth Amendment." University of Georgia Law School Forum, Athens, GA, September 30, 1968. *Georgia Law Review* 3 (1968): 1–10.

"Group Action in Pursuit of Justice." James Madison Lecture, New York University School of Law, New York, NY, April 17, 1969. *New York University Law Review* 44 (1969): 661–672.

"Remarks on the Death Penalty." Second Circuit Judicial Conference, Hershey, PA, September 7, 1985. *Columbia Law Review* 86 (1986): 1–8.

"Reflections on the Bicentennial of the Constitution." San Francisco Patent and Trademark Law Association Seminar, Maui, HI, May 6, 1987. PTM, Box 574, Folder 11; *Harvard Law Review* 101 (November 1987): 1–5.

ROBERT PARRIS MOSES
(1935–), civil rights activist, social activist, professor

RICHARD J. JENSEN AND JOHN C. HAMMERBACK

In *Dreams Die Hard* David Harris described a speech that Robert Moses delivered on April 24, 1964, at Stanford University:

> Every seat in the auditorium was taken. From the balcony, Bob Moses looked frail, generating an immense, almost Zen presence as he talked. He made no attempt to work anyone up. Each word had clearly been considered and was said with the rhythms of a man crossing a stream, hopping from rock to rock. The audience grew increasingly intent as Moses proceeded. . . . When Moses was finished, the hall was absolutely quiet for almost a minute as more than 400 continued to listen. Then a five-minute standing ovation began.

Harris presented an intriguing portrait of a rhetor who differed sharply in method and manner from most activist orators of the 1960s. Moses had less confidence in the power of public discourse than in the deeds that frequently spoke far louder than did one's words. By deemphasizing the role of public persuasion in his campaign to reform the established order, he separated himself from the dominant rhetorical tradition of American protest and seemed out of place amidst the outspoken advocacy of the 1960s. Thus it may seem unsurprising that he has not been the subject of study by scholars of rhetorical discourse. Yet a close examination of his public address reveals him to be a skillful, if somewhat unconventional, rhetor who combined a complementary mix of rhetorical elements into a powerful message that helped him achieve his militant goals. His was a quiet but important voice in the civil rights movement of the 1960s.

Robert Parris Moses was born in Harlem in 1935 and grew up in a housing project. A sensitive and intellectually gifted child, he passed a citywide competitive exam as a teenager and was admitted to Stuyvesant High School, a school for gifted students in Manhattan. Upon graduation he won a scholarship to Hamilton College in upstate New York. One of only three black students at Hamilton, he was active in sports and student politics. He joined a Christian study group that commuted to New York City on weekends to preach on Times Square but failed as a preacher, according to Taylor Branch, because "his voice was much too soft for the task."

In his studies, Moses emphasized philosophy and mathematics. He read Camus, Eastern philosophers, and pacifist thought on issues connected with war and peace. His pacifist interests led to his participation in Quaker workshops in France and Japan. In 1956 he entered Harvard to begin graduate study of philosophy, with an emphasis on mathematical logic. He finished his M.A. in 1957 and began work on a Ph.D. but soon dropped out of school because of the sudden death of his mother and his father's poor health. He then accepted a position teaching mathematics at Horace Mann High School, a private school in New York City.

Moses's public activism began in 1959 when he helped organize the second Youth March for Integrated Schools in Washington, D.C. The student sit-ins in 1960 intensified his commitment, and while visiting an uncle in Virginia, he participated in a demonstration in Newport News that inspired him to join the civil rights movement in the South. During the summer of 1960 he worked in the Southern Christian Leadership Conference (SCLC) office in Atlanta, where he met leaders of the Atlanta student movement as well as members of the Student Nonviolent Coordinating Committee (SNCC), which shared an office with SCLC. He was recruited to travel throughout the South as an organizer for SNCC. During a trip in Cleveland, Mississippi, he met Amzie Moore, who convinced Moses to begin recruiting students to travel to Mississippi to register blacks to vote.

In the summer of 1961 Moses returned to Mississippi to begin the registration drive. He had hoped to initiate the drive in Cleveland, but dangerous conditions forced him to launch his movement in McComb, Mississippi. He and a group of volunteers began organizing blacks by offering classes designed to prepare individuals to register. The drive soon encountered serious obstacles: Moses was beaten when he accompanied local residents who sought to register, SNCC leaders were jailed, and fellow activists were killed. In spite of these obstacles, Moses and other members of SNCC continued to work in McComb and surrounding areas through 1961 and 1962.

In 1962 several groups in Mississippi joined to form an umbrella organization, the Council of Federated Organizations (COFO), and Moses was chosen to lead the group. COFO initiated its first major project, Freedom Vote, in the fall of 1963. Moses organized the project around a simple premise: because blacks were excluded from voting, there would be a statewide mock election in which candidates ran for major offices in Mississippi in order to prove that blacks would vote if given the opportunity. Moses recruited white students from Yale and Stanford to inform potential voters about the election. Although many of these students were arrested and beaten, they contributed significantly to a successful campaign.

The result of Freedom Vote inspired Moses to create Freedom Summer in 1964. This ambitious project employed a large number of students from the North who volunteered to expand voter registration, to operate Freedom Schools that taught reading and math to black students, and to open community centers that gave legal and medical assistance to poor blacks. Moses and his followers also organized the Mississippi Freedom Democratic party (MFDP), a group that hoped to challenge the Mississippi Democratic party's right to represent the state at the 1964 Democratic National Convention in Atlantic City. He carefully organized a process of choosing delegates that paralleled the Democratic party's usual pattern. Although members of the MFDP failed to unseat the regular Democrats, they created an awareness of the unfair political system in the South. This new awareness led to many significant changes in the party's process of choosing delegates in 1968.

In the mid-1960s Moses expanded his agenda of social activism, participating in and helping to organize several demonstrations against the Vietnam War. He believed that the attitudes that led to U.S. actions in Vietnam were similar to those held by Southern whites who oppressed blacks. Thus his antiwar actions were a natural outgrowth of his work for civil rights.

Tom Hayden observed that people who met Moses knew that "they were in the presence of a special leader." Hayden added that Moses's "specialness" was unusual for a militant protestor: "Rather than preach and arouse people, rather than make himself the visible leader, Bob set an example through practice, gaining loyalty by listening, helped individuals empower themselves." Quiet and unassuming by nature, Moses believed that the nation's news media presented a distorted picture of who he was. "If you let it," Mary King quotes him as warning, "the news media will tell you who your leaders are instead of your telling the news media who your leaders are." In the fall of 1964, frustrated with being depicted as a heroic leader by the media and disturbed by the almost Jesus-like aura that he and his name had acquired, Moses started to withdraw as a leader in SNCC. In December he resigned as director of COFO because he believed that the staff and residents were overly awed by his image and too dependent on his leadership. He even changed his last name, taking his middle name, Parris, as his last. He no longer wanted to be identified as Moses or be seen as a Moses.

From 1966 to 1993 Moses underwent dramatic changes in his life. Increasingly bitter over social conditions in the United States, he broke off all relations with whites in 1966 and withdrew from all political activity. In 1966 he left the country to avoid the draft. After leaving the United States he lived in Canada for a while and then settled in Tanzania, where he taught in a small village. His absence from the United States further added to his status as a myth. In 1977 he returned to the United States under the amnesty program offered by the Carter administration. He settled in Cambridge, Massachusetts, and eventually completed his Ph.D in mathematics. In 1980 he won a prestigious five-year Mac-Arthur Fellowship that allowed him to start the Algebra Project in Boston. That program, which teaches higher math to inner-city youth, had spread to ten states by 1992.

THE PHILOSOPHER AS ACTIVIST

As an activist for civil rights for African-Americans, Moses combined his keen intellect, clear commitment, quiet manner, hard work, and discomfort with being a hero into an unusual but effective set of qualities for a leader. His rhetorical prowess, an important part of his success in inspiring followers and bringing about change, relied on these same qualities. His persona was at the center of his persuasion. Those who knew him described him as a "murky, moody intellectual"; a "northern intellectual" who "evinced a patient pragmatism and an overriding commitment to humanist values"; being "original in his thinking and invention"; "a legend in his own time"; and the "ad hoc theoretician, general idea man and Moses of the Mississippi freedom movement." Mary King, who worked with Moses in the South, depicted his rhetorical persona in these words:

> Bob was reserved. He showed his immense personal power and strength through a quiet, monotonal tranquillity. In the same way that one listens more attentively to a whisper, people were drawn to Bob—he was so obtrusive that in his quiet, self-possessed stillness, he fixed additional attention to himself. He seemed entirely nourished from within.

Other observers of his speaking centered on his calm assurance, quiet manner, profound depth, and impressive efforts: "[Moses] speaks very calmly, in a voice that is rather soft and slow but with enunciation almost pedagogically careful, as though he were teaching a foreign language"; "his rhetoric was poetic, his moral stance defiant"; audiences became "absorbed in him, an extension of his soft voice"; and he "managed to communicate a soothing, spiritual depth."

Moses's persona clearly affected his coworkers and others who knew him. In some local areas he was characterized as "Moses in the Bible." Sally Belfrage, a student volunteer in Freedom Summer, stated that on a wall in the house where she lived there was a picture of Moses from the *Saturday Evening Post* hanging next to one of Christ (74). SNCC workers copied both his appearance and public address, wrote Doug McAdam, as they wore his uniform of "a T-shirt and denim overalls, in the bib of which he [Moses] propped his hands" and emulated his "slow, thoughtful manner of speaking."

One source of Moses's image among SNCC organizers was his legendary lack of fear. Two instances are often cited. On one occasion he and two other SNCC organizers were being followed by a carload of unfriendly riders armed with guns. Moses was in the back seat lying down trying to sleep when the

SNCC car began to accelerate. His response to being told why the driver was speeding was often repeated: he looked at the car behind, said that its occupants would not bother them, and promptly went to sleep. On another occasion Moses and other volunteers rushed to Greenwood, Mississippi, after receiving a call that the SNCC office was being attacked by a mob. When they arrived at two o'clock in the morning, the staff had escaped and the office was empty. Moses entered, checked the deserted premises, made a bed on the couch, and immediately went to sleep. One of his companions commented: "I was scared. I just couldn't understand what kind of a guy this Bob Moses is, that could walk into a place where a lynch mob had just left and make up a bed and prepare to go to sleep, as if the situation was normal."

Moses's quiet persuasion was effective for students at elite colleges as well as with activists in the field. On April 24, 1964, he addressed students at Stanford University in his characteristic informal manner, eschewing the platform-speech format for a lengthy session of questions and answers. The strength and depth of his ideas emerged clearly, delivered in his usual soft voice and deliberate pace. His address captivated his listeners.

The language of his Stanford speech, and indeed of all his speeches and writings, was consistent with his delivery and persona. It avoided any display of flamboyance or rhetorical excess and focused attention on his ideas rather than on himself. His words were plain and easily understood, and his stories illustrated his substantive points. Often his anecdotes and examples illuminated the problems blacks faced in the South and particularly the violence he and other SNCC volunteers confronted and eventually conquered. In several places in the speech his language gained impact from its arrangement into parallel structure. For example, he instructed:

> The questions that we think face the country are questions which in one sense are much deeper than civil rights. They're questions which go very much to the bottom of mankind and people. They're questions which have repercussions in terms of a whole international affairs and relations. They're questions which go to the very root of our society. What kind of society will we be?

Elsewhere in the speech he used a similar pattern but concluded with a brief statement rather than a question: "Most of them say they don't have telephones. They don't have newspapers. They have very little contact with the outside world. They do have radios. They do have televisions. So they have contact."

In addition to his simple, clear language and parallel structure, Moses relied on memorable imagery to communicate his ideas. These vivid images are well illustrated by an often-quoted letter he wrote on November 1, 1961, while in jail in Magnolia, Mississippi. He began his letter "from the drunk tank of the county jail" by describing his cellmates:

> Later on Hollis will lead out with a clear tenor into a freedom song. Talbert and Lewis will supply jokes, and McDew will discourse on the history of the black

man and the Jew. McDew, a black by birth, a Jew by choice, and a revolutionary by necessity, has taken the deep hates and loves of America, and the world, reserved for those who dare to stand in a strong sun and cast a sharp shadow.

After recounting how he was harshly treated by the judge who sentenced him to jail and lamenting the poor food and accommodations, he concluded with an inspiring peroration:

> This is Mississippi, the middle of the iceberg. Hollis is leading off with his tenor, "Michael row the boat ashore; Christian brothers don't be slow, Alleluia; Mississippi next to go, Alleluia." This is a tremor in the middle of the iceberg—from a stone that the builders rejected.

Even as Moses shifted attention from himself to his ideas through his language and delivery, his training in philosophy surfaced in his themes, arguments, and explanations. During the training of volunteers for Freedom Summer, for example, he used Tolkien's *Ring Trilogy* to express how he felt in sending volunteers to their possible death. King captured his meaning and manner: "His point was that the power to make such decisions is corrupting, just as the ring which Frodo carried so far to destroy affected him to the point where he almost failed to destroy it. At such moments Bob would speak very slowly, sometimes simply standing quietly before a large group for many minutes before the words came." He sometimes referred to Camus in his public discourse, revealing his study of the author in college and his rereading of *The Rebel* and *The Plague* while in jail. For example, he told volunteers who were training for Freedom Summer:

> There is an analogy in *The Plague* by Camus. The country isn't willing yet to admit it has the plague, but it pervades the whole society. Everyone must come to grips with this, because it affects us all. We must discuss it openly and honestly, even with the danger that we get too analytic and tangled up. If we ignore it, it's going to blow up in our faces.

The broad theme of Moses's discourse was that society needed to be dramatically altered through a careful analysis and concerted effort by all of its members. In "Moses of Mississippi Raises Some Universal Questions," an interview in *Pacific Scene*, he made clear his underlying optimism about people:

> I have certain feelings about people in general. I feel that they've [been] manipulated. I don't happen to believe that they, if they were presented with real information about people and how they live, if they weren't forced to live under myths about themselves and other people, that they would consciously choose to isolate other people. To force them into ghettos. To restrict their participation in society.

Thus the public would make needed reforms once informed of the truth and freed from a false set of myths about humans. The country could overcome its problems, he believed, by engaging in a critical dialectical process. He explained: "The question before this country really is: does it have the ability to probe deeply into any issue? And does it have the stamina once it starts probing to keep going until it gets to the bottom of the problem?"

The needed study of national problems required the full involvement of oppressed people, particularly the people of the South. To begin with, he said, "certainly one of the most basic rights we have been seeking is the right to participate fully in the life of this country." To achieve this right, blacks and whites must suppress their differences and work together. Such cooperation would be difficult, he added, but in the end the two groups must live together cooperatively and peacefully—and "the less overlay of bitterness, the more possible to work out a reconciliation."

Historian Clayborne Carson has written that Moses taught that the South was the natural place to initiate change. The solving of problems in that region would establish a model for solving problems throughout the country. The biggest obstacle to change in the South was the fear that gripped its residents, a fear that would be removed by sustained efforts of organizers: "The deeper the fear, the deeper the problems in the community, the longer you have to stay to convince them." Volunteers from the North could reduce such fears by linking the Southerners' battle to the rest of the country. Moses explained: "They [the Southern residents] look upon the [summer] volunteers and the people from all over the country like the coming of the country. They bring the country with them. This country couldn't come if they didn't come." Once the nation came to the South, an entire country's strength would permeate the region's oppressed blacks.

When blacks lost their fear, they would need two tools to transform their lives: the right to vote, and the opportunity for an excellent education. The first tool was denied them by registration procedures. Rather than allowing Southern officials to administer literacy exams, federal officials should oversee the tests. In 1963 testimony before a congressional subcommittee, Moses discussed how Southern institutions had linked voting and education to bar blacks from participating in democracy: "I still think that the country owes it to the Negroes who have been denied the right of an education to offer them an alternative. That either they be registered without a literacy test or they be provided with a massive education program because there is no adult education program in Mississippi."

The lack of education damaged blacks economically as well as politically. Workers driven off Southern plantations because of automation were often forced to leave the South and migrate to the North. In his speech at Stanford, Moses traced this migration: "They're gonna go to Chicago; they're gonna go to St. Louis and Detroit; they're gonna come to California and Los Angeles and

San Francisco.'' Whatever their destination, these uneducated blacks faced a
bleak future in the new culture they would enter.

Moses saw his movement achieve many of his goals. In his ''Letter to
Northern Supporters,'' he cited one immediate effect:

> This is a new dimension for a voting program in Mississippi; Negroes have been
> herded to the polls before by white people but have never stood en masse in protest
> at the seat of power in the iceberg of Mississippi politics. Negroes who couldn't
> read and write stood in line to tell the register they still wanted to vote, that they
> didn't have a chance to go to school when they were small and anyway Mr. John
> Jones can't read and write either and *he* votes.

Beyond such tangible successes, Moses and the other volunteers forced Americans to question fundamental assumptions and practices in their society. He
helped people in the South to overcome fear and begin to challenge the entrenched power structure; and he educated them on their basic rights as citizens
and on how to express those rights through voting and through protesting against
the status quo.

Although Moses is not as well known as many African-American leaders and
rhetors, he played an important role at a crucial time in the formative years of
the recent protest movement for civil rights for America's ethnic minorities. As
a theorist, organizer, and activist, he contributed significantly to the drive for
justice for blacks. As a rhetor, he merged his persona, language, delivery, and
ideas into a moving message that emphasized his substantive thought rather than
his rhetorical performance. This rhetorical profile was appropriate for a spokesman who believed that the general public, once it was informed, would respond
to efforts by blacks to end injustice. He thus sought to teach, rather than to
incite, trusting his calmly presented facts and arguments to accomplish his goals.
He put his faith in careful reasoning and pragmatic activism and illustrated that
faith in his thoughtful public address and energetic organizing. His ideas and
character merged to make him an effective, if unusual, voice of protest.

INFORMATION SOURCES

Research Collections and Collected Speeches

The only speech in an archive is a cassette recording of Moses's speech at Stanford
University on April 24, 1964. The recording is located in the Stanford University Archive
of Recorded Sound. An interview with Moses is located in the Anne Romaine Oral
History Collection, King Library and Archives, the Martin Luther King, Jr., Center for
Nonviolent Social Change, Atlanta, Georgia.

''Letter from Magnolia, Mississippi, Jail, November 1, 1961.'' Forman, 233; Grant, 303.
''Interview with SNCC Leader: Voter Registration Drive Moves Forward Painfully.''
    New America, February 6, 1963: 5.

"Letter to Northern Supporters, February 27, 1963." Grant, 299–300.

"Only the Literate." *Southern Patriot*, May 1963: 1, 3.

"Negroes Would Still Be Marching." *Southern Patriot*, June 18, 1963: 4.

"Moses of Mississippi Raises Some Universal Questions." *Pacific Scene*, February 1965: 1–5.

". . . . One Freedom Worker's Views." *Southern Patriot*, October 1965: 3.

"Interview with Robert Penn Warren." Warren, 89–99.

"Mississippi: 1961–1962." *Liberation*, January 1970: 6–17.

"Civil Rights at the Grass Roots." *Christian Science Monitor*, January 17, 1992: 19.

Selected Biographies

Atwater, James. "If We Can Crack Mississippi." *Saturday Evening Post*, July 25, 1964: 16–19.

Belfrage, Sally. *Freedom Summer*. New York: Viking, 1965.

Branch, Taylor. *Parting the Waters: America in the King Years, 1954–63*. New York: Simon and Schuster, 1988.

Burner, Eric. *And Gently He Shall Lead Them: Robert Parris Moses and Civil Rights in Mississippi*. New York: New York UP, 1994.

Carson, Clayborne. *In Struggle: SNCC and the Black Awakening of the 1960s*. Cambridge, MA: Harvard UP, 1981.

Forman, James. *The Making of Black Revolutionaries: A Personal Account*. New York: Macmillan, 1972.

Grant, Joanne, ed. *Black Protest: History, Documents, and Analyses, 1619 to the present*. New York: Fawcett, 1968.

Harris, David. *Dreams Die Hard*. New York: St. Martin's, 1982.

Hayden, Tom. *Reunion*. New York: Random House, 1988.

Jacobs, Paul, and Saul Landau. *The New Radicals*. New York: Vintage, 1966.

Jetter, Alexis. "Mississippi Learning." *New York Times Magazine*, February 21, 1993: 28–32, 35, 50–51, 64, 72.

King, Mary. *Freedom Song*. New York: William Morrow, 1987.

McAdam, Doug. *Freedom Summer*. New York: Oxford UP, 1988.

Warren, Robert Penn. *Who Speaks for the Negro?* New York: Random House, 1965.

We Accuse. Berkeley, CA: Diablo, 1965.

CHRONOLOGY OF MAJOR SPEECHES

"Testimony on Civil Rights." *Hearings before Subcommittee No. 5 of the Committee of the Judiciary*, House of Representatives, 88th Cong., 1st Sess., May 28, 1963, 1248–1263.

"Speech at Stanford." Palo Alto, CA, April 24, 1964.

"Questions Raised by Moses." Jacobs and Landau, 123; *Movement* (SNCC California newspaper), April 1965.

"Speech at Vietnam Days." Berkeley, CA, May 22, 1965. Petras, 148–153.

ELEANOR HOLMES NORTON
(1937–), lawyer, professor, U.S. representative

VANESSA WYNDER QUAINOO

Eleanor Holmes Norton has been called a woman of extraordinary vision and grace. As a young, brilliant African-American attorney, she championed the fight for civil rights and racial equality in the 1970s and 1980s. Eleanor Holmes Norton is distinctly a woman of profound rhetorical vision who has dedicated her life to the ideals of justice and equality. While her major contributions have been in the area of racial equality, she has also fought for the equal rights of women and for the protection of free-speech rights for all citizens of the United States.

Born on June 13, 1937, in Washington, D.C., to Coleman and Vela Holmes, Eleanor was a fourth-generation Washingtonian and a precocious child of sharp intellect and varied interests. Holmes's upbringing affected her sense of self-esteem and firm determination. One of three daughters in an upper-middle-class African-American family, Holmes said of education, "[it] was like bread—life did not proceed without it." She explained that her parents had themselves undergone continuous schooling for many years during her childhood. She remembered her father remarking that while she was entering the first grade, he was entering a first grade also—the first year of law school. Her mother, a teacher, returned to school to complete her master's degree.

Holmes was clearly motivated by parental role models who measured the value of education in the highest terms. Glimpses of her sense of esteem can be seen when she speaks of her years at Dunbar High School, a prestigious African-American public school: "I never felt I was the inferior one." Active in school and civic activities, Holmes remarked that along with her classmates she felt strong and complete in her African-American community. She did not have a sense of isolation or a sense of being excluded from the mainstream. She even had sympathy for Euro-Americans who lived close by Dunbar, but, purely because of race, chose to attend predominantly white schools far from their homes.

After graduating from high school, Eleanor attended Antioch College, where she earned a B.A. in 1960. She then attended Yale University, where she was awarded an M.A. in American Studies in 1963 and a J.D. from the Law School in 1964. After completing her formal education, Holmes began her legal career as a law clerk for the presiding justice of the Federal District Court in 1964, and from 1965 through 1970 she served as the assistant legal director of the American Civil Liberties Union (ACLU). In 1965, she married Edward W. Norton, also an attorney, and they have two children, Katherine and John.

In 1971, Eleanor Holmes Norton assumed the position of executive assistant to the mayor of New York City. Returning to Washington in 1977, she joined the office of the Equal Employment Opportunity Commission (EEOC). According to historian Peggy Lamson, she significantly reformed the EEOC. In 1981–82, Norton was a senior fellow at the Urban Institute, and 1982 marked the beginning of a professorship at Georgetown University Law Center. A brief hiatus from her faculty position was devoted to serving as the representative from Washington, D.C., to the U.S. Congress. She has currently returned to her professorial duties at Georgetown and is the recipient of over twenty-five honorary doctorate degrees from colleges and universities across the country.

ELEANOR HOLMES NORTON: POLITICAL ORATOR

Norton's professional development correlates with her thematic delivery throughout the last two decades. She has been consistent and direct in confronting social concerns. Her discourse can be divided into three general categories: the delineation of an African-American rhetoric of civil rights, an explanatory embrace of the women's liberation movement, and the advocacy of a legal and political agenda for human rights. Norton seems to have devoted equal intensity to each area, and most of her writings and speeches incorporate these themes from beginning to end. She is also adamant about articulating the loss of dignity African-Americans have incurred because of the slavery legacy, and this dominant and emotive factor is intricately woven throughout much of Norton's thinking.

When considering Norton as an orator who is committed to an African-American rhetoric, it is important to examine her purpose. When asked in a 1975 interview for *Civil Liberties Review* why she fought so hard against injustice, Norton noted that "to undo the handicaps that the slave culture worked on black family and the black psyche takes more than just handing out resources." As a political orator, Norton is driven toward enactment of policy that, ideally, culminates in tangible social change. Making a universal appeal to all women to eradicate male dominance and the abuse of women, she wrote in "For Sadie and Maude" that "we have a chance to make family life a liberating experience instead of the confining experience it more often has been. We have a chance to free woman and, with her, the rest of us.'' Part of the strength of Norton's appeals is that, previous to writing that essay, she had established herself as a human rights attorney with the ACLU. Her work had crossed several taboo boundaries as she had defended those who were unpopular or extremist.

In 1968, Holmes argued the case of *George Wallace v. the People,* in which she defended Wallace's plea to speak at Shea Stadium in New York City. She had also argued ACLU court cases filed for the protection of the rights of the Ku Klux Klan to demonstrate peacefully. Explaining her position, Norton linked her commitment to universal rights back to her Yale Law School days when she was one of just fourteen women in her graduating class. She recalled that the fourteen were very concerned with the First Amendment. In subsequent comments, she reminded her audience that the right of someone like Stokely Carmichael to speak out against racism was only as secure as the right of George Wallace to also speak in public. For Norton, human rights included freedom of speech and freedom from oppressive lifestyle.

When asked by Alan Westin how the African-American community responded to her ACLU tenure, she noted that ''blacks felt proud that the principled person turned out to be black in America.'' The dominant themes in Norton's oratory are, in kaleidoscope fashion, different angles of a single essential edict: all human beings have the right to exist and live free of oppression. Women and African-Americans happen to represent two groups who are urgently in need of civil and human rights enactment. Norton, being African-American and a woman, is herself a symbol of both movements. She lends credibility to the movements because of what she has been able to accomplish despite opposition.

As she rhetorically opposes the oppression of minorities, Norton typically begins by confronting the assumptions currently in vogue. For example, in her speech ''Population Growth and the Future of Black Folk,'' Norton attacked the racist thinking that advocated excessive population controls against people of Color and the poor. Speaking as the chairman of the Human Rights Commission of New York City, Norton noted that ''the [Commission's] report rejects the notion that minorities are primarily responsible for the bulk of the population growth.'' Norton then created a confrontational dialectic by imposing a specific position on the underrepresented group, a position that in turn illuminated the root problem. ''The real issue for Black people,'' Norton went on to tell her audience, ''is how to improve their quality of life . . . getting better education, jobs, and social services.''

Eleanor Holmes Norton's speeches reveal a sensitive communicator, one whose oratory is particularly informed by an African-American rhetoric of civil rights. Two ideological principles guide her rhetoric, principles which are grounded in the tradition of African-American civil rights. The first may be termed ''core symbols.'' These are expressly demonstrated as values which connect the importance of family relationships, individual uniqueness, optimism, and a circular world view in respect to the politics of equality.

The African-American context is a confluence of complex institutional and social elements under siege and plagued by an all-encompassing canopy of race and race relations. Issues such as unemployment and the lack of empowering employment are inextricably linked to symptomatic practices such as teenage pregnancy, generational welfare dependency, and substance abuse. Although these practices are not unique to the African-American community, their presence in the African-American context are the catalyst for orators who try to articulate agendas which would impact all Americans and invariably liberate African-Americans. The African-American who speaks out of this tradition is expected to address such concerns by appealing to the core values of that community.

In her 1995 House speech on the Republican Welfare Reform Bill, for example, Norton declared employment a universal need and then personalized this need by pointing to the lack of jobs in ''the District,''—her district—and in effect the African-American community in which she was raised. She personalized the individual through statements such as ''Sister, can you get me a job?'' This posture of self-reliance is emphasized and then juxtaposed with the stereotype of the welfare recipient who supposedly begs ''Brother, can you spare a dime?'' Ultimately, Norton's circular world view which purports equality comes in conflict with the linear, hierarchical world view of Republican conservatism.

The second principle present in Norton's ideology is what Cornel West, in *Keeping Faith*, calls an insurgent progression away from the status quo ideals and policies, beliefs and practices that sustain the elite at the expense of marginal groups and their urgent need for restored dignity. Norton's 1995 ''Statement Introducing the District of Columbia Federal Tax Equity Act'' illustrated this principle in action. On its face, the statement was a typical congressperson's defense of her constituency's interest. In defense of the bill, which would have exempted District of Columbia citizens from paying federal income, gift and estate taxes, Norton argued that federal taxation of her constituents violated their right to fair and equitable taxation. Federal taxation is unfair, she noted, because the District of Columbia has no outlying counties or state government to share the burden of taxation. The maintenance of the city rests squarely on the shoulders of the city, and no one else. Further, past Congressional discrimination is, she argued, partly to blame for the city's current fiscal woes. Federal taxation is also inequitable, she declared, because District residents do not have full representation in the House and Senate.

There were no racial appeals or directives in the text of her speech. Norton's speech argued only to that which would be universally equal and fair. There was irony, of course, in an African-American woman articulating resistance to taxation. This resistance, however, was simply what one may call ''critical negation'' of the institutions which, historically, have discriminated against African-Americans. Norton critically evaluated current policy, practices which, if altered, would make African-Americans the indirect beneficiaries of an improved system.

Eleanor Holmes Norton is a woman of remarkable vision and political savvy. Perhaps her oratory is as revealing to us as she is herself, for it contains themes that are transcendent and timeless. Norton's commitment to racial justice is not stymied by ethnocentrically narrowed claims of racial exclusivity. Her commitment to an agenda of civil rights is intricately connected to her political stand for human rights. During Norton's tenure as the District of Columbia representative, she was considered an expert in the political intricacies of Congress and the federal government. Born out of a universal appeal for human rights is her women's liberation rhetoric. Together, her arguments for race, gender, and human rights form a powerful discourse.

Norton's articulate and graceful style is augmented by a tough-minded reserve that confronts faulty assumptions and strikes hard at the center of any argument. She is unusually calm when facing the struggles of injustice and inequality. When asked by Westin "How do you stay optimistic?" she responded: "It's almost existential—some people derive their energy from struggle, other people derive theirs from achievement. I'm someone who just is moved by struggle." It requires a unique kind of grace and resolve to stay focused when struggling against odds. Eleanor Holmes Norton is extraordinary because she not only beats the odds, but she articulates, with passion, the sentiments of a generation. She is a political orator with a rhetorical vision.

INFORMATION SOURCES

Research Collections and Collected Speeches

Related papers may be found at the Library of Congress, the Georgetown University Center of Law, the Brown University Library, Yale Law School, and the University of Rhode Island Library.

Norton, Eleanor Holmes. "For Sadie and Maude." *Sisterhood Is Powerful: An Anthology of Writings from the Women's Liberation Movement.* Ed. Robin Morgan. New York: Random House, 1970, 353–359.

Selected Critical Studies

Cheatham, Cheryl Smith. *African American Women in the Legal Academy: Selected Bibliography of Patricia Harris, Lanni Guinier, Patricia Williams, Emma Coleman Jordan, and Eleanor Holmes Norton.* Cleveland, OH: Case Western Reserve UP, 1994.
Gordon, Ed. "A Dialogue with Eleanor Holmes Norton." *Emerge,* August 1990: 11–12.
Lamson, Peggy. "Eleanor Holmes Norton Reforms the Equal Employment Opportunity Commission." *Women Leaders in American Politics.* Ed. James David Barber and Barbara Kellerman. Englewood Cliffs, NJ: Prentice-Hall, 1986.
Westin, A. "Some People Derive Their Energy from the Struggle." *Civil Liberties Review,* Winter 1975: 90–110.

Selected Biographies

"Eleanor Holmes Norton." *Current Biography,* November 1976:15–17.

CHRONOLOGY OF MAJOR SPEECHES

"The Law School Curriculum and the Legal Rights of Women" (Symposium address to the Association of American Law Schools and the New York University School of Law). New York, NY, October 21, 1972. Reprinted in a pamphlet of the same name.

"Population Growth and the Future of Black Folk." *Crisis,* May 1973: 151–153.

"National Women and the Law" (Keynote address to the Seventh National Women and the Law Conference). Washington, DC, 1976. Audiocassette. Dub-L-Tape: 1976.

"Unity, Reaching In, Reaching Out" (Keynote address to the Black Perspectives in Contemporary American Studies Symposium). Ames, IA, September 22, 1981. Audiocassette. Ames: Iowa State University Media Resources Center, 1981.

"The Constitutional Stimulus and the New Equality" (Albert Blumenthal Memorial Lecture, Hunter College). New York, NY, 1988. Reprinted in a pamphlet of the same name by Hunter College of New York, 1988.

"Culture and Gender Relations in the Black Community: Re-opening a Discourse on Some Very Dirty Linen" (Address to the Conference on Race, Gender and Power in America, Georgetown University Law Center). Washington, DC, October 16, 1992. Reprinted in *Race, Gender, and Power in America*. Washington, DC: Georgetown University Law Center, 1992; Videocassette. Georgetown University Law Center, 1992.

"Statement Introducing the District of Columbia Federal Tax Equity Act." Washington, D.C., January 31, 1995. Available through Rep. Norton's Congressional office.

"Remarks on the Republican Welfare Reform bill." Washington D.C., March 24, 1995. *Congressional Record*, March 24, 1995, H3766.

ADAM CLAYTON POWELL, JR.
(1908–1972), minister, U.S. representative

ENRIQUE D. RIGSBY

Adam Clayton Powell, Jr., was the first of the great preacher-politicians to emerge from the African-American community. From his base as pulpit minister of the Abyssinian Baptist Church in Harlem, Powell rose to become the single most powerful voice on behalf of equal rights for black Americans at the mid-point of the twentieth century. Before Montgomery, before Martin Luther King, Jr., or Malcolm X, before the Equal Rights Act or the Voting Rights Act, there was Congressman Adam Clayton Powell, Jr.

Adam Clayton Powell, Jr., was known by numerous titles, including "Mr. Civil Rights," "King of the Cats," "The Father of Black Power," and "The Flaming Tongue." Most notably, Powell will be recorded in history as the flamboyant politician from New York whose fiery rhetorical style filled the halls of Congress and captured the attention of congregants at his Harlem church. Powell made history by becoming, in November 1944, only the fourth African-American since the Reconstruction era to be elected to Congress. The election culminated years of activism throughout Harlem.

Upon graduation from college, Powell succeeded his ailing father as pastor of Harlem's Abyssinian Baptist Church. When not preaching, Powell organized attacks against segregated practices in and around Harlem. As his small following grew, so too did Powell's reputation as a dynamic and powerful speaker. Such lines as "don't buy where you can't work" were stock phrases used by Powell that later served as rallying cries during the civil rights era. In fact, Powell's work with another civil rights activist, A. Philip Randolph, resulted in the redistricting of Harlem, which produced a gerrymandered district without incumbent representation. In 1944, Powell successfully ran for election from the newly created congressional district and thus began twenty-six years of a successful, though stormy, tenure in public office.

Adam Clayton Powell, Jr., was born on November 29, 1908, in New Haven, Connecticut. He was the youngest child of Mattie Fletcher Schafer Powell and Adam Clayton Powell, Sr., who held a pastorate in New Haven. In 1909, the family moved to an upper-middle-class, predominantly Jewish area of New York known as Harlem. Powell, Sr., served as pastor of Abyssinian Baptist until Adam, Jr., took over for his ill father in 1930. Franklin noted that 1930 was the year Powell received his "political baptism" as well. A group of Harlem physicians, banned by a white hospital administration from practicing medicine, went to Powell for assistance. Powell eventually led a march of over six thousand to city hall in protest over the segregated practice. The victory resulted in integrated status for practicing physicians and convinced Powell of the power of mass support. A series of community victories as minister and as a New York City Council member yielded tremendous popularity for the tall, handsome, silver-tongued Powell. As Haskins noted, "Black people loved Powell." African-Americans were impressed by the way Powell stood tall against racist and segregated power structures.

By the mid-1940s, Adam Clayton Powell, Jr., had a reputation for a fiery style of oratory with a disdain for vacillation. Powell's image was larger than life among African-Americans not just in Harlem but throughout America. Powell was known as the pastor of the largest African-American church in America and the man who would stand up "for his people" against the white power structure. When the new congressional district was formed in 1944, Councilman Powell became Congressman Powell. Powell's autobiography made little mention of his four-year term as councilman, perhaps because so few of his proposals were enacted into law. Such would not be the case in Congress.

As a freshman congressman, Powell fought against discriminatory practices throughout Washington, D.C. He demanded that African-American reporters be allowed to sit and work in the congressional press gallery, which, to this point, had been segregated. Powell used his position to exert great pressure before Congress for the desegregation of the armed forces.

His first chair assignment was to head the Mines and Mining Committee. Although Powell claimed to know little about the mining business, his committee produced safety-standard measures that were passed by Congress and are still in effect today. His most notable congressional work came as chair of the powerful Education and Labor Committee. Among the major pieces of legislation drafted by this committee and eventually passed into law were the minimum-wage law and the War on Poverty bill (eventually signed by President Lyndon B. Johnson). President Johnson commended Powell's achievement, stating that "only with progressive leadership could so much be accomplished by one committee in so short a time." Powell's committee was a powerful one, and through it Powell pushed scores of bills before legislators aimed at destroying segregation strongholds. For example, a rider that appeared on numerous bills, known as the Powell Amendment, stipulated that federal funds would be withheld should segregated practices be revealed in the implementation of a bill.

By the mid-1960s, America's civil rights movement was in full swing, and Adam Clayton Powell, Jr., was considered the most powerful African-American politician in the United States. Ironically, the mid-1960s also represented the beginning of the end for the fragile civil rights coalition and for the political career of Adam Clayton Powell. Various allegations, including charges of misuse of campaign funds and the use of congressional funds for family travel, began what Powell would refer to as "The War on Powell." In 1967, Powell was removed from his seat as chair of the Education and Labor Committee, and one day later, it was voted that he be removed from Congress pending a committee hearing.

When it was time for Powell to address Congress in his defense, he was as defiant as ever as he scolded congressmen for their hypocrisy and accused members of "having skeletons in their closet." He told congressmen that he knew that pressure was on them to offer the harshest punishment possible, and that if they could vote secretly he would be vindicated. When the House vote was tabulated, Powell had lost 363 to 65, causing him to shout, "You are looking at the first black man who was ever lynched by Congress!" Congress condemned Powell publicly, stripped him of his power, and fined him forty thousand dollars.

Powell assembled a cadre of attorneys and challenged congressional actions all the way to the U.S. Supreme Court. On June 16, 1969, the Supreme Court ruled that Powell had been unconstitutionally excluded from Congress. However, the validation was too little, too late. In practice, Powell had resigned from Congress, seeking instead to labor effortlessly on a fishing boat in Bimini. Although renominated for his congressional seat, he campaigned little and, on June 23, 1970, lost in a primary election to opponent Charles Rangel.

By this point, Powell's health was deteriorating rapidly. A decrease in public appearances was preceded by the announcement of his retirement from the Harlem pastorate. On April 4, 1972, Adam Clayton Powell, Jr., died from cancer.

ADAM CLAYTON POWELL, JR., AND THE RHETORIC OF REVOLT

Scholars investigating civil rights history have noted that, generally, three protest strategies have been available to African-American agitators: assimilation, separatism, and revolt. The "King of the Cats," Adam Clayton Powell, Jr., was unmistakably an employer of revolt rhetoric. Whether Powell was preaching at Abyssinian Baptist Church in Harlem, volleying salvos with legislators on Capitol Hill, or wooing college students from coast to coast, Powell's rhetorical tone suggested an arrogant disdain for what he called the "American way."

In a 1968 speech delivered before the student body at the University of California, Berkeley, Powell condemned America with alarming defiance: "The old order is dead . . . gone with the wind. And people like you here on this campus have blared the trumpet and rolled the drums, and sent a call out to the world that we are searching for a new way . . . because we're tired . . . we're tired of the American way.'' Powell's defiance was shaped by the tones of an East Coast accent and the rhythms of a Black Southern Baptist preacher. The product was a loud, rich, melodic text that simultaneously riveted his words to his listeners' hearts and made them tap their feet.

Powell said, ''Every human being has a right to protest. This is what I have been doing and why I am in the place that I am in today.'' The ''place'' Powell found himself in for most of his public career was at the opposite end of America's established order. However, writers such as Wil Haygood have contended that regardless of the place in which Powell found himself, he felt that it was his obligation both as an elected official of a voiceless district and a spokesperson for African-Americans that he protest with all the vehemence and venom he could muster. As these observers have noted, Powell's community style of address and general oratorical ability rarely avoided leaving an everlasting impression, regardless of how one felt about the individual. Referring to a series of speeches in Panama during 1949, Haygood chronicled reports from U.S. diplomats who witnessed Powell's rhetorical abilities: ''There can be no question . . . that Powell's evident interest in Panama, his personal charm, his adroit use of flattery, and his showmanship made a favorable impression not only on political leaders but on the Panamanian public in general.''

Powell's rhetorical strategy to condemn the America whose freedoms he enjoyed seems contradictory. However, historical accounts of Powell's personal and professional endeavors reveal a lifestyle of contradictions (see especially Hamilton and Haygood). For example, although he was a minister, Powell did not believe in the Virgin Birth or in heaven and hell as literal places. Despite overwhelming popularity among congressional district constituents, his ''Christian lifestyle'' alienated many, including some who sat in the pews of Abyssinian Baptist Church, who, from the beginning, had viewed Powell as a young, headline-seeking playboy who did not believe or teach the entire Bible. Wrote Haygood:

> His personal life was a bundle of ironies and contradictions. It was not merely that he frequented nightclubs and drank liquor with obvious relish and enormous capacity. These things were debatable, to some, as sinful. But his continuing to see other women shortly after he was married, arranging rendezvous with the aid of friends—such activities could hardly be condoned. He lived, in other words, the hypocritical, dilemma-filled life he so forcefully condemned in America's racial system.

Despite such obvious contradictions in his personal and public life, few can deny the rhetorical power Adam Clayton Powell managed to generate as minister, congressman, and advocate for African-Americans.

Powell's rhetorical stance was significant in that it allowed him to perform a dualistic role in the American system. By definition, Powell was a legitimate member of the established order; for twenty-six years he served as a U.S. congressman. However, his use of language and rhetorical style allowed Powell to comfortably vacillate from establishment agent to agitator. Powell's use of language served to create divisions between Powell and other members of Congress and to keep him close to constituents. For example, a serious transgression within the African-American community is to "forget where you've come from." Adam Clayton Powell, Jr., never forgot. Stock phrases such as "We are developing a new breed of cats," "Keep the faith, baby," "When you have black power you don't need violence," and "Keep on fighting" worked to keep Powell close to those he advocated for, despite being part of a union he believed was racist. Additionally, the use of slang words such as "baby" and "chick" reinforced Powell's purposeful desire to remain in the congressional minority and close to the cries of dissenting Americans.

Arguably, Powell's most powerful rhetorical tool was his voice. Powell's tone spoke more than the words contained in his speech. Powell's tone of voice seemed to say, "America, I dare you to act right. In fact, America, I don't think you're capable of behaving on your own, so Adam, the King of the Cats, will keep check on you." Whether he was in church or on campus, Powell was always lecturing. Whether he was admonishing African-Americans to embrace black power or scolding white college students for their reluctance in choosing African-Americans as leaders, Powell never wavered from his indignant fervor. In each public speech, Powell left no doubt that he was not pleased with the status quo. It was a kind of polarizing rhetoric, particularly toward the end of his life, that united Powell with the Black Panthers and the extreme factions of numerous agencies, including the Student Nonviolent Coordinating Committee. The same rhetoric, however, alienated him from others within the African-American community, such as the mainstream civil rights organization, the Southern Christian Leadership Conference (SCLC). During his Berkeley speech, Powell referred directly to the SCLC's president, Martin Luther King, Jr., stating, "One day we might make a man out of him . . . might take the halo off his head."

But Powell's rhetorical goal was not to make friends. Throughout his public life, he seemed to have the uncanny ability to state exactly what he felt, and not in tones that might reflect reconciliation. His was a militant rhetoric, an annoying rhetoric, that could not be ignored. Even if words were ushered aside, there was no escape from the unmistakable speaker who was Adam Clayton Powell, Jr. In his autobiography *Adam by Adam*, a chapter entitled "First Bad Nigger in Congress" offers insight into his rhetorical style:

> There was only one thing I could do—hammer relentlessly, continually crying aloud even if in a wilderness, and force open, by sheer muscle power, every closed door. Once inside, I had to pierce the consciences of men so that somewhere someone would have to answer, somewhere something would have to be done.

Adam Clayton Powell, Jr., was many things to many cadres of publics. He was Mr. Civil Rights to those who loved him in Harlem; he voiced the fears, concerns, and demands of African-Americans throughout America; he championed causes and pushed for reforms in areas such as labor, health, and education; he was the outspoken, radical, and agitating senior pastor to congregants at Abyssinian Baptist Church; he was a supporter of the young militancy of the 1960s and a foe to those who might oppose such a position; and he was the flamboyant, outspoken, and defiant congressional representative from Harlem.

However, the constant variable among his public roles was Powell's rhetorical style. His was a style that combined the smooth rhythm and cadence of the Southern black preacher with the sophisticated streetwise slang of a Harlemite. The product was a rhetoric that cut to the heart of the matter with indignant precision. Powell's uncanny ability to speak in tones of arrogant disdain about topics ranging from the minimum-wage issue to why Martin Luther King, Jr., was an ineffective leader produced both cheers and condemnation. One thing was certain. Adam Clayton Powell, Jr.'s, rhetorical ability—conveyed largely through language and style—stirred the consciousness of the American public and produced memorable speeches worthy of continued investigation.

INFORMATION SOURCES

Research Collections and Collected Speeches

Powell's sermons have been reprinted in his book, *Keep the Faith, Baby!*, but no similar anthology of his political oratory has been published. No central collection of Powell's work is available, according to Esther McCall, who coordinates the Adam Clayton Powell, Jr., Memorial Room located at the Abyssinian Baptist Church. Speeches, bills and amendments, and voting records compiled during Powell's congressional years (1945–67) are located in the records of the National Association for the Advancement of Colored People (NAACP), housed in the Library of Congress, Washington, DC. A variety of material is found in the Library of Congress collection, most notably Powell's congressional administrative papers (Group 4A, Containers 58 and 59). Contents include papers on his expulsion from the House of Representatives (1967), the black power movement (1966), NAACP involvement (1966–67), and general materials (1966–67). Additionally, Powell's public speeches in Congress are contained in volumes of the *Congressional Record.*

Additional collections of Powell materials are located in the Adam Clayton Powell, Jr., Collection at the Schomburg Center for Research in Black Culture in the New York Public Library and at the National Archives in Washington, D.C., filed under the Select Committee of the House Administration Committee Pursuant to House Resolutions, 1967. The Western Reserve Historical Society's collection (Cleveland, OH) includes some of Powell's materials in the Cyrus Eaton Papers collection. The Lyndon Baines Johnson Library at the University of Texas, Austin, holds Powell materials in several files: the White House Central Files; the White House Central Files, Confidential File (Box 7); and the LBJ Archives, Congressional File (Box 52).

Finally, some of Powell's personal papers, memos, letters, and personal belongings are available and on display at the Adam Clayton Powell, Jr., Memorial Room, located at Abyssinian Baptist Church in New York, New York.

[ACP] Adam Clayton Powell, Jr. Collection. Schomburg Center for Research in Black Culture, New York Public Library, New York, NY.
[*CR*] *Congressional Record*, 1945–1967.
Powell, Adam Clayton. *Adam by Adam: The Autobiography of Adam Clayton Powell, Jr.* New York: Dial, 1971.
———. "Black Power in the Church." *Black Scholar* 2 (December 1970): 32–34.
———. *Keep the Faith, Baby!* New York: Trident, 1967.

Selected Critical Studies

Hamilton, Charles. *Adam Clayton Powell, Jr.: The Political Biography of an American Dilemma.* New York: Maxwell Macmillan International, 1991.
Haygood, Wil. *King of the Cats: The Life and Times of Adam Clayton Powell, Jr.* Boston: Houghton Mifflin, 1993.

Selected Biographies

Coleman, Emmett. *The Rise, Fall, and . . . ? of Adam Clayton Powell.* New York: Bee-Line Books, 1967.
Dionisopoulos, P. Allan. *Rebellion, Racism, and Representation: The Adam Clayton Powell Case and Its Antecedents.* Dekalb: Northern Illinois UP, 1970.
Gunther, Lenworth. *Flamin' Tongue: The Rise of Adam Clayton Powell, Jr., 1908–1941.* Ann Arbor, MI: University Microfilms International, 1986.
Hampton, Henry and Steve Fayer with Sarah Flynn. *Voices of Freedom: An Oral History of the Civil Rights Movement from the 1950s through the 1980s.* New York: Bantam, 1990.
Hapgood, David. *The Purge That Failed: Tammany v. Powell.* New York: Holt, 1959.
Hickey, Neil. *Adam Clayton Powell and the Politics of Race.* New York: Fleet, 1965.
Jacobs, Andy. *The Powell Affair: Freedom Minus One.* Indianapolis, IN: Bobbs-Merrill, 1973.
Lewis, Claude. *Adam Clayton Powell.* Greenwich, CT: Fawcett, 1963.
Salley, Columbus. *The Black 100: A Ranking of the Most Influential African-Americans, Past and Present.* New York: Citadel, 1993.

CHRONOLOGY OF MAJOR SPEECHES

[See "Research Collections and Collected Speeches" for source codes.]

"Campaign Radio Address." New York, NY, October 10, 1944. ACP, Reel F1, 1944–1946, dated October 10, 1944.
"Speech on the Red Scare." Washington, DC, February 18, 1947. *CR (House of Representatives)*, February 18, 1947: 1132.

"Speech on Segregation in Washington, D.C." Washington, DC, March 2, 1949. *CR (House of Representatives)*, March 2, 1949: 1744.

"Speech on the Fair Employment Practices Committee." Washington, DC, June 29, 1949. *CR (House of Representatives)*, June 29, 1949: 8657–8658.

"Speech to the Panamanian National Assembly." Panama City, Panama, December 19, 1949. U.S. Department of State Records, 033.1119, dated December 19, 1949.

"Speech on Civil Rights." Washington, DC, February 2, 1955. *CR (House of Representatives)*, February 2, 1955: 1084–1085.

"Speech for the Anti-Segregation Amendment." Washington, DC, January 24, 1956. *CR (House of Representatives)*, January 24, 1956: 1191–1193.

"Speech for the Desegregation of Schools." Washington, DC, June 29, 1956. *CR (House of Representatives)*, June 29, 1956: 11472–11474.

"Speech on Discrimination in the New York City Police Department." Washington, DC, February 25, 1960. *CR (House of Representatives)*, February 25, 1960: 3526–3528.

"Speech of Apologia." Washington, DC, February 18, 1965. *CR (House of Representatives)*, February 18, 1965: 3006–3038.

"Can There Any Good Thing Come Out of Nazareth?" (Commencement speech delivered at Howard University). Washington, DC, May 29, 1966. *The Voice of Black America: Major Speeches by Negroes in the United States, 1797–1971*. Ed. Philip S. Foner. New York: Simon and Schuster, 1972, 1027–1033.

"Speech to Berkeley Students." Berkeley, CA, 1968. "Adam Clayton Powell in Berkeley," audio recording, Pacifica Tape Library, 1968.

COLIN LUTHER POWELL
(1937–   ) four-star general

RICHARD W. LEEMAN

In many regards, perhaps more so than with most other speakers, the oratory of General Colin Powell is a reflection of who he is as a person. His is a discourse that sounds the themes of pride, hope, strength, determination, and the value of hard work. Whether he is speaking to high-school students at his alma mater in the Bronx or business leaders at a conference in Los Angeles, Powell's is a problem-solving oratory. What problems do we face? he asks the audience. How can we solve them? What can you, the audience, do about them? Occasionally, his speaking style soars and he demonstrates a capacity for eloquence, but generally he prefers the direct and clear over the flowery and poetic. As with his life itself, his public speaking is businesslike; one always has a sense that his speech is prefatory to some sleeve-rolling, let's-get-down-to-work time.

Colin Luther Powell was born in Harlem, New York, on April 5, 1937, to Luther and Maud Ariel Powell. Both of his parents were Jamaican immigrants who worked in the apparel industry, his father as a shipping clerk and his mother as a seamstress. With his sister Marilyn, six years older than he, he was part of a tight-knit family that stressed hard work and education. "Until the day [my parents] died," Means quoted Powell as saying, "I was never able to convince them that it would never be possible for me to do better than they did in providing their children with values and goals. It wasn't a matter of spending a great deal of time with my parents discussing things. . . . It was just the way they lived their lives."

In 1940, the family moved to an apartment on Kelly Street in the Hunts Point area of the South Bronx, and there Powell attended elementary school and junior high, graduating from Morris High School in early 1954. Educationally, Powell performed well enough, even if he did not excel academically. Most remember him as quiet, mild-mannered, and a hard worker. He worked summers in a bottling plant, beginning the first summer mopping floors and by the third summer working as a deputy foreman. In addition, he was employed year-round at Sickser's baby-furniture store, two blocks from the Powells' apartment.

After high school, he enrolled as an engineering major at the City College of New York. Although his initial grades were B average, he quickly abandoned engineering and eventually graduated in 1958 with a B.S. in geology. After his first semester he enrolled in the Reserve Officers' Training Corps (ROTC), and it was there that he excelled. In addition to straight-A work in his ROTC classes, he joined the elite Pershing Rifles, became the company commander by his senior year, and graduated at the top of his ROTC class with the rank of cadet colonel.

After boot-camp training at Fort Benning, Georgia, Powell was assigned to infantry duty as a platoon leader in Gelnhausen, Germany, about fifty miles from the East German border. During his next assignment at Fort Devens, Massachusetts, Powell met Alma Vivian Johnson, an audiologist and graduate student at Emerson College from Birmingham, Alabama. They were married on August 25, 1962, after Powell received orders to go to Vietnam to work as one of the U.S. "military advisors" to the Army of South Vietnam.

Powell began his first Vietnam tour of duty in December 1962, stationed in the A Shau Valley near the Laotian border. There he learned about the birth of the first of his three children and his only son, Michael. On this tour, he also received the Purple Heart for a foot injury from stepping on a punji-stick trap. Despite this wound, he continued his work at A Shau until late 1963.

After a series of stateside assignments, including Advanced Infantry Officers Training, Powell returned to Vietnam in 1968 for a second tour of duty. Now a major, he worked first as a battalion executive officer and then as a division planning and operations officer. While he was on reconnaissance in November of 1968, his helicopter crashed, and he made four trips to pull fellow soldiers out of the smoldering wreckage. For that action, he received the Soldier's Medal, and he received the Bronze Star for his overall service in Vietnam.

Back in the United States, Powell continued his education, earning an M.B.A. from Georgetown University in 1971, and he was then awarded one of the prestigious White House Fellowships in 1972. Under that fellowship, he worked for Frank Carlucci, deputy director of the Office of Management and Budget. Throughout the 1970s and early 1980s, Powell was primarily assigned to a series of positions in the Pentagon in Arlington, Virginia. In 1983, he became the senior military assistant to Secretary of Defense Caspar Weinberger. He was named the commanding general of the Fifth Corps, stationed in Frankfurt, Germany, in 1986, and only after President Reagan himself called did Powell accept yet another "desk" assignment in 1987 as deputy national security advisor to his old mentor, Frank Carlucci.

In December 1987, Powell succeeded Carlucci as national security advisor when the latter became secretary of defense. As director of the National Security Council (NSC), Powell worked with the U.S. effort to aid the contra fighters in

Nicaragua, the negotiation of a nuclear arms agreement with the Soviet Union, and the U.S. naval escort of Kuwaiti ships through the Persian Gulf. After one more brief military post at Fort McPherson, Georgia, Powell became the chairman of the Joint Chiefs of Staff (JCS) on October 1, 1989.

His position as chairman of the JCS is, of course, the one that provided him the greatest fame. In that position, he presided over the 1989 U.S. military effort in Panama that removed Manuel Noriega from power, and over the U.S.-Allied troops in the 1991 Persian Gulf War against Iraq. At a Pentagon press conference, Powell demonstrated the lesson he had learned from Vietnam. After describing the general military plan of action, he announced the strategy behind U.S. tactics: "Our strategy for going after [the Iraqi] army is very, very simple. First we are going to cut it off, and then we are going to kill it."

His four-year term as chairman of the JCS ended in September 1993, at which time he retired after thirty five years in the army. As of this writing, he is working on his memoirs and doing some public speaking and has continued his public service by being part of a three-man negotiating team sent by President Clinton to Haiti in 1994. Speculation continues as to whether he will run for public office—including perhaps the presidency—and if so, which party he would join. A registered independent, Powell is usually identified with the Republican party on issues of the military and defense, and with the Democratic party on social issues.

COLIN POWELL: THE ORATORY OF A GENERAL

If Colin Powell chooses to continue his career of public service in the political realm, his style of speaking will stand him well, for his oratory never strays far from the identity of the speaker himself. It is an oratory that sounds like a general's and represents a general's problem-solving view of the world. While Colin Powell undoubtedly spoke in public long before he became a general and was thrust into prominence as the director of the NSC, the speech texts available are those that coincide with the increasing influence of the positions he held and the corresponding importance of the speeches themselves.

Broadly, Powell's speeches can be grouped into two types: policy speeches and ceremonial speeches. Policy speeches were those that addressed issues directly related to his official position. Ceremonial speeches were those in which he addressed concerns of the audience, ones not directly drawn from his office. Some speeches, such as his commencement speech at Harvard University in 1993, blended both types of messages fairly equally, and most speeches had some references to policy issues and audience concerns, but usually one message or the other was predominant.

There are certain characteristics of Powell's content and style that are constant across these two speech types, however. First, his speeches almost always focus on solving a problem. Second, in developing his solutions, Powell typically looks to history, experience, and traditional values. Finally, whether discussing the problem, the solution, or both, his speeches always display a keen awareness of the audience and the occasion.

As problem-solving oratory, Powell's speeches are always tightly organized. His policy address of December 12, 1988, before the Economic Club of Detroit is typical. He began by announcing that "East-West relations are clearly in a new era," as *perestroika* was opening up the Soviet Union and Communist-bloc nations. There were signs of hope in the world—increasing democracy and free-market economies—but also signs of concern—U.S. economic decline, energy problems, and, most of all, the need to balance economic and military strength. Powell then previewed the topics he would consider in the speech as they related to the "place economics has in our national security strategy": relations with Communist countries, industrialized democracies, developing nations, global challenges, and domestic economic policies.

Within each of these sections Powell laid out the challenges he saw and the administration's responses to those challenges. For example, in discussing U.S. "economic partnership with our allies," Powell noted that "the days of American economic hegemony . . . are over." The United States was faced now with economic disagreements that could impact its national security, as when Japan refused "to open its agricultural market to foreign competition, [which is then] frustrating to American farmers whose perception is that their tax dollars are helping ensure Japan's military successes." Powell argued that while multilateral talks could be useful, most negotiation with powerful democratic U.S. allies must be bilateral. There the United States could concentrate on "our common political values and security interests that give both sides a powerful, overriding incentive to resolve the disputes fairly."

Throughout the speech, Powell used clear transition statements to delineate his structure: "This means, first of all, that trade must be limited," "This brings me to the next set of issues," "Let me give a few less anecdotal examples," and "Having surveyed these international economic issues, I come back, finally, to economic issues at home." In his conclusion, he wove together the individual strands he had developed, noting that the challenge Gorbachev faced in the Soviet Union "goes to the essence of a system that is inherently unworkable," while "the challenges we face are challenges to policy." Despite the difficulties posed by those problems, the Soviets' experience "can only give us a renewed appreciation for the blessings of our own political and economic freedom." It was within that freedom, Powell contended, that Americans would find their political and economic security.

Within his tight organizational structure, Powell's oratorical approach to solving problems is a rational one. Powell first identifies the problem and any knowledge we have that might aid in solving that problem, and then enumerates the steps of the solution. While describing the problem and specifying the solution are both important components, there is a sense in which the key task seems to be in identifying the lessons we have learned elsewhere and properly applying them to the problem at hand. Throughout Powell's speeches, there is a distilling of the lessons learned, some recent and some very old.

Clear-sighted lessons are important, for example, in Powell's speech, "U.S. Foreign Policy in a Changing World," delivered to the Town Hall of California in Los Angeles on March 23, 1990. The first lesson Powell drew from world events was a lesson of firmness. In a typical blending of past and present, Powell identified the source of American success in winning the Cold War: "Almost half a century ago, George Kennan advocated a policy of containment. If we held firm, he said, the inherent weaknesses of communism would bring it down. We held firm. And the walls of communism are coming down."

Amid this welter of changes, Powell summarized the critical importance of discerning the true lessons from the false: "As Clausewitz said, 'Beware the vividness of transient events.' Amidst these incredible changes, we have to identify the principal factors that affect our interests and sort them out from the cascade of more glamorous but essentially transient events." Powell "sorted out" three such factors. First, America must understand that "yes, the Soviet army is going home" as it withdrew from Eastern Europe, "but it is not disbanding," he warned. Second, Powell noted that, while current U.S.-Soviet relations were friendly, "we have no way of knowing what is in store for the Soviet Union." Third, he observed that "the world has not ceased being a place where America's interests are sometimes threatened." Drawing upon these truths, Powell returned to George Kennan's lesson: "These three factors remind us of the importance of the strength that brought the Free World this victory in the first place."

Other lessons followed. For example, Powell noted that "superpower status imposes responsibilities on us. Our outlook must be global and it must encompass the strong alliances that are critical to the future peace of the world." In solving U.S. budget problems "we must find the balance between our superpower base force requirements and what the American people are willing to pay." Americans should also realize that the end of the Cold War had shifted their strategic task. "Now," Powell said, "the task is keeping democracy alive, not fighting and containing communism. Now the task is helping the dozens of democracies that are just being born." Within these changing tasks, however, the lesson of military strength and resolve remained constant: "No one is better fitted for these tasks than America and her allies. If we stay strong and lead, the world will follow. Of that I am sure."

Many of Powell's lessons are drawn from history, and especially from that history that he himself has witnessed. Indeed, he often begins his speeches by drawing comparisons between current and historical events. For example, in his West Point commencement speech, he contrasted the Cold War world of the newly commissioned "Second Lieutenant Powell" of thirty-two years ago with the post–Cold War world confronting the newly commissioned second lieutenants he was addressing. In his Harvard commencement speech of June 10, 1993, Powell made reference to General George Marshall's 1947 commencement speech delivered at Harvard, which announced the Marshall Plan for rebuilding war-torn Europe. "In perhaps the most famous speech ever delivered here," Powell told the audience, Marshall "committed America's wealth and leadership to the task of rebuilding Europe and ensuring its peace and prosperity." Again, Powell drew from that work a lesson: "There could be no going back after that. . . . We had to be *of* this world, not just *in* it." Powell used that lesson to justify maintaining a strong U.S. military posture in the post–Cold War world.

In his April 16, 1991, speech to the Association for a Better New York, Powell spoke in celebration of the Gulf War victory and applied the lessons learned there to the urban problems that concerned the New York City organization he was addressing. The lessons were partly historical and partly personal. The success of the volunteer army and other branches of service, Powell said, could be attributed to (1) having the highest expectations, (2) imposing discipline and standards, (3) stressing teamwork and family, (4) stressing self-responsibility and accountability, (5) allowing no tolerance of drugs, and (6) believing in each and every soldier. In testifying to the lack of tolerance for drug use, Powell related how, as he was leaving Fort McPherson to assume the duties of chairman of the JCS, it was his turn to be tested for drug use: "And the young lieutenant had his duty to do and he didn't care if I was going to be Chairman of the Joint Chiefs of Staff, my name had come up on the roster and he was there with his kit and his rubber gloves."

"Is all this transferable?" Powell asked rhetorically. He answered directly and simply: "You bet your life it is." Employing description, Powell sketched out what would happen if these lessons were applied in civilian life:

> As I drove through the Bronx yesterday, I asked myself what if we used in our schools the same general approach to our children that we use in our Armed Forces? What if, for example, our inner cities were as free of drugs as your Armed Forces? What if the children of our inner cities learned, trained, and worked hard together for a common purpose? . . . What if, black, white, yellow or brown; Muslim, Jew or Christian; Irish, Polish, Italian or African, they all felt as if they were *family*?

Powell answered his question indirectly: "If we could ever reach that goal . . . pretty soon the Association For a Better New York would have other things to do."

In many cases, the lessons Powell learns from history or personal experience can be labeled "traditional." His Fisk University commencement speech, delivered on May 4, 1992, in Nashville, Tennessee, is representative of the values he displays throughout his speeches. For example, Powell fervently articulated the belief that America is the land of opportunity: "America is the only country in the world that strives incessantly to make the dream of America the reality of America." He acknowledged the limitations, as documented by the Rodney King beating, trial, and subsequent rioting in Los Angeles, but Powell went on to avow that "if I didn't believe to the depths of my heart that we could work it out, I wouldn't be able to call myself an American." The solution to these problems lay again in traditional values such as hard work. "Believe in yourself," Powell told the graduates, for "there is nothing—NOTHING—you cannot accomplish by hard work and commitment." You must also believe in America, he told them, for "I've travelled around this world and I've seen a hundred countries and I've got to tell you there is no better place or system on earth than that which we enjoy here in America." "Third," he said, "find strength in your diversity. . . . Let it be someone else's problem, but never yours. Never hide behind it or use it as an excuse for not doing your best." Finally, he told them, remember to "raise strong families." In language as traditional as the values he espoused, Powell insisted that "the worst kind of poverty is not economic poverty, it is the poverty of *values*. It is the poverty of *caring*. It is the poverty of *love*." Hard work, determination, confidence, family, and America: these are the values that Powell learned and profited by in his own life, and they are the values that he preaches throughout his speeches.

These "traditional" values are traditional across ethnic lines in America; they are the same values one hears in the speeches of Frances Harper, Booker T. Washington, Martin Luther King, Jr., and a host of other African-American orators. In his speeches, Powell sounds another "traditional" theme that is particularly unique to African-American oratory: remembering where you came from. This theme can be found in any speech Powell delivers to a predominantly black audience. In his August 10, 1991, speech to the national convention of the Tuskegee Airmen in Detroit, Michigan, Powell recalled the military contributions of African-Americans from the Revolutionary War through the 54th Massachusetts in the Civil War, from the Buffalo soldiers in the West to the Tuskegee Airmen in World War II. "I never forget for a day, or for an hour, or for a minute," Powell told his audience, "that I climbed to my position on the backs of the courageous African-American men and women who went before me." In fact, Powell used almost identical language to make this same observation in his commencement speeches at Fisk University in 1992 and at Howard University in 1994. In the Howard speech as well as that given at Fisk, Powell explained the responsibility that goes with the memory: "They would say to me now, 'Well done. And now let others climb up on your shoulders.' " The Howard graduating class he addressed faced the same dual responsibility of achieving for themselves and helping those who came behind: "You can now continue climbing to reach the top of the mountain; while reaching down and back to help those less fortunate." "You face great expectations," Powell challenged the students; "much has been given to you and much is expected from you."

While most of Powell's speeches can be characterized as businesslike, discussing problems and solutions using a relatively plain style, he is capable of being eloquent as well. Typically, his eloquence can be found in the introductions or, more commonly, the conclusions of his speeches. Perhaps his most eloquent address, however, is his Memorial Day speech of 1991, delivered at the Vietnam Veterans Memorial in Washington, D.C. It is also, indirectly, evidence of the personal nature that is characteristic of his speaking. With a skillful use of metaphors, parallel structure, and personal reminiscences, Powell paid homage to the sacrifices of America's soldiers and to the idea of freedom for which they fought and died.

He began the address by noting all that Americans had "to be thankful for." In a community-building litany, this Vietnam veteran general said that "we are thankful for the contributions of all our brave veterans of wars past, . . . World War II, Korea, Operation Just Cause, and *especially from Vietnam*. We know what sacrifices they made." Americans were thankful, he went on, for the "clear victory of American arms" in the Gulf War and the "blessedly small number of casualties," and "we are also thankful that Americans are not in combat on this Memorial Day." Describing the military's humanitarian missions in Kurdish Iraq and Bangladesh, Powell introduced a particularly American vision of the military: "What you've seen over and over in these scenes is American troops bringing hope back to people who had lost hope."

Powell then told a story about a visit by General Mikhail Moiseyev, Powell's military counterpart in the Soviet Union, a story that had caused him to realize "how much we have to be thankful for." In order to bring the general to a tour of the Vietnam Veterans Memorial "Wall," Powell said that "I first had to show him what America was really about, what we really stood for. I had him look into the very crucible where America's values were fired."

He took Moiseyev first to the Jefferson Memorial, where he showed him Jefferson's "nation-building words about our Constitution"—"his freedom-loving words" and "ageless words from the Declaration of Independence." Pointing later to the more quoted words about equality, Powell first singled out the Declaration's conclusion, that to the purpose of freedom "we mutually pledge our lives, our fortunes, and our sacred honor." Moving next to the Lincoln Memorial, Powell showed Moiseyev the words of the Gettysburg Address, words that noted that Americans fought the Civil War so that the nation could have a "new birth of freedom," so that "government of the people, by the people, and for the people shall not perish from the earth."

"And I believe General Moiseyev began to realize how sacred these words and these ideas are to Americans," Powell said. Only then, he noted, could he walk the general to the "Wall." There they looked up the name of Major Tony Mavroudis, a boyhood friend of Powell's who had died in Vietnam in 1967. Powell pointed out the statue of the three soldiers: "They pay homage to their buddies and they guard the Wall. They symbolize the eternal vigilance of America's warriors, of America's Armed Forces."

The story ended as General Moiseyev "reached out and gently touched the Wall." Powell said, using the parallel structure of antithesis, "On this Memorial Day we again reach out and touch the Wall. We again run our fingers softly over the names. We again draw near to feel its grief and its dark pain. We again experience the terror and the horror of war—all war." Returning to the Gulf War, Powell personalized that horror by describing his encounters with wounded soldiers, but he also recalled the principle that guided that war: when war becomes necessary, you must shoulder that burden and ''do it right.''

In the peace that follows war, ''you must never forget'' the soldier's sacrifice and the soldier's duty. It is within this history of the American soldier that the Vietnam veteran must place himself or herself. In a climactic conclusion, Powell noted that the Vietnam veteran will be at ''every parade and at every celebration'' of the Gulf War, because the celebration of the American military is his celebration, too. As one such veteran himself, Powell spoke with a prideful camaraderie.

> The parades and celebrations are not needed to restore our honor as Vietnam veterans because we never lost our honor. They're not to clear up the matter of our valor because our valor was never in question. Two hundred and thirty-six Medals of Honor say our valor was never in question. Fifty-eight thousand, one hundred and seventy-five names on this Wall say our valor and the value of our service were never in question.

Echoing the words of Jefferson's Declaration and the history of American arms, Powell concluded his memorial to the American soldier.

> My friends, Americans have placed their lives, their fortunes, and their sacred honor in harm's way from Concord Bridge to Gettysburg, from Normandy to Pork Chop Hill, from the A Shau Valley to the Valley of the Euphrates. And today, we are proud of all who served. Today, we remember and honor all who gave their lives for our beloved America. Today—we remember. Thank you.

At six feet one inch tall, weighing about two hundred pounds, and with a strong baritone voice, Colin Powell looks and sounds like the general he is. His approach to speaking seems to closely reflect his approach to life. He confronts problems directly and searches actively for solutions to them. He applies lessons quickly, especially those learned from history or personal experience or drawn from traditional values. He is generally a plain-styled speaker but can, when the occasion demands, speak eloquently as well. Wherever future public service may lead him, Colin Powell's oratory will probably serve him well, for his public speaking seems fully a part of him, rather than apart from him.

INFORMATION SOURCES

Research Collections and Collected Speeches

There are no archival collections or published sources of collected speeches at this time. Transcripts of speeches delivered while General Powell was chairman of the Joint Chiefs of Staff can be obtained from the Office of the Chairman, Public Affairs, 9999 Joint Staff, Pentagon, Washington, DC 20318.

Powell, Colin L. *My American Journey*. New York: Random House, 1995.

Selected Critical Studies

Booker, Simeon. "Colin L. Powell: Black General at the Summit of U.S. Power." *Ebony*, July 1988: 136–142.
Brown, Luther. "Powell Ascends to Center of Political Prominence." *Black Enterprise*, February 1988: 36.
Brown, Marshall. "Powell Reaches the Pinnacle of Pentagon Power." *Black Enterprise*, October 1989: 22.

Selected Biographies

"Colin Luther Powell." *Current Biography*, June 1988: 46–49.
Means, Howard. *Colin Powell*. New York: Donald I. Fine, 1992.
Roth, David. *Sacred Honor: A Biography of Colin Powell*. San Francisco: Harper, 1993.

CHRONOLOGY OF MAJOR SPEECHES

"U.S. Foreign Policy in a Time of Transition" (Address to the National Press Club). Washington, DC, October 27, 1988. *Department of State Bulletin*, January 1989: 30–32.

"Economics and National Security" (Address to the Economic Club of Detroit). Detroit, MI, December 12, 1988. *Vital Speeches of the Day*, January 15, 1989: 194–197.

"U.S. Foreign Policy in a Changing World" (Address to the Town Hall of California). Los Angeles, CA, March 23, 1990. *Vital Speeches of the Day*, May 1, 1990: 418–421.

"Commencement Address." U.S. Military Academy, West Point, NY, May 31, 1990. Available through the Office of Public Affairs, U.S. Military Academy, West Point, NY 10996.

"Remarks to Morris High School." Bronx, NY, April 15, 1991.

"Remarks to the Association for a Better New York." New York, NY, April 16, 1991.

"Memorial Day Speech" (Address to the ceremony at the Vietnam Veterans Memorial). Washington, DC, May 27, 1991.

"Remarks at the 20th Annual National Convention of the Tuskegee Airmen." Detroit, MI, August 10, 1991.

"Commencement Address." Fisk University, Nashville, TN, May 4, 1992.

"Remarks Introducing President Bill Clinton at the Memorial Day Ceremonies." Washington, DC, May 31, 1993.

"Commencement Address." Harvard University, Cambridge, MA, June 10, 1993.

"Remarks at the Groundbreaking Ceremony for the Vietnam Women's Memorial." Washington, DC, July 29, 1993.

"Commencement Address." Howard University, Washington, DC, May 14, 1994. Available through the Public Relations Office, Howard University, Washington, DC 20059.

ASA PHILIP RANDOLPH
(1889–1979), labor leader, civil rights activist

EDWARD M. PANETTA

The civil rights tactics A. Philip Randolph originated and his dual citizenship in organized labor and the African-American community provided him with a unique perspective on race relations in America. For Randolph, the liberation of African-Americans from racial and economic oppression was inextricably linked to improved economic conditions for workers of all colors. A civil rights pioneer in the 1930s and 1940s, Randolph developed a framework for mass political action that would ultimately succeed in the 1960s. He was a major twentieth-century figure in the struggle for freedom and social justice.

Asa Philip Randolph, born in 1889, was the second child of James and Elizabeth Randolph. Randolph spent his formative years in Florida, where his father, a minister, was one of the three major influences on his oratorical skills. The elder Randolph was a self-trained African Methodist Episcopal preacher whose own rhetorical skills were shaped by the Bible and the Reconstruction rhetoric of the Reverend Henry McNeal Turner. The two other formative influences on A. Philip Randolph's oratorical skills were the study of Shakespeare and elocution during a fledgling acting career in New York, and the abolitionist speeches of Frederick Douglass and Wendell Phillips.

A. Philip Randolph delivered his high-school valedictorian address, "The Man of the Hour," in 1907 at the Cookman Institute. He left Florida for Harlem, New York, in 1911. During his initial years in New York, Randolph pursued a college education at City College, where he refined his speaking skills and was introduced to socialist ideology.

In the tradition of leftist political activists of that era, Randolph first made a name for himself in Harlem as a soapbox orator. As a result of his commitment to leftist politics, Randolph, along with Chandler Owen, established a political magazine, the *Messenger*. In the introductory issue, he described it as "the first voice of radical, revolutionary, economic and political action among Negroes in America.'' Randolph's editorials were largely socialist critiques of the liberal capitalist system. The *Messenger* called for solidarity among African-American and white workers, exposed the inadequacies of elected political leadership, and highlighted African-Americans' ability to respond to exploitation with boycotts.

This presence in the Harlem community led to Randolph's appointment as the leader of an organizational effort for the Brotherhood of Sleeping Car Porters (BSCP) in 1925. It was as head of the BSCP that Randolph first achieved prominence as a leader in the African-American community. After a protracted twelve-year labor battle, the Pullman Company signed a collective bargaining agreement with the BSCP in 1937. The BSCP, the first African-American union to sign a major labor contract, became the most influential black labor union in the United States. According to Randolph, the BSCP was a movement that stood ''for the self-expression and interest of Negroes by Negroes for Negroes.''

As a result of leading the BSCP, Randolph developed followers in both the African-American and white press. He became ''Mr. Black Labor'' and ''a great leader.'' Because of the symbolic importance of the BSCP victory over the Pullman Company, Randolph and the union acquired a stature that surpassed that normally accorded a union or the leader of a union with a membership of less than fifteen thousand. Randolph found himself speaking in public venues that had previously neglected African-American participation. He spoke to American Federation of Labor (AFL) meetings in an effort to integrate unions, articulated the ''black opinion'' before governmental committees, and served on blue-ribbon committees charged with assessing urban problems in New York City.

Randolph's career reached its greatest heights in the 1940s. Capitalizing on his reputation and an economy in transition from depression to war, Randolph proposed a mass march on Washington for integration of the armed forces and employment opportunities in defense industries for African-Americans. In response to this pressure, President Roosevelt signed Executive Order 8802, which called for the creation of a Fair Employment Practice Committee. The objective of this government agency was to place minority workers in defense industries and to raise the morale of those who had been discriminated against by those industries. While calling off the march on Washington, Randolph attempted to keep the coalition alive by establishing the March on Washington Movement.

The issue of segregated armed forces, shelved in response to FDR's compromise in 1941, was later resolved in 1948. During Senate testimony on the establishment of a peacetime draft, Randolph threatened to lead a campaign of civil disobedience and to encourage young African-Americans to refuse to register for a ''Jim Crow'' army. Randolph's public posture impacted President Truman's decision to desegregate the armed forces with Executive Order 9981. During the 1950s and the 1960s Randolph became a ''senior statesman'' for the civil rights movement, a political leader who worked to unify the often-disparate groups in the movement. During these last two decades in public life Randolph often worked within the framework of the National Association for the Advancement of Colored People (NAACP) to pursue shared political interests, a collaboration that differed from Randolph's pursuit of an individual agenda in the 1930s and 1940s.

A. PHILIP RANDOLPH AS A LABOR AND CIVIL RIGHTS ORATOR

While the rhetoric of A. Philip Randolph evolved throughout his life, one constant in his discourse was the belief that African-Americans should organize into unions to achieve both economic and social justice. Randolph's early labor rhetoric appeared mostly in pamphlets and editorials in the *Messenger*. In one essay, "How to Stop Lynching," Randolph called for African-Americans to be "thoroughly organized into unions, whereupon they could make demands and withhold their labor from the transportation industry and also from personal and domestic service and the South will be paralyzed industrially and in commercial consternation."

Randolph's first effort to organize African-Americans into a political movement occurred in the late 1930s. The National Negro Conference (NNC), an organization dedicated to bringing together the diverse elements of the African-American community into a movement that could pressure government to institute change, elected Randolph as its head. While Communist infiltration ultimately destroyed the NNC, the organization did provide Randolph with a platform for the espousal of his civil rights agenda. His 1937 address to the NNC, "The Crisis of the Negro and the Constitution," defined a new method for African-American protests that would be followed in the 1940s. "True liberation," Randolph argued, "can be acquired and maintained only when the Negro people possess power; and power is the product and flower of organization—organization of the masses." This speech contained a theme prevalent in Randolph's rhetoric: the "power" of African-Americans was grounded in their own ability to fight and persevere. Declared Randolph, "Assuring full citizenship rights to [the] Afro-American is the duty and responsibility of the state, but securing them is the task of the Negro; it is the task of Labor and the progressive and liberal forces of the nation. Freedom is never given; it is won. And the Negro people must win their freedom. They must achieve justice. This involves struggle, continuous struggle." Throughout this period of his career, Randolph sought to redefine the African-American as a member of an ethnic group with political power and aspirations, rather than as a dependent class.

Following the demise of the NNC, Randolph achieved his greatest political accomplishments in the 1940s. He successfully pressured both Presidents Roosevelt and Truman to capitulate to his political demands and desegregate the defense industries and the armed forces. No other African-American leader had ever successfully pressured a president of the United States into taking a political action. This achievement contributed to the emergence of civil rights on the national political scene.

In the "Keynote Address to the Policy Conference," delivered to the members of the March on Washington Movement planning conference in Detroit, Michigan, on September 26, 1942, Randolph outlined the potential of mass political action. He stated, "Thus our feet are set in the path toward equality— economic, political and social and racial. Equality is the heart and essence of democracy, freedom and justice." Randolph defiantly rejected the second-class citizenship status that had been accorded African-Americans and reminded his audience that "rights must be taken." Borrowing from Gandhi, Randolph argued that "we must develop huge demonstrations because the world is used to big dramatic affairs." Proposed specific actions included "the picketing of the White House," the development of education programs, and the marshalling of forces to develop "mass plans to secure mass registration of the Negro people for the primaries and elections."

When engaged in nonviolent civil disobedience, "the Negro masses will be disciplined in struggle. Some of us will be put in jail and court battles may ensue but this will give the Negro masses a sense of their importance and value as citizens and as fighters in the Negro liberation movement." Randolph believed that nonviolent mass action was the best hope to blunt the forces of racism. In the 1940s, the threat of such action alone influenced the policy decisions of the Roosevelt and Truman administrations.

According to Paula Pfeffer, Randolph exhibited the qualities of a charismatic rhetor during this period of time. He was an imposing physical figure with a remarkable voice and delivery skills that were honed as an actor, street-corner orator, and labor spokesperson. For example, in "Call to the March" Randolph stated: "What shall we do? What a Dilemma! What a runaround! What a disgrace! What a blow below the belt! 'Though dark, doubtful and discouraging, all is not lost, all is not hopeless. 'Though battered and bruised, we are not beaten, broken or bewildered." This rhetoric exhibited Randolph's effective use of light and dark metaphors as well as repetitive phrases and cadence. As he had in his "radical" period, Randolph continued to borrow noted phrases from other rhetors in his address. From Roosevelt he adapted the phrases "Freedom from want! Freedom from fear! Freedom from Jim Crow!" and "Dear fellow Negro Americans, be not dismayed by these terrible times. You possess power, great power."

Beyond his creative use of language and delivery, Randolph exhibited a sense of pageantry in his mass rallies. At a Madison Square Garden gathering, hundreds of Pullman porters in dress uniform escorted Randolph to the podium. Paula Pfeffer described the applauding audience that greeted Randolph in Madison Square Garden while the BSCP played the union song "Hold the Fort For WE Are Coming." In this rally Randolph prompted his audience to be active participants in the struggle for civil rights. They should "Fight for Freedom" and "Pay for Equality of Rights." He urged them to exhibit "Courage," "Guts," and "Determination."

In testimony before the Senate Armed Services Committee, Randolph called for the use of nonviolent civil disobedience in response to the existence of a "Jim Crow" army. Said Randolph, "So long as the Armed Services propose to enforce such universally harmful segregation not only here but also overseas, Negro youth have a moral obligation not to lend themselves as world-wide carriers of an evil and hellish doctrine." The African-American youth would carry out this obligation by engaging in "mass civil disobedience along the lines of the magnificent struggles of the people of India against British imperialism." As in the case of labor's struggle, Randolph attempted to identify the African-American struggle for full citizenship with other public struggles. "In resorting to the principles of direct-action techniques of Gandhi, . . . In refusing to accept compulsory military segregation, Negro youth will be serving their fellow men throughout the world." By linking the "Jim Crow" struggle with that of Gandhi, Randolph hoped to blunt criticism that such action was wrong or unpatriotic. For Randolph the "Negro youth" would be "serving a law higher than any decree of the Supreme Court."

Additionally, Randolph's Senate testimony made a direct appeal to white youth to join the protest against a segregated army. "I shall appeal to the thousands of white youth in schools and colleges who are today vigorously shedding the prejudices of their parents and professors. I shall urge them to demonstrate their solidarity with Negro youth by ignoring the entire registration and induction machinery." Such an appeal to the use of nonviolent protest by both African-Americans and whites became a cornerstone of the civil rights movement in the 1950s and 1960s.

In Randolph's speeches and essays from the 1940s, there are several recurrent arguments. First, Randolph held that African-Americans must themselves fight and persevere to achieve freedom and justice. Second, he maintained that African-Americans would benefit socially and economically if they were integrated into mainstream society. Third, Randolph argued that the civil rights movement did "not involve opposition of Negroes to whites or whites to Negroes." Rather, it was a manifestation of the failure of the capitalist revolution. Fourth, he held that organized labor was the best vehicle for political reform and the enhancement of the civil rights agenda. In a 1956 address to the NAACP, Randolph proclaimed that "without the support of the trade union movement, it will be increasingly difficult to effect the implementation of the United States Supreme Court decision for the desegregation of public schools."

As the civil rights movement gained public attention and support, Randolph found himself delivering speeches to an assortment of public audiences. Although an atheist himself, Randolph articulated a variety of religious appeals for these audiences. He employed a plethora of biblical references, perhaps attributable to the influence of his father. One of the more noteworthy speeches of this period was the "Statement to the Prayer Pilgrimage for Freedom at the

Lincoln Memorial'' delivered on May 17, 1957. The Prayer Pilgrimage was a mass youth rally held to publicize the need for voter registration in the South. In his speech, Randolph's biblical references included "By this will all men know that you are my disciples, if you love one for another," "I am the way, the truth and the light," and "I will lift up mine eyes unto the hills from whence cometh my help." Beyond reflecting the use of religious imagery in Randolph's speech, the Prayer Pilgrimage was an important moment in the civil rights movement. While Randolph had successfully used the threat of mass action in the 1940s to desegregate the defense industries and the military, the 'Prayer Pilgrimage' was the first event that hinted at the movement's ability to organize a peaceful mass movement in a short time period.

Throughout his career Randolph spoke to various labor groups, including the American Federation of Labor (AFL), calling for African-Americans to become "first-class" economic citizens in the movement. In a 1936 address to the AFL convention, "Protesting Discrimination against Negroes," Randolph stated: "And so in raising the question to abolish discrimination, it is in the interests of greater solidarity, it is for the purpose of making a stronger labor movement in the nation. You can't do it by putting your foot down on one worker, because he happens to be black or white." Although his speeches of the 1930s and 1940s were impassioned, they accomplished little toward integrating unions. However, the argument that discrimination and racism undermined labor solidarity and denied workers power was a constant in Randolph's rhetoric, and by the 1950s he had successfully influenced the politics of the AFL-CIO to the point that the union became a powerful public voice in support of civil rights legislation.

The July 15, 1959, address "The Civil Rights Revolution and Labor," delivered before the NAACP convention, reflects Randolph's pragmatic approach during this period. Randolph stressed the need for workers of all colors to advance their self-interest by collaborative efforts. For Randolph, the "revolution" to empower African-Americans was not an innovative one, but rather was a continuation of labor's struggle to improve unions: "The transformation of relationships of Negro workers in the house of labor will constitute the second phase of the moral revolution which labor initiated in the drastic program of expulsion of national and international unions under corrupt influences."

In this and many of his speeches, Randolph often concluded by providing the audience with "Steps of Progress." "The Civil Rights Revolution and Labor" concluded with a call for the implementation of previously adopted segregation resolutions, the election of African-Americans to AFL-CIO oversight boards, expanded hiring of African-Americans at the national office, and participation in the labor struggle of Third World nations. His speeches inspired individuals to act by combining eloquent prose with a pragmatic agenda for action.

A. Philip Randolph delivered his last major public address at the civil rights March on Washington on August 28, 1963. At that moment, the protest movement had enacted the "political threat" Randolph first identified in the 1940s.

Randolph's vision, nurtured in the conflict with Presidents Roosevelt and Truman, reached fruition on that August day in Washington. As he looked out on the crowd of more than 200,000, Randolph proclaimed, "Let the nation and the world know the meaning of our numbers. We are not a pressure group. We are not an organization or group of organizations. We are not a mob. We are the advance guard of a massive moral revolution for jobs and freedom." In 1963, as he had in 1919, Randolph outlined an agenda that merged the interests of African-Americans and labor in an effort to blunt the systemic abuses of capital.

The March on Washington was an instance in which a prophet lived to participate in his dream. At the march, Randolph presented Martin Luther King, Jr., to the crowd and proclaimed him "the man who personifies the moral leadership of the civil rights revolution." These were words that could be used to describe Randolph himself. Following his death in 1979 at the age of ninety, the AFL-CIO established a committee to build a monument to Randolph in Washington. At that time, the AFL-CIO Executive Council hailed Asa Philip Randolph as "a symbol to all minority and oppressed workers of the promise the labor movement holds for them in their struggle for a piece of the American Dream."

INFORMATION SOURCES

Research Collections and Collected Speeches

The Manuscript Division of the Library of Congress holds a thirteen-thousand-page A. Philip Randolph collection (su 83-49775). This is a complete, but not fully indexed, collection of Randolph's work. Other pertinent document collections include the Brotherhood of Sleeping Car Porters Papers at the Library of Congress, the Congress of Racial Equality Papers in Madison, Wisconsin, and Joseph F. Wilson, *Tearing Down the Color Bar: A Documentary History and Analysis of the Brotherhood of Sleeping Car Porters.* New York: Columbia UP, 1989.

[PF] Foner, Philip S., and Ronald L. Lewis, eds. *The Black Worker from the Founding of the CIO to the AFL-CIO Merger, 1936–1955.* Philadelphia: Temple UP, 1983.
[BPT] Meier, August, Elliott Rudwick, and Francis L. Broderick, eds. *Black Protest Thought in the Twentieth Century.* 2nd ed. Indianapolis, IN: Bobbs-Merrill, 1971.
[NC] National Association for the Advancement of Colored People. Papers. Library of Congress, Washington, DC.
[APR] Randolph, A. Philip. Papers. Library of Congress, Washington, DC.

Selected Critical Studies

Garfinkel, Herbert. *When Negroes March: The March on Washington Movement in the Organizational Politics for FEPC.* New York: Atheneum, 1969.
Harris, William H. *Keeping the Faith: A. Philip Randolph, Milton P. Webster, and the Brotherhood of Sleeping Car Porters, 1925–1937.* Urbana: U of Illinois P, 1977.

Morris, Aldon D. *The Origins of the Civil Rights Movement.* New York: Free Press, 1984.

Pfeffer, Paula F. *A. Philip Randolph, Pioneer of the Civil Rights Movement.* Baton Rouge: Louisiana State UP, 1990.

Santino, Jack. *Miles of Smiles, Years of Struggle: Stories of Black Pullman Porters.* Urbana: U of Illinois P, 1989.

Selected Biography

Anderson, Jervis. *A. Philip Randolph: A Biographical Portrait.* Berkeley: U of California P, 1986.

CHRONOLOGY OF MAJOR SPEECHES

[See "Research Collections and Collected Speeches" for source codes.]

"How to Stop Lynching." August 1919. *BPT,* 95–97.

"Protesting Discrimination against Negroes." 1936. *PF,* 429–433.

"The Crisis of the Negro and the Constitution" (A. Philip Randolph Calls for a United Front). 1937. *BPT,* 204–212.

"Call to the March" (A. Philip Randolph Calls for a March on Washington). July 1, 1941. *BPT,* 221–224.

"Keynote Address to the Policy Conference of the March on Washington Movement" (Address to Policy Conference). Detroit, MI, September 26, 1942. *BPT,* 224–233.

"Testimony of A. Philip Randolph before the Senate Armed Services Committee" (A. Philip Randolph Urges Civil Disobedience against Jim Crow). Washington, DC, March 31, 1948. *BPT,* 274–280.

"Address of A. Philip Randolph at the Third Annual Conference of the National Trade Union Committee for Racial Justice." November 11–12, 1955. APR.

"Bill of Rights Day." Philadelphia, PA, December 15, 1955. APR.

"Address by A. Philip Randolph on Civil Rights and the Negro." Chicago, IL, May 17, 1956. APR.

"Statement of A. Philip Randolph to the Prayer Pilgrimage for Freedom." Washington, DC, May 17, 1957. APR.

"Statement to the Labor Conference on Human Rights." Los Angeles, CA, October 3, 1958. APR.

"The Civil Rights Revolution and Labor" (Address to the NAACP Convention). New York, NY, July 15, 1959. NC.

"Why the National Negro Labor Council?" (Statement to the Steering Committee of the Proposed National Negro Labor Council). Cleveland, OH, November 14, 1959. APR.

"The Struggle for the Liberation of the Black Laboring Masses in This Age of a Revolution of Human Rights" (Keynote Address at the Second Negro American Labor Council). Chicago, IL, November 10, 1961. APR.

"Address of A. Philip Randolph at the March on Washington." Washington, DC, August 28, 1963. APR.

CHARLES LENOX REMOND
(1810–1873), abolitionist, reform activist

PATRICK G. WHEATON AND CELESTE M. CONDIT

Charles Lenox Remond of Salem, Massachusetts, was the first African-American to become a regular lecturer in the cause of antislavery. For ten years, Remond occupied a position of prominence in the Northern abolition societies. After the emergence of Frederick Douglass in 1842, Remond's popularity as a speaker diminished. Douglass overshadowed Remond because, unlike Remond, he was a former slave. The historian Carter Woodson noted that due to the unusual career of Douglass, Remond "has been all but forgotten as an anti-slavery orator."

Charles Lenox Remond was born in Salem, Massachusetts, on February 1, 1810. He was the second of eight children and the eldest son born to John Remond and Nancy Lenox. John Remond was originally from Curaçao, an island in the Caribbean. He emigrated to the United States in 1798 at the age of ten and became a naturalized citizen in 1811. Nancy Lenox was the daughter of a prominent Bostonian who had served in the Continental army.

Remond began his career as an abolitionist as a young man. In 1831, he heard William Lloyd Garrison speak, and the following year he became an agent for Garrison's abolitionist newspaper, the *Liberator*. As an agent, Remond solicited subscriptions for Garrison's weekly publication and collected donations for the antislavery cause. In 1833, Remond, Garrison, and twelve other men formed the New England Anti-Slavery Society. Remond was also a founding member of the American Anti-Slavery Society. He spent the next several years as an agent for these societies and for the *Liberator*.

Hired in 1838 by the American Anti-Slavery Society as an agent-lecturer, Remond became the first African-American to be employed as an abolitionist speaker. For the next two and one-half years he traveled throughout Maine on behalf of the national society, collecting membership fees and other financial contributions to the organization. Salary payments were unreliable, however, and Remond eventually terminated the tour due to a lack of funds. Remond was plagued by poor finances throughout his public speaking career. His annual salary never exceeded one hundred dollars, and he was, wrote historian William Ward "often compelled to appeal to his white friends for funds." Unfortunately, Remond did not make a record of his speeches during this first tour.

In June 1840, Remond attended the annual meeting of the American Anti-Slavery Society held in New York City. At this gathering, he was chosen as one of eleven delegates to the World Anti-Slavery Conference to be held in London. On the voyage to England, Remond was compelled to travel in steerage and was subjected to continual abuse by the ship's Southern crew. When he arrived at the convention, he joined the other American delegates who were seated in the gallery as a protest against the convention's refusal to recognize women as delegates. Following the conference, Remond remained in England and spent the next eighteen months touring the British Isles soliciting financial aid for the American Anti-Slavery Society.

When he returned to America, Remond delivered his first major address to an influential American audience. On February 22, 1842, he became the first African-American to testify before the Legislative Committee of the Massachusetts House of Representatives. He was enraged at being forced to travel in a "Jim Crow" car on the railroad. He protested the discriminatory policies of the railroads and claimed equal rights for all persons regardless of color.

Remond spent the next twenty-seven years speaking on a broad range of reform topics, always relating them to slavery and racial prejudice. In 1852, he opposed the attempts of Douglass and other prominent African-American leaders to create a "black-only" movement. Remond felt that segregation was counterproductive and that equality would be achieved through a "unity of forces." During the 1850s, Remond attempted to maintain his devotion to the moral campaign of the Garrisonians. He became increasingly frustrated with the sluggish progress and grew both more political and more militant as time passed.

During the Civil War, age and declining health restricted Remond's activities to Massachusetts. He was less active, but remained visible by attending numerous state and local antislavery meetings. In 1863, he became critical of praise afforded the Emancipation Proclamation, arguing that emancipation without equality was meaningless. Remond's activities increased slightly following the war as he became an active advocate of suffrage and attended the first Equal Rights Convention in May 1867. Earlier in the year Remond had traveled to suffrage meetings in western New York, but once again ill health forced him to abandon his efforts and return home. After the passage of the Fifteenth Amendment, Remond retired from the public eye. He died at the age of sixty-three in 1873.

THE EMERGENCE OF A MILITANT CIVIL RIGHTS ACTIVIST

Although Charles Lenox Remond began his public career in 1838, it was not until his tour of the British Isles that he emerged as a prominent antislavery orator. During his tours he had the opportunity to address many British audiences. Four of these speeches were recorded by reporters for publication in Garrison's *Liberator*. William Ward contended that Remond's lectures to English audiences secured his role in the abolition movement and "proved him to be a capable and astute orator." The primary theme of these addresses included the evils of slavery, the inconsistency between the practice of slavery and American democratic principles, the effects of slavery on the free African-Americans, and the virtue of abolition.

Remond's first speech before a British audience was delivered at the anniversary meeting of the British and Foreign Anti-Slavery Society in 1840. In this address he began his critique of slavery by arguing that it was "a system of lust and cruelty and blood." The analysis of America's "peculiar institution" found in this lecture was less developed than that in Remond's final speech before returning to the United States. In the latter speech, "Slavery and the Irish" (1841), Remond devoted considerable effort to more vividly explicating the malicious nature of slavery. He referred to it as "the unholy cause of bondage" that victimized the slave with "heartless cruelty." He highlighted the "atrocities" and "horrors" of an inhuman system that "pours blood like mountain streams." The image conjured by a river of blood suggested that slaveholders were murdering men for economic and social gain. In addition to this physical reference to bloodshed, Remond asserted that slavery was synonymous with murder because of its denial of basic human or civil rights. He argued that the slave was "murdered piecemeal in being condemned to a hateful, lingering existence, from which man would be relieved by death, and whereof the only solace is the hope of the grave." Remond believed that telling these tales of cruelty was critical to the abolition of slavery. He hoped that by viewing the inhuman nature of American slavery, an individual could do nothing but "turn away in disgust and indignation, and vow himself from that moment out the inveterate and implacable enemy of that atrocious system."

The inconsistency between the principles of American democracy and the practice of slavery represents the second point articulated by Remond during his British lectures. In "Slavery and the Irish," he declared that the U.S. flag should be torn down because it "flaunts absurdly over a recreant land which . . . makes liberty a mockery." Similarly, in "Slavery As It Concerns the British" (1841), Remond argued that "Liberty" was alive in principle, "but in practice it is completely dead." The spirit of liberty was extinguished by the practice of racial bondage. He told his Irish audience that American democracy was a "republicanism . . . whose deeds belie their splendid promises and whose actions are those of oppression and persecution." As a result of this betrayal, Remond declared that he preferred despotism to "that which is in itself, a lie."

To further illustrate the duplicity of slavery and American republicanism, Remond referenced the documents revered as the bulwarks of the young nation. In his speech to the British and Foreign Anti-Slavery Society (1840), he noted that the rights and privileges guaranteed by the Constitution and the Declaration of Independence were "withheld from" African-Americans. Remond considered this dichotomy between ideology and practice as "the inconsistency" of his fellow Americans. In "Slavery and the Irish," he declared that the unequal application of the principles of the Declaration of Independence was an embarrassment because the fingers of the wise and good of the world "pointed ignominiously at that glorious charter which she pretends to have adopted as the rule of her life, but which, day by day, desecrates and dishonors."

The third argument prominent in Remond's British tour consisted of the effect of slavery on the free African-Americans of the North. In the first speech before the British and Foreign Anti-Slavery Society, he noted that the free men and women of color were not the only slaves in America. Remond argued that they were all enslaved because the fugitive slave laws created the risk that any African-American "was liable to be seized and bound and thrown into prison . . . For no other reason than this, that African blood flowed in his veins." Speaking to the Glasgow Emancipation Society, he told his Scottish audience that "500,000 men of color, who were nominally free, were condemned to suffer as part and parcel of the system, which . . . ground the colored man to the dust."

After establishing the ills of slavery, Remond proceeded to praise the efforts of the abolitionists. While he professed the virtues of the antislavery cause and praised its advocates in each of his addresses, he did so with particular clarity in "Slavery and the Irish." He applauded all abolitionists, regardless of nationality, because abolition was "an employment more dignified, more noble, more exalted than any other whatsoever in which man can be engaged." He claimed that their work was sacred because their object was "none other than that holy and godlike one of elevating" the slaves "to the station and glorious dignity" of humans. Remond asked the Irish to extend to the slaves the same sympathy and affection that they would wish for themselves were they "in similar circumstances."

Remond's speaking tour in Britain not only allowed him to articulate a cogent antislavery platform, it offered him an excellent opportunity to mature as an orator. The early speeches on the tour were all solid and intelligent. By the time he spoke to the Hibernian Anti-Slavery Society, however, he had achieved mastery of his medium. "Slavery and the Irish" reaches that rare level of eloquence in which serious substance fuses with artistic form to provide a moving and powerful statement that rings through the ages.

Remond's speaking continued to evolve when he returned to the United States. The most noticeable change was a gradually increasing militancy. For example, in 1840 he downplayed the possibility of disunion. By 1847 he had adopted disunion as a rhetorical tool for provoking emancipation. By the eve of the Civil War he welcomed violence if it would bring an end to slavery. This increasing intensity extended in three major directions: first, with regard to his natural-rights argument; second, the addition of a critique of racism that extended beyond slavery; and third, with regard to the means to be used for liberation.

Remond's "Independence Day Address" (1857) represents the militant culmination of his position on natural rights. In his early speeches, Remond had been content to assert and to insist that African-Americans were entitled to natural rights, while pointing out that America had failed to respect those rights. By his "Independence Day Address," Remond no longer merely pointed to the contradiction, expecting his audience to see and to act upon the racial discrepancy. Instead, he excoriated the audience, proclaiming Fourth of July celebrations to be "mockeries" of liberty. He denounced the false talk engaged upon during such ceremonies, challenging his audience:

> Talk to me of Bunker Hill, and tell me that a fugitive passed through Boston today! Talk about Lexington, and tell me a slave mother must be secreted in Boston! Talk to me of commemorating the memory of Joseph Warren, while thirty thousand fugitive slaves are in Canada! I will scout the memory of Washington, and Adams, and Hancock, until the soil of Massachusetts shall be as free to every fugitive, and as free to me, as it is to the descendants of any of them.

This emotionally potent speech followed a well-established genre of anti–Fourth of July addresses given by African-American antislavery advocates, of which those by Frederick Douglass are the most famous. Remond's speech was an excellent and forceful specimen of the genre. Through this speech and others such as that to commemorate the Boston Massacre (1858), Remond evolved from a position that called on America to live up to its revolutionary natural-rights doctrine to a position denouncing that revolution as a betrayal.

Remond's discourse became more militant over time not simply because it intensified the application of natural-rights doctrines, but also because he extended his critique from natural rights to civil rights. In the British tour, Remond had argued that slavery had negative impacts on free African-Americans. Later, he broadened this argument to note and to attack the common racism that underwrote both slavery and persecution of free African-Americans. Before the Massachusetts legislature ("The Rights of Colored Citizens in Travelling," 1842), he attacked the discriminatory laws and practices that barred free African-Americans from the use of public facilities. In his address commemorating the Boston Massacre, as well as the "Independence Day Address," he attacked race prejudice in all of its manifestations. Moreover, he asked his white audience members to try to take off the racial mask and to imagine how the issues would look were the slaves white men or were the white audience members themselves black. He urged, "If you could only be black, friends, for eight and forty hours, how would you reason on this question?" ("Speech at the New England Anti-

Slavery Society Convention,'' 1854). Remond thus extended the scope of his concern from slavery per se to racism and prejudice in general.

The third major argumentative evolution in Remond's American speaking pertained to the means for achieving abolition. In earlier speeches, Remond had argued for a gradual evolution, using peaceful, moral persuasion. He took the classic Garrisonian antipolitical position. By 1854, however, he vehemently urged the political activist position of separation of the North from the South. In defending dissolution to the New England Anti-Slavery Society Convention, he challenged his Boston audience, ''Tell me what reward you are receiving for this almost idolatrous advocacy and defense of the American Union? Has the South honored you? When and where? Has she given you office? When?'' Further, after admonishing his audience for the prevalent ''spirit of Negro hate,'' he maintained, nonetheless, that ''even in the humble position I occupy as a black man in the State of Massachusetts, I would rather be ten thousand times blacker than I am than to be the proudest pale face that walks State Street to-day, doing the bidding of the slaveholder.''

Not only did Remond come to advocate dissolution of the Union, he also urged immediate, local civil disobedience. In his New England Anti-Slavery Society Convention address, he urged his audience to rescue a fugitive slave from the courthouse the next morning, prompting them:

> Let them go there to-morrow; and then, if the victim is brought out, let some one cry out, ''Rescue that man!'' and I believe, as if by magic, he will be rescued. All that is wanted is the right voice, at the right time, and in the right place, and the work will be done.

In this speech Remond sanctioned even the fullest range of violence, lamenting only the inability of African-Americans to use violence effectively: ''I tell you, my friends, if we were equal in numbers to-morrow, we should not ask your aid, into our own hands we would take the vindication of our rights.''

Over time, therefore, Remond's oratory had substantively evolved. Remond began as one who had faith in the power of reason and rights, but as the years wore on, he lost faith in their sufficiency. He did not abandon arguments of reason and rights, but he supplemented moral agency with political activism, emotional challenge, and the threat of violence in situations where right actions were not taken.

Remond's style also evolved. In the early years, he was almost shy, a polite and dignified ambassador. In the later years, he used a broader emotional range, freely challenging his audiences, berating them, or shaming them. At the 1854 New England Anti-Slavery Society Convention, Remond questioned the character of his fellow abolitionists when he asserted that ''the courage and patriotism of the colored man is of higher character than that of the white man.'' In his ''Independence Day Address,'' he chastised the members of his audience for their complacent acceptance of the Dred Scott decision:

> I look at Massachusetts, and I see our State, as an entire State, silently acquiescing in the recent disgraceful decision given by Judge Taney in the United States Supreme Court, whereby it is declared that the black man in the United States has no rights which the white man is bound to respect! Shame on Judge Taney! Shame on the United States Supreme Court! Shame on Massachusetts.

On other occasions he urged them to laugh with him, albeit bitterly ("Speech at the Commemorative Festival of the Boston Massacre"). In the early years, Remond used long, complex clauses and classical allusions. In the later years, he used more short, forceful sentences and more phrases of simple form that were emotionally potent. His allusions began to refer primarily to American history and contemporary activities.

Despite these shifts, throughout his career four stylistic markers distinguished Remond's eloquence. He was fond of triplets, as this double sequence from "Slavery and the Irish" reveals: "It is an employment more dignified, more noble, more exalted than any other whatsoever in which man can be engaged. It is not because the slave is a poor man, nor an ignorant man, nor a lowly man." Remond also used rhetorical questions frequently and to great effect, as in the "Independence Day Address," when he queried his audience, "I ask you if I say too much when I say, that to a slave, the popular Fourth of July in the United States is an insult?" Third, Remond used metaphor far more sparingly than orators such as Frederick Douglass or Martin Luther King, Jr., but those he chose were fitting and potent. In one instance, for example, he balanced "eyes" against "fingers," using corporal metaphors often associated with slavery to move his argument forward: "While eyes of the whole world are directed to my guilty country, the fingers of the wise and of the good in all lands are also pointed ignominiously at that glorious charter which she pretends to have adopted" ("Slavery and the Irish"). Finally, Remond was skilled at catching truths squarely and building them toward an expressive climax, as in the final paragraph of his Boston Massacre oration:

> I believe, my friends, that we have rights in this country, in spite of slavery and negrophobia, in spite of the American Constitution,—I believe we have rights against the world in argument, and believing this, I hold it to be our right and duty to defy the men and the bodies who shall, at this late hour, undertake still to crush us in the dust. The time is coming when this battle is to be fought. As I said before, let us resolve, in this Hall, that when the hour comes, we shall be found in the foremost ranks, with our faces, not our backs, to the foe.

Charles Lenox Remond had a long and important speaking career. He grew from a technically solid ambassador for abolition to a militant and forceful representative of African-Americans among American whites. His oratory grew from a narrow, moral consideration of slavery to a broad politicized consideration of human rights. We have no reports about most of his speeches, and only fragmentary accounts of others, but of those surviving, the most eloquent at stating these self-evident truths were "Slavery and the Irish" (1841), "Speech at the New England Anti-Slavery Society Convention" (1854), "Independence Day Address" (1857), and "Speech at the Commemorative Festival of the Boston Massacre" (1858). In all of his extant speeches, however, one finds Remond ably advocating the cause of abolition and forwarding the rights of African-Americans, free and slave alike.

INFORMATION SOURCES

Research Collections and Collected Speeches

Because Remond did not record his orations, no speech manuscripts are known to exist. The texts of his speeches, however, were recorded in various newspapers of the time, primarily the *Liberator*.

[RP] Remond Papers. Essex Institute, Salem, MA.
[*JNH*] Woodson, Carter G., ed. "The Letters of Charles Lenox Remond." *Journal of Negro History* 10 (1925): 477–512.
[*CGW*]———. *Negro Orators and Their Orations*. 1925. New York: Russell and Russell, 1969.

Selected Critical Study

Usrey, Miriam L. "Charles Lenox Remond, Garrison's Ebony Echo, World Anti-Slavery Convention, 1840." *Essex Institute Historical Collections* 106 (1970): 112–125.

Selected Biographies

Porter, Dorothy Burnett. "The Remonds of Salem, Massachusetts: A Nineteenth-Century Family Revisited." *Proceedings of the American Antiquarian Society* 95 (1985): 259–295.
Ward, William Edward. "Charles Lenox Remond: Black Abolitionist, 1838–1873." Ph.D. diss., Clark U, 1977. Ann Arbor: UMI, 1978. 783414.

CHRONOLOGY OF MAJOR SPEECHES

[See "Research Collections and Collected Speeches" for source code.]

"Speech to the British and Foreign Anti-Slavery Society." London, England, June 24, 1840. *Liberator,* July 31, 1840, 122.
"Speech to the Glasgow Emancipation Society." Glasgow, Scotland, August 7, 1840. *Liberator,* August 28, 1840, 138.
"Speech at the Second Anniversary of the British and Foreign Anti-Slavery Society

(Slavery As It Concerns the British).'' London, England, May 14, 1841. *CGW,*
    127–130; *Liberator,* July 9, 1841, 110.
''Speech to the Hibernian Anti-Slavery Society (Slavery and the Irish).'' Dublin, Ireland,
    November 1841. *CGW,* 131–143; *Liberator,* November 19, 1841, 185.
''Speech to the Legislative Committee of the Massachusetts House of Representatives
    (The Rights of Colored Citizens in Travelling).'' Boston, MA, February 22, 1842.
    CGW, 144–149; *Liberator,* February 25, 1842, 30.
''Speech at the Business Meeting of the American Anti-Slavery Society.'' New York,
    NY, May 9, 1844. *National Anti-Slavery Standard,* May 16, 1844, 198.
''Speech at the Anti-Fugitive Slave Law Meeting of the Colored Citizens of Boston.''
    Boston, MA, October 4, 1850. *Liberator,* October 11, 1850, 162–163.
''Speech at the Meeting of the Colored Citizens of Boston to Welcome George Thomp-
    son.'' Boston, MA, November 18, 1850. *Liberator,* November 29, 1850, 189.
''Speech at the New England Anti-Slavery Society Convention.'' Boston, MA, May 30,
    1854. *CGW,* 229–237; *Liberator,* June 23, 1854, 100.
''Speech to the Massachusetts Anti-Slavery Society at the Anti-Slavery Celebration of
    Independence Day (Independence Day Address).'' Framingham, MA, July 4,
    1857. *CGW,* 237–241; *Liberator,* July 10, 1857, 110.
''Speech at the Commemorative Festival of the Boston Massacre.'' Boston, MA, March
    5, 1858. *Liberator,* March 12, 1858, 43.
''Speech at the New England Anti-Slavery Society Convention.'' Boston, MA, May 25,
    1859. *Liberator,* June 3, 1859, 85.

MARIA W. MILLER STEWART
(1803–1879), essayist, educator

HALFORD ROSS RYAN

Maria Stewart is regarded as the first woman to address publicly both males and females, African-Americans and whites. "Prejudice, ignorance, and poverty," she held, were the troika that enslaved black Americans in the nineteenth century. Through religious writings and oratory, Stewart tried to redress that troika.

By her account in *Religion and the Pure Principles of Morality*, Stewart was born in Hartford, Connecticut, in 1803. She was orphaned at age five and bound out, which meant that she performed services for room, board, and schooling to a clergyman's family, which she left at fifteen. In 1826, she married James Steward [*sic*] in Boston and was widowed in 1829. In 1830, she turned to Jesus. From 1831 through 1833, she produced two religious tracts and four speeches. Owing to pressures from blacks against a woman's speaking in public, Stewart ceased her public persuasions and moved to New York City. She then devoted her life to teaching in New York City schools, 1833–52; in Baltimore, 1852–61; in her own school in Washington, D.C., 1861–65; and in her Sunday school, opened in 1871, for blacks in Washington, D.C., where she died on December 17, 1879.

As a communicator in the 1830s, Stewart faced two rhetorical obstacles. Her first handicap was her sex. In the nineteenth century, women were excluded from the public platform, for that was beyond a woman's sphere. Her second impediment was color. Whites believed in the nineteenth century that blacks could not be eloquent. Henry Gates, Jr., noted in *Spiritual Narratives* that ever since whites had encountered blacks in the sixteenth century, they wondered whether the "African 'species of men,' as they were commonly called, *could* ever create formal literature, could ever master 'the arts and sciences,' '' (emphasis in original). If blacks could, then they were like whites; if not, then blacks were destined by nature to be slaves. Stewart's essays and speeches were read in the *Liberator*, which had around three thousand subscribers in the 1830s. Although whites subscribed to the *Liberator*, its predominant readership was black.

STEWART'S JEREMIADS TO BLACKS AND WHITES

Based on the preaching of the Biblical prophet Jeremiah, the Jeremiad is an American form of discourse that can innervate secular topics, although it was originally intended for sermons. As practiced by Puritan preachers, the jeremiad (1) assumed that colonial Americans were God's chosen people with a special destiny—Stewart treated blacks as God's people with a mission to overcome slavery; (2) stressed a sequence of sin, repentance, and redemption—Stewart entreated blacks to acknowledge their faults, to repent, and then to gain salvation/freedom; and (3) applied religious doctrines to secular affairs—Stewart implored blacks to get right with God and whites in order to obtain freedom.

Stewart's *Religion and the Pure Principles of Morality* was published by Garrison and Knapp in Boston in 1831. William Lloyd Garrison was the famous abolitionist, and Isaac Knapp was Garrison's copublisher of the *Liberator*, the major abolitionist newspaper that was founded in 1831. Stewart concisely advanced her thesis: "Feeling a deep solemnity of soul, in view of our wretched and degraded situation, and sensible of the gross ignorance that prevails amongst us, I have thought it proper thus publicly to express my sentiments before you . . . in order to arouse you to exertion, and to enforce upon your minds the great necessity of turning your attention to knowledge and improvement." This theme, running through all her persuasions, assumed that whites enslaved blacks because they were debased; therefore, blacks could redeem themselves by becoming godly and learned. Thus white–like, blacks would be accepted as equals by whites. This idea was embodied in her favored stanza of poetry:

> Though black your skins as shades of night,
> Your hearts are pure, your souls are white.

From a modern perspective, we know that Stewart's conviction was mistaken and her solution was constrained by color prejudice; however, she did not have the benefit of historical hindsight to realize that her reliance on white humanitarianism was misplaced.

Utilizing the Biblical vocative, "O, ye daughters of Africa," Stewart supplicated blacks to become pious. If blacks heeded the call, then "their souls would become fired with a holy zeal for freedom's cause. . . . Knowledge would begin to flow, and the chains of slavery and ignorance would melt like wax before the flames." Refuting the charge that most blacks could not send their children to schools, Stewart told African-American parents to teach their offspring "useful knowledge" in the hope that they would "attain to higher advantages." She summarized her ineluctable conclusion: "I am of a strong opinion that the day we unite, heart and soul, and turn our attention to knowledge and improvement, that day the hissing and reproach amongst the nations of the earth against us will cease." Exhorting blacks to be white–like, Stewart prodded her readers: "The Americans have practised nothing but head-work these 200 years, and we have done their drudgery. And is it not high time for us to imitate their examples, and practise head-work too, and keep what we have got, and get what we can?" The obvious reply to Stewart's rhetorical question was the reader's affirmation.

Whereas the body of the tract had been aimed primarily at blacks, Stewart turned to white America in its denouement. She used the vocative, "O, ye great and mighty men of America," to prophesy retribution: "You may kill, tyrannize, and oppress as much as you choose, until our cry shall come up before the throne of God; for I am firmly persuaded, that he will not suffer you to quell the proud, fearless and undaunted spirits of the Africans forever; for in his own time, he [will] . . . pour out upon you the ten plagues of Egypt." The extract is also an example of what Wilson Moses termed the "Black Jeremiad," in which blacks warned whites of the impending judgment for the sins of slavery. Stewart's theological exegesis of slavery presciently predated President Abraham Lincoln's assessment of the Civil War as expiation. The sixteenth president said in his Second Inaugural Address in 1865 that American slavery was an offense for which God gave "to both North and South this terrible war as the woe due to those by whom the offense came."

In 1832, Stewart published through the auspices of Garrison and Knapp her *Meditations from the Pen of Mrs. Maria W. Stewart*, which she dedicated to the First African Baptist Church of Boston. This work comprised fourteen meditations, many of which had a prayer affixed to them. The efficacy of such a religious autobiography, Sue Houchins believed, was that a black's experience of sin and repentance "could produce both a comparable spiritual and a political" transformation in other blacks.

To be sure, Stewart reiterated in her introduction the necessity for a Christian life, which resonated with her earlier *Religion and the Pure Principles of Morality*. But the precept had evolved to all sinners: "I am more and more convinced that the cause of Christ will never be built up, Satan's kingdom will never be destroyed, the chains of slavery and ignorance will never burst, and morality and virtue will never flourish, till pure and holy examples are set at home." Meditations II, VII, and IX are exemplars of the jeremiad form of sin, repentance, and salvation by getting right with God.

Although undated, Stewart's first speech is held to be an address delivered before the Afric-American Female Intelligence Society of Boston in the spring of 1832. Mindful of charting a new course for women orators, Stewart allowed in her introduction that "the frowns of the world shall never discourage me" and that she could weather the "assaults of wicked men." The address was mostly a jeremiad, replete with scriptural quotations, to call black women to God.

Yet Stewart did urge some secular solutions for her female audience. First, she assayed what would not work: "It is useless for us any longer to sit with our hands folded, reproaching the whites; for that will never elevate us." Rather, she posited black self-help on the rhetorical examples of contemporaneous peoples: She listed Greeks, Frenchmen, Poles, and even American Indians, all of whom commanded more respect than blacks did because they had "contended for their rights and privileges."

In her conclusion, Stewart reminded her audience that she had exerted herself "both for your temporal and eternal welfare." She twice employed the anaphora, or parallelism, of "O woman, woman!" which is also the vocative, in order to impel African-American women to improve their sacred and secular situation.

Stewart's second speech was a lecture delivered in Boston's Franklin Hall on September 21, 1832. The speech has a refutative style. Doubtless she wanted to dispute white misconceptions about black people. First, she countered a suggestion that a woman should not address an audience by stating that she was executing God's will. Next, she contended against color prejudice. Stewart related how she had often asked white businesspeople if they would employ qualified blacks. The whites replied that they had no personal objection, but feared that "they would be in danger of losing the public patronage." "And such is the powerful force of prejudice," Stewart exclaimed.

Stewart turned to the belief that blacks were "lazy and idle." Cleverly turning the tables, Stewart claimed that most blacks were industrious, but did admit that some blacks were not; then she administered the coup de grace, a rhetorical question to whites: "And have you not a similar class among yourselves?"

Stewart quickly dispatched a white aspersion that blacks were a "ragged set, crying for liberty." If whites had to work as hard for so little, she countered, then whites would find themselves in exactly the same situation as blacks: "Most of our color have dragged out a miserable existence of servitude from the cradle to the grave." Accordingly, she abjured white women, using the vocative of "O, ye fairer sisters," to admit that blacks could be like whites if blacks possessed the advantages that belonged alone to whites. Although Stewart's excoriation of racism was uttered 160 years ago, it is as relevant now: "Look at our young men, smart, active and energetic, with souls filled with ambitious fire; if they look forward, alas! what are their prospects? They can be nothing but the humblest laborers, on account of their dark complexions; hence many of them lose their ambition, and become worthless."

Stewart used her conclusion to complete the logic of her lecture. She urged black political activism by a compelling analogy. Colonial Americans had raised themselves up against British tyranny. She clinched her appeal with a rhetorical question: "And, my brethren, have you made a powerful effort?" Thus the audience members would realize the analogous steps they should take to secure black liberties in the United States.

Stewart's third speech was "African Rights and Liberty." The jeremiad suited Stewart's persuasive purposes, for she urged her audience to recognize its calling as African-Americans, to acknowledge their shortcomings, and to seek a secular salvation through political activism. "Where are the names of our illustrious ones?" Stewart entreated her predominantly black audience at the African Masonic Hall, Boston, February 27, 1833.

Combining anger and guilt to stir her listeners, Stewart reminded them that blacks had suffered insults at the hands of whites, who argued that if blacks had a natural spirit of independence, then surely "some one of our sable race" would have achieved eminence. Stewart was particularly harsh on black males, whom she castigated: "Talk, without effort, is nothing; you are abundantly capable, gentlemen, of making yourselves men of distinction; and this gross neglect, on your part, causes my blood to boil within me. Here is the grand cause which hinders the rise and progress of the people of color. It is their want of laudable ambition and requisite courage." Reiterating the theme that blacks could improve themselves, she opined, "Had the men amongst us, who have had an opportunity, turned their attention as assiduously to mental and moral improvement as they have to gambling and dancing, I might have remained quietly at home, and they stood contending in my place." One understands why Stewart, with such unequivocal rhetoric, met resistance from blacks, especially males.

Then Stewart urged a secular salvation. First, she excoriated a white-sponsored colonization program for American blacks to emigrate to Liberia. Stewart sarcastically skewered white hypocrisy: "But ah! methinks their hearts are so frozen towards us, they had rather their money should be sunk in the ocean than to administer it to our relief." Rather, Stewart beseeched blacks to sign a petition to abolish slavery in the District of Columbia as a first step in attaining their full rights as free, black citizens of the United States.

Stewart's *elocutio*, the classical canon of style or word choice, was also remarkable. Consider the following extract: "We have pursued the shadow, they have obtained the substance; we have performed the labor, they have received the profits; we have planted the vines, they have eaten the fruits of them." Stewart used antithesis in each clause to stress the disparity between blacks and whites ("we" versus "they"); anaphora of "we have" and "they have"; alliteration of "p" for verbs and nouns; and asyndeton, or leaving out the connective, in order to make all three clauses vocally equal.

In her peroration, Stewart recapitulated the theme of a black jeremiad. She warned whites that God would soon judge them for enslaving blacks and entreated whites "to awake and save our sons from dissipation, and our daughters from ruin." Her last paragraph was the most damning. She recounted how whites first drove the native American from the land, then stole blacks from Africa and enslaved them, and now would drive blacks back to Africa. Rather, Stewart urged blacks to secure their liberty in the United States, which was their right and their land.

Stewart's fourth speech, a swan song, was "Mrs. Stewart's Farewell Address to Her Friends in the City of Boston." The date was September 18 or 21, 1833.

The address, akin to an apologia, was arranged with an introduction, body, and conclusion.

Stewart's introduction recounted her religious experiences. She quoted Biblical passages that functioned as proof texts, thus warranting her special calling, and she credited Garrison and Knapp for recognizing that "female influence was powerful."

However, the body of her speech contained the most important rhetoric. First, skillfully warming to her subject, Stewart allowed that Christ had helped her to speak (implicit in her argument was the warning that blacks who opposed Stewart also opposed God); thus Stewart sought sympathy when she protested the reproaches she received. She broached her chief issue—"What if I am a woman?"—by refuting reservations about the rhetorical role of women. Although she acknowledged that St. Paul believed that women should not speak in public, Stewart countered with a plausible rebuttal: "Did St. Paul but know of our wrongs and deprivations, I presume he would make no objections to our pleading in public for our rights." She argued by using historical examples to demonstrate that women had successfully functioned in the religious and political affairs of their times.

Her second point was targeted to the lack of black unity. She was leaving Boston because she could no longer "make myself useful among my color in this city." The reason was that blacks needed to close ranks behind blacks in order to challenge whites. Stewart used the hortatory subjunctive: "Let us no longer talk of prejudice, till prejudice becomes extinct at home. Let us no longer talk of opposition, till we cease to oppose our own."

Her third point replied to criticisms that she talked too much about religion, which people did not want to hear, and not enough about black greatness, which the audience preferred. But Stewart refused, as she believed that such talk accomplished little. Only individuals, with God's help, could gain spiritual and temporal salvation.

"But I draw to a conclusion" was Stewart's oral signpost of her epilogue. She recounted her religious beliefs, acknowledged that she had "made myself contemptible in the eyes of many, that I might win some," which she admitted was "like a labor in vain," and stated that she was closing her role as a "prophet," which was to comfort her people.

Maria Stewart was a prototypical black American orator. Although she addressed primarily African-Americans, her charges against the white racism and hypocrisy that she found in the nineteenth century are still relevant. Her call for black self-help, black education, and black unity still seeks satisfaction. That she posited these ideas in a religious matrix—that God would eventually extend his hand to Ethiopia—was as problematic then as it is now. Nonetheless, Stewart's archetypal rhetorical role as a Jeremiah to her fellow citizens remains her everlasting contribution as an American orator.

INFORMATION SOURCES

Research Collections and Collected Speeches

[*OW*] Anderson, Judith, ed. *Outspoken Women: Speeches by American Women Reformers, 1635–1935*. Dubuque, IA: Kendall/Hunt, 1984.
[*MCSFH*] Campbell, Karlyn Kohrs, ed. *Man Cannot Speak for Her*. vol. 2. New York: Praeger, 1989.
[*MWS*] Richardson, Marilyn, ed. *Maria W. Stewart, America's First Black Woman Political Writer: Essays and Speeches*. Bloomington: Indiana UP, 1987.
[*SN*] *Spiritual Narratives*. Foreword by Henry Louis Gates, Jr. Introduction by Sue E. Houchins. New York: Oxford UP, 1988.
Stewart, Maria Miller. *Meditations from the Pen of Mrs. Maria W. Stewart*. Boston: Garrison and Knapp, 1832.
————. *Meditations from the Pen of Mrs. Maria W. Stewart*. 2nd ed. Washington, DC: np, 1879.
————. *Productions of Mrs. Maria W. Stewart*. Boston: Friends of Freedom and Virtue, 1835.
————. *Religion and the Pure Principles of Morality, the Sure Foundation on Which We Must Build*. Boston: Garrison and Knapp, 1831.

Selected Critical Studies

Campbell, Karlyn Kohrs. *Man Cannot Speak For Her*. Vol. 1. New York: Praeger, 1989.
Moses, Wilson Jeremiah. *Black Messiahs and Uncle Toms: Social and Literary Manipulations of a Religious Myth*. University Park: Pennsylvania State UP, 1982.
Sells, Laura R. "Maria W. Miller Stewart." *Women Public Speakers in the United States. 1800-1925: A Bio-Critical Sourcebook*. Ed. Karlyn Kohrs Campbell. Westport, CT: Greenwood, 1993.

CHRONOLOGY OF MAJOR SPEECHES

[See "Research Collections and Collected Speeches" for source codes.]

"Address." Afric-American Female Intelligence Society. Boston, MA, Spring, 1832. *MWS*, pp. 50-55; *SN*, pp. 56-63.
"Lecture." Franklin Hall, Boston, MA, September 21, 1832. *MCSFH*, pp. 3-10; *MWS*, pp. 45-49; *SN*, pp. 51-56.
"African Rights and Liberty." African Masonic Hall, Boston, MA, February 27, 1833. *MWS*, 56–64; *OW*, 169–173; *SN*, 63–72.
"Mrs. Stewart's Farewell Address to Her Friends in the City of Boston." Boston, MA, September 21, 1833. *MWS*, 65–74; *SN*, 72–82.
Religion and the Pure Principles of Morality. MWS, 28–42; *SN*, 3–22.
Meditations from the Pen of Mrs. Maria W. Stewart. SN, 23–51.

MARY ELIZA CHURCH TERRELL
(1863–1954), educator, writer, lecturer

RUTHLEON W. BUTLER AND A. CHEREE CARLSON

Mary Church Terrell was an ardent believer in the American dream. She was an educator, writer, political reformer, and lecturer who, for more than sixty-six years, utilized various forums in a struggle to reconcile the contradiction between America's principle of justice for all and its practice of discrimination against women and citizens of African descent. She supported studies of education, woman suffrage, civil rights, and social reform. Today, she is highly respected within the African American community and is often referred to by teachers and community leaders as an example of unswerving determination and commitment to the cause of justice and equality. The scope of her influence, however, extended beyond her own race and nation to the international public. Numerous awards, commendations, and tributes are testimony to her outstanding achievements and fine qualities as a true humanitarian. Among them are induction into the Washington, D.C., Women's Hall of Fame, honorary doctoral degrees from three universities, the Diamond Cross of Malta, and the Seagram's Vanguard Award.

Mary Eliza Church was born on September 23, 1863, in Memphis, Tennessee, nine months after her young parents, Robert Reed Church and Louisa Ayres Church, were emancipated from slavery. She grew up in a postwar decade marked by racial conflict and violence. As her African American community tried to establish its independence, seeking the prosperity promised by the American dream, it was raided by a hostile white populace determined to continue to hold African Americans in servitude. Despite the fact that her family and community were continuously assaulted, Mollie, as she was called, enjoyed the privileges of America's elite. She grew up in an elegant home, had the finest clothing and toys money could buy, enjoyed an exclusive elementary, high-school, and college education, and traveled extensively throughout America and Europe.

During slavery, her parents, favored by their owners, had been allowed many privileges denied to most slaves, including education, mobility, and exposure to the world of business. Once emancipated, they used their entrepreneurial skills to amass a fortune and were the first ex-slaves to become millionaires in the nineteenth-century South. In *A Colored Woman in a White World*, the first published full-length autobiography of a black woman, Terrell recalled, "Mother's hair store was in the most exclusive business section of Memphis . . . [and] it was she who bought the first home and the first carriage we had." Later, Robert Church purchased real estate made available by an outbreak of yellow fever, which subsequently brought him and his family substantial financial wealth.

Biographer Beverly Jones noted the impact of the family's wealth on Mollie's childhood: "The Churchs' world functioned to isolate Mollie from the realities of being black in a white world, but, of course, the isolation could not be complete." She was first exposed to "the darker side of slavery" through the tearful remembrances of slave brutality told to her by Aunt Liza, her maternal grandmother, a trusted healer in their Memphis community. Later, when Mollie was sent to a "model" integrated elementary school in Yellow Springs, Ohio, some white peers and teachers treated her as "beneath" them because of her race. Mollie was offended and disappointed, but as she progressed through elementary and high school, her study of African, American, and world history reinforced her sense of racial pride, for she discovered, as she later wrote in her autobiography,

> that with a single, solitary exception, and that a very small one, no race has lived upon the face of this earth which has not at some time in its history been the subject of a stronger. . . . This fact not only comforted and consoled me, but it greatly increased my self-respect. I felt I had the right to look the world in the eye like any other free woman and to hold my head as high as anybody else.

Mollie Church was determined to counter the undeserved stigma of racial inferiority by providing living proof that a woman of African descent is the intellectual equal of those of other races. With this impetus, she excelled in her studies throughout high school and college. When she graduated in 1884, she was one of a still-small group of college-educated women, the third African American woman to graduate from Oberlin College, and the only African American woman in a class of forty men to graduate with an A.B. (master's) degree in the classics, having chosen the "gentleman's classical" rather than the ladies' curriculum.

Mollie took her first job teaching at the foremost school for "colored" students in the country, Wilberforce University in Ohio. Within a few years she moved to Washington, D.C., to teach in the classical department of a well-known colored high school. At her father's request, she took a hiatus from teaching, traveling and studying abroad for two years, and completed her mastery of German, French, and Italian by living with families abroad. She returned to Washington to teach, but her career ended when she married Robert H. Terrell, a Harvard honors graduate who would later preside as judge over the Municipal Court of the District of Columbia, but who at the time was her supervisor at the high school.

Through the prestigious Church family and her marriage to Judge Terrell, Mary Church Terrell developed many influential political connections at home and abroad. She attended gala affairs such as presidential inaugural balls, was the welcomed guest of literary greats such as H. G. Wells and Paul Laurence Dunbar, and on several occasions dined with royalty, including Lady Asher of London, Prince Henry of Prussia, and Emperor Haile Selassie of Ethiopia.

While she enjoyed a great deal of social mobility, she was also actively involved in civic duties and the politics of her times. In 1895, she was one of two women appointed to the District of Columbia Board of Education. There she had the demanding responsibility of overseeing the administration of the "colored" schools, with a population of over eighty thousand African Americans living in Washington, D.C. While serving in this distinguished capacity, she earned a reputation as one who stood for equal opportunity and quality education for all children in the District of Columbia. Terrell was active in the suffrage movement, was appointed director of the Eastern Division among Colored Women of the Republican National Committee in 1920, campaigned for Presidents Harding and Coolidge, and in 1929 and 1930 directed the senatorial campaign of Ruth Hanna McCormick of Illinois. She was a prolific writer whose articles about current events, though considered "too controversial" for most of the white press, were widely circulated in African American newspapers and magazines across the nation. She traveled north, south, east, west and overseas as a professional lecturer, hoping to better relations between the races. Even in her senior years, she headed campaigns to save Rosa Lee Ingram and her sons (an African American family accused of murdering a white farmer) and the Rosenbergs (a white married couple accused of espionage) from execution because she believed them to be victims of injustice. She lived to the age of ninety-one, and on July 24, 1954, she died at her summer home in Highland Beach, Maryland.

Mary Church Terrell's years of struggle are represented in her more than thirty years on the lecture platform. Wealth, education, travel, and political exposure combined with her experiences as a member of a devalued racial and sexual group to form a unique voice empowered to speak on many fronts. Hers was the well-trained voice of an ambassador, one whose primary mission was to represent the interests of citizens of African descent. As a lecturer, she was known for her elegance, candor, and ability to articulate her concerns, not only in her native tongue, but in three foreign languages.

Terrell's concerns—the progress and problems of African Americans, woman suffrage, lynching, and disfranchisement—were commonly found in the rhetoric of her African American and white female contemporaries. A masterful, informative, persuasive, and evocative speaker who used a variety of rhetorical strategies, her central theme was the contradiction between American principle and practice. She relied heavily upon the eternal principles of liberty, justice, and equality for all citizens. Clarity, precision, boldness, and grace were the distinguishing characteristics of her language. Benjamin Brawley, her turn-of-the-century contemporary, described her eloquent manner:

> Her words bristle with earnestness and energy, quickly captivating an audience. . . . Her gestures are frequent, but always in sympathetic harmony. Her face is inclined to be sad in repose, but lights quickly and effectively to the soul of whatever subject she touches. Her voice is singularly clear and free from harsh notes. She exhibits no apparent effort in speaking, and at once impresses an audience by her ease, her courage, and her self-abnegation.

While her message and masterful style remained consistent, Terrell's oratory evolved in its central approach. She initially believed that the great portion of the dominant race, as she often referred to the white American majority, were basically good people kept ignorant of the fact that their fellow citizens of African descent had dreams similar to their own, but did not have equal opportunities to realize their dreams. Hence, she later wrote that she began her career by appealing "to the sense of justice of broad-minded generous-hearted" white Americans, those who would be friends of the oppressed. When such "friends" proved indifferent to the increased persecution of the African American community, she altered her rhetorical strategies, moving from education to confrontation.

MARY CHURCH TERRELL ON THE LECTURE PLATFORM

Speaking from the podium was far more significant at the turn of the century in the world of Mary Church Terrell than it is in today's world of televised oratory. The lecture platform was the primary source that connected the public with current events and international affairs. As Dorothy Sterling pointed out, "Lectures then were a form of popular entertainment, as well as education; people attended Lyceums and summertime Chautauquas to hear explorers, authors, and all kinds of celebrities." The formation of African American and of white middle-class women's clubs and the increasing acceptability of women speakers afforded Mary Church Terrell many opportunities to lecture. A highly respected leader among African American women, well acquainted with the issues in her community and in the vanguard of its struggles, she traveled as a professional lecturer at three-week intervals, speaking at leading forums in Washington, D.C., New York, Boston, Chicago, Cleveland, Memphis, and other parts of the South.

Mary Church Terrell and other African American women created women's clubs not out of leisure, but out of necessity—as a way to address the community's circumstances of poverty, illiteracy, violence, and disfranchisement. In

1896, Terrell and others, among them Mrs. Booker T. Washington, Rebecca Cole, Ida Wells-Barnett, Rosa D. Bowser, Frances Jackson, and Frances Ellen Watkins Harper, formed the National Association of Colored Women (NACW), the largest federation of African American women's clubs in the United States. Terrell was nominated president and one year later, in September 1897, in a tone similar to that set forth in the Declaration of Independence, gave the "First Presidential Address to the National Association of Colored Women" in Nashville, Tennessee. Although this ceremonial speech was delivered to an immediate audience of African American women reformers, Terrell actually addressed herself to all who would listen:

> We proclaim to the world that the women of our race have become partners in the great firm of progress and reform. We denominate ourselves colored, not because we are narrow, and wish to lay special emphasis on the color of the skin . . . but because our peculiar status in this country at the present time seems to demand that we stand by ourselves in the special work for which we have organized. For this reason it was thought best to invite the attention of the world to the fact that colored women feel their responsibility as a unit, and together have clasped hands to assume it.

The NACW took on the practical work of cleaning up, educating, and nurturing its struggling African American communities, many of which were still recovering from destitution brought on by slavery. Terrell encouraged NACW members not to focus upon the limited financial and material resources available to meet their awesome task, but to be inspired with the knowledge that their love, commitment, and willingness to sacrifice were their most valuable assets: "It is not by powerful armies and the outlays of vast fortunes that the greatest revolutions are wrought and the most enduring reforms inaugurated. . . . the heaviest blows are struck for virtue and right."

The following year, Terrell delivered a speech at the 1898 biennial session of the National American Woman Suffrage Association, held in Washington, D.C. Asked to speak "as a colored woman about colored women," she delivered a speech on "The Progress and Problems of Colored Women." Terrell's style in this speech was delicate and optimistic, as she assumed that her audience, white middle-class women, were ignorant of the facts, yet of benevolent spirit. Attempting to educate her audience, she informed them that in every capacity— nursing, teaching, and various vocations, homemaking, business, even literature and the arts—women of the African American community were quite capable and already accomplishing much. She illustrated their achievements:

> Some years ago a large number of young men and women of the dominant race and only one colored person—a colored girl—competed for a scholarship which entitled the successful competitor to an entire course in the Chicago University. As a result of the examination which was held the only colored person among

those who took it stood first and thus captured this great prize. . . . Many years ago the Phyllis Wheatley Club of New Orleans undertook a task that was herculean indeed. This group of colored women had the courage to attempt to establish a Sanitarium with a Training School for Nurses and they had phenomenal success. . . . During an epidemic of yellow fever in New Orleans . . . Phyllis Wheatley nurses rendered such excellent service that . . . proved to be such a blessing to the city as a whole, without regard to race or color, that the municipal government voted it an annual appropriation of several hundred dollars.

By citing such examples of African American women's outstanding progress since their emancipation from bondage thirty-five years prior, Terrell indirectly refuted prevailing myths that African Americans were inherently uneducable, immoral, uncultured, inartistic, and inarticulate. Employing a method of argument standard in her lecture style, Terrell used example after example of women's success in order to replace the myths with a truer picture of the potential and character of citizens of African descent. In a manner appropriate to her educational style, Terrell sought to clarify the full significance of these accomplishments: "If judged by the depths from which they have come rather than by the heights those blessed with centuries of opportunities have attained colored women need not hang their heads in shame."

Using an educator's tact, Terrell cordially acknowledged that "the story of the Progress and Problems of Colored Women can never be truthfully told without referring to the invaluable assistance rendered by so many of their white sisters both before and after the Civil War." However, she carefully balanced this sense of indebtedness with a clear statement that the African American community asked for nothing more than equal opportunity: "Seeking no favors because of their color they knock at the gates of justice asking nothing except permission to work and achieve according to their ability and merit." The African American community praised this early oratorical effort. Wrote the *Colored American*, "She made a most magnificent appeal for the assistance of white women in breaking up the obnoxious systems in the South that tend to degrade colored women—the Jim Crow car, the convict lease system and other unsavory institutions."

Two years later, Terrell received a second invitation to address the National American Woman Suffrage Association at its 1900 biennial session, also held in Washington, D.C. Terrell delivered her speech, "The Justice of Woman Suffrage," not as a "colored" woman, she wrote, "but as a woman without regard to race." Here she argued that "the nation is deprived of its best when one segment is flagrantly excluded." In a rhetorical strategy typical of her oratory, Terrell held the entire nation accountable for all of its citizenry. Significantly, laying the responsibility on the "nation" generally, but not on her audience specifically is representative of Terrell's early use of indirection.

Throughout the speech, drawing upon America's founding principles, Terrell turned well-known arguments against woman suffrage into fallacious abandonments of justice and good sense. She proclaimed in a tone that would shame the offenders: "To assign reasons in this day and time why it is unjust to deprive one-half of the human race of rights and privileges freely accorded to the other, which is neither more deserving nor more capable of exercising them, seems like a reflection upon the intelligence of the audience." Again using a technique typical of her oratory, Terrell amplified this contradiction between principle and practice by noting:

> Before the world we pose as a government whose citizens have the right to life, liberty, and the pursuit of happiness. And yet, in spite of these lofty professions and noble sentiments, the present policy of this government is to hold one-half of its citizens in legal subjection to the other, without being able to assign good and sufficient reasons for such a flagrant violation of the very principles upon which it was founded.

Despite Terrell's and other African American orators' attempts to educate America, prejudice and racial discrimination became increasingly codified in Jim Crow laws. Flagrant lies appeared almost daily in the white press, and the nascent white film industry took pleasure in unbridled ridicule of African American women, men, and children. In turn, Terrell became more direct and assertive in her oratory, in tones less informative and more persuasive. For example, in a later version of "The Progress of Colored Women," delivered for the Chautauquas around 1904, she ended the speech not with a tone of gratitude, but with a challenge. Terrell's message was that the African American community needed only opportunity and facility to accomplish its goals. However, the white community had a responsibility to turn toward its own communities and families, its sons and husbands and fathers, and to teach them that racism is wrong. The white community must teach itself that it had a moral obligation before God and country to render justice to others based solely on the ability and merit of the person.

Although "The Progress of Colored Women" challenged its white audience, Terrell continued to seek friendship between the white and African American communities. When she lectured for the Chautauquas, she also spoke on the life of Harriet Beecher Stowe, in which she defined and measured that friendship. She established deep commitment in the historical relationship of friends of the African American community. She characterized Stowe as the epitome of a true friend of the downtrodden, one who had the courage and good sense to practice her Christian beliefs. Terrell said that through hard times and great sacrifice, Stowe persevered to write a literary piece that fired the sentiments of white Americans and brought about the Civil War that brought slavery to an end. Terrell also noted that Stowe lived in the past and that the current tide of friendship toward the African Americans was waning.

In another speech, "Uncle Sam and the Sons of Ham," also delivered for the Chautauquas, Terrell began to question the allegiance of those once very visible friends of her community who now watched silently while the tortured bodies of innocent men, women, and children swung from Southern trees: "In some sections the colored man is the victim of both lawlessness and law, and everywhere of prejudice. And where, pray, are the men and women who but a few years ago, so courageously advocated the colored man's cause?" Despite her query, Terrell was still convinced of the white community's ultimate benevolence and ended the speech with an appeal to her audience's sense of justice:

> In the race problem there is much that is complicated, but I believe the American people will break these bonds as they did those of slavery, and afford the colored man an opportunity of reaching the point it is possible for him to attain. . . . Uncle Sam is still being trusted and loyally served by the faithful, trusting, grateful sons of Ham.

During the same year, at the Cooper Union, Terrell delivered "Lynching from a Negro's Point of View," an effort to stop the wave of press reports that blamed African American men for an increase in lynching. Here, Terrell was combative rather than educational. Using evidence from prominent, reputable sources, such as eyewitnesses, ministers, and professors from Southern white communities, the usually genial Terrell denounced the press accounts as bald-faced lies. She set forth the legacy of slavery and illiteracy as the true culprits:

> Lynching is the aftermath of slavery. The white men who shoot negroes to death and flay them alive, and the white women who apply flaming torches to their oil-soaked bodies today, are the sons and daughters of women who had but little, if any, compassion on the race when it was enslaved. . . . According to the reports of lynchings sent out by the Southern press itself, mobs are generally composed of the "best citizens" of a place, who quietly disperse to their homes as soon as they are certain that the negroe [*sic*] is good and dead. . . . If the children of the poor whites of the South are the chief aggressors in the lynching-bees of that section, it is because their ancestors were brutalized by their slaveholding environment.

Finally, she not only questioned the friendship of the white community, but she began to challenge its patriotism and commitment to justice:

> There seems to be a decline of the great convictions in which this government was conceived and into which it was born. Until there is a renaissance of popular belief in the principles of liberty and equality upon which this government was founded, lynching . . . and similar atrocities will continue to dishearten and degrade the negroe [*sic*], and stain the fair name of the United States.

Indeed, Terrell challenged the hypocrisy of a country quick to condemn others' acts of injustice, but blind to its own:

> For there can be no doubt that the greatest obstacle in the way of extirpating
> lynching is the general attitude of the public mind toward this unspeakable crime.
> The whole country seems tired of hearing about the black man's woes. The wrongs
> of . . . every other oppressed people upon the face of the globe, can arouse the
> sympathy and fire the indignation of the American public, while they seem to be
> all but indifferent to the murderous assaults upon the negroe [sic] in the South.

One year later, in her "Address Delivered at the National Council of Women
Convention," Terrell was even more unequivocal in her condemnation: "As
long as the evil nature alone is encouraged to develop while the higher nobler
qualities of little ones are deadened and dwarfed by the very atmosphere with
which they breathe, the negligent pitiless public is responsible for the results
and to a certain extent is partner of their crimes." A dialectical relationship is
established between the ills in the African American community and the indifference of the white community. Significantly, while she did not blame all white
people, she did now hold them all accountable. She disapproved of "undesir-
ables" in the African American community, but she refused to allow her white
audiences to ignore the fact that they had created the very conditions they now
criticized.

As the struggle against violence and discrimination continued and escalated,
Terrell's oratory became increasingly ironic. In "What It Means to Be Colored
in the Capital of the United States," a 1906 speech given to the United Women's
Club in Washington, D.C., Terrell disputed the prevalent characterization of the
nation's capital as "the colored man's paradise." Constructing her speech in a
series of examples, Terrell described multiple incidents of highly qualified, morally upstanding African Americans denied access to jobs, education, restaurants,
theaters, and housing—unable to fulfill their personal dreams and duties to their
country—simply because of the color of their skin. Terrell pointed out that even
as a citizen with wealth and prestige, she was denied the most basic privileges
afforded all Americans:

> As a colored woman I cannot visit the tomb of the Father of this country, which
> owes its very existence to the love of freedom in the human heart and which
> stands for equal opportunity to all without being forced to sit in the Jim Crow
> section of an electric car which starts from the very heart of the city—midway
> between the Capitol and the White House.

Terrell's examples reflected the purest of intent on the part of the victimized,
and, in sarcastic overtones, she described the worst form of uncalled-for offenses
on the part of the perpetrators. For example, she pointed out that a common
occurrence in churches where "only the fair of face are expected to worship
God" was that a visitor of African descent would be ushered to "a seat in the
rear, which is named in honor of a certain personage, well known in this country,

and commonly called Jim Crow.'' Terrell concluded the speech with a metaphor illustrating how far removed the nation was from its founding principles:

> And surely nowhere in the world do oppression and persecution based solely on the color of the skin appear more hateful and hideous than in the capital of the United States, because the chasm between principles upon which this Government is founded, in which it still professes to believe, and those which are daily practiced under the protection of the flag yawns so deep and wide.

Mary Church Terrell had a long history as a political reformer and public speaker throughout her life. She represented African American women abroad at the International Congress of Women in Berlin, Germany, in 1904, at the International Congress of Women for Permanent Peace in Zurich, Switzerland, in 1919, and at the World Fellowships of Faith in London, England, in 1937. She surfaced over several decades as a principal agitator for woman suffrage, civil rights, and educational and social reform, sharing the podium with prominent figures such as Susan B. Anthony, Jane Addams, Frederick Douglass, Ida B. Wells-Barnett, Booker T. Washington, W. E. B. DuBois, and Thurgood Marshall. There were a few short periods of absence from public activity from 1938 to 1946 due to illness, along with the death of her husband in 1944. According to Jones, after her illness and the death of her husband,

> She did not resume her activism until 1946. But it was a different Mary Church Terrell who returned to the fray. She shifted her tactics from pursuing interracial understanding through attacks on the press and through her writings and speeches to a militant approach that attacked discrimination first through the American court system and later through such direct-action tactics as picketing, boycotting, and sit-ins.

For more than five decades, Terrell campaigned, boycotted, picketed, and appealed to the Congress and the highest court, accomplishing significant victories, such as the passage of the Nineteenth Amendment, and continuing the struggle against racial discrimination. In the midst of struggles over the desegregation of restaurants, theaters, housing, and public schools, Terrell's rhetorical strategies changed from appealing to the goodwill and understanding of her audiences to direct confrontation. According to Jones, ''Her battle for justice . . . against the segregation of public accommodations marked a person who had moved from the use of such strategies as moral suasion and interracial dialogue to boycotting, and sitting-ins.''

In 1951, Terrell headed a committee of distinguished citizens to demand enforcement of a seventy-five-year-old ''Lost Law'' banning racial discrimination of ''respectable persons'' from restaurants. It was a great victory for supporters from all walks of life, and one of Mary Church Terrell's proudest moments, when the Municipal Court of Appeals declared that the ''Lost Law''—the Anti-

Discrimination Law—was still in effect, and that restaurants in Washington, D.C., could no longer legally discriminate on the basis of race. On June 15, 1951, Terrell delivered an address at a mass meeting in Washington, D.C., a would-be celebration of the victory. It was a hollow festivity, however, because Corporation Counsel West, charged with enforcement of the Anti-Discrimination Law, sent messages to proprietors throughout the District of Columbia that he would not prosecute them, ostensibly fearing that his office would be over-whelmed with cases. Terrell directed her full sense of irony and sarcasm toward this injustice, using "loud talkin'," the black signification strategy in which comments about the affairs of one person are openly directed to a third party within the hearing of the party concerned. For example, Terrell ridiculed West's tortured logic:

> Mr. West predicted that if he enforced the law, his office would be piled up with cases mountain-high. So he fled from such a catastrophic multitude of cases as he would have fled from a hungry lion. . . . The only laws which Mr. West seems to like to enforce are the laws which are never broken at all and do not need to be enforced. Mr. West seems to forget that straightening out difficult and annoying laws is part of the job for which the District pays him his salary.

Although West was probably not seated in the immediate audience, the message was clearly meant for him. Terrell continued:

> By the stand Mr. West has taken in this . . . He has nominated and unanimously elected himself as Dictator. Somebody should write to Franco of Spain and advise him to get in touch with Corporation Counsel West immediately, so as to get some good points on how to be metamorphosed quickly into a successful Dictator—for Corporation Counsel West has shown he knows all the answers.

Terrell's tone was very different in this speech. Her examples were no longer ones of how hard African Americans were working to better themselves, but were instead examples of the calculated discrimination endemic to American society. Terrell ended this speech with a sad tone, one that revealed her disap-pointment that the white community never had lived up to the principles of liberty and justice for all with which she had challenged them forty-five years earlier.

> It pains me greatly to think that the Capital of my own country, the Capital of the United States of America—is the only capital in the whole wide world in which restaurants refuse to serve colored people on account of their race. . . . When I came here sixty years ago I did not dream that sixty years from that date colored people here would still be subjected to practically the same discrimination and segregation as they were at that time.

Terrell did live to see the U.S. Supreme Court uphold the Anti-Discrimination Law on June 8, 1953.

As a woman of "fair" complexion, Mary Church Terrell could easily have "passed" into white society and avoided the stigma of racism. Instead, she immersed herself in struggles against injustice and turned her oratorical talents to the problems of race and gender in America. Recognized as an accomplished orator, Sterling wrote that Terrell was "handsome, fashionably dressed, speaking in a deep, resonant voice which carried to the far reaches of an auditorium, she made a striking impression on her listeners." While African Americans were caricatured as lazy, ignorant, and barbaric, Mary Church Terrell proved by example that "colored" people were hardworking citizens who valiantly faced odds they would ultimately overcome. While women were demeaned and woman suffrage scoffed at, Terrell demonstrated through her oratory that women were responsible American citizens who needed to become empowered to carry out their duty to the nation. Displaying the full range of rhetorical prowess from educational to confrontational, Mary Church Terrell's was a powerful voice for justice. With the passage of time her voice grows even more resonant and continues to stand for the eternal principles of liberty, justice, and equality for all citizens.

INFORMATION SOURCES

Research Collections and Collected Speeches

Few published manuscripts of speeches still exist, but unpublished manuscripts and related archival materials can be found in two collections. Commentary on several of her speeches can be found in Terrell's autobiography, *A Colored Woman in a White World*.

[*OSW*] Anderson, Judith, ed. *Outspoken Women: Speeches by American Women Reformers, 1635–1935*. Dubuque, IA: Kendall/Hunt, 1984.

[*QFE*] Jones, Beverly W. *Quest for Equality: The Life and Writings of Mary Church Terrell*. Brooklyn, NY: Carlson, 1990.

[*BWWA*] Lerner, Gerda, ed. *Black Women in White America: A Documentary History*. New York: Pantheon, 1972.

[LC] Terrell, Mary Church. Papers. Library of Congress, Washington, DC. This collection is available on microfilm.

[MSRC] Terrell, Mary Church. Papers. Moorland-Spingarn Research Center, Howard University, Washington, DC.

[*TRS*] Walker, Robbie Jean, ed. *The Rhetoric of Struggle: Public Address by African American Women*. New York: Garland, 1992.

Selected Critical Studies

Brawley, Benjamin G. *Women of Achievement*. Chicago: Woman's American Baptist Home Mission Society, 1919.

Campbell, Karlyn K. "Style and Content in the Rhetoric of Early Afro-American Feminists." *Quarterly Journal of Speech* 72 (1986): 434–445.

Jones, Beverly W. "Mary Church Terrell and the National Association for the Advancement of Colored People, 1896–1901." *Journal of Negro History* 67 (1982): 20–33.

Leone, Janice. "Integrating the AAUW." *Historian* 51 (1989): 423–445.

Neverdon-Morton, Cynthia. *Afro-American Women of the South and the Advancement of the Race, 1895–1925.* Knoxville: U of Tennessee P, 1989.

Peebles-Wilkins, Wilma, and E. Aracelis Francis. "Two Outstanding Black Women in Social Welfare History: Mary Church Terrell and Ida B. Wells." *Affilia* 5 (1990): 87–95.

Render, Sylvia. "Afro-American Women: The Outstanding and the Obscure." *Quarterly Journal of the Library of Congress* 32 (1975): 306–321.

Sterling, Dorothy. *We Are Your Sisters: Black Women in the Nineteenth Century.* New York: W. W. Norton, 1984.

White, Gloria. "Mary Church Terrell: Organizer of Black Women." *Integrated Education* 17 (1980): 5–6.

Selected Biographies

Jones, Beverly W. *Quest for Equality: The Life and Writings of Mary Church Terrell.* Brooklyn, NY: Carlson, 1990.

Shepperd, Gladys B. *Mary Church Terrell: Respectable Person.* Baltimore: Human Relations Press, 1959.

Sterling, Dorothy. *Black Foremothers: Three Lives.* New York: Feminist Press, 1988.

Terrell, Mary C. *A Colored Woman in a White World.* 1940. Reprint. New York: Arno, 1980.

CHRONOLOGY OF MAJOR SPEECHES

[See "Research Collections and Collected Speeches" for source codes.]

"First Presidential Address to the National Association of Colored Women." Nashville, TN, September 15, 1897. *QFE*, 133–138.

"The Progress and Problems of Colored Women," Speech to the Biennial Session of the National American Woman Suffrage Association. Columbia Theatre, Washington, DC, 1898. MSRC, Box 102-3, Folder 96.

"The Justice of Woman Suffrage," Speech to the Biennial Session of the National American Woman Suffrage Association. Universalist Church, Washington, DC, February 1900. *Crisis* 90 (1983): 6; *History of Woman Suffrage*, Ed. Susan B. Anthony and Ida Husted Harper, vol. 4, New York: Arno, 1969, 358–359.

"Harriet Beecher Stowe." Speech for the Chautauquas. c.1904. MSRC, Box 102-5, Folder 145.

"The Progress of Colored Women." Speech for the Chautauquas. c.1904. *QFE*, 183–187; *TRS*, 205–210.

"Uncle Sam and the Sons of Ham." Speech for the Chautauquas. c.1904. MSRC, Box 102, Folder 153.

"Address to the International Congress of Women." The Philharmonie, Berlin, Germany, June 13, 1904. *QFE*, 189–196; LC, Microfilm Reel 21.

"Lynching from a Negro's Point of View," Speech to Cooper Union. *BWWA*, 205–211; *North American Review* 178 (June 1904): 853–868.

"Address Delivered at the National Council of Women Convention." Washington, D.C. April 9, 1905. LC, Microfilm Reel 21.

"Citizenship from a Woman's Point of View." Speech to Cooper Union, March 10, 1906. LC, Microfilm Reel 21.

"What It Means to be Colored in the Capital of the United States" (also "The Colored Man's Paradise"), Speech to the Washington, DC, United Women's Club. Washington, DC, October 10, 1906. *BWWA*, 378–382; *OSW*, 191–196; *QFE*, 283–291; *TRS*, 83–93.

"Frederick Douglass and Woman Suffrage," Speech to the Political Equality Club in Celebration of the Sixtieth Anniversary of the First Women's Rights Convention. Rochester, N.Y, May 27, 1908. LC, Microfilm Reel 21; *TRS*, 117–120.

"Statement to the Senate Judiciary Committee on the Equal Rights Amendment." U.S. Senate, Washington, DC, 1945. *Congressional Record*, 40.

"Statement to the House Judiciary Committee on the Equal Rights Amendment." U.S. House of Representatives, Washington, DC, 1948. *Congressional Record*, 38–39.

"Statement to the House Judiciary Committee on the Mundt-Nixon Bill (H.R. 7595)." U.S. House of Representatives, Washington, DC, May 5, 1950. *Congressional Record*, 2360–2361.

"Mass Meeting." Washington, DC, June 15, 1951. LC, Microfilm Reel 23, 1–8.

SOJOURNER TRUTH
(c.1797–1883), lecturer, abolitionist, women's rights speaker

ROBBIE JEAN WALKER

African-American women orators during the nineteenth century were generally women of privilege or extraordinary educational and cultural status. Sojourner Truth, however, could claim none of these attributes usually associated with the limited number of women who took to the public platform during this period of history. Although she was unable to read or write, Sojourner Truth's legacy has nonetheless remained intact due to the very audacity that empowered her to speak out on the prevailing issues of the day, especially women's rights, African-American rights, and temperance.

Biographers and historians have used at least three years in chronicling Sojourner Truth's year of birth: 1797, 1798, and 1799. McKissack and McKissack fixed the year more precisely, asserting that "Sojourner was born sometime in 1797, the same year John Adams became the second president of the United States, and George Washington warned the nation in his farewell speech that regional bickering would one day 'disrupt the Union.' " She was born Isabella, sometimes recorded as Isabelle, in the state of New York to slave parents. Biographical references to her as Isabella Baumfree recognize the name of her father, James Baumfree, although last names were not usually recorded for slaves. During the years of her enslavement, Isabella served at least four masters: Hardenbergh, Neely, Schryvers, and Dumont, her last official owner. Isabella cared deeply for Bob, a slave on another plantation, but Bob's master, disapproving of close relationships between his slaves and slaves from other plantations, successfully sabotaged the relationship. Sometime around 1814, Dumont deemed her to be of breeding age and selected an older slave, Thomas, for her husband. Isabella and Thomas became the parents of five children, four of whom survived.

Isabella was known variously by the names of her slave owners over the first four decades of her life. In the early 1840s, she reputedly sought divine guidance for a new name befitting her changed status as a free woman. Thereafter Isabella was known as Sojourner Truth, both parts of her name appropriately prophetic of the nature and substance of what she believed to be her preordained mission in life.

Sojourner Truth left New York in June 1843, leaving behind two of her daughters who chose to remain at the Dumont farm, the last of several places she inhabited during slavery. She took her youngest daughter with her, still hoping that one day her entire family would be reunited. Her son Peter had been sold to another New York farm and later illegally sold to slavery in Alabama at the age of five, a transaction Isabella had vigorously protested. Her triumphant efforts in rescuing Peter from slavery in Alabama typify the courage that would inform her philosophy and work from that time forward.

Her first contact with the outside world occurred a few days after her departure from New York at a religious camp meeting of the 'Millerites,' a religious denomination that later evolved into the Seventh-Day Adventists. The religious fervor and air of anticipation prevailing among the Millerites, who were awaiting the second advent of Jesus, comported well with the zeal dramatized by Truth's optimism and determination to be free. Association with this group provided a forum for her to articulate messages emphasizing the essence of hope and freedom, although her philosophy of agitation was not an articulated tenet of the Millerite doctrine. The group nonetheless respected her ability to inspire and granted her permission to speak on various occasions.

Sojourner Truth's earliest speaking engagements were essentially confined to religious gatherings. However, around 1843 or 1844, while in Massachusetts, she learned that there were people who openly opposed slavery and who were committed to the abolition of this affront to human dignity. Following a brief trip to New York to see her children once more, she became actively engaged in the mounting crusade against slavery. Speaking to mixed audiences at this time in history was indeed rare, but Truth's commitment to the cause and her courage defied threats, mobs, and tradition. She became a famous, sought-after public advocate for human rights.

Another dimension of human rights would soon claim her attention and receive equal effort and passion: the struggle for the rights of women. What Mary Church Terrell and others termed the ''double cross'' became an increasingly concrete reality for Truth as she learned that the battles for racial freedom and women's rights were not always harmonious. Sometimes at odds with her African-American brothers and at other times with white women, she experienced the agony of witnessing one of the causes to which she had devoted her life being forced into a subordinate position because of the other. Her efforts to explain that both causes—the race struggle and the gender struggle—were indeed based on the same ideals of justice failed to receive unanimous endorsement from either group, but her more global concept sustained her efforts and prevented complete discouragement on her part.

Sojourner Truth indeed lived true to both parts of her new name as she jour-
neyed across the nation espousing the causes of human dignity and fairness. By
1882, her travels became exhausting and illness overtook her. Olive Gilbert, to
whom Truth dictated her life's story known as *Narrative of Sojourner Truth*,
recalled that at this time, "her life's forces were spent." Sojourner Truth died
on November 26, 1883, at the age of eighty-six.

SOJOURNER TRUTH: BOLD ACTIVIST FOR HUMAN RIGHTS

Several biographers and critics refer to numerous speaking engagements of
Truth. Complete texts, however, exist for only three of her public speeches, one
the famous "Woman's Rights" ("Ain't I a Woman?") speech delivered in
Akron, Ohio, in 1851 at the Woman's Rights Convention and two 1867
speeches. The latter speeches, sometimes presented under the general rubric
"When Woman Gets Her Rights Man Will Be Right," were delivered at the
annual meeting of the American Equal Rights Association. Numerous quotations
from speeches or sustained comments on other occasions receive attention in
the literature, but these speech texts are not available in their entirety.

The famous "Woman's Rights" speech was an extemporaneous response to
the arguments of several preachers who attended the Woman's Rights Convention with an ostensibly concerted view toward intimidating the women in their
bid for equal rights. Truth's speech enumerated the ministers' assertions: the
need of women to be assisted, women's inferior intellect in relation to the intellect of men, the demonic nature of Eve that translated to all women, and the
gender of Christ. In her response, Sojourner systematically challenged all the
enumerated claims, employing traditional rhetorical arguments belying the colloquial language in which the speech was presented.

The speech by Truth, often referred to as the first feminist speech by a woman
of color and categorized as a gender defense, inevitably embodies clear and
compelling references to the implications of race as well. Her message conveys
more than the rightful place of women in the affairs of society; it also points to
the respect and expectations accorded women based on race. Her retort, especially to the ministers' first argument, notes that their logic had failed to take
into account women like her. As a woman of African descent, she had never
enjoyed the privileges to which the speakers alluded. The central importance of
race to her argument underscores Mabee's point about the relative emphasis on
race and gender in Sojourner Truth's rhetoric: "During all the years she spoke
publicly as a reformer, from 1850 on, she advocated improving the condition
of blacks in 136 speeches, but advocated improving the condition of women in
only 28."

The compelling refrain "And ain't I a woman?" dramatizes through its description and repetition the vast discrepancies between the treatment of white
women and women of color. Her analysis of these discrepancies achieves a dual
effect, that of allowing the men to hear the shallowness of their own arguments

and that of dramatizing how her experiences differed so significantly from those described. Thus her argument not only rejects the claim that women must be treated "specially," but vividly reminds the audience of the inhumane treatment suffered by African-Americans of both genders.

She dismissed the assumption of superior male intellect with some sarcasm: "If my cup won't hold but a pint, and yourn holds a quart, wouldn't ye be mean not to let me have my little half-measure full?" Her argument here is powerful, implying that even if the assumption of male intellectual superiority were valid, the men so blessed were behaving inappropriately by restricting the exercise of abilities women did possess. Paula Giddings, in her now-classic work *When and Where I Enter*, described Truth's rhetorical triumph: "Raising herself to her full height of six feet, flexing a muscled arm, and bellowing with a voice one observer likened to the apocalyptic thunder, Truth informed the audience that she could outwork, outeat, and outlast any man." In the Akron speech, Truth calmed the fear of white women suffragists that the battle for gender rights would suffer if racial concerns were introduced. Truth effectively communicated her commitment to fight for gender rights as a cause sufficient in itself. She also effectively challenged the specious arguments upon which the men based their claims of male superiority.

Victoria Ortiz, in *Sojourner Truth, A Self-Made Woman* quoted Frances Gage's assessment of the effect of the speech on the female audience in particular:

> She had taken us up in her strong arms and carried us safely over the slough of difficulty, turning the whole tide in our favor. I have never in my life seen anything like the magical influence that subdued the mobbish spirit of the day and turned the jibes and sneers of an excited crowd into notes of respect and admiration.

Mabee noted that Frances Gage's soaring testimonial about the impact of Truth's speech on the convention is not supported by newspaper accounts published soon after the time of the speech. Statements from the Akron *Summit Beacon* and the *Anti-Slavery Bugle* suggest that Truth's impact was less than phenomenal. The coverage devoted to the speaker in the *New York Daily Tribune* seems to corroborate the *Bugle*'s assertion that among the speakers at the 1851 Woman's Rights Convention, "no mighty sun eclipsed all lesser lights."

Across time, however, Sojourner Truth's speech indeed has drawn unto itself all the attributes of a "mighty sun." The popular refrain has an almost immediate identity quotient in rhetorical parlance and African-American culture. Current topics and titles attest to the continuing influence of Truth as a champion of women's rights. This unlettered orator's combined message and essence seem to strike a responsive chord in the American psyche, subtly conferring a sense of empowerment to diverse groups in their struggle for dignity and equality.

Sojourner Truth spoke before the 1867 annual meeting of the American Equal Rights Association, delivering speeches on May 9 and May 10. In these speeches, she implicitly developed two traditional arguments. Comparing gender rights with the newly won civil rights of African-American males and examining the advantages equal rights would provide to men, Truth dramatized problems and concerns common to striving humanity. Through her arguments and her rhetorical style, she called forth the cultural values of independence, courage, and confidence.

Truth opened the first speech before the Equal Rights Convention on May 9, 1867, with a comparison of the race problem and the gender problem. She was emphatic in her declaration that women of color would not be satisfied with equal rights for only men of the race. She warned: ''There is a great stir about colored men getting their rights, but not a word about the colored women; and if colored men get their rights, and not colored women get theirs, there will be a bad time about it.'' The speaker commented on the subordinate status of women in the courts, urging the audience to consider that matter seriously. The speech also contained Truth's speculation that espousing the cause of women was perhaps her preordained mission in that she had lived for eighty years and stood as the exception among women of color in exposing the status of women and crusading for reform. She stated her position in her typical colloquial language, but the thought embodied was profound and moving. She reminded her audience: ''I am above eighty years old; it is about time for me to be going. But I suppose I am kept here because something remains for me to do. I suppose I am yet to help break the chain.''

In a strong rhetorical comparison, she equated the attitude of men to that of the ruling majority. Her condemnation of limiting or withholding rights that women deserved dramatized her belief that subordination from any source— even from men of color—was unacceptable. Such conditions were no less reprehensible than those imposed by slave masters. Just as slavery was, by law, now condemned, so did Truth deem any attempt by any group to impose any form of subordination to be both disappointing and wrong.

Truth interspersed her speech with the hymn ''We Are Going Home'' and concluded with a compelling articulation of her determination to complete the work she had begun. Referring to the ''home'' mentioned in the hymn, she emphasized the importance of doing what one had to do while time remained. She then communicated her determination ''not to stop till I get there to that beautiful place.''

In the second speech, presented before the convention on May 10, 1867, Truth continued her analysis of the prevailing attitudes among men of her generation. Early in the discourse, she emphasized the point that some rhetoricians and historians have used as the title of the speech, ''When Woman Gets Her Rights Man Will Be Right.'' A central theme in this part of her presentation was that men applied quite different standards in considering their own concerns and the concerns of women.

An effective passage in her argument dealt with the phenomenon of the moment of opportunity. Her prediction was that the realization of equal rights by women would come soon. An important prerequisite of that realization, however, was that agitation must be continued now that attention was focused on the subordinate status of women. She used the metaphor of troubled waters to communicate the possibility that if action were not taken at the moment, the momentum gained to this point might thereby be diminished. Her assertion that "now is the time to step into the pool" clarified her perception of the importance of taking advantage of current opportunities to keep the issue before thinking men and women.

Truth enhanced the rhetorical effectiveness of her address through images of agitation and dissatisfaction. Word choices such as "stirring troubled waters," "breaking the ice," and "shaking every place" to which she traveled conveyed the notions of tension and flux. This state of affairs stood in direct contrast with complacency and enjoyed general acceptance, if the agitation manifested itself in socially acceptable actions. When conditions became intolerable, she suggested, the hope for change expressed through agitation was an effective strategy for motivating concerted efforts directed toward achieving a more satisfactory status.

The orator posited another argument based on a theme introduced early in this speech, the inclination of men to support their own views and perceptions with little discrimination while almost automatically rejecting similar consideration for the views and status of women. She then alluded to a common tendency of men to dismiss women's competence or "fitness" to rule by invoking negative portrayals of women. She asserted that men, for example, often invoked the biblical account of Mary Magdalene's being possessed by seven demons as evidence against women's right, or ability, to rule. To counteract this line of reasoning, she used another biblical allusion dramatizing a man with a "legion" of demons. Her comparison was compelling: " 'Seven devils is of no account. . . . Just behold the man had a legion.' They never thought about that."

She extended her argument by noting how the cleansing affected Mary Magdalene, who was later commended for her faithfulness and love for Jesus. Truth challenged the audience to find comparable behavior on the part of men, the group who went away before realizing that Jesus was no longer in the place of entombment. Truth's comparison reinforced the appropriateness of women's right to equality. Women had, she implied, demonstrated courage and responsibility in affairs of great import, vastly exceeding the courage and responsibility exhibited by men.

The speaker's communication of her perception that her role was significant, indeed even imperative, not only enhanced her ethical appeal but conveyed hope to numerous women with less initiative. Evident throughout her addresses was Truth's belief that she possessed the ability to make a difference in the current social battle, a battle that she hoped would be the last. Her confidence in herself extended to others. She admonished the women to be strong, to fight to the finish, and to be courageous. Significantly, these positive characteristics of strength and boldness were intrinsically linked to the concept of human rights.

Invoking values esteemed by the dominant group, the speaker exploited the potential of these referents to disturb the conscience of her audience.

The hortatives with which Truth concluded her speech are compelling. The structure of these hortatives in themselves supports the argument that the speaker possessed a sense of empowerment. She was not making a meek appeal that women be accorded equal rights. She was, instead, communicating to them that it was their battle and was suggesting the possibility of ultimate transcendence. Her determination was evident and unequivocal.

Several excerpts from other speeches reinforce positive assessments of Sojourner Truth's rhetorical powers. For example, in a speech delivered in Rochester, New York, on January 1, 1871, she made a plea to the government on behalf of disenfranchised and dependent African-Americans. The thrust of her plea was that the government set aside land in the West to provide homes and employment for disadvantaged groups living near the nation's capital in Washington, D.C.

Truth chided her audience for seeking solutions from her and challenged them to accept responsibility commensurate with their preparation and power: "You ask me what to do for them? Do you want a poor old creature who doesn't know how to read to tell educated people what to do? I give you the hint, and you ought to know what to do." With audacity and confidence typical of her speaking, Truth challenged the audience's conscience.

> You owe it to them . . . because you took away from them all they earned and made them what they are. You take no interest in the colored people. . . . You are the cause of the brutality of these poor creatures. For you are the children of those who enslaved them. . . . You are ready to help the heathen in foreign lands, but don't care for the heathen right about you. I want you to sign the petition to send to Washington.

Another example of Truth's rhetoric was recorded by McKissack and McKissack in *Sojourner Truth: Ain't I A Woman?* On this occasion, Truth was introduced by William Lloyd Garrison simply as "Sojourner" at a meeting in late 1850. After singing several verses she herself had authored, she opened her speech with the following words: "I was born a slave in Ulster County, New York. I don't know if it was summer or winter, fall or spring. I don't even know what day of the week it was. They don't care when a slave is born or when he dies . . . just how much work they can do." The silence and weeping that followed demonstrated the poignancy evoked when an audience is confronted with the reality that even ordinary celebrations accorded the lowliest of society have been categorically denied to one segment of its populace solely on the basis of color.

McKissack and McKissack eloquently captured the essence of Truth's comprehensive influence:

Whenever people speak out against injustice and scorn oppression, Sojourner Truth is in their midst. Whenever people are working to make conditions better for the weak and downtrodden, Sojourner Truth is there rejoicing. Whoever believes in equality, freedom, and justice keeps the spirit of Sojourner Truth alive and well.

Their claim was echoed by Margaret Washington in *Narrative of Sojourner Truth* with her observation that had the circumstances been different, the world might have witnessed another Joan of Arc. Like the Maid of Orleans, a "fearlessness and childlike simplicity . . . untrammelled by education or conventional customs—purity of character . . . unflinching adherence to principle—and . . . native enthusiasm" were embodied in the life, labors, and speeches of Sojourner Truth.

The oratory of Sojourner Truth belies the lack of formal education possessed by the speaker. In all its colloquial linguistic features and simplicity, it dramatizes the eloquence and profundity that inhere in fidelity to truth and the articulation of the ideals of simple justice and human rights. This reality explains, at least in part, how the oratory of an unlettered woman of African descent has survived as a pivotal symbol of the racial and cultural legacy. But the oratory has done more than survive. Its ideas have prevailed, and its eloquence has placed the name of Sojourner Truth—unlettered and without privilege—in a rhetorical tradition synonymous with privilege and power.

INFORMATION SOURCES

Research Collections and Collected Speeches

No speech manuscripts are known to still exist, but related materials may be found in the Sojourner Truth Collection at the Library of Congress, Washington, D.C., and the Bernice Lowe Collection, Bentley Historical Library, University of Michigan at Ann Arbor.

Selected Critical Studies

Fauset, Arthur Huff. *Sojourner Truth: God's Faithful Pilgrim.* Chapel Hill: U of North Carolina P, 1938.

Giddings, Paula. *When and Where I Enter.* New York: W. Morrow, 1984.

Mabee, Carleton. *Sojourner Truth: Slave, Prophet, Legend.* New York: New York UP, 1993.

Ortiz, Victoria. *Sojourner Truth, a Self-Made Woman.* Philadelphia: J. B. Lippincott, 1974.

Stanton, Elizabeth Cady, Susan B. Anthony, and Matilda Joslyn Gage, eds. *History of Woman Suffrage.* Vol. 1. 1881. Reprint. New York: Arno, 1969.

Washington, Margaret, ed. *Narrative of Sojourner Truth.* New York: Vintage, 1993.

Selected Biographies

Gilbert, Olive. *Narrative of Sojourner Truth*. New York: Arno, 1968.
Krass, Peter. *Sojourner Truth*. New York: Chelsea House, 1988.
McKissack, Patricia, and Fredrick McKissack. *Sojourner Truth: Ain't I A Woman?* New York: Scholastic, 1992.

CHRONOLOGY OF MAJOR SPEECHES

A general chronology of Truth's speaking tours is provided in Mabee, xiii–xvi.

"Woman's Rights" ("Ain't I A Woman?"). Delivered before the Woman's Rights Convention, Akron, OH, May 28–29, 1851. Stanton, Anthony, and Gage, eds., *History of Woman Suffrage*, 1:115–117.

Antislavery Speech. Salem, OH, August 1852. Confronted Frederick Douglass, asking "Is God Gone?" Described in Mabee, 83–92.

Antislavery Speech. Silver Lake, IN, October 1858. When proslavery opponents accused her of being a man in disguise, she bared her breasts to the audience. Described in Fauset, 138–140.

Antislavery Speeches. Sterben County, IN, May–June 1861. Threatened with violence and arrested. Described in Mabee, 91.

Women's Rights Speeches (2). Delivered at the annual meeting of the American Equal Rights Association, New York, NY, May 9–10, 1867. *National Anti-Slavery Standard*, June 1, 1867, 3.

Speech on behalf of Petitioning for Land for African-Americans. Rochester, NY, January 1, 1871. Described in Ortiz, 123–124.

BOOKER T. WASHINGTON
(1856–1915), educator, community leader

STEPHEN E. LUCAS

Lauded by his supporters as a pragmatic, farsighted leader who struck the best possible bargain for American blacks in a time of pronounced racial backsliding, reviled by his adversaries as a weak-kneed accommodationist who sold out the best interests of his race to white supremacists, Booker T. Washington is among the most enigmatic of all African-American leaders and orators. A master of subtlety and indirection, he learned at an early age how to talk and act so as to ingratiate himself with white people, and every major step in his remarkable public career was predicated upon the patronage and support of influential whites. To maintain his power base in the South, he seldom spoke harshly against racial injustice, and the criticisms he did advance were often squeezed between other passages in such a way that it was easy for listeners to overlook them. A loyal son of the South, he did the best he could to reconcile the needs of his race to the region's commercial, social, and political mores.

Yet behind his public mask of affability and acquiescence, Washington was well aware of the injustices facing African-Americans, and he went as far as he thought he could in condemning those injustices. A persistent spokesman for racial power, esteem, and solidarity, he often stated that he was proud to be a black person and that other blacks should feel the same way. He lent his support to a wide range of black educational and economic enterprises, and he expended considerable time and money behind the scenes working against such evils as vote fraud, lynching, the convict lease system, segregated railway facilities, and the exclusion of blacks from jury panels. No less an authority than W. E. B. Du Bois averred that "actually Washington had no more faith in the white man than I do." According to Du Bois, many of the differences between the two men could be traced to the fact that he, unlike Washington, had never felt the lash.

The son of a black plantation cook and an unidentified white man, Washington was born in Franklin County, Virginia, in April 1856. After spending the first nine years of his life in slavery, he passed the remainder of his childhood in the small town of Malden, West Virginia, where he worked in the mines and attended a one-room school. In the fall of 1872 he enrolled at Hampton Institute, a normal and agricultural secondary school founded three years earlier by General Samuel G. Armstrong. A dedicated exponent of industrial education for blacks, Armstrong stressed the virtues of hard work, frugality, discipline, and self-improvement. Washington learned his lessons well, and to the end of his life he regarded Armstrong as the finest man he had ever known.

Fired with the ideals he had internalized at Hampton, Washington graduated in 1875 and went back to Malden, where he taught school for three years. He also tried his hand at the study of law and the ministry, but found neither to his liking. In 1879 he returned to Hampton as a postgraduate student and a part-time teacher. Two years later, on Armstrong's recommendation, he was appointed head of Tuskegee Institute, a new school in Macon County, Alabama. During the next thirty-four years, Washington built Tuskegee into the nation's most prominent black vocational college. By the time of his death in 1915, Tuskegee owned more than 2,000 acres of local land and an additional 25,000 acres in northern Alabama, enrolled 1,537 students and employed 197 faculty members, had an annual operating budget of $290,000, and boasted an endowment of nearly $2,000,000. Had Washington done nothing else in his life, his work at Tuskegee would have made him a consequential figure in the history of American education.

In September 1895 Washington vaulted to national prominence as a result of his speech at the Cotton States and International Exposition in Atlanta, Georgia. Lauded by prominent whites throughout the nation for advancing what they regarded as an ideal solution to the conundrum of Southern race relations, he quickly became the most prominent and powerful African-American in the United States. His fame spread around the world after publication of *Up from Slavery*, his Horatio Alger–like autobiography that was translated into more than a dozen languages. Preaching the gospel of hard work, self-reliance, and individual initiative, he acquired funds for Tuskegee Institute from a host of wealthy benefactors, including John D. Rockefeller, George Eastman, Henry H. Rogers, Julius Rosenwald, and Andrew Carnegie. In 1900 he founded the National Negro Business League and served as its president until his death. Dedicated to promoting black commercial enterprise, this organization also provided Washington a core of loyal supporters in towns and cities across the nation. From 1901 to 1913 he served as an advisor to presidents Theodore Roosevelt and William Howard Taft, in which capacity he worked to maintain a solid Republican majority among black voters, to weaken the hold of lily-white forces on the party's Southern wing, and to secure federal posts for worthy blacks who stood behind his position on racial matters. Facing increasingly strident challenges to his leadership within the black community after publication of Du

Bois's *Souls of Black Folk* in 1903, he warded off his opponents with a combination of public insouciance and ruthless behind-the-scenes maneuvering. Although his historical reputation has suffered vis-à-vis that of Du Bois, he was such a dominant figure during his lifetime that the years 1895–1915 continue to be known in African-American history as the age of Booker T. Washington.

Washington's achievements as an educator and a race leader were intimately bound up with his career as an orator. Active as a speaker from the time of his arrival at Tuskegee, he became, in the two decades after the Atlanta Exposition Address, one of the most sought-after public figures in the United States. In his estimation, had he accepted even one-third of the speaking invitations he received, he would have hardly ever been at Tuskegee. As it was, he spent about half of his time on the road raising funds for his school and addressing a wide range of audiences—Northern and Southern, black and white—on his approach to race relations. Seemingly indefatigable, he sometimes presented as many as four speeches a day, and it has been estimated that he delivered approximately four thousand over the full course of his public career. Virtually everywhere he went, he was greeted by large and enthusiastic auditories. He loved being on the platform, and he exulted in the "combination of mental and physical delight . . . which comes to a public speaker when he feels that he has a great audience completely within his control." So great was the demand to see him and to hear him that on some occasions he would have to speak twice— once to the people fortunate enough to get seats inside the auditorium and a second time to those, at times numbering in the thousands, waiting for him outside or at nearby venues.

Given the number of speeches Washington delivered, it is not surprising that he often repeated the same ideas and echoed the same language. As he stated in 1913, "I sometimes change my text, but usually preach the same sermon." Yet he was exceptionally adroit at tailoring his general message to specific audiences. "I always make it a rule to make especial preparation for each separate address," he explained in *Up from Slavery*. "It is my aim to reach and talk to the heart of each individual audience, taking it into my confidence very much as I would a person." Speaking in a direct, lively, conversational mode, he seldom memorized his addresses or read them from manuscript. Most he presented extemporaneously in a personal, straightforward manner that conveyed a strong sense of sincerity and conviction. A master storyteller, he frequently spiced his remarks with humorous anecdotes and illustrations, which he used both to establish common ground with white listeners and to make by indirection points that he believed might not be well received otherwise. But he also knew how to make a case, and many of his addresses were filled with facts and figures supporting his point of view.

Perhaps most remarkable was his ability to generate positive reactions from all three major groups to whom he spoke—Southern whites, Northern whites, and blacks of both sections. As he stated in 1911, the overriding rhetorical problem he faced throughout his career was "how best to win and hold the respect of all three of these classes of people," each of whom looked at his efforts "with such different eyes and from such widely different points of view." Although Washington has often been accused of achieving his popularity by obsequiously acceding to second-class citizenship for his race, such a charge does not do justice to his rhetorical genius, to his program for racial advancement, or to the millions of black men and women who were devoted to him. If we are to understand, much less appreciate, his rhetorical achievements and his approach to solving the problems facing black Americans, we must learn to read his speeches in the language of the Gilded Age, and we must work to get behind the mask of his conventional utterances. When we do, we find an orator of much greater depth and complexity than conventional wisdom would suggest.

WASHINGTON'S ORATORY OF RACE LEADERSHIP

Bright, responsive, and verbally adroit from childhood, Washington received his first formal training in speech at Hampton Institute, where he excelled as a debater and received private lessons in breathing, emphasis, and articulation. As part of his graduation ceremonies in 1875, he was chosen to participate in a debate on the annexation of Cuba. According to the *New York Times,* which had a correspondent at the event, Washington presented his points with "great vigor," was "enthusiastically applauded," and "carried the whole audience." By 1877 he had developed enough of a reputation as a speaker to be invited by a committee of white citizens to spend the summer of that year stumping black communities around Malden in behalf of efforts to locate the West Virginia state capital at Charleston. The campaign was successful and enhanced Washington's stature as a young man of special ability and promise. So, too, did his presentation of the Post-Graduate Essay at the Hampton commencement exercises in May 1879. The address, which Washington spent three weeks preparing under the tutelage of his former teacher Nathalie Lord, was titled "The Force That Wins." It was so well received that a reporter from the *Boston Congregationalist* commented, "The Institute that can develop such a man, and send him out, may well take credit to itself for doing good work."

Unfortunately, there are no known surviving texts of these early speeches. The first address by Washington of which we have a reasonably complete text is his April 7, 1882, presentation to the Alabama State Teachers' Association, in which he made clear his commitment to the Hampton model of industrial education he hoped to develop in the heart of Alabama's Black Belt. In his view, there were three principal advantages of industrial education: it aided students in acquiring mental training, it taught them how to earn a living, and it instilled respect for the dignity of labor. Citing the success of industrial education in England, Washington claimed that it provided the majority of young blacks in the post-Reconstruction South "the only alternative between remaining ignorant and receiving, at least, a common practical education." Such an education, he argued, could be a powerful engine for racial advancement by training men and women whose knowledge and skills would provide "a central light whose rays will soon penetrate the house of every family in the community." Rehearsing a theme he would repeat often in subsequent years, Washington also held that industrial education was vital if Southern blacks were to maintain their edge in skilled labor against competition from European immigrants. "When the day comes," he said, "as it evidently will, when that great train of sturdy Englishmen and Germans begins to fill up the South, unless the Negro prepares himself thoroughly for the conflict, during the interim, his only resort will be in the cotton field." Washington did not deny the value of academic training, but he held that the immediate need of the race was for inventors, machinists, planters, and merchants. "Such persons," he said, "will do more to banish prejudice than all the laws Congress can pass."

As Washington's 1882 speech makes clear, Tuskegee Institute was, in his mind, considerably more than an educational institution. From the outset he conceived of it as a model for elevating the condition of blacks throughout the South. When he received an invitation from Thomas W. Bicknell, president of the National Educational Association, to explain his ideas at the organization's national meeting in July 1884, he quickly accepted. His speech, delivered in Madison, Wisconsin, was so important to Washington that he described it in *Up from Slavery* as marking, "in a sense, the beginning of my public speaking career." Addressing an audience of more than four thousand persons, including a fair number from Alabama, and even some from the town of Tuskegee, Washington asserted that any plan for the elevation of Southern blacks "must have to a certain extent the cooperation of the Southern whites. They control the government and own the property." Knowing the opposition of white Southerners to mandates for racial change dictated by the federal government, he held that the best course was to leave the question of civil rights to the South and to trust in the power of education to bring the needed changes. "Good school teachers and plenty of money to pay them," he declared, "will be more potent in settling the race question than many civil rights bills and investigating committees." Using words he would repeat many times in the next three decades, he claimed that harmony between the races would come "in proportion as the black man gets something that the white man wants, whether it be of brains or of material." Although Washington did not discuss industrial education at length in this speech, he was candid in stating that his advocacy of it was based partly on the fact that it was the only kind of schooling for blacks that white Southerners would support: "It 'kills two birds with one stone,' viz.: secures the cooperation of the whites, and does the best possible thing for the black man." So satisfied was Washington with this early statement of his approach to "the broad question of the relations of the two races" that he could declare, almost two decades later, "since that time I have not found any reason for changing my views on any important point."

Although Washington's best-known addresses are those he delivered to predominantly white audiences, throughout his career he spoke regularly to black educational, religious, literary, and civic organizations. From the earliest stages of his career, these speeches reflected his concern with racial pride and solidarity. Notable in this regard is his address to the Philosophian Lyceum of Lincoln University on April 26, 1888. Taking as his topic "The South as an Opening for a Career," he sought to show why young blacks of talent and industry should look to the Southern states as a land of special opportunity. In doing so, he had "no sympathy with those who would stoop to sacrifice manhood to satisfy unreasonable whims of the South, but would advise you to be there as here a man—every inch a man." Indeed, he held, the most effective ammunition with which to fight prejudice was the kind of "men who are before me—men who in every act, word and thought give the lie to the assertion of his enemies North and South that the Negro is the inferior of the white man."

Dropping the mask that he wore when addressing white audiences, Washington told his listeners at Lincoln that "In any business enterprise requiring push, snap, tact, and continual and close attention, the wide awake Negro has an immense advantage, for the Southern white man evades as a rule any occupation that requires early rising or late retiring, that removes him very far from a shade tree or the sunless side of a house." Sounding more like a twentieth-century black nationalist than a nineteenth-century accommodationist, he lamented the fact that for centuries black people had "been taught by precept and example that everything great has its origin in the white man and that Negro is a synonym for dishonesty, degradation and incapacity . . . that the Devil is black, that the devil's angels are black, that sin is black, and that it is a sin to be black." The way to destroy this "false teaching," he said, was to produce successful teachers, planters, doctors, merchants, and manufacturers who would lead the race into a glorious future in which black men and women, twelve million strong and "daily growing in wealth, experience and intelligence," would no longer submit to "oppression, political disfranchisement and taxation without representation." This is hardly the language of a latter-day Uncle Tom.

Far and away the most important speech of Washington's career was his Atlanta Exposition Address of September 18, 1895. Although often belittled by scholars as a collocation of bland, tactful bromides calculated to please the white South, the address becomes more richly textured the more closely it is examined. Washington knew that "by one sentence I could have blasted, in a large degree, the success of the Exposition." His purpose, however, was to gain a hearing for himself and his program. "I was determined from the first not to say anything that would give undue offense to the South," he said later. "And at the same time I was equally determined to be true to the North and to the interests of my own race." This would have posed a formidable challenge in the best of circumstances, but Washington did not have that luxury. He faced a situation in which one false step could have been calamitous for him, for his program, even for Tuskegee Institute itself. At Atlanta, as in other speeches to racially mixed audiences, he walked what Rebecca C. Barton called "the razor's edge between Negro pride and white prejudice." Having only one month to prepare, he composed an oratorical masterwork that outlined a comprehensive, far-reaching plan for improving the lot of Southern blacks and creating harmonious racial relations while at the same time balancing the conflicting goals, interests, and attitudes of different groups in his audience.

Dramatizing his remarks with an allegory about a ship lost at sea, Washington urged Southern blacks to cast down their buckets where they were "by making friends in every manly way of the people of all races by whom we are surrounded." Friendship, however, was far from his ultimate objective. Believing that economic power was the controlling factor in social and political relationships, he urged blacks to remain in the South, not because of any special bond between the races, but because "when it comes to business, pure and simple, it is in the South that the Negro is given a man's chance in the commercial world." Washington did not have any special faith in the inherent goodness of the white race; nor did he naively assume that the American political system was uniquely responsive to the moral dimensions of the struggle for racial justice. He did believe, as he stated at Atlanta, that "No race that has anything to contribute to the markets of the world is long in any degree ostracized." To Washington, this principle was as much a matter of natural law as the operations of the physical world. Believing that true social and political progress was a slow, evolutionary process of "severe and constant struggle rather than of artificial forcing," and convinced that economic advancement was the most important element in that process, he was willing to exchange immediate civil rights for economic opportunity, confident that such opportunity would lead ultimately to the complete civil and political empowerment of his race.

This is the bargain Washington sought to strike at Atlanta. To make it attractive to Southern whites, he abjured social equality between the races, stating, in the most famous words of the speech, "In all things that are purely social we can be as separate as the fingers, yet one as the hand in all things essential to mutual progress." Although many students of the address read "social equality" as roughly equivalent to "civil rights" or the abolishment of segregation, such a reading reflects late twentieth-century sensibilities rather than the linguistic world of Washington's time. "Social equality," in the language of the 1890s, meant intimate social relationships, and it tapped into the white South's perennial phobia about miscegenation and racial amalgamation. As Washington explained in a letter to Edna Dow Cheney one month after his Atlanta address, "the southern people often refrain from giving colored people many opportunities that they would otherwise give them because of an unreasonable fear that the colored people will take advantage of opportunities given them to intrude themselves into the social society of the south." By disavowing any intentions of social equality on the part of blacks, Washington aimed to eliminate the issue as a barrier to his agenda for racial advancement. He had no intention of relegating his race to second-class citizenship. Indeed, as he told his audience at Atlanta, the "industrial, commercial, civil, and religious life" of blacks and whites should be interlaced "in a way that shall make the interests of both races one." By disavowing social equality, which he did not regard as essential to racial progress, he was trying to buy time for the implementation of a program that he believed would eventually guarantee Southern blacks complete citizenship rights.

Just as there is a persistent tension in the Atlanta Exposition Address between Washington's short-term methods, which entailed renunciation of social equality and accommodation with the white South on immediate civil rights, and his ultimate objectives, which envisioned the full participation of blacks in every facet of American life, so is there a disjuncture between the ingratiating tone he adopted in much of the speech and his vision of the disastrous consequences that would follow if the oppression of Southern blacks were allowed to continue. The language of ingratiation was part of Washington's mask in dealing with whites, and it was imperative for survival in the mine field of Southern race relations during the 1890s. Although Washington knew full well the indignities and injustices imposed daily on blacks in the South, his program for racial advancement depended on the cooperation of influential whites, and he could not risk their disaffection with a frontal attack on established attitudes or institutions. Yet he did weave into the Atlanta Exposition Address a number of allusions to the mistreatment of Southern blacks. He also issued a powerful warning that the needs of his people could not be ignored without jeopardizing the prosperity and progress of both races. "No effort seeking the material, civil, or moral welfare" of the South, he said, could succeed without encouraging "the highest intelligence and development" of all its people. Blacks, he prophesied, "shall constitute one-third and more of the ignorance and crime of the South, or one-third its intelligence and progress; we shall contribute one-third to the business and industrial prosperity of the South, or we shall prove a veritable body of death, stagnating, depressing, retarding every effort to advance the body politic." There is no ingratiation here, no hint of genuflection. This is some of the strongest imagery in all of Washington's public discourse.

As matters turned out, the white South did not heed Washington's warning. It was pleased to take the renunciation of social equality and immediate civil rights he proffered in the Atlanta Exposition Address, but it was not willing to provide the opportunity for economic advancement he asked for in return. By the time Washington died two decades later, Southern blacks were almost universally stripped of their citizenship rights and were no better off economically than they had been in 1895. But Washington could not have foreseen these developments when he took the platform in Atlanta. It may be that he should have spoken out more vigorously against racial injustice in later years, but we need to be wary of deflecting criticism of his rhetoric after 1895 back onto the Atlanta Exposition Address. When seen in its original context, the address emerges as an estimable effort to deal with what proved to be an intractable problem. Even Du Bois, who would later become Washington's keenest adversary, heartily congratulated him at the time for his "phenomenal success at Atlanta—it was a word fitly spoken."

A rhetorical triumph of the first order, the Atlanta Exposition Address gave Washington access to platforms he could not have ascended before. In June 1896 he received an honorary master's degree from Harvard, the first New England college to accord such recognition to a black person. Greeted with what the *New York Times* called "vociferous and long-continued" applause, his speech at the alumni dinner "carried off the oratorical honors." It is best known today for Washington's statement about the "severe American crucible" that faced all groups seeking upward progress: "In the economy of God there is but one standard by which an individual can succeed—there is but one for a race. This country demands that every race measure itself by the American standard. By it a race must rise or fall, succeed or fail, and in the last analysis mere sentiment counts for little. . . . This, this is the passport to all that is best in the life of our republic, and the Negro must possess it, or be debarred." Perfectly in tune with the Social Darwinist assumptions of the age, Washington's words are sometimes interpreted to mean that he put the full burden of responsibility for racial progress on the shoulders of blacks themselves. In fact, however, he was careful, at Harvard and in other speeches, to affirm the interdependence of the races and the need for "the help, the encouragement, the guidance that the strong can give the weak." Thus aided, Washington assured his listeners, Southern blacks were coming up "through oppression, unjust discrimination and prejudice," and "there is no power on earth that can permanently stay our progress."

Washington returned to the Bay State in May 1897 to speak at the unveiling of the Robert Gould Shaw Monument. Addressing a packed house in Boston's Music Hall, he used the occasion not just to apotheosize Shaw and the black soldiers of the Massachusetts 54th Regiment who fell at Fort Wagner, but to call the nation to complete the work begun by those heroic souls. "The full measure of Fort Wagner," he declared, "will not be realized until every man covered with a black skin, shall, by patience and natural effort, grow to that height in industry, property, intelligence and moral responsibility, where no man in all our land will be tempted to degrade himself by withholding from his black brother any opportunity which he himself would possess. Until that time comes this monument will stand for effort, not victory complete." Coming from Washington, these were forceful words. Although they appear to have been largely overlooked in the hoopla and emotion of the ceremonies in Boston, the speech as a whole was so well received that Washington was emboldened to take an even stronger stand a year later in his October 1898 address at the Chicago Peace Jubilee.

A celebration of victory in the Spanish-American War, the jubilee presented Washington with an audience of sixteen thousand people, including President William McKinley and a host of other dignitaries. In one of the finest speeches of his career, he took as his text the words of Jesus that "Mary hath chosen the better part." Applying these words to African-Americans, he found that in every crisis of the republic they, too, had chosen "the better part." Praising the honor and heroism of black soldiers in the war with Spain, he challenged his listeners to "decide within yourselves whether a race that is thus willing to die for its country, should not be given the highest opportunity to live for its country." The United States, he said, had "succeeded in every conflict, except the effort to conquer ourselves in the blotting out of racial prejudices." There was no better way to celebrate the coming of peace "than by a firm resolve on the part of the Northern men and Southern men, black men and white men, that the trench which we together dug around Santiago, shall be the eternal burial place of all that which separates us in our business and civil relations. . . . Until we thus conquer ourselves, I make no empty statement when I say that we shall have, especially in the Southern part of our country, a cancer gnawing at the heart of the Republic, that shall one day prove as dangerous as an attack from an army without or within."

Washington's listeners greeted his speech with applause and cheers that "made the very columns of the massive building tremble," while the *Chicago Times-Herald* deemed it "one of the most eloquent tributes ever paid to the loyalty and valor of the colored race, and . . . one of the most powerful appeals for justice to a race which has always chosen the better part." But the address received a very different response in the South, partly because of its explicit criticism of the region, partly because many whites interpreted "business and civil relations" as including social relations. Facing a torrent of criticism from the *Atlanta Constitution* and other newspapers that usually supported him, Washington beat a strategic retreat and was more guarded in his future statements.

The reaction to Washington's Peace Jubilee speech is symptomatic of how little margin for error he had in dealing with the white South. It is easy to find fault with him today for not mounting a frontal assault against the Southern racial system, but he had little to gain and much to lose by such a course. When it came to the subject of education, however, his position at Tuskegee gave him more rhetorical leeway than he had on many other issues. Although best known for his advocacy of industrial training, he championed all forms of schooling for his race, and he consistently used the public platform to further the cause of black education. Thus when Mississippi governor James K. Vardaman, in his January 1904 inaugural address, alleged that efforts to educate Southern blacks had failed to elevate the race intellectually or morally, Washington took the occasion of a Lincoln's Birthday celebration in New York City to present a spirited response. Using a dextrous blend of striking examples, telling statistics, and authoritative testimony, he systematically cut the ground out from under Vardaman and those of similar persuasion by demonstrating that education for his race had produced positive results morally, religiously, and economically. Among blacks who had received schooling, he demonstrated, crime rates were down, life expectancy was up, and material prosperity was growing daily. "Often hungry and in rags, making sacrifices of which you little dream," Washington told his predominantly white audience, "the Negro youth has been determined to annihilate his mental darkness."

But Washington did not stop there, for he did not want to leave the impression that educational opportunities for his race were anywhere near adequate. He noted that per capita spending on education for blacks in the ex-slave states was less than half of that for whites, and expenditures for both races were beggarly in comparison to the North. In fact, he proclaimed in a line he would use in many other speeches, when people "are bold enough to claim that the education of the Negro is a failure, I reply that it has never been tried." Although reaffirming the need for blacks to progress slowly "one step at a time through all the constructive grades of industrial, mental, moral and social development," he put an equal burden on whites to use their prosperity and power to help lift up his race. "All the Negro asks," he explained, "is that the door which rewards industry, thrift, intelligence, and character be left as wide open for him as for the foreigner who constantly comes to our country. More than this, he has no right to request. Less than this a republic has no right to vouchsafe." Issuing one of his strongest public challenges to the forces of white supremacy, he declared that the elevation of his race was an issue of vital importance for the entire nation: "In the last analysis it means that we shall have in this country either a democratic form of government or a mere sham and semblance of the same." So effective was Washington's argument that the *New York Daily Tribune* opined that it "completely refuted Governor Vardaman's libels on the colored race."

Another issue on which Washington spoke consistently throughout his career was the importance of economic development for the long-term progress of his race. Believing that economic power was the entering wedge to equal partnership in all aspects of American life, he called upon blacks to acquire the mechanical training and habits of character requisite for a proficient, reliable work force. His ultimate economic aspirations, however, went well beyond the acquisition of job skills. Although he anticipated, as he said in the Atlanta Exposition Address, that the masses were going to labor in "the common occupations of life," above all he looked forward to the creation of a powerful black entrepreneurial class that would provide economic leadership for the race as a whole and, in the process, create a lasting foundation for genuine progress in civil and political rights.

In all of Washington's speeches there is no more emphatic statement on this issue than his 1912 presidential address to the National Negro Business League. Speaking with an almost visionary fervor, he warned that if the current generation did not do its duty "in laying the proper foundation for economic and commercial growth, our children, and our children's children will suffer because of our inactivity." Blacks, he argued, needed to act now "to lay hold on the primary sources of wealth and civilization" by "owning, developing, manufacturing, and trading in the natural resources of our country." Rather than being content with "merely skimming around . . . securing odd and uncertain jobs," Washington argued, blacks should "get in at the bottom of these fundamental industries and stand among the leading producers." By doing so, the race would acquire "influence and usefulness that no political party can give us or take from us." Washington also counseled blacks to organize among themselves if they wished to increase their commercial strength in the modern age of economic specialization: "Organize, organize, locally in the state and nation. Work together and stick together. . . . In racial unity, racial peace and coadhesiveness and organization will be our strength and life." Responding to those who decried his emphasis on economics, he explained that his program did not relegate blacks to being "merely breadwinners or hewers of wood and drawers of water," but would create owners, producers, manufacturers, and distributors of goods and services. Rather than limiting the race mentally, morally, or civilly, it would produce "real growth and real independence."

Washington's detractors have disagreed, of course, arguing that he committed a grave error by not giving priority to issues of civil and political rights. Yet Washington's emphasis on economics was located solidly in the mainstream of African-American opinion when he first developed his program. The orthodox view among black leaders during the 1880s and 1890s—including Du Bois and many others who would emerge as opponents of Washington after the turn of the century—was that economic, mental, and moral improvement, given circumstances at the time, would be more efficacious than political agitation in securing the race its full citizenship rights. Moreover, although the dominant strain of black thought since Washington's time, and especially since the civil rights movement of the 1950s and 1960s, has privileged political activity as the primary path to racial uplift, there are those who point convincingly to the necessity of complementing political empowerment with corresponding advances in the economic sphere for genuine progress in a capitalist society. In their view, Washington recognized the fact that any group in the United States that is marginalized economically will remain marginalized in other respects as well. Broadus Butler, for example, praises Washington as a bold visionary who articulated a crucial point, "not yet well learned, . . . that political and social gains not grounded in commensurate economic gains are like geegaws which are superficial and easily lost." So, too, does Harold Cruse, who places Washington within the black nationalist tradition for his efforts to develop a powerful African-American economy. Ultimately, Cruse acknowledges, Washington failed, but he had "a longer-range view than most of his contemporaries," and his failure was "no greater than that of those who sought equality through politics."

Just as we can understand why Washington took the course he did, so can we comprehend the frustration of other blacks when he did not speak vehemently against such injustices as disfranchisement and Jim Crow laws as the troubles of African-Americans multiplied in the opening decade of the twentieth century. Although Washington continued to work privately on a number of fronts, he did little in his public discourse to defuse the charge of his critics that he was too cautious, too accommodating, too beholden to rich and powerful whites to represent the best interests of his race. Particularly troubling to other blacks was his refusal to denounce Theodore Roosevelt for discharging, without trial, three companies of black soldiers from the 25th U.S. Army Regiment in the wake of a racial melee in Brownsville, Texas, in August 1906. Constrained by his role as a presidential advisor and by his personal loyalty to Roosevelt, Washington did all he could behind the scenes to dissuade Roosevelt from his high-handed action, but publicly he remained silent. For many blacks the Brownsville incident was a turning point in their views of white society and in their relations with Washington.

Washington's opponents were also infuriated by his habit of lauding the United States as a land of opportunity for blacks despite the obviously deteriorating state of race relations after 1900. There seemed to them little basis for Washington's repeated declarations that African-Americans were living in the midst of "the most progressive and highest type of white man that the world has seen." Nor could they countenance his relentlessly optimistic public statements about hopeful signs of racial progress in the face of overwhelming evidence to the contrary. This issue came to a head in late 1910, after Washington's return from his second European tour, when Du Bois and thirty-one others issued a manifesto censuring Washington for "giving the impression abroad that the Negro problem in America is in process of satisfactory solution." It was one thing, said the manifesto, "to be optimistic, self-forgetful and forgiving, but it is quite a different thing, consciously or unconsciously, to misrepresent the truth." Elevated in tone and uncompromising in argument, the manifesto cut short efforts to produce a rapprochement between Washington and the newly formed NAACP and helped fuel a spirit of animosity that became increasingly acute in the years ahead.

It is more than a bit ironic that as the rift between the two camps widened, events were converging that would lead Washington, during the final three years of his life, to alter some of his public pronouncements in the direction of being more forthright about the injustices facing his race. One of those events was a March 1911 incident in which Washington was physically attacked in New York City by a white man named Henry Albert Ulrich. Although the evidence against Ulrich was overwhelming, when the case came to trial eight months later, he was acquitted by a panel of three white judges after five minutes of deliberation. According to Washington's biographer Louis R. Harlan, the Ulrich affair made inescapably clear "what being a black man, even Booker T. Washington, really meant in a society dedicated to white supremacy." The second event affecting the tone of Washington's discourse was the ascendancy to the White House of Woodrow Wilson and the Democratic party. Freed of his perceived duty to remain publicly loyal to a Republican administration, Washington could now express himself more openly than at any juncture since 1900.

The result, as Harlan notes, was a series of public statements denouncing the discriminatory treatment of blacks by Southern railroads, opposing the growth of urban residential segregation, and calling for a boycott of the racist film *Birth of a Nation*. The two most important documents were magazine articles. The first, "Is the Negro Having a Fair Chance?" appeared in the November 1912 issue of *Century*, while the second, "My Views of Segregation Laws," was printed in the *New Republic* three weeks after Washington's death. Neither was written in the idiom favored by more strident African-American leaders, but both were noticeably more pointed than Washington's usual public discourse, and the latter was reprinted by the NAACP in a pamphlet on the evils of segregation. For the most part, however, Washington's speech texts from this period do not reflect the sharper tone of his *Century* and *New Republic* articles, though traces are evident in such addresses as his January 1914 presentation to the National Conference on Race Betterment and his lecture four months later to the Southern Sociological Congress. He may have concluded that the medium of print allowed him greater latitude to express himself with relative candor on sensitive issues than did the highly personal and potentially volatile medium of a public speech.

On October 25, 1915, Washington addressed a meeting of the American Missionary Association and National Council of Congregational Churches on the campus of Yale University in New Haven, Connecticut. The speech focused on education and called for a comprehensive effort by religious associations, educational boards, and people of both races to raise the funding and quality of all levels of black schooling to the same level as existed for whites. It was not an exceptional address, but it requires comment because it was widely reported to be Washington's final public speech. Suffering the cumulative effects of a lifetime of compulsive overwork, Washington died twenty days after his appearance at Yale. But contrary to press accounts and to Ernest Davidson Washington's anthology of his father's speeches, it was not the Tuskegeean's last address. Seldom did Washington journey to a city without speaking in the black community. After his presentation at Yale's Woolsey Hall, he went to New Haven's AME Zion Church to speak with members of his own race. This was his last speech. As with so many of Washington's presentations to African-American audiences, there is no text of his remarks, but the subject was education, and at least part of the speech urged local blacks to avail themselves of the opportunities for higher schooling available in New Haven. According to a black auditor who attended both speeches, Washington's "heart to heart talk" at Zion Church was preferable to his "eloquent" address at Yale because, he wrote Washington, "you were among your own people and you could appeal direct to them in a confidential manner better than you could in a great meeting."

It is interesting to surmise what might have occurred had Washington, who died at the age of fifty-nine, lived for another decade. Given the personal enmity between him and his adversaries in the NAACP, it seems unlikely that the chasm separating them could have been bridged. Yet stranger things have happened. Had Washington continued in the years ahead to express himself publicly with greater candor about the problems facing his race, it is not inconceivable that he and his critics could have found enough common ground to bring about, if not a perfect peace, at least an uneasy truce, thereby allowing the race to speak with a more unified voice. One also wonders how Washington would have responded to American entry into World War I, to the shameful treatment of blacks after the war, and to the resulting increase in racial tension and violence. Had he staked out a forward position on these issues, he might have enhanced both his moral authority and his historical reputation.

But this is idle speculation mixed with a healthy dose of wishful thinking. It is hard enough to come to terms with Washington as he was without trying to imagine what he might have been under different circumstances. There was always a substantial degree of opacity in Washington's rhetoric—indeed, in every aspect of his public persona. Living and working in the Byzantine world of Southern race relations during the late nineteenth and early twentieth centuries, he was never free to speak his mind fully on issues of public consequence. It took a black person with Washington's singular personality and special brand of rhetorical genius to attain such remarkable success within that world. His speeches, like other aspects of his life, were replete with tensions, crosscurrents, and overlapping layers of meaning that reflected his constant struggle to balance the conflicting exigencies faced by an African-American leader seeking racial justice in a society dominated by white attitudes and institutions.

INFORMATION SOURCES

Research Collections and Collected Speeches

The major collection of Booker T. Washington's private papers, containing more than one million items, is housed at the Library of Congress. *The Booker T. Washington Papers*, edited by Louis R. Harlan, is the authoritative published collection of Washington's speeches and writings. Twenty-nine of Washington's major addresses are reprinted in *Selected Speeches of Booker T. Washington*, edited by his son Ernest Davidson Washington. A number are also available in Washington's two autobiographies, *The Story of My Life and Work*, written primarily for a black audience, and *Up from Slavery*, which was designed to promote Washington's image among white readers. Two of Washington's books—*Character Building* and *Putting the Most into Life*—are anthologies of Sunday Evening Talks to the students at Tuskegee Institute.

[*BTWP*] Washington, Booker T. *The Booker T. Washington Papers*. Ed. Louis R. Harlan et al. 14 vols. Urbana: U of Illinois P, 1972–89.
———. *Character Building: Being Addresses Delivered on Sunday Evenings to the Students of Tuskegee Institute*. New York: Doubleday, Page and Company, 1902.
———. *Putting the Most into Life*. New York: Thomas Y. Crowell and Company, 1906.
[*SSBW*]———. *Selected Speeches of Booker T. Washington*. Ed. Ernest Davidson Washington. Garden City, NY: Doubleday, Doran, and Company, 1932.
[*SML*]———. *The Story of My Life and Work*. Toronto: J. L. Nichols, 1900.
[*UFS*]———. *Up from Slavery*. New York: Doubleday, Page and Company, 1901.

Selected Critical Studies

Bruce, Dickson D., Jr. "Booker T. Washington's *The Man Farthest Down* and the Transformation of Race." *Mississippi Quarterly* 48 (1995): 239–253.

Butler, Broadus N. "Booker T. Washington, W. E. B. Du Bois, Black Americans, and the NAACP—Another Perspective." *Crisis* 85 (1978): 222–230.

Cruse, Harold. *Rebellion or Revolution?* New York: William Morrow, 1968.

Gibson, Donald B. "Strategies and Revisions of Self–Representation in Booker T. Washington's Autobiographies." *American Quarterly* 45 (1993): 370–393.

Heath, Robert L. "A Time for Silence: Booker T. Washington at Atlanta." *Quarterly Journal of Speech* 64 (1978): 385–399.

King, Andrew. "Booker T. Washington and the Myth of Heroic Materialism." *Quarterly Journal of Speech* 60 (1974): 323–327.

McElroy, Frederick. "Booker T. Washington as Literary Trickster." *Southern Folklore* 49 (1992): 89–107.

Thornbrough, Emma L. "Booker T. Washington As Seen by His White Contemporaries." *Journal of Negro History* 53 (1968): 161–182.

Wallace, Karl R. "Booker T. Washington." *A History and Criticism of American Public Address* Vol. 1. Ed. William Norwood Brigance. New York: McGraw-Hill, 1943.

Selected Biographies

Harlan, Louis R. *Booker T. Washington: The Making of a Black Leader, 1856–1901.* New York: Oxford UP, 1972.

———. *Booker T. Washington: The Wizard of Tuskegee, 1901–1915.* New York: Oxford UP, 1983.

Scott, Emmett J., and Lyman Beecher Stowe. *Booker T. Washington: Builder of a Civilization.* Garden City, NY: Doubleday, Page and Company, 1916.

Spencer, Samuel R., Jr. *Booker T. Washington and the Negro's Place in American Life.* Boston: Little, Brown, 1955.

CHRONOLOGY OF MAJOR SPEECHES

[See "Research Collections and Collected Speeches" for source codes.]

Speech before the Alabama State Teachers' Association. Selma, AL, April 7, 1882. *BTWP,* 2:191–195.

Speech before the National Educational Association. Madison, WI, July 16, 1884. *BTWP,* 2:255–262; *SSBW,* 1–11.

Speech before the Philosophian Lyceum of Lincoln University. Lincoln University, PA, April 26, 1888. *BTWP,* 2:439–451.

Atlanta Exposition Address. Atlanta, GA, September 18, 1895. *BTWP,* 3:583–587; *SSBW,* 31–36; *SML,* 165–171; *UFS,* 218–225.

Address at the Harvard University Alumni Dinner. Cambridge, MA, June 24, 1896. *BTWP,* 4:183–185; *SSBW,* 51–53; *SML,* 210–212.

Speech at the Unveiling of the Robert Gould Shaw Monument. Boston, MA, May 31, 1897. *BTWP,* 4:285–289; *SSBW,* 54–59; *SML,* 236–242.

Address at the National Peace Jubilee. Chicago, IL, October 16, 1898. *BTWP*, 4:490–493; *SML*, 263–267.

Lincoln's Birthday Address. New York, NY, February 12, 1904. *BTWP*, 7:429–440; *SSBW*, 118–134.

Address before the National Negro Business League. Chicago, IL, August 21, 1912. *BTWP*, 11:578–586.

Address at the First National Conference on Race Betterment. Battle Creek, MI, January 8, 1914. *BTWP*, 12:406–417; *SSBW*, 218–234.

Address before the Southern Sociological Congress. Memphis, TN, May 8, 1914. *BTWP*, 13:16–21; *SSBW*, 235–242.

Address before the American Missionary Association and National Council of Congregational Churches. New Haven, CT, October 25, 1915. *BTWP*, 13:410–414; *SSBW*, 277–283.

ALYCE FAYE WATTLETON
(1943–   ), nurse, public health official, Planned Parenthood president

LORRAINE D. JACKSON

Throughout her tenure as the president of the Planned Parenthood Federation of America (PPFA) from 1978 to 1992, Alyce Faye Wattleton emerged as a leading spokesperson for the pro-choice movement. She redefined the abortion controversy from a moral question into an issue about personal choice and control. Her messages focused on reproductive planning and health and on the rights of women as autonomous decision makers. Wattleton's leadership ability, talent for debate, and public speaking skills gained respect from supporters and adversaries alike. Lois Romano, writing in *Glamour,* remarked that "even pro-life activists concede she is everything you don't want in an opponent—articulate, strikingly telegenic, bright, and most importantly, messianic on this subject."

Faye Wattleton, as she prefers to be called, was born in St. Louis, Missouri, on July 8, 1943. Her father, the late George Wattleton, worked in a factory, while her mother, Ozie, was a minister in the fundamentalist Church of God. In an interview with Nancy Rubin for *Savvy Woman,* Faye disclosed: "I was raised by my parents to believe that it was my obligation to help those with less than I had. Although we were materially poor, the value of my family life was that there was a sense of achievement." Her drive to achieve was apparent at an early age. She entered Ohio State University at the age of sixteen with the goal of becoming a missionary nurse and graduated in 1964 with a bachelor's degree in nursing. In 1966, after working for two years as a maternity instructor, Faye entered Columbia University in New York. While working toward an M.S. in maternal and infant care, she completed an internship at Harlem Hospital. During that time, she was particularly affected by the suffering that faced disadvantaged women, many of whom tried to terminate pregnancies themselves in the absence of safe, legal abortions. For example, Wattleton observed a seventeen-year-old die of kidney failure after the victim's mother injected a combination of Lysol and bleach into the adolescent's uterus. Not surprisingly, incidents such as these had a profound effect upon Faye Wattleton's development.

After completing her M.S., Faye moved to Dayton, Ohio, where she became assistant director of the Montgomery County Combined Public Health District. Once again, she was confronted by frightened young women, maladministered abortions, and neglected children. As a result of these experiences, Faye turned her attention to becoming a different type of missionary. While in Dayton, she served on the board of directors for Planned Parenthood of Miami Valley and two years later was asked to serve as executive director, a position she held for seven years. When asked by a reporter for *USA Today* why she joined Planned Parenthood, she replied, "Is it better to continue trying to save these children and those people who are injured and vulnerable, or to work for a world in which these conditions don't occur?"

The 1970s brought new personal and professional responsibilities for Wattleton. In 1973 she married social worker Franklin Gordon. Two years later, while pregnant with her daughter Felicia, she was elected chairperson of PPFA's National Executive Director's Council. In January of 1978, she was chosen from among over two hundred applicants to assume the presidency of PPFA, a position previously held only by white men. Faye Wattleton became the first African-American, the first woman, and the youngest president in the history of the organization. She set out to change the organization's image from one of conservatism to one of advocacy for women's reproductive freedom. During her first year, antiabortion extremists increased their firebombing attacks on abortion clinics, and Wattleton herself received death threats.

The 1980s were marked by continued struggles. In 1981, under the pressures of her new role, her marriage ended in divorce. In legal assaults on Planned Parenthood services, the Reagan administration was cutting funding to family-planning services, requiring parental consent for contraceptives, and imposing a "gag rule" that prevented federally funded clinics from counseling women on abortion, even if withholding such information endangered the woman's health. The Reagan administration also attempted to restrict access to reproductive services by forbidding foreign recipients of general family-planning funds to offer abortion counseling, referrals, or abortions, even when the abortion-related efforts were funded separately by private funds. Perhaps the most damaging legal attack for the pro-choice movement occurred in July 1989, when the Supreme Court's *Webster* ruling referred the issue of abortion to the state legislatures. Although this did not reverse *Roe v. Wade,* it meant that a woman's right to abortion would have to be argued state by state. During this time, in her efforts to counter these legal rulings, Wattleton made public appearances on television and radio shows to debate right-to-lifers, established an Action Fund to increase lobbying efforts against the anti-choice movement, and mobilized high-profile pro-choice celebrities.

She continued during President Bush's term to fight the erosion of women's reproductive rights by challenging women to become involved in the political process and to protect their reproductive freedom. As she explained to reporter Elizabeth Kolbert, writing for *Vogue,* ''I think the pro-choice movement has done a good job of articulating the dangers . . . but how can you make people feel that those dangers imminently affect them? I don't know, except for women to start dying and filling up the hospital wards. I say to women all day long, 'you have a special responsibility.' I don't know how much plainer that can be.''

Faye Wattleton resigned from Planned Parenthood in 1992. Under her leadership, the organization's budget tripled to approximately 380 million dollars. At present, she continues to speak to various groups about women's health, reproductive rights, and feminist issues and is working on a book about how national politics are shaped by American attitudes toward sexuality.

FAYE WATTLETON: SETTING THE AGENDA FOR WOMEN'S HEALTH

Faye Wattleton's competence is evidenced by her ability to adapt her message appropriately. On some occasions, her arguments are marked by emphatic, metaphorical examples and language; at other times, emphasis is placed on neutral language and well-informed, carefully reasoned arguments. Her ability to remain confident, focused, and unwavering in light of powerful opposition is impressive. Additionally, her substantive messages are complemented by her elegance. Standing almost six feet tall, Wattleton's beauty, style, and poise captured the attention of the media, and through her oratory she has developed into an influential political force. Today, she remains an articulate role model for feminists.

The themes of Wattleton's speeches were influenced by external political, social, and legal events. In a speech titled ''The End of the Reagan Era: The State of Worldwide Reproductive Rights,'' delivered in 1988 to the Commonwealth Club in San Francisco, Wattleton outlined the need for and status of family-planning efforts throughout the world. The speech demonstrated both the family-planning successes in developing countries such as Thailand and the necessity for efforts to be expanded in places like sub-Saharan Africa, where it is not uncommon for women to have eight to ten unplanned children in their lifetime. After comparing various countries' infant and maternal mortality rates, Wattleton explained that with adequate access to family planning, many unplanned pregnancies and maternal deaths would be preventable. Moreover, she explored the suffering that accompanies being unable to plan and support a family.

Statistical evidence reinforced her main point as she illuminated the irony of the Reagan administration's antiabortion effort. The ''crippling restrictions'' imposed on family-planning programs abroad, she argued, undermined the very programs that provided contraceptives and prevented unwanted pregnancies and, ultimately, abortions. Through her skillful use of logical appeals and dramatic metaphors she depicted the gravity of the situation: "Three and a half to four million people we serve are hanging by a thread. . . . if Planned Parenthood's program is de-funded, there will be 400,000 additional unwanted pregnancies, 70,000 additional abortions, and over 1,200 deaths from abortions." Both directly and through metaphors, she indicted the administration for violating human rights: "Many millions of people who suffer these horrors have been turned into political hostages by our own federal government," she noted and she then warned that Planned Parenthood would pursue legal action.

Wattleton's word choice, or diction, was deliberate. In one passage, she charged that "these regulations . . . are nothing more than transparent attempts to pay off the administration's debt to a handful of anti–family planning extremists, whose lust for sexual repression remains unfulfilled." As in the majority of her speeches, she did not refer to the opposition as "pro-life," but instead used descriptors such as "anti–family planning extremists" or "anti-abortionists."

Ultimately, the purpose of this speech was to actuate the members of her audience into lobbying their public officials. She effectively compelled the audience to feel compassion and, more important, "to speak out for those who are too weak, too young, too far away—or just too desperate and dispirited—to make their voices heard." The speech concluded with an affirmation of teamwork: "If we are willing to work together on behalf of common sense and common human decency, we cannot help but win the many other struggles before us."

Wattleton strove to win the battle for reproductive freedom by mobilizing support. In a 1989 speech, "March and Rally for Women's Equality/Women's Lives," delivered in Washington, D.C., she employed a poignant metaphor to magnify the restrictions on freedom: "And as a woman, I know that the power of the government to control women's reproduction is more frightening than any other tyranny, more binding than any other prison." In this speech, she also used repetition to emphasize the importance of privacy: "In a pluralistic nation, private morality must be just that—private! . . . Let privacy be the bedrock of our freedom!" She concluded with an emphatic reference to specific individuals: "And to the Bushes, the Thornburghs, and the Falwells of the world, it is we who say 'Read our lips. No more back alleys!' "

Her impassioned delivery and provocative content are also evidenced in her speech, "Remarks at Central Park Rally," made on Earth Day in 1990, characterized by several stylistic and poetic devices. The ancient Greeks coined the word *ecphrasis* to describe a stylistic device whereby speakers use vivid descriptions to make a thought "stand out" in the minds of listeners. Wattleton declared vividly: "200,000 women die every year from sharp sticks, from drinking bleach, from horrifying means of abortion." She also contrasted President Bush's words with those of her own in the following rhetorical question: "What could be *less* kind or gentle—what could be more cruel and illogical—than trying to reduce abortion by curbing contraception?" Wattleton also incorporated rhyme into this speech, asserting: "It is high time our government created a foreign policy that responds to *compassion for distress—not* a *compulsion to oppress.*" Once again, her purpose was to motivate her audience to participate in political processes, and she ended her Earth Day speech with a specific plea for action to benefit "all the Earth's people."

In "Guaranteeing the Promise of Roe," delivered in 1991 to the Family Planning Advocates of New York State, Wattleton commended her audience for working to defeat abortion-restrictive bills. At the same time, she discussed the difficulties still facing freedom regarding parental-notification policies and the gag rule that prevented practitioner/patient discussion of abortion options. Her style was personal as she talked about her own teenaged daughter. Through personal references she stressed the importance of voluntary communication in families while rejecting the compulsory communication associated with parental notification. Her goal in this speech was to revitalize and reinforce the concerns of an audience already in agreement with the need for reproductive liberation. Again, her proficiency was apparent. She commonly employed "military" metaphors such as "Our opponents won't give up . . . we can expect major battles to continue . . . I know I can count on you to be my partners in this fight" in order to energize her audience. Her inventive use of rhyme and alliteration added notable form to her points: "By forbidding practitioners to provide complete, accurate health information, the gag rule turns *doctors* into *indoctrinators,* and *patients* into *pawns.*"

In the speech "African-American Reproductive Choices," delivered to the National Medical Association Council on the Concerns of Women Physicians in Indianapolis on July 28, 1991, Wattleton attempted to increase active involvement and support from health professionals. She first asserted that maladministered abortions particularly affected minority women: "Before 1973, 80% of deaths from illegal abortions occurred to minority women! The mortality rate from illegal abortion for minority women was 12 times the rate for white women!" Resuming her criticism of the gag rule, she made convincing use of analogy:

> If *your* pregnant patient asks about abortion, even if continuing the pregnancy threatens her health, the government has decreed what you must tell her—"The project does not consider abortion an appropriate method of family planning." Imagine a gag rule applied to other areas of medical care: "You have emphysema, Ms. Smith, but the government subsidized tobacco industry doesn't think that stopping smoking is an appropriate matter for discussion in a federal clinic." This is larger than "abortion." This is censorship. This is government mind control. This is government propaganda in physicians' examining rooms.

In addition to the use of analogy, this excerpt also employs *anaphora,* a scheme of repetition in which successive sentences begin with the same language. Again, Wattleton's use of repetition lent emphasis to her assertions.

Wattleton adapted this speech to a primarily female audience by making specific references to issues of gender inequality: "This debate is about controlling women by controlling our fertility! I am aware of *no proposals* in this country aimed at regulating *men's* fertility." In her conclusion, she urged women to join her in the struggle for reproductive freedom by becoming involved in political processes.

Two speeches from 1992, "Planned Parenthood and Pro-Choice: Sexual and Reproductive Freedom" and "Sacred Rights: Preserving Our Reproductive Freedom," provide representative examples of Wattleton's advocacy of reproductive freedom. Although both speeches are similar in content and purpose, the latter is worthy of particular attention because it required special audience analysis and adaptation. In this speech, delivered at Marble Collegiate Church in New York City, Wattleton developed the argument that fundamental rights to the individual, including religious freedom, need to be protected from intrusive government involvement. Initially, she did not mention "abortion" directly, but instead referred to autonomous decision making: "The freedom to practice the religion of our choice and serve the God of our beliefs is inextricably tied to our right to think and speak for ourselves, without the government telling us what to do." Wattleton also made a personal reference to her mother's occupation as a fundamentalist Protestant preacher and went on to say: "We don't quite agree on many issues! But we respect each other's convictions, and we feel no need to impose them on each other." This admission appeared near the beginning of her speech and was important because it established a connection with the audience by decreasing polarization on the abortion issue while emphasizing similarities and issues of respect. In this speech, Wattleton developed anecdotes rather than statistical evidence and focused on personal choice and reproductive freedom. The following passage depicted her beliefs:

> Like religion, questions of reproductive choice are deeply *personal*. No one group has a monopoly on *truth*. No one group has a lock on morals and ethics for all time. The promise of the First Amendment is that Americans need *never* fear that they will be *governed* by a *religious* doctrine! . . . A government that can mandate *prayer in the schools* is a government that can mandate *which prayers* we say! How would Christian Fundamentalists like it if government forced their children to recite daily hymns to the Krishna or the Earth Goddess? A government that can compel women to *have* children is a government that can force them *not* to have children.

In a later passage of this speech, Wattleton addressed the firebombings of abortion clinics that were carried out on religious grounds:

> In the *Bray* case before the court, the Bush administration and the terrorist mobs of Operation Rescue have entered into an unholy alliance. They say that a law enacted in 1871 to protect blacks against the Ku Klux Klan does *not* protect

women against the attacks of Operation Rescue. In other words, as an African
American, I am protected from mob violence, but as a woman, I enjoy no such
protection! . . . The flames of intolerance still burn brightly in our nation.

By comparing Operation Rescue with the Ku Klux Klan, she portrayed extremists as violent and intolerant. Later, she asked rhetorically: "And isn't true Christianity based on compassion and tolerance?" This juxtaposition, along with her
poise and reason, defined Wattleton's influence strategies. Near the end of this
speech, Wattleton mentioned abortion directly and offered a rejoinder:

I have no quarrel with those who oppose abortion and contraception and try to
convince others of their views. That's what religious liberty and free speech are
all about. But the danger is translating *personal morality* into *public* law, imposing
a single standard of morality by force of law—the kind of tyranny, denial of
choices, and choking off of dissent, that the founders of this nation were *escaping*
when they first came to these shores.

In closing this speech, Wattleton asked the audience to support and preserve
individual freedoms.
    Two later speeches delivered by Wattleton after her resignation from Planned
Parenthood and after Bill Clinton was elected president are noteworthy. In both
the 1993 speech "Equality, Liberty, and Justice: Women's Unfinished Agenda"
and "The Future of Women's Health," delivered in 1994, abortion-related
themes were diminished and emphasis was placed upon broader feminist issues.
In the former speech, she explained: "There is a bigger issue of which we must
not lose sight. The big picture is that *reproductive health care* is at the center
of women's struggle to achieve social, economic, and political equality." In the
latter speech, Wattleton acknowledged political changes, but suggested that
women's health needs continued to be a priority. She explained:

Some things have changed now that Bill Clinton is in the White House. But as
Will Rogers warned us, "Even if you're on the right track, you'll get run over if
you just sit there." Because reproductive rights and reproductive health are inextricably joined, this will be the arena in which the political struggle in the health
care debate will be most intense. Even beyond the politically charged issue of
abortion, women's health has not been given the priority it deserves.

"The Future of Women's Health" was delivered at Salem College in March
1994 and drew heavily upon recent research affecting women's health. This
speech represented a shift in her use of persuasive appeals. In order to adapt to
her college-educated audience, she relied on research evidence in the place of
emphatic, metaphorical language. Wattleton explained that prior to 1993, the
Food and Drug Administration did not publish guidelines recognizing that
women and men may react differently, in hormonal responses, to drug tests. She
warned that AIDS is expected to become one of the five leading causes of death

among women aged 15–44, yet little research explores women and AIDS. Wattleton wanted to see more research centered around screening for ovarian cancer. She also noted major studies of heart disease that found that women were less likely to be treated as aggressively as men, even though heart disease is a leading killer of women. She wanted to see more birth-control options for men explored so they could share ''the burden and responsibility of birth control.'' Wattleton also cited research indicating that women's and men's wishes regarding the termination of treatment are not given equal respect.

Underlying all of these health controversies were issues of gender bias and discrimination. Reporting the number of women and men in various elected positions, Wattleton noted that between 1776 and 1992, men outnumbered women 1,733 to 16 in the U.S. Senate, and 4 of the 16 women were elected in November 1992. Wattleton went on to cite research indicating that society tends to stifle young girls' sense of power for the sake of acceptance and approval, and that gender bias in schools and society accounts for a measurable loss of self-esteem in adolescent girls.

In a reflective narrative, Wattleton explained how her own background represented an enriching departure from cultural and gender norms and, in simple diction, explained her perception of her mission: ''The richness of my career is a blessing beyond all my expectations. I have been praised—and vilified,—but whatever I faced, it was not intimidating, because I stood for what I believed was right. I am the daughter of a woman. I stood for women. I stood for the future of my child—a woman.'' The speech concluded with quotations by the founder of Planned Parenthood, Margaret Sanger, and abolitionist Soujourner Truth that promoted empowerment. Like these women, Faye Wattleton is, and will continue to be, recognized for helping women.

An uncommon kind of power is unleashed when a passionately determined, competent orator leads a cause. Faye Wattleton's oratory is characterized by deeply held convictions, confidence, and commitment. Her speeches are often marked by stirring accounts of injustice and inequality, and she consistently challenges her audience to take specific action to promote personal choice. Although she is primarily known for her pro-choice message regarding abortion, her speeches touch on broader, yet related, themes. Through skillful oratory, Faye Wattleton has provided leadership for several consequential issues involving the role of the government and personal autonomy, gender equality, and other equally vital matters relating to equality and women's health.

INFORMATION SOURCES

Research Collections and Collected Speeches

Speech texts are available from the Planned Parenthood Federation, 810 7th Avenue, 12th Floor, New York, NY 10019. I thank Ellen Schorr and Alywnn Wilbur for their assistance.

Selected Biographies

Current Biography Yearbook, 51. Bronx, NY: H. W. Wilson, January 1990, 610–614.
Hine, Darlene, ed. *Black Women in America: An Historical Encyclopedia.* Brooklyn, NY:
    Carlson, 1993, 1239–1240.

CHRONOLOGY OF MAJOR SPEECHES

"The End of the Reagan Era: The State of Worldwide Reproductive Rights" (Speech
    to the Commonwealth Club). San Francisco, CA, January 21, 1988.
"March and Rally for Women's Equality/Women's Lives." Washington, DC, April 9,
    1989.
"Remarks by Faye Wattleton: Earth Day Central Park Rally." New York, NY, April
    22, 1990.
"Guaranteeing the Promise of *Roe*" (Speech to the Family Planning Advocates of New
    York State). Albany, NY, January 28, 1991.
"African-American Reproductive Choices" (Speech to the National Medical Association
    Council on the Concerns of Women Physicians). Indianapolis, IN, July 28, 1991.
"Sacred Rights: Preserving Our Reproductive Freedom" (Speech at the Marble Colle-
    giate Church). New York, NY, February 4, 1992.
"Planned Parenthood and Pro-Choice: Sexual and Reproductive Freedom" (Speech to
    the Columbus Metropolitan Club and Planned Parenthood of Central Ohio). Co-
    lumbus, OH, March 9, 1992.
"Equality, Liberty, and Justice: Women's Unfinished Agenda" (Speech at the Jewish
    Community Center of Norwalk). Westport, CT, May 6, 1993.
"The Future of Women's Health" (Speech at Salem College). Winston-Salem, NC,
    March 23, 1994.

IDA BELL WELLS-BARNETT
(1862–1931), journalist, civil rights activist, antilynching crusader

VIRGIE NOBLES HARRIS

Historians, political scholars, and rhetorical critics agree that Ida Wells-Barnett figured prominently in what has been frequently referred to as a one-woman campaign against lynching. The journalist-orator's investigative reporting, speeches, interviews, and publications shared one common objective, as Wells explained in *A Red Record*: to provide "a record which shows that a large portion of the American People avow anarchy, condone murder and defy the contempt of civilizations." Frederick Douglass's assessment of Wells's style and her astuteness as a journalist-orator is exemplary of contemporary as well as modern critical estimations. Claiming that "there has been no word equal to it in convincing power," Douglass said that Wells "dealt with the facts with cool, painstaking fidelity and left those naked and uncontradicted facts to speak for themselves." Wells's speaking and writing, argued Campbell, avoided the "stylistic markers indicating attempts by a woman speaker to appear 'womanly,' " instead developing strong logical arguments documented with irrefutable evidence from traditional Euro-American sources.

Born in Holly Springs, Mississippi, on July 16, 1862, Wells was the eldest of eight children. After the Emancipation Proclamation and the Civil War, Wells's parents became leaders in the Southern town. Her father, a successful contractor who restored many of the homes, factories, and civil buildings destroyed in the war, was elected to the board of Shaw University. During a yellow-fever epidemic, however, her parents and her younger brother died. At sixteen, Wells dropped out of Shaw University and assumed the responsibility for her surviving siblings. Without difficulty, Wells passed the teacher's examination and was employed as a schoolteacher in a one-room school in a nearby rural community. Later, Wells taught in Tennessee, California, and Missouri.

In 1884, while teaching in Memphis, the twenty-two-year-old Wells sued the Chesapeake and Ohio Railroad for not allowing her to use her first-class ticket to ride in the ladies' car. As white passengers cheered, the conductor and two cohorts lifted Wells, who refused to move, and deposited her in the smoking car. The headline in the December 25, 1884, edition of the *Memphis Daily* announced the outcome: "A Darky Damsel Obtains a Verdict for Damages against the Chesapeake and Ohio Railroad—What It Cost to Put a Colored School Teacher in a Smoking Car—Verdict for $500.00." Subsequently, however, the decision was reversed in the Supreme Court of Tennessee. Twelve years later, Duster recorded, Wells learned that her case "had attracted so much bitter attention and was fought so bitterly by the Chesapeake and Ohio Railroad" because "it was the first case in which a colored plaintiff of the South had appealed to the state court since the repeal of the Civil Rights Bill by the United States Supreme Court."

Undaunted by the Tennessee Supreme Court's decision, Wells used the case to launch a newspaper campaign for human rights. Wells's articles first appeared in the *Evening Star* and were later reprinted in the *Living Way*. Using the pen name "Iola," Wells became known as the "brilliant Iola" and the "Princess of the Press" because she "could handle a goose quill with a diamond point as easily as any man in newspaper work," wrote Thomas Fortune, editor of the *New York Age*.

In *The Afro-American Press and Its Editors*, I. Garland Penn expressed a similar view. Penn explained that Wells was not only a "writer with superb ability," but that she was also considered a member of "the newspaper fraternity." As a member of that "fraternity," Wells was elected assistant secretary at the 1887 National Afro-American Press Convention, held in Louisville, where she delivered her womanist speech, "Women in Journalism or How I Would Edit." At the March 4, 1889, National Press Association Convention held in Washington, D.C., Wells was elected secretary.

Wells earned the respect of the newspaper fraternity and that of her reading audience when she was editor and one-third owner of the *Free Speech and Headlight*. While working on this Memphis-based organ, Wells exposed both the inadequate education provided to African-Americans and the unjustifiable violence perpetrated against them. In an article on the Memphis lynching of Thomas Moss, Calvin McDowell, and Henry Stewart, successful African-American businessmen, Wells established that these men were not lynched in the defense of white womanhood, but, rather, their murder was a "barbaric" attempt to ensure white economic hegemony. For this factual account about the true cause of lynching, Wells's life was threatened, her business was destroyed, and she became an exile from the South. Still, neither the lynchers nor the white press could silence Ida Wells-Barnett.

In the years that followed, Wells worked as a journalist and a lecturer in New York, Chicago, and abroad. Traveling to Europe in 1893 and 1894 to gather support for the cause, she told her audiences that she had come to them because her race could not obtain a hearing in the United States. Neither the press nor the pulpit had spoken out against the shocking statistics that proved that lynchings were increasing, she said. Throughout Europe, Wells received a positive response, and she helped organize a Society for the Recognition of the Brotherhood of Man in several communities in Scotland and England.

On June 27, 1895, Wells married Ferdinand Lee Barnett, the famous editor of the Chicago-based newspaper, the *Conservator*. Although he was considered one of the best journalists in the nation, black or white, Barnett left journalism to become a successful attorney and politician. Prior to the marriage, Wells had purchased the *Conservator* and had become its new editor.

Throughout the 1890s and the first decade of the twentieth century, Wells exposed and attacked the evils of lynching with the publication of numerous books: *Southern Horrors: Lynch Law in All Its Phases* (1892), *The Reason Why the Colored American Is Not in the World's Columbian Exposition* (1893), *United States Atrocities* (London, 1893), *A Red Record: Tabulated Statistics and Alleged Causes of Lynching in the United States* (1895), *Lynch Law in Georgia* (1899), *Mob Rule in New Orleans: Robert Charles and His Fight to the Death* (1900), and *How Enfranchisement Stops Lynching* (1910). These volumes, combined with her numerous newspaper articles, lectures, and interviews in the United States and Europe, demonstrate Wells's commitment to exposing the atrocities of the mob that she described in *Southern Horror* as more brutalizing than slavery.

During a lifetime marked by achievements, Wells was also a charter member of the National Association for the Advancement of Colored People and was the founder of the first African-American female suffrage organization. In 1930, a year before her death, Wells ran for the state senate against Warren Douglass. Wells was defeated, but she continued her civil rights works. After a long and fruitful public career, impacting the national conscience during both the nineteenth and the twentieth centuries, Wells died on March 25, 1931, in Chicago.

EXPOSING THE TRUTH: WELLS AS JOURNALIST-ORATOR

Unmistakably, Ida Wells-Barnett's success as a journalist and as an orator was largely influenced by her commitment to truth. This commitment led her to develop the androgynous, deliberative style that she skillfully cultivated, in which her primary mode of persuasion was logos. Wells's style was androgynous in that it employed gender-inclusive language and was crafted to appeal to male and female audiences. In May of 1893, the editors of the *Manchester Guardian*, for example, opined that the "refined" orator's "intelligence and earnestness, her avoidance of all oratorical tricks and her dependence upon the simple eloquence of facts make her a powerful and convincing advocate."

While Wells left behind a voluminous library of her journalism and writings, few speech texts survive, despite her extensive lecture tours of the 1890s. Two major rhetorical artifacts, "Southern Horrors" and *A Red Record*, are probably representative of Wells's oratory generally. The former is a speech delivered early in her career, when she was first lecturing in the East and gaining national fame for her antilynching crusade. The latter was, according to Trudier Harris, Wells's most "inflammatory" publication and probably grew out of her experiences on her British and American speaking tours of 1894–95.

In "Southern Horrors: Lynch Law in All Its Phases," a speech delivered at Lyric Hall in New York City on October 5, 1892, Wells developed her argument first by reviewing the history of the subject and then proceeded to cite voluminous evidence to support her characterization of its present usage. Throughout the speech, she employed an androgynous deliberative style of address.

First, Wells reviewed the history of race relations in America and challenged Americans and the world to ask why the crime of rape was not a topic of discussion during the Civil War. Here was a period when Southern white women had to depend solely on black men and women, yet "the world knows that the crime of rape was unknown during the four years of the Civil War, when white women of the South were at the mercy of the race which is all at once charged with being a bestial one." Quoting J. C. Drake's article in the *Herald*, a Montgomery, Alabama, newspaper, Wells explained "that white women attract Negro men" because there was a "growing appreciation of white Juliets for colored Romeos." Bluntly, Wells argued that "white men lynch the offending Afro American, not because he is a despoiler of virtue, but because he succumbs to the smiles of white women." She followed this forthright assessment with several specific cases involving white women whose concupiscence for black men had been documented in the white press.

Continuing to construct her argument based on the facts of psychogenetic attractions, Wells noted that black women had been victims for four hundred years of rape by white men: "The miscegenation laws of the South only operate against the legitimate union of the races; they leave the white man free to seduce all the colored girls he can, but it is death to the colored man who yields to the force and advances of a similar attraction in white women." Proceeding then to statistical data recorded in the *Chicago Tribune*, Wells observed "the fact that only one-third of the 728 victims of the mob had been charged with rape, to say nothing of that one-third who were innocent of the charge." Wells cited the *Baltimore Sun*'s report that an African-American had been lynched even though he had been declared innocent by the victim. The girl had been raped instead by a white man. In most cases, Wells noted, white women were victims of intraracial rape.

Wells argued that "the malicious and untruthful white press"—for example, the *Daily Commercial* and the *Evening Scimitar*—made unscrupulous use of sensationalism and fostered unrest between the races. "In spite of the fact that there had been no white women outraged by an African-American," Wells said, headlines still read "More Rapes, More Lynchings." More often than not, she explained, African-Americans in Memphis were middle-class, "law-abiding, property owning and thrifty which was the reason this new cry of rape stalks

in broad daylight in large cities, the centres of civilization, and is encouraged
by the 'leading citizens' and the presses.''

In *A Red Record*, Wells continued to attack the alleged causes of lynching
and to expose the real ones. Wrote Trudier Harris, ''Wells refuted the charges
of rape through evidence and exposed the reason that the white man 'was compelled to give excuses for his barbarism.' '' Again taking a historical perspective,
Wells agreed with Frederick Douglass that there were three distinct eras of
''southern barbarism'' and that three distinct excuses had been made to defend
the ''appalling slaughter'' of African-Americans during these periods.

During the first period of Southern barbarism, occurring immediately after
the Civil War, the white man used ''race riots'' to explain his savagery. Not
only was there ''no proof of insurrections or riots,'' but there were also no
''apprehended'' or ''convicted rioters'' and no confiscated ''dynamite.'' Sus-
piciously, while blacks were routinely killed in these ''riots,'' whites escaped
unharmed: ''From 1865 to 1872, hundreds of colored men and women were
mercilessly murdered and the almost invariable reason assigned was insurrection
or riot.'' Recounting case after case and supplying provocative statistical data
to accompany the retelling, Wells explained that the second barbaric era took
place ''during the turbulent times of reconstruction.'' In a quest for white supremacy, ''the Ku Klux Klan, the Regulators, and the lawless mobs . . . [led a]
long, gory campaign.''

> The blood chills and the heart almost loses faith in Christianity when one thinks
> of Yazoo, Hamburg, Edgefield, Copiah and the countless massacres of defenseless
> Negroes, whose only crime was the attempt to exercise their right to vote. . . .
> Scourged from his home, hunted by midnight raiders, and openly murdered in the
> light of day, the Negro clung to his right of franchise with a heroism that would
> have wrung admiration from the hearts of savages.

Human rights as well as civil rights for African-Americans became a ''barren
ideality.''

Arguing that a psychological addiction to bizarre acts of violence took hold,
Wells said that the third barbaric era took place during the years of lynching in
''defense'' of white womanhood. Challenging the white man's ''chivalry,''
Wells recalled that after the Civil War ''thousands'' of white women came from
the North to teach black children, but had never been raped by black men.

> And yet these northern women worked on year after year, unselfishly, with heroism
> which amounted almost to martyrdom. Treading their way through dense forests,
> working in schoolhouses in the cabin and in the church . . . thousands of them
> have spent more than a quarter century [among] the colored people without pro-
> tection, save that which innocence gives every good woman, they went about their
> work, fearing no assault and suffering none. . . . They never complained of assaults
> and no mob was ever called into existence to avenge crimes against them.

With disquieting facility, Wells reminded her audience that indeed it had been the "chivalrous white men" who had insulted, persecuted, and ostracized these Northern white women. Millions of blacks, however, had respected and protected these white female teachers and missionaries. The journalist-orator scrupulously constructed her arguments to encourage a previously unthinking audience to consider the illogic of the Southern claim:

> To justify their own barbarism they assume a chivalry which they do not possess. True chivalry respects all womanhood, and no one who reads the record, as it is written on the face of the millions [of] mulattoes in the South, will for a minute conceive that the Southern white man had a very chivalrous regard for the honor due to women of his own race or respect for the womanhood which circumstances placed in his power. . . . Virtue knows no color line and that chivalry which depends upon complexion . . . can command no honest respect.

After carefully constructing the logic of her case, Wells cited statistics that were, again, recorded in the white presses, primarily by the *Chicago Tribune*. Wells persistently labored to expose the truth. The lynching of black men and women was not in the defense of white womanhood, but was instead a tactic designed to ensure white hegemony. For example, when whites were unable to pay black laborers, they often cried rape. When blacks owned successful businesses that took black income from the white business community, lynchings resulted. When white women and black men shared mutual relationships, mobs engaged in "bestial" acts. When black women and girls were raped by white men, however, the state police were called in to protect the rapists. Wells noted that in Tennessee, for example, one white rapist had become a detective with the police department.

Wells was equally appalled that whites considered lynching a social event and that they brought their children to witness the most inhumane acts of violence ever recorded in human history. Her concerns and arguments, she said, were "not for colored people alone," they were for all humanity. As Wells sought to free African-Americans from the crime of lynching, she simultaneously attempted to free the lyncher by exposing his psychopathic behavior to the nation and to himself.

Unlike most women during this period in history, Wells spoke and wrote with the authority of a leader. Wells not only stated the problem, cited examples, and cultivated an androgynous style that appealed to both genders, but she also provided workable solutions to the problem. Relentlessly, Wells argued that everyone was entitled to a trial. She challenged blacks to investigate lynching for themselves and to determine the facts. She encouraged economic boycotts and urged blacks to move west. Equally important, Wells encouraged blacks to arm themselves to protect their families and businesses. Here again, Wells presented evidence of examples where these methods of self-protection had been used successfully.

Wells's appeals did not go unnoticed. Publicly, white Southern women began to doubt the Southern justification of lynching. Like Wells, Jessie Daniel Ames realized that among whites a "fear of the future and a definite hopelessness in the present prevailed throughout the country." Surreptitious organizations like the Klan, these women began to admit, were organized to uphold white supremacy, which translated into "jobs for white men before Negroes" and, as Wells had postulated, ensured white economic hegemony. In 1930, Ames founded the Association of Southern Women for the Prevention of Lynching.

Campbell argued that Wells was successful in persuading people like Ames because her arguments "rested on kinds of evidence that made the problem vivid, demonstrated its scope [and] supported the speaker's analysis of its causes." As early as 1882, Frederick Douglass had written, "Brave woman! You have done your people and mine a service which can neither be weighed nor measured."

"Nobody in this section of the country believes the old threadbare lie that Negro men rape white women," Wells argued, and it was this daring candor that marked her success. The rhetorical power of Wells's argument lies in her commitment to the truth, her objective use of the facts, and her androgynous style. Wells's stylistic approach has rarely been mastered by modern rhetors, male or female. By tenaciously challenging the moral fabric of both continents, Wells crafted a place for herself in American and European history.

INFORMATION SOURCES

Research Collections and Collected Speeches

[*SWW*] Harris, Trudier, ed. *Selected Works of Ida B. Wells-Barnett*. New York: Oxford UP, 1991.

[*CFJ*] Wells, Ida B. *Crusade for Justice: The Autobiography of Ida B. Wells*. Ed. Alfreda M. Duster. Chicago: U of Chicago P, 1970.

———. *Our Day: A Record and Review of Current Reform*. Boston: Our Day Publishing, 1893.

Wells-Barnett, Ida B. *Lynch Law in Georgia*. Chicago: Chicago Colored Citizens, 1899.

[*OLS*]———. *On Lynchings*. Ed. August Meier. New York: Arno, 1969.

Selected Critical Studies

Campbell, Karlyn Kohrs. *Man Cannot Speak For Her*. Vol. 1. New York: Praeger, 1989, 145–150.

———. "Style and Content in the Rhetoric of Early Afro-American Feminists." *Quarterly Journal of Speech* 72 (1986): 434–445.

Tucker, David M. "Miss Ida B. Wells and Memphis Lynching." *Phylon* 32 (Summer 1971): 112–122.

Selected Biographies

Aptheker, Herbert, ed. *A Documentary History of the Negro People in the United States*. New York: Citadel, 1951.

Brawley, Benjamin. *Negro Builders and Heroes*. Chapel Hill: U of North Carolina P, 1937.

Gosnell, Harold F. *Negro Politicians: The Rise of Negro Politics in Chicago*. Chicago: U of Chicago P, 1935.

Hold, Thomas C. "The Lonely Warrior: Ida B. Wells-Barnett and the Struggle for Black Leadership." *Black Leaders of the Twentieth Century*. Ed. John Hope Franklin and August Meier. Chicago: U of Chicago P, 1982. 39–61.

Penn, I. Garland. *The Afro-American Press and its Editors*. New York: Arno, 1969.

Thompson, Mildred I. *Ida B. Wells-Barnett*. Brooklyn, NY: Carlson, 1990.

Van Deusen, John G. *The Black Man in White America*. Washington, DC: Associated Publishers, 1938.

CHRONOLOGY OF MAJOR SPEECHES

[See "Research Collections and Collected Speeches" for source codes.]

"Southern Horrors: Lynch Law in All Its Phases" (Address at Lyric Hall). New York, NY, October 5, 1892. *SWW,* 14–45; *OLS,* 4–24. Described in *CFJ,* 78–80.

"Lynch Law in All Its Phases" (Address at Tremont Temple). Boston, MA, February 13, 1893. *Our Day*, May 1893, 333–337; Thompson, 171–187.

"United States Atrocities." London, England, 1893. No copy extant.

"Lynching, Our National Crime." New York, NY, May 31–June 1, 1909. *Proceedings of the National Negro Conference 1909*. New York: n.p., 1909, 174–179, 197–206.

"How Enfranchisement Stops Lynching." 1910. No copy extant.

WILLIAM WHIPPER
(c.1804–1876), businessman, abolitionist, reform activist

Thomas M. Lessl

William Whipper earned his place in the history of the abolition movement as an orator, editor, and active participant in the Underground Railroad. Although much less remembered than such African-American orators as Frederick Douglass, Sojourner Truth, and Henry Highland Garnet, Whipper was widely recognized as an intellectual spokesperson for African-Americans in the nineteenth century. His prominence as a writer, speaker, and editor grew out of his active involvement with the African-American convention movement of the 1830s and 1840s. He was especially well known during this time for his Christian idealism and his firm commitment to nonviolence and to the abolition of all distinctions based on race. Twelve years before the publication of Thoreau's essay on civil disobedience, Whipper had already taken a position in favor of nonresistance to aggression, and more than a century before the civil rights career of Martin Luther King, Jr., he was expounding arguments in favor of racial integration. Although these two positions were not always preeminent in the rhetorical struggles of African-Americans before the abolition of slavery, their pronouncement in Whipper's discourses provides a unique opportunity to observe how they compare with competing rhetorics in another age.

Few details are available with which we can piece together a picture of Whipper's life. We know that he was the offspring of an African-American servant girl and her white master, and that he worked in and eventually inherited his father's lumber business in Columbia, Pennsylvania. Whipper used his considerable wealth and influence to advance the cause of his people. His generosity and compassion, abetted by the tactical location of his business along the Susquehanna River in southern Pennsylvania, enabled him to become one of the foremost actors in the Underground Railroad movement. Whipper gave not only food and shelter to the hundreds of fugitive slaves who passed through his home on their way to freedom in Canada but also his riches. Whipper's livelihood was itself greatly endangered after the passage of the Fugitive Slave Law of 1850, and he gave serious thought to the prospect of following into Canada those he had helped to escape slavery. But the outbreak of the Civil War encouraged the hope that a new civilization might be established on American soil, and he remained until his death in 1876.

Whipper's rhetorical efforts on behalf of his race were centered largely in the city of Philadelphia, which was the most prominent community for free African-Americans in the 1830s. It was here that Whipper opened a free-labor grocery store in 1834, not only as an economic measure designed to provide goods not produced by slave labor but also as an outlet for abolitionist and temperance books and pamphlets.

Most of what can be known of Whipper's career as an abolitionist speaker and writer must be drawn from a handful of addresses and published essays that were recorded in the pages of the influential African-American newspaper, the *Colored American*. As a rhetorical figure, Whipper was often at the center of controversy, not so much for his commitment to nonviolent resistance, which he shared with the Garrisonians, as for his rather extreme integrationist stance. Whipper wished to banish all linguistic demarcations of race and was resistant to the formation of any institutions that were exclusively African-American. The reality of his people's plight and the intractable opposition of the majority of abolitionists made it necessary for him to soften this position later in his life. He would also eventually modify his belief that the emancipation of African-Americans could be accomplished by self-improvement alone. This belief had been key to his important role in the founding of the short-lived Moral Reform Society and to his service as the editor of that society's organ, the *National Reformer*.

NONVIOLENCE AND INTEGRATION: WILLIAM WHIPPER'S CHRISTIANITY

No historical records exist that provide a window through which to examine the education or development of William Whipper as a writer and speaker. However, in the earliest of his published speeches, made in 1828 to inaugurate the Colored Reading Society of Philadelphia, Whipper revealed some aspects of his own oratorical training. He did this in part by example, but he also did so by virtue of the speech's topic—the advancement of African-Americans through the liberal arts—which necessitated some comment on the requirements of a rhetorical education. By virtue of this concern, this particular speech provides us with some insight into Whipper's own rhetorical tastes. He began his address by expressing his modest antipathy for what he called the "fastidious" style of his age that "demands eloquence, figure, rhetoric, and pathos." But as Whipper turned to his description of such popular ornamentation, we can see that his own style was by no means plain:

> Such high-wrought artificial lectures, however, are like beautiful paint upon windows, they rather obscure than admit the light of the sun. Truth should always be exhibited in such a dress as may be best suited to the state of the audience, accompanied with every principle of science and reason.

The alternative notion of eloquence that Whipper demonstrated, with its measured dignity, its invocation of science, and its concrete sensibilities regarding the audience, is suggestive of the Scottish rhetoricians. He explicitly acknowledged his allegiance to the philosophy of the mind that most influenced the rhetorical theories of George Campbell and Hugh Blair.

If any teacher of rhetoric left a mark on Whipper, one would have to speculate that this would be Blair, for Whipper attached considerable importance to the individual's development of those powers of judgment that Blair had popularly associated with the notion of "taste." Thus he urged his friends to understand that "learning must furnish the material; taste must give the polish, and in many cases the capacity of useful application. It is therefore not without good reason that in a system of education so much attention is required to the study of belles lettres, to criticism, to composition, pronunciation, style, and to everything included in the name of eloquence."

These reflections of Whipper's give some indication of the advantages he enjoyed as an African-American orator and essayist who clearly benefited from a mainstream education. He reads also as one imbued with a substantial measure of Enlightenment faith in the emancipatory powers of reason. This faith may account for his optimism about the prospects of education that are heralded in his early speeches as the means for eliminating prejudice. Whipper believed that the emancipation of African-Americans, both free and slave, could be accomplished through moral and intellectual development alone. Somewhat naively, at least in the view of most of his peers, Whipper believed that the ability of his race to show forth its moral and rational integrity would demonstrate the futility and error of all prejudice.

However, Whipper's faith in reason was only one leg of his abolitionism; the other more powerful leg was Christianity. Whipper's oratory is permeated by Christian symbolism and ideals, and in all of his speeches religious conviction provides the premises that drive his arguments. In this regard, Whipper evinced a form of Christianity that was prominent in the early nineteenth century, one that had appropriated Enlightenment notions of the emancipatory power of rationality, but firmly grounded these ideas in the concept of Divine Providence. It was Christian belief that ultimately authorized Whipper's vision of interracial harmony and that underscored in his rhetoric the unity of human beings as children of one God.

The influence of Enlightenment ideals in Whipper's oratory, at least during the earlier part of his career, is most evident in his argument that the oppression of African-Americans was a product of their condition rather than their complexion. This theme constituted the basis of much of the discourse that he produced during the 1830s, his most active years as an abolitionist speaker and writer. However, a letter written to Frederick Douglass in 1854 indicates that his perspective on this issue had been modified by this time. In this case, Whipper's Christian conviction of an entrenched sinfulness in human nature superseded his earlier optimism about the liberating power of reason. Prejudice, Whipper concluded, was simply too deeply rooted in human beings as an effect of "man's selfish nature, pride and ambition" to be quickly eradicated.

> It grows spontaneously, inflates the instincts of the ignorant, and directs the minds of the learned. It has a home at the fireside and the altar. It follows men to the loftiest heights of ambition, and down to the deepest grave.

The pessimism that Whipper expressed in this letter to Douglass would never deter his belief that the "moral improvement" proffered by education would help African-Americans to surmount prejudice. Rather, the older Whipper would choose to augment his program of moral improvement with more concrete policies such as Canadian emigration and the establishment of African-American churches.

The most prominent of Whipper's religious beliefs were responsible for his position favoring nonaggression. Whipper's pacifist convictions provided the theme of his best-known and most impressive oration, "Non-Resistance to Offensive Aggression." Whipper gave this speech in 1837 at the convention of the American Moral Reform Society in Philadelphia, where he spoke to the resolution that "non-resistance to physical aggression, is not only consistent with reason, but the surest method of obtaining a speedy triumph of the principles of universal peace." Although supporting the resolution, Whipper also wished to protest its insinuation that

> if there were no God to guide and govern the destinies of man on this planet, no Bible to light his path through the wilds of sin, darkness and error, and no religion to give him a glorious and lasting consolation while traversing the gloomy vale of despondency ... mankind might enjoy an exalted state of civilization, peace and quietude in their social, civil and international relations, far beyond that which Christians now enjoy, guarded and protected by the great Author of all good and the doctrines of the Prince of Peace.

Whipper's position was clearly the inverse of this allegation, and his "Non-Resistance" speech was an affirmation and defense of pacifism as something that could be sustained only by a rationality expressed through Christian principles. In affirming the Christian position, and perhaps in deference to the many ordained clergymen in the abolitionist ranks, Whipper did not undertake a biblical exegesis. Instead he labored within a Christian frame to forge an understanding of the connections that bind faith and reason together. Whipper accomplished this not so much by attacking the rationalistic assumptions of his opponents as by endeavoring to Christianize their understanding of reason.

Whipper asked his audience to recognize that reason is not the source of truth itself and that it cannot empower human beings to do what is right:

> There is a right and a wrong method of reasoning. The latter is governed by our animal impulses and wicked desires, without regard for the end to be attained. The former fixes its premises, in great fundamental and unalterable truths—surveys the magnitude of the objects and the difficulties to be surmounted, and calls to its aid the resources of enlightened wisdom as a landmark by which to conduct its operations.

The thesis that Whipper spoke against here was a commonplace of the prevalent Enlightenment thought of his day, the supposition that reason is itself capable of making provision for a just society. Reason, Whipper's message contended, may bear witness to the futility of violence, but it is not capable of overcoming the "spirit of conquest" that feeds our thirst for blood. Reason may bear witness to the truth of pacifism, but it has no power to enforce it. Peace is only fostered when humans reason within the framework of revelation and a devotion to the "will of their Author."

Whipper reminded his audience that an abolitionism that rejected the Christian principle that evil must not be repaid in kind might instead adopt the premise that "resistance to tyrants is obedience to God." In alluding to the concept that had recently inspired France's Reign of Terror, Whipper was warning against any philosophy of political action that wandered too far from Christian morality.

In this speech Whipper addressed two problems that were as evident in the abolition movement's early struggles as they have been in struggles for African-American emancipation ever since. The first issue is the ethical dilemma of trying to overcome violence without also becoming a party to violence. The second issue is a problem of social attribution, the problem of determining which elements of a society should be held accountable for the evils of slavery and prejudice. The second problem bears on the first to the extent that while Whipper founded his commitment to nonresistance on Christian principles, it was also clear to him—as already indicated—that many of his contemporaries regarded Christian beliefs as the social factor that accounted for the violence and perpetuation of slavery.

Whipper responded to this exigence by asserting that Christian principles are the sole means by which human beings may overcome oppression. Whipper did not directly undertake the construction of an apologetic for Christianity; instead he put Christian ideas to work in his speech in an effort to demonstrate their liberating potentiality.

An interesting and important feature of the "Non-Resistance" speech is Whipper's determination to construct an understanding of the problems of racism and slavery from the vantage point of a much more general theory of evil.

In this sense slavery and the abolitionists' response to it were only secondary topics of the oration. Its primary topics were sinfulness in the human condition and the requirements that God imposes upon human beings who wish to have done with evil. In the popular language of faculty psychology that Whipper so often used to articulate his theology, we see that the eradication of evil requires that the individual allow "reason" to rule over the "passions." Reason is put forward as the faculty through which the nature of God is most clearly manifested in human beings, and thus any policy that is an expression of the irrational side of our humanity, namely the "passions," is evil. If the violence of slavery is to be overcome, human beings must "be ready to sacrifice on the altar of principle the rude passions that animate them. This they can only perform by exerting their reasoning powers." But above all, humanity must place its faith "in Him who is able to protect them from danger or they will soon fall a prey to the wicked artifices of their wicked enemies."

Whipper took the position that the eradication of evil is only truly accomplished when it begins inwardly, in the subjection of one's soul to the law of God. Rather than struggling to eradicate racism through force or even through legislation—which he regarded as powerless in the face of inward bigotry—Whipper envisioned a program of education for African-Americans that would enable them, by morally perfecting themselves as individuals, to lay the foundation of a just government. "The power of reason," Whipper declared, "is the noblest gift of Heaven to man, because it assimilates man to his Maker. And were he to improve his mind by cultivating his reasoning powers, his acts of life would bear the impress of the Deity indelibly stamped upon them."

While his arguments against violence were based on the principle that "what is scriptural is right," Whipper also recognized the practical rhetorical power of nonresistance. He regarded nonresistance as right because it expressed the highest principles of morality, but it was rhetorically powerful for the same reason. The power of the antislavery position becomes self-evident, Whipper stated, when the enemies of abolition "frequently muster a whole neighborhood of from 50 to 300 men, with sticks, stones, rotten eggs and bowie knives, to mob and beat a single individual . . . whose heart's law is nonresistance."

It is Whipper's commitment to what is "eternal" and "immutable" as the bases for the abolition movement that appears to be most central to his rhetorical career. Thus in the first of three letters responding to the separatist motions of the Albany Convention of Colored Citizens of 1841, he wrote that he could accept actions and ideas only if he believed that they "emanated from the pure foundation of heaven-born truth." Whipper could not reconcile the growing popularity of separatism and African nationalism to an understanding of African-American emancipation based on Christian principles. Thus in these three letters, published in the *Colored American* during January 1841, he took the Albany Convention of Colored Citizens to task for simultaneously passing resolutions that deplored distinctions of "complexion" while also excluding white membership. It was not merely hypocrisy that Whipper protested against; rather, it was the fact that the convention was operating outside the bounds of a Christian principle that he regarded as unassailable—the fundamental equality of human beings as children of God. This Whipper regarded as "a detestable prejudice" and no less an "infringement of the 'divine law' " when practiced by African-Americans than when practiced by whites. Thus Whipper deemed it

> peculiarly appropriate for any people that have long been trodden under foot by the "iron heel" of any peculiar despotism that when they appeal to the rectitude of just principles in behalf of their deliverance, that they should first exhibit to the world, that they were not only prepared to act upon those principles themselves, but that they had hurled that principle of despotism from their own borders.

The strict integrationist stand that arose from this opposition to all forms of hypocrisy never became popular among the abolitionists of Whipper's generation. Indeed, it often caused Whipper to be regarded as a radical. Nevertheless, it is interesting that Whipper protested against reverse discrimination not only on principle but also on rhetorical grounds. While he firmly believed that the human family was one and that any representation of it as otherwise was a basis for oppression, he also believed that the purposes of the abolitionist conventions could not be achieved if African-Americans were found to perpetuate the same racial distinctions that their white oppressors employed. A strong integrationist position safeguarded against any appearance of contradiction and was thus regarded by Whipper as a necessary basis for the movement's ethos.

Arguably, the prescience of Whipper's integrationist beliefs may reflect the uniqueness of his own position as a free African-American living within a white society that was still a long way from granting such privileges to ethnic minorities more generally. Among the people of color living in the early nineteenth century, Whipper was one of a handful of individuals who enjoyed a degree of liberty that can only be purchased by wealth. While we have no record of Whipper's treatment at the hands of his white Pennsylvania neighbors, the fact that he owned and ran a successful lumber business and was involved in a number of other entrepreneurial pursuits indicates that he was integrated into mainstream society, at least in an economic sense. The quality and style of his writing and speaking also indicate that he had been integrated into the educational mainstream of white society.

Because he was devoted to the principle that human conduct ought to derive from what Scripture reveals, Whipper was as uncompromising in his devotion to racial integration as he was to nonviolence. On both of these counts, one cannot help but notice the extent to which the views adopted and expressed in Whipper's messages presage those of Martin Luther King, Jr. This is not entirely surprising, despite the fact that their lives were separated by a full century. Like King, Whipper employed New Testament principles not only to expose the immorality of white behavior toward African-Americans but also, and perhaps

more importantly, to safeguard the moral witness of the movement he represented.

INFORMATION SOURCES

Research Collections and Collected Speeches

No manuscripts of Whipper's speeches are known to still exist, but some biographical
information may be found in the Leigh Whipper Papers in the Moorland-Springarn Research Center at Howard University.

[*NPU*] Aptheker, Herbert, ed. *A Documentary History of the Negro People in the United
States*. New York: Citadel, 1951.
[*VBA*] Foner, Philip S., ed *The Voice of Black America: Major Speeches by Negroes in
the United States, 1797–1971*. New York: Capricorn, 1972.
[*ENW*] Porter, Dorothy, ed. *Early Negro Writing, 1760–1837*. Boston: Beacon, 1971.
[*BAP*] Ripley, C. Peter, ed. *The Black Abolitionist Papers*. Vol. 3, *The United States,
1830–1846*. Chapel Hill: U of North Carolina P, 1991.
[*IOB*] Stuckey, Sterling. *The Ideological Origins of Black Nationalism*. Boston: Beacon,
1972.
[*NOO*] Woodson, Carter G., ed. *Negro Orators and Their Orations*. Washington DC:
Associated Publishers, 1925.

Selected Biographies

Logan, Rayford W. and Michael R. Winston, ed. *Dictionary of American Negro Biog-
raphy*. New York: W. W. Norton, 1982.
McCormick, Richard P. "William Whipper: Moral Reformer." *Pennsylvania History* 43
(1976): 23–46.
Quarles, Benjamin. *Black Abolitionists*. New York: Oxford UP, 1969.
Still, William. *The Underground Rail Road*. Philadelphia: Porter and Coates, 1872. Re-
print. New York: Arno, 1968.
Stuckey, Sterling. *The Ideological Origins of Black Nationalism*. Boston: Beacon, 1972.

CHRONOLOGY OF MAJOR SPEECHES

[See "Research Collections and Collected Speeches" for source codes.]

"An Address Delivered before the Colored Reading Society of Philadelphia." Philadel-
phia, PA, June 1828. *ENW*, 106–119.
"First Annual Negro Convention," June 1831. *NPU*, 115–118; *Liberator*, October 22,
1831. (This message is signed by Belfast Burton, Junius C. Morel, and William
Whipper.)
"To the Honorable the Senate and House of Representatives of the Commonwealth of
Pennsylvania." *NPU*, 126–131. (This is signed by William Whipper, Robert
Purvis, and James Forten.)

"Eulogy on William Wilberforce." Philadelphia, PA, December 6, 1833. *VBA,* 71–78. Published originally as a pamphlet by the Historical Society of Pennsylvania.

"An Address Delivered before the Colored Temperance Society of Philadelphia." Philadelphia, PA, January 1834. *BAP,* 119–129; *Liberator,* June 21, June 28, July 5, 1834.

"To the American People." Philadelphia, PA, June 3, 1835. *BAP,* 146–151; *Minutes of the Fifth Annual Convention for the Improvement of the Free People of Color in the United States, 1835.* Philadelphia: np, 1836. (The names of Alfred Niger and Augustus Price are added to Whipper's in this document, but Whipper himself is regarded as the primary author.)

"Non-Resistance to Offensive Aggression." September 1837. *NOO,* 104–118; *BAP,* 238–251; *Colored American,* September 9, September 16, September 23, September 30, 1837.

"Three Letters in Opposition to Black Separatism." January 3, January 10, January 17, 1841. *IOB,* 252–260; *Colored American.*

LAWRENCE DOUGLAS WILDER
(1931–   ), lawyer, politician, governor

NINA-JO MOORE

In their book *Speech Criticism*, Lester Thonssen, A. Craig Baird and Waldo W. Braden noted that the "speaking accomplishments of a public figure are often interwoven with the story of his life." These writers also contended that while the history of a person's life is important to the way he or she chooses to speak, one needs to examine the social patterns in which the speaker's thoughts were expressed and not just the sequence of events in his or her life. The oratory of Lawrence Douglas Wilder illustrates that view. Raised from a young age to speak clearly and cogently, Wilder has always seen public speaking as an avenue of advancement rather than an obstacle to progress. He is the successful son of a Depression-era family, and the economics of poverty and the ethics of work have always been central to his oratory.

Wilder, a child of the Great Depression, was born on January 17, 1931, in Richmond, Virginia. His father, Robert, was an insurance salesman, while his mother, Beulah, worked as a maid. In an interview the author conducted with Wilder, he reminisced about being raised in the "poor and segregated Church Hill section," the son of a poor African-American family and the grandson of slaves. He came from what he called "very humble beginnings." It was in these early years of his life, within the confines of his own family, that he began his public speaking experiences. His great-aunt helped his mother a great deal in those years in the matter of finances as well as in raising the children. His aunt would hold what she called "Silver Teas," and the children were expected to attend and participate. There they were to "speak properly" or be punished severely if they did not. In addition to some "proper speaking," the eight Wilder children performed at these teas, some playing the piano, while others sang. Douglas could do neither very well, so he took to "reciting things." These private experiences gave him confidence for speaking publicly; in fact, he believed that he was an outstanding speaker at this point in his life. It was only much later, when he actually received some instruction and watched some highly accomplished speakers, that he realized that he was still a beginning public speaker.

Wilder's formal introduction to public speaking came when he attended Virginia Union University, where he majored in chemistry. He credits his speech professors, E. Paul Sims and Edwin McCrary, with providing him with an understanding of the importance of good public speaking skills. In his interview, Wilder smiled as he recalled this first public speaking instruction. Better than forty years had passed, yet the memory of these two instructors was as vivid to Wilder as if it had been the previous year. Wilder said that what he most appreciated about these professors was their "crisp and clear style" and their ethics. Wilder's speaking style exemplifies these qualities as well: he uses a clear, concise organizational pattern in addition to clear signposting and transitions, and he speaks his mind as clearly as he organizes his thoughts.

During this time, Wilder also became fascinated with people he thought communicated well and with teachers who could "hold you in the palm of their hand." Wilder readily named speakers whom he believed had this ability, especially ones from his college years. Three he named were Sam Proctor, E. Paul Sims, and Mordecai Johnson, who had been administrators, professors, and preachers from his days at Virginia Union and whose communication skills had obviously left a lasting impression on him.

After graduating from college in 1951, Wilder was drafted into the army, where he was sent to fight in the Korean War. There he received a Bronze Star for valor after seeing action near Pork Chop Hill. While in the army he filed a formal complaint regarding the slow pace of integration, a legal action that resulted in speedier recognition for African-American servicemen.

After working in the state medical examiner's office as a chemist, Wilder used the GI bill to enroll in the Howard University Law School in 1956. Wilder's days at Howard Law School in the 1950s gave him a new and different view of public speaking. His focus turned to how to speak effectively in front of judges and juries. Wilder admitted that he found it hard to keep quiet at this time in his life, perhaps setting the tone for his later years in the political arena.

Wilder graduated with his J.D. in 1959 and returned to Richmond to establish a private practice. In 1969, he ran for the state senate and became the first black elected to the Virginia legislature when his two opponents split the white vote. Early in his legislative career he was confrontational and flamboyant, using his maiden speech to denounce the legislature for its racist policies. Behind the scenes, however, he also became known for his hard work and diligence, so that by the end of his tenure he had been named one of the five most influential state senators.

In July of 1984, a more moderate, more pragmatic Wilder announced, to the surprise of many, that he was running for the Democratic nomination for lieutenant governor. In November of 1985, Wilder was elected lieutenant governor with 51 percent of the vote and became the first African-American to hold a statewide office in the South since Reconstruction. Despite some professional and personal controversy with the governor, Gerald Baliles, and one of Virginia's U.S. senators, Chuck Robb, Wilder won the Democratic nomination for governor in 1989 without opposition. Wilder won the general election by 6,741 votes—one-third of 1 percent of those cast. In 1992 he made a short run at the Democratic presidential nomination, but withdrew early in the primary season. The Virginia Constitution limits governors to one four-year term, which forced Wilder's retirement—perhaps only temporarily—from public office. In the summer of 1994, he made a brief run as an independent candidate for the U.S. Senate, campaigning in a four-way race against Chuck Robb (Democrat), Oliver North (Republican), and Marshall Coleman (independent). He withdrew, however, when it became clear from the polls that the race was a tight one between Robb and North, with little chance for either of the independents to win.

DOUGLAS WILDER: SPEAKING FROM THE HEART

It is perhaps uncharacteristic for a politician to "speak from the heart," but in matters of content and style, not only has Douglas Wilder done so, he has done so successfully. He talks about those issues that concern him, and he frames those concerns in arguments that speak simply and directly. Stylistically, he avoids excessive imagery and flowery phrases, choosing instead a delivery that reflects the "crisp and clear" style that he admired in his speech professors.

Wilder firmly believes that a person should take a position and "stick with it," and his oratory has typically reflected this debate-style approach. Wilder often contextualizes his issues by referring to arguments that have been made or to those that he anticipates will be made. For example, responding to media criticism that he had been an absentee governor while campaigning for the Democratic presidential nomination, in his 1992 State of the Commonwealth Address Wilder argued that "I recognize that there are a number of Virginians whose only opinions about my tenure are based on news reports that speak of my being outside the Commonwealth. So perhaps this is a good time to boast a bit where before I have been too modest." He continued:

My administration has worked hard to prepare our Commonwealth for the future, and I say to you again today that Virginia is my top priority. I understand the concerns of those who question my role in national politics, but I stand firm before you tonight on the pledge I have taken—to serve the people of this Commonwealth. I invite you to study my tenure and look at what we have achieved.

Wilder then enumerated the accomplishments of his office in the two years of his tenure as governor. He returned to the issue in his closing statements:

> Long before I announced for President, I said that if it became too difficult for me to govern the Commonwealth and conduct a Presidential Campaign, I would terminate one endeavor. I was left with a choice, either to devote all my energies to delivering that message or to guiding Virginia through these difficult times. I have chosen the latter, as my pledge and responsibilities demand. Therefore, I stand before you to state that I am hereby withdrawing from the Presidential race.

It is representative of Wilder's debate approach that his response to the criticism of absenteeism was to first argue for his position but to then accede to the general thrust of the criticism. He was not adverse to having people argue against him, but he was going to make sure that his side of the argument was understood before he made any changes himself.

Perhaps one of the best examples of Wilder's tactics of argument occurred in his 1993 State of the Commonwealth Address response to those who criticized his gun-control plan. Despite the volatility of the issue, and knowing that many Virginians would not support his plan to "place a one gun per month limit on firearm purchases" or "allow the State Police to retain record of instant background approvals for twelve months," Wilder still presented his position clearly and concisely. Challenging the legislators directly, Wilder framed the issue as one of ethical responsibility:

> There's not a legislator among you who does not think of him or herself as a friend of law enforcement. But when a majority of those who put their lives on the line every day plead through their representatives for your help, will you substitute your judgment for theirs? These are commonsense measures that a majority of Virginia gun owners will support if they are given the correct information. Certain organizations have an interest in misleading the voters and members of the General Assembly, and will rely on spreading fears, using slogans, and making threats. Maybe these special interests can offer you something, something you may believe you cannot do without. As an alternative, I can offer you nothing . . . nothing but a clear conscience. One day, when you leave these halls, will you be able to say with confidence and pride that you did everything you could to protect Virginia's good name and heritage?

Wilder then moved from an ethical appeal to an emotional one.

> Will you be able to visit an inner-city school and say that you did everything in your power to keep stray bullets from the playground? Will you be able to pick up the newspaper and say you made your best effort to keep teenaged boys and girls off the obituary pages and away from trafficking in guns and drugs? . . . I welcome any constructive amendments and changes to this legislation, as long as it has the effect of increasing the peace. Credit and acclaim is not important to me, what is important is being able to say "enough."

Of Wilder's political positions, state finances and the economy took the forefront during his tenure as governor; indeed, he began every State of the Commonwealth address by discussing the financial issues facing Virginia. Wilder's concern with the economy probably results from his roots as a poor child of the Great Depression era. In his State of the Commonwealth addresses, one finds that Wilder suggested that he had the answers to the questions on how to solve the problems of the economic recession Virginia was suffering from in 1990–92. Just as he had been able to pull himself from poverty to wealth, there was a confidence that the same qualities of hard work, diligence, and fairness would be successful for him as governor.

As one who speaks his mind and his heart, Wilder has championed the cause of equal treatment for all people. He set that tone of equality in his Inaugural Address, delivered in January 1990:

> In the coming years, we must persist and make every citizen of our Commonwealth the subject of our interest and concern. We must insist that every agency of our government utilize every proper and effective instrument to carry out the will of the people—for, as with any democracy . . . the will of the people is supreme. An administration can only be effective when it works for the people . . . all of the people.

Wilder especially reached out to touch those who had endured hardship, had been oppressed, or had experienced discrimination:

> If these words about freedom are to be heard today, I hope they will be heard by the young people of this Commonwealth. I want them to know: . . . that oppression can be lifted; . . . that discrimination can be eliminated; . . . that poverty need not be binding; . . . that disability can be overcome.

Within this litany of the disenfranchised, of course, Wilder was describing himself. He had loosed the bonds of poverty and lifted the oppression. If he had not eliminated discrimination, he had at least overcome it to rise from the Church Hill section of Richmond to the governor's mansion itself. Others, too, could overcome oppression, discrimination, poverty, and disability, and state government should help provide them the opportunity to do so.

But while Wilder sounded the themes of equality and opportunity, he was also criticized by many African-American minority groups because he was not more vocal about their plight in American society generally and Virginia specifically. He was accused by many of not being proactive in this area. Wilder, however, did not move from his position that equality and opportunity brought with them responsibility. The close of his Inaugural Address is representative:

> The idea . . . that all men and women are created equal; . . . that they are endowed by their Creator with certain inalienable rights; . . . the right to life . . . lib-

erty . . . and the pursuit of happiness. . . . [These rights] that offer the opportunity in a free society carries with it the requirement of hard work, the rejection of drugs and other false highs, and a willingness to work with others whatever their color or national origin.

If equal opportunity generally meant individual responsibility, for state government it particularly meant fair treatment in education. In Wilder's 1990 State of the Commonwealth Address, delivered less than one month after he took office, he created a Governor's Commission on Educational Opportunity for all Virginians that would examine "the issue of disparity in education." Each subsequent State of the Commonwealth address returned to this issue. Each year Wilder called on the legislature to enact measures to ensure an equal education for all students in Virginia. In his 1991 State of the Commonwealth Address, he revealed some of the wellsprings of his concern: "Perhaps more than some, I know about the educational disparity one may face in their youth. . . . Even in 1991, circumstances of birth play far too great a role in determining whether *all* children get the education needed to develop their potential."

Wilder is not only straightforward about his political positions and personal beliefs, but he is always unembarrassed by his civic pride, especially regarding his native state. His speeches are replete with numerous historical references, particularly involving Virginia. Wilder obviously believes in Cicero's conception of a commonwealth, a conception Wilder quoted in his Inaugural Address: "A Commonwealth is not any collection of human beings . . . but an assembly of people joined in agreement on justice and partnership for the common good, and a community where civility must reign and all must live peacefully together."

It is unsurprising, given this view of a commonwealth, that Wilder especially preferred to reference Virginia's role in the founding of the country. In his Inaugural Address, he challenged his audience: "Let us fulfill the perfect promise of freedom and liberty left as legacy for us by those who founded this Commonwealth." In his 1992 State of the Commonwealth Address, Wilder again used history to frame his present-day call: "The power of our forefathers' words put a special responsibility on us, those who represent Virginia's interests. We must be responsive to our people, while leading them toward excellence."

When Wilder turned to more recent history, he called on the history of his youth:

As a young boy I remember hearing Franklin D. Roosevelt on the radio, and although I was still a little too young to understand what a depression was, I knew times were hard and that our President told us to keep faith and be of stout heart. He didn't tell us he had the answer to everything, he told us not to be afraid of the future, and that government was on our side.

Representing a state so steeped in history allowed Wilder to draw rhetorically on the history of Virginia and America, but it was a rhetorical move that seemed to come naturally to him.

Wilder's language is as heartfelt as his messages. In talking about his style, Wilder said in the interview that he started with a "grander style" using "fancy words." Somewhere early on in his career, however, he found that a "simple speaking style" was best, using "words that are clear and understood by all— not fancy language." True to his word, all of Wilder's State of the Commonwealth addresses are written in common, everyday language. Although he employs some imagery, metaphors, and similes, most of his points are made with plain and simple statements. For example, throughout his speeches one can find statements of clarification, such as in his 1990 State of the Commonwealth Address, when he noted that "a biennial budget is a budget for two years—not one." Wilder also reported that he aims to avoid "jargon and acronyms," although he has sometimes used them in manuscript speeches that had to do with what he called "clinical issues" such as financial issues, social services, or other topics of a more technical nature. Again, a study of his speeches bears this out; they are remarkably void of the specialized language, often found in political rhetoric, that confuses more than it clarifies.

While his language is generally simple, there is often a ministerial tone to his speeches. Many of those whom Wilder recalled as outstanding speakers were preachers, an influence that seems to manifest itself in many of his own speeches. Religious references can be found in his Inaugural Address as well as his four State of the Commonwealth addresses. Sounding as much like a minister as a politician, Wilder said in his Inaugural Address: "We mark today not a victory of party or the accomplishments of an individual, but the triumph of an idea—an idea as old as America; as old as the God who looks out for us all." He closed the Inaugural Address by saying: "I ask for your energy; for your understanding; for your dedication; for your patience; and yes—for your prayers. . . . [My] pride does burst forth, and lifts my voice and my spirit to proclaim, 'I am a son of Virginia.' I thank you all. And may God be ever with us."

Wilder closed all four of his State of the Commonwealth addresses by petitioning for God's help and blessings on all those listening. In two of those speeches he asked for a moment of silence and for prayers, in 1991 for those serving in the Persian Gulf and in 1993 for the victims of the Southmountain mining accident. Wilder's religious beliefs were not allowed to fall victim to the separation of church and state; he spoke from his heart because God was an important part of his belief system. Regardless of the criticism this might engender from potential allies, Wilder's style was not clear for the sake of clarity, but clear about what he felt and believed.

Consistent with the plainness of his style and his objective of clarity, Wilder prefers the extemporaneous style of speaking over the more formal use of a manuscript. He feels that he can respond more easily to the feedback of his audience when he speaks extemporaneously, but he also knows that when one must be precise and establish a written record for future reference, a manuscript delivery is required. His Inaugural Address and the State of the Commonwealth addresses, then, did not reflect his preference for an extemporaneous delivery. On the campaign trail, however, and in other less formal settings, one would see that he has a remarkable ability to relate to his audience because of his effective use of an extemporaneous delivery.

While governor, Wilder often found the more formal demands of delivery to be difficult, frequently because of constraints placed upon him due to the demands of media coverage. For example, Wilder likes to gesture, but the media told him that he should not. He found using a teleprompter easy, but it did mean that he had to remain in one place when speaking. Watching him campaign, however, one sees a far more dynamic speaker in the extemporaneous setting than was possible in the more formal delivery style he had to use as governor.

Wilder can use an extemporaneous delivery in part because he does not suffer from stage fright. His real apprehension, he notes, comes from the thought that he might not reach his audience or that he might be misunderstood, not from fear of standing up in front of them. His choice of clear, plain, conversational language, combined with his preference for the more communicative style of extemporaneous delivery, illustrates that concern. Douglas Wilder speaks from the heart because it is the hearts of the audience that he hopes to reach.

Wilder's upbringing and history have been influential in many of his oratorical choices. His debater's method of argument, his approach to the issues of fairness and equality, his choice of plain language style, and his extemporaneous delivery all reflect his background and experiences. In today's age, where many politicians mold themselves to a telegenic image, Douglas Wilder stands apart in his reliance on who he is and where he has been to shape his public presence as the first elected African-American governor of this nation.

INFORMATION SOURCES

Research Collections and Collected Speeches

There is no current collection of papers available. As of this writing, however, copies of speeches may be obtained by writing to Gov. L. Douglas Wilder, P.O. Box 1354, Richmond, VA 23211.

Selected Critical Studies

Barnes, Fred. "Mild Wilder." *New Republic,* August 13, 1990:27–29.

Bennett, Lerone, Jr. "Inaugurating the Future." *Ebony,* April 1990:27–28.

Dingle, Derek T. "A New Force in the Old Dominion." *Black Enterprise,* January 1989: 36–44.

Holden, Matthew, Jr. "The Rewards of Daring and the Ambiguity of Power: Perspectives on the Wilder Election of 1989." *The State of Black America 1990.* Ed. Janet Dewart. Washington, DC: National Urban League, 1990, 109–120.

Meyerson, Adam. "Low Tax Liberal." *Policy Review,* Winter 1991:26–31.

Poinsett, Alex. "Who Will Be the First Black Elected Governor?" *Ebony,* November
    1989:38–46.
Randolph, Laura B. "The First Black Elected Governor." *Ebony*, February 1990:22–26.

Selected Biographies

Edds, Margaret. *Claiming the Dream: The Victorious Campaign of Douglas Wilder of
    Virginia*. Chapel Hill, NC: Algonquin, 1990.
"L. Douglas Wilder." *Current Biography Yearbook 1990,* 622–626.
Yancey, Dwayne. *When Hell Froze Over: The Untold Story of Doug Wilder*. Dallas, TX:
    Taylor, 1988.

CHRONOLOGY OF MAJOR SPEECHES

"Announcement Speech for Lieutenant Governor." Richmond, VA, July 1984.
"Inaugural Address." Richmond, VA, January 13, 1990.
"State of the Commonwealth." Richmond, VA, January 15, 1990.
"Remarks Made to the Yale Political Student Union." New Haven, CT, April 30, 1990.
"Commencement Speech at Norfolk State University" (Announcing Virginia's disin-
    vestment in South Africa). Norfolk, VA, May 12, 1990.
"Remarks Made for the Mount Vernon Slave Memorial Wreathlaying Ceremony."
    Mount Vernon, VA, September 22, 1990.
"Winning the White House: A Fiscally Responsible 'New Mainstream' for a Democratic
    Victory in 1992" (Address to the John F. Kennedy School for Government).
    Cambridge, MA, October 19, 1990.
"State of the Commonwealth." Richmond, VA, January 9, 1991.
". . . Liberty and Justice for All" (Address to the Detroit Chapter of the NAACP). De-
    troit, MI, April 28, 1991.
"Remarks Made to the People of the Commonwealth." Richmond, VA, September 13,
    1991.
"State of the Commonwealth." Richmond, VA, January 8, 1992.
"Cato Institute Address." Washington, DC, April 20, 1992.
"Remarks to the NAACP 57th Annual State Convention." Alexandria, VA, October 30,
    1992.
"Remarks Made at Top Management Luncheon." New York, NY, November 5, 1992.
"State of the Commonwealth." Richmond, VA, January 13, 1993.
"Frederick Douglass Memorial Convocation" (Morgan State University). Baltimore,
    MD, February 18, 1993.
"Address to the Democratic State Convention." Richmond, VA, May 7, 1993.
"Commencement Address." Howard University Law School, Washington, DC, May 8,
    1993.
"African Summit Remarks." Libreville, Gabon, May 26, 1993.

FANNIE BARRIER WILLIAMS
(1855–1944), writer, lecturer, community activist

Best known for her club work during the late nineteenth and early twentieth centuries, Fannie Barrier Williams was also a talented orator and writer. She became a prominent spokesperson during the Progressive Era in which the women's reform movement gained momentum, race relations reached their nadir, and black migration to Northern and Midwestern cities peaked. To serve the needs of African-Americans, Williams championed the development of a national association for African-American women that would unite grass-roots clubs throughout the nation and pushed for economic advancement for blacks. Through her assistance, in 1896 the largest African-American female organization, the National Association of Colored Women (NACW), was established.

Williams was born ten years before slavery officially ended, on February 12, 1855. Yet her childhood experiences never resembled those of the majority of African-Americans during that decade. She was the eldest of two daughters and one son of a prominent free African-American family in Brockport, New York. Her father, Anthony Barrier, was a barber, coal merchant, homeowner, and active leader in the predominantly white community. The Barriers often fraternized with their white acquaintances. Fannie attended the local schools and the State Normal School at Brockport, where she graduated in 1870.

After graduation she devoted her time to teaching. Inspired to help educate the newly freed people, she joined with black and white Northern females who ventured South during Reconstruction. The experience was anything but pleasant. Influenced by her sheltered middle-class life in Brockport, she strongly believed that class distinctions outweighed race delineations in relationships. Outside the borders of her Northern haven, however, Southern racism forced her to confront the painful knowledge that race overrode economic standing. In her autobiography, she lamented that while there she "began life as a colored person, in all that term implies."

Anger, frustration, and indignation compelled her to move to more hospitable surroundings. Washington, D.C., offered a large African-American elite community and respectable employment. She became a teacher in the city, socialized with other middle-class blacks, and met a promising young law student, S. Laing Williams. Upon completion of his law degree in 1887, the couple married and moved to Chicago, where the Williamses moved up the social ladder quickly. He became a prominent lawyer and was later appointed the first black assistant district attorney in Chicago. She became an active progressive reformer and club woman.

Throughout her life, she held membership in several organizations, including the Phyllis [Phillis] Wheatley Home Association, the Prudence Crandall Study Club, the Chicago Women's Club, the NACW, and the Illinois Federation of Colored Women's Clubs. In addition, she chaired the Committee on State Schools for Dependent Children for the Illinois Woman's Alliance.

As a reporter for the *Woman's Era*, a monthly newspaper that disseminated news to African-American women nationwide and a writer of numerous essays and journal articles, she championed the cause of African-Americans and African-American women. Economic exploitation, political disfranchisement, and social segregation necessitated the full participation of women like Williams in the movement toward black equality.

FANNIE BARRIER WILLIAMS AS A VICTORIAN PROGRESSIVE REFORMER

Only a few of Williams's speeches are available, but a study of her discourse shows that it echoed the central themes of the era: racial tolerance, Christian benevolence, Victorian morality, and economic opportunity. An attractive and cultured woman, she pacified her white audiences with a noncombative style that gained her distinction among blacks and whites. Her oratorical presentation reflected a public persona of refined gentility. When she was addressing the evils of racism, her language was polished and nonthreatening.

Her style closely resembled that of Booker T. Washington, the head of Tuskegee Institute and the most prominent African-American spokesperson of the era. Although he was attacked by many other prominent black leaders for his appeasing tone and acquiescence to Southern white demands of social segregation and political disfranchisement, Williams remained loyal, praising his effort whenever possible. It was Washington, she told a Memphis audience, "who has done more for practical education of the colored people in all things than any other one man in America." He in turn played a significant role in the appointment of her husband as an assistant district attorney in Illinois and invited her to write in several journals favorable to his cause.

Like Washington, Williams cautiously balanced her rhetoric, never intending to put the audience on the defensive. She discussed the disgrace of slavery within the context of the strides African-Americans had made since servitude. She acknowledged that African-American women shouldered the burden of race and sex discrimination, but contended that they had advanced despite their hardships and would continue to do so. She argued for equal economic opportunities, not because whites owed them to blacks, but because African-Americans could excel if given the chance. Moreover, she insisted that the responsibility of uplift rested on the race, particularly its women.

A religious woman, Williams believed that religion provided one of the answers for eradicating racial problems. In "What Can Religion Further Do to Advance the Condition of the American Negro?" delivered in 1893 at the World's Parliament Of Religions held during the Columbian Exposition in Chicago, she chastised religious officials for abdicating their duty in improving relationships between the races. Probably because of her own Southern experience and the overt, divisive discriminatory message sent by white Christians, she contended that "it is a monstrous thing that nearly one-half of the so-called Evangelical churches of this country, those situated in the South, repudiate fellowship to every Christian man and woman who happens to be of African descent." Distorted interpretations of the Bible, she continued, formed the basis of the hatred: "The golden rule of fellowship taught in the Christian Bible becomes in practice the iron rule of race hatred. Can religion help the American people to be consistent and to live up to all they profess and believe in their government and religion?" "What we need," she concluded, "is such a reinforcement of the gentle power of religion that all souls of whatever color shall be included within the blessed circle of its influence. It should be the province of religion to unite, and not to separate, men and women according to superficial differences of race line."

Williams was unwavering when she spoke about the dual burdens of racism and sexism that African-American women faced. "To be a colored woman," she asserted, "is to be discredited, mistrusted and often meanly hated." As an example, she recalled her own experience with the elite white Chicago Women's Club in 1894. After her nomination for admission to the club by several prominent white female friends, for fourteen months the organization deliberated on admitting an African-American woman. Her controversial admission caused some members to withdraw from the club and forced the General Federation of Women's Clubs to confront the issue of black female membership. For her, the agony over the debate surrounding her confirmation resembled the "anti-slavery question" because it "was fought over again in the same spirit and with the same arguments." "This simple question," she concluded, "was the old bugbear of social equality." Ultimately, Williams was admitted and suggested that "the common sense of the members finally prevailed over their prejudices."

In her appeals to the common sense of all, she consistently challenged white women to recognize the contributions of African-American women. In "The Intellectual Progress and Present Status of the Colored Women of the United States since the Emancipation Proclamation" to the 1893 World's Congress of

Representative Women held in Chicago, Williams emphasized the dual burden of racism and sexism that black women faced while also championing the advances they had made. She challenged her predominantly white female audience, first, to acknowledge the existence of black women and second, to understand that the commonality of gender played a much greater role in all of their lives than the divisive factor of race. In a piercing indictment, she lamented that "less is known of our women than of any other class of Americans. No organization of far-reaching influence for their special advancement, no conventions of women to take note of their progress, and no special literature reciting the incidents, the events, and all things interesting and instructive concerning them are to be found among the agencies directing their career." She found it curious that for African-American women "there has been no special interest in their peculiar condition as native-born American women. Their power to affect the social life of America, either for good or for ill, has excited not even a speculative interest."

Stressing their commonality as women, she argued that "the exceptional career of our women will yet stamp itself indelibly upon the thought of this country." Like white women, African-American women saw "social evils" as "dangerously contagious": "The fixed policy of persecution and injustice against a class of women who are weak and defenseless will be necessarily hurtful to the cause of all women. Colored women are becoming more and more a part of the social forces that must help to determine the questions that so concern women generally."

On employment, Williams begged for fairness. "In their complaint against hindrances to their employment colored women ask for no special favors. They are even willing to bring to every position fifty per cent more of ability than is required of any other class of women. They plead for opportunities untrammeled by prejudice. They plead for the right of the individual to be judged, not by tradition and race estimate, but by the present evidences of individual worth."

Another theme that she wove throughout her speeches concerned issues of morality. As a Victorian progressive woman, Williams accepted the ideology of separate spheres that blended the mores of chastity, purity, and femininity. She expected African-American women to live within the confines of "acceptable" behavior. Black women of the last decade of the nineteenth century, she told the World's Congress,

> the daughters of women who thirty years ago were not allowed to be modest, not allowed to follow the instincts of moral rectitude, who could cry for protection to no living man, have so elevated the moral tone of their social life that new and purer standards of personal worth have been created, and new ideals of womanhood, instinct with grace and delicacy, are everywhere recognized and emulated. This moral regeneration of a whole race of women is no idle sentiment—it is a serious business; and everywhere there is witnessed a feverish anxiety to be free from the mean suspicions that have so long underestimated the character strength of our women.

She coupled her idea of an umbrella association with the theme of Victorian motherhood. As morally superior to men and the mothers of the race, African-American women, she argued, held the future of the race in their hands. In her 1895 speech "Opportunities and Responsibilities of Colored Women," Williams told the Ladies' Auxiliary of the Whittier Association in Memphis that "if I can say anything that is helpful it is not to suggest problems and difficulties, but to suggest duties and responsibilities that our women must begin to feel and exercise if we would become a part of the forces that are working everywhere about us for the things that deeply concern the kingdom of womankind." "Organized womanhood to-day, the world over," she continued, "is the spirit of reform incarnate. It impresses its reforming influence upon every existing evil, and its protecting power of love hovers over every cherished interest of human society. All combined institutions of Church, State, and civic societies do not touch humanity on so many sides as the organized efforts of women."

To lead black women in significant reform efforts, she supported female suffrage and promoted the creation of a national women's organization to develop strategies, promote moral values, and answer the needs of the African-American community. "In order to equip ourselves with knowledge, sympathy, and earnestness for this work, we need the soul strengthening influences of organization," she argued. In her straightforward, penetrating style, she lauded the Victorian idealism of women's moral responsibility while insisting that "women unorganized in the presence of the heart-stirring opportunities are narrow, weak, suspicious, and sentimental. Women organized for high purposes, discover their strength for large usefulness, and encircle all humanity with the blessedness of their sympathy."

Williams sought to influence whites throughout her life, but she never forgot that it was African-American women that she wanted to lead. She offered women a solid program of development in the struggle for equality through her oratory, her organizational skills, and her writings, and she presented that audience with a viable strategy for seeking equality.

By the turn of the century, Williams's public speaking career seems to have ended as she devoted most of her time to writing essays and articles. The message, however, remained the same. In the *Colored American* (1903), she wrote that "slavery in America was debasing, but the debasement of the Negro woman was deeper than that of the Negro man. Slavery made her the only woman in all America for whom virtue was not an ornament and a necessity. What a terrible inheritance is this for the women of a race declared to be emancipated and equal sharers in the glories and responsibilities of the Republic!" Nevertheless, she continued, "In spite of some of the unspeakable demoralizations of slavery, the womanhood of the race was marked by many of the virtues, mental and social, that are characteristic of the women of all races who are capable of a high state of development."

The following year, in "A Northern Negro's Autobiography," she recounted the story of her life and chastised white women for discrimination. Though she had white friends and did not feel victimized as an individual, she nevertheless recognized that "it was much easier for progressive white women to be considerate and even companionable to one colored woman whom they chanced to know and like than to be just and generous to colored young women as a race who needed their sympathy and influence in securing employment and recognition according to their tastes and ability."

As increasing numbers of blacks fled the oppressive Jim Crow system of the South, Williams wrote more articles on the problems plaguing the urban ghettos of Chicago. "The Need for Social Settlement Work for the City Negro" (1904), "Social Bonds in the Black Belt of Chicago" (1905), and "Colored Women in Chicago" (1914) were a few of the articles that reflected her concerns.

In 1905, the Frederick Douglass Center opened as a settlement project under the auspices of a white Unitarian minister, Celia Parker Woolley, with the aid of several prominent black families, including the Williamses. The center, located on the fringes of the predominantly black Second Ward, was an interracial experiment dedicated to promoting amicable relations between blacks and whites.

From 1924 to 1926, Williams served on the Chicago Library Board. As the first black woman to hold that position, she was a trailblazer. In 1926, Williams returned to her home in Brockport to live with her sister. She died of arteriosclerosis at the age of eighty-nine in 1944.

Few scholars have written about Williams, and there is no full-length study of her life. Though she is often referred to in historical works about African-American women, she remains an obscure figure. Reared in the North, devoted to a Washingtonian self-help philosophy, and confined by elitism, she was shielded from overt racism throughout much of her life. Williams's convictions were grounded in traditional mainstream values. She did not seek a shift in basic attitudes but attempted instead to overcome the barriers that separated black from white, and she expected the largest segment of the black populace, those in the lower class, to abide by those rules. Her devotion to traditional values notwithstanding, her work as a champion of civil rights for African-Americans reflected her commitment to creating a just society.

INFORMATION SOURCES

Research Collections and Collected Speeches

There are no research collections or collected speeches, but Williams's articles are representative of her oral discourse as well.

Williams, Fannie Barrier. "The Club Movement among Colored Women of America."
    A New Negro for a New Century: An Accurate and Up-to-Date Record of the
    Upward Struggles of the Negro Race. Ed. Booker T. Washington. Chicago: American Publishing House, 1900, 379–428.
———. "Club Movement among Negro Women." *Progress of a Race; or, The Re-*

markable Advancement of the Colored American. Ed. John W. Gibson and W. H. Crogman. Naperville, IL: J. L. Nichols, 1902, 197–231.

———. "The Colored Girl." *Voice of the Negro* 2 (June 1905): 401–403.

———. "Colored Women in Chicago." *Southern Workman* vol. 4 (October 1914): 564–566.

———. "Frederick Douglass." *Woman's Era* 2 (April 1895): 4.

———. "The Frederick Douglass Centre." *Voice of the Negro* 1 (December 1904): 601–604.

———. "The Need for Social Settlement Work for the City Negro." *Southern Workman* 33 (September 1904): 501–506.

———. "The Negro and Public Opinion." *Voice of the Negro* 1 (January 1904): 31–32.

———. "A Northern Negro's Autobiography." *Independent,* July 14, 1904: 91–96.

———. "Social Bonds in the Black Belt of Chicago." *Charities* 7 (October 1905): 40–44.

———. "The Woman's Part in a Man's Business." *Voice of the Negro* 1 (November 1904): 543–547.

———. "Women in Politics." *Woman's Era* 1 (November 1894): 12–13.

Selected Biographies

David, Jay, ed. *Black Defiance: Black Profiles in Courage.* New York: William Morrow, 1972.

Davis, Elizabeth Lindsay. *Lifting As They Climb.* Washington, DC: National Association of Colored Women, 1933.

———. *The Story of the Illinois Federation of Colored Women's Clubs.* Chicago np, 1922.

Gatewood, Williard B. *Aristocrats of Color: The Black Elite, 1880–1920.* Bloomington: Indiana UP, 1990.

James, Edward T., Janet Wilson James, and Paul S. Boyer, eds. *Notable American Women, 1607–1950: A Biographical Dictionary.* Cambridge, MA: Belknap Press of Harvard UP, 1971.

CHRONOLOGY OF MAJOR SPEECHES

"The Intellectual Progress and Present Status of the Colored Women of the United States since the Emancipation Proclamation." Chicago, IL, May 15–22, 1893. *The World's Congress of Representative Women.* Vol. 2. Ed. May Wright Sewall. Chicago: Rand, McNally, 1894, 696–711.

"What Can Religion Further Do to Advance the Condition of the American Negro?" Chicago, IL, 1893. *The World's Parliament of Religions.* Chicago: Parliament Publishing Co., 1893, 1114–1115.

"Opportunities and Responsibilities of Colored Women" (Speech to the Ladies' Auxiliary of the Whittier Association). Memphis, TN, 1895. *Afro-American Encyclopaedia; or, The Thoughts, Doings, and Sayings of the Race.* Nashville, TN: Haley and Florida, 1895, 146–161.

WALTER EDWARD WILLIAMS
(1936–   ), professor, editorialist

RONALD F. REID

Although Walter Williams is not a "stem-winder" like highly publicized contemporary speakers such as Jesse Jackson, he is one of the most active black polemicists of our time. Born in 1936, Williams was reared in a poor section of Philadelphia that, as he frequently tells audiences, had not yet succumbed to the now-current problems of crime, teenage pregnancy, family breakdown, and poor schooling. He speaks nostalgically about how his family instilled a sense of pride for his race and a strong work ethic. He also praises the black neighborhood, which had strong family values, a sense of community, and a deep-seated religious commitment. As a youngster, Williams did odd jobs, such as sweeping stores and caddying at the golf course. After army service, he earned a bachelor's degree from California State University in 1965 and a Ph.D. in economics from the University of California at Los Angeles in 1972. Although he worked with juvenile delinquents for the Los Angeles County Probation Department from 1963 to 1967 and was on the research staff of the Urban Institute from 1971 to 1973, most of his career has been in academe. He was on the faculties of Los Angeles City College (1967–69), California State University (1967–71), and Temple University (1973–80). Since 1980 he has been at George Mason University, where he is now the John M. Olin Distinguished Professor of Economics.

Unlike many distinguished professors, Williams does not confine his discourse to classroom teaching and scholarly writing. In a November 2, 1993, interview with the author, he estimated that he delivers thirty to forty speeches a year. Half are given to student groups on college campuses. Most of the remainder are delivered to business associations, but a few are motivational speeches to disadvantaged youngsters who are predominantly but not exclusively black. He also lectures occasionally on economic topics at workshops for high-school teachers and testifies on economic policy to congressional committees. He appears frequently on public television programs, such as the "MacNeil/ Lehrer News Hour," and occasionally on commercial television and radio programs, such as ABC's "Nightline." In 1984–85 he was featured in two television documentaries. As a writer, he has published several books aimed at the general public. While at Temple, he wrote a weekly editorial for the *Philadelphia Tribune*; and since 1980 he has written a weekly column that is carried in approximately one hundred newspapers.

Although his audiences are varied, all except the disadvantaged youngsters can be classified broadly as "opinion leaders": Congress, business executives, college students, high-school teachers, viewers of public television, and readers of the editorial pages. In short, he sometimes speaks to the black community, but more often for the black community when addressing opinion leaders who are mostly white.

Despite his extensive rhetorical activity, Williams has not been the subject of previous rhetorical critiques. Nor does he publish his speeches, which are delivered extemporaneously from what he calls "cryptic notes." Consequently, this essay must be considered a preliminary exploration into his rhetorical work. Although it focuses on speaking, his spoken and written rhetoric are integrated so closely that separating them is somewhat artificial. His ideological themes, rhetorical methods, and illustrative material are essentially the same irrespective of whether he is writing or speaking. He often refers to one mode of communication when he is engaged in the other, as for example during the last week of 1993, when he summarized some of his newspaper columns while speaking as the guest host of the Rush Limbaugh radio talk show.

MINORITY ADVOCATE FOR THE BLACK MINORITY

Another example of Williams's integration of the written and oral media is his editorial follow-up of a speech delivered in mid-1993 to the Wichita, Kansas, branch of the privately funded National Foundation for Teaching Entrepreneurship to Handicapped and Disadvantaged Youth (NFTE). He spoke as a member of NFTE's Advisory Board to an audience of three hundred people, which included teachers and parents, and his primary goal was to congratulate and inspire the teenage listeners. This discourse falls within the genre of what he calls his "motivational speeches," which are designed to instill a social ethic that puts high values on thrift, ambition, and hard work.

Shortly after the speech, Williams publicized NFTE to a wider audience in one of his weekly newspaper columns. He wrote in the *Conservative Chronicle* that with branches in ten cities, "NFTE teaches [disadvantaged] youths how to develop a business plan and market a product or service. Under its auspices, businesses started by at-risk youngsters include: stereo component installers, desktop publishing, magicians and baby-sitters. The kids are excited, energetic, enthusiastic and learning practical lessons."

The editorial was more than simply a report of NFTE's work. Williams pointedly narrated the story of one NFTE participant, a black fifteen-year-old high-school student. She had started a part-time business washing and braiding hair called A Touch of Class. It attracted enough customers to earn her a profit of one hundred dollars per month, and her success prompted NFTE to honor her as one of five Outstanding High School Entrepreneurs. After hearing about the award and receiving complaints from over one hundred licensed cosmetologists, the Kansas State Cosmetology Board warned her that she would be subject to a fine and/or imprisonment unless she acquired a license, which was dependent on her completing a year-long course at a certified cosmetology school. Williams indignantly pointed out that cosmetology schools, which charge tuitions ranging from $2,500 to $5,500, do not admit students under seventeen years of age and that most of them do not teach hair braiding. More important, he argued, ''Since braiding hair involves no use of chemicals, there is no public health issue. The customer's hair is washed, and the braider spends anywhere from two to eight hours weaving intricate patterns. The real issue is monopoly.''

The girl's ''experience,'' Williams argued, ''is simply the tip of the ugly occupational licensing iceberg that cuts off the bottom rungs of the economic ladder. . . . More and more states legislate against private, unlicensed, small-scale day care services. Civil rights organizations and black politicians are silent and often support denial of opportunity. But they beg for handouts.'' He concluded his editorial with a rhetorical question: ''Wouldn't it be great if civil rights organizations focused attention on economic liberties instead of constantly begging?''

This speech-editorial, like his appearance on the Rush Limbaugh show, demonstrates that Williams's rhetoric does not fit the stereotype of contemporary black orators. The publicity given to speakers such as Jesse Jackson and Angela Davis helps perpetuate a stereotype that all black polemicists are ''liberal'' or ''radical,'' but Williams's rhetoric is generally called ''conservative.'' The ''conservative'' image is reinforced by his serving on executive boards of organizations such as the National Tax Limitation Committee and the Hoover Institution and being an Adjunct Scholar of the Cato Institute and the Heritage Foundation.

Unfortunately, ''conservative'' is an ambiguous word that American society uses in contradictory ways. It sometimes is used to label people who wish to retain the status quo; but it is also used to label proposals for significant departures from the status quo, such as the proposed voucher system for parents who wish to send their children to private schools. ''Conservative'' is also used to label a big-government ideology that favors business and farm subsidies, protective tariffs, and other policies in the tradition of Alexander Hamilton; but it is also used to label the small-government philosophy of Hamilton's leading opponent, Thomas Jefferson.

Williams is well aware of the ambiguities surrounding the word ''conservative,'' but he is equally cognizant of the ambiguities encompassing the word "liberal." Turning to American history, as he does frequently in his speeches and writings, he points out that "liberal" was used originally to label men such as Thomas Jefferson who believed in limited government. He regards himself as a "liberal" in that classic sense of the word. Unfortunately for him, the word "liberal" is now associated with a commitment to big government; and despite his objections, he has joined many other classic liberals in becoming identified as a "conservative."

Williams's classic liberalism, or "conservatism," emphasizes a free-market economy and opposes governmental programs unless they are (1) consistent with the "explicit powers" interpretation of the Constitution propounded by Jefferson (and now abandoned by so-called "liberals," who favor Hamilton's "implicit powers" doctrine) and (2) absolutely necessary for the public good (as distinguished from helping special interests). It is an ideology consistent with that of economic theorists such as Friedrich A. von Hayek and Joseph Schumpeter, both of whom he cited in a speech entitled "The Legitimate Role of Government in a Free Economy" delivered on May 24, 1993, as the annual Frank M. Engle Lecture at American College in Bryn Mawr, Pennsylvania. Although a little more "academic" than many of his speeches, it serves as an excellent statement of his basic ideology, illustrates his characteristic rhetorical methods, and is easily available because it is one of his few speeches to have been published.

Williams began the speech by alluding to some contemporary economic phenomena, such as high unemployment, huge government deficits, and "a growing and seemingly endless national debt." These phenomena, he emphasized, were "symptoms," not "causes" of the basic problem, which was "a significant departure from the principles of individual liberty that made us a rich nation in the first place." He went on to define the "principles of liberty" as (1) "self-ownership" and (2) "what classical liberals like John Locke, William Blackstone and Adam Smith called natural, or God-given, rights to life, liberty, and property." After a brief digression to condemn slavery and rape for violating "self-ownership," he continued clarifying the term's meaning by specifying its economic attributes: "Self-ownership also implies that one must own what he produces" and "that two or more individuals should be free to engage in peaceable, voluntary exchange without interference by third parties." By defining terms, Williams's introduction functioned rhetorically to summarize the thesis of the speech and to set the stage for its amplification. Aristotelian critics will readily observe that his definitional method was to move from the general to the specific, and disciples of Richard Weaver will admire his establishing a definitional base for his subsequent line of argument.

Williams opened his line of argument by turning to history. He said that the writers of the Constitution, although not forming a government that was perfect in sustaining liberty, believed that limiting governmental power was essential to protect liberty. Early political leaders, he said, had learned from history that governments tend to increase their power at the expense of individual liberty, and he quoted Thomas Jefferson, one of his favorite sources, to that effect.

Consistent with this historical view, "The [constitutional] powers of the state are limited to national defense, enforcing constitutional order, adjudication of disputes, at some level police protection, and the provision of certain public goods."

The meaning of the term "public goods," Williams argued, has been perverted, thereby causing an "erosion of liberty." The perversions, which he documented at length in his speech, are of two types. One is governmental coercion to further what Williams sarcastically called the " 'new' human rights." These are efforts to equalize income, protect the environment, and other so-called "public goods" that are initiated by what Williams variously called the "elite" or the "do-gooders." Even though well intentioned, such policies inevitably reduce liberty by increasing taxes and governmental regulations. The second type of perversion is when so-called "public goods" actually serve self-interest groups. He said:

> Almost every group in our nation has come to feel that the government owes them a special privilege or favor. Conservatives are by no means exempt from the practice, nor are the following:
>
> • Manufacturers think that the government owes them protective tariffs to keep out foreign products and charge higher prices.
>
> • Farmers feel that the government owes them crop subsidies.
>
> • Organized labor wants the government to protect their jobs from competition from those who are not union members. . . .
>
> • Intellectuals—college professors—feel the government should give them funds for research.
>
> • The unemployed and the unemployable feel the government owes them a living.

Running through Williams's condemnation of these perversions was a well-integrated combination of statistical evidence, humorous analogies, and illustrations. One statistic contrasted the average tax paid by Americans in 1902 ($60 a year) and 1993 ($8,000). In another contrast he said: "The average taxpayer works from January 1st to May 6th to pay federal, state, and local taxes. Last year it was from January 1st to May 4th." Relating these statistical data to his definitions, he said: "Keep in mind that the working definition of slavery states that one works all year and does not have rights to the fruit of his labor. Somebody else makes the decision about how it's used. We are approaching handing over five months' worth of our labor to somebody else to decide how the money we earn is spent." He declared that this is inconsistent with the proper definitions of both "self-ownership" and "liberty."

One of Williams's best analogies was drawn from Leonard Read's remark "that if you wanted to take freedom away from Americans, you had to know how to cook a frog. Dr. Read warned that a frog cannot be cooked simply by putting on a pot of boiling water and then tossing in the frog. The frog's reflexes are so quick that the instant his feet touch the water he leaps out and is free. In order to cook a frog, you must put the frog into a pot of cold water, and then heat the water bit by bit. By the time the frog realizes he is being cooked, it is too late." Williams analogized the frog to a key term in his speech, "erosion of liberty." By adding a day or two to the labor that Americans must expend each year to pay the government, their liberty is not being taken away suddenly. It is being eroded. Analogically, they are being cooked without realizing it, just like the frog.

A touch of humor also pervaded a hypothetical example that Williams used to illustrate how governmental policies are coercive even when they are designed to accomplish good:

> Suppose I see a homeless person in desperate need of medical care, housing and food. Suppose further, I walk up to Professor White [who had introduced Williams to the audience] with a gun in my hand and say, "Mike, give me your $200." Then, having gotten his $200, I go downtown and buy the lady some food, medicine, and housing. I take by force, threat or intimidation, money that rightfully belongs to another in order to assist the homeless. . . . Regardless of what I did with the money, the average person, were he on a jury, would most certainly find me guilty of having committed a crime. Is there a conceptual distinction between that act whereby I walked up to Mike and forcibly took his money, and one wherein a group of people, represented by government, takes property that rightfully belongs to one and gives it to another to whom it does not belong? No, the conceptual distinction is absent. Each of these two acts constitutes confiscation of one person's property for the benefit of someone else.

Williams said that the only difference is that one theft is legal whereas the other is illegal; and he used historical examples of legal theft, such as slavery and the Stalinist purges, to show that legality "cannot be the talisman" of morality. He concluded his speech by reiterating that the "legal" erosion of liberty is leading to catastrophe and urging support for a constitutional amendment to require a balanced budget.

This speech exemplifies Williams's basic ideology and rhetorical method, but it is atypical in one respect: except for a few brief remarks about slavery and unemployment, it is devoid of references to racial problems or poverty. However, the problem of black poverty is central to much of his rhetorical discourse, and this makes him a "conservative" spokesman for the black community instead of just a "conservative."

Because Williams's other speeches are unpublished, all except brief quotations must be taken from his writings or congressional testimony. In both his oral and written discourse he applies his "classic liberalism" to the problems of the black poor while relying heavily on the same rhetorical methods exemplified in the American College lecture: he establishes a definitional base for his argument; he looks carefully at cause-effect relationships; he uses historical evidence; and he amplifies arguments with a combination of statistical data, detailed illustrations, and humorous analogies.

Williams frequently reminds audiences of a fundamental distinction between "good intentions" and "actual effects." He acknowledges that most do-gooders intend to help the poor when they support "liberal" legislation such as minimum wages; but the actual effects hurt poor people, especially poor blacks. However, he makes one exception: labor unions do not even have "good intentions." They support self-interest legislation that protects their members from the competition of nonmembers. This hurts many Americans, but blacks especially are injured because unions support a seniority system, and blacks were excluded from unions until recently.

Equally fundamental to his rhetoric is Williams's analysis of causality. Contemptuous of the liberals' frequent assertion that black poverty is caused by "racism" and "discrimination," he refutes it in many of his discourses, and this refutation is the centerpiece of one of his most frequently repeated speeches, "How Much Can Discrimination Explain?" Although acknowledging that "residual discrimination" still adversely affects blacks, he denies that it is the basic cause of present-day black poverty. Part of his denial consists of asking rhetorical questions about the definition of "discrimination." For example, after presenting statistical evidence showing that black baseball players in the major leagues have higher batting averages than whites, he asks whether this difference means "discrimination." He also presents examples of minority groups, such as the Japanese-Americans, who have prospered despite being discriminated against, and asks why the alleged cause-effect relationship between discrimination and poverty does not hold up in these situations. His most devastating refutation of the liberal assertion is when he turns to a statistical analysis of black economic improvement prior to the advent of civil rights legislation. He emphasizes that despite discrimination, blacks were actually improving economically as much as, and in some cases more than, whites. For example, writing in the *Conservative Chronicle* he drew upon Bureau of Labor statistics to show that "in 1948, white teen unemployment was 10.2 percent, and black teen unemployment was 9.4 percent. At the same time, black teens, as well as blacks in general, were more active in the labor force than whites."

If racial discrimination is not the major cause of black poverty, what is? It is the " 'rules of the game' . . . [which Williams defines as] the many federal, state and local laws that regulate economic activity." Many laws, he claims, "systematically discriminate against the employment and advancement of people who are outsiders, latecomers and poor in resources." Williams agrees that many groups suffer from the "rules of the game," but, he wrote in *The State Against Blacks*, "because of their history in the U.S., blacks are disproportionately represented in the class of people described as outsiders, latecomers and resourceless." One of his most oft-used illustrations of this point is the taxi business. Whereas many ethnic groups had enough resources in the 1920s to buy a used car and become an owner-operator of a taxi, blacks usually lacked the resources for taking this route to upward mobility. Today, increased resources have led to blacks owning three-quarters of the taxis in Washington, D.C. Licenses in Washington cost approximately $100, depending on the weight of the vehicle, but there are almost no black-owned taxis in other cities because of the high licensing fees. The license, or ''medallion,'' in New York City costs $125,000. Williams usually concludes this example by emphasizing that the high license fees are not for the public good. They are to protect a monopoly.

Another oft-repeated illustration was first used when Williams testified against affirmative action before the U.S. Senate Labor Committee in 1981. He narrated the example of a black trucker, Ward Smith, who submitted the low bid on a government contract to ship household goods for air force personnel. The contract went to a competitor whose bid was $80,000 higher because Smith did not have an Interstate Commerce Commission (ICC) license to ship goods across state lines. Williams concluded the example by saying, ''Many people seeing few blacks with federal contracts will say quotas and set-asides are needed. Ward Smith did not need a quota; he needed the government . . . off his back. But the quota approach ignores this monopoly problem, a monopoly set up for the Teamsters and big trucking companies. There are *white* truckers in the same situation as Smith. They cannot get ICC authority either. How do you think a white trucker who can't get ICC authority, who differs from Ward Smith *only* in color, feels when a quota is set up favoring Smith? What does this do for race relations? Congress sets the basis for conflict.''

Affirmative-action programs do more than create racial conflict by embittering whites; they undermine black self-esteem and social values. Prior to affirmative action, Williams maintains, blacks who advanced economically knew that it was due to individual merit; but when a minority person now gets a good job, he or she can no longer be sure that it was obtained on the basis of merit rather than his or her minority classification.

Williams used similar arguments against minimum-wage laws in testimony prepared for Congress in 1977; but the committee staff, composed of ''liberals,'' refused to let Congress see his testimony unless he deleted sections. He reluctantly agreed, but an unedited version was privately published. Since then, he has often attacked minimum-wage laws. He updates factual data, but his basic arguments do not change. He argues that minimum-wage laws discourage employers from hiring marginal workers; and blacks, being ''latecomers,'' have an unusually high percentage of marginal workers. However, the real problem is one that confronts black teenagers. Williams presents statistical data to show that most adult workers earn more than the minimum wage, which in actuality makes the laws applicable almost exclusively to teenagers. Minimum-wage laws keep teenagers out of the labor market; and because black teenagers living in ghettos are ''outsiders'' who are less well educated than their suburban peers, they are even less likely to get a job. Then the ''government reinforces his disadvantage by sending him to a school where he has a good chance of graduating semiliterate.'' Getting a job is important for poor youngsters, not only because it brings in money, but also because it raises self-esteem and instills virtues of punctuality, ambition, work, and responsibility.

In short, Williams's discourse is built around opposition to "liberal" legislation that allegedly helps poor people but actually hurts them. Such legislation, to use his favorite phrase, "cuts off the bottom rungs of the economic ladder." Arguing that the poor must begin at the bottom, Williams often quotes his stepfather as saying a poor job at a poor wage is better than no job at no wage.

"Liberal legislation," in Williams's outspoken style, is "race hustlers' pablum." He frequently attacks black "leaders" for supporting such legislation while failing to support black "self-help" groups who have established private schools, set up anticrime watches, and worked against labor-union monopolies. He contrasts the "poverty pimps," who have done little to eradicate drugs, with the Black Muslims who get rid of drug dealers without bothering "to give Miranda warnings." No wonder, he says, that the "self-appointed" black "leaders" are unrepresentative of their black "followers." He notes that more blacks identify themselves as "conservative" than "liberal," whereas the reverse is true of the "leaders." He also points out that 70 percent of blacks sympathized with Clarence Thomas during his Senate "trial," whereas the "leaders" tried to ignore the subject.

An increasing number of black "leaders" have begun expressing concern about the collapse of social values that has torn inner-city families apart and is destroying the work ethic. Although few have yet accepted Williams's assertion that a major cause of the collapse is so-called "liberal" legislation, perhaps they will in the future. If that happens, Williams will become a representative speaker of the black minority instead of a minority spokesman for the black minority.

INFORMATION SOURCES

Because Williams has not yet been the subject of scholarly studies, information sources are limited to his own publications. His weekly editorials, 1980–present, carried in approximately one hundred newspapers, were originally entitled "A Minority View" and syndicated by Heritage Features. Since 1991, they have been syndicated by Creators Syndicate. The following is a list of his books and a selected group of his articles:

All It Takes Is Guts. Washington, DC: Regnery-Gateway, 1987.

America: A Minority Viewpoint. Stanford: Hoover Institution Press, 1982. Collected editorials reprinted from *Philadelphia Tribune.*

"False Civil Rights Vision." *Georgia Law Review* 21 (1987): 1119–1139.

"False Civil Rights Vision and Contempt for Rule of Law." *Georgetown Law Journal* 79 (1991): 1777–1782.

"Freedom to Contract: Blacks and Labor Organizations." *Black America and Organized Labor: A Fair Deal?* Eds. Walter E. Williams, Loren A. Smith, and Wendell W. Gunn. Washington, DC: Lincoln Institute for Research and Education, n.d. [c.1980], 10–32.

"Good Intentions—Bad Results: The Economy Pastoral and America's Disadvantaged." *Notre Dame Journal of Law, Ethics, and Public Policy* 2 (1985): 179–199.
"Higher Education and Minority Opportunities." *Howard Law Journal* 21 (1978): 545–557.
"Legal Restriction on Black Progress." *Howard Law Journal* 21 (1978): 47–71.
South Africa's War against Capitalism. New York: Praeger, 1989; revised edition: Cape Town, South Africa: Juta Publishers, 1990.
The State against Blacks. New York: McGraw-Hill, 1982.
(With Gregory B. Christiansen) "Welfare, Family Cohesiveness, and Out-of-Wedlock Births." *The American Family and the State.* Eds. Joseph R. Peden and Fred R. Glahe. San Francisco: Pacific Research Institute for Public Policy, 1986, 381–424.
"Why the Poor Pay More: An Alternative Explanation." *Social Science Quarterly* 54 (1973): 375–379.
Youth and Minority Unemployment. Commissioned by United States Congress, Joint Economic Committee, 95th Congress, 1st session. Washington, DC: U.S. Government Printing Office, 1977. Edited version.
Youth and Minority Unemployment. Stanford: Hoover Institution Press, 1977. Unexpurgated version of testimony to the Joint Economic Committee.

CHRONOLOGY OF MAJOR SPEECHES

"The State against Blacks." Produced by the Manhattan Institute. PBS. Fall 1984. Oral version of the book with the same title.
"Good Intentions: A Personal Statement." Produced by Amagin, Inc. PBS. 1985.
"The Legitimate Role of Government in a Free Economy." The 1993 Frank M. Engle Lecture of the American College, Bryn Mawr, Pennsylvania. May 24, 1993. Published by the college. Copies are available from Dr. Michael D. White, Frank M. Engle Distinguished Chair, The American College, 270 South Bryn Mawr Avenue, Bryn Mawr, PA 19010.
Guest host, Rush Limbaugh radio talk show, December 27–31, 1993.
"Be Somebody." A motivational speech given to young blacks. Says that opportunities for black upward mobility were increased markedly by civil rights legislation and urges young blacks to keep faith with the leaders of the 1960s civil rights movement by taking advantage of current opportunities through ambition, thrift, and similar social values. Recurring extemporaneous lecture.
"Government Intervention and Individual Freedom." Expounds Williams's "limited-government" philosophy. Recurring extemporaneous lecture.
"How Much Can Discrimination Explain?" Argues that although racial prejudice and discrimination against women exist, discrimination is not the major cause of income differentials and similar phenomena. Recurring extemporaneous lecture.
"South Africa's War against Capitalism." An oral version of the book with the same title. Recurring extemporaneous lecture.

MALCOLM X
(1925–1965), religious leader, civil rights activist

MARK BERNARD WHITE

Surely the most controversial African-American orator in history, Malcolm X was perhaps reviled and revered in equal measure during his public life. Exalted to the status of icon decades after his death, Malcolm stands as one of the most virtuosic, significant, and influential speakers in the African-American rhetorical tradition.

Malcolm's life was a series of abrupt and pivotal transformations, thrust upon him in his youth, chosen by him as an adult. He was born Malcolm Little in Omaha, Nebraska, in 1925, the son of Earl and Louise Little. His earliest memory recalled racist terrorism, his family's home being torched by night riders. Malcolm's father was a carpenter and a Baptist preacher who included in his preaching the separatist ideology of Marcus Garvey, for whose Universal Negro Improvement Association he was an organizer.

Malcolm's parents subjected their children to harsh chastisement that apparently fell somewhat short of cruelty, but that was meted out in such manner as to expose the problems of complexion that marred their family relations. Malcolm, the palest of the children, was treated with favoritism by his very dark father, who, despite preaching black pride, still displayed symptoms of the acculturated self-loathing among African-Americans that exalts and values pigmentation the further from black and the closer to white it is. His mother, conversely, despising her own paleness that was the inheritance of her mother being raped by a white man in her native St. Lucia, treated Malcolm more harshly than she did the other children. He recalled in his *Autobiography*: ''[J]ust as my father favored me for being lighter than the other children, my mother gave me more hell for the same reason.''

Settling his family in East Lansing, Michigan, Earl Little continued his Garveyist preaching. White racists likely murdered him for his efforts; Little's body was found with his head bashed in, apparently thrown onto trolley tracks, and nearly cut in half by a trolley. The family, deprived of its provider, fell into desperate poverty, suffering hunger, cold, raggedness, and the indignities of intrusions by social workers into the affairs of the family. Under the pressure, Louise Little slowly disintegrated into mental illness, and Malcolm's becoming a petty thief and general miscreant no doubt added to her distress. Eventually she was institutionalized, and the children dispersed. Malcolm blamed the system: "I truly believe that if ever a state social agency destroyed a family, it destroyed ours."

Placed in the home of white foster parents who boarded troubled boys, Malcolm experienced a degree of stability unknown since the death of his father and began to excel as a student in his class, which was, except for himself, all white. Among the top three students in his class and elected class president, Malcolm aspired to become a lawyer. One day, however, his English teacher told him, "Malcolm . . . you've got to be realistic about being a nigger. A lawyer—that's no realistic goal for a nigger." "It was then," said Malcolm in his *Autobiography*, "that I began to change—inside."

This began Malcolm's second transformation, marked by his move to Boston to live with his half-sister Ella Collins and his indoctrination into big-city living and petty-criminal hustling. Moving on to Harlem, New York, where he was known as "Detroit Red"—both for his Michigan origins and his complexion and hair—Malcolm became involved in a variety of criminal activities, including numbers running, procuring, narcotics peddling, and thievery. Having made potentially fatal enemies in Harlem, Malcolm fled back to Boston, where he led a burglary ring, a criminal enterprise that eventuated in his arrest. A first-time offender, twenty-year-old Malcolm and his partner Malcolm Jarvis received sentences of eight to ten years, nearly five times longer than usual for a first offender, probably as retribution for what he believed to be their real crime against white society—sexual liaison with the white women who were their confederates in crime.

Impressed by an inmate named Bimbi, who was, he said, "the first man I had ever seen command respect . . . with his words," Malcolm became reawakened to the importance of learning, especially learning to use language to gain respect and status and to wield rhetorical power. Bimbi convinced Malcolm to make use of the prison library. He had not been a reader in the years of his descent from honor student to convict, but now he resumed his reading with an almost obsessive devotion to self-education, including a laborious copying of every definition in the dictionary.

Malcolm exhibited such disrespect for religion that inmates nicknamed him "Satan." But family members soon introduced him to "the black man's natural religion," the Nation of Islam, a sect associated with the Muslim religion more in name than in doctrine. The sect was founded in 1930 as the 'Temple of Islam.' Its founder, W. D. Fard, disappeared mysteriously in 1934, and after a brief power struggle the Honorable Elijah Muhammad ascended to leadership of the "nation." Muhammad afterward claimed that Fard had been Allah himself, incarnated on earth to rescue his true people "lost in the wilderness of America." This visitation by God and his association with the former Elijah Poole conferred upon the now-renamed Elijah Muhammad the status of God's prophet, foretold in the Bible to appear during the final days before the end of the world. Elijah Muhammad thus superseded the authority of previous prophets, including the original prophet Muhammad, whom orthodox Islam believes to be the last of God's line of prophets.

Elijah Muhammad taught that black people were the "original" humans, an Asiatic (not African) race, that ruled the world in peace and harmony until an evil scientist named Yacub invented white people by first producing genetic mutations and then through selective breeding. White people, according to this story, are genetically evil, natural "devils," whom God eventually granted the temporary privilege of ruling the world for six thousand years. The twentieth century marks the end of their rule, and God intends to redeem his true people from the devils who snatched them away from their home and brought them to the "wilderness" of America. This apocalyptic story can have only one outcome unless the white man repents his evil ways, as appropriately evidenced by separating from the black man and giving the black man a geographic domain of his own. The rhetorical mission of the Nation of Islam, and especially Malcolm's mission as its chief public spokesman, was twofold: to "wake up" black people into racial consciousness, pride, and true redemptive religion, and to denounce white people and warn them to change their evil behavior (resisting their nature) before it was too late to avoid God's judgment. Taught also that black people had been stripped of everything that defined them as human, including their history, religion, language, and culture, Elijah Muhammad's followers rejected their European "slave names" and replaced them with an X to represent the unknown original family name that white men had robbed them of.

Religious nationalism of this type has never enjoyed popular success among African-Americans, but secular versions of territorial separatism have been an important part of the ongoing nationalist-integrationist dialectic at least since Martin Delany. The assertion that black people and white people cannot possibly coexist, that whenever black people have encountered white people the result has been disastrous for black people, squares with the centuries-old common experience of African-Americans.

Intensified by his zeal now to evangelize on behalf of Elijah Muhammad, Malcolm focused his self-education on developing rhetorical weapons for his holy cause. At this point his passion for rhetoric became reanimated, and his career as an orator actually began. Born into the home of a preacher and exhorter, and into a culture that values masterly and artistic use of language and rhetorical power, Malcolm enjoyed debate as an adolescent, and he prepared self-consciously for rhetorical combat while still a prisoner. Immediately upon parole in 1952 he became an activist with the Nation of Islam, initiating aggressive evangelizing strategies that eventually increased adherents from about

400 to perhaps as many as 40,000. Impressive though this growth was, the Nation of Islam and Malcolm were still largely unknown even among African-Americans. All this changed in July 1959 with the television broadcast of the documentary "The Hate That Hate Produced," a program that featured the Nation of Islam and especially Malcolm. Hearing Malcolm, Elijah Muhammad, and other Muslims describe the collective white man as evil and as the devil incarnate shocked, frightened, and fascinated its audience. Overnight, Malcolm became one of the most sought-after interviews and one of the most popular speakers in America, particularly in demand on university campuses.

This attention, far eclipsing the attention given even to Elijah Muhammad himself, aroused fierce jealousy among other ministers in the Nation of Islam, who began to persuade Elijah Muhammad that Malcolm harbored ambitions to take over the organization. At this same time, Malcolm found out that the man he revered as God's agent of moral redemption had fathered several children with young church secretaries. Malcolm thus reached a crisis of faith that was to lead to his final significant personal transformation. Feeling threatened, Elijah Muhammad seized upon an opportunity to suppress Malcolm, ostensibly punishing him for having made some imprudent remarks about the assassination of John F. Kennedy (Malcolm asserted that Kennedy's assassination was "a case of the chickens coming home to roost," by which he meant to suggest a cycle of violence in which American militarism and racial oppression redounded against the nation's leader). The punishment of "silencing" Malcolm, prohibiting his public speaking even in his home mosque, was announced to last a period of ninety days, but Malcolm, convinced finally that Elijah Muhammad would never let him resume his functions in the Nation of Islam, reluctantly declared his independence from Elijah Muhammad in March 1964. He had less than a year to live.

The pivotal event in Malcolm's final year was his "hajj," the Islamic pilgrimage to the holy city of Mecca that Muslims are commanded to make, if they can, at least once in their lives. His acceptance into the holy city signaled his legitimacy as an orthodox Muslim. Even more, it inspired another transformation in his perspective and belief structure. People back home were startled when they received letters from Malcolm renouncing racism. As he recounted in his *Autobiography*:

> During the past eleven days here in the Muslim world, I have eaten from the same plate, drunk from the same glass, and slept in the same bed (on the same rug)—while praying to the *same* God—with fellow Muslims, whose eyes were the bluest of blue, whose hair was the blondest of blond, and whose skin was the whitest of white.

Malcolm had traveled to Africa and the Middle East before, but while under the sway of the doctrines of Elijah Muhammad he was apparently incapable of reconciling the racial diversity of Islam with what he had been taught. Now, though, given a new perspective, Malcolm became an ardent internationalist, spending much of the last year of his life abroad absorbing the ideologies of emerging African nations and their leaders, as well as Islamic leaders.

Although Malcolm never became an integrationist, he eventually expressed a tolerance for interracial association and even declared it none of his business who married whom. The organizations that he established, Moslem Mosque Inc., his new religious base, and the Organization of Afro-American Unity, his secular base (modeled on the Organization of African Unity), were racially exclusive. But Malcolm spoke more and more before white audiences during this period, and most of the texts of his speeches that we have are from this time.

The enmity between Malcolm and Elijah Muhammad and his followers grew fiercer, with the Nation's newspaper, *Muhammad Speaks*, calling in coded terms for Malcolm to be put to death for being a ''hypocrite'' and slandering, as it claimed, Elijah Muhammad. Malcolm's last months were spent under threat of death, which spurred him to accelerate his activities even more. On February 14, 1965, his Queens, New York, home was firebombed in the early morning hours, while his wife Betty, and his four young daughters were asleep. A week later, at the Audubon Ballroom in Harlem, just as he was beginning to speak, assassins opened fire, killing him instantly in the presence of his wife and children. He was thirty-nine years old. Three men were eventually convicted of the murder, but it seems likely that more men were involved in the conspiracy to murder Malcolm.

MALCOLM X AS A MAN OF HIS WORDS

Malcolm X is a historical figure defined by rhetoric, the legacy of his career being exceptionally narrow in its scope. Unlike, for example, Booker T. Washington, Mary McLeod Bethune, Martin Luther King, Jr., and other leaders who were renowned for their speaking but who could also show a connection between their rhetorical leadership and some concrete social actions, Malcolm is more akin to Jesse Jackson, also defined more by his speech than any concrete actions or accomplishments. Malcolm did not build an institution of lasting significance, nor did he influence legislation, nor did he leave behind treatises that explain a coherent political or philosophical point of view. His legacy is a collection of speeches, debates, and interviews and an autobiography published posthumously. That Malcolm continues to be an object of fascination is a tribute to the enduring power of his rhetoric.

Malcolm's rhetoric can be bisected twice: into two phases, Nation of Islam rhetoric and post–Nation of Islam rhetoric; and also into two rhetorical missions, waking up black people and denouncing white people. Leaving the Nation of Islam and its teachings helped to secularize his speeches, and his waking up black people became at this time more political than religious. His denunciation of white people became more selective at this time as he came to believe that not all whites worldwide were implacable enemies. Nonetheless, Malcolm's characteristic rhetorical strategies remained consistent even through the drastic changes in his ideas, beliefs, and perspectives.

"Message to the Grass Roots" is the best known and probably the best of his Nation of Islam speeches. Delivered to an audience of militant black activists in Detroit, Michigan, on November 10, 1963, it provides a striking demonstration of Malcolm's adjustment to a black audience already "awake" and leaning toward Malcolm's own version of black nationalism. He articulated themes common to many of his speeches at this time: the need to unify diverse black activists against a common enemy, criticism of a unilateral commitment to nonviolence as inconsistent and impractical, and definition of the true nature of revolution.

His emphasis on a need for unity was based upon sharing a common enemy:

> What you and I need to do is learn to forget our differences. . . . We have this in common: We have a common oppressor, a common exploiter, and a common discriminator. But once we all realize that we have a common enemy, then we unite—on the basis of what we have in common. And what we have foremost in common is that enemy—the white man.

This appeal, repeated frequently throughout Malcolm's career in speeches to non-Muslim African-American audiences, has immediate power but underlying weaknesses, demonstrating the rhetorical strengths inherent in Nation of Islam discourse as well as the weakness of Elijah Muhammad's understanding of the character of African-American culture. Social identification cast in negative terms, defined by a common enemy, creates a strong sense of "us versus them" and therefore intensifies a feeling of solidarity. This was especially important for Malcolm, whose religion and attacks on Christianity would tend to alienate black people generally even when they agreed with him on non-religious points. But it defines what one is against without emphasizing what one is for and makes African-American unity and identity dependent upon the enemy. This perspective is consistent with the Nation of Islam's portrayal of African-American culture as pathological and desperately in need of a salvation that only Elijah Muhammad can provide.

Malcolm's criticism of a unilateral commitment to nonviolence was rooted in pragmatic social and political behavior as well as principles of ethical consistency and reciprocity:

> How can you justify being nonviolent in Mississippi and Alabama, when your churches are being bombed, and your little girls are being murdered, and at the same time you are going to get violent with Hitler, and Tojo, and somebody else you don't even know?
>
> If violence is wrong in America, violence is wrong abroad. If it is wrong to be violent defending black women and black children and black babies and black men, then it is wrong for America to draft us and make us violent abroad in

defense of her. And if it is right for America to draft us, and teach us how to be violent in defense of her, then it is right for you and me to do whatever is necessary to defend our own people right here in this country.

His definition of revolution served to undercut and reduce to absurdity the claims of mainstream civil rights leaders that they were conducting a "Negro revolution":

There's no such thing as a nonviolent revolution. The only kind of revolution that is nonviolent is the Negro revolution. The only revolution in which the goal is loving your enemy is the Negro revolution. It's the only revolution in which the goal is a desegregated lunch counter, a desegregated theater, a desegregated park, and a desegregated public toilet; you can sit down next to white folks—on the toilet. That's not revolution. . . . Revolution is bloody, revolution is hostile, revolution knows no compromise, revolution overturns and destroys everything that gets in its way.

"The Ballot or the Bullet," delivered in Cleveland, Ohio, on April 3, 1964, shortly after the break with Elijah Muhammad, and Malcolm's stump speech for the last year of his life, demonstrates some of the changes in his perspectives, particularly his turn toward political activism, his conception of black nationalism, and his turn away from blanket condemnation of whites. Malcolm used "the ballot" and "the bullet" metonymically to characterize antithetical strategies for changing American society, either by working within the system of representative government, or else, failing that, by violent resistance against a system that could not be reformed. Clearly he preferred a political solution, reserving violent resistance as a last resort, and even then expecting that violence could be used to spur political reformation without necessitating a commitment to the complete overthrow of the government. Still, Malcolm was pessimistic about political processes, asserting that the system was corrupted by racism and the hypocritical violation of its own laws and declared principles.

These senators and congressmen actually violate the constitutional amendments that guarantee the people of that particular state or county the right to vote. . . . If the black man in these Southern states had his full voting rights, the key Dixiecrats in Washington, D.C. . . . would lose their seats. . . .

You and I in America are faced not with a segregationist conspiracy, we're faced with a government conspiracy. Everyone who's finagling in Washington, D.C., is a congressman—that's the government. . . . The same government that you go abroad to fight for and die for is the government that is in a conspiracy to deprive you of your voting rights, deprive you of your economic opportunities, deprive you of decent housing, deprive you of decent education.

His articulation of black nationalism partook of traditional definitions:

> The political philosophy of black nationalism means that the black man should control the politics and the politicians in his own community.... The economic philosophy of black nationalism ... means that we should control the economy of our community.... The social philosophy of black nationalism only means that we have to get together and remove the evils, the vices, alcoholism, drug addiction, and other evils that are destroying the moral fiber of our community.

Malcolm's rhetoric here was preeminently ethical. He presented himself as an ethical exemplar in arguing for societal change that began with the transformation of individual character. In contrast to his Nation of Islam rhetoric, Malcolm's post–Nation rhetoric urged action, so the ethical transformation was not static, as with true believers waiting for the millennium, but rather a prelude to informed and effective action, based upon education and uplifting of the individual, the family, the community, and the African-American "nation."

> [B]lack nationalism ... is not designed to make the black man re-evaluate the white man—you know him already—but to make the black man re-evaluate himself. We've got to change our own minds about each other. We have to see each other with new eyes. We have to see each other as brothers and sisters.

"The Ballot or the Bullet" is also marked by Malcolm's attempts to dissociate himself from past racist statements and blanket condemnations of all whites:

> Now in speaking like this, it doesn't mean that we're anti-white, but it does mean we're anti-exploitation, we're anti-degradation, we're anti-oppression. And if the white man doesn't want us to be anti-him, let him stop oppressing and exploiting and degrading us.

Malcolm's arguments are marked by frequent antitheses and figures of speech and strategies of argument that evidence antithetical thinking. This places him squarely in the tradition of the African-American cultural predilection for antithetical thought and expression, itself a response to being surrounded by a hostile culture that historically has denied its humanity, worth, intelligence, and creativity, while also defining African-Americans as ugly, stupid, dishonest, and lascivious. Even more, the professed ideals of American democracy, fair play, and freedom have so blatantly been ignored and transgressed as regards African-Americans that historically there has been a large gap between what is professed and promised and what is delivered, between official appearance and rank reality. The historic response has been discourse that exposes the hypocrisy and the disparity between what is real and what is declared. Malcolm's frequently used antitheses not only function in the usual way of antitheses, to emphasize by contrast and juxtaposition, but they also suggest a refutation of the audience's habits of thought and expectation and social identification:

> [In a revolution] You don't do any singing, you're too busy swinging.

We didn't land on Plymouth Rock . . . Plymouth Rock landed on us.

No, I'm not an American. I'm one of the 22 million black people who are the victims of Americanism.

I don't see any American dream; I see an American nightmare.

Likewise, Malcolm's frequent use of chiasmus—the reversal of grammatical structures in successive clauses—reflects the belief that black people's sense of reality is distorted, reversed, oriented in a way opposite to realistic, self-interested, and advantageous thinking. Underlying all of this is a sense that the influence of white supremacy imposes a reversal of proper moral order, a reversal of reality.

[Y]ou end up hating your friends and loving your enemies.

[P]eople accept wrong as right and reject right as wrong.

[P]eople actually think that the criminal is the victim and the victim is the criminal.

Focusing often on the easy-to-expose hypocrisy of white America, Malcolm's rhetoric also functions to diminish conventional authority by exposing its weaknesses and dishonesty and by challenging its rhetorical power with his own, which, because of the built-in hypocrisy that he so easily exposes and debunks, actually gives him, discursively at least, power comparable to the power of institutions. Thus he could point out the gaps between the declared ideals of the founding fathers and the Christian churches in comparison with their actions toward Americans of African descent.

Indisputably powerful though it is, Malcolm's rhetoric presents some problems, most particularly as regards the numerous inaccuracies, misstatements, errors, and exaggerations that mark his speeches. A representative example is his discussion (from ''Message to the Grass Roots'') of the ''house Negro'' and the ''field Negro'':

There were two kinds of slaves, the house Negro and the field Negro. The house Negroes . . . lived near the master; and they loved the master more than the master loved himself. . . . And if you came to the house Negro and said, ''Let's run away, let's escape, let's separate,'' the house Negro would look at you and say, ''Man, you crazy. What you mean, separate?'' That was the house Negro. In those days he was called a ''house nigger.'' And that's what we call them today, because we've still got some house niggers running around here.

On that same plantation, there was the field Negro. . . . The field Negro was beaten from morning to night. . . . He hated his master. I say he hated his master. He was intelligent. . . . If someone came to the field Negro and said, ''Let's separate, let's run,'' he didn't say ''Where we going?'' He'd say, ''Any place is better than here.'' You've got field Negroes in America today. I'm a field Negro.

As a rhetorical tool, Malcolm's contrast effectively derides the ''house'' attitude, compelling the audience to choose to identify with the field Negro. The concept clearly and vividly describes opposing sets of value, self-interest, and social identity. By personifying the ethic of the field Negro, Malcolm invited his audience to share in his own ethos, to become what he was in an act of emulation, identification, and communion. This particular exercise of Malcolm's rhetorical power has been persistently influential for nearly thirty years.

However compelling, Malcolm's characterization of the house slave and the field slave simply is not true. The historical truth is that, apart from the occasional Judas or slave snob, the slaves in the master's house were most often conduits of vital information to their field counterparts. They were often spies in the homes of their enemies, using the intelligence they gathered to help other slaves escape, or at least to help them better cope with their burdens. Malcolm's description offers not only inaccurate history but slander as well. It is false teaching. Moreover, because it may work ultimately to narrow rather than to broaden the range of strategies available to his followers in their struggle for liberation, this rhetoric potentially diminishes the members of his audience in the very act of trying to edify them.

Such misstatements can be found in nearly every one of his speeches, but it is difficult to call these misstatements of facts ''lies.'' Evidence suggests that Malcolm not only meant what he said but also genuinely meant well. Further, he aimed to enlighten and elevate his audience by helping them to discover truth. Although ignorance is no excuse, nor is it especially a virtue in those who would be leaders, neither does it deserve the degree of censure we diligently accord cynical manipulation and outright dishonesty. In fact, Malcolm's career encourages tolerance for his being misinformed, both because of the circumstances of his intellectual growth and because whenever he discovered his errors he immediately and publicly corrected himself. In his descriptions of the house and the field slaves, for instance, he was trying earnestly to teach his audience on the basis of history. He was always at least a seeker of truth, if not always a finder of it. It is neither too generous nor too romantic to believe that, had he not been murdered in the middle of his self-education, he likely would have combined knowledge with his formidable intellect and good sense to produce something like ''wisdom.'' So while one cannot blithely ignore defects in argumentation, including conclusions drawn from premises that are demonstrably false, analogies in which one term has no basis in reality, or lessons drawn from history that never happened, dwelling on these deficiencies seems almost beside the point in attempting to understand Malcolm's rhetorical power.

Ultimately, any impartial assessment of Malcolm's career as an orator demands something of the intellectual and analytical flexibility that Malcolm himself displayed. His rhetoric deserves respect for its persuasive power, its humor, its frequent analytical sharpness and constant lucidity, its vigorous arguments, and its capacity for exposing hatred and hypocrisy. It also deserves some reproof for its frequent, if inadvertent, misstatements of fact. Finally, Malcolm commands honor for the relentless honesty that impelled him to search for and to articulate the truth as he understood it, even when to do so meant severe disadvantage for him. He was a good man who tried his best to uplift his society by speaking well.

INFORMATION SOURCES

Research Collections and Collected Speeches

No collection of speeches exists because Malcolm did not speak from written texts, but the most extensive collection of tape recordings of his speeches may be found in the Malcolm X Collection at the Schomburg Center for Research in Black Culture, the New York Public Library.

[*WWG*] Lomax, Louis. *When the Word Is Given*. New York: Signet, 1964.
[*AMN*] X, Malcolm. *By Any Means Necessary: Speeches, Interviews, and a Letter, by Malcolm X*. Ed. George Breitman. New York: Pathfinder, 1970.
[*WWS*]———. *The End of White World Supremacy; Four Speeches*. Ed., introd. by Goodman Benjamin. New York: Merlin House, 1971.
[*TES*]———. *February 1965: The Final Speeches*. Ed. Steve Clark. New York: Pathfinder, 1992.
———. *Malcolm X on Afro-American History*. New York: Merit Publishers, 1967.
[*AAH*]———. *Malcolm X on Afro-American History*. Expanded and illustrated ed. New York: Pathfinder, 1970.
[*MXS*]———. *Malcolm X Speaks: Selected Speeches and Statements*. Ed. George Breitman. New York: Merit, 1965.
[*TYP*]———. *Malcolm X Talks to Young People: Speeches in the U.S., Britain, and Africa*. Ed. Steve Clark. New York: Pathfinder, 1991.
[*TLS*]———. *Malcolm X: The Last Speeches*. Ed. Bruce Perry. New York: Pathfinder, 1989.
[*SAH*]———. *The Speeches of Malcolm X at Harvard*. Ed. Archie Epps. With an introductory essay. New York: William Morrow, 1968.

Selected Critical Studies

Benson, Thomas W. "Rhetoric and Autobiography: The Case of Malcolm X." *Quarterly Journal of Speech* 60 (1974): 1–13.
Breitman, George. *The Last Year of Malcolm X: The Evolution of a Revolutionary*. New York: Merit Publishers, 1967.
Campbell, Finley C. "Voices of Thunder, Voices of Rage: A Symbolic Analysis of a Selection from Malcolm X's Speech, 'Message to the Grass Roots.' " *Speech Teacher* 19.2 (1970): 101–110.
Flick, Hank, and Larry Powell. "Animal Imagery in the Rhetoric of Malcolm X." *Journal of Black Studies* 18.4 (1988): 435–451.
Illo, John. "The Rhetoric of Malcolm X." *The Columbia University Forum* 9 (1966): 5–12.

Leader, Edward Roland. *Understanding Malcolm X: The Controversial Changes in His Political Philosophy.* New York: Vantage, 1993.

Paris, Peter J. "Malcolm X." *Black Religious Leaders: Conflict in Unity.* 2nd ed. Louisville, KY: Westminster/John Knox, 1991, 183–222.

Rich, Andrea Louise, and Arthur L. Smith, assisted by Elizabeth Barry. "Malcolm X: Architect of Black Revolution." *Rhetoric of Revolution: Samuel Adams, Emma Goldman, Malcolm X.* Durham, NC: Moore Pub. Co., 1970, 143–212.

Sales, William W., Jr. *From Civil Rights to Black Liberation: Malcolm X and the Organization of Afro-American Unity.* Boston: South End, 1994.

White, John. "Malcolm X: Sinner and Convert." *Black Leadership in America: From Booker T. Washington to Jesse Jackson.* 2nd ed. Studies in Modern History. London and New York: Longman, 1990, 145–171.

Wolfenstein, E. Victor. *The Victims of Democracy: Malcolm X and the Black Revolution.* Berkeley: U of California P, 1981.

Selected Biographies

Goldman, Peter Louis. *The Death and Life of Malcolm X.* 2nd ed. Blacks in the New World. Urbana: U of Illinois P, 1979.

Perry, Bruce. *Malcolm: The Life of a Man Who Changed Black America.* Barrytown, NY: Station Hill Press. 1991.

X, Malcolm. *The Autobiography of Malcolm X.* With the assistance of Alex Haley. Introd. by M. S. Handler. Epilogue by Alex Haley. New York: Grove Press, 1965. New York: Ballantine, 1973.

CHRONOLOGY OF MAJOR SPEECHES

[See "Research Collections and Collected Speeches" for source codes.]

"Malcolm X at Yale." New Haven, CT, n.d. *WWG,* 179–195.

"Malcolm X 'On Unity.' " Harlem, NY, 1960. *WWG,* 128–135.

"The Harvard Law School Forum of March 24, 1961." Cambridge, MA, March 24, 1961. *SAH,* 115–131.

"Black Man's History." Harlem, NY, December 1962. *WWS,* 23–66.

"The Black Revolution." Harlem, NY, June 1963. *WWS,* 67–80.

"The Old Negro and the New Negro." Philadelphia, PA, fall 1963. *WWS,* 81–120.

"Message to the Grass Roots." Detroit, MI, November 10, 1963. *MXS,* 4–17.

"God's Judgment of White America (The Chickens Are Coming Home to Roost)." New York, NY, December 4, 1963. *WWS,* 121–148.

"The Leverett House Forum of March 18, 1964." Cambridge, MA, March 18, 1964. *SAH,* 131–160.

"The Ballot or the Bullet." Cleveland, OH, April 3, 1964. *MXS,* 23–44.

"The Founding Rally of the OAAU." Harlem, NY, June 28, 1964. *AMN,* 33–68.

"The Second Rally of the OAAU." Harlem, NY, July 5, 1964. *AMN,* 75–107.

"At the Audubon." Harlem, NY, December 13, 1964. *MXS,* 88–104.

"The Harvard Law School Forum of December 16, 1964." Cambridge, MA, December 16, 1964. *SAH,* 161–182.

"At the Audubon." Harlem, NY, December 20, 1964. *MXS,* 115–136.

"The Oppressed Masses of the World Cry Out for Action against the Common Oppressor." London, England, February 11, 1965. *TFS,* 46–64.

"There's a Worldwide Revolution Going On." Harlem, NY, February 15, 1965. *TFS,* 106–142.

"Not Just an American Problem, But a World Problem." Rochester, NY, February 16, 1965. *TFS,* 143–170.

ANDREW JACKSON YOUNG

(1932–   ), minister, civil rights activist, U.S. representative, U.S. ambassador, mayor

CAL M. LOGUE AND JEAN L. DEHART

Andrew Jackson Young has been successful as minister, civil rights worker, representative to Congress from Georgia, mayor of Atlanta, United Nations ambassador, and corporate executive. Young's early training prepared him well for these diverse tasks. Because of his rearing, Young gained an appreciation for reading, became secure in his convictions, and learned to communicate well with diverse audiences. Born on March 12, 1932, in New Orleans, Louisiana, the son of Andrew J. Young, a dentist, and Daisy Fuller Young, a teacher, as a child Young was "encouraged" to "express himself well." By joining in "adult conversation," he gained personal confidence and better awareness of others' motivations. Through these experiences, he acquired the art of adjusting to others, a skill that later enabled him to mobilize many African-American citizens and to negotiate with selected white segregationists.

In school, Young studied a varied curriculum that eventually led to the ministry and active participation in street protests for civil rights for African-Americans, politics, and business. After finishing his program of study at Gilbert Academy, a private school in New Orleans, in 1947 and studying for two years at Dillard University, he was graduated with the B.S. degree in biology from Howard University, Washington, D.C., and from Hartford Theological Seminary, Connecticut. As a member of the United Church of Christ, during the 1950s he pastored a church in Marion, Alabama, the Bethany Congregational Church in Thomasville, Georgia, and the Evergreen Congregational Church in Beachton, Georgia. Even in this early ministry, Young broadened his sacred mission to include remedies for alcoholism, unemployment, teenage pregnancy, and lack of voter registration.

Early experiences dealing with hostile audiences prepared Young well for participation in the civil rights movement. When Young was minister of the church in Thomasville, African-Americans were not allowed to go to the front door of a white person's house. As cochair of the March of Dimes drive in that community, however, Young did just that. Also, as he described to newspaper editors at a 1989 meeting in Atlanta, when he organized a campaign to register blacks to vote in south Georgia, four hundred members of the Ku Klux Klan attempted to intimidate him to cease that work. As associate director of youth with the National Council of Churches from 1957 to 1967, Young gained knowledge and skills working with television that were invaluable in attracting national media coverage of civil rights protests. In 1978, Young explained to a University of Georgia Law Day audience how the "mass media made possible the reeducation of the American people along new concepts of justice."

During the 1960s, Young was executive director and executive vice president of the Southern Christian Leadership Conference (SCLC), an organization led by Dr. Martin Luther King, Jr. Being a "superb organizer," Young often researched conditions and issues and negotiated behind the scenes. Young helped draft legislation for the voting rights bill of 1965 and prepared the way for King's arrival for protest efforts in communities throughout the South and beyond. While greatly valued by King as a strategist for the movement, Young was also effective as mobilizer and protester, marching arm in arm in the streets of the South and beyond with King, Reverend Ralph Abernathy, and others. In 1963, Young spoke in African-American schools to mobilize children to march and sing against discriminatory segregationist laws in the streets of Birmingham. On three occasions he was jailed for protesting discriminatory practices. In St. Augustine, Florida, in 1964, while promoting a "crisis of conscience," Young was knocked unconscious. In Memphis, at the time King was murdered, Young appeared in court to remove obstacles to the SCLC's initiatives.

After King was assassinated, Young worked for equal justice and advancement for all through public office. He was defeated in his first campaign for the U.S. House of Representatives from Georgia. However, in 1972, he won election to the House, becoming the first African-American from Georgia to be elected to Congress since Reconstruction. Serving in Congress from 1972 to 1976, Young fought successfully to protect the peanut subsidy for Georgia farmers, the Talmadge Bridge in Savannah, the state's interstate highway system, Atlanta's rapid rail-transit network, the international airport in Atlanta, and preservation of the Chattahoochee River as a national recreation area. From 1977 to 1979, Young served in the Jimmy Carter administration as ambassador to the United Nations. As ambassador, Young helped introduce American businesses to the markets of the world. In 1980, President Carter awarded him the Presidential Medal of Freedom. From 1980 to 1981, Young was president of Young Ideas, Inc., and wrote for the *Los Angeles Times*. He was mayor of Atlanta from 1982 to 1989, an achievement he used in speeches to illustrate the social progress made in the South since the 1950s, when he had been threatened for merely assisting African-Americans to register to vote. In 1990, although unsuccessful in becoming the Democratic candidate for governor, Young was the first

African-American in Georgia to make it past the initial primary and into a runoff. Later, Young became executive consultant for the Law Companies and worked to bring the 1996 Olympics to Atlanta.

ANDREW YOUNG AS POLITICAL PREACHER

With his own experience in Atlanta in mind, Young explained to newspaper editors convened in Atlanta in 1989 that ''a Mayor is basically a preacher with a big pulpit.'' By temperament and actions, Young has been more mentor and instructor to followers and opponents than agitator. Motivated by an idealistic view of life, in his discourses Young inquires and teaches more than he rebukes. ''You never know it all,'' he cautioned a graduating class at Oglethorpe University in Atlanta in 1990. We must ''understand the past so that we might be able to shape the present and dream about the future.'' Recognizing the constant ''struggle'' fought ''between . . . good and evil within'' each person, in 1990, Young warned soldiers at Fort Stewart, Georgia, that correcting social abuses is ''not something you can do once and for all.'' Rather, he indicated during an ''honesty campaign'' in Columbus, Ohio, that same year, one must be vigilant to oppose social evils confronted by ''every generation.''

Young's political theology is firmly grounded in a personal commitment to moral integrity. In 1978, he told the Georgia Law Day audience that ''noncooperation with evil is as important as cooperation with good.'' In a time when many are cautious to separate religious beliefs from public life, Young often fuses sacred and secular values. While speaking about health care and social problems to a graduation exercise at Georgia College in 1990, Young advised those present to ''work out your own salvation with fear and trembling under the watchful eye of a liberating God.'' Young frequently stresses ''the spiritual values which hold our country together.'' In early 1990, during Martin Luther King Week at the University of Georgia and at a Fort Stewart prayer breakfast, Young lamented the ''aimlessness'' and ''lack of discipline'' among the youth of the United States. As a remedy to these ills, he recommended that young citizens be taught that ''their bodies are the temple of the holy spirit.'' Thus they should gain ''respect'' for ''themselves'' and discover the ''meaning of prayer.'' Young reflected that he applied these same ideals to himself when he expressed remorse over the increased crime rate in Atlanta during his term as mayor. At a 1990 Georgia Professional Crime Fighters Association meeting in Atlanta, Young explained that he was ''ashamed that as a result of my struggle'' crime had increased.

An offshoot of Young's pledge to principle is his personal optimism about life. Despite the racial discrimination he has experienced and observed, Young urges citizens to, as Gardner quotes him, ''see hope where there is none.'' However, he combines idealism with realism in arguing for a ''realistic hope,'' as when in 1977, while United Nations ambassador, Young told the United

Nations Economic Commission for Latin America that "hope must have a basis or it is not hope, but an illusion."

Young translates religious values into political practice. In his optimistic statement to the United Nations Economic Commission, Young explained that his faith might stem from "the preacher in me." Young recalled for the Honesty Campaign audience in Columbus, Ohio, in March 1990 how hard experience in the trenches of the civil rights movement had convinced him that basic values are "essential to a survival of any civilized . . . society." "Unless we find a way to maintain a level of honesty and fairness," he reminded the leaders in Ohio, "the values of our society will not be able to survive." He called for a return to communities "undergirded by a basic foundation of morality" and "respect." "One of the nicest compliments people paid to us in the civil rights movement," Young continued, was "that we were able to treat people better than they really were. . . . We expected them to respond to our initiative of love and forgiveness for racial segregation . . . and they did."

To Young, communal integrity branches from raw courage. "If you let people stop you," Schulke and McPhee quote him as saying, "it only encouraged them to kill you. . . . So we were morally obligated to . . . continue march[ing]." Young explained to soldiers and their families at Fort Stewart that during the civil rights movement, he and fellow activists "found the wisdom, the faith, the courage, and the determination" required in the "religious undergirding of our political process," when "human rights became a part of the national politics."

Young's faith in the human spirit's potential for good is reflected in his speaking strategies. Ultimately Young believes that one must do what is morally right. When translated into street protests, this means acting nonviolently for a defensible cause. For example, in Birmingham in 1963, Young faced the formidable trial of convincing many African-Americans not to retaliate against whites' bombings with violent acts of their own. Initially, when one talked "in terms of nonviolence in Birmingham," he recalled to Schulke and McPhee, "folks would look at you like you were crazy because they had been bombing black homes." Although involved in dangerous activities about volatile issues, Young exercised more personal "control" than many. On most occasions, when plotting protests for particular communities, Young counselled King to take a judicious approach to problem solving, a view King came to expect and appreciate. Rather than alienate supporters and opponents, Young attempted to find common ground for progress.

Young's brave work for civil rights has enhanced his credibility throughout his career of private and public works. To the March 2, 1990, Council on Foreign Relations meeting to honor Franklin H. Williams of the Harlem Boys Choir, Young explained the special credentials of civil rights workers. What gave these protesters their "intensity" and "passion," he stated, "comes from being black, and being oppressed . . . the humiliation, the frustration, the experiences . . . and having to . . . overcome it." This background "also gives you a kind of identification with the oppressed, and it gives the oppressed an identification with you.''

Young's belief in honest citizenship is reflected in the singular candor with which he speaks publicly, a practice that angers some and gratifies others. Young's public address is distinguished by its forthrightness. For example, Stone records that Young accused the British of ''invent[ing] racism'' and criticized Swedes as being ''terrible racists.'' He opposed the Vietnam War and was willing to talk with leaders of the Palestine Liberation Organization (PLO) as well as segregationists in the deep South. Although some critics perceived him to be impulsive, many who disagreed with Young respected his frank counsel. For example, because of his ''gentle, intelligent tone of voice and his hard working ethics,'' colleagues in the Congress ''liked him.'' With ''humor'' and ''candor,'' Stone says, Young could ''win'' over hostile audiences. They ''listen[ed] to him.'' Usually at least once during a speech, Young will needle himself to make a point. To the 1990 Georgia College graduates, Young admitted that ''I graduated not *cum laude*, but 'Oh Thank you Lord-ie' [extended laughter and applause].'' ''When *Ms. Magazine* said that I was one of the people in the Carter administration who was most sensitive to the rights of women,'' Young told the 1978 University of Georgia Law Day audience, ''the women in my household said the Carter administration is in terrible shape!'' Young often extends wit to support a claim. In many speeches, when marvelling at his own election as mayor of Atlanta, he describes how, when driving through Georgia in the 1950s, he ''stopped for a rat in the road,'' maintaining that the rat ''had more rights'' in the South than African-Americans.

Young is able to unite individuals with differing opinions for a common cause. In the King Week speech at the University of Georgia, Young stressed how ''Martin always said you have got to find a way to give your opponent a face saving way out.'' ''Celebrat[ing] diversity,'' he argued in the King Week address that ''nonviolence is not one side trying to overcome the other side. Nonviolence is both sides coming together . . . where both can be free.'' Persons of diverse backgrounds, Young advised his Columbus, Ohio, listeners, can ''maintain'' their ''identity . . . sense of heritage and pride, and learn from each other.'' Young perceived the law to be a complementary instrument to nonviolence. In his University of Georgia Law Day address, Young envisioned law as ''a creative dialogue'' between individuals and government. He said that law helps citizens ''come to an understanding of new ways of relating to each other which provides justice and equality and human opportunity to all citizens.''

Through his tenure as ambassador to the United Nations, Young applied his faith in diversity when calling for cooperation among nations. In the 1990 Columbus, Ohio, address, he advocated peace and prosperity through ''respect'' of ''each other's culture.'' ''Foreign policy,'' he explained to the Council on Foreign Relations, ''is about reconciliation, and reconciliation is about bringing together opposite cultures.'' He was particularly pleased, as he observed at the 1990 Oglethorpe University commencement, that ''almost anywhere in the world that people have come to rise up to be free . . . they always sing 'We Shall Overcome.' '' This ''ideal . . . of social change that evolved from Georgia . . . helped transform the world . . . without violence.''

While some African-American leaders have advocated a separatist approach to abolishing racial inequities, Young works within the framework of the body politic. He advocated to his Fort Stewart, Georgia, listeners that people should ''disagree without being disagreeable.'' Before the Council on Foreign Relations in New York City, Young recommended that minority advocates ''be able to get along with the brothers on the street in Harlem, and . . . in the forums of the Supreme Court or in the boardrooms of corporate America and the forums of the United Nations, and do it equally well.'' While refusing to sacrifice principle for effect, when appropriate, he adapted skillfully both to African-Americans angered by constant abuse and to white leaders hampered by racist traditions. He was comfortable reaching out to rural and urban African-Americans and whites. While recognizing that racist attitudes ''are still there,'' he informed the Columbus, Ohio, honesty campaigners that when he had been campaigning for governor throughout Georgia, he had received a ''very positive'' response from audiences ranging from members of the Confederate Civil War Service to African-American and white farmers convened at country stores.

In his transformation from the pulpit to government, Young has balanced commitment to integrity with the necessity of money and the importance of education. During the civil rights movement, he discovered the value of economic boycotts. In his Law Day speech at the University of Georgia, he reasoned wryly how it only takes ''about a 10 percent minority to bring about a new sensitivity . . . in the business community.'' In 1974, as a member of Congress, Young predicted that ''the battleground of the future is the world marketplace.'' At the Oglethorpe University graduation in 1990, Young posited that citizens would be increasingly preoccupied with ''the struggles between the haves and the have-nots'' and ''amongst the genders.'' ''I don't care what you do with race relations,'' he argued to newspaper editors, ''it's economics that are vital. In order to make the politics of the South work, it's got to translate economically'' and ''through education'' to ''wiping out poverty'' and ''educational inadequacies.'' If the nation educates its youth, he told Georgia College graduates, then those persons will not be ''on welfare, not in jail, not burdens.''

Increasingly, Young has contended that equitable economic opportunity is the basis for more stable institutions and better living conditions for all, nationally and internationally. In 1973, he argued before the U.S. House of Representatives that the ''worst energy crisis'' is ''the waste of energy by idle people who want jobs.'' As mayor of Atlanta, Young placed great emphasis upon economic prosperity and job growth. His administration attracted billions of dollars of new investments and half a million new jobs to Georgia, brought the Democratic National Convention to Atlanta, and amassed 142 million dollars to redevelop Underground Atlanta, a potentially flourishing shopping area. Later, Young was personally instrumental in attracting the 1996 Summer Olympic Games to Atlanta, winning the day with a ringing appeal to the decision-making authority.

Communities "must generate wealth," he advocated to newspaper editors in 1989, "not just redistribute it." Young often traveled to Africa and other countries in search of reciprocal investing of resources. In his 1990 speech to the Council on Foreign Relations, Young reiterated his belief in the importance of economics by stressing that U.S. "foreign policy in the 21st century will be overwhelmingly economic policy."

Whether speaking on human values or economic prosperity, Young's delivery style confirms his preference for informed instruction over oratorical bombast. He addresses African-American students, racially integrated audiences, and white auditors in the mode of a reasonable instructor. Video recordings of speeches show him speaking in a businesslike demeanor, patiently explaining the causes and implications of social, economic, and educational wrongs and opportunities. While carefully laying the groundwork that enables audiences to comprehend a subject, Young stands calmly with hands moving for emphasis, continuously searching for understanding in the eyes of his audiences. Seldom referring to prepared notes in his speeches, Young exhibits a superior memory and an unusually keen command of thought and language needed to dissect complex and controversial issues. Although not overbearing, Young speaks with confidence, decisiveness, and authoritativeness, refusing to compromise basic values of decency and character.

Motivated by personal integrity and a desire that all citizens have a fair chance for advancement in life, as minister, congressional representative, ambassador, mayor, and business executive, through an enlightened, uplifting, and judicious discourse and organizational prowess, Andrew Young has contributed substantially to the extension of civil rights to all residents of the United States and beyond. In 1989, looking back at advances made, Young concluded that "law enforcement, voting rights, educational opportunity for all by and large have been guaranteed in my life time." With justifiable pride he counted twenty-three Georgia towns with African-American mayors. In Thomasville, for example, although the majority of voters were white, citizens there elected an African-American mayor. While aware of progress, Young explained to newspaper editors gathered from throughout the United States and a few other countries that much remained to be done. He noted that children "move into Atlanta from rural areas with little or no preparation." Many of the elderly were in need of services, and 30 percent of citizens "live below the poverty line," he reminded. Great strides had been taken, he praised, but "we still are struggling" for "economic development."

INFORMATION SOURCES

Research Collections and Collected Speeches

Andrew Young's papers are housed at the Martin Luther King, Jr., Center for Non-violence in Atlanta, Georgia. Many of his papers are still uncatalogued, but a number are available in the collection on the Southern Christian Leadership Conference at the King Center.

Andrew Young at the United Nations. Ed. Lee Clement. Salisbury, NC: Documentary Publications, 1978.

Selected Critical Studies

Gardner, Carl. *Andrew Young: A Biography.* New York: Drake Publishers, 1978.
Haskins, James. *Andrew Young: Man with a Mission.* New York: Lothrop, Lee, and Shepard Co., 1979.
King, Coretta Scott. *My Life with Martin Luther King, Jr.* New York: Holt, Rinehart and Winston, 1969.
Oates, Stephen B. *Let the Trumpet Sound: The Life of Martin Luther King, Jr.* New York: Harper and Row, 1982.
Schulke, Flip, and Penelope O. McPhee. *King Remembered.* New York: W. W. Norton, 1986.
Simpson, Jan. *Andrew Young: A Matter of Choice.* St. Paul, MN: EMC Corporation, 1978.
Stone, Eddie. *Andrew Young: Biography of a Realist.* Los Angeles, CA: Holloway House, 1980.

CHRONOLOGY OF MAJOR SPEECHES

Remarks on the Comprehensive Manpower Act of 1973. U.S. House of Representatives, Washington, D.C., November 28, 1973. *Congressional Record*, 38425–38426.
Extension of remarks on "Going to War without an Army." U.S. House of Representatives, Washington, D.C., July 1, 1974. *Congressional Record*, 21971–21972.
"Law Day Address." University of Georgia, Athens, GA, April 29, 1978. Audio recording provided by the University of Georgia, Athens, GA.
"Speech to Annual Conference of the International Society of Weekly Newspaper Editors." Oglethorpe University, Atlanta, GA, July 12, 1989. Video recording provided by the International Society of Weekly Newspaper Editors, Santa Fe, NM.
"Martin Luther King Week Speech." University of Georgia, Athens, GA, January 17, 1990. Audio recording provided by the University of Georgia, Athens, GA.
"Prayer Breakfast Speech." Officers' Club, Fort Stewart, GA, February 22, 1990. Video recording provided by the Chaplin, Fort Stewart, GA.
"Minority Involvement in Making Foreign Policy Speech." Council on Foreign Relations, luncheon honoring Franklin H. Williams of the Harlem Boys Choir, New York, NY, March 2, 1990. Video recording provided by the Council on Foreign Relations, New York, NY.
"Honesty Campaign Speech." Honesty Campaign Luncheon, Columbus, OH, March 9, 1990. Video recording provided by the Mayor's Office, Columbus, Oh.
Speech to Georgia Professional Crime Fighters Association. Atlanta, GA, May 4, 1990. Excerpts in *Atlanta Constitution*, May 5, 1990: C3.
"Oglethorpe University Commencement Address." Atlanta, GA, May 13, 1990. Video recording provided by Oglethorpe University, Atlanta, GA.
"Georgia College Commencement Speech." Milledgeville, GA, June 9, 1990. Video recording provided by Georgia College, Milledgeville, GA.

INDEX

ABOUT THE CONTRIBUTORS

HAL W. BOCHIN, Professor of Speech Communication, California State University, Fresno, teaches courses in rhetorical criticism and the history of American public address. He is the author of *Richard Nixon: Rhetorical Strategist* and coauthor of *Hiram Johnson: A Bio-Bibliography* and *Hiram Johnson: Political Revivalist.*

DETINE L. BOWERS, Assistant Professor of Communication Studies, Virginia Polytechnic Institute and State University, teaches courses in African-American rhetoric, rhetorical theory, and rhetorical criticism. Her research specialization and publications focus on African-American rhetoric and Afrocentrism. The author wishes to express her gratitude to Desta D. Daggett for her research assistance on this essay.

BERNARD L. BROCK, Professor of Speech Communication, Wayne State University, teaches courses in rhetorical criticism, political communication, and contemporary public address. He has published widely on rhetoric and public address and is coauthor of *Methods of Rhetorical Criticism: A Twentieth-Century Perspective.*

CARL R. BURGCHARDT, Associate Professor of Speech Communication, Colorado State University, teaches and publishes in the areas of critical methodology and the history and analysis of American public address. He is the author of *Robert M. La Follette, Sr.: The Voice of Conscience* and articles on Communist pamphlets, William E. Borah, Henry Clay, and Herbert Hoover.

RUTHLEON W. BUTLER, Faculty Associate, Department of Communication, Arizona State University, teaches courses in performance studies and intercultural communication. She studies African-American women's rhetoric from an indigenous perspective and wrote her M.A. thesis on "Double Voice in the Rhetoric of African American Women."

A. CHEREE CARLSON, Associate Professor of Communication and Women's Studies, Arizona State University, is a rhetorician with a long-standing interest in the history of women's issues. She has written several articles on women's rhetoric in the nineteenth-century United States.

DANIEL ROSS CHANDLER, a United Methodist minister, is a Post-Doctoral Research Scholar in the Divinity School of the University of Chicago. He is the author of *The Reverend Dr. Preston Bradley, The Rhetorical Tradition*, and *The History of Rhetoric* and has published articles on American public address.

CELESTE M. CONDIT, Professor of Speech Communication, University of Georgia, teaches courses in rhetorical criticism and theory. She is the author of *Decoding Abortion Rhetoric: Communicating Social Change* and coauthor (with John Louis Lucaites) of *Crafting Equality: America's Anglo-African Word* and has published several articles on civil rights and African-American rhetors.

MELBOURNE S. CUMMINGS, Professor and Chair of the Department of Human Communication Studies at Howard University, teaches courses in African-American rhetoric and public address, rhetorical theory and criticism, and intercultural/interracial communication. She is the coeditor of the *Handbook on Communication and Development in Africa and the African Diaspora* and has written several essays on African-American rhetoric and rhetorical figures.

JEAN L. DEHART, Assistant Professor of Communication, Appalachian State University, teaches courses in political communication, rhetorical and communication theory, and persuasion. Her research interests include contemporary political conflict and the rhetoric of education reform.

LEROY G. DORSEY, Assistant Professor of Speech Communication, Texas A&M University, teaches courses in presidential rhetoric, argumentation and debate, and American public address. His work has appeared in the *Western Journal of Communication*.

GERALD FULKERSON, Professor of Communication and Chair of the Department of Communication and Literature, Freed-Hardeman University, teaches courses in oratory of Western civilization, argumentation, rhetorical theory, and Frederick Douglass. He is the textual editor of the speech and autobiography volumes of *The Frederick Douglass Papers* and has written several articles for communication journals.

CINDY L. GRIFFIN, Assistant Professor of Speech Communication, Colorado State University, teaches courses in contemporary rhetorical theory, rhetorical criticism, women's communication, and business and professional speaking. Her research focuses on women's rhetoric and the development of feminist rhetorical theory.

JOHN C. HAMMERBACK, Associate Dean and Professor of Speech Communication, California State University, Hayward, teaches classes in rhetorical theory and criticism. He has coauthored *A War of Words: Chicano Protest in the 1960s and 1970s*, has coedited *In Search of Justice: The Indiana Tradition in Speech Communication*, and has written articles and book chapters on Chicano rhetoric, African-American rhetoric, and political communication.

VIRGIE NOBLES HARRIS, Associate Professor of Fine Arts, Fort Valley State College, teaches courses in public speaking and drama. Her research interests include many forms of African-American discourse, including public address.

ROBERT L. HEATH, Professor of Communication, University of Houston, teaches courses in criticism of public speaking, rhetorical theory, persuasion, activist rhetoric, and corporate rhetoric. He is the author of *Realism and Relativism: A Perspective on Kenneth Burke* and several books on issues management, public relations, and corporate communication. He has also authored articles on Malcolm X, the Black Panther party, Alexander Crummell, and the controversial "Cotton States Exposition Address" by Booker T. Washington.

WANDA A. HENDRICKS, Assistant Professor of History, Arizona State University, Tempe, teaches courses in African-American history, African-American women's history, and civil rights. She has contributed entries to several African-American reference works and is currently completing a monograph on African-American women in Illinois from 1890 to 1920.

ROBERT INCHAUSTI, Professor of English, California Polytechnic University, San Luis Obispo, teaches courses in American and Russian literature and critical theory. He is the author of *The Ignorant Perfection of Ordinary People, Spitwad Sutras: Classroom Teaching as Sublime Vocation*, and *Thomas Merton: American Dissident*.

LORRAINE D. JACKSON, Assistant Professor of Speech Communication, California Polytechnic University, teaches courses in health communication, gender and communication, and communication theory. She has published several articles on communication and health issues.

RICHARD J. JENSEN, Professor of Communication, University of Nevada, Las Vegas, teaches courses in protest rhetoric, rhetorical criticism, and public address. He has written *Clarence Darrow: The Creation of an American Myth*, has coauthored *A War of Words: Chicano Protest in the 1960s and 1970s*, has coedited *In Search of Justice: The Indiana Tradition in Speech Communication*, and has written articles and book chapters on Chicano rhetoric, African-American rhetoric, and protest rhetoric.

CYNTHIA P. KING, doctoral candidate, University of Maryland, College Park, teaches courses in African-American rhetoric and basic principles of speech communication. Her dissertation examines nineteenth-century histories as rhetorical discourse.

DALE G. LEATHERS, Professor of Speech Communication, University of Georgia, Athens, publishes in the areas of impression management, nonverbal communication, and rhetorical criticism. He is the author of *Successful Nonverbal Communication* as well as recent articles and book chapters on impression management in the Anita Hill–Clarence Thomas hearings and the William Kennedy Smith trial.

RICHARD W. LEEMAN, Associate Professor of Communication Studies, University of North Carolina, Charlotte, teaches courses in rhetorical theory, political communication, and African-American oratory. He is the author of *The Rhetoric of Terrorism and Counterterrorism* and *"Do Everything" Reform: The Oratory of Frances E. Willard* and has published several articles on African-American discourse.

THOMAS M. LESSL, Associate Professor of Speech Communication, University of Georgia, teaches courses in rhetorical criticism, rhetorical theory, and religious communication. He is the author of several articles on the nature of religious speech and on the rhetoric of science.

DREMA R. LIPSCOMB, Assistant Professor of English, University of Rochester, teaches courses in women's and African-American feminist literature. Her scholarly work focuses especially on the discourse of early American feminists.

CAL M. LOGUE, Professor of Speech Communication, University of Georgia, teaches courses in blacks' discourse, women's discourse, and rhetorical criticism. He is the author of *Eugene Talmadge: Rhetoric and Response* and coeditor (with Howard Dorgan) of *The Oratory of Southern Demagogues* and *A New Diversity in Contemporary Southern Rhetoric*. He has also written articles on communication during slavery, Reconstruction, and the Civil War.

STEPHEN E. LUCAS, Professor of Communication Arts, University of Wisconsin, teaches courses in the history of American public address. His book *Portents of Rebellion: Rhetoric and Revolution in Philadelphia, 1765–76* was nominated for a Pulitzer Prize and received the Speech Communication Association Golden Anniversary Award. He is currently working on a book-length study of Booker T. Washington's oratory.

MARK LAWRENCE MCPHAIL, Associate Professor of Communication, University of Utah, teaches courses in the rhetoric of race relations, language and power in society and education, and rhetorical theory and epistemology. His poetry has been featured in the *American Literary Review* and *Dark Horse Magazine*, and he is the author of *The Rhetoric of Racism* and *Zen in the Art of Rhetoric*.

NINA-JO MOORE, Associate Professor of Communication, Appalachian State University, teaches courses in communication theory and persuasion. Her scholarly interests include communication theory, persuasion, and American public address.

CARLOS MORRISON is a doctoral candidate at Howard University, with research interests in African-American public address.

LYNDREY A. NILES, Professor of Human Communication Studies, Howard University, teaches courses in rhetorical theory, intercultural communication, and African-American rhetoric. He is the editor of *African American Rhetoric: A Reader*.

WARREN OBERMAN, graduate student in English, California Polytechnic University, San Luis Obispo, has written on Samuel Beckett, Marguerite Duras, and Kathy Acker.

EDWARD M. PANETTA, Associate Professor of Speech Communication, University of Georgia, teaches courses in argumentation, rhetorical theory, and political communication. He is the author of several articles related to forensic theory and the study of public argument.

JOHN H. PATTON, Associate Professor of Communication and Fellow at the Newcomb College of Communication, Tulane University, teaches courses in persuasion, political communication, and communication in Caribbean cultures. Recent publications include articles on the rhetoric of Martin Luther King, Jr., and on calypso and cultural identity in the Caribbean.

GARTH PAULEY is a doctoral student in the Department of Speech Communication at Pennsylvania State University. He is the author of a chapter on civil rights oratory in *Lone Star Voices: Studies of Great Texas Orators* and has presented papers on rhetoric and public address.

VANESSA WYNDER QUAINOO, Assistant Professor of Speech Communication, University of Rhode Island, teaches courses in oral interpretation and race, media, and politics. Her scholarly interests include African-American public address.

RONALD F. REID, Professor Emeritus of Communication Studies, University of Massachusetts, previously taught courses in argumentation, debate, and the history of rhetorical theory and public address. He is the author of *Edward: Everett: Unionist Orator, The American Revolution and the Rhetoric of History*, and *Three Centuries of American Rhetorical Discourse: An Anthology and a Review*. He received the Winans-Wichelns Award for Distinguished Scholarship in Rhetoric and Public Address in 1977 and is a two-time recipient of the Speech Communication Association Monograph Award.

ENRIQUE D. RIGSBY, Assistant Professor of Speech Communication, Texas A&M University, teaches courses in rhetorical theory, civil rights studies, and media studies. His publications have examined the protest movement of the civil rights era, focusing especially on the role of the black church and the rhetoric of mass meetings.

KURT RITTER, Professor of Speech Communication, Texas A&M University, teaches courses in American public address, political rhetoric, and religious communication. He is the coauthor of *Ronald Reagan: The Great Communicator* and *The American Ideology: Reflections of the Revolution in American Rhetoric* and editor of *The 1980 Presidential Debates*. His scholarship has earned him the Speech Communication Association's Winans-Wichelns Award and Karl Wallace Award and the Western States Communication Association's Aubrey Fisher Award.

HALFORD ROSS RYAN, Professor of Speech, Washington and Lee University, teaches courses in the history and criticism of American public address and in feminist rhetoric. He is the author, editor, or coeditor of eleven books, the most recent being *The Inaugural Addresses of Twentieth-Century American Presidents*.

STACY L. SMITH is a Graduate Fellow in the Department of Speech Communication at the University of Maryland, College Park. Her primary interests are social movement rhetoric, rhetorical criticism, and American public address.

STEPHEN A. SMITH, Professor of Communication, University of Arkansas, Fayetteville, teaches courses in American public address, political communication, and freedom of speech. His publications include *Myth, Media, and the Southern Mind* and *Bill Clinton on Stump, State and Stage: The Rhetorical Road to the White House*.

MARY ANNE TRASCIATTI, graduate student in Speech Communication, University of Maryland, College Park, has research interests in the history of radical American public discourse. Her dissertation is an analysis of Italian immigrant rhetoric in the late nineteenth and early twentieth centuries.

MINA A. VAUGHN, Lecturer of Speech Communication, California Polytechnic State University, teaches courses in speech communication and critical thinking. She has written articles on Father Divine and on organizational symbolism.

BETH M. WAGGENSPACK, Associate Professor of Communication Studies, Virginia Polytechnic Institute and State University, teaches courses in persuasion, argumentation, and rhetorical theory, criticism, and practice. She is the author of *The Search for Self-Sovereignty: The Oratory of Elizabeth Cady Stanton* and coauthor (with Samuel Wallace) of *Communicating in Context: A Handbook for the Basic Course.*

ROBBIE JEAN WALKER, Professor of English, Auburn University, Montgomery, teaches courses in written composition, African-American literature, and rhetoric and style. She is the editor of *The Rhetoric of Struggle: Public Address by African American Women* and has written extensively on writing pedagogy and African-American literature. She is currently working on an archetypal analysis of the fictional treatment of slavery in novels by African-American women.

EDE WARNER, JR., Assistant Professor of Communication, Louisville University, teaches courses in argumentation, debate, and communication in the black community. His research interests include forensics and American public address.

MARTHA SOLOMON WATSON, Professor of Speech Communication and Associate Dean of the College of Arts and Humanities, University of Maryland, College Park, teaches courses in the rhetoric of woman's rights, suffrage, and civil rights as well as textual analysis. She is the author of *Emma Goldman: A Critical Biography* and *Anna Howard Shaw: Suffrage Orator and Social Reformer* and the editor of *A Voice of Their Own: The Woman Suffrage Press, 1840–1910* and is currently writing a book on the autobiographies of late nineteenth- and early twentieth-century women who were active in social movements.

JAMES K. WEST, graduate student in English, California Polytechnic University, San Luis Obispo, teaches courses in composition. He writes reviews of jazz and classical recordings and has written extensively on Miles Davis, Glenn Gould, and Henry James.

PATRICK G. WHEATON, doctoral candidate in Speech Communication, University of Georgia, is the Assistant Director of Debate and teaches public speaking. His research interests include argumentation, American public address, and political communication.

MARK BERNARD WHITE, Assistant Professor of Communication Arts, Baylor University, teaches courses in African-American rhetoric, rhetorical criticism, and speech composition. He is the author of *Palpable Designs: Wordsworth's Rhetorical Stance and the Ethics of Lyric* and has written several articles on African-American discourse and rhetoric and poetics. He is currently writing a book on the rhetoric of Malcolm X.

ISBN 0-313-29014-8

9 780313 290145

HARDCOVER BAR CODE